War and Human Progress

An Essay on the
Rise of Industrial Civilization

John U. Nef

The Norton Library

W · W · NORTON & COMPANY · INC ·

NEW YORK

TO ELINOR
Vingt-neuf ans après

Introduction to the Paperback Edition

THE COMPOSITION OF THIS ESSAY WAS BEGUN DURING THE AUTUMN OF 1941, just before the United States entered the Second World War. The book was released for publication by the Harvard University Press nine years afterwards, in the autumn of 1950, when this country had embarked on the Korean War.

The subject matter on which I drew for knowledge of the past was derived from old books, documents and historical monuments which I had been examining as the basis for a project that I had had in mind ever since 1932, when I finished my first book, *The Rise of the British Coal Industry*. Starting with my special researches into European industrial history, my intention had been to weave those into a scheme touching all phases of the general history of Western Civilization since the Renaissance.

I had come to realize that all sides of human endeavor are interrelated, and that the very specialization which for a century had been opening new avenues to information concerning many facets of history was blinding historians to the consideration of history as a whole and from views of the nature and extent of historical interrelations. These fascinated me, and I wanted to reveal those suggested to my mind. I had touched on them in lectures to students. Yet I felt the lack of any principle that would enable me to present historical interrelationships to the reader in the form of history filled with concrete examples.

My aim was to help others understand how this planet has become the industrialized world of the twentieth century, and I suspected that a probing of the connections between industrial history and other kinds of history might reveal new explanations of this industrialization and so provide fresh knowledge of its consequences in the development of human societies. Preliminary articles and papers written during the nineteen-thirties were beginning to give me an impression (which I was able to convey only dimly for want of deeper experience) that in the times I mainly wrote about—the age of Columbus' voyages and, still

more, the hundred years following the Reformation—important changes
occurred in the nature of the visions and beliefs of individuals which
guided their work and determined their actions. I was eventually to see
that these changes had much to do with the course of history during
the past four centuries. Yet, in spite of all I was learning, I still supposed
that an account of the coming of industrialism should be built around
changes in the empty forms of economic enterprise, of economic growth,
or of price history, which had been treated by Marx and by so many of
his followers and critics as determining historical factors. My essay
"Industrial Europe at the Time of the Reformation," published in 1941,[1]
was mainly concerned, as had been most of my earlier essays which
covered years from about 1540 to 1640,[2] with economic growth, with
changes in the price level and in the technology and the administrative
organization of industrial enterprise. Until 1942 all these articles represented for me drafts of chapters which might eventually appear in the
long historical book I planned to publish.

What brought me to turn from a specialized and conventional career
in economic history as the basis for excursions into other aspects of
history, to the subject of war and peace? What brought me to recognize
that human nature (in which the animal is mingled with spiritual forces
of good and evil, faith and fear, delight and messy cruelty) is behind
peace or war more than economic conditions or processes? What led me
to make these forces—playing about in the inner lives of men and women
—the central theme of this book?

At the beginning of the nineteen-forties a number of external circumstances drew me to war as a subject. The period from about 1540 to 1640,
with which I had planned to begin my book, was an age marred by
terrible wars fought partly over religious issues. Among the many
chapters of historical interrelations which I planned to write, one,
which I had on the stocks, dealt with connections between those wars
and economic history. As war was very much in the air from 1939 to

---

[1] In *The Journal of Political Economy*, XLIX, 1 and 2.

[2] See John U. Nef, "The Progress of Technology and the Growth of Large-Scale
Industry in Great Britain, 1540-1640," in *Economic History Review*, V, 1 (Oct.
1934); "A Comparison of Industrial Growth in France and England from 1540 to
1640," in *The Journal of Political Economy*, XLIV, 3, 4, and 5 (June, August,
and October 1936); "Note on the Progress of Iron Production in England, 1540-
1640," in *The Journal of Political Economy*, XLIV, 3 (June 1936); "Prices and
Industrial Capitalism in France and England, 1540-1640," in *Economic History
Review*, VII, 2 (May 1937); *Industry and Government in France and England,
1540-1640*, American Philosophical Memoirs, Vol. XV, 1940 (paperback edition:
Great Seal Books, Cornell University Press).

1942, I found it natural to draft versions of that chapter. Two were published.[1]

External circumstances by themselves, however, would never have led me to make the problem of peace or war the unifying theme of a general history. The main reason for the change in my purpose, which created this book during the years 1943 to 1950, came from a sense of mission born in me much earlier. It is expressed in the dedication.

For a brief period of weeks I had been in training as an infantry soldier for service in the First World War. The Armistice which we still commemorate had delivered me from actual participation in those mass slaughters on what had been called the western front. The gratitude I felt for this deliverance surged up in me as never before three years later as part of a great happiness that came into my life in the autumn of 1921, at the time the President of the United States called a conference for naval disarmament. That meeting of statesmen of what had been the chief allied powers aroused my hopes for the permanent peace which Woodrow Wilson's words, "a war to end war," had convinced me was the purpose for which the older members of my generation had fought. As I look back, it seems to me I was vaguely aware forty years ago of what is now clear to all sensitive persons who love their neighbors, that men must find some way of mastering war, or war will bring us collectively to commit the suicide which, as individuals, some of us believe will deny us all hope of Eternity! I sensed already in 1921 that the need of human beings for great striving, for exaltation, expressed so devastatingly in war, must somehow be transferred from war to peace if the dignity of God in man is to be retained, if civilization is to prevail. In my imagination I anticipated as Samuel Johnson had much earlier in *Rasselas,* the appearance of swarms of airships blotting out the sun as they obliterated us and, along with us, all that our forebears managed to create and leave behind in enduring beauty.

In the nineteen-forties an old yearning, aroused first twenty years before, came back to me in a new form in connection with the life of historian which I had since adopted. Might not my search for historical truth reveal some of the forces within individuals responsible for the unprecedented conditions of peace and gentle manners that had prevailed, as it seemed, among the Europeans and Americans at the time I was born? In writing history might I not do something to repay the

---

[1] See John U. Nef, "War and Economic Progress, 1540-1640," *Economic History Review,* XII, 1, 1942; "War and the Early Industrial Revolution," in *Economic Problems of War and Its Aftermath,* ed. C. W. Wright, Chicago, 1942.

debt I owed for a decent life, and for the beauty which had come into it, by helping human beings in the future to diminish the violence and suffering that war always brings?

Far from turning me away from my plan to consider the general history of Western Civilization since the Renaissance, this renewal in the nineteen-forties of my early inspiration led me toward that general history. I discovered that peace, which is an absence of war, and war, which is an absence of peace, were closely related to every facet of historical development during the past four or five centuries in Europe, in America and indeed, in the whole world. In the drama that determined peace or war, I discovered a human principle capable of giving cohesion to the many sides of history that had concerned me ever since 1929, when I had begun to lecture to students, most of whom were studying economics.

That is how this book came to be written. I am told that soon after it appeared, a news agency in Russia seized upon the four words of the title as evidence of the belligerent temper of Americans! But the book is in no sense a work of propaganda. It is a part of a search for truth, guided by certainty that history is rich in many-sided truths, and that in the writing of history, as in all artistic efforts, the results can never be clear and precise in quite the same way as scientific statements can be. Once it is finished, a history book like mine, which aims to make a small contribution to art, no longer belongs to its author, but is open at many places to divergent interpretations, all of which may be legitimate. Yet there are also illegitimate interpretations of such a work.[1] And the view that the story I have related could incite persons to the mutual suicide which total war has now become seems to me altogether illegitimate. Perhaps I may be permitted to refer in support of what I say to the opinion of a reviewer who is not always given in his criticism to such warming enthusiasm, Professor Hugh Trevor-Roper.

This is what he wrote in *The Sunday Times* of London in 1951 about *War and Human Progress*:

Is war or is it not a means of progress? Does it—quite apart from the cost of fighting or the spoils of victory—hasten commercial and industrial development? In 1913 Werner Sombart, a German

---

[1] See John U. Nef, *A Search for Civilization*, Chicago, 1962, pp. 75-78.

economic ideologue, argued that it does; that the centralization and standardization which it entails, the demands which it creates, and the invention which it stimulates cause inevitably an economic advance. This argument has now been examined by a far profounder scholar than Sombart ... [Nef] shows that the industrial revolutions of both the Elizabethan and of the Napoleonic periods were developed not in warring Europe but in peaceful England; that the invention of gunpowder and of many other weapons of war was a by-product not of military need but of peaceful industry, and that certainly pure and possibly even applied science has flourished most in peace and least in war. In short [he] demolishes Sombart, learnedly, logically, completely.

Trevor-Roper goes on to say: "that is by no means all he does. This is not only an historical but—in the best sense—a philosophical book. It provokes numerous trains of thought and fertilises many fields of study which it only incidentally touches."

These are the sides of the book which make it a general history for the ordinary reader, in no sense dependent upon a special concern with war for the public it is designed to reach. War alas, and peace also, have been fundamental parts of history; to leave them out of my story would have been to renounce the attempt to write a general history. Not to relate them as truthfully as possible to the other sides of history, about which I had been lecturing for years, would have simply added to the innumerable available studies of war as a special subject.

When I was in the early stages of composition, and the Second World War was ending in Europe and was about to end in the Far East, a friend of mine, who had generously sponsored my researches from 1942 to 1945, commiserated with me. It was a pity, he said, that I had not finished before the coming of peace, or that the war had not continued until I had finished! As a specialist, my friend, who had not seen my book, assumed that I had specialized on the subject of war and economic progress (as in the two essays I had published), and that economists (at whom he assumed my book was aimed) would not in time of peace be interested in interrelations between *wars* and industrial development. Everyone was going to forget about war as fast as possible. He feared my book might be already obsolete when it appeared!

Today his political miscalculation strikes us as droll. During the seventeen years that have followed the first dropping of the atomic bomb, we have lived continually under the threat of wars and not infrequently under the threat of total war. It is doubtful whether at any time in history people generally have thought more about organized war.

So my book remains timely in the sense my friend feared it would be out-of-date. Yet it does not depend for its audience on this kind of timeliness. Even if my friend's happy dream had been realized, even if it should (to our infinite relief) be realized in the immediate future, even if peace were to become the normal condition for human societies, as I have always longed to have it, the story I try to tell in this book would not be obsolete. This book is less about war than about the search for peace and for the fruits of peace. Its central subject matter is how Western society has developed since the times of Columbus' voyages. I am concerned with the coming of what in the eighteenth century some Europeans began to call "civilization." They meant by the word an order of relationships between individuals and groups such as they believed had never existed, and they meant by it a society in which gentle manners and peaceful commerce counted as never before in history.[1]

My book describes some of the ways in which civilization, in that eighteenth-century sense, came into being. Further it aims to describe how industrialism, which now envelops most of the people living on this planet, emerged out of civilization. It tries to show how this emerging industrialism has made total war for the first time possible, and how total war makes it possible for men to destroy themselves and their history.

My object has been to present a different, and I hope a truer, view of Western history during the age of European expansion than has yet appeared. So this is a new story not to be found in the scores of popular histories and textbooks of history, which purport to sum up the existing state of our historical knowledge, and which have provided hitherto the historical diet of the young. The story I have told here is that of some twenty generations of human effort, which began in Europe in the times of Columbus. This effort has left Damocles' sword hanging over our heads. If the thread that holds the sword should break, no one may be left to read my story. If, as we must hope, humankind manages to remove that sword before it falls, some such story as the one I have told may prove true enough and dramatic enough for our children's children to remember.

JOHN U. NEF

July 1, 1963

---

[1] John U. Nef, *Cultural Foundations of Industrial Civilization*, Harper Torchbooks, 1960.

Preface

THIS ESSAY WOULD HARDLY HAVE APPEARED BUT FOR THE encouragement, support, and criticism of two persons. To one the book is dedicated; all my published historical work has been in a sense a joint enterprise in which she is the silent partner. The other is my colleague and friend, Professor Earl J. Hamilton. From the time in 1941 when I began to compose essays dealing with the historical interrelations between war and industry, he took an interest far more generous and sustained than any historian has the right to hope for from another member of the craft. At a difficult point during the last war, his enthusiasm for the subject, and the financial support which he obtained for my research into it, kept me at work upon it. Since that time he has combined critical interest with friendly indulgence in the proportions most likely to stimulate an author to stay at his last. I only regret that the work itself is not more worthy of his generous and constant intellectual and moral support.

Other colleagues and friends have given me most constructive advice and encouragement. Among them are H. S. Bennett, A. L. Castle, Mrs. M. W. Castle, S. C. Gilfillan, Waldemar Gurian, Victor Hammer, Jean Hugonnot, H. A. Innis, Jacques Maritain, Jean Meynaud, Gerald Mignot, William Pullin, Artur Schnabel, R. H. Tawney, A. P. Usher (who helped me to bring into relief the central thesis of the essay), and John B. Wolf.

My debt to my colleagues of the Committee on Social Thought is beyond acknowledgment, both for their help in operating the enterprise and for their particular favors in connection with composition. The essays which led to the writing of this book were begun at the time when the Committee was formed. For that reason and also because I have tried in writing the book to serve one of the purposes of the Committee — to draw together historical knowledge which has been kept in separate compartments — the two enterprises have been inseparable from the start. I am deeply grateful to the colleagues who are my contemporaries for founding and sustaining the Committee on

Social Thought and to my younger colleagues and student associates for making it into something worthy to endure. During the past eight years a number of other books have appeared by members and associates of the Committee. These demonstrate far better than this book how the purposes for which the Committee exists should be served.

The preparation of my own essay has involved, in small ways, many of the difficulties which are likely to beset all who turn toward what seems to us of the Committee on Social Thought a major task of our time, that of bringing some sort of unity and order out of the masses of knowledge discovered by specialists during the last century and a half. I have in mind especially the difficulty of treating several subjects together with the same competence that is rightly expected from the scholar or the man of letters who treats only one. Drawn to consider not only military history but industrial and constitutional history, the history of science, of art, and of manners, I have become as I worked increasingly conscious of how much I ought to know that I do not know. In military history alone the bibliographic material available is overwhelmingly vast, and I am troubled by the reflection that there is much I ought to have studied that I have been unable even to read. My task both here and in connection with possible ways of treating the subject of war, has been facilitated by the comprehensive book of my colleague, Professor Quincy Wright. Though our treatment of the subject is different, I have had occasion to make frequent use of his two-volume *A Study of War*.

I should have done very much worse in this matter of bibliography had I not had the advantage in the early stages of my research of the enterprise and precision of Miss Stella Lange, who ran down a great deal of material for me. Since the war her place was taken by Mrs. Netabel Rice, whose skill and devotion to her work have saved me from many errors. In rewriting, preparing the manuscripts and the typescripts for the press, I have been helped for more than five years by Mrs. R. Armour, whose admirable accuracy, efficiency, and discretion are beyond praise.

Funds to finance much of the research have come from two sources. First, from the Social Science Research Council through the initiative of Dr. Hamilton and on the recommendation of Dr. Innis and Professor A. H. Cole of the Committee on Research in Economic History, founded by The Rockefeller Foundation. Second, from the Social Science Research Committee of the University of Chicago and The Rockefeller Foundation, through the initiative of my friend Professor Robert Redfield. I wish to express my warm thanks to these bodies and these gentlemen for their heartening encouragement.

Some of the material in this book appeared, in a different form, in *The Review of Politics; The Economic History Review; The Journal of Economic History; Measure; The Canadian Journal of Economics and Politics,* published by the University of Toronto Press; in a book, *Economic Problems of War and Its Aftermath,* published by the University of Chicago Press in 1942; in *The Constitution Reconsidered,* edited by Conyers Read and published in 1938 by the Columbia University Press; and in *La Route de la guerre totale* (Cahiers de la Fondation Nationale des Sciences Politiques, no. 11). For permission to make use of the material I have to thank the various editors.

I have a special sense of gratitude and obligation to my publishers. Everyone knows they are good publishers. They are more; they are kind and sympathetic and understanding ones.

J. U. N.

Chicago
January 1, 1950

Contents

PART THREE

INDUSTRIALISM AND TOTAL WAR

Circa 1740 to Circa 1950

PART ONE

THE NEW WARFARE AND THE GENESIS OF INDUSTRIALISM
Circa 1494 to Circa 1640

CHAPTER ONE

A Tripartite Division of European History

· IN 1660, OR THEREABOUTS, THE CELEBRATED CHEMIST ROBERT BOYLE observed that "the invention of gunpowder hath quite altered the condition of martial affairs over the world, both by sea and land." [1] Until the twentieth century no other product of man's ingenuity effected such a change in warfare.

The change which drew Boyle's comment had taken place mainly during the preceding century and a half, beginning with a French invasion of Italy in 1494. For Western Europe that period, which followed Columbus' voyages, was of decisive importance in the genesis of modern industrial civilization. How was the growing command which the Europeans exercised over their industrial resources connected with their growing power of destruction? What relations had the new warfare to the employment of human talents and energies in ways leading toward the industrialism which now dominates the lives of most men and women on this planet?

During the fifteenth century the Europeans became more concerned than their medieval ancestors had been with the actual condition of human bodies, of animals, of landscapes and skies, of all that they could see, hear, touch, smell, and taste. The intensity of the human desire to probe the world directly accessible to the senses led men to seek new objects to satisfy old needs. The discovery of the Americas and of new sea passages to India and China were two among many results of this interest in the fresh exploration of nature. Nearer at hand the same interest led people to re-examine and to exploit anew the natural resources of Europe, to cross glaciers and climb mountains, to dig stones and mine ores in larger quantities; to design and create new kinds of dress, furniture, tapestries, and a bewildering variety of other sumptuous works of decorative art — paintings, statues, objects in glass and iron — all conceived in the same spirit and sometimes by the same artists as the new styles of architecture which were spreading from Italy over the Alps, as new towns and new parts of old towns were planned and built. For some three generations following the Hundred Years' War, which ended in 1453, industrial growth, striking increases in the yield of the land and striking commercial prosperity were frequent on the Continent — all the way from Poland and the Balkans to the toe of Italy and the Portuguese coast of the Spanish peninsula, whence many discoverers set out on their voyages. The banqueting tables of princes, nobles, and rich churchmen were heaped with meats, fishes, fruits, and other delicacies which had never been seen in such profusion in Western Europe — not, at any rate, since the second century of our era, when the Antonines ruled over the vast, unified Roman Empire.

It was mainly for the rich, above all for the great establishments from churches to mansions, maintained by bishops and princes, lesser priests and nobles, and some municipal authorities, that craftsmen and artists produced commodities in larger quantities than before. Yet most ranks of the growing population, even poor journeymen and an increasing number of other wage earners, had access to some of the durable goods which were being manufactured, especially to the quantities of printed matter turned out by the presses installed in such towns as Basel, Frankfurt, Nuremberg, Augsburg, Paris, Lyons, and Antwerp. After 1520 pamphlets were issued in many tens of thousands by the German religious reformers who supported Luther in his opposition to the ancient Roman Church and to the forms of dogma and worship which it prescribed, to the images and the saints which their ancestors had venerated. Without the new means of reaching the people provided by the printing press, without the new wealth, and the jealousy which wealth frequently bred in those who felt themselves to be less wealthy and less fortunate, Luther's doctrines and those of Calvin could hardly have gained so enormous a following. By the 1540's the support of discontented elements, of sovereign princes of the old Holy Roman Empire, and of the kings of Sweden, England, and Denmark, had established a future for the principal reformed religions. During the next hundred years, from about 1540 to 1640, Europe divided in Christian worship — after nearly a millennium when notwithstanding frequent heresies, almost all the Western peoples had belonged to one church, had gone to mass, and had received the sacraments.

These momentous divisions in the Christian faith were accompanied by geographical divisions in the industrial history of Europe which seem in some ways to complement the religious ones. The economy under which a large part of the earth's inhabitants live in the twentieth century is unique. In order to establish it, a break was inevitable with older civilized ideas of the appropriate ways to exploit the world's natural resources. Certain parts of Europe made such a break during the late sixteenth and early seventeenth centuries, but most parts moved in other directions. After the mid-sixteenth century striking differences appeared in the rate and the nature of industrial progress in the various countries.

Of course the economic experiences of these countries had not been identical before the Reformation. Remarkable diversities in ways of measuring, in ways of manufacturing, in ways of handling money and financing economic ventures had been characteristic of late medieval Europe. Each region had had its own weights and coins, which are the despair of the modern statistician when he tries to obtain any general figures for production and trade. Regional individuality in the methods by which men and women performed essential daily tasks was more pronounced from the late eleventh through the thirteenth century than in modern times. Medieval Europe at its best was an approach to unity in diversity; the modern civilization which has taken possession of the globe during the past hundred years is nearer disunity in standardization.

From the late eleventh to the early sixteenth century, there were other differences in the kinds of economy prevailing in various parts of Europe. Life among the townsmen was much more industrialized, more commercially and financially sophisticated, than life among the great majority, which was composed of husbandmen tilling the soil, tending vines and fruit-bearing trees, or shepherding flocks. There were differences too in the degree of economic development, between one town and another and among the towns of different countries. To citizens of Florence, Genoa, Barcelona, or Bruges, with their use of credit, the ways of doing business in contemporary Edinburgh, Coventry, York, or even London, must have seemed backward. The creation of deposits without any exchange of cash, as a means of lending money, was an innovation of bankers in Spanish and Italian towns at least as early as the thirteenth century. But such methods of lending were apparently little practiced in Great Britain until three centuries afterward.

What is meant by saying that the Reformation was followed by divisions in economic history that were new, if conditions before the Reformation had been so diverse? In spite of the wide differences in the degrees of economic development, from the late eleventh to the early fourteenth century all Europe participated in the development. The long age which began on the eve of the first crusade, in 1096–1099, and lasted through the lifetime of Dante, who died in 1321, left every country — one could almost say every region — more populous and wealthy. Everywhere the volume of industrial output, the yield of minerals and manufactured articles, notably increased.

Almost all Europe also shared in the comparatively stationary conditions of production and trade which prevailed during the last three-quarters of the fourteenth century and the first half of the fifteenth — the period of the Black Death, with its tremendous toll of lives, and the Hundred Years' War. There was temporary local prosperity in Bohemia and Franconia in the third quarter of the fourteenth century, and in the southern Low Countries under the government of the Burgundian duke, Philip the Good, from 1419 to 1467. But in Europe as a whole, the output of most agricultural and industrial products grew little, if at all, from about 1325 to about 1460; the output of ores probably declined.

Again, most countries shared in the remarkable renewal of industrial expansion and the growth of trade which began in the late fifteenth century, which accompanied the discoveries and the new interest in nature. For a period of several decades, between about 1470 and 1540, continental Europe grew prosperous as rapidly as at any time during the twelfth and thirteenth centuries.

It was only after the mid-sixteenth century that European industrial history divided sharply along geographical lines. The principal divisions were three. In the first there was a marked decline in the volume of output, a diminution in the scale of industrial enterprise, and a shrinkage in the relative importance of industry as compared to agriculture. In the second there was a notable growth in the products of the artistic and the luxury industries, a fresh development of art and artisanry, but only a slight increase in the output of the heavy industries, and consequently no remarkable change in the volume of output. In the third there was an expansion of the heavy industries, and consequently of output, for which there had been no precedent.

The first of the three divisions comprised a large part of Europe, the Imperial and the Spanish dominions, including Franche-Comté and the southern Netherlands — all territory which had been nominally united for a generation under the Emperor Charles V, who was also King of Spain and who abdicated these great offices in 1555 and 1556. In Franche-Comté, and probably also in Spain itself, the volume of production continued to mount, though slowly, after the middle of the sixteenth century until at least 1590. But the forty years from 1550 to 1590 were disastrous for the economic fortune of the Spanish Netherlands, and hardly less so for that of central Europe. After the decade 1591–1600 the prosperity of Spain and Franche-Comté collapsed. Neither Velasquez nor Murillo painted, as El Greco had, in an age of affluence. Spain was probably less populous when Velasquez died in 1660 than it had been a hundred years earlier when El Greco was a child. The Spanish textile and metal manufactures had grown under Ferdinand and Isabella and their grandson, Charles V, until they were among the most productive in Europe. But during the first half of the seventeenth century industrial output shrank rapidly, as is indicated by the great decline in the population of many Spanish towns. By 1660 Spain seems to have reverted to a more rural economy than had prevailed since Charles V was crowned as king of Spain in 1520.

In southern Germany and adjacent Bohemia and Austria, the decline in prosperity began soon after Luther's death, in 1546, earlier than in Spain and Franche-Comté. The economic collapse, which followed the outbreak of the Thirty Years' War in 1618, was even greater in central Europe than in Spain. According to the most reliable estimates, the number of persons living in those regions which were to form the German Empire of 1871–1919 diminished in the hundred years 1550–1650 from almost twenty-one millions to about thirteen and a half millions.[2] Some towns lost practically all their inhabitants. For example, near Karlsbad in western Bohemia, Joachimstal, the most productive of all the German copper and silver mining centers in the decade 1530–1539, then had nearly twenty thousand people. A century later a few hundreds remained. The work of an ardent disciple of Luther, Johann Mathesius (1504–1565), in converting the mining community to Protestantism was undone.[3]

For some decades in the mid-seventeenth century it seemed that Germany and the regions of German settlement to the east and south, bristling with sturdy little towns at the time of the Reformation, might again become lands of peasants almost denuded of the urban life that had been an integral part of developing Western civilization since the eleventh century. Almost everywhere industrial production had shrunk even more than had population. Central Europe produced hardly one-fifth as much silver in 1650 as in 1540.[4] Only a strip of coast along the North Sea, where Hamburg was the principal port, escaped economic disasters.

Outside the Imperial and the Spanish dominions economic fortune presented different faces during the hundred years from 1540 to 1640. Conditions were much better in Italy, France, and Switzerland. During

the early sixteenth century parts of northern and central Italy ceased
to prosper industrially, especially after about 1525. But there was extensive economic progress throughout the Italian peninsula and in
Sicily during the sixteenth century, especially during the second half.
Italy was more prosperous when Palestrina and Veronese were at the
height of their powers than when they were born; more prosperous in
Titian's old age than during his middle years, when he was painting his
remarkable portraits of the Emperor Charles V; more prosperous in the
youth of Galileo (1564–1642), before he had worked out his laws of
motion, than when Machiavelli died in 1527 after bemoaning the fate
Italy was suffering from French, German, and Spanish invaders. Between the thirties and the eighties of the sixteenth century the output
of fine woolen cloth in Venice nearly quadrupled.[5] In Sicily and the
Kingdom of Naples the population grew rapidly from 1500 until 1570,
nor was there any falling off in the number of Italians during the first
half of the seventeenth century. The population of Rome, which had
declined during the early part of the sixteenth century, more than
doubled in the second half. Rome had over 100,000 inhabitants in the
early seventeenth century and was among the largest cities of Europe.[6]
Paris, London, Amsterdam, Naples, Venice, and possibly also Palermo,
and Seville, alone were larger.

While the position of London and Amsterdam as leading cities was
novel, Paris had been in front for centuries. In its main lines French
industrial development resembled Italian between the mid-sixteenth
and the mid-seventeenth centuries, though progress did not take place
simultaneously in the two countries. The late sixteenth century, when
economic enterprise thrived in Italy, was not a prosperous time for
France. From 1562 to 1589, until Henry IV's accession helped to pacify
much of the country, France was swept by religious civil wars. While
the damage done to industry was exaggerated by contemporary writers,
the volume of national production undoubtedly diminished. But from
1595 to 1620, there was a notable expansion of industrial enterprise,
above all of the luxury and artistic industries. France was bringing into
the modern world a technical and administrative genius of her own,
modeled on the experience of earlier civilizations, especially those of
the Italian Renaissance and of classical Rome and Greece. French industry maintained and developed the values of beauty and splendor;
French civilization gave these values an order, a moderation, and a
tenderness which were new and which were of help in the pacification
of Europe.

Early in the seventeenth century Francis Bacon remarked of the
Swiss: They "last well, notwithstanding their diversity of religion and

of cantons: for utility is their bond, and not respects." [7] If one judges from the experience of Basel and the rest of northern Switzerland, the late sixteenth century was for the cantons a time of industrial prosperity equal to that of contemporary Italy. While the expansion which characterized the period roughly from 1550 to 1595 hardly continued thereafter, Switzerland generally suffered relatively little in her trade or industry from the Thirty Years' War, especially by comparison with Germany, Austria, and Bohemia. In addition to the expansion of the printing and papermaking industries, established before the Reformation, there was a striking increase in the production of woolen cloth, buttons, and leather.

It was not on the basis of utility alone, as Bacon's remark might suggest, that the manufactures of Basel and the north thrived. Italian influence, which was hardly less strong in Switzerland than in France, led mainly in other directions than utility. At the end of the sixteenth century, by all odds the leading manufacture in Basel was the production of silk and silk wares, work which the French crown was doing everything possible to encourage in France.[8] Silk is not a product which contributes primarily to the kind of economic expansion characteristic of modern industrialism. It is scarce and exclusive, an aristocrat among fabrics, much as gold is an aristocrat among metals. The delicate process of silk-making, by which worms have to be nourished on the leaves of a special tree, the mulberry, to produce the cocoons from which authentic silk thread can be manufactured, is hardly better suited by nature to unlimited multiplication than gold. A philosopher's stone would be needed to produce either as cheaply and plentifully as paper or iron. It has not been alchemy but science which has created the industrialized world of the twentieth century.

While the hundred years which followed the 1540's were not as a whole very prosperous for Italy, Switzerland, and France — while there was little increase in the production of heavy products, such as coal and iron — these countries were, by comparison with Spain and central Europe, well off in the mid-seventeenth century. As a young man John Evelyn, most known to posterity through his diary, toured France and Italy, to return home in 1645 by way of southern Switzerland. "Divers experienced and curious persons" assured him "there was little more to be seen in the rest of the civil world, after Italy, France, Flanders, and the Low Countries, but plain and prodigious barbarism." [9] Active soon afterwards in the scientific movement that resulted in England in the founding of the Royal Society, Evelyn was deeply interested in new kinds of machinery and other curiosities of engineering. He was led to suppose that there was little in Germany or Spain to interest him.

It was in the north of Europe — in Sweden, Denmark, and Scotland, above all in England, where Evelyn had come from, and in the Dutch Republic, founded by William the Silent during his struggle to hold back the Spanish armies of Philip II — that the age was marked by a striking growth in the volume of production. In those northern parts the prosperity was very great.

> *England's a perfect World! has Indies too!*
> *Correct your Maps! New-castle is Peru.*

So run two verses by the irrepressible author of a poem to coal, printed in 1651.[10] Figures of shipments kept in port books by the toiling customs officials prove that the English had actually begun during the previous hundred years to build their civilization upon a black El Dorado. Within the span of seven decades from 1564 to 1634, the recorded shipments of coal from the Tyne increased nearly fourteen times over, from 32,952 tons to 452,625 tons.[11] The indications are that shipments of coal from ports on the Firth of Forth expanded almost as rapidly.[12]

Other British industries besides coal mining — for example salt manufacturing, brickmaking, brewing, and metallurgy — were growing as never before.[13] Plain glass for ordinary windowpanes first came into widespread use in southern England during Elizabeth's reign. In 1608 Thomas Coryat, a parson's son from Somerset, made his way all about the Continent, and was surprised to find as he moved south in France that in good houses many of the windows were covered entirely with paper, and that glass was put only in the upper portion even in the most pretentious residences in the rich town of Lyons, with its financial barons versed in the latest banking practices.[14] Plain glass, a mark of substantial new comfort, was moving south from England as, to Coryat's astonishment, the fork, a symbol of new table manners, moved north from Italy. He had never seen the delicate little two-pronged instrument in his native land.

Coal was coming to serve increasingly the British manufacturers of salt, bricks, and even beer. At about the time of Coryat's travels the English discovered how, by means of covered crucibles, to separate the materials for making glass from direct contact with the flames in the furnaces.[15] This enabled them to substitute coal for wood as fuel in glassmaking. Had they been equally successful in finding a satisfactory method of smelting ores with coal, metal production might have grown as rapidly as coal production during the seventeenth century.

As it was, the output of iron in England apparently increased some five- or sixfold from 1540 to 1620,[16] when the shortage of timber had led in some places to a rationing of tree cutting.[17] The discovery in

Somerset in the 1560's of calamine, the ore of zinc, hitherto little known in Great Britain, led to the first development of brass-making there, and helped to bring about a remarkable expansion in the mining and smelting of copper ore.[18] There was also a rapid increase in the smelting of lead ore, which required less fuel than iron or copper.[19] While the progress of copper as well as of iron production was arrested early in the seventeenth century by the increasing shortage of wood for fuel, and while the lead-making industry also suffered from the shortage, the manufacture of metal commodities continued to expand because of a rapid increase after 1620 in the imports of iron and copper from Sweden.[20]

Machinery, driven by horse and water power, and large-scale industrial enterprise under the control of private capitalists, made more remarkable progress than ever before in any European country. Hammers weighing two hundred pounds and more, moved mechanically by the force of water falling on overshot wheels, smote the metal in the furnaces and forges. In once quiet valleys these hammers caused a commotion of sound which travelers, like Camden (1551–1623), the historian, called a bedlam, because the noise resembled the cries of lunatics in the London asylum. Four-wheeled, horse-drawn coaches were introduced to move about the island of Great Britain and alarm the foot travelers by the clouds of dust which they raised and by the dead or mutilated bodies which they sometimes left behind as they dashed ahead like modern motorists. Along narrow causeways of stones many trains of pack horses — laden with bags of coal, wool, or cloth — were conducted by mounted boys, who rang bells as they turned hilly corners to warn other trains approaching in the opposite direction. Herds of cattle, some brought in boats from Ireland, were driven along old roads and paths, especially down Watling Street from Chester to London, where they were slaughtered to feed the rapidly growing population. Scores and later hundreds of hoys, many of them three-masted, filled with coal, salt, and cases of sheet glass, set out in large fleets from the mouths of the Tyne and the Wear.

Middlemen multiplied in many trades. In the coal trade, for example, after delivery to the hoys, the coal might pass through the hands of as many as three different dealers before it found its way into the cellars of London householders — first merchants who owned the ships, then woodmongers with large storage yards, and finally retailers in a smaller way of business. Each middleman expected a profit. Combinations were formed to keep up the price; the cartels of the Newcastle "hostman," who owned the collieries near the Tyne, and the rings of the London "woodmongers," who sold it wholesale in the capital, became a public scandal with which the king's Privy Council dealt as best it could but never to the satisfaction of the increasingly numerous consumers. Parts in new industrial enterprises — the collieries, the iron mills, the textile firms — were exchanged, sold, and willed like shares in the new joint-stock companies organized for foreign trade. Merchants found an ever more lucrative business in lending money at interest to straitened landlords and industrialists throughout England and Wales. Lands and industrial plants were mortgaged to obtain the loans. As mortgages were foreclosed for failure to pay debts, as old landed families disposed of their properties to meet their mounting expenses, as crown lands were sold to meet the increasing costs of government, representatives of the rising mercantile classes, who had the means, came into possession of many new lands in every shire. It was from the returns on the investments made by his father — a London "scrivener" or ancestor of the modern banker — that Milton was able to keep himself and his three daughters, while he devoted his time to writing his magnificently brocaded poetry for which there was no such lucrative market as for cloth, coal, money, or credit.

Beginning in the early seventies of the sixteenth century, before Milton was born and before Shakespeare started his career in London, the balance of economic power in Europe had begun to shift from the Continent to England. Between 1570 and 1640 an early "industrial revolution" occurred on the island. For the character of modern civilization in Great Britain, her dominions, and the United States, this "industrial revolution" was no less important than that of the eighteenth century.[21]

In the decade 1631–1640, which preceded the English Civil War, the contrast between the wealth of England and the relative poverty of those parts of continental Europe which had been in the vanguard of economic progress for some six hundred years escaped no discerning observer. Traveling through the length of England and Wales in 1635 with two soldier companions, an army lieutenant commented upon the "remarkable singular Blessings" of the English nation. These were such "as make all Strangers over the whole face of the Universe to gaze and wonder."[22] The first Earl of Clarendon, who was chief adviser to Charles II and Lord Chancellor after the Restoration of 1660, began his history of the great rebellion by describing the extraordinary prosperity of the English people before they fought among themselves in the 1640's. They "enjoyed . . . the fullest measure of felicity, that any people in any age, for so long time together, have been blessed with." They were "the wonder and envy of all the parts of Christendom."[23]

In the United Provinces the expansion of industry was nearly as rapid as in England, after the successful resistance of the Dutch in the 1580's to the attempts of the Spaniards to conquer them. The output of cloth at Leiden increased some fourfold in thirty-five years, from 26,620 pieces in 1584 to 109,560 pieces in 1619,[24] two years after the ten-year-old Rembrandt had left this town of his birth for Amsterdam. Leiden was swelled correspondingly with people who crowded looms and dyeing vats into newly built houses. Hollanders became the great carriers in the growing commerce by sea between the countries of northern Europe. Shipbuilding and the auxiliary manufactures to provide anchors, sails, and ropes, grew almost as fast in Holland from 1580 to 1640 as did coal mining in Great Britain.

Under the direction of a fabulously successful Calvinist capitalist, Louis de Geer, with his headquarters at Amsterdam, iron and copper metallurgy developed at an even more rapid rate in Sweden than in England. Swedish iron exports increased more than tenfold, from some 1600 tons in 1548 to approximately 5000 tons annually in the early 1620's and then to some 20,000 tons in the early 1650's.[25] Swedish copper exports increased from 100 tons in 1548 to 2,600 tons in 1650.[26] For the first time Sweden was entering fully into the framework of Western economic civilization. Roads were improved. The bank of Stockholm imitated the bank of Amsterdam. Swedish ships were sent out, after the example of the English, the Dutch, and the French, to establish colonies along the Atlantic coast of North America.[27]

De Geer developed the Swedish metallurgical industry with the help of experts whom he brought to Sweden from Liége, the land of his birth. That little state at a great bend in the river Meuse formed a kind of bridge between the Low Countries of the north, which escaped Spanish domination, and those of the south, which were forced to submit. An independent principality of the ancient Empire, governed by a prince-bishop, Liége was perhaps the most progressive region in Europe for mining and metallurgy during the first sixty years of the sixteenth century. Again in the first half of the seventeenth century there was a revival in the prosperity of metallurgy, not only at Liége but in the open country of Hainaut and Namurois and in the regions of Vervins and Chimay.[28] Nevertheless, this improvement was not accompanied by any restoration of prosperity in the towns of the Spanish Netherlands. Urban industry suffered the same fate there as in Spain and central Europe.[29]

In the 1620's and 1630's the borderland separating unprecedented prosperity from poverty lay between the lower Rhine and the lower Meuse, as these large rivers turn and flow parallel to each other straight west to the sea, cutting the Low Countries into two parts. North of the Rhine all was busy commercial and industrial activity. South of the Meuse cities and towns had lost more than half their inhabitants since the mid-sixteenth century. In 1627 one of the most widely traveled observers of the age, the Abbé Scaglia, who undertook delicate diplomatic missions for the Spanish king, Philip IV, described the contrasts as he traveled from Brussels into Holland. "I have come on to Amsterdam where I now am," he wrote, "and [I] find all the [Dutch] towns as full of people as those held by Spain are empty, and on my way from one to the other of these [Dutch] towns which lie two or three leagues apart, I met such throngs of people that there are not as many carriages in the streets of Rome as there are carts here crowded with passengers, whilst the canals which run through the country in every direction are covered with . . . numberless vessels." [30]

The block of countries along the northern seas — Great Britain, the United Provinces, Sweden, and Denmark — had become for the first time in history the hub of European commercial and financial activity, the storehouse of coal and metal, the home of ships, the chief center of heavy industry. Their combined population had probably risen from some six to some ten or eleven millions. More rapid still was the growth of the industrial population, and of wageworkers in particular, especially in England. Never before had so large a proportion of the inhabitants of any nation earned a living in specially built establishments for mining and manufacturing, financed by private capitalists who took no part in the manual labor, and who made their business decisions independent of governmental authority, lay and ecclesiastical. In the use of water power and horse power for driving machinery at mines and small factories, England had come to lead the world. For the first time in history coal was consumed in large quantities. The annual output in Great Britain already approached two million tons in the decade 1631–1640, while the rest of the world combined probably produced less than one-fifth as much. A leadership in heavy industry under the control of private capital, which Great Britain was not to relinquish until the late nineteenth century, dates from the age of Elizabeth and her first two Stuart successors, James I and Charles I. Both the emergence and the eclipse of Great Britain as the leading industrial power of the world have been closely related to the use made of the coal resources of the island.

How, and how far, can these contrasts in the course of economic development in three parts of Europe between 1540 and 1640 be ex-

plained by military history? How, and how far, can contrasts in the
military history of these same three parts of Europe be understood in
terms of economic history? What in particular had war and peace to
do with the genesis of industrial civilization, marked by the early
English "industrial revolution" which prepared the way for the eventual
industrialization of the world? The five chapters that follow this one
aim to supply tentative answers to these questions.

The answers have to be sought, to no small extent, outside both
economic and military history, as these subjects are usually understood. Governments were growing more despotic during the late fifteenth and early sixteenth centuries. The rulers, lay and ecclesiastical,
of the many states into which Europe was divided were taking an
increasingly active part in regulating and even in operating industrial
enterprises, and in raising revenue at the expense of the third estate,
which consisted of merchants and industrialists of some means, along
with all the privileged classes of society other than the clergy and the
nobility. The subsequent course of events from 1540 to 1640 shows
that these economic policies met with considerable success in France,
where the power of the crown to tax the third estate, to regulate and
to participate in industrial enterprise grew stronger than ever during
the seventeenth century after the worst phases of the French religious
wars had ended. In England the attempts of the crown to exercise
similar authority were much less successful. During the reigns of
James I and Charles I, from 1603 to 1642, the policies of industrial
regulation and direct taxation of property practically broke down because of the resistance of leading English merchants and industrialists.
They used their growing influence as justices of the peace, as municipal
officials, and as members of the House of Commons to defeat policies
which seemed unfavorable to their interests. The inability of the Stuart
kings and their privy councils to enforce unwelcome proclamations,
orders, and other regulations which were issued without the support
of Parliament, gave the English merchants and industrialists advantages
over the French in developing heavy industry. A weakening of effective
administrative control over economic life facilitated the early English
"industrial revolution." [31]

It is equally clear that Henry VIII's break with Rome (followed
soon by the dissolution of the monasteries and other religious gilds)
and the resulting reduction in the number and wealth of the clergy,
provided conditions which were favorable to industrial expansion on
the eve of the Elizabethan age, long before the constitutional struggle
became acute. The proportion of the national income required to maintain ecclesiastical foundations was much smaller in England after the
dissolutions of 1536 and 1539 than it had been for some eight hundred

years. This was by no means true of the countries which remained
Roman Catholic. In France the clergy retained their hold over property
and remained as numerous as ever. In Spain and the Spanish Netherlands the combined number of priests, monks, and nuns increased.

The partial dispossession of the clergy in England (and in other
Protestant countries — Sweden, Denmark, Scotland, and Holland in
particular) made it easier than during the Middle Ages for private
businessmen to get possession of land and mineral resources on advantageous terms. Fewer opportunities were presented for a priestly
life; almost none for monastic contemplation. While ecclesiastical
foundations had exploited the natural wealth of their estates during
the Middle Ages, the nature of the religious offices of priests and monks
was not likely to encourage ingenuity and drive in developing new
means of working coal and ores at greater depths. By reducing the
number of the religious, the Reformation released human intelligence
and human energy for the single-minded pursuit of profit and the
earning of wages by the production and distribution of useful commodities — coal, bricks, metalwares, and clothing of all kinds from
hats to shoes. In these ways, as well as by the encouragement which it
gave businessmen and industrial workers to better their station, the
Reformation fostered industrial progress in Great Britain and also in
Sweden, Denmark, Scotland, and Holland. In all these countries the
government deprived the Roman Catholic ecclesiastical foundations
of rights which they continued to possess in those German states and
Swiss cantons which retained the ancient worship.

While constitutional and ecclesiastical history help to explain the
prosperity of northern Europe during the hundred years following the
Reformation, taken together they fall far short of providing the explanation of this prosperity. How were they related in their economic
influences to the history of war, whose place in the rise of industrial
civilization since the discovery of America is the subject of this book?

The most elementary acquaintance with Europe in early modern
times indicates that war and religion were not kept in closed compartments. Disputes concerning the terms on which eternal life in Christ
is to be attained were among the principal causes for the religious wars
between Europeans from 1562, when the Huguenots fell to fighting
with the Catholics in France, until 1648, when the Peace of Westphalia
brought an end to the most destructive of all these wars — the Thirty
Years' War.[32]

As religious disputes were a potent cause for war, it is not surprising
that on some occasions the forms of worship were determined, at least
temporarily, by the results of war. In varying degrees, all sides in the

armed religious struggles aimed either to extend or to maintain by force their conceptions of religion. Although no side managed to conquer the others, although force failed in the end to settle religious controversy, as it has always failed to decide any important issue of belief, the battles, the auto-da-fé, together with the threats of torture and of burnings, were naturally not without influence upon the religious avowals of men and women. Unusually strong convictions or an unusually powerful conscience, combined with physical heroism, are required in order to avoid outward conformity to orders which are backed up inexorably by prison, torture, and death. When the Austrians invaded the Engadine early in the Thirty Years' War, they saw to it that the local Swiss population adhered to Roman Catholicism. Then in 1633, after the Austrians were driven out by the French under a former Huguenot leader named Rohan, who had fought earlier in the religious wars of southern France, the outward forms of religion completely changed. Everyone was expected to attend Protestant worship. Not a single Catholic was to be found either in the Prätigau or at Davos. In the Lower Engadine the number of Roman communicants fell from 6000 to 280! [33]

If, then, we are concerned with the relations between military and industrial history, we have to recognize that the religious dissensions had a strong influence upon the wars fought during the century following the Reformation. We have to recognize also that the course of military events influenced religious and ecclesiastical history. By itself and without its relations to the entire story of an epoch, war can no more be properly the subject of history than economic development.

It is no less unhistorical to keep military history separate from the history of political authority than to keep either separate from ecclesiastical history. During the sixteenth and early seventeenth centuries the Christian religion had a strong hold upon statesmen and upon legislative, administrative, and judicial officers. Ecclesiastical foundations (ranging in scope from a small monastery to the papacy) exercised political authority — legislative, administrative, and judicial.

Authority is a source both of strength and of weakness. Its possessors are almost always concerned over the precarious nature of their possession, for authority is no less at the mercy of circumstance than is the worldly wealth of an individual. Just as the inordinate pursuit of wealth makes for the insecurity of wealth, so the inordinate pursuit of political authority makes for the insecurity of that authority. As the political rulers of Europe grew more despotic — especially the kings of Spain, France, and England, the Emperor and the Pope — the ever stronger, yet ever more ephemeral, quest for power increased their thirst for larger territorial dominions. They sought to acquire more territory at the expense of one another and still more at the expense of the small and weak sovereign states which abounded in Europe at the close of the Middle Ages. Conquests of these small states — especially those of Italy — were not unopposed. A determination arose among many Italians to expel the invaders. This found its most famous expression in Machiavelli's celebrated book, *The Prince*. Like the growing dissension concerning the true nature of the Christian faith, the growing despotism of European governments increased the motives for war.

It is even clearer that military history influenced constitutional history. The wars of the sixteenth and early seventeenth centuries imposed large financial burdens on the states of Europe. These burdens were heaviest among the states which engaged most extensively in the wars. The cost of maintaining soldiers is no more economically constructive than that of maintaining priests, monks, and nuns. Soldiers — fighting, pillaging, and destroying — do not add to the national dividend of consumable goods any more than do architects, artists, craftsmen, and unskilled laborers employed in building, repairing, and decorating cathedrals and churches.

The dissipation of energies in fighting and in preparations for fighting, partly for religious motives, encouraged despotic government, partly because war brought with it increasing state interference with the fortunes and the private initiative of industrial adventurers and traders. If the French crown was more successful than the English in enforcing its policy of direct taxation, in regulating and even participating in economic enterprise, this was partly because France was more heavily engaged in war. In Western history war has always made it necessary, to a lesser or greater extent, for the governments which wage it to control or seize the sources of trade and production. It has become almost a historical truism that the French religious wars helped to make possible the absolute rule of the Bourbon monarchs, the first of whom was Henry of Navarre who came to the throne in 1589 as Henry IV. After the anarchy of thirty years of civil conflict, the people longed for order. Absolute government seemed a small price to pay for it, especially with so conciliatory, so sympathetic, and so witty a prince, whose flexibility in the matter of religion enabled him to rejoin the church of his fathers and yet to make a gesture, by the edict of Nantes in 1598, of protecting the Huguenots, with whose cause he had been associated in his earlier years.

It would be obviously unrealistic to consider military history, any more than religious, constitutional, or industrial history, as a separate entity. The same is true — as we try to show in later chapters — of the history of invention, of science, and of art. The tripartite division of European industrial history from 1540 to 1640 can be understood only in terms of the entire history of the age. It is important to insist on this, because military history from 1494 to 1640, in its broad outlines, might seem almost to explain by itself the remarkable differences between the economic fortunes of the various European countries.

The general prosperity which characterized most of continental Europe at the close of the Middle Ages was first interrupted in Italy early in the sixteenth century, when the Italian peninsula became the principal battleground for the great powers of Europe.[34] Charles V and Francis I, king of France from 1515 to 1547, kept up an intermittent struggle in the small Italian states for political power and for the political support of the papacy. For five decades much of the serious fighting among European armies was on Italian soil. Then, by the middle of the sixteenth century the scene of the worst battles began to shift over the Alps. Religion was replacing politics as the major cause for wars, and religious dissension was much more serious in central Europe, France, and the Low Countries than in Italy. Italy recovered a considerable prosperity after the mid-sixteenth century, when fighting grew fiercer and more continuous almost everywhere on the Continent except in the Italian and the Spanish peninsulas, the two bastions of the ancient Roman Catholic Church. During the long religious wars, which broke out in the 1560's in France and the Low Countries, all the continental countries, large and small, suffered heavily from the fighting. Spain, though not much invaded, was continually engaged. Many more Spanish than Italian soldiers battled for the Pope outside their native lands. Among the countries least affected by the fighting were Italy, Switzerland, and also France after the establishment of the Bourbon dynasty in 1589 — in short those parts of continental Europe which more than held their own industrially between 1540 and 1640. War was most frequent and devastating in the countries of the Spanish Netherlands and central Europe. These countries — Belgium, Austria, Bohemia, and most of Germany — had been in the flood of industrial progress at the time of the Reformation; when the wars of religion came to an end in the middle of the seventeenth century, all of them were in an industrial backwater.

The most impressive of the contrasts in the military history of this early modern era were those between the Continent and England. The hundred years from 1540 to 1640 formed a century of almost uninterrupted warfare for continental Europe. The only comparatively peaceful decade was from 1609 to 1618, when a truce was declared in Spain's long struggle to conquer the Low Countries. Only four years — 1548, 1549, 1550, and 1610 — were without organized fighting on the Continent or in the Mediterranean.[35] During long stretches of time few men in the leading countries — in France and the Spanish Netherlands, in Germany and the rest of central Europe — trusted their neighbors or even their relatives. For suspicion and hatred, devastation and hardship, there was to be nothing like it again until the twentieth century.

To the amazement of Philip IV, who reigned in Spain from 1621 to 1665, the Spanish authorities in the Netherlands chose the great Flemish painter Rubens as one of the diplomats to negotiate with England for a cessation of the sporadic naval battles fought from 1626 to 1630 between Spain and France on one side and England on the other. Rubens was friend and trusted servant of the Infanta Isabella, Philip IV's aunt and the widow of the Archduke Albert, who had helped her to govern the Netherlands for Spain. The artist's aim was the pacification and general unification of Europe.[36] His missions and his advice seem to have had some influence in holding back Spain from attempting under Philip IV any serious naval attack on England.

When Rubens crossed the Channel and visited London, he found what seemed to him a rich and luxurious people. He found them, as he expressed it, "in the very depths of peace."[37] He seems to have forgotten that he was actually in London on behalf of a power with whom England was at war! The naval encounter with France and Spain was not really war for most of Rubens' hosts. But it was the only kind of war that England knew for more than two generations. While the continental fields, hillsides, and towns were continually overrun and ravaged by armies — marching, camping, and fighting — peace ruled within the island of Great Britain.

In his *Sidelights on the Thirty Years' War*, Hubert Reade, an enterprising researcher in archives, summed up England's position in the fighting of a destructive age. For seventy years, "between 1569 when Elizabeth reduced the Catholic North to obedience forever, and 1639, when the Covenanters of Scotland forced their way across the Tweed, scarce a shot, if we except the Spanish raid upon Newlyn, was fired in anger upon English ground." The professional political historian might object that plots to restore the Roman Catholic communion did not end with 1569. The historian of crime could point to many murders and much highway robbery in an age when men and women were well aware of an underworld of rogues and vagabonds.[38] Total peace has hardly ever existed on this planet and even England was much farther from total peace under Elizabeth and James I than under Victoria. Yet it cannot be denied that the contrasts, which Reade emphasized, between English and continental history were real.

British isolation from European war was in some ways more pronounced than American isolation in the less warlike period of the nineteenth century. While English and Scottish leaders could not remain indifferent to the outcome of the religious and political struggles on the Continent, the people generally heard much less about the actual battles that were taking place in Europe than Americans heard about the Crimean War or the wars fought by Prussia against Denmark, Austria, and France between 1864 and 1871. There were no newspapers to report engagements at sea or to send correspondents to describe in 1586 the death of a fine poet, Sir Philip Sidney, in the battle of Zutphen in the Netherlands, or the unsuccessful attempt of the Duke of Buckingham, in 1627, to relieve the Isle of Rhé, off La Rochelle, held by French Protestants. Knowledge of such exploits on foreign soil filtered through only slowly to the thriving English towns. Some villages never heard of them.

In the early sixteenth century the English had been invariably described, whether by friend or foe, as "the fiercest people in all Europe." Benvenuto Cellini (1500–1571), out of his Italian experience which was hardly devoid of violence, called them "wild beasts." [39] During the last half of the sixteenth century they became increasingly pacific in their outlook and habits, until they had less relish for fighting than any of the continentals.[40] In the Elizabethan age, and even more in the reign of James I, businessmen in England were able to devote themselves to the pursuit of economic gain with fewer distractions, either religious or political, than ever before in English history. In 1627, two years after the death of James I, Sir Edward Cecil, Viscount Wimbledon, long a colonel of an English regiment in the Dutch service, jotted down the relative advantages to the English of relieving the Huguenot garrison of La Rochelle, which Richelieu was attacking. An ardent military man who had recently raided Cadiz, Wimbledon made no attempt to conceal his enthusiasm for getting the English more actively engaged in fighting, nor his contempt for their slothful materialistic habits which he attributed, without hesitation, to the long years "without the practise and knowledge of warr. And that peace hath soe beesotted us," he added, "that as wee are altogither ignorant, soe are wee soe much the more, as not sensible of that defect, ffor wee thinke if wee have men and shipps our kingdome is safe." [41]

Except for the defeat of the Spanish Armada in 1588, English men-of-war and armed merchantmen took part in no vital naval battles between 1558 and 1640. To the satisfaction of the two unwarlike sovereigns, Elizabeth and James I, the Spanish proverb, "Peace with England and war with all beside," was almost a literal description of the foreign relations of the great powers of Europe.[42] While eight wars raged on the Continent, the English farmed, mined, manufactured, and traded peacefully. For generations the intoxication of the English with peace, which worried Lord Wimbledon, served Great Britain well.

CHAPTER TWO

Invention and Firearms

· WITHOUT THE EXTRAORDINARY TECHNOLOGICAL PROGRESS OF THE past four centuries, the triumph of large-scale industry would have been impossible. So would have been the progress of large-scale war. The Renaissance, in its later phases, beginning in the mid-fifteenth century at the end of the Hundred Years' War, and the spread of the reformed religions during the hundred years following 1540 were accompanied by many important industrial inventions. The printing press; the blast furnace; the furnace for separating silver from argentiferous copper ore with the help of lead; boring rods for discovering the nature of underground strata; powerful horse- and water-driven engines for draining mines; railed ways with large horse-drawn wagons for carrying coal; the stocking-knitting frame; the so-called "Dutch" or "engine" loom for weaving ribbons, garters, tape, and other small wares; new furnaces permitting the use of coal instead of wood in glassmaking, steelmaking, and brickmaking; coke for drying malt; sheathing of the planks of ships with thin sheets of lead to cheat the ravages of worms — these are only a few examples of European inventions between 1440 and 1640. These technological improvements played an essential part in the early English "industrial revolution" [1] of the late sixteenth and early seventeenth centuries. They cheapened the costs of production and so made feasible the production of coal, glass, metal, and many other commodities in much larger quantities than ever before. They were preceded and accompanied by other technological developments which made possible, after the fifteenth century, the general use in war of novel weapons based on gunpowder. To what extent was the ingenuity which went into productive inventions, a by-product of the ingenuity which went into destructive ones? How far and in what sense was the invention of firearms and explosives a necessary part of the historical process that led eventually to the industrial civilization of the twentieth century?

(1) *The Revolution in the Art of War*

The invasion of Italy in 1494–95 by the young French king, Charles VIII, was a turning point in the kinds of weapons upon which captains of armies and navies depended for victory. The French assembled for the first time numerous trains of horse-drawn artillery, mostly of shining bronze, about eight feet in length.[2]

This artillery was prepared, in part at least, during the reign of Charles VIII's father, Louis XI (1461–1483), who was the first king to provide a number of readily movable cannon of the new type.[3] From 1482 to 1492, in Charles' youth, the Spaniards had made some use of artillery in the wars which their rulers, Ferdinand and Isabella, had waged to drive the Moors back into Africa. But this Spanish ordnance was far more clumsy in construction than that which Charles VIII put into execution. Made of iron bars two inches in breadth and held together by iron bolts and rings, the Spanish guns were incapable of either horizontal or vertical movement. They hurled mostly balls of heavy marble, and these, while deadly and destructive enough at the spot they hit, were too expensive to supply and too difficult to aim, to be effective against moving troops on a field of battle.[4]

Just before Charles' army, with its new guns, tramped and rode over the Alpine passes into Italy, a large French warship (commanded by the Duke of Orléans, the king's cousin and future successor as Louis XII) was fitted out with the new cannon and sent as part of a fleet to the Italian coast near Genoa. There King Alfonso of Naples, the eldest son of Ferdinand and Isabella, had dispatched an army. The guns protruding from the French warship at Spezzia and Rapallo alarmed the enemy, for their like had never been seen in Italy. In the shadow of these cannon, the French landed troops at Rapallo. There on September 5, 1494, they won a skirmish with King Alfonso's forces, which included a number of Swiss mercenaries.[5] A year later, in 1495, as the main French army was returning home after its long, unopposed march to Naples, a battle was fought at Fornovo, some ten miles southwest of Parma between Florence and Milan. As the French successfully met their Italian opponents commanded by Rudolf di Gonzaga, uncle of the Marquis of Mantua, the new guns began to shoot on land against fellow Christians. The terror which they spread resulted more from the noise they made than from the damage they caused. According to Comines, the great historian who accompanied Charles VIII, only ten men were killed by the artillery.[6] Yet the battle portended the shooting wars which were to follow. Twenty years afterwards, at Marignano, the French cannon actually killed and wounded a substantial proportion of the enemies' best soldiers.

After Fornovo the tempo of technical innovation in weapons increased. This, combined with the multiplication of the new weapons, continually upset the calculations of captains in the field. In almost every campaign they were confronted with enemy armies whose equipment and tactics were novel. It was up to them to outwit their opponents in the range and violence of their own instruments of war.[7]

The changes in the weapons used were the result in large measure of the ingenuity of men who died before the slaughter with gunpowder began. How was this ingenuity aroused, how was it turned in destructive directions?

The basic discoveries and inventions behind the change in the character of war were gunpowder and firearms of various kinds, first of all cannon. Roger Bacon wrote of gunpowder as early as 1248.[8] Albertus Magnus had heard of it before his death in 1280. How they had come by their knowledge is uncertain. Apparently they did not derive it from the Chinese, the Arabs, or even the Hindus, though these peoples seem to have known of the explosive properties of gunpowder. Saltpeter is the essential element in its manufacture, and in Europe saltpeter is said to have been first differentiated from other salts during the second quarter of the thirteenth century.[9] Scholars have hardly proved that saltpeter had no earlier history, but they have proved that both saltpeter and gunpowder had a history during the thirteenth century.

In that age philosophy was based on Christian theological foundations and it comprehended the whole of knowledge. Among the famous learned men Roger Bacon and Albertus Magnus were perhaps the most interested in the study of natural phenomena — in science in the modern English sense of that word. Both seem to have had an extensive knowledge of mineral substances and of industrial processes in which these substances were used. Both lectured at the University of Paris during the reign of the saintly Louis IX (1236–1270), when the university became the first and perhaps the only true institute of wisdom in Western history. Both gave to and took from this common fount at a time when learned Europeans were filled with a confidence in the intellect that their descendants were hardly to have again until the great renewal of intellectual inquiry during the late fifteenth century.

The reign of Louis IX was one of those rare periods in European history when wars among the Christian peoples of the West were few and moderate. Early in his reign, in 1240, the terror engendered by the approach of the armies of the Great Khan had united the whole of Germany against the East.[10] The French king was the motivating spirit in the last two of the eight crusades to provide pilgrims' progresses toward Christ's sepulcher, and to reclaim the sacred objects of the Holy Land from the Mohammedan infidel — the crusades of 1248–1254 and 1270. In his final crusade, Louis died of disease in Carthage. The crusades, which had begun at the end of the eleventh century, diverted the fighting instincts of the European knights overseas. These holy wars emphasized the highly imperfect, but existent, solidarity of the Christian West. They were the only wars in which there was even the pretense that the Western European states acted as a unit. However nationalistic and selfish were the armed forces which undertook the last two crusades, and however political the papacy was becoming in its motives for supporting these armed pilgrimages, Louis IX was the embodiment of this universal Christian spirit.[11]

Six centuries later, at the time of the Congress of Vienna in 1814, when the Count of Saint-Simon sought to establish permanent peace, he drew a lesson from the Middle Ages and from the thirteenth century in particular. In spite of his own confidence in the future benefits to man of industrial progress, in spite of what he called "the superb distrust we affect for the Middle Ages," Saint-Simon saw that the conception of European spiritual unity, which prevailed in the era of the crusades and which was expressed through imperial and especially papal authority, had made it possible for the political system of Europe to rest on its true base, on a superstructure transcending all particular boundaries, spiritual and territorial. As long as allegiance to the sovereign principle of religious unity and universal government subsisted, wrote Saint-Simon, "there were few wars in Europe and these wars had little importance." [12]

It was during those relatively peaceful times for Western Europe, during the age of the crusades, that gunpowder was discovered. Notwithstanding the views of modern authorities, a tradition lingers that it was used in the twelfth century to blast through stone encountered at the lead and silver mines of the Rammelsberg in the Hartz Mountains of Germany.[13] Whether or not that is true, the "invention" had clearly nothing to do with war. Robert Boyle, whose historical knowledge was considerable, wrote of the "antipathy between salt-petre and brimstone," which causes an explosion, as "a casual discovery — giving an occasional rise to the invention of gunpowder." [14] Until metallic tubes were devised through which the explosive could drive projectiles, gunpowder could be used for no more destructive purpose than to shatter the rocks which increasingly hindered the European miners during the rapid development of mining in the late twelfth and thirteenth centuries. It was not for at least two generations after the first firmly established references to gunpowder, possibly not until 1313, that we have firmly established references to cannon.[15] In the thirteenth century the pressure to exploit gunpowder for military purposes could not have been great, even with the motives which the crusades provided for more powerful weapons. The Church was ready to sanction against Mohammedans the use of what were considered weapons unfit for Christian fighting; for example, the crossbow, whose use among Christians was contrary to papal enactment. But it was after the crusades were over that guns were invented. While the crusades gave an impetus to the manufacture of military equipment, the movement was more in the direction of improving old weapons than of introducing new ones.[16] In Europe great advances were made in the building of fortifications; there were no comparable advances in offensive weapons.

Saltpeter and gunpowder appear in Western history as by-products of remarkable general progress in knowledge for peaceful purposes. As we know, the thirteenth century was especially rich in creative thought and in art. It was also rich in new knowledge of the properties of nature and many remarkable technical improvements were made in connection with industry and transport. Some of these improvements had their origins in the twelfth and even in the eleventh centuries. Machinery driven by the wind or by moving water, more efficient kilns and furnaces, more powerful bellows, reduced the costs of manufacturing. Improved harnesses and stronger breeds of horses reduced the cost of hauling stone and ore. The primary interest of Europeans during the twelfth and thirteenth centuries in the use of newly discovered substances and new technical processes was in the service of peaceful building. The Europeans were also seeking to advance the practice of medicine and surgery (in which at this time the Europeans began to go beyond the ancients) or to perfect the sport of falconry (about which one of the most warlike among the powerful rulers of the age, the Emperor Frederick II of Hohenstaufen, wrote a remarkable treatise).

Tin and copper ore liquefy at a lower temperature than iron ore, and the foundry, where the liquid hardens in prepared molds in the ground, was first employed for casting bronze. A method of running liquid bronze into church bells was described at the end of the eleventh century by a German Benedictine monk named Theophilus,[17] a younger contemporary of the founder of scholastic philosophy, Saint Anselm of Canterbury.

During the great age of cathedral and church building that followed in the twelfth and thirteenth centuries, the bronze foundry produced a large number of these beautiful sounding instruments in all the European countries. The term "bell-metal" became a synonym for bronze, and this suggests that the original, and long the principal, use of bronze was in bell casting. Then, at the beginning of the fourteenth century, at the time Dante wrote the *Divine Comedy*, when the Western peoples became increasingly disposed to war upon one another, it was discovered that the method of casting bells would lend itself with comparatively little change to the casting of guns. Liquid metal derived from tin and copper ore was run into the form of a hollow cylinder to make the first bronze cannon. The early founders, whose task had been to fashion bells which tolled the message of eternal peace from Sweden and Poland to Spain, and from Ireland to the Balkans, contributed unintentionally to the discovery of one of man's most terrible weapons.[18]

These cannon were expensive to make. They were either so small and weakly built that they caused little damage, or they were so cumbersome to move as to be of no practical use except in battering down buildings and weak fortifications after complete victories had been won in the field. Without any knowledge of gunpowder, the ancient Mediterranean peoples of the Hellenistic and Imperial Roman periods had become masters of siege-engines capable of hurling stones and other heavy missiles of hard wood. A skillful combination of lever, balance, steelyard, winch, roller, inclined plane, capstan, and so forth — combined with the practical application of geometrical principles — had enabled the ancient peoples by their ingenuity and careful calculations to achieve remarkable results.[19] Their most destructive engines had been more effective than were medieval cannon. Even in the early seventeenth century, when cannon had been much improved and had come into widespread use, there were some Europeans who doubted, perhaps mistakenly, whether European artillery could defend forts more effectively than the classical engines. These, it was said, had been capable in their day, without gunpowder, of heaving stones and long pieces of timber which sank ships and carried some men's heads off their shoulders. Sir Walter Raleigh gave it as his opinion that, in defending Syracuse against the Romans, Archimedes "had framed such engines of war as . . . did more mischief than could have been wrought by the cannon or any instruments of gunpowder, had they in that age been known."[20]

However that may be, cannon were used very sparingly through the period of the Hundred Years' War, from the mid-fourteenth to the mid-fifteenth century. Hand guns, while used at least as early as 1364, were little more than clumsy tubes stuck on the end of a stick. In tapestries and other works of art of the fifteenth century, they are difficult to distinguish from firebrands. They lacked precision of aim, took an intolerably long time to load, and were no match for either the crossbow or the longbow. In close combat they could serve only as clubs.[21]

Arrows remained the most common projectiles throughout the period of the Hundred Years' War. The success in 1415 at Agincourt of Henry V's English archers, who stopped the charging French knights, was achieved with the help of a newly devised arrow, so forged that it could go through the small space between the loops in the combination of mail and plate armor still worn by many knights. After Agincourt the increasing use of full plate armor, introduced much earlier and first extensively used in Italy and Germany,[22] made arrows less and less effective against an offensive of charging knights. Plate armor was even fashioned to protect the breasts, the faces, and the front legs of their thoroughbred mounts. The mounted knight had gained the ascendancy over foot soldiers on European battlefields more than four hundred years before, and it was the superior striking power of the thoroughbred horse, achieved earlier on the Continent than in England, which had enabled William of Normandy to conquer England in 1066,[23] the only serious invasion of the island during the past nine hundred years. As suits of full plate armor came into wider use than ever before during the fifteenth century, and the mounted knights were better protected, it seemed that they would retain their ascendancy.

In his massive and careful work on the history of the art of war, published as a series of volumes early in the twentieth century, Hans Delbrück, the most learned German student of the subject, showed that firearms had no serious influence on the issues of battles before the last quarter of the fifteenth century.[24] If gunpowder was to have a decisive effect in determining a closely contested action, it was necessary to produce cannon which were much more mobile and many times more numerous than those in use before the late fifteenth century. That was done between 1494 and 1529 partly by mounting cannon on horse-drawn gun carriages, partly by the construction both of lighter artillery (culverins, sakers, falcons, and falconets) and of small firearms (merlons, hand arquebuses, muskets, and pistols) which were given to both the infantry and the cavalry. Firearms were also made more effective in the late fifteenth century by the introduction of granulated gunpowder, which exploded with more violence than the fine dust previously used.[25] Balls of iron were fired out of the cannon, though lead was used for smaller missiles. Then, in order to do even greater mischief, to tear the flesh of many soldiers at one swoop, hollow iron balls filled with gunpowder were introduced. These shells exploded on the targets and so struck many blows at a time. Sometimes explosive balls were made also for smaller pieces than cannon — for arquebuses and even for pistols. Writing in the 1530's Biringuccio, an Italian master craftsman in metal and an authority on the new weapons, observed that arquebuses and pistols were doing "in battle what the archers used to do, both on foot and on horse." [26]

These and many more developments in weapons based on explosives occurred in rapid succession in the space of a generation following Columbus' discovery of America and the first ascent, in 1492, of what appeared to be an unclimbable needle of rock, the Mont Aiguille near Grenoble.[27] Like the new warfare, both exploits were examples of a fresh spirit of expansion which was at work in many directions. Hernán Cortés followed Columbus to the New World. His use of the improved firearms helps to explain his astonishing conquest of Mexico, from 1519 to 1521, when with a small band of a few hundred men he won easy victories over thousands and even tens of thousands of civilized Indian defenders.[28]

A celebrated statesman of the next generation, Antoine Perrenot de Granvelle (1517–1586), Bishop of Arras and one of the ablest and most influential princes of the Roman Church, made some striking remarks in 1559 about the shattering effects of the new weapons on the older habits of conducting war. He had already served Charles V as secretary of state, and he was about to govern the Netherlands for Charles' son, Philip II, as prime minister to the regent, Philip's half-sister, Margaret of Parma. At the ripe age of forty-two, Granvelle had helped to negotiate with France and England the Treaty of Cateau Cambrésis, which left the French in possession of Calais and deprived the English of their last firm hold of territory in continental Europe, after centuries of fighting to retain or add to the possessions of the English crown in France. The continuous experience with the problems of war and peace made Granvelle one of the most acute observers of his time.

An agent of Queen Elizabeth asked Granvelle whether England could look for help from Spain if the English were to renew their quarrel with France. His reply was discouraging. The whole world, he suggested, knew of England's "weakness." "Your men are hardy and valiant," he said, "but what discipline have they had these many years? and the art of war is now such that men be fain to learn anew at every two years' end." [29]

The weakness on which Granvelle put his finger might have been fatal to a land power; to a wealthy nation surrounded by seas, it could actually become a source of strength, if England refrained from exhausting its military and economic forces on behalf of either side in the continental wars. Granvelle may have failed to see this; if he *had* seen it he was too skillful a diplomat to have helped the English to recognize their advantage. By 1559 England had already increased considerably its output from mines and manufactures since the dissolution of the monasteries some twenty years before. But it was mainly during the three decades following 1559, especially from 1570 to 1588, that the English began to wax exceedingly fat in material possessions. Their resources in ships, guns, and gunpowder increased.

In 1512, eighteen years after the appearance of the new guns on the French warship at Rapallo, cannon first played a dominant role in naval war in a battle between French and English sailing squadrons.[30] After that, maneuvering at sea, like maneuvering on land, changed with the multiplication of firearms. The new guns were mounted on more warships during the later years of Henry VIII's reign (1509–1547)[31] and the royal navy expanded rapidly during the late sixteenth century; both developments helped the English make the most of the opportunities which cannon along the coasts and on warships gave them for holding off an invader. Then, before Queen Elizabeth's death, the obsolete bill and bow were abandoned by the local trained bands, whose preparation for fighting was far from complete, but who were available for defense in each county under the supervision of a lord lieutenant.[32] In 1596 the crown issued instructions that all local forces throughout England should convert billmen into pikemen and bowmen into musketeers.[33] Thus the English "home guard" of footmen and horsemen tardily adopted weapons, muskets and pistols in particular, which the Spaniards had exploited nearly eighty years earlier and which continental infantry and cavalry were coming to use extensively after the middle of the sixteenth century.[34]

If Philip II, who married Elizabeth's predecessor and Roman Catholic half-sister, Mary, had attacked England at once, as Granvelle suggested either France or Spain could have done successfully, Spain might have won. Instead Philip waited thirty years and lost.

The rapid changes in weapons and in methods of warfare, to which Granvelle referred, continued through the eighty years following 1559, as battles were waged more frequently in France and the Low Countries and then, with even greater intensity, all through central Europe. "We see the face of war and the forms of weapons alter almost daily," wrote an English soldier when the Civil War broke out in 1642, "every nation striving to outwit each other in excellency of weapons."[35] Tactics were revolutionized. The mounted knight enveloped in armor and his majestic and stationary counterpart, the fortified castle, with its moat

and its massive walls (some fifteen or twenty feet thick), were unable
to withstand the musket and the cannon.[36] An end was put to the reign
of those stately monuments, slow moving or at rest, representing, as
each had, an exceedingly heavy investment of capital and labor.

Chivalry had long been on the wane,[37] particularly during the
fifteenth century, when men and women outdid themselves in crafty
cruelty and disgusting vices, in cowardly murders, as they had outdone
themselves in the tenth century and were again to outdo themselves in
the twentieth. The new weapons and tactics hastened the destruction
of ancient scruples and conventions concerning combat. War became
less chivalrous and sporting; more bloody and calculating. After the
sixteenth century the knight lingered only in the mysterious world of
the imaginative mind; a lean quixotic figure, created by Cervantes, he
rode about on an emaciated horse, without protection, to tilt at windmills and to capture the fancy of many generations of excited readers.

(2) *The Expansion in Metal Production*

When we consider the "art of war," as contemporaries called it,
which evolved with such remarkable speed after the French invasion
of Italy in 1494, when with the help of contemporary descriptions we
examine the new guns, the new projectiles, and their manufacture, we
are struck by one capital fact. The whole series of developments depended upon a large increase in the supplies of metals, above all copper
and iron.

While armor was of little help in battles after about 1525, it continued to be worn by princes, nobles, and men-at-arms who were not
generally exposed to the hardships of the common soldiers. William
the Silent, the savior of Dutch independence, was wearing armor in
1566, when he rode through the streets of Antwerp to calm the revolt
of the Calvinists, to announce a temporary accord between the local
nobles and the Spaniards, and to utter for the last time the words, "long
live the king." To judge from the armor preserved in museums, no
medieval ruler had more suits than this same king, Philip II, who occupied the Spanish throne from 1556 to 1598. Unlike his father, Charles
V, Philip was seldom active on the field of battle. Armor was immensely
esteemed for show, and it was relinquished by princes and nobles with
reluctance.

More armor was being produced during the early sixteenth century
than ever before. Full armor gave the soldier who wore it and the horse
that carried him an additional burden often as heavy as the man's
body. Even pikemen, billmen, and arquebusiers, who fought on foot,
wore half armor.[1] With the growth of armies and the increase in fight-

ing, the demand for the extensive and expensive metal needed to fashion a suit increased, at the very time when there arose a great new demand for metal to make firearms and missiles.

Biringuccio's account of the manufacture of guns, written about 1535, shows that even after many efforts to make cannon lighter and cheaper, between three and four tons of bronze still went into one of the largest pieces.[2] No appreciable reduction was effected in the weight of artillery during the hundred years that followed. Copper was the principal ingredient in the bronze. In addition the gun carriages, though of wood, were armored with bands of iron, especially the great wheels. They had heavy iron bolts, a chain, and a stout iron hook above the axle to help hold the cannon from slipping downhill. All told, the iron in one of these gun carriages was almost as heavy as the bronze in the gun itself. The iron parts of the carriage weighed rather more than two tons — between 4500 and 5000 pounds.[3]

Some of these large cannon fired cast-iron balls almost as large as a man's head, and there were actually occasions when these monstrous missiles took some poor creature's head off his shoulders before he had time to cry for God's mercy. In 1582 Philip II's famous general — and through the Duchess Margaret his nephew — Alexander Farnese, Duke of Parma (1545–1592), was besieging Oudenarde. West of Brussels on the Schelde, Oudenarde was a place of considerable military importance, then held by the Protestant forces in the Low Countries. One day in early spring Farnese had a table laid for himself and his staff, to dine in the open air near to the entrenchment. "Hardly had the repast commenced, when a ball came flying over the table, taking off the head of a young Walloon officer who was sitting near Parma . . . A portion of his skull struck out the eye of another gentleman present. A second ball . . . destroyed two more of the guests as they sat at the banquet . . . The blood and brains of these unfortunate individuals were strewn over the festive board, and the others all started to their feet, having little appetite left for their dinner. Alexander alone remained in his seat. . . Quietly ordering the attendants to remove the dead bodies, and to bring a clean tablecloth, he insisted that his guests should resume their places."[4]

According to Biringuccio an iron ball discharged from a medium-sized cannon weighed 25 to 30 pounds, while a ball discharged from the largest cannon might weigh up to 120 pounds.[5] Even in the mid-seventeenth century, after many attempts had been made to economize on metal, a missile for the larger cannon apparently weighed 64 pounds.[6] If many rounds were fired, more metal was soon consumed in balls than went into the manufacture of the piece.

The high cost of hauling the larger cannon, with the wagon loads of heavy ammunition which they required, put a premium on smaller pieces and smaller balls. It was mainly firearms under six feet in length — particularly arquebuses, pistols, and muskets — that were turned out in ever larger numbers. Their barrels were generally of wrought iron, obtained from the new rolling mills in sheets to be formed into metallic tubes.[7] Behind the barrel was a sunken wooden butt.

These new smaller firearms, the arquebuses in particular, were so heavy that it was difficult for a soldier to lug one on a march [8] or to hold one in his hands while he aimed and fired. The heavier pieces were sometimes brought in carts to be distributed to the soldiers and mounted at the time of battle.[9] Crotched rests, making it possible to pose the gun when shooting, are said to have been invented in 1521.[10] At the beginning of the seventeenth century, in spite of improvements from ten minutes to a quarter of an hour were sometimes required to reload and fire. Very wet weather might dampen the powder so seriously that it became impossible to fire at all.[11] Like the big guns of the age, these "hand pieces" are bound to strike a twentieth-century man as primitive. To those of his ancestors who four hundred years ago dreaded war (and the proportion of the population who dreaded it was perhaps as large then as now), the guns seemed powerful enough, and very easily movable. They were all too accurate in aim to suit the many who suffered wounds and the many others who lost brothers, husbands, or sons in battle. It would have been difficult to convince the civilized Aztecs that the guns of the great Cortés were primitive.

Muskets had greater killing power than the other early firearms, including cannon.[12] It was the general use of firearms by foot soldiers — particularly the use of the musket, introduced by the Spaniards in 1521 with telling effect in their Italian campaigns against the French, and widely adopted late in the sixteenth century by the French themselves — which made the infantry the decisive striking arm in war. Small firearms, first used by the infantry, spread to the cavalry. During the second half of the sixteenth century the riders made an increasing use of pistols, especially of the heavy pistol called a petronel, which, though large, was easy to carry compared to the arquebus and even the musket. Every branch of a fighting army had to have guns, and all the guns required metal for their manufacture and still more metal for their use. In the case of the bullets and various other missiles of iron and lead, the eagerness of the soldiers on campaign for munitions knew no limit. The hunger of a man for food is as nothing to his hunger for ammunition when the enemy is attacking.

Warfare based on gunpowder involved a waste in metal which

might have shocked the ancient Greeks and Romans. The idea of ransacking the subsoil for base ores seemed unhealthy to them, if we can judge from the writings which have come down to us, for example those of the celebrated naturalist of the first century, Pliny the Elder (23–79 A.D.). All civilized peoples have made some use of metal; it was reserved for the Western Europeans and their descendants in America to make the first extravagant use of it. In spite of the extensive development of industry in the early Roman Empire, Pliny remarked that it was still the custom for young men to give their fiancées iron rings as tokens of their engagement.[13] Today the iron, once so scarce, pours in flaming cascades from furnaces which at night light up the skies for miles in every direction.

Modern war and modern industrialism alike have been based upon the production of tremendous quantities of metal — above all iron and steel. The origins of what eventually became a deluge of base metal can be traced back in central Europe to the late fifteenth and early sixteenth centuries. Between about 1460 and 1540 the output of iron in Germany, Bohemia, Hungary, and the Eastern Alps grew several times over — possibly as much as four- or even fivefold.[14] In the Low Countries, northeastern France, Spain, and probably in northern Italy, the increase in the production of iron was hardly less striking than in central Europe. There the production of copper — the most essential element in the new cannon — grew at an even more rapid rate than the output of iron. As the spread of new artillery was followed by the rapid multiplication of smaller firearms during the sixteenth century, a large portion of the much increased output of metal must have gone into the manufacture of guns, gun carriages, balls, and bullets. The mounting volume of iron and copper, and also of lead, calamine, and tin, provided the sinews of the new warfare based on gunpowder.

By the 1520's and 1530's the output of iron and copper had grown prodigiously, as it would seem to ancient peoples, though not to the modern public, which has been drilled by newspapers, magazines, and broadcasts to think in millions. After the remarkable expansion of the metallurgical industries on the eve of the Reformation, the annual output of iron and steel in Western Europe from 1530 to 1540 was perhaps not much more than 100,000 tons, or at the outside 150,000 tons.[15] The output of copper was perhaps some 15,000 tons a year.[16] In 1910, just before the First World War, the European output of iron and steel had reached 60,000,000 tons. There has been no such overwhelming expansion since the Reformation in the production of copper. In 1913 Europe produced about 100,000 tons — only six or seven times as much as in 1540. The world output of copper amounted to about a million tons.

If guns were to become the principal means of winning battles, they had to be abundant. The conditions which facilitated an expansion in the output of metal on the eve of the Reformation were hardly less responsible for modern warfare than the discovery of gunpowder and of cannon. The inventions which cheapened the costs of making copper and iron preceded by many years and even decades the development of the new firearms and of the metal missiles which they fired — so much more numerous and deadly than the balls of marble, granite, and other kinds of expensive stone which had been wafted through the air by the earliest cannon. In order to get at the sequence of developments that helped produce the slaughters of the sixteenth and early seventeenth centuries, it is necessary to seek for the motives which led to the inventions.

Towards the middle of the fifteenth century it was discovered that the separation of silver from the argentiferous copper ores, which abounded in central Europe, could be accomplished with the help of lead. The new method was apparently introduced about 1451 by a man named Johannsen Funcken. The spark he struck much reduced the cost of copper, partly because of the new manufacturing establishments, the *saigerhütte*, which were built as a result of the invention. These large establishments made a more efficient and extensive use than heretofore of water power for driving machinery and bellows.[17]

Seams of rich argentiferous copper ores, particularly those in central Europe, could now be mined not only to produce copper and bronze, but also silver and brass. Both were in growing demand: silver because of its value, brass because of its cheapness as compared with bronze. As a consequence the economic advantages of exploiting copper mines greatly increased. By adding to the revenues from mining and metallurgy, the new alternative uses for copper ores helped to make it economically practicable, even at a heavy cost, to install more powerful and efficient machinery to drain and to exploit the mines. The successful use of this machinery further lowered the price of copper ores. It increased still further the demand for all the products of these ores.

The expense of making iron was reduced by a number of less spectacular developments in metallurgy. These began long before the widespread exploitation of copper ores and calamine. They culminated in the invention of the blast furnace.

During and after the eleventh century water-driven machinery, little used by the ancient Greeks or Romans, was developed in Western

Europe for many purposes, among them grinding grain and fulling cloth.[18] Before the end of the twelfth century and during the thirteenth the use of water power was spreading to metallurgy, especially to the production of silver from argentiferous lead ores. In the most advanced ironmaking districts of central Europe, such as Styria, water power was sometimes employed for driving the bellows and the hammers used in converting ore directly into wrought iron by the age-old process of earlier civilizations, without the reduction of the ore to liquid. While the processes were old, the extensive use of water power in them was probably new. It encouraged craftsmen to make both the bellows and the hammers larger and more powerful instruments, such as could not be operated by the hands and feet. By the beginning of the fourteenth century the Europeans had invented a heart-shaped bellows more effective than any used by the ancients.[19] When driven by the force of moving water, released from specially constructed dams, such bellows sometimes generated so fierce a flame that even the intractable ore of iron ran before the eyes of the astonished ironmasters. As the casting of bronze had long been practiced, it was natural that the new discovery should open the way to the casting of iron. Iron being cheaper than bronze, there were obvious advantages in substituting it in the manufacture of cannon. Cannon made of cast iron appeared before the middle of the fifteenth century at Dijon, in the dominions of the enterprising dukes of Burgundy, and somewhat later, about 1460–1464, in the Alps and northern Italy.[20] But the early cast-iron cannon were too breakable to enter extensively into practical use.

When brass was first made into cannon is uncertain, but brass cannon were known in England by 1535.[21] About a decade later, after a striking revolution in the weapons of war had already been effected on the Continent, cast-iron cannon were devised to stand up under repeated shooting. The improvements in the process of casting occurred in southeastern England in the 1540's.[22] While it was apparently a French founder who taught an Englishman, Ralph Hogge, to make the new guns,[23] the English quickly improved on the work of their teachers. With the use of cast iron for cannon, a change was made from breech to muzzle loading; there was some slight reduction in the caliber and weight of the pieces, accompanied by an increase of muzzle velocity and gun power. Many cast-iron cannon were shipped from England to the Continent, especially during the early seventeenth century, for use in the Thirty Years' War. During that war, which broke out in 1618, Swedish iron ore began to be used for the founding of guns.[24] Cannon made of brass were mounted on the increasingly numerous ships of the English Royal Navy.[25]

Although the manufacture of bronze guns was not abandoned in the northern countries,[26] cheaper cannon of iron and brass largely superseded them. The chief significance of the change was that it gave the northern countries increased protection in an age when they were growing rich much faster than the rest of Europe. The new guns reinforced the natural frontiers provided by water. They helped make Great Britain and Holland into fortresses. Within them it became possible for merchants and other industrial adventurers to develop economic enterprise more extensively and to make a fuller use than ever before of coal.

The discovery that iron ore, like bronze, could be reduced to liquid had much importance in increasing the supply of metal available for the multiplication of firearms, even when the actual cannon were of bronze, as most of them continued to be on the Continent. The cannon balls which came into use during the early sixteenth century were almost always made of cast iron. These balls were cast in molds, and already by the 1530's in Italy, as Biringuccio explained, the molds themselves were made of iron, instead of bronze, "in order to save expense." [27]

Furthermore the cost of the wrought iron, needed for small firearms and various auxiliary parts for the new weapons, was reduced by the widespread use of a more powerful blast and of larger furnaces. The principal reduction in the expense of producing wrought iron came with the development of a novel roundabout process of manufacturing it. A beginning had been made before the invention of the new method of extracting silver from copper ore — which is to say before 1450.[28] A few genuine blast furnaces, with auxiliary forges, were built in northeastern France and northern Italy before the new warfare began.[29] Cast iron replaced wrought iron as the primary product. The liquid iron was tapped from time to time at the bottom of tall furnaces and run into large molds, which came to be called pigs. As a result a far smaller portion of the ore mined was lost in the manufacture. At nearby forges cast iron, in the form of pigs, was given subsequent treatments of heating and hammering to decarbonize it. In modern times the new product, generally cheaper, eventually replaced the older wrought iron made directly from the ore, without melting.

In spite of the introduction of the new method of manufacturing iron, blast furnaces with auxiliary forges were not at all common in Europe until after 1540.[30] During the next hundred years the roundabout process of treating iron ores spread rapidly in the north, first in the Spanish Netherlands, in the region of Namur, where there were said to be thirty-five blast furnaces in 1560, and in the prince-bishopric of Liége.[31] Before the middle of the seventeenth century the blast furnace had come into general use in England and Wales (where there were probably between 100 and 150 furnaces in blast on the eve of the Civil War);[32] it had made headway in Scotland and Sweden.[33]

Among the motives behind these various metallurgical inventions, which helped to increase the output of copper, bronze, brass, and iron, was the desire for more weapons. But the demand for metal during the fourteenth and fifteenth centuries, when the decisive steps were taken which led to cheaper metal, by no means came only from warring princes, nobles, and the persons they employed to fight for them. There was an increase in the variety and quantity of artistic metal work, both in connection with the religious buildings and the castles and lesser mansions of the nobility and the rising mercantile classes. In the new luxury of the Renaissance, metal of various kinds — including iron — was an essential material for embroidering the merchants' houses, their strong boxes and furniture, for making some of their doors and the grills for their gardens. The development of the new styles of architecture, influenced by the classical architecture of the Greco-Roman world, led during the fifteenth and early sixteenth centuries to a need for new objects of art in new styles. Metals, which had been much used by artists as materials in Greco-Roman times, were now wanted more than ever for artistic purposes. In the fifteenth century there was also a great unfilled demand for precious metal — especially silver — among all the European princes, lay and ecclesiastical, who minted coins and who wanted more money to meet their expenses. The expansion of industry and trade during the relatively peaceful decades following the Hundred Years' War, increased the need for every kind of cash and credit.

In all probability the predominant motive behind the new process which revolutionized copper mining and metallurgy in the late fifteenth century was the expanding demand for silver. Funcken's invention, which opened a rich new source of silver supplies, had probably no military purpose.

While the demand for weapons had more influence upon the changes in the ironmaking industry, it is reasonably certain that most of the craftsmen who worked with ore and metal had no idea that inventions to cheapen iron would help to make *firearms* the decisive weapons in war. The men who first developed the more powerful furnaces and forges in ironmaking were probably thinking, as men are always prone to think — even in the twentieth century when industrial and military changes are obviously more rapid than ever before — in terms of an older warfare which proves to be out of date when the new warfare comes. In the older warfare of the late Middle Ages iron was already, according to a modern student of the Hundred Years' War, "the most essential material." [34] It was needed for swords, lances, daggers, arrows, and above all for the plate armor that was capable of blunting the force of these weapons. As we have seen, the demand for armor went on increasing not only during the fifteenth century but in the early part of the sixteenth. The use of larger quantities of iron, copper, bronze, brass, and lead for firearms, and for the projectiles which they hurled in ever greater profusion during the sixteenth century, was not brought about by premeditated design on the part of the miners, craftsmen, and engineers whose inventions increased the supply of metal. When they discovered more efficient methods of exploiting the ore resources of the earth, they had in mind other goals than the spread of fighting with gunpowder and explosives.

The basic inventions behind the revolution in the art of war were not made predominantly in response to military needs. Nor were the novel military needs which accompanied the new warfare of the sixteenth and early seventeenth centuries a factor of predominant importance in the technological changes which were an essential part of the early "industrial revolution." Certain inventions of the sixteenth century, for example portable mills of various types for grinding grain, were made for the convenience of the armies,[35] which were larger and moved about more than had medieval armies. According to a German scholar, Bernard Hagedorn, the English had outstripped all other nations in warship construction by the time of Queen Elizabeth, when English merchant ships could not bear comparison with Dutch and German vessels. In 1582 a bluff English sailor wrote that the King of Denmark "has English shipwrights that build him goodly ships and galleys after the English mould and fashion. I would they were hanged." Hagedorn suggested that important innovations, such as very large sails, were made first on warships because the expense was of less concern than in merchant shipbuilding, where the essential object was to obtain a profit on the investment.[36] Nevertheless, the Dutch *flüte*, which had considerable influence upon shipbuilding in all the northern countries in the early seventeenth century, seems to have been invented for commercial purposes. A swift sailing vessel which could be handled by fewer seamen, but which had much hold space, the *flüte* cheapened the cost of carrying bulky commodities, like coal, salt, and sheet glass in heavy cases. [37]

What is striking not only in the later Middle Ages but during the hundred and fifty years which followed Columbus' voyages is that the inventive ingenuity of the Europeans was manifested, in the main, independently of military requirements. During the sixteenth century the increase in fighting was not a major cause for harnessing the intelligence to technological improvement. Indeed the developments which were essential in the genesis of industrial civilization — the introduction of larger, more efficient furnaces, the substitution of coal for wood fuel in manufacturing, the use of "railways," and the spread of horse- and water-driven machinery for draining mines and driving bellows and hammers — were most remarkable in Great Britain, within whose shores peaceful relations prevailed.

War was calling forth inventive ingenuity which the Western Europeans were interested in exercising even without war. A revolution in weapons was a necessary part of the revolution in tools only in the sense that the Western peoples had not managed to break away from the traditional attitude of civilized as well as of primitive peoples — the attitude that weapons are one indispensable kind of tool. An inquiry into the history of technology in Europe from the eleventh to the middle of the seventeenth century hardly suggests that the Western peoples, compared with other civilized peoples, were giving an especially large share of their inventive talents to military technology, or that the key to the early English "industrial revolution" can be found in a new enthusiasm for military engineering. Yet it shows that, as long as war remains a part of human experience, peoples cannot change their methods of producing without also changing their methods of destroying.

CHAPTER THREE

The Birth of Modern Science

· IF ONE CAN JUDGE FROM THE COMMENTS UPON GUNPOWDER AND cannon during the century and a half of bitter wars which followed the battle of Fornovo, most writers were horrified by the discoveries which had helped bring on a new era of destruction. For the work of their fellow human beings who bore the original responsibility for the explosions, they expressed unreserved disgust and remorse.

The sense of sin was deep in the sixteenth century, perhaps as deep as during the times of Francis of Assisi, Thomas Aquinas, and Dante. Calvinist dogma, which was spreading rapidly through Europe (in spite of the efforts of defenders of the ancient faith to shoot, torture, poison, and burn out the heresy), was among the most terrifying versions of Christian other-world reality in the emphasis which it laid upon the predestination of most individuals to damnation. A consciousness of sinful responsibility weighed on our sixteenth-century ancestors far more heavily in connection with firearms than in connection with old accepted weapons, such as bows, lances, and swords. The peculiar violence with which cannon balls and bullets sped through the air led some men, among them Galileo, to suppose that the speed obtained by a missile fired from a musket or a cannon was supernatural in origin.[1] Consequently it seemed rational in an age of strong Christian belief to conclude that the invention of the gun was work of the devil. A modern, who no longer believes in the devil, ejaculates "the son of a gun" without realizing the meaning of his curse.

An English historian, Polydore Virgil (c. 1470–1555), born in Italy and whose life (like the lives of Erasmus and Thomas More) spanned the revolution in the art of war, remarked in a widely read work of the time, *De inventoribus rerum* (1499), "of all other weapons that were devised to the destruction of man, the gones be most devilische." Virgil attributed their invention to "a certaine Almaine" and continued: "For this invencion, he received this benefit that his name was never knowen lest he might for thys abhomynable devise, have been cursed and evil spoken of whilest the worlde standeth." [2] The culprit was soon deprived of that benefit, such as it was! His name was found to be Schwartz. Some said he was a monk. The sixteenth century saw Schwartz in the inkiest black; by inveighing against him, men seem to have found some slight consolation for the damage his invention had done and continued to do.

There are many examples of the fanciful flights taken at the expense of poor Schwartz. Among them is a quaint account by an Elizabethan *Of the First Invention of That Horryble Instrument of Gonnes*. This Englishman wrote:

In the year of our Lord God 1380 . . . one Bertholdus Swartz, an Almayne, did first invent the makying of Gonnes by the putting of the powder of brimstone in a mortar for a medicine, who covered the mortar by a stone, and striking fyer it so fortuned that a sparke fell into the said powder, whereby there arose a very sudden flame . . . and herewith lifted upp the stone . . . a great hight, which thing the said Bertholdus perceiving did this devise by the Suggestion (as it was thought) of the Devyll himself, a Pipe of iron, and loaded it with the powder, and so finished this deadlye and horryble Engine, and then taught it to the Venecians when they had warres against the [Genoese], which was in anno domini 1380. [3]

Much history has been crammed into this imaginary episode of a single fanciful life. (The Venetians are said to have obtained from Germany the cannon which they used in 1380 against the Genoese at Chioggia on the Gulf of Venice.) [4] All these things happened, even if not to one man and not all at once. Humanity cannot evade the responsibility, though it appears less grievous when it is distributed, as it should be, among many men and over several centuries.

Some persons there were — most of whose names are lost — who used their ingenuity to devise ways of doing ever worse mischief with the diabolical new explosives. One of these men, who discovered extensive and formidable uses for the explosive mine and the floating battery, is well known for his exploits as a general. Pedro Navarro (*c.* 1460–1528) has been called the leading military engineer of his age. Nothing is known of his birth and parentage, except that they were considered by his contemporaries to be obscure and base. He began active life as a sailor and then became a footman, running errands for a Spanish cardinal. In 1485 he enlisted as a mercenary soldier in one of the small inconsequential Italian wars of the time and learned his profession during the next fifteen years in piratical fighting, of the coarsest and most unscrupulous kind, between the Genoese corsairs and the Mohammedans of northern Africa. From 1500 to 1503 his actual experiments in laying mines for the Spaniards in Sicily and southern Italy led to the production of a species of explosive that changed little during four hundred years.[5] In 1515 Navarro betrayed the Spanish cause and went into the service of the French king, Francis I.

If Navarro is representative of military inventors in his time, then the frightful new engines were often devised by actual soldiers, often soldiers of fortune of an unsavory kind who worked out their tricks on the field of battle. Technical advance in offensive weapons had not yet become, as it was to become later, a field for specialists in which the inventors were professional technicians and even scientists. The instruments for inflicting pain and destruction were not prepared in laboratories as in our mechanical age; they were often improved with the enemy before the inventor's eyes; the mingled physical horror and perverse pleasure entailed in their use was more obvious.

Yet behind the development of artillery and small firearms at the end of the fifteenth century was a movement of scientific inquiry in Italy, south Germany, and the rest of central Europe, including Hungary and Poland. Between the end of the Hundred Years' War, in 1453, and the French invasion of Italy, in 1494, the Continent enjoyed a longer respite from serious and extensive warfare than it was to have again for more than two hundred years.[6] Machiavelli has given his numerous modern readers the impression, indeed, that such organized fighting as took place in fifteenth-century Italy resembled comic opera. He described several engagements. One was the battle over a bridge near Anghiari in Tuscany, in which a soldier of fortune, Niccolo Piccinino, in the employ of the Duke.of Milan, pitted his hired soldiers unsuccessfully against the Florentines. According to Machiavelli, the struggle lasted four hours, but only one man was slain, "and he not by any Wound or honorable Exploit, but falling from his Horse he was trodden to Death."[7] Machiavelli's picturesque pen, employed to show how unwarlike the Italians had become on the eve of the foreign invasions, and how ineffective it was to confine fighting to mercenaries, is said to have ensnared modern historians into exaggerating the peacefulness of the late fifteenth century. Even in Italy much blood was drawn when troops actually fought.[8] Yet the bands of soldiers were not large — a few thousands at the most — and in comparison with the troublous times of the Hundred Years' War, there were during the second half of the fifteenth century so few serious battles between Christians in continental Europe, and so little plundering by armies, that the tranquillity and felicity seemed great. Contemporaries were even disposed to believe that fighting among civilized peoples might disappear altogether. In 1474 the Duke of Ferrara's ambassador to Florence reported: "Stability has increased so much that, if nothing unexpected happens, we shall in future hear more about battles against birds and dogs than about battles between armies." [9] To the unwary these peaceful conditions seemed as promising for the ultimate tranquillity of the human race as those which prevailed toward the end of the nineteenth century, when the generation called to fight in the First World War was born.

What absorbed European minds during the late fifteenth century was the making of beautiful objects and the closely related task of expanding and even rebuilding towns and villages in a new style of architecture, inspired partly by classical models and classical treatises, of which the most read was that of Vitruvius, architect of the early Caesars.[10] If war had been the principal spur to invention and scientific discovery, we should expect to find many of the new weapons in England, where Englishmen were pitted against Englishmen in fierce dynastic struggles. Yet in England this was a barren period both for science and for invention. The technical changes which revolutionized warfare were wholly of continental origin. According to the leading English historian of the subject, the late Professor Oman, "It is not too much to say that for over fifty years, from 1455 to 1509, England was completely out of touch with the modern developments of the art of War." [11]

The English dynastic wars, like the Hundred Years' War, had less to do with technical improvements in the guns and explosives than the new interest taken by the Italians and other continentals in luxury and delight. The revolution in weapons, which made firearms decisive in battle, occurred at the end of a comparatively peaceful period. The new weapons were largely by-products of the Renaissance spirit, the main *intention* of which was a fuller, more delightful worldly existence within the framework of the Christian faith. If one were prompted, after the fashion of our Christian ancestors, to draw a Biblical parallel, it might be suggested that the Europeans tasted anew of forbidden fruit and paid the penalty in the sting of new weapons.

Once the wars with the new weapons got under way on the Continent, the relation of distinguished European minds to military engines seems to have altered. As war became more prevalent and devastating than in the past, as troops became more numerous, campaigns and battles more frequent, as the religious issues of the wars touched the lives of everyone from the most powerful to the humblest, the number of Europeans diminished who stood aloof from war, who felt no concern about the instruments of attack and especially about the instruments of defense. Many of the men who played a part from 1500 to 1650 in the scientific revolution which proved essential to the later triumph of industrial civilization showed much curiosity concerning the nature and properties of the new weapons.

While still only thirty, Leonardo da Vinci (1452–1519) vaunted his skill as a destructive inventor in a letter which has become famous. It was prepared for one of his patrons, Ludovico Sforza (1451–1508),[12] who was later responsible for the entry into Italy in 1494 of the French king, Charles VIII, with his artillery. The novelty which Leonardo claimed for his methods, and still more the novelty claimed for him by his modern admirers, seems to be exaggerated. According to one of his most recent and informed biographers, Sir Kenneth Clark, "Leonardo's knowledge of military engineering was not in advance of his time." [13]

Like some others among his contemporaries, who looked back with interest and admiration on the civilized thought and life of the Greeks and Romans, Leonardo was impressed by the war engines of these ancient peoples. Among their engines were scythed war chariots, which were used by armies during the Hellenistic period.[14] Leonardo made drawings of a car with projecting sickles.[15] Wagons of a similar kind (without the macaberesque sickles) were known to John Ziska, the Czech leader, aged and blind but full of ingenuity, who had used them two generations earlier in the Hussite wars in Bohemia. Ziska's skill consisted in mounting small cannon on horse-drawn wagons, thus giving guns more mobility than before. Ziska's wagons were not, as has been suggested,[16] true ancestors of the tank; they were more directly ancestors of the horse-drawn artillery, and their function was primarily defensive, unlike the function of the tank which is to break through the enemy's lines.[17]

Whether Ziska's "chariots" were known to Leonardo, it is not possible to say. But Leonardo's sketches of war scenes and his remarks about them hardly suggest that his conception of a battle was in advance of the battles that were actually taking place during the later years of his life. Of his concern over the consequences of the new warfare in spurting blood and mangled flesh, there is no doubt. War was one of many theaters in which he studied actual material conditions.[18] Some of his suggestions for the painting of a battle scene are extremely gruesome, yet they never anticipate the kinds of battles which developed after his death. His notebooks contain references to missiles which were becoming obsolete in his later years — pieces of rock, small stones, even darts and arrows.[19]

In Leonardo's time and during part of Charles V's imperial reign which followed from 1519 to 1555, older tactical traditions of medieval warfare with ancient weapons died hard. The same campaign, even the same battle, might provide a confusing, picturesque mixture, in which archers and charging knights were intermingled with moving artillery and with infantry, equipped with arquebuses and eventually pistols and muskets.[20] Arrows, lances, and swords have a prominent place in Leonardo's idea of a picture. After talking about drawing the smoke from the artillery, Leonardo proceeds: "Let the air be full of arrows going in various directions, some mounting upwards, others falling, others flying horizontally, and let the balls shot from the guns have a train of smoke following their course. . . If you represent any one fallen you should show the mark where he has been dragged through the dust, which has become changed to blood-stained mire . . . Put all sorts of arms lying between the feet of the combatants, such as broken shields, lances, broken swords, and other things like these." [21]

Leonardo's picture is a mixture of the old war with the new. It resembles descriptions of the terrible struggle at Marignano, near Milan, fought by the French against the Swiss in 1515. After serious casualties from the fire of French cannon and arquebus had demoralized the Swiss, lancers encased in armor struck the decisive blow which won complete victory for the young French king, Francis I.

Much confusion exists concerning Leonardo's place in both technology and science. One of the most dramatic and arresting figures in intellectual history by virtue of the astonishing range, originality, and penetration of his mind, Leonardo's life has attracted many historical writers. Most of them have written largely in ignorance of the remarkable capacity of some other men besides Leonardo in the late fifteenth century, as well as during the sixteenth and early seventeenth centuries, to visualize and even to draw not only the guns and missiles which actually came into use, but also tanks, submarines, and airships which were not to play any role in war for several hundred years. Leonardo's biographers have found references to all these destructive engines, often accompanied by drawings, in the notebooks which he kept throughout his later life, beginning about the time he wrote to Sforza. Manuscripts of Leonardo's less famous contemporaries have not cast the same spell as have his over modern writers.

For that reason Leonardo has been frequently credited with the original conception of many destructive engines; he has even been treated as the inventor of some. Yet, "before Leonardo's time," as Clark has explained, "other Renaissance artists had set out the result of their inquiries into machinery, architecture, and fortification in the form of treatises: such, for example, is a manuscript in the Laurentian Library . . . attributed to Francesco di Giorgio, which actually belonged to Leonardo and is annotated in his handwriting. It contains plans of churches, drawings of weapons and machinery — everything, in fact, which we find in the early manuscripts of Leonardo, and although the style of drawing is more primitive the technical knowledge displayed is hardly inferior." [22] During the two centuries following the Hundred Years' War, which ended in 1453, ideas for all the remarkable engines of destruction and locomotion found in Leonardo's notebooks were becoming the staple of a considerable number of ingenious minds. What is likely to puzzle a twentieth-century historian, in possession of this evidence that Leonardo's writings and drawings were not the source of these remarkable early notions about military engineering, is why, if so many men had ideas that seem precocious and modern, relatively few of the murderous engines were actually realized. In later chapters we discuss some of the material, intellectual, and spiritual reasons which delayed their realization. [23] A clue to one of the reasons is provided by the widely expressed horror for the inventor of the gun. Skill in contriving more effective means for murder was less esteemed then than in modern times; pressure from tradition and political authority to realize such means was lacking. [24]

What was much more remarkable about Leonardo's mind than his information concerning military operations, or even his grasp of the technique of military engineering, was his insight as a self-educated natural scientist. Under the influence of the ancients, Archimedes in particular, he began to ask questions about the first principles of dynamics, about motion in itself, and he then went on to ask questions which had never been asked before concerning nonmilitary matters — concerning winds, clouds, the process of generation, the age of the earth, and the physical structure of the human heart. The turning point in his scientific self-education toward creative originality came in his early forties, about the year 1494 (not, be it added, as a result of the French invasion of Italy!). At that time the mere curiosity of his earlier years merged into profound scientific research. [25]

While no definitive statement has yet been made concerning Leonardo's position in the history of natural science, it has been established that his notebooks actually provided a valuable quarry for a few influential scientists. Among them was Girolamo Cardan (1501–

1576), a learned and widely traveled Italian, whose interests ranged from mathematics through medicine and physics to astrology. Cardan's statements on the subjects of statics and dynamics were largely derived from Leonardo.[26] Through his influence on Cardan and on a younger Italian scientist with equally wide interests, Bernardino Baldi (1533–1617), Leonardo made an important contribution to the awakening of natural science in France.[27] By way of Cardan, he contributed to the geological theory of the formation of fossils, set forth by a modest but remarkably gifted Frenchman, Bernard Palissy (c. 1510–c. 1589),[28] whose capacity for combining the genius of the artist, in his ceramics, with that of the scientist resembled Leonardo's. By way of Cardan, too, Leonardo contributed to the mechanics of Salomon de Caus (c. 1576–1626),[29] a more obscure and much younger Frenchman than Palissy, who published in 1615 a theory of the expansion and condensation of steam, which has led some later writers to claim him as the inventor of the steam engine. By way of Baldi, Leonardo's questions and theories concerning dynamics influenced the great French geometers of the early seventeenth century — Mersenne (1588–1648), Roberval (1602–1675), and Descartes (1596–1650).

Pierre Duhem, a modern French authority on the history of science, has called the sixteenth century and the first half of the seventeenth the epoch "when plagiarism was practiced with the most cynical impudence."[30] But the modern notion that ideas are a man's personal property was then imperfectly developed. Men looked on the intellectual life more as artists than as scientists, and for the artist the laurels rest less with him who says it first than with him who says it best. "Truth in a raw state," as the distinguished French poet, the late Paul Valéry, reminded us in his own study of Leonardo, can be "more false than falsehood."[31] For the artist the impulse to exploit, without acknowledgment, anything that his predecessors can give him is irresistible, and it is no cause for a scandal. In the late fifteenth and early sixteenth centuries the artist's view of the world and of knowledge, which, as we shall see, is fundamentally different from the modern scientist's view,[32] had a more notable influence upon the development of science than at any later time.

However extensive may have been the plagiarizing by later men of Leonardo's ideas, scientific knowledge made enormous strides which cannot be attributed to his genius in the hundred and thirty years following his death in 1519. It was during this period, especially at the end of the sixteenth century and in the early seventeenth, that those discoveries were made concerning the nature of the body and the physical world which properly mark the birth of modern science.

There was an immense advance in the knowledge of physiology between the time of the great French Renaissance physician, Jean Fernel (1485–1557), and the great English physician, William Harvey (1578–1657), the true discoverer of the circulation of the blood.[33] The understanding achieved by Galileo (1564–1642) and Kepler (1571–1630) of the motions of the heavenly bodies and of dynamics and statics generally was of fundamental importance to the later universal physics of Newton (1642–1727). Neither their discoveries nor those of their principal predecessors can be traced to the notebooks of Leonardo.

It is obviously grotesque to attribute a major part of the extraordinary scientific advance during the late sixteenth and early seventeenth centuries to the influence of Leonardo. Would it not be almost equally grotesque to attribute this advance mainly to the influence of military engineering and war?

After the initial revolution in methods of destruction during the first three or four decades of the sixteenth century, warfare, as it came to be conducted, raised almost endless fresh technical problems. The solution of one problem generally gave rise to many others. The destruction produced by the new weapons could not be met by the old methods of healing wounds and of defending towns and cities against onslaughts with arrows, lances, swords, and battle axes. According to the prevailing views of European thought in the sixteenth century, healing and even defending were humane, to some extent charitable, objectives as contrasted with killing and destroying. Contributions to healing and to the art of defense consequently freed the contributors from the stigma which was attached to those who made direct technical contributions to engines and missiles dealing out death and ruin. The distinctions between the two kinds of contributions in war — to the attack and to the defense — were clearer than they have since become.

Firearms caused wounds that neither Hippocrates nor Galen had had to treat. In spite of his humble origin, a remarkable Frenchman named Ambroise Paré (c. 1517–1590) rose to the occasion. The idea that pure thought had a dignity which was denied the mind employed in the manipulation of matter, had kept the surgeon, during the Middle Ages, from occupying a place in learning comparable to that of the physician, who for the most part assiduously avoided all direct contact with the bodies of his patients. As a surgeon of the lowest order, a barber-surgeon, Paré was despised by the physicians who belonged to the faculties of French universities. But four French kings, who cared more for their health than for ossified conventions, made him their principal medical adviser and left the faculties to the sterile disputes, for which faculties are apt to have a predilection. When Paré accompanied Francis I to the renewed Italian wars of the 1540's, it had become the accepted practice to pour hot oil on the gunshot wounds which had become so common and so horrible. But in one of the battles the wounds were too numerous for the supply of oil. Finding the next day that the soldiers he had failed to treat were better off than those he had treated, Paré abandoned hot oil.[34] Like so many great discoveries in science and medicine, including some of those of Claude Bernard (great French medical genius of the nineteenth century), this was the product of what seems to posterity, looking back, the simplest common sense. History also teaches us that the courageous and persistent use of common sense to break through old habits is rare. Paré claimed no special merit for the novel methods of dressing wounds which he later developed. "I dressed him and God cured him," was the laconic comment that he repeated all his life when, as happened miraculously often, his patients got well.

The growing use of firearms also made it necessary to reconsider the methods of defending strong places. Forts were now needed to protect harbors from the guns of warships and to meet the onslaughts of the new and more effective field artillery, which could be massed in some force in favorable positions for attack. Even when the medieval attackers had managed to scale the thick lofty walls of mighty places, the structures themselves remained and could be used as defenses again and again. But at the end of the fifteenth century, majestic heights and thicknesses like Carcassonne, one of the artistic glories of the Middle Ages and perhaps the most perfect example of the defensive works completed in the late thirteenth century,[35] became obsolete. The new destructive culverins and other cannon were capable of reducing to rubble the walls of castles which once were virtually impregnable, and which had withstood strong land forces until the end of the fifteenth century.[36] It was found that the only successful way of meeting the new bombardment was by counter-bombardment. Fortifications were needed for accommodating guns.

The first steps towards making a new type of fort, with bastions and with guns to answer the attackers, were taken in Italy, Germany, and the Low Countries in the early sixteenth century. In the new architecture of fortification, two Italian architects, Michele Sanmichele (1484–1559) and Antonio da Sangallo the Younger (c. 1483–1546), were the leaders. In his celebrated *Lives*, Vasari gave an account of Sanmichele's study and development of fortifications in Dalmatia and the island of Corfu (against the Turks) as well as in Italy. Charles V and Francis I sought in vain to enlist his services. Sanmichele preferred to fortify places on behalf of his native Italy. The military discoveries of such an architect were closely allied with the general development of his architectural styles. Michelangelo's and Dürer's principal services to the military art also seem to have been connected with improved forts.

The new fortifications spread slowly both in Italy and beyond the Alps.[37] Important improvements began to be made nearly a century later. First a German named Daniel Speckle, who was an architect for the city of Strasbourg until his death in 1589, published a treatise full of novel ideas for more defensible forts.[38] Soon therafter further advances were made by a famous Dutch man of science, Simon Stevin (1548–1620), who served the prince Maurice of Orange (1567–1625), second son of William the Silent. Although Stevin's very original ideas concerning the defense of strong places were not all adopted in his time, his contributions to the building of more effective forts were important in defending Holland against the Spaniards.[39] His fortifications also helped to stabilize European warfare during the seventeenth century, by giving the defenders advantages once again after a long period of increasingly terrible pitched battles and increasingly frequent sacks of towns.

Stevin's leading principle was to destroy by concentrated cannon fire the trenches and other preparations which the besiegers made to cover their advance, rather than to slay as many of the besiegers as possible. He built four stories on each flank of his fortifications. He was anxious to strengthen the firing power from the various stories as the occasion demanded, by mounting additional artillery drawn by horses. Accordingly he constructed a series of ramps similar to those used earlier for industrial purposes in central European mines, where horses were driven down ramps winding into the earth like a screw to operate drainage machinery several score feet below the surface.[40]

Stevin's contributions to military technology, unlike those of the inventors of the guns, balls, and explosive missiles that made new fortifications necessary, were of little or no help in the seventeenth century to rulers bent on conquest — political or religious. Like England, Holland with its new-found riches was mainly interested in holding potential invaders at bay, while its industrious people developed industry and trade at home and, above all, on the sea. Even in the midst of the bitter religious wars, it was still possible to defend a country without retaliating to destroy the nation which attacked.

Stevin lectured during the early seventeenth century at the recently formed University of Leiden. He introduced the decimal system for representing fractions, and he has a firm place in the scientific revolution of his age because he helped to render science more amenable to a mathematical mode of treatment.[41] It is difficult to determine how far his scientific knowledge was increased by practical experience with the problems of war. That such experience helped him seems more than probable. But it would be exaggerated to regard it as the main source of his scientific discoveries.[42]

At the beginning of the seventeenth century France had begun to share with Holland the leadership in the development of fortifications. Jean Errard (1555–1610) has been considered the founder of the French school of defense, which became by all odds the most important in Europe during the next two hundred years. In 1594 he published a treatise whose title, *Fortification reduicte en art*, indicates that his inspiration was not altogether scientific, in the modern sense of that word. Only one French natural scientist of the front rank seems to have made any significant contribution to fortress building before the middle of the seventeenth century. This was Gérard Desargues (1593–1662), who had been a soldier and had taken part in the siege of the Protestant stronghold of La Rochelle. He soon turned away from military engineering to abstract mathematical speculations. The French school of fortifications seems to have renewed in a form of its own the older Italian association of warlike preparations with art. Though he fancied himself to be a serious natural scientist, Blaise de Pagan (1604–1665), whose ideas about forts dominated in France toward the mid-seventeenth century, was not even a practical engineer.[43]

As had been true of the Dutch and the Italians in their small states, the French had as their main object in building fortifications the guarding of their territory against attack. In the case of France the country to protect was the largest and most populous in Western Europe; consequently its policy in fortifying, and the methods employed by its experts in building fortifications, had a predominant influence among the Europeans for a long time.

The remarkable progress of natural science in the sixteenth and early seventeenth centuries, the growing use after about 1575 of the experimental method as the decisive test of the validity of any scientific theory, combined with the new disposition to treat natural phenomena mathematically, owed something to the acute problems raised by the new and more deadly warfare. Perhaps for the first time in history, treatises were devoted exclusively to metallurgy, and in at least two of them (that by the Italian Biringuccio,[44] already referred to, and one completed in 1603 by a Spaniard, Diego de Prado y

Tovar) [45] the technology of weapons — guns in particular — occupied
a leading place. Yet the space given to military engineering was no
greater than in the technical treatises of antiquity, which, while
generally less concerned with mechanical improvement, were no less
concerned with weapons of war.[46] War was only one of many stimuli
to modern scientific and technical progress. It was no more important,
relative to other stimuli, than in earlier civilizations before the use of
gunpowder and cannon. The absence of industrialism in these earlier
civilizations can hardly be explained on the ground that they missed
the exhilarating experiences of battle, the lust for conquest, the fear of
subjection.

Throughout the sixteenth century and at the beginning of the
seventeenth, the Italians made perhaps more advances in the natural
sciences than any other people. War left a mark on the body of at least
one of the leading Italian mathematicians, Niccolò Tartaglia, who was
born about 1506 during the period of the foreign invasions of Italy.
As a child he was mutilated by some French soldiers at the sack of
Brescia. His first published work, *Nuova scienzia,* appeared in 1537. It
was concerned with the theory and practice of gunnery. Modern students have considered Tartaglia's treatment of the subject a landmark
of change from the mysterious to the scientific, from ritual to em-
piricism, from the medieval to the modern view of artillery.[47] It can
be plausibly suggested that his interest in problems of artillery and
fortification resulted from bitterness over his wounds, and that these
problems helped to furnish him with material for his mathematical
speculations.

Other Italian scientists also devoted time to the study of the motion
of projectiles and contributed to knowledge of this science of ballistics.
Among them was Galileo, who has been called the founder of the
experimental method in physics. A study of artillery was one source
of Galileo's formulation of the laws of the interdependence of motion
and force. By watching the flash and hearing the report from cannon,
he was able to prove that the movement of sound took time.[48] The
setting for the dialogue of his *Two New Sciences,* first published in
1638, was the Venetian arsenal, long a center for outfitting men-of-war.

Yet a close reading of this work, combined with a study of Galileo's
life, indicates that he derived most of his knowledge from observations
and experiments of a nonmilitary nature. His father, Vincenzo Galileo,
had made a name for himself in the history of music, a subject which
deeply interested the son. He learned more about the nature of sound
from the study of musical instruments, including the spinet, than from
the study of artillery.[49] After 1609 the telescope provided him with a

device for inspecting the stars and the sun, and he made observations which were of decisive importance in the development of his theory of motion.[50] Casual circumstances of daily life provided him with material upon which to speculate concerning movement, and daily life for him and most of his Italian contemporaries had in it more religion than war. While at mass in the cathedral of Pisa, a town whose leaning tower offered him special advantages for experimenting with falling bodies, Galileo hit upon the idea of the law of the pendulum by observing a swinging lamp.[51]

Galileo's early intention of becoming a monk, the fascination which intellectual problems had for him in his younger years, when he was educated in a monastery near Florence, his talents for music and painting, his lectures on Dante's *Inferno*, his fine literary style, the charms of geometry for his youthful mind, all suggest that nature and a peaceful early environment conspired to endow him with habits of application, such as a combination of broad culture with speculative genius alone can establish. Military problems were only one of many experiences to which he turned for positive data to support his speculations. It would be even more one-sided to treat war than to treat music as the principal source of his knowledge. It is difficult to believe that the results which flowed from his mind would have been notably impoverished if he had been left without such nourishment as the observation of guns and gunpowder offered.

The great scientific movement of which Galileo's work formed part was, to some extent, an outgrowth of the new interest in man and the physical world which became most ardent in Italy during the relatively peaceful times preceding the French invasion. The more strictly scientific genius of the Italians first reached a fullness after the frightful Italian wars of the early sixteenth century were over. The naval victory of Lepanto in 1571 — commemorated by Titian, then ninety-four, in a celebrated painting — left Venice and Italy free from serious fear of the Turk. Three years later, when Galileo was a boy of ten, the Spanish and French troops finally evacuated the cities of Piedmont. The military maneuvers of the dukes of Savoy, which preceded and accompanied during his later years the Thirty Years' War, affected mainly the slopes of the Alps. The development of natural science in Italy in Galileo's lifetime probably owed something to the relative tranquillity which came when the country ceased to provide frequent battlefields for European rulers, but provided better conditions for speculative thought.

The importance of Italian scientific achievement in Galileo's time should not obscure a movement of even greater importance for the rise of modern science. A shift was occurring in the centers of progress in both industrial technology and science from south and central Europe to Holland and above all to Great Britain. The possible utility of scientific knowledge for the increase in riches and the improvement of health, was first given philosophical significance by Francis Bacon (1561–1626), and then by Descartes (1596–1650) during his long sojourn in the economically progressive United Provinces, more advanced in material conveniences than his native France, and fuller of the bustle and noise portentous of the coming industrial civilization. The change in outlook, the new emphasis on the physical services which scientific speculation and discovery were capable of rendering mankind, had a profound influence on the development of modern science. The change can be traced back in England at least as far as the late years of Elizabeth's reign.

The early "industrial revolution" in England brought with it more new kinds of machinery and furnaces than in any other country. Few of the industrial methods which spread through the island of Great Britain before the Civil War were exclusively British in origin. But the concern of Englishmen and Scotchmen with reducing the costs of production by substituting machinery for hand labor, by burning coal instead of wood, and by constructing furnaces which would consume less fuel, together with their eagerness to derive instruction both from experiences abroad and experiments at home, prepared the ground for later English inventions and helped to kindle an enduring interest in natural science such as no earlier people had possessed. When Voltaire turned to the subject of science, in his *Siècle de Louis XIV*, he wrote that with respect to the inventions in which he put high hopes for humanity, the period of Louis XIV's reign from 1643 to 1715 might be most appropriately called "the century of the English." [52] England replaced Italy as the leading scientific country in the later decades of the seventeenth century, partly because of the exceptional interest which the early "industrial revolution" aroused not only in technology but in the scientific experiments and observations which were destined to provide a new basis for technological improvement. The interest in observation and experiment — in the experimental method as the basis for all scientific knowledge — was exemplified first by William Gilbert, the discoverer of magnetism and electricity, and then by Harvey, during an age which was for Great Britain a long era of peace.

One condition of this peace, as it seemed to the British, was preparation for defense. It would be a mistake to assume that the problems of warfare were of no concern, in the Elizabethan age, to the men who laid the foundations for the later scientific and technological leadership of Great Britain. On the outskirts of Edinburgh, in the midst of coal-bearing properties, a considerable landlord, John Napier of Merchiston — a Scot of genius, full of learning and many-sided in his interests, a passionate Calvinist in his beliefs — besides inventing machinery to drain coal mines, spent a certain amount of time on death-dealing engines, and apparently with some remarkable results. He possessed one of the great scientific minds of his age, fit to place beside those of his slightly younger contemporaries, Galileo and Kepler.

The threats, repeated after the failure of the Armada in 1588, of a Spanish invasion drew Napier's attention to weapons. These threats caused considerable alarm during the fifteen years that followed the Armada. Kinsale, in Ireland, was actually taken by the Spanish in 1601 and held for a year. Napier left behind a signed manuscript, dated June 7, 1596, in which he described several "Secrett Inventionis, proffitabill and necessary in theis dayes for defence of this Iland, and withstanding of strangers, enemies of God's truth and religion." The most momentous was what he called "a piece of artillery," whose nature is considered in a later chapter. In addition to this weapon, for which we have discovered no precedent, Napier described several other war engines, all of which had been frequently conceived in one form or another during the previous century and a half. Among these was a "chariot" which seems to have resembled very closely, in its form and military purpose, a twentieth-century tank.

In his letter to Sforza, Leonardo da Vinci had written about armored cars (*carri coperti*) equipped with cannon, "safe and unassailable," capable of breaking through "the serried ranks of the enemy," and providing undefended paths for the infantry to follow.[53] While Leonardo's early drawings of war chariots do not fit this description, in a drawing of his preserved in the British Museum a prototype of the tank actually appears — an armored car with holes for the guns and an opening at the top to admit air. "One may hold bellows in them to spread terror among the horses of the enemy," Leonardo observed, "and one may put carabiniers in them to break up every company." [54] In order to avoid using horses as draught animals, presenting a vulnerable target, this vehicle was to be moved by eight men inside, by means of crank handles attached to horizontal trundle wheels. The trundle wheels turned the circular spindles of pin wheels, and these in their turn drove the wheels of the car.[55]

Plans for horse-drawn vehicles, encased in metal and armed with guns, go back in England at least to 1523, when Sir William Bulmer (1465–1531), sheriff of county Durham, wrote to the Earl of Surrey about six carts covered with steel and brass, each with eight men and guns.[56] But Napier's vehicle, like Leonardo's, had no horses. From Napier's description, it seems to have been even more formidable and modern than Leonardo's. Napier wrote "of a round chariot of mettle made of the proofe of double muskett." The musket, unknown in Leonardo's time, had since become the most deadly weapon in the field. Napier evidently intended to make his tank impregnable. The motion, he explained, "shall be by those that be within the same, more easie, more light, and more spedie by much than so manie armed men would be otherwayes. The use hereof as well, in moving, serveth to breake the array of the enemies battle, it serveth to destroy the environed enemy by continuall charge and shott of harquebush through small hoalles; the enemie in the meanetime being abased and altogether uncertaine what defence or pursuit to use against a moving mouth of mettle." Here was an artfully propelled fortress bristling with guns! It only lacked the internal combustion engine to make it move at prodigious speed.

Napier also referred in his manuscript to "devises of sayling under the water." [57] Here was a conception that many others, among them Leonardo,[58] had had before this time. But more was done at the beginning of the seventeenth century than before to realize the underwater boat. Shortly after Napier's death in 1617, crude submarines were apparently built and launched. The Spanish dramatic poet, Calderón, invoked one in connection with the Dutch attempt to relieve the siege of Breda in 1625.[59] If this ship existed outside Calderón's imagination, it may have been prepared in England. Shortly before 1625 a Dutch mechanic and chemist, Cornelius Drebbel, seems to have discovered a fluid for preserving human respiration in a vessel below the surface. He made a trial in the Thames for the learned king James I. The submarine is reported to have carried twelve rowers besides passengers. According to a far more distinguished chemist than Drebbel, Robert Boyle, who was born in 1627, the vessel was an "admired success." Writing in 1662, Boyle remarked that one of the passengers in this undersea boat was still alive and had given his account "to an excellent mathematician that informed me of it." [60]

When need arose in peaceful Britain there was evidently no lack of inventive ingenuity directed toward defense. Yet the early British scientists derived their stimulus toward speculative thought and the application of the experimental method mainly from other sources than military engineering. As we shall see, Napier's war inventions were a sideline.[61] He took no pride in them and he was alarmed over their possible consequences. His life was wrapped up in general theological, scientific, and mathematical speculations. He is remembered as the discoverer of logarithms — an invention conceived wholly in his remarkable mind, and one destined to have a far-reaching influence on astronomy and every science involving calculations. There is no evidence that his logarithms had their origin in his work with war engines.

As conceived by Scotchmen, Englishmen, and Dutchmen, submarines and chariots were wanted for many other purposes besides defense. In a book called *Mathematicall Magick*, published in 1648, after the long peace in Great Britain had been broken and the interest in engines of war had perhaps increased, John Wilkins, the celebrated English divine and scientist, showed much enthusiasm for wind-driven chariots, submarines, and flying machines. Wilkins had begun his publications in 1638 with a plan for journeying to the moon.[62] Some years later he was one of the founders of the Royal Society, which became later in the seventeenth century the greatest center in Europe for the discussion of natural philosophy and for the exchange of knowledge gained from observation and experiment. He regarded the wind-driven chariot, which was invented in Holland by Simon Stevin, as an economical means of traveling and transporting goods. Unlike horses, Wilkins remarked, the wind "costs nothing and eats nothing." Flying "chariots" had for him various uses, none military. They might convey men quickly "to any remote place of this earth: as suppose to the Indies or Antipodes." Of the three new means of conveyance, Wilkins spoke only of the underwater "ark" as a valuable weapon. But that was not its only or perhaps even its main purpose. Wilkins considered it of much potential value as a means of traveling across the oceans independent of storms and tides and of carrying out scientific observations and discoveries "at the bottom of the sea." [63] It is proper, therefore, to regard much of the work done in the sixteenth and early seventeenth centuries on submarines, as well as on "chariots," as arising not from war but from the vision expressed in Francis Bacon's *New Atlantis* of man's power peacefully to conquer the earth.

Problems of warfare seem to have occupied a smaller place in English scientific and technical treatises than in those written by continental scientists and engineers. England was the first nation to develop a system of patents, of the kind that became general in the nineteenth century, to protect inventors and insure them a reward by granting them exclusive privileges to exploit a new technological process for a period of fourteen years. Some of the specifications for patents granted by the English crown from 1561 to 1640 have been preserved. Almost all of the processes were recommended by their sponsors for the improvements they promised to bring about not in destruction but in mining, manufacturing, transportation, and agriculture.[64] We may perhaps assume that a market arose only much later for the profitable sale of such discreditable products as new destructive engines, that only later, when fear of the devil diminished, inventions "of the devil" were thought to deserve protection. In any event, if the urgency of problems of war and a concern with weapons had been the chief factors in the progress of natural science and technology, we should hardly have had in the late sixteenth and early seventeenth centuries so striking a shift in the centers of observation and experiment, as well as of practical invention, away from those parts of Europe where wars were fiercest, to the island of Great Britain whose insularity helped to shield it from battle.

It is true that there were branches of science in which the French, as well as the Italians, excelled the English during the hundred years from 1540 to 1640, when France was engaged in wars so much more than England. Mathematics was one, and the study of ballistics, with its mathematical issues, might be expected to help explain why the French made more fundamental contributions than the English or any other people to mathematical theory. But apart from Desargues' experience with the art of fortification, there is apparently little evidence of a direct relation between the problems of military engineering and the speculative achievements of any first-rate French mathematician of the early seventeenth century. The discoveries in mathematics which led to the invention of analytical geometry and the differential calculus were associated primarily with Frenchmen, of whom the most famous is Descartes. Sitting in his slippers beside his warm Dutch stove, Descartes became in middle life almost a disembodied intellect. Descartes' parents, like those of other great French mathematicians of his time, belonged to the class of civil servants who worked with their heads rather than their hands. As the attitude of the French university faculties towards Paré's surgical discoveries shows, it was traditional for the learned to regard labor with matter as less excellent than more pure labor of the mind — a conception derived from medieval thought and practice, as well as from Greek tradition as formed especially by Plato and his followers. Descartes reacted against instruction in mathematics received in his youth from a Jesuit teacher, a certain Father François, in the college of La Flèche. In the late sixteenth century, in the early years of Father François, mathematicians in France had been mainly interested in applied mathematics, and Father François had talked to Descartes about land surveying, topography, hydrography, and hydrology. Descartes and most of the great

French mathematicians who were his contemporaries sought for mathematics what was still considered a nobler destiny. They sought to lead it in those more purely speculative directions which had appealed not only to the scholastic mathematicians but to the mathematicians of the antiquity for which Renaissance Europeans had so great an admiration. Descartes' personal interest in mathematics arose entirely from what he called "the certainty of its demonstrations and the evidence of its reasoning." For him its proper application was not to mechanics, but to philosophy, starting with metaphysics.[65]

In striving to renew the dignity of mathematics and to give the subject the cosmic, universal significance to which they thought it was entitled, the French were actually moving away from the practical, and even from the direct study of matter. Gilson has suggested that Descartes' principal philosophical error consisted in trying to make mathematics almost coextensive with philosophy, a kind of substitute for it, concerned as philosophy was with ultimate reality, with the most general causes and principles of all things. Descartes' overwhelming early interest in pure thought seems to have interfered with the success of his later attempts to experiment with matter,[66] when a reading of Harvey's work on the motions of the heart revealed to him the benefits which humanity might derive from the practical applications of new scientific discoveries.

War itself is a material experience, whatever heroism and romance may surround it. The construction of effective modern weapons is a material process. Mathematics had become too mechanical, too much concerned with practical problems, such as the moving of heavy objects, cannon among them, to suit Descartes. The turn taken by French mathematics in the early seventeenth century towards pure speculation was no response to war needs. The French mind was diverted at this time from the direct study of matter and of physical forces, which was destined to contribute to more destructive warfare but which early modern wars did little to encourage in France. In England, where the dangers of war were less continuous and less imminent, scientists, university men in particular, were much more willing than in France to avail themselves of material evidence and to devote themselves to gathering it by means of the new experimental method.

Partly perhaps on that account the French made less notable contributions in the seventeenth century than the English to physiology. They contributed less to the invention of labor-saving machinery driven by horses or water power, and to furnaces designed to cheapen the cost of fuel in manufacturing. While the English had no surgeon to match Paré, the French had no natural scientist to match William Harvey, with his epoch-making discovery of the circulation of the blood. This discovery was based on vivisection and experimental science of the kind that had not yet come into favor among French learned men, who spurned the handling of matter as "servile labor," suitable only for barber-surgeons, like Paré. The conclusions of Harvey's treatise, *Exercitatio anatomica de motu cordis et sanguinis in animalibus* (An Anatomical Disquisition on the Motion of the Heart and Blood in Animals), were generally rejected by the French university faculties. Not until 1649, more than two decades after its publication, did the member of an important school of medicine in France, Lazarus Riverius, of the University of Montpellier, venture to defend and teach Harvey's theory. This created such a scandal that he was called upon by an adherent of the old school of physiology to resign his chair.[67]

While constant warfare, such as was waged on the Continent, created new and intriguing problems for the scientists, the surgeons, and the industrial technicians, French thought failed to show a predilection for the solution of these problems. In so far as continentals were drawn to such problems under the stress of war, they were obliged to push aside matters relating to the improvement of health or wealth. Serious wars interfered with scholarship of every kind, including pure speculation, the study of the basic theoretical issues upon the discussion and solution of which the rise of modern science depended. During the French religious wars from 1562 to 1589, hardly a man was born in France who made his mark as a first-rate philosopher, scientist, or even as a mathematician.[68] It was in the comparatively peaceful period which followed, that the French intellect resumed its place in the front rank of European science.

The Thirty Years' War was even more damaging to the progress of natural science in Germany than the earlier religious wars had been to the progress of natural science in France. That long war helped to bring to an end a brilliant period for the study of the natural sciences in central Europe, a period which began with the discoveries of Copernicus (1473–1543). It was primarily the achievements of Copernicus and his successors in Poland, Austria, and Germany, especially Kepler, which revolutionized man's view of the movements of the earth and the heavenly bodies.

As court mathematician and astronomer since 1601 to successive emperors, Kepler had not much concern with any problem of military engineering. An abundant vintage in 1613 drew his attention to the defective methods used in estimating the cubic content of vessels, and led to an essay which helped prepare the way for the discovery of the infinitesimal calculus.

When the Thirty Years' War broke out Kepler was in Vienna, a center of European cultural life since the mid-fifteenth century. He had already discovered the third and last of his famous laws of planetary motion. His misgivings concerning the effect of the coming struggle upon science and learning generally, were expressed in his letter of dedication to Book V of the *Epitome of Copernican Astronomy*, first published in 1620. By that time soldiers were beginning to fight on behalf of the Roman Catholic worship, which the Emperor Ferdinand II set out to reëstablish in the states which had gone over to the Reform nearly a century before. In the famous battle of the White Mountain, the forces of the Empire were about to strike a successful blow against the armies defending Prague. This has been classed as one of the decisive battles of history. It actually decided nothing in the realm of the spirit, unless it was the dismal, if temporary, fate of learning in the German countries, which Kepler foresaw. This is what he wrote: "If I regard the circumstances of the time, this publication, alas! arrives in town late, after a very destructive war has arisen and the assemblages of students for whom these things are written have either been dispersed by the confusions of war or thinned out and wasted away by the expectation of war; after Austria, hitherto my nurse and benefactor, has struck against a very hard reef and seems to be called away from the guardianship of these beauties to serious care for her own safety." [69]

Let us recapitulate the argument of the last two chapters. The progress of practical technology and the rise of modern science, in their relations to the early history of war with gunpowder, divide into three fairly well-defined periods. In the working of copper and iron, all the basic metallurgical discoveries which led to an increased output of metal, indispensable for a widespread use of firearms, were made before 1490, when the first period may be said to have ended. The half century which followed, especially the years 1494–1529, brought into use new kinds of firearms and missiles. The captains of the leading continental armies began to depend on cannon, and still more on pistols, arquebuses, and muskets, as the decisive weapons in battle. The consequences of the revolution in weapons and in tactics, which began in this second period, were felt mainly during the third period, the hundred years or so following 1540 — the period which culminated in central Europe in those war decades that proved as unfavorable for the progress of natural science as Kepler had feared.

During the first of the three periods — and in some parts of Europe during the second — relatively peaceful conditions, which encouraged invention, observation, and experiment, helped to provide a favorable setting for the progress of industrial technology and for the birth of new concepts concerning natural phenomena. The ingenuity which led to the increase in the supply of metals, needed for the production of more guns and ammunition, was aroused mainly by efforts to build rather than to destroy, or at least to protect men and horses with armor from destruction. While next to nothing is known about the actual inventors of the destructive engines and the diabolical missiles which replaced bows, lances, and swords, the most fundamental inventions seem to have come as by-products of the Renaissance spirit of inquiry. Military engineering was hardly responsible for the astonishing master-pieces in the visual arts and the remarkable new interest in the nature of the body and of the physical world. This spirit of inquiry, expressed simultaneously and almost interchangeably in art and science, came to fruition during the late fifteenth century, in Copernicus' early years, before heavy fighting became at all general in Europe.

As wars grew more serious and widespread, inventive ingenuity was focused more than in earlier, relatively peaceful times upon meeting practical problems of attack or defense. Scientific speculation derived some of its material from the experiences of the new warfare, particularly from the shooting of balls and bullets, the treatment of new kinds of wounds, and the building of new fortifications.

Yet the more acute and general the new warfare became, the more it interfered with technical inventions and improvements of all kinds, and with the revolutionary scientific work of the late sixteenth and early seventeenth centuries: the methodical application of the experimental method (combined with mathematics) to the study of natural phenomena. War interfered because of the destruction of life which it caused through casualties, starvation, and disease, and also because of the disruption of the peaceful conditions necessary to original thought and to the practice of any new constructive skill. Heavy fighting on the Continent was a factor in moving the centers of technical development and scientific progress to the north of Europe, where there was less war.

For considerable stretches of time between 1450 and 1640 parts of Europe were relatively peaceful. It was then and there that the greatest advances took place in natural science, and few of these advances can be attributed to efforts to solve problems raised by warfare. If all the Western people had been engulfed in destruction during the Thirty Years' War, as the people of central Europe were engulfed, science would in all probability have suffered a general eclipse.

CHAPTER FOUR

Progress of Capitalist Industry

· IN A STUDY OF INTERRELATIONS BETWEEN EUROPEAN MILITARY AND
economic history since the Middle Ages, Werner Sombart (1863–1941)
deliberately ignored the destructive aspects of modern war on the
ground that these aspects were obvious and had received much attention from writers on political history.[1] Sombart was a prominent professor of Kaiser Wilhelm II's generation, who lived on to accept Hitler
and national socialism. He set about to emphasize what might be
called the "constructive" sides of war.

In an age of increasing specialization such a procedure was in the
best repute. "Search for the new," scholars were told; "study what has
not been examined and assume that you and your readers will remember what was known before." It was a procedure which helped
to destroy the scholar's view of history, and so of life as a whole.

The "constructive" aspects of war were likely to strike especially a
German historian of Sombart's age, because his country, during the
seventy-eight years of his life, was busy invading foreign territory,
without the more disagreeable experience of having its enemies
spread havoc in Germany itself, as they were destined to do on a
colossal scale shortly after he died. Sombart's argument is that, after
guns became the decisive weapons, the growth in the number of men
under arms and the increasing cost of supplying them made it necessary to assemble capital in large units and led to the development of
large-scale enterprise in industry, commerce, and finance. Thus, in
spite of the destruction it caused, modern war, based on gunpowder,
played a prominent part (like the less destructive growth of luxury)
in the rise of "modern capitalism" during the sixteenth, seventeenth,
and eighteenth centuries.[2]

Within the limits which Sombart imposed on the subject, his thesis is sound enough. During the sixteenth and early seventeenth centuries, changes in the weapons and in the scope of warfare brought about some concentration of industry in large establishments, which anticipated the factories of the nineteenth century, though such machinery as there was in them was turned not by steam or hydroelectric power, but by the pull of horses or the rush of water. War promoted large-scale industry both directly and indirectly: directly, because it led to the building of extensive plants for the production of the new armaments; indirectly, because the growing military demands for supplies of ore and metal (especially iron and copper) stimulated the mining and metallurgical industries, which, like the armament industries proper, could often be carried on with more economic efficiency in larger more expensive establishments, employing many workers.

What makes Sombart's thesis concerning war and capitalism false is the limits he imposed on the subject. Problems essential to an inquiry into the origins of industrialism are hardly touched by his evidence. How important was the demand for new arms, as compared with other new, nonmilitary demands, in changing the forms of industrial organization, in encouraging the progress of capitalistic mining and manufacturing? What effects did fighting with the new weapons have upon industrial development? To discuss the economic consequences of the production of the instruments of war as if this could be kept separate from the economic consequences of their use is of little service to truth.

(1) *Armies and Large-Scale Industrial Enterprise*

The arsenal at Nancy, which belonged to the dukes of Lorraine, was among the largest of the new armament works. It was appropriately called "l'Artillerie," and it was already of some importance early in the sixteenth century. It was expanded several times during the next hundred years and was equipped for the manufacture and the repair, as well as for the storage, of weapons and munitions of every description. Here, gathered together, were furnaces, forges, cannon foundries, gunpowder mills, and saltpeter shops, and also mills for grinding grain, apparently to supply the numerous working population with flour.[3] Within the town the arsenal with its buildings occupied several acres of ground, as thickly populated as many of the compact villages in the open country, which are said to have had normally from fifty to five hundred inhabitants in the later Middle Ages.[4]

From the beginning, foundries for producing cannon seem often to have required the services of a number of workers. In a drawing Leonardo da Vinci made of a foundry we see several groups, each of eight to ten men.[5] The strength of their muscles is aided in moving and placing cannon by an elaborate system of pulleys. There is no horse or water power. Both kinds of power (which had been employed industrially during the Middle Ages) came into wider use during the hundred and fifty years following the times of Leonardo, especially in Great Britain and in Sweden, where the manufacture of guns flourished so remarkably during the Thirty Years' War. As machinery, set in motion by the push of running or falling water or the tug of horses, became more common in metallurgy, the cost of establishing cannon foundries increased. At the same time, with the spread of fighting and with the growing use of cannon which accompanied the spread of fighting, these foundries multiplied. The new warfare brought about a concentration of industrial plant and industrial labor in larger units.

Extensive and varied establishments, employing scores and even hundreds of workers under a single administration, did not originate with the general use of firearms and explosives. Industrial enterprises requiring much capital and hundreds of hands were far from unknown in the time of Caesar, or perhaps even in the Hellenistic world.[6] The prevalence of slave labor encouraged them in the mining industry [7] and in some manufactures; for example, in the production of red-glazed pottery and of bronze- and copperwares at Capua in Italy.[8] Before the general use of gunpowder and firearms, the European peoples had had establishments for shipbuilding at least as large as the sixteenth-century armament plant at Nancy. Perhaps the largest was the "arsenal" at Venice, founded in 1104. Its primary purpose was to build and outfit the Venetian war fleet, although some merchant galleys were built at least from the middle of the fourteenth century. With its wharves, launching yards, workshops, and storage houses, the arsenal enclosure already occupied about thirty-two acres, with additions begun in 1325, four years after the death of Dante.[9] That was long before the time when, according to our anonymous Elizabethan, the Venetians learned from Schwartz how to make cannon! To Dante, this establishment at Venice had seemed so dark, so noisy, so filthy, and so vast, that he compared it to the Fifth Chasm of the Inferno, where the barterers in public offices and authority lay expiating their sins in a bath of the foulest pitch. Dante's description reminds us that it is a questionable assumption which men have been prone to make in recent times, the assumption behind works like Sombart's on modern capitalism that the appearance of any new, large plant, with machinery to abridge manual labor, is necessarily a contribution to human happiness.

The large plant, then, was not the *creation* of modern war with gunpowder. Nor did the new warfare of the sixteenth century lead *invariably* to the concentration of the armament industries in large plants. In saltpeter and gunpowder making in France, for example, the crown fostered small units of production, scattered all through the country. An inventory was taken after the death of one gunpowder maker at Barjols, near Aix-en-Provence, in 1626, when the Thirty Years' War was raging in central Europe. This gunpowder maker's possessions in his tiny cottage consisted of one foul bed, two much-worn coats, four plates, and three spoons, besides some crude furniture. In the room where he had manufactured powder were a few tools, two scales, and an old arquebus.[10] This was domestic work of a type that had predominated in industry as far back as the twelfth century. There was nothing about this little man's craft, as it appears in the book of the local notary who took the inventory, which seems to point the way towards industrial civilization.

While saltpeter and gunpowder were often manufactured in France during the reign of Louis XIII (1610–1643) on a larger scale than at Barjols, these munitions were still produced for the most part within the precincts of old homes. Domestic manufacturers, who entered into contracts for the delivery of their products to officials representing the crown, remained the rule.[11] It was in England, isolated from the continental wars and so relatively freer than France from the urgent direct pressure of military requirements, that a substantial part of the gunpowder-making industry came to be concentrated in a single enterprise, consisting of several mills at scattered spots near London. For sixty-five years or so this enterprise was in the hands of the family of John Evelyn, whose grandfather had been granted an exclusive patent by Queen Elizabeth for the manufacture of gunpowder. It would have been much more dangerous for the French kings, exposed as their country was to invasion, to have concentrated the industry in one region, subject to capture by an enemy army.[12]

In France in the early seventeenth century even the making of artillery was often carried on (as the making of armor had been) [13] by scattered craftsmen in small units, sometimes as domestic enterprise, under contracts like those which predominated in the saltpeter and gunpowder manufactures. In Languedoc in 1621 and 1622, when, in spite of the crown, the Huguenot forces still retained political control, and when they were preparing to hold the Cévennes and the strip of towns along the coast from the Rhone valley to Toulouse against threatened attack from the royal forces, the officials who were in charge of the municipal government at Nîmes, a Protestant stronghold, put out the manufacture of cannon to a founder in Montpellier, thirty-five miles to the southwest. This they did in the autumn of 1622, on the very eve of the surrender of Montpellier to the armies organized for the king by Richelieu to eradicate all independent Protestant armed authority. The same officials at Nîmes put out the manufacture of cannon balls to two citizens of Alais, thirty miles to the north in the Cévennes. Alais had become a center for the manufacture of arms in southern France during the religious wars, and there the production of cannon, like the making of muskets and other firearms, was apparently in the hands of smiths, working in their homes with only a few helpers, usually members of their families.[14]

Numerous survivals of small enterprise do not show, of course, that the manufacture of gunpowder and firearms exerted no pull in the direction of the factory form of production. But they put us on guard against exaggerating the force of the pull. During the first half of the seventeenth century the only large manufacture of guns in central Europe, aflame with war, was that at Suhl, in the Thüringerwald of Saxony. This town was long known as "the armory of Germany." Its gun factory not only produced firearms for Germany; pieces were exported to Hungary, Italy, Spain, Switzerland, Russia, Poland, Denmark, and France. Cannon, muskets, and pistols from Suhl served the armies fighting on both sides in the Thirty Years' War. Not until after that war ended in 1648, were further large gunmaking factories started in Germany.[15]

Small and large forms of industrial enterprise existed side by side in the new armament industries, as they had long existed in the textile manufactures with their innumerable ramifications. Clothmaking was not, as historians once supposed, the first Western European industry to adopt the factory form of enterprise. It was among the last.[16] While the armament manufactures, generally speaking, lent themselves more readily to factory enterprise than did the textile manufactures, there were other early modern industries more susceptible to industrial capitalism than either. Among these was salt production, when climatic conditions made it necessary to use fuel in heating the salt solution, instead of depending on the natural heat of the sun for evaporation — the method employed with sea water at the marshes along the coasts of the Mediterranean and the Bay of Biscay. Alum making and coal mining were two other industries which proved even better suited than salt manufacturing to the development of expensive plants, staffed by many workmen. Large establishments, similar in scale to the arsenal at Nancy, were developed in connection with all these industries during the sixteenth and early seventeenth centuries and even before.

Neither salt nor alum nor coal was valuable at this time as a war material. Before the extensive use of ice, salt provided the chief pre-servative for perishable foods, particularly fish. The demand for salt grew notably after the mid-fifteenth century, with the increase in the size of markets and in the length of sea voyages. In the sixteenth century fleets of little fishing ships began to set out on long summer voyages for the Newfoundland banks from the ports of Holland and western France,[17] and during the early seventeenth century the fishing trade in the North Sea grew very rapidly under Dutch leadership, so that there was an almost continuous increase in the market for salt, especially in the north of Europe. Alum was indispensable for dyeing. There was a rapid expansion in the demand for it during the late fifteenth century and afterwards, brought about by the spread of elaborate and rich clothing, bedding, table coverings, and hangings — luxuries with which no military officer could afford to supply his soldiers. Coal had been used in small quantities in the Middle Ages by lime burners and smiths, who lived near to outcropping seams. A new market was created for coal in Great Britain in the late sixteenth and seventeenth centuries, mainly by the shortage of firewood and char-coal. But on the Continent, where large armies were on the move, there was still no general shortage of timber. Soldiers were beginning to carry with them small stoves for baking bread and for cooking, but they almost invariably burned firewood or charcoal. As coal was not yet successfully used in smelting ores even in Great Britain, it was still of little importance compared to charcoal and firewood in providing the supplies of metal so essential for warfare.

Salt making, alum making, and coal mining, therefore, were not war industries during the sixteenth and seventeenth centuries. All of them thrived on peace. But the expansion of these industries led more frequently than the expansion of the armament industries to the build-ing of costly plants and to the concentration of workers in large establishments. The saltworks built early in the sixteenth century at Salins in Franche-Comté, and those belonging to the dukes of Lorraine at Dieuze, were hardly less extensive and monumental than the arsenal at Nancy. They involved a scarcely less heavy investment of capital. At Salins salt manufacturing was carried on in an enclosure which occupied an irregular strip of land three hundred yards long and one hundred wide. Some of the buildings had towers, arcades, and Doric columns. Fountains played in the squares.[18] To Gollut, the sixteenth-century historian of Franche-Comté, these saltworks were one of the architectural wonders of the country.[19]

In 1461, when Leonardo was still a child, alum making on a large scale was introduced to Europe from the Near East, a generation

before any great extension took place in the armament manufacture
at Nancy. The first large alum making plants in Western Europe were
in the papal estates, at Tolfa, near Rome. In the late fifteenth century
the alum works there apparently employed scores (possibly hundreds)
of workers. During the next hundred and fifty years, similar alum
manufactures were founded at several places north of the Alps, in
spite of the efforts of the popes to monopolize the supply of alum for
Europe, by threatening with excommunication princes and other
buyers who got this dyeing material from enterprises nearer home
than the one at Tolfa.[20] Among the largest of all the alum works was
the one established in Yorkshire during the reign of James I (1603–
1625). A contemporary described it as "a distracted worke in severall
places and of sundry partes, not possible to bee performed by anie
one man nor by a fewe. But by a multitude of the baser sort, of whom
the most part are idle, careless and false in their labour."[21] In 1619
this Yorkshire alum venture comprised some six or seven houses for
manufacturing. Each was furnished with large brick furnaces and
cisterns, piles of alum stone, coal and wood fuel, and about ten massive
metal pans for heating the liquid derived from the alum stone. Each
house cost thousands of pounds sterling to build and equip and each
employed regularly about sixty workmen. The annual expense of the
fuel and other materials needed to keep one house in operation exceeded £1000, equivalent to some $50,000 or more in American money
of 1950. The capital invested in these Yorkshire works by the English
crown during the five years from 1612 to 1617 came to nearly £70,000,
the equivalent of about $4,000,000 today. In addition many private
persons put large sums into them.[22]

By the reign of Charles I (1625–1642) there were several extensive
collieries in Great Britain, each with a hundred or more men on its
pay roll. The largest, the Grand Lease Colliery at Whickham, across
the river from Newcastle, probably employed nearly five hundred
laborers above and below ground.[23] A few miles away, at the mouth
of the Tyne, the sea-salt works at South Shields were even larger than
the brine-salt works at Salins. They employed many hundreds of
workers.[24]

As England became the chief country in Europe for technological
improvements of a utilitarian kind during the peaceful reigns of
Elizabeth and James I, it also became the chief country for the expansion of most heavy industries. Peace was not the only or even the
principal explanation. Alum making developed because of the presence
of raw materials. Rich beds of alum stones were found in Yorkshire
and other counties. Coal mining expanded because of the unrivaled

supplies of thick coal seams outcropping in many parts of Great Britain, often close to navigable water, which facilitated the carriage of so heavy and bulky a commodity. But it would be no less one-sided to argue that peace contributed nothing to the prosperity of heavy industry in England than to argue that the new warfare had no influence upon the size of the enterprises producing arms. What made possible the rise of industrial capitalism in the north of Europe — what made possible the early English "industrial revolution," with an extensive use of horse- and water-driven machinery and with a remarkable concentration of capital in mines and manufacturing ventures under the control of private businessmen — was peace combined with abundant natural resources, with good harbors for coastwise commerce, and with the natural isolation provided by the seas, an isolation without which peace would have been more difficult to keep. Toward the end of the sixteenth century a historian of Devonshire remarked, "England maye better lyve of selffe without any other nation then any other nation without it." [25] This self-sufficiency in the essential commodities of life was to last England more than two hundred years, until the nineteenth century.

England derived many industrial advantages from the peaceful conditions which prevailed in the island of Great Britain, set off from a warring Europe. For example, the expansion during Elizabeth's reign of the new draperies in East Anglia was based on the skill of Huguenot refugees, driven out of northern France and the southern Low Countries by the religious wars. Foreign refugees played an indispensable part in the progress of the woolen and worsted industries in and about Norwich.

In point of numbers employed, textiles — with spinning, carding, weaving, fulling, dyeing, steaming, hat making, sailcloth making, tapestry making, and so on — was the largest of all European industries. While it was late in becoming a stronghold of factory enterprise, it lent itself from medieval times to another capitalistic form of organization. This has been frequently called the "putting-out system," because the workers labored in their own homes — in cellars, garrets, or cottages — and sometimes, when water power was used, as in fulling, at little mills built along the streams. In the rooms where they cooked and slept and lived with their wives and children, these men worked on raw materials and partly finished cloths, which were "put-out" to them by merchants, some of whom were in a considerable way of business. The system involved some concentration of capital, because the materials — wool, flax, cotton, yarn, and cloth in various stages of manufacture, together with fuel, alum, and other substances needed in fulling, dyeing, and pressing — were kept in one or more warehouses. Sometimes these were an annex of the home of one of the capitalists, sometimes they were specially built. The workers either went to the warehouses for their materials, or received them in their homes at the hands of the entrepreneurs who owned the enterprises, or from their agents. When the workers had performed their special tasks in clothmaking, they returned the pieces and claimed their wages.

Neither capitalists nor the "capitalist spirit" were innovations of the Renaissance or the Reformation. They were already important elements in economic life during the twelfth and thirteenth centuries, as the great Pirenne and his pupils have taught. In the age of the crusades, however, the large majority of master craftsmen retained financial independence, in the sense that they not only owned the tools and the other equipment with which they labored, but bought their materials (sometimes on credit) and sold their partly finished products. By the time of the Reformation, when the new warfare was beginning, the proportion of these independent or semi-independent craftsmen in the textile industry was still large everywhere in Europe, even in the most advanced regions for clothmaking — northern Italy, Flanders, and Brabant. In the English textile industries independent craftsmen probably far outnumbered wageworkers. The spread of wagework, where the craftsman was usually paid so much a piece by the capitalist who furnished the materials, did not transform the conditions of labor. But the craftsman ceased buying and selling. Wagework made him an employee even though he stayed at home. The spread of wagework was also frequently accompanied by some growth in the scale of the commercial enterprise undertaken by a single capitalist trader or a group of traders joined in partnership. As the opportunities to employ workers for wages multiplied, such capitalists needed raw materials in larger quantities — for example, alum and other dyestuffs and many varieties of wool. They needed larger quarters for storage and wider connections with landlords who raised sheep and with merchants and financiers in centers for selling cloth such as Florence.

Karl Marx called this form of capitalism "manufacture," as distinguished from "machinofacture." He traced its great expansion from the mid-sixteenth to the late eighteenth century.[26] Marx leaned heavily for his historical generalizations on English experience. He settled in London in 1849 at the age of thirty-one and lived there for the remainder of his sixty-five years. Even this intellectual giant of the nineteenth century was not entirely independent of special circumstances in his researches. He could not always rise above the atmosphere of readily accessible books and documents, as provided by the

British Museum, where he worked when he was composing *Das Kapital*.

It now appears that neither the late sixteenth nor the early seventeenth century was a period of marked growth for "manufacture" in most of continental Europe. There the rapid development of this form of capitalist enterprise had taken place, first, in the late twelfth and thirteenth centuries, and then again in the late fifteenth and early sixteenth. Yet Marx's insistence on the capitalistic character of what he called "manufacture" and what we here call, somewhat arbitrarily, the "putting-out system," was an important contribution to historical truth.[27] The *late* sixteenth century, which he thought of as a decisive time for the progress of this form of capitalistic enterprise, actually marked the beginning of a remarkable expansion of "putting-out" in most branches of clothmaking (and also in the working of metal by smiths of many kinds) both in England and Holland. A notable increase took place in the division of labor, in the amount of industrial wagework, and in the openings for capitalists capable of coördinating the labor of many different kinds of craftsmen.

In England, at least, there seems to have been a growth of larger units of putting-out enterprise than had been at all common heretofore in continental countries. Sometimes hundreds and possibly, in an exceptional case, more than a thousand workpeople — living in scattered cottages in the country surrounding a small town or in several growing villages — labored (as spinners, carders, weavers, fullers, dyers, scourers, dressers) for a single concern, or for persons supplied with credit by a single concern. Many of the workers served alternately several textile firms of different sizes, so that their names might be found now on one payroll, now on another. Some of the textile firms assembled as much as ten or twenty thousand pounds sterling, or even more capital, the rough equivalent in present-day American money of many hundreds of thousands of dollars. Taken altogether, the new opportunities for investment in capitalistically organized textile enterprises may have exceeded those in mining.[28]

The growth of cloth manufacturing in England and Holland was encouraged by the partial immunity which these countries were able to maintain from the bitter fighting, above all from the civil war which smoldered in France and Germany during years of nominal peace and put citizen against citizen and even brother against brother. Toleration of rival religious beliefs, first established as a principle in Holland during the 1580's by William the Silent to unite the Dutch in their struggle against the attacking armies of Philip II, helped the textile industries to thrive.

Progress of Capitalist Industry

Protestant worship, especially in its Calvinist f~~orms~~
found fertile soil in the towns and expanding industr~~ies, among~~
the numerous mechanics, as well as among the ri~~ch~~
traders who were frequently their employers. Prot~~estantism had~~
an attraction for cloth merchants, who coördinated the w~~ork of~~
out craftsmen, and for numerous craftsmen who made and finished the
cloth, whether they were wageworkers or independent masters buying
their materials and selling their products. As the Inquisition spread
from Spain through much of Europe in the late sixteenth century, it
created difficult conditions for the men engaged in the cloth trade and
in the making of cloth, especially when they were devout Calvinists
and tenacious in their faith.

The case of Bertrand le Blas, a velvet worker, apparently a small
independent master, in the ancient town of Tournai on the river
Scheldt in Flanders, is illustrative of the difficulties which beset the
Protestant industrialist with a strong conscience, when he lived in a
community which was being reclaimed for the Pope of Rome. According to Le Blas's biographer, his horror of the "idolatry of Popedom"
had led him in the summer of 1555 to leave his work in Tournai and
go to Wesel, more than a hundred and fifty miles northeast across the
Rhine, where the Protestants were able to worship in their own ways.
But he was unable to persuade his wife, with their little children, to
join him. After making in vain three special trips from Wesel, he
settled again in December in his home in Tournai. His mind was more
troubled than ever by the religious conditions there. On Christmas day
he betook himself to the cathedral. In one of the smaller chapels he
stood upright, hat on head, without attracting any attention, so large
was the crowd on this day of days. Then, as the parish priest lifted
the sacrament in the mass, Le Blas dashed through the kneeling men,
women, and children. Snatching the wafer, he threw it on the floor,
crushed it to pieces under his shoe, and shouted at the top of his
voice: "Do you believe, ill-advised humans, that this is Jesus Christ,
the true God and Savior?"

The same action committed today in a Catholic church in the
United States would be treated as that of a crank. It would be
punished, if at all, only by committing its perpetrator to a home for
the mentally deranged! In the late sixteenth century, in territory
claimed by the militant counterreformers, it could have, as Le Blas
knew, only one result. Three days later, refusing to repent, the velvet
worker was bound to the chains of a strappado. Horribly tortured, he
was drawn up and down over a little fire until, fried and roasted, he

ıed his last. The flames having consumed his body, his ashes ɹe scattered in the river Scheldt.[29]

The records of the Protestant martyrs indicate that, among the textile workers, there were many men and women hardly less determined than Le Blas. And for every person so physically heroic, there were scores, even hundreds, whose nights and days were troubled with the conflict which religious war created between their hopes for eternal life and the pursuit of a tranquil worldly existence in the midst of the enemies of their consciences. These were not conditions under which they could work most effectively at their trades. It is evident that in the north — not only in Holland but in England, where after the accession of Queen Elizabeth in 1558 the religious issues were seldom so desperate as on the Continent — the textile workers (including those who preferred the Roman Catholic to the Anglican worship) were much better able to turn their minds to the problems of business and workmanship than in France, Franche-Comté, Flanders, Brabant, or in most of the small sovereign states into which the Holy Roman Empire was divided from the Vosges to the Oder, the Eastern Alps, and the Carpathian Mountains.

Religious toleration and peace acted as magnets drawing skilled textile craftsmen away from persecution and out of the war zones, over the Rhine into Holland and across the Channel into England. The road taken by Le Blas, in a preliminary effort to escape his dilemma, was followed during the next decades by tens of thousands of Protestants, many of them textile workers. Other thousands took to ships, which carried them to England and Scotland. In these countries they found more favorable conditions than they had been accustomed to for innovations such as more efficient looms and for the concentration of larger stocks of materials in the warehouses of a single enterprise. Holland, and still more England and Scotland, had been hitherto relatively backward industrially, and the regulations were often lacking which interfered in old industrial centers with such technical innovations as the Dutch engine loom for weaving ribbons and other small wares. There were fewer rules restricting the scale of enterprise. This helps to explain why the expansion of textiles in the peaceful north provided opportunities for the development of larger units of putting-out enterprise than had been common in Italy, Flanders, and France.

England owed the first notable progress of a sugar-making industry partly to the fierceness of the continental wars. Sugar was apparently not used in classical times by the Greeks and Romans, who depended for sweetening mainly on honey. During the later Middle Ages sugar was derived by the Europeans in small quantities from cane planted in the islands of the Mediterranean. After the discovery of America, the cane was planted successfully on island after island of the Atlantic. Before the middle of the seventeenth century plantations had been started in Barbados.[30]

Some of the cane was brought to Europe for refining. During the industrial expansion of the late fifteenth and early sixteenth centuries on the Continent, sugar making came to be carried on in sizable buildings, especially at Antwerp, where the industry prospered as nowhere else during a stretch of some forty years following 1520. The work required a capital outlay which, though inferior to that in alum making or large-scale coal mining, might amount to the Flemish equivalent of several thousand pounds sterling.[31] Sugar refining often called for larger investments in room space, iron rollers, and other machinery and equipment than were common on the Continent in saltpeter and gunpowder making. While saltpeter and gunpowder making were nourished by war, the war which Philip II began to wage in the 1560's against the Protestants almost destroyed the sugar manufacture in the Spanish Low Countries (modern Belgium).

What brought sugar refining to England was the collapse of the industry at Antwerp. That city had been the hub of economic activity for the European world from about 1520 to 1560,[32] when the merchants of the leading towns of Italy, Spain, Portugal, and southern Germany transacted much of their business along its streets and in its houses. During the early years of Elizabeth's reign, there were only two small sugar refineries in London; England got most of its sugar from Antwerp.[33] But few, if any, of the large Antwerp refineries survived the sack of that cosmopolitan city by Spanish and French troops in 1576 and in 1583. The markets which Antwerp had supplied were thrown open to new producers. Sugar making took the same passages north as cloth manufacturing. It moved to Amsterdam, Hamburg, Middleburg, and London, and also west over the French border to Rouen.

During the sixteenth and early seventeenth centuries the Europeans developed a taste for sugar that had not existed among earlier civilized peoples. That is partly explained perhaps by the growth of economic civilization in the north. The northern fruits and vegetables had less natural succulence than those growing in the Mediterranean soil. To make them palatable it was necessary to sweeten them. Since the Reformation there has never been enough sugar in time of war. So the shortage created by the destruction of Antwerp only served to encourage sugar making elsewhere. In London several large refineries were built during the decade following the second sack of Antwerp.[34] English haberdashers, ironmongers, grocers, and merchant tailors, whose capital was derived from their success in these other businesses, combined with Dutchmen of experience in the sugar-making industry, to develop the London sugar manufacture. In a document written in 1593, Richard Carmarden, perhaps the best informed and most reliable of Queen Elizabeth's later customs officials, observed: "Now the English can supply Germany and the Low Countries [with sugar] better cheap than they can supply us." [35]

The fate of the sugar makers of Antwerp is a further illustration of the way in which fighting in the Spanish Netherlands, perhaps the leading manufacturing area of Europe from about 1540 to 1560, pushed industrial capital and large-scale industry across the Channel and northeast along the coasts of the Continent, leaving the potentially rich industrial country of modern Belgium lean of active town life, at the time when Rubens and the Abbé Scaglia were trying, by diplomatic negotiations, to bring the wars to an end. With one hand, the continental war lords and their marching armies created a need for large new establishments to furnish war materials; with the other, they interfered with the progress of large new establishments designed to cater to peacetime markets. In some cases, they drove rising capitalistic manufactures out of the war zones and even across the Channel. In a variety of ways the industrial losses of the warring countries were gains for peaceful England. The spectacle of war and peace during the hundred years following the Reformation casts doubt on the notion that large-scale industrial enterprise would have made less progress if Western civilization had been spared the curse of gunpowder and firearms. But could we expect that the quest for new industrial riches would free civilized men from their propensity to fight?

For the continental peoples — especially those of central Europe and the Spanish Netherlands — the decades from 1560 through 1640 were a period of more organized fighting, more devastation, and more misery bred of both, than any earlier age since the Western Europeans had begun to advance economically in the eleventh century. The only previous period at all comparable was that of the Hundred Years' War,[36] from the mid-fourteenth to the mid-fifteenth century, when the English fought in France to win and hold territory, and when there were sporadic battles and plundering almost everywhere in Europe, including Great Britain. Then the armies raised were very much smaller and most of the guns were lacking. The only effective pistol was the bottle of sack which Falstaff offered Prince Hal in preparation for his combat with Hotspur. "Take my pistol, if thou wilt." "Give it me. What, is it in the case?" "Ay, Hal; 'tis hot, 'tis hot. There's that will sack a city." [37]

In spite of the long campaigns and the fearful battles waged with guns and metal missiles almost continuously from 1560 to 1648, there was no notable increase in the output of metal on the Continent. In central Europe and perhaps also in the Spanish Netherlands there was a falling off in the production of copper. Even the output of iron apparently diminished in these countries,[38] though there was a temporary revival of the Belgian iron manufacture in the first quarter of the seventeenth century.[39] In France and Spain iron production grew slowly, if at all. At the end of the sixteenth century, and again in the thirties of the seventeenth, the fighting and the movement of troops in Franche-Comté and across the French border in Champagne and Burgundy caused the temporary cessation of labor at many ironworks and the complete destruction of some.[40] The distress of the ironmaking industry of Champagne on the eve of Louis XIV's accession to the French throne in 1643 was hardly offset by increased production in provinces which escaped the fighting of the Thirty Years' War. While the demand for arms had stimulated iron metallurgy in the neighborhood of Saint Etienne, the number of ironworks in the Cévennes seems to have declined between 1540 and 1640.[41] The spread of large new blast furnaces, with substantial auxiliary forges such as were already common in England early in the seventeenth century, hardly began in France before 1645.[42]

Like sugar refining, metallurgy was prominent among the industries pushing north. As early as 1624, if not before, many workers from the metallurgical manufacture in the Spanish Netherlands were induced by Dutch factors to emigrate to Sweden and help exploit the rich Scandinavian mineral resources.[43] In Sweden the prodigious manufacture of guns — especially of powerful new iron cannon — under the direction of Louis de Geer came at a critical time. This extraordinarily enterprising merchant was able to supply Gustavus Adolphus' armies for the invasion of Germany in 1630–1632 — an invasion which ended the power of the two Roman Catholic generals, Tilly and Wallenstein, who had won sweeping victories during the early phases of the Thirty Years' War. The great Swedish warrior-king routed Tilly at Breitenfeld, north of Leipzig, and then met Wallenstein at Lützen in the less decisive action in which Gustavus Adolphus lost his own life driving back the enemy in a mist that obscured the course of the battle.

De Geer seems to have always had cannon to spare for the Netherlands. He shipped some four hundred great guns from Swedish ports

to the United Provinces by 1627,[44] on the eve of battles which
were to drive back over the Rhine-Meuse delta the Spanish armies,
which had advanced under another Roman Catholic general, the
Marquis of Spinola. United in an unholy alliance with France, whose
foreign policies were in the hands of Cardinal Richelieu, the new
Dutch stadholder, Frederick Henry of Orange (youngest child of
William the Silent), conducted successful campaigns against the
Spanish armies, culminating in 1637 with the recapture of Breda beyond the Meuse in Brabant. These victories of the Dutch, following
those of Sweden in Germany, were decisive in turning the war against
the Imperial, the Spanish, and the papal cause.

At the same critical juncture of the Thirty Years' War, during the
late 1620's and the early 1630's, the English were shipping cast-iron
cannon to the United Provinces from large foundries in the once
thickly wooded "Weald" of Sussex and Kent. Arms formed a substantial proportion of the ironwares exported from England in the 1630's.[45]
Competition from Sweden seems to have troubled at least one prominent English ironmaster, John Browne of Brenchley, who is said to
have employed two hundred men in manufacturing cannon.[46]

As long as the three great powers of northern Europe — England,
Sweden, and the United Provinces — could keep peace among themselves, avoid civil strife, and ship cannon and other firearms to each
other and to their friends on the Continent, they possessed a force of
resistance in metal, guns, and ammunition which it was increasingly
difficult for the larger continental states, under representatives of the
imperial house of Hapsburg, once so much wealthier, to match. Even
France began to get warships, cannon, and war materials from Sweden,
at least as early as the 1630's.[47] It is not improbable that Richelieu,
who was astute in economic matters, was influenced after 1628 in his
increasingly pro-Protestant foreign policy by knowledge of the great
military resources which the Protestant states of the north were beginning to exploit.

On the eve of the English Civil War, which broke out in 1642,
Sweden and Great Britain, between them, were producing nearly as
much iron as the rest of Western Europe. Together their output was
perhaps in the neighborhood of 75,000 or 80,000 tons a year. To appreciate the significance of this figure, we have to realize that at the
beginning of the eighteenth century the entire iron production of
Europe, including not only Great Britain and Sweden but also European Russia (hitherto of little or no importance in the iron manufacture), has been estimated at between 145,000 and 180,000 tons per
annum.[48] Apparently there had been little increase in European pro-

duction in more than one hundred fifty years, since the 1530's.[49] The change had been in the location of the principal metallurgical establishments. Between them Great Britain and Sweden, with a population of hardly eight millions, had come to produce as much metal as the other states of Europe combined, with their population of at least sixty millions.

Was the demand for munitions the principal cause for the rapid growth in metal production in northern Europe? While this was probably the principal cause in Sweden, in Great Britain it was not. During the sixteenth century Sussex was the chief center in Great Britain for the manufacture of the new cannon. It was a county rich in iron ore and favorably placed for the transport of guns to the English naval arsenals or to ports for shipment to warring countries across the Channel. Yet Rhys Jenkins, an enterprising engineer turned antiquarian, an authority on the ironmaking industry in the Elizabethan era, writes that even in Sussex "guns [never] became at any period the largest item of production." [50] During the early seventeenth century the English ironmaking industry grew, not in Sussex or in the adjacent counties of Surrey and Kent, but in the Midlands and Gloucestershire,[51] where the manufacture of cannon was of much less importance than in southeastern England.

What was done in Great Britain with the iron and other metals which did not go into guns and ammunition? There was a remarkable increase in the domestic demand for metals, to equip the new industrial enterprises, to supply new conveyances, and to provide commodities for ordinary living and even for ordinary dying.

Sugar refining, brewing, soap boiling, the dyeing and carding of wool and cloth — all manufactures which grew rapidly — required metal parts such as rollers, boilers, stoves, and tools. Mining machinery, driven by horse or water power, was installed for draining and also for lowering pitmen into the earth, especially at the new collieries in the north of England, in Scotland, and in the Midlands. This machinery had metal parts. Many hundreds of salt pans with coal-burning furnaces were installed at the mouths of the rivers Tyne and Wear and along the coasts of the Firth of Forth in Scotland. These pans were made of iron pieces riveted together into a metal floor, which was sometimes twenty by twenty-five feet across, with iron walls two or three feet in height. The pans were filled with sea water, which was gradually cooked to salt by means of a furnace underneath. A large salt pan probably required as much metal as a cannon. The ironwork was in need of continual repair and eventually of replacement.

Changes were occurring in the peaceful domestic habits of the

British which, taken altogether, also added substantially to the per capita demand for metal. Most men and women had to have pins and nails, many men had to have steel razors. Scissors were coming into increasing use. So were knives, particularly table knives. Forks made their way onto the tables of the pretentious, and the number of the pretentious grew as never before — new knights and baronets and peers and still more persons who aped their habits. With the growth of wealth among the middle class, iron gates, bolts, locks, and keys were wanted in greater numbers as protection against thieves. Lead increasingly replaced thatch or shingle for roofing, as much of England was rebuilt in a new architectural style and with novel domestic conveniences. New hearths with chimneys were constructed to accommodate the new sea-coal fires. They had iron grates and iron firebacks.

John Taylor, a humble waterman turned poet, who made a *Pennyles Pilgrimage* on foot from London to Edinburgh in 1618, remarked: "This is the rattling, rowling, rumbling age, and *The World runnes on Wheeles.*" He declared that in 1564 a Dutchman, William Boonen, one of Queen Elizabeth's coachmen, had introduced the coach into England, "a strange monster in those dayes." Since then everyone, it seemed, had taken to these great four-wheeled "beasts," which resembled the quadrupeds, in place of the manly two-wheeled carts, symbolizing the dignity of the upright human being. The rapid growth in wheeled travel had increased the demand for horses, with their shoes and bits, and for the nails and other small metal parts of the coaches which Taylor so abhorred. Together with the multiplying trains of pack horses and the wagons for hauling coal and ore, these coaches increased the demand for metal.[52]

Iron in the form of slabs was coming to be widely used in England for marking the graves of the dead. On the Continent war and violence increased the death rates, above all in central Europe during the Thirty Years' War. But battles and butchery, together with the starvation and pestilence bred of both, often mowed men and women down too fast for Christian burial. The tens of thousands who were put to death by the inquisitors or poisoned and assassinated by persons feeling, or at least professing, religious zeal, could not expect Christian burial. It was part of the purpose of a religious zealot to destroy the body that had harbored a heretical soul, as Le Blas's body was destroyed. Peace more than war led to the kind of commemoration which required metal. Of all the peoples of Europe, the British most often died respectably in their beds. As the population of Great Britain increased, the good earth of the island was sown with the flesh and bones of ever larger numbers of those bodies which Hobbes expected to rise to their full stature beside the iron slabs which marked their graves, when the trumpets blew on the Day of Judgment.

The peace which prevailed gave the English their opportunity to make use of metal more extensively than other peoples before them. And no industry of the age lent itself more readily than metallurgy to capitalistic forms of enterprise. Smelting furnaces, forges, cutting mills, and wireworks, with dams for storing water to drive machinery and buildings for storing materials and housing workmen, were built at scores of places in England and Wales. The capital invested in one of these metallurgical establishments often amounted to several thousand pounds. It sometimes ran into tens of thousands of pounds.[53] The workers frequently numbered several dozens; in some cases, for example at the celebrated wireworks at Tintern in Gloucestershire in 1581, a hundred persons were on the pay roll.[54] At Keswick, in the north of England, the Society of Mines Royal operated an even larger enterprise, combining the mining of copper ore with smelting. According to a contemporary writer, "the smelting houses were so many that they looked like a little town." [55]

Until the early English "industrial revolution," the working of metal had been primarily artistic labor. Works of art take a great deal of time and thought. Almost infinite pains are required to achieve the best results, in planning and preparing the materials as well as in fashioning the masterpiece itself. So long as beauty remained the primary concern in working metals into finished objects, fairly rigid limits were set to the demand for metal, because of the time, thought, and labor required in using even a small quantity.

The shift in the centers of metal production to the north of Europe foreshadowed a change in these conditions. At the beginning of the sixteenth century, Great Britain had been backward in artistic craftsmanship as compared with Italy, France, Belgium, southern Germany, and Spain; consequently the traditions of artistic work were less deeply entrenched in connection with metalwork in Great Britain than on the Continent. The rapid growth in demand which followed from 1540 to 1640 in England and Scotland was especially for crude metal objects, such as iron pans, which were not required for salt making along the coasts of the Mediterranean and the Bay of Biscay. The manufacture of these crude wares helped orient the metal manufacture towards the guiding principle of profits in place of the older guiding principle of beauty. Quantity was beginning to assume more prominence in metalwork in Great Britain than on the Continent. What held back the expansion of metallurgy in England and Scotland was a shortage of timber. Once means were found of smelting ores with cheap coal, in place of dear firewood and charcoal, there would be no longer any effective restraint upon the production of metal except that imposed by the scarcity of the ore available in the earth.

(2) *Navies and Large-Scale Industrial Enterprise*

Great Britain, Sweden, Holland — with their long coasts and numerous harbors — were all natural sea powers. As these powers rose to greater importance in the history of Europe, they outfitted more men-of-war than any other European countries. By the late 1570's the strength of English sea power seems to have made it difficult for the Spaniards to send ships through the Channel with money to pay the soldiers that they kept in the Netherlands,[1] and the famous Armada itself was partly a desperate gamble of the Spaniards to regain commercial control of these seas. The demand made upon industry for native warships increased notably in Great Britain during the peaceful reigns of Elizabeth and James I, when there was no comparable increase in the demand for equipping native armies.

After the decline during the sixteenth century of the navies of Venice and later of Spain, the rising naval powers were Holland and England, the two principal carrying nations of the age. In the case of England, the coastwise trade (particularly in coal) became of vital importance to the economic life of the metropolitan city of London. A growing need was felt, especially on the outbreak of naval war with Spain and France in 1626, to protect the colliers from hostile raids by arming them and providing convoys. There was much pressure from the crown to get warships for convoy duty, as well as for the battle squadrons needed to engage enemy vessels at sea and even to attack continental ports. Battleships of a thousand tons and over, armed with two or three tiers of guns, were coming into use during the prosperous reign of Charles I. Consequently the growth of the English navy led to the establishment and the expansion of large industrial plants, such as those at Chatham, Portsmouth, and Woolwich.[2]

Yet the production of many naval supplies, like the manufacture of saltpeter and gunpowder in France, was not centralized. Sometimes it was not even subject to government control. In the spring of 1666, after England's many decades of peace were over and in the midst of naval war with Holland — which was complicated by the fearful London plague of the previous year — sailcloth and cordage in Dorset were made for the navy by "poore men, that cannot forbeare theire moneys, but must be payd on delivery." They apparently worked in their homes with looms and other equipment, as we learn from letters written from Weymouth by a captain in the naval service, George

Pleye, to young Samuel Pepys, who was engaged in the administration of affairs at the navy office in London. The workmen at Weymouth were independent of the naval administration. Pepys's correspondent was at his wits' end, because he could not get regularly from the crown the cash he needed to buy their products. He feared they would stop making sailcloth and that warships would be left without sails. "If once they should . . . let fall theire Loomes," Pleye wrote to Pepys, "it would be a very difficult thing to revive that manufacture againe, when once they are necessitated to betake themselfs to other Callings." A week later Pleye feared that the workers would sell the cloth they had already made, and which he had no money to buy, to private persons in Bristol, where "they may have 1d. and 2d. per yard for it more . . . than the King gives." "Theire they were at a certainty for theire moneys on delivery." [3]

The correspondence suggests that the laborers were not even wage-workers, let alone factory hands. They could not be compelled to labor for the government when they could find a better price in the open market. The only way in which the English crown could get either materials or labor for war work was to bid for them. That was the situation not only in the preparation of sailcloth but in the manufacture of anchors for the navy. [4]

The existence of craftsmen who worked at home and who were free alike from government coercion and the coercion of capitalist masters should not blind us to the influence of shipbuilding upon industrial capitalism. But to what extent was modern war a cause for the growth of shipbuilding?

Two history scholars, Bernhard Hagedorn and Walter Oakeshott, have made much of the part played during the sixteenth century by the requirements of naval war with guns in stimulating sea commerce. They have drawn attention to the role of war in bringing into being a new kind of warship, which, unlike the earlier Venetian galleass, relied entirely upon sails. This warship was of great length in proportion to its beam, with places for cannon and storage space for ammunition — a type of vessel which could be readily adapted for trading purposes by skillful shipbuilders. [5] But while the building of warships provided models for building more commodious merchant vessels, one reason new warships were built was to protect the expanding commerce of the prosperous countries of northern Europe. Has enough attention been paid to the influence exercised by the progress of commerce by sea, coastwise as well as foreign, in the development of large-scale shipbuilding from the mid-sixteenth to the mid-seventeenth century? It is still a matter for debate whether the

influence of sea power upon the growth of commerce has been greater
than that of sea commerce upon the development of navies.

In one of the few books written concerning war which puts the
subject in its larger setting, as part of the history of civilization, Admiral Mahan (1840–1914), who after active service in the American
navy became a historian, took the position that in marine matters the
flag is inclined to follow the merchant and his dollars, rather than the
merchant and his dollars the flag.[6] This generalization is doubtless
applicable only to a civilized existence where people generally accept
the exchange of goods between private merchants for profitable advantage as the first purpose of economic relations, international as well
as national, and where they acknowledge the welfare of the private
merchant as a leading object of political policy. "The growth of sea
power in the broad sense," wrote Mahan, ". . . includes . . . the
peaceful commerce and shipping from which alone a military fleet
naturally and healthfully springs, and on which it securely rests." [7]
What the Admiral mistook for normal conditions, of the kind on which
sensible political rulers might base their calculations in a world of
independent sovereign states, have not always been dominant as they
were in the Victorian world. These conditions grew partly out of the
peculiar circumstances of isolated security and power, possessed by
Great Britain and the United States during the centuries when the
entire globe was first opened for commerce. Both the circumstances,
and the conditions which they bred, are ceasing to prevail in the
twentieth century. But in Elizabeth's reign, English civilization was
bending to this mercantile outlook on life. Sir Walter Raleigh remarked, "Who rules the trade of the world rules the wealth of the
world and consequently the world itself." [8] Guns, and the new security
they gave England, helped to change the ancient conception that it
was necessary to conquer and hold peoples in subjection in order to
gain the fat of foreign lands. The long years of peace at home permitted
the English to think, as Raleigh thought, in terms of trade. More and
more they submitted questions of policy to the test of material economic calculations.

An older contemporary of Sir Walter by the name of Hooker, a
native of Exeter, devoted much pains to describing the condition of
Devonshire in the late sixteenth century. He wrote with enthusiasm
of its rich havens and creeks. "And the coastes lykewyse be inhabited
and replenyshed with great housholdes and famylies of sea faringe
men: which Do travell farre and neere as well in marchundyse as in
fyshinge in all places bothe farre and neere in deepes and places of
the best fyshinge. And with theire sayde fyshe so taken they do not

onely furnishe this theire countrie and the whole Realme but also by waye of marchundyse they do transporte the same into foreyn nations by which meanes the navie is meanetened, they and theire famylies sustened and the whole comon welthe inriched and bettred." [9] The opinion was widespread, it was stated in many documents which have survived, that the fishing trade and the coastwise coal trade were the two grand nurseries of English seamen; that it was trade and particularly these two trades, because they required so many ships, which sustained the navy.

Such figures as are available concerning English ships and shipbuilding seem also to support Mahan's thesis that it has not been war but commerce which has set the pace for shipwrights, carpenters, smiths, sail- and ropemakers. During the reigns of Elizabeth, James I, and Charles I there were many growing shipyards in the island of Great Britain, such as those at Yarmouth, Harwich, Ipswich, and other commercial ports. While the tonnage of the Royal Navy little more than doubled,[10] that of the merchant marine increased nearly fivefold between 1560 and 1629.[11] Progress was more rapid in the next decade. An incomplete list of English ships for 1629 enumerates 355 merchant vessels of more than one hundred tons' burden. During the five years 1629 to 1634, at least ninety-five new ones were completed in English yards.[12]

Sombart's notion that what he calls the "craftsman type of shipbuilding" (*handwerksmässige Schiffbauerei*) would have satisfied the requirements of the merchant marine for centuries after about 1520, when cannon were beginning to be widely used in naval fighting,[13] does not hold even for a hundred years. A great expansion in the commercial traffic in heavy commodities was probably behind the Dutch invention in the sixteenth century of a new type of vessel, the *flüte*. The twelve-year truce declared in 1609 between Spain and the United Provinces gave impetus to the spread of this swift vessel,[14] which could be managed at sea by a relatively small number of sailors. Its commercial success impressed the English. What were for the age relatively large ships, of more than one hundred tons' burden, were needed especially in the coastwise coal and salt trades. With the very rapid expansion of both trades, English shipbuilders probably followed Dutch designs. At any rate, during the reigns of James I and Charles I, many colliers capable of carrying from 100 to 500 tons of coal were launched from privately owned shipyards at such ports in East Anglia as Harwich, Ipswich, and Yarmouth. These ships went to sea with about half as many sailors as had been needed to manage a ship of the same size fifty years before.[15] In England, as in Holland, most of the vessels for commerce and fishing were coming to be built in sizable shipyards owned by private capitalists. Although the supply of accessories, such as sailcloth, nails, and perhaps anchors, came often from independent craftsmen outside the yards, this procedure was also true of accessories for naval construction, as Pleye's letters to Pepys show. The opportunities for investment in commercial shipbuilding, especially in connection with the fishing and the coal trades, exceeded in all probability those for investment in naval arsenals.

The remarkable development of commercial shipbuilding — which was still more striking in Holland — added largely to the demand for metal. Even a wooden vessel could not be constructed and launched without nails to hold the planks together, wire for the masts, and heavy keels of lead and metal sheets to sheath the hulls in order to gain speed and to prevent the ravages of worms. Each of the large ships had two or three bulky iron anchors, equipped with iron chains.[16] Like salt pans, anchors, chains, and keels were crude heavy objects, wanted in large numbers and calling in their manufacture for little of the artistic craftsmanship which predominated in metalwork on the Continent during the Middle Ages and the Renaissance, and which continued to predominate during the period of religious wars that followed.

On the sea, as well as on land, it was peace more than the preparation for war which stimulated the progress of heavy industry both directly and indirectly. The close interdependence of peace and felicity is apparent in the celebrated lines which the supreme English poet, writing in the midst of the early "industrial revolution," put into the mouth of John of Gaunt, in *Richard II*:

> *This fortress built by Nature for herself*
> *Against infection and the hand of war.*

CHAPTER FIVE

Progress of Capitalist
Commerce and Finance

MUCH HAS BEEN WRITTEN ABOUT A COMMERCIAL REVOLUTION, little about an industrial revolution, during what is called "early modern times" — often meaning the two hundred years and more from the late fifteenth to the mid-eighteenth century. The two "revolutions" were complementary and interdependent. The priority given in historical textbooks to the commercial revolution has been responsible for a one-sided view of economic history and so of general history.

Of immense importance in the life of the Europeans were the new routes to the Orient, the opening of trading relations with the Americas, so rich in silver and all the natural resources on which industrial civilization has been built. The historical drama of Western civilization would be incomprehensible without the discoveries. They gave man a new world. They gave him a sense of possession of the planet he had circled, a progressiveness he lacked when what lay beyond the horizon was a mystery. Yet it may be doubted whether between the mid-fifteenth century, when the voyages of discovery began to affect European economic life, and the mid-seventeenth, when traffic with American colonies had become an established part of European experience, the volume of foreign trade of the European countries actually grew much more rapidly than their industrial output. In the case of Great Britain, which became by 1640 the leading state of Europe for heavy industry, the volume of foreign trade appears to have increased less rapidly than the products of mines and manufactures which found their principal markets within the island. It may be doubted whether the changes in navigation were more astonishing to the Europeans than the changes at home in mining and manufacturing. The new varieties of plants, ores, animals, and fish in distant lands and waters may have been more intoxicating to those who saw them, and to those with imagination who read about them, than the new varieties of minerals unearthed in the Alpine regions of Europe, which offer some of the most dramatic and enchanting scenery in the world. But more men and women saw and lived among the fresh wonders near at hand.

Foreign commerce, by sea in particular, has left much more obvious traces in readily accessible records than domestic commerce. Harassed by toilsome problems of research, students of history have been prone, not unnaturally, to follow the line of least resistance, to use the data that are relatively abundant and easy to find, and to neglect the unrecorded traffic by mule and pack horse, by cart and wagon, even to neglect the traffic by river barge or trow and by coasting ship which was sometimes recorded, but usually in such a form that the record searcher must expend long, arduous labor in order to obtain statistical results that have any general interest.

Between 1540 and 1640 in England and Wales the growth in coastwise trade was apparently much more rapid than in foreign trade. Historians have been attracted by the exciting spectacle of sailing vessels, piloted by captains (such as Drake, Hawkins, or Frobisher) full of courage and glamour, moving in strange seas and reaching strange lands of which the Christian peoples and the pagans before them had been ignorant. Therefore students of the economic past have made little effort to recreate the more prosaic picture of expanding traffic nearer home, in ores, other minerals, metals, and manufactured commodities such as metalwares, soap, sugar, paper, shoes, and other leather work. As some of the products of newly discovered lands — notably the silver which poured into Europe from America during the late sixteenth century — were relatively little used in manufacturing, the close connections between commerce and industry have been often overlooked. It has even been assumed that European commerce, which now tapped new continents, was expanding very rapidly, while European industry was stagnant.

As a partial corrective to special commercial studies, the work of Sombart is valuable. According to him, modern war encouraged the concentration of capital in trade and finance at the same time that it encouraged such concentration in industry. Conditions of industry, trade, and finance are obviously interdependent. A movement towards large-scale operations in one is likely to encourage large-scale operations in all.

In what ways was the new warfare with gunpowder affecting commerce and finance before the English Civil War, during the hundred and fifty years which began with Charles VIII's invasion of Italy? Were the influences likely to encourage progress toward the industrial civilization which has transformed the life of many parts of the earth?

The careful researches of Hans Delbrück and Ferdinand Lot indicate that during the first five hundred years of advancing Western civilization, from the eleventh through the fifteenth century, no reliable evidence exists of a European army of more than 10,000 or at the outside 12,000 combatants. Five or six thousand soldiers was a large force to send into battle as late as the fifteenth century. Henry V's English army, which won the celebrated victory at Agincourt in 1415, had scarcely six thousand men. Contrary to the general impression, the defeated French army was somewhat inferior in numbers.[1]

Exaggerated reports of casualties and of numbers engaged are part of the ordinary currency of battle experience and war observation; such reports have by no means disappeared with the novel development in modern times of an interest in accurate statistical statement. When the science of statistics was coming into being during the late seventeenth century, a French marshal, the duc de Villars (1653–1734), after dictating a report that his men had met three thousand enemy soldiers, claimed that they had killed four thousand. When his secretary called his attention to the discrepancy, he changed the figure to twenty-five hundred.[2] In the twentieth century, when all students of economics in the universities were expected to gain a knowledge of statistics, the war correspondent of an English newspaper, who reported battles during the First World War from the Hotel Ritz in Paris, is said to have recorded the death of more than a hundred million Germans!

Estimates by contemporary writers of the numbers who took part in engagements during the hundred and fifty years which ended in 1648, with the Peace of Westphalia, can hardly be treated much more seriously than those for the Middle Ages. As Professor Lot's meticulous care to rid the statements concerning the size of armies from every bit of stuffing has not extended beyond the late fifteenth century, it is possible that more unverified figures retain credit among experts for the sixteenth and seventeenth centuries than for the preceding five hundred years. Yet, even when allowance is made for errors in the figures which are now regarded as reliable, it seems clear that the forces thrown into battles grew much larger between 1494 and 1648.

The Thirty Years' War really got going in 1620 with the battle before Prague, known as the battle of the White Mountain. After his already long career as a soldier in the Roman Catholic cause, the Count of Tilly (1559–1632), who commanded the force which overran Bohemia, is reliably reported to have had about 31,000 fighting men at his disposal. His slightly younger contemporary, the Marquis of Spinola (1569–1630), the Genoese-born Spanish general, had 26,000 foot and 4,500 horse in the army that besieged Breda in 1624–1625.[3] The size of these armies of Tilly and Spinola suggests that the forces which were put into action had nearly tripled during the hundred and fifty years since firearms had become the decisive weapons in war.[4]

Battles were more frequent and often resulted in much heavier casualties than during the Middle Ages. This was true already in the early sixteenth century in Italy, northern France, and the Low Countries in the political duels between Francis I, the French king, and Charles V, whose dominions, as inherited and consolidated, surrounded France. Nor was there any lessening in the frequency or the deadliness of engagements after the abdication of Charles V. His son, Philip II, who succeeded in 1555 to his Spanish dominions, including Franche-Comté and most of what is modern Belgium, set out to subdue the entire Netherlands to Spain and the Catholic faith. Armies were continually being organized and marched north from the Mediterranean through the Western Alps into what had been the Burgundian dominions but had come into the hands of Spain. In the same period of the late sixteenth century, Huguenots and members of the Catholic League fought many pitched battles in the French civil wars. During the first half of the seventeenth century the Spanish struggles were resumed by Philip's successors, especially his grandson Philip IV (1621–1665), against both the increasingly wealthy United Provinces and France. After 1620, a blaze of battles flared up in the German-speaking countries such as had not been seen before in Christian Europe. The Thirty Years' War made overwhelming demands for soldiers upon almost every ruler, great and small, in divided Germany, Austria, and Bohemia. It taxed the manpower available to most European kings. In 1627 the Duke of Wallenstein (1583–1634), on whom the waning hopes of a complete counterreformation were centered, now that both Tilly and Spinola were old, is said to have had subject to his orders about 100,000 men in various contingents scattered over Germany and neighboring countries.[5]

In continental Europe the sixteenth and early seventeenth centuries were obviously times of notable increase in the proportion of all men who engaged in military service on behalf of one prince or another.

Consequently the commercial and financial problems connected with war grew in magnitude and in complexity.

With the decline during the later Middle Ages of the system of knight-service — in which princes relied on their landholding vassals and subvassals to supply them with fighting men, horses, armor, and other military equipment — the practice of hiring soldiers to fight, already of some importance in the period of the crusades, became ever more common. During the fourteenth and fifteenth centuries military service claimed a far larger proportion of the male population in Switzerland than in any other country, partly because of the efforts of the three cantons (Uri, Schwyz, and Unterwalden) to establish their independence within the Empire. These had been the first cantons to unite in resisting the soldiers sent by the Hapsburgs, those traditional enemies of William Tell and his countrymen. The astonishing later success of Swiss soldiers against the fiery and ruthless Duke of Burgundy, Charles the Bold, whom his enemies called "the terrible," made an impression throughout Europe. He aimed to make Burgundy into the largest and most powerful state in Europe and he wanted to be emperor himself. After the Swiss had defeated the Burgundians in 1476 and 1477 in the three battles of Grandson, Morat, and Nancy (in the last of which Charles was left lying in the field, an almost unidentifiable corpse), the French and Spanish kings and also the popes turned more than ever to Switzerland for recruits to wage war on each other. Two decades later, after the battle of Fornovo, Swiss mercenary service, which had been mainly a process of voluntary enlistments by individuals, became mainly a collective system. A young scholar has recently called it "war for export." Foreign powers entered into treaties of military capitulation with the Swiss diet, with particular cantons or with groups of cantons. Swiss magistrates and statesmen supplied the troops in return for the payment of pensions. Parts of the pensions were usually distributed yearly among the citizens who entered the foreign military service. But of course the magistrates, who acted as middlemen in this traffic, retained a profit on the transactions, and so had a strong interest in providing as many mercenaries as possible.[6]

Switzerland was not alone in supplying hired soldiers for the wars of the sixteenth and early seventeenth centuries. The proverb *Point d'argent, point de Suisse* (no cash, no Swiss) could have been extended to the recruits from most European states. In other countries than Switzerland soldiers of fortune, often with considerable wealth, entered into contracts with the principal European rulers to supply mercenaries — in the case of the Empire *landsknechts*, or infantrymen, and *reiters*, a new kind of cavalry armed with pistols. Unlike most of the

Swiss magistrates, whose interest in providing mercenaries was almost exclusively financial, these soldiers of fortune, who were in the pay of some sovereign ruler, acted as captains in the field, sometimes as commanding officers.

On the eve of the Reformation venal methods of providing warriors were already a scandal, against which men as different in their aims and temperaments as Machiavelli and Zwingli protested. The influential Swiss reformer actually served for a time as a hired soldier, as many famous men of intellect were destined to do. As the Pope was one of the offenders in hiring Swiss, Zwingli used the mercenary system as a part of his indictment of the papacy. Was it not a greater sin "to sell human flesh for slaughter," he asked, than to taste animal flesh on fast days?

Of all the nations of Europe, France was the worst offender in so far as the hiring of Swiss was concerned. Zwingli's English contemporary, Thomas More, drew his readers' attention in *Utopia* (1516) to the "plage" with which the French kingdom was "troubled and infected." "The whole royalme," he continued, "is fylled and besieged with hiered souldiours in peace tyme (yf that bee peace)." [7]

With the growth in the population of continental Europe at the juncture of the fifteenth and sixteenth centuries, the proportion of the young men with no settled occupation increased, and the increase was even more remarkable in the last half of the sixteenth century, a period when "rogues and vagabonds" became an acute problem in most countries.[8] War offered employment. But once started, wars have a dialectic of their own; they drag in members of the population who are engaged in other work that is both necessary and absorbing, work that people have little inclination to forsake. During the era in European history which lasted from about 1520 to 1650 political and religious disputes provided issues that made fighting itself seem to many a necessity. This helped the Europeans to swallow the iniquities of mercenary armies. As national feeling grew, and still more as religious division and controversy put people into the curious state of mind in which they were determined both to die and to kill for their conception of Christ and of the terms on which salvation through Him could be obtained, spiritual motives for raising soldiers were added to material ones. The view of armed service as a virtuous calling made some headway, especially when, as in the case of the United Provinces, the motives seemed to be clearly defensive. In the late sixteenth century a number of Englishmen joined the Dutch forces as volunteers. In Holland, Spain, and France, a nucleus was prepared for the later standing armies by the provision of a small number of professional native troops. Yet in order to fill the ranks under the stress of war, with its mounting casualties, the sovereign princes had always to fall back upon mercenaries in large numbers.

While there were occasions when independent commanders, like Coligny in the French religious wars or Wallenstein in the German, paid some of these fighting men out of the wealth of their own estates, the cost of hiring mercenaries fell mainly on the leading princes of Europe with their increasingly centralized governments.

Once in the army, the soldier's needs had to be provided for. Sovereign states escaped, nevertheless, a considerable part of the expense of supply which they were obliged increasingly to assume after the middle of the seventeenth century.[9] Like many workmen of the epoch in peaceful occupations, like for example the miners in the multiplying English collieries (who were hired by foremen under contract to work pits for the colliery owners), the soldiers during the sixteenth and early seventeenth centuries were expected to supply their own equipment in large part, though not their pikes, arquebuses, pistols, and ammunition. Uniforms began to be worn by common soldiers only after 1640, when they were introduced in the parliamentary army organized by Oliver Cromwell to fight against Charles I and his troops. Until that time each soldier was fitted out according to his means and fancy. He presented an appearance which would seem odd and undisciplined to our standardized, mechanical age.

Armies carried some equipment with them on campaigns; for example, stoves for baking bread and tents to provide a covering when no way was found of billeting the soldiers. But there were no special supply services,[10] and army affairs were administered almost exclusively by the fighting officers.[11] The soldiers lived for the most part off the country, taking what they needed in the way of lodging and food where they could get it.[12] It was not until the campaigns of 1630 to 1632 in Germany, led by Gustavus Adolphus, that much fighting was attempted during the winter months. Prior to that time armies had been frequently disbanded in winter; the soldiers were left to look out for themselves. Some returned to labor they had abandoned in the fields or at looms, others to the vagabondage or banditry in which they had been brought up.

It had been an ancient custom in armies, a custom which Tacitus described in the first century of the Christian Era, for the women to accompany their men on military campaigns. In the early seventeenth century the custom persisted. As the English dramatist, Thomas Dekker, wrote in 1608, "The Switzer has his wench and his cock with him when he goes to the wars." [13] It was the same with soldiers of all nationalities. Conjugal relations were not yet generally interrupted by military service. At the beginning of the seventeenth century a majority of the veteran Spanish soldiers in the Low Countries were married and had their wives with them. As not infrequently happened, more women than men were attached to the Spanish regiments.[14] In addition to wives and children every considerable army had thousands of hangers-on. There were servants, grooms, hawkers, tricksters, prostitutes, and vagabonds, as well as cattle and mules.[15] It was not the task of these auxiliaries to fight; they trudged along with the armed forces to minister to the needs of the fighters. In a crude and sometimes unsavory way they relieved governments and commanding officers of functions and expenses which, in later times of war, states have undertaken. In the absence of a regular hospital system the women, besides cooking and mending for their men, took such care as they could of the wounded,[16] before and after the intervention of the barber-surgeons who went on the campaigns. In the absence of organized entertainment such as is provided in the twentieth century, the hangers-on kept the soldiers amused by tricks and games and gave them the rather desperate joy which soldiers have always been prone to demand.

Although most of the soldiers or the captains who assembled them were left in these ways to shift for themselves when it came to clothes, food, nursing, and pleasure, the provision of the new weapons, particularly the firearms and ammunition and the new forts, fell heavily on the sovereign princes who hired the armies. Military preparations called for organizing skill much greater in scope than in the past. Traders had to be engaged to deliver much larger quantities of munitions. Officials were confronted with new problems of coördinating the supplies of cannon, arquebuses, muskets and pistols, saltpeter and gunpowder, bullets, balls, and explosive missiles so that they would be available to the various branches of the new armies — the infantry, cavalry, and artillery — at the time of battle. Other traders, as well as state officials and experts in engineering, had to supply materials and superintend the building of the new forts which cost more money than any except the richest princes were prepared to pay.[17]

In this age the storage and transport of the new kinds of munitions were in their infancy. There was an immense variety in the guns turned out and in the balls and bullets manufactured, a variety which was ill suited to the military objective of killing and destroying as effectively as possible; a variety which, in consequence, tried the ingenuity, the powers of improvisation, and the resourcefulness of the administrator. Rules of thumb for meeting the problems of supply hardly existed.

In France the provision of cannon, smaller firearms, and ammuni-

tion came into the hands of the crown. For assembling munitions of
war a hierarchy of state officials chosen by the king and his ministers
treated with local authorities, traders, and producers in the various
provinces. Nothing resembling the independence which the manufacturers of gunpowder and cannon were allowed in England was
permitted in the French kingdom.[18] An important step toward the
centralized control of munitions is said to have been taken as early
as the reign of Louis XI (1461–1483), when the provision of arms and
ammunition was confided to an official called the *grand-maître de
l'artillerie*. This system of managing supplies was strengthened by
ordinances, which Francis I promulgated in 1546 at Saint-Germain-en-
Laye. The crown assumed control over the supplies of cannon, as it
had done already over the supplies of gunpowder.[19] During the reign
of Henry IV (1589–1610), the administration of munitions was given
a form which endured almost down to the French revolution. The
office of *grand-maître de l'artillerie* was held by the king's principal
minister, the duc de Sully, a great statesman who shared with his
royal master the major responsibility for the destinies of France, and
who delegated the management of military supplies to subordinate
officers. It was not until the later seventeenth century that the armament administration came to be parceled out at all generally among
private merchants and financiers, to whom the crown confided independent powers of judgment and decision.

During the sixteenth and early seventeenth centuries the burdens
of war — administrative, commercial, and financial — increased for
all the principal European states and especially for the continental
powers — France, Spain, and the Empire — which engaged in frequent
and extensive military campaigns. What were the consequences for
national economic policies and, through the policies, for the economic,
social, and political position and influence of the mercantile classes
whose members lived by their business profits?

Half a century ago a German history scholar, Richard Ehrenberg,
suggested that the increased burdens of the new warfare played into
the hands of private merchants and financiers who had large sums to
lend.[20] According to Ehrenberg, Charles V owed his election as
emperor in 1519 partly to money lent him by Jacob Fugger of Augsburg (1459–1525). Fugger has become the most famous, perhaps he
was the richest, of all the merchants alive at the time of the Reformation. The loans which he made to the future emperor have been
represented as giving him considerable political influence. He wrote to
Charles V in a plain and outspoken manner about getting back his

money. It has been inferred that, by increasing the needs of princes for financial support, the more extensive military campaigns of the sixteenth century added much to the prestige and political influence of capitalists who were in positions to engage in large-scale lending operations.[21]

The notion that the wars of the sixteenth and early seventeenth centuries strengthened the social and political influence of the private capitalist on the Continent rests partly on an old impression that earlier conditions of trade and finance were more elementary than is now known to have been the case. Extensive commercial and financial operations by private persons were no novelty at the time of the Reformation. During the twelfth and thirteenth centuries a remarkably wide international trade had grown up, not only in cloth and various luxury commodities, but also in metals such as tin, copper, and even iron.[22] This international commerce had provided opportunities for merchants who were sometimes in a large way of business. They combined extensive trading with extensive financial operations. There had been a development of credit and even of deposit banking — especially in Italy, Spain, and the Low Countries — during the late thirteenth, fourteenth, and fifteenth centuries.[23] The practice of royal borrowing from the mercantile classes had become fairly common in the thirteenth century, if not before.

On the eve of the Reformation, south German merchants like Jacob Fugger surpassed all others in the magnitude and complexity of their commercial and financial interests. They operated on a larger scale than the leading merchants of the late thirteenth century, another period of remarkable prosperity. But their success was not mainly a result of war. Their immense fortunes were founded in the first place upon the peaceful development of the mining and metallurgical industries during the late fifteenth century. Their commercial and financial empires extended through much of central Europe, where they had large interests in the ores and metals produced in the Tirol, Carinthia, and Hungary, as well as in Germany. Their interests even stretched to Sweden and Spain, where they also dealt in the products of mines, forges, and furnaces.[24]

Although war was probably the major stimulus to larger state budgets in Europe during the sixteenth and early seventeenth centuries, the policies of most of the continental princes of this age were not in the main favorable to the political strength, the social prestige, or even the material wealth of the mercantile classes. Kings and princes took money where they could get it. In France and most continental states, particularly those which were subject to the supremacy of

Rome, the nobility and the clergy managed to escape paying most of the taxes. Private merchants and financiers, who were unable or unwilling to subordinate their interests to those of the state and to abandon their vocation of merchant for that of civil servant, were subject to impositions no less than peasants. Heavy levies on the mercantile classes worked to dry up the springs of private capital which kings and other sovereign authorities, of which there were many scores, could count on for loans. For a time this caused the royal advisers little concern. In France the revenue from taxes and impositions rose much faster than the value of money fell.

Resort was had also to borrowing. But security was lacking for the lender, in case a powerful sovereign chose to default. It may be doubted whether the financiers or the large-scale traders of the Middle Ages would have had much to learn from the merchants who lent money to princes to meet the new military needs of the sixteenth century, or from the merchants who served the military supply services which were expanded in France, Spain, and central Europe as a result of the religious wars. In France, at any rate, the merchants who served the royal administration seem to have operated on a smaller scale than the leading merchants had done on the eve of the Reformation in south Germany, Italy, and Spain. The French merchants of the early seventeenth century seem to have been subjected, more than the Fuggers and their ilk had been, to control and regulation by a prince through his officers and advisers. Leopold von Ranke observed that the mid-seventeenth century was an especially favorable period in continental Europe for the aristocracy. He was thinking mainly of the influence of the nobility over the decisions of sovereign princes.[25] In France, Spain, and Italy the nobility were placed in a relatively strong position as compared with the mercantile classes. This is partly explained by the religious wars of the period 1562–1648. These wars did not contribute to an increase in the social and political influence of mercantile classes on the Continent. The growing fierceness and seriousness of warfare caused close regulation of economic life, and this was unfavorable, as it almost always is, to private enterprise. Thus the wars of the sixteenth and early seventeenth centuries moved most of continental Europe less in the direction of nineteenth-century capitalism than away from it.

The partial control over the national receipts and expenditures in seventeenth-century England, which the mercantile interests succeeded in establishing by their votes in the House of Commons, provided private merchants in England with new opportunities to seek their advantage without respect for the economic rules and regulations which the crown tried to impose. Eventually the power of the House of Commons over the national budget gave the capitalist, whose only passport was his money, an influence in politics for which there are few, if any, historical precedents. This influence reached its zenith in the industrialized world of the peaceful nineteenth century.

There was no parallel during the seventeenth century in the countries of continental Europe, other than the United Provinces, for the effective refusal then made by the English House of Commons to permit the crown to collect new and heavy taxes from the mercantile classes. Nor was there a parallel for the ascendancy which the Dutch merchant, Louis de Geer, gained in the counsels of Gustavus Adolphus. It was not in France, Spain, Italy, or Germany, but in the states of northern Europe — above all in England, the most peaceful state of the period 1558–1640 — that the private merchant gained an independence, an economic security from princely rule, and a consequent influence in government which were novel.

What part did military needs play during the century which followed the Reformation in this strengthening of the economic, social, and political position of the mercantile classes in the north of Europe? In Sweden the career of De Geer, who was perhaps the most powerful and wealthy European merchant-financier of the early seventeenth century, was inseparable from the development of the munitions industries. In all the leading northern countries, with their rising sea power, the growth of navies seems to have provided less restricted opportunities for the initiative of private merchants than the expansion of the military establishments on the Continent. Unlike armies, navies could not live off the country. The general supply by national governments of food and stores other than munitions for considerable forces of men first assumed an importance in connection with preparations for naval wars. According to records of Admiralty stores, preserved in English archives, the service of food for seamen and building materials for warships came to provide concentrated and fairly steady demands during the late sixteenth and early seventeenth centuries. In Elizabeth's reign food was already purchased in large quantities for the navy.[26]

While the expansion of war establishments in Holland and Sweden and the growth in the services supplying munitions, fuel, and foodstuffs for the Dutch, Swedish, and English navies offered the mercantile classes in northern Europe new opportunities for gain, the sums actually required in England for military purposes were small compared to those in continental states which (like Spain, France, and Germany) were continually at war. Far from increasing, the number of Englishmen kept under arms was greatly reduced as peace became an English habit and from the viewpoint of enthusiastic soldiers a canker of the commonwealth.

On one occasion during the later years of Henry VIII's reign the crown is reported to have had some 120,000 armed men at its command, when, in the summer of 1545, the French threatened not only to attack the English garrisons across the Channel at Calais, Guisnes, and Boulogne, but to invade Great Britain.[27] More than half a century later during the reign of James I (1603–1625), when the population of England had increased probably by more than a million, the number of sailors in the expanded Royal Navy does not appear to have exceeded seven or eight thousand.[28] There was no army in England comparable to the armies maintained by the leading continental states. Theoretically all the inhabitants who were able to bear arms had to be trained for military service in their counties, under the authority of the leading county officials, the lord lieutenants, who were chosen from the nobility rather than from the increasingly commercialized gentry. It is not possible to estimate how many persons were actually trained under the lord lieutenants. In Gloucestershire, a relatively populous county, the armed bands apparently shrank from some 3,500 in 1588, under the threat of the Spanish Armada, to little more than 2,000 two decades later. Whenever the danger of a Spanish invasion was felt, as in 1588, 1598, and 1618, there was an increase in the numbers who were prepared, though most inadequately, for fighting. But such a crisis was always followed by a decline in the numbers. From 1558 to 1640 the trained bands never smelt battle powder and experts regarded them as unfit for active military service. It was only the few men who were forced into service for special occasions from among the untrained in the counties — the so-called "pressed levies" — who actually saw fighting on sea or land.[29]

The financial burdens of the inadequate English militia system fell largely on the county and the local population. From the careers of leading local merchants, it appears that the openings for traffic in weapons and equipment provided by the armed bands were of little consequence compared to those offered by the continually increasing local commerce in peaceful commodities such as cloth and the materials needed to make it, timber and coal, metal and other manufactured goods, and foods of all kinds for the multiplying inhabitants.

The expansion of military supply services in England does not provide an important explanation for the increasingly powerful position which the mercantile classes were coming to occupy. The new opportunities for trade in supplying the navy with food, fuel, and other stores [30] were not nearly so extensive as the new opportunities offered by the peaceful London metropolitan market. The growth of this market was first called to our attention by Professor Gras, whose description was later amplified by Mr. F. J. Fisher.[31] In the hundred years from about 1540 to 1640, the population of London increased from some 50,000 or 60,000 to more than 300,000 inhabitants.[32] The city, which had once depended for its necessities upon the surrounding counties, came to draw its fuel from the Tyne and Wear basins and its food from the whole of England and even from Ireland. The supply of coal, grain, meat, vegetables, building materials, fish, and clothing gave a great many wholesale dealers new openings for profitable trade, which dwarfed those provided private merchants anywhere on the Continent by the numerous moving armies.

In all civilizations an increase in war orders has produced, in the first instance, fresh opportunities for capitalists seeking profits from trade. This was the case, for example, in the ancient Roman Republic in connection with the preparations for the Second Punic War late in the third century B.C.[33] The religious wars of the sixteenth and early seventeenth centuries were no exception to this rule. But if we are considering the effects of war on commercial development, we have to take account of its destructive as well as its constructive sides. As conducted on the Continent, the frequent military campaigns and battles provided the merchant with little scope for supplying in any orderly way the elementary economic needs of armies in the field. The very fact that the soldiers, together with camp followers and other hangers-on, were left largely on their own to satisfy their imperative wants made them a special menace to the maintenance of orderly trading relations. In the fourteenth century, with the outbreak of the Hundred Years' War, military campaigns are said to have become more cruel than they had been before, especially after about 1355.[34] It is questionable whether the armies of the sixteenth and early seventeenth centuries were more ruthless and beastly than their predecessors, though we now know that the sixteenth century was extraordinarily productive of banditry and piracy on the Continent and in the Mediterranean.[35] Even if the armies in the religious wars were no worse than those of the Hundred Years' War, they were larger. The numbers engaged had increased several fold, and in consequence a greater strain was imposed on the economy to meet their lawless demands for food, lodging, clothing, and other commodities. In the forces swarming about France during the 1570's and 1580's ruthless pillaging was taken for granted; even the officers encouraged it and engaged in it. The same was true in the Low Countries, where the Spanish army divided itself into "republics" of pillagers, who sometimes took perverse pleasure in living at the expense of the local inhabitants. Conditions were no better a generation later. During the Thirty Years' War the foreign troops in the Low Countries "were utterly without discipline, robbed the whole countryside, and spared neither the women, the churches nor the houses of the gentry." [36] These mercenary forces did very much more damage to economic life than the larger armies of the late seventeenth and early eighteenth centuries, when the need of the soldiers to live off the country they passed through was reduced by the development of supply services.[37] During the period of religious wars, battles and movements of troops reduced the volume of trade in France and still more in Flanders, Brabant, and central Europe.

Records of shipments through the Danish Sound from the Kattegat, show that the French salt trade to the Baltic almost collapsed during the last half of the sixteenth century largely as a result of the civil wars.[38] Salt and wine had been the staple exports from southwestern France during the later Middle Ages. At the outbreak of war in 1562, shipments from the salt marshes along the coasts between Bordeaux and Nantes had never been larger, and for a few years the fighting within France seems to have had little effect upon this ancient commerce. But after the five-year period 1562–1566 there was a disruption of the trade in salt at home and a precipitous drop in exports.

The marshes along the Bay of Biscay were cultivated mainly for the French domestic market, not for the export market in salt. Salt was collected in royal storehouses, where the commodity was subject to the *gabelle*, a tax which came to be regarded as infamous, especially because it obliged the peasants to buy salt which they did not need. From the *gabelle* the crown derived a notable portion of the revenues to supply its armies. In the civil wars it became a part of rebel strategy for the Protestant forces to interfere with the movement of salt to the royal storehouses. In 1568 the Huguenot leaders, in their efforts to defeat their enemies, seized the entire salt production of the Biscayan provinces.[39] Even after the worst phases of the French religious wars had ended in 1589, the Huguenots apparently continued to harass the salt trade. In 1594, in order to thwart the crown, Protestant garrisons at Rochefort and at other places along the Bay of Biscay levied prohibitively high taxes of their own on the salt made locally by the evaporation of sea water. As a result the officials in charge of the royal storehouses at Le Mans and La Ferté Bernard (which had usually received their supplies from Nantes by way of the rivers Loire and

Sarthe) could not afford to pay the price necessary to buy Biscayan salt. As an alternative, they asked the crown for permission to bring salt overland some hundred miles from Caen in Normandy.[40] Salt was not yet manufactured from sea water in large plants in France as it was beginning to be manufactured in England, and consequently the cost of making salt along the coasts of Normandy was very high because of the niggardliness of the sunshine. The appeals of the officials at Le Mans and La Ferté Bernard suggest how difficult the Protestants had made their position by blocking the natural channels of supply.

This tussle in the French civil wars for the control of Biscayan salt proved most unfavorable to the orderly shipment of the commodity by sea. Exports to the Baltic were down by at least four-fifths in the five-year period 1574–1578 as compared with the period 1562–1566. Even as late as the period 1595–1599, after peace had been largely restored within France, there had been small improvement in the foreign salt trade. Little more than a third as much salt was being shipped to the Baltic as at the beginning of the religious wars. Not until the period 1605–1609, when French economic life generally had begun to thrive again, was there a real recovery.[41]

The proportion of the French country seriously affected at any given time by battles, by the movements and the extraordinary demands of armies, or by preparations for war was probably small. There was generally a recovery after the troops disbanded or moved on. In spite of the interference with the salt trade of southwestern France during the last thirty-five years of the sixteenth century, the trade in cloth and leather guods in the adjacent province of Poitou apparently grew substantially at this very time of civil strife.[42] While the great decrease in the acta, entered from 1575 to 1595 in the books of Parisian notaries,[43] suggests that there may have been a startling decline in the business transacted in the capital during the civil wars, the transatlantic commerce from Le Havre and Honfleur, at the mouth of the Seine, was greater during the wars than after Henry IV had established more peaceful conditions at the beginning of the seventeenth century.[44] While the towns of Languedoc, especially Montpellier and Aigues Mortes, seem to have declined in commercial importance during the last half of the sixteenth century, Marseilles had an expanding traffic at least well into the eighties, both up the Rhone valley and by sea with other Mediterranean ports.[45] The economic self-sufficiency of local areas which still prevailed in France during the sixteenth and seventeenth centuries, prevented the religious wars from causing a national economic collapse.

In the smaller and industrially more developed Spanish Low

Countries the economic consequences of war were more serious. A learned French historian, Professor Emile Coornaert, has provided statistical evidence concerning the harm done to commerce by the religious wars in Flanders. The town of Hondschoote, a few miles from Dunkirk, had become a populous weaving center in the late fifteenth century. Between the 1480's, when the textile industry there was already of some importance, and the 1560's the annual traffic in cloth increased from some 15,000 to approximately 90,000 pieces.[46] The collapse of the textile trade in the hundred years that followed, during which the traffic was reduced to a figure inferior to that of the late fifteenth century,[47] was brought about in part by the movements of troops in the neighborhood, first in the 1580's and later in the 1640's.

Of the direct harm done by military campaigns to orderly economic relations we have proof. Pillage and the commercial anarchy encouraged by pillaging were the price of invasion. In 1582 hundreds of French troops occupied Hondschoote. At that time, and again half a century later during the war between France and Spain, soldiers ransacked and set fire to most of the houses; they partially destroyed the cloth and woolen markets and even the church. For years after these catastrophes, commercial life in Hondschoote and the neighborhood was continually disrupted by the presence of armed forces on their way to and from battle. The troops demanded food and lodging from the inhabitants; forced some of them to leave their looms, spinning wheels, dyeing vats, and fulling mills to labor for the army; stole cloth and other stores from the warehouses; and robbed messengers and traders carrying stocks of goods. The traffic in cloth dropped from more than 80,000 pieces annually in the 1570's to less than 12,000 pieces annually from 1585 to 1589. After a substantial recovery in the second and third decades of the seventeenth century, when the district had a respite from war, the traffic fell from about 55,000 pieces in the early 1630's to less than 8,000 pieces from 1646 to 1649. This time there was no revival. [48] In 1657 and 1658 numerous French regiments of infantry and cavalry again lacerated the region with the scourge of war.

It would be rash to assume that the trade of most, or even many, industrial and commercial centers in the Low Countries and elsewhere west and south of the Rhine suffered as much from the wars as the trade of Hondschoote. Dunkirk and its environs have had more than their share of fighting in the course of the warlike history of Europe; by its situation, Hondschoote was on the route of passing armies and more vulnerable to attack and occupation than most textile centers even in Flanders. During the early seventeenth century the place might have partly recovered its position in the cloth trade, in spite of all these disadvantages, had it not been for increasing competition — especially from the Dutch towns of Leiden, Haarlem, and Delft — in the production of says, fine thin woolen cloths, used especially for outer garments. Hondschoote lost the advantages it had possessed earlier as a rapidly growing commercial center, largely free from the heavy taxes and the regulations imposed on cloth manufactures in ancient towns. The place developed a corporate egotism of its own. The local government became far more regulative in character than it had been; the local aldermen, who were known as *échevins*, interfered increasingly with the freedom of enterprise upon which the cloth trade of the place had thrived in the early sixteenth century.[49] Yet so complete was the collapse of commerce at Hondschoote in the wake of armed violence that we are safe in treating war as the major explanation for the decline, as war was indeed a major cause for the less overwhelming disintegration of the commerce in cloth, metalwares, and foodstuffs in the Spanish Netherlands generally.

The damage done by war to trade was most pronounced in the eastern Rhineland and in the German principalities all through central Europe as far as the eastern slopes of the Alps and the Carpathian Mountains. Fighting over religion began to interfere with commercial progress from the middle of the sixteenth century. But it was mainly the campaigns of armies during the Thirty Years' War which reduced the volume of trade, in foodstuffs as well as in manufactured goods, all through Germany, Austria, and Bohemia. We may select one among scores of accounts of the suffering caused by these campaigns. In 1638, Bernhard, Duke of Saxe-Weimar, a brilliant Protestant general, who had joined Gustavus Adolphus and who was now egged on by Richelieu, besieged the strong fortress on the right bank of the Rhine at Breisach, held by the Imperialists. So fearful became the plight of the defenders that one of the inhabitants gave a diamond ring for three pounds of bread and a glass of wine. Cats and rats were for the feasts of the rich; the people descended to cannibalism.[50]

Such horrors were not new. There had been precedents in earlier European wars. What was new during the 1620's and 1630's was that these horrors ceased to be mere episodes. They became almost a yearly experience in most regions all the way from Franche-Comté to Bohemia and from Carniola to Brandenburg. In some places the inhabitants diminished by a third, in other places by half and even more.[51] Whatever the tenacity of those who remained, not enough people were left to keep commerce at anything approaching the levels which had still prevailed at the beginning of the seventeenth century. For nearly two generations after the Peace of Westphalia in 1648 central Europe failed to recover even the moderate prosperity which had existed in some regions on the eve of the Thirty Years' War.

If England had been heavily dependent upon continental countries for markets, the European wars might have interfered very seriously with economic progress in Great Britain. But the island was always able to fall back either on a fresh development of foreign markets beyond the range of the wars, or on markets within Great Britain itself, with its increasing population and the increasing eagerness of the inhabitants for larger quantities of commodities, especially for the products of the expanding mines and manufactures. The Duke of Alva, who was becoming notorious for his cruelty as Spanish governor of the Netherlands from 1567 to 1573, tried to keep the British from helping the Protestant elements by prohibiting the provinces he governed from trading with England and by placing an embargo on English property in the Low Countries. As measures designed to cripple England itself, these acts of Alva's failed of their purpose. English statesmen and merchants, working together, were clever in opening rival trade routes. In London the Spanish ambassador wrote, "The Hamburg business is turning out well for them; and, although they feel the stoppage of trade with Flanders, this outlet prevents the people from raising a disturbance." [52]

The Thirty Years' War had much to do with a sharp depression in the English textile industries — especially those of East Anglia — a depression which lasted from 1618 until 1624 or 1625. But after 1625, especially during the decade 1630–1639, there was a notable recovery in the English cloth trade in spite of the war. While the trade in heavy cloth from London had not regained its old position, the trade of the outports in lighter fabrics, for which there was a large demand in the Mediterranean countries, was greater than before the depression. [53] The curtailment of the market for cloth in central Europe gave the English producers an incentive to experiment with new methods and materials in order to find substitute markets. In the west country and in Lancashire these efforts met with much success; new kinds of woolen and cotton cloth were produced and sold in England, without reference to the materials or the sizes prescribed by statute. [54] In so far as the Thirty Years' War affected English commerce and finance directly, it hindered the progress of private capitalist enterprise in both. Yet, while the war continued, England not only recovered from the great depression in the cloth trade, but enjoyed an expansion in shipbuilding, in coal mining, in salt and alum manufacturing, and in several other industries — an expansion which raised the country to a pitch of prosperity unequaled even during the remarkably prosperous decade which preceded the outbreak of the Thirty Years' War in 1618.[55]

It would be easy, but false, to attribute this mounting prosperity and the remarkable progress from 1540 to 1640 of large-scale economic enterprise under private control mainly to the peace which was so precariously maintained for so long a time by England's rulers. There were other countries that had peace but no prosperity and that made no appreciable headway toward the industrialized civilization of the nineteenth century. Iceland was at peace from the fifteenth down into the eighteenth century, except for periodic raids of English, Gascon, and Algerine pirates, who caused some devastation in 1579, 1613–1616, and 1627.[56] If peace had been the only essential requirement for the extraordinary economic progress which led to the eventual triumph of industrial civilization, Iceland should have moved more rapidly than Great Britain towards industrialism during the past five hundred years.

Iceland lacked the mineral resources, coal and iron ore in particular, upon which industrialism was built. The history of Sweden from the accession of Gustavus Vasa in 1523 to the abdication of Gustavus Adolphus' daughter Christina in 1654 shows what abundant resources, in iron and copper ores and timber, could accomplish for a backward country, even when it engaged heavily in foreign military campaigns. The Swedish kings frequently went to war with Poland, Russia, and Denmark. But, being skillful in diplomacy, they managed to maintain relatively peaceful conditions at home, except for the struggle precipitated by King Sigismund (1566–1632), who for a time held simultaneously the crowns of Sweden and Poland. Sigismund sought to become the Philip II of the north and, with Catholic Poland as a base, to restore the Roman worship throughout Scandinavia. But the resistance to Sigismund of the Swedes themselves under Gustavus Vasa's fourth son, Duke Charles (1550–1611), was successful as a result of the battle of Stångåbro in 1598, which was followed by the deposition of Sigismund as king of Sweden and the succession of the duke as Charles IX.

Holland offers another example of a country which was more or less continuously at war, yet which grew very prosperous from about 1585 to 1665. The United Provinces rivaled England in the extent of their commercial and financial progress and in the development of large-scale enterprise by private capitalists. Two circumstances largely explain the extraordinary economic success of Holland in the midst of warring Europe. First, sea trade was a vital matter in Dutch prosperity. After 1585 the sea trade of Holland actually drew special advantages from the openings war provided for bringing commodities by water to regions which were cut off temporarily, as a result of the fighting, from receiving their accustomed supplies by land. Secondly, the Dutch were able to limit their participation in the wars almost entirely to an amazingly successful defense based, in so far as the Spanish enemy was concerned, on the natural water barriers formed on the southern border of the United Provinces by the Rhine and the Meuse. As a result Holland managed to establish within her small territory the peace essential to economic prosperity, as is shown by the testimony of the greatest philosopher of the age, who had served as a soldier in his youth.

Descartes lived in Holland during the last two decades of the Thirty Years' War, which the Dutch by no means escaped. Eight years after his arrival, he explained his choice of this residence in the *Discours de la méthode* (1637). What he sought was tranquillity for the development of his thought. This desire, he wrote, "constrained me to remove from all those places where interruption from any of my acquaintances was possible, and betake myself to a country in which the long duration of the war has led to the establishment of such discipline, that the armies maintained seem to be of use only in enabling the inhabitants to enjoy more securely the blessings of peace." [57]

If the blessings of peace should be regarded as only one among many causes of economic prosperity in northern Europe, war should not be regarded as the only cause of the poverty which descended in the seventeenth century upon the dominions that had been united a hundred years before under Charles V. During the period of the religious wars Spain was hardly invaded. In terms of direct harm done by armies, Spain got off more easily from the wars than France, a country which fared better than Spain economically and which by 1660 had added to her territory by the acquisition of such provinces along the Spanish border as Navarre, Béarn, and Roussillon. The economic collapse of Spain in the first half of the seventeenth century was as complete as that of the Spanish Netherlands where, it may be said, the people lived under invasion for more than two generations after the Duke of Alva arrived at Brussels in 1567.

Nevertheless war cannot be overlooked as a cause for Spanish economic decadence, any more than peace can be neglected as a cause for English prosperity. It may almost be said of Spain that her military efforts were devoted wholly to attack in an age when the military efforts of Holland were limited almost entirely to defense. The drains imposed on Spanish resources by the belligerent policy of the Spanish kings in waging battles on foreign soil — in Italy, in America, and then in the Low Countries — interfered increasingly with economic development at home. Eventually the Spaniards paid the price of aggression. The Spanish war with France from 1635 to 1659 has been called "perhaps the most disastrous conflict since the Moors overran the Peninsula in the eighth century." [58]

Voltaire wrote of the early seventeenth-century warfare in which France engaged as resembling all the wars of Christian princes during centuries of time. He remarked that these wars added at best a few frontier towns whose possession rarely compensated for the costs of the conquest in dead men and ravaged provinces. It was during the intervals of peace in the hundred years from 1540 to 1640 that France progressed economically. A well-informed French observer, Mont-chrétien, who has been considered a chauvinist in foreign policy, remarked in 1615, "Since we have enjoyed peace, the people of this kingdom have multiplied infinitely." [59] In sober fact the increase had been finite and limited since internal peace had been largely reëstablished about 1595, but the multiplication was sufficient to offset most of the losses from civil strife between 1562 and 1589. Though France became the most powerful nation of Europe at the end of the Thirty Years' War, Voltaire was essentially correct in his view of the consequences of military campaigns. France owed its ascendancy not to any positive economic improvements resulting from waging war, but to the collapse of Spain and the Empire.

What made the long years of peace within Great Britain from 1558 to 1640 tell mightily in England's favor was the island's growing economic independence of the warring areas. England owed this independence to several conditions. She owed it partly to the opening up of ocean trade with the fisheries and islands of the Atlantic, with the American colonies, and with the East Indies. She owed it partly to growth of trade with the Mediterranean. She owed it still more to the trade by way of the North Sea and the Baltic, to the rising industrial and commercial importance of the group of northern Protestant states along the sea — Holland, northern Germany, Denmark, Sweden, and Scotland. With all of them English trade multiplied. Together they formed a block of countries with many common economic and religious interests, such as the strength and independence of the private merchant and the strength and independence of the reformed worships, which left both economic enterprise and religious conformity more to the discretion of the individual.

These northern countries of Europe were growing in population and in wealth, especially in the wealth of the middle and upper middle classes of tradesmen and merchants, who exhibited an enthusiasm that was new for the substantial material comforts so necessary to civilized living in a cool, rainy climate. At this particular juncture of history, in the early seventeenth century, it would have been virtually impossible for the United Provinces, and difficult even for England, to have developed into great commercial states without Swedish timber, iron, and copper. As long as the nations of the north remained at peace with one another they were all defended by spearheads of Dutch soldiers and seamen along the lower Rhine and by Swedish armies which resisted invaders and later invaded Germany.

England owed her increasing economic independence and power most of all to the phenomenal expansion of coastwise trade and of trade by land and river. That expansion was made possible by the vigorous exploitation of the natural resources and markets within the island of Great Britain, so rich in minerals and good soil and so well provided with harbors that made possible shipment of commodities by water at relatively low costs to every port in the British Isles.

Peace, combined with exceptional geographical advantages and with rich, hitherto largely unexploited mineral resources, provided the foundation for the genesis of industrial civilization in Great Britain. Without that foundation the constitutional and religious changes which put businessmen in a favorable position to make the most of natural resources, as well as the new interest in technological developments which provided more efficient means for exploiting the resources, would not have met with sufficiently favorable conditions to have created in embryo an industrial state — a prototype for the larger and much more industrialized states which rose in the nineteenth century.

The driving forces behind England's industrialization from 1540 to 1640 were also multiple. One was the rapid increase in prices which began in the 1540's and 1550's.[60] During the fourteenth and fifteenth centuries prices in England had remained remarkably stable, and during the first four decades of the sixteenth century the rise brought about by the increasing productivity of the silver mines in central Europe had been slight. Then, in 1542–1544, Henry VIII's extravagant expenditures led him and his advisers to debase the silver content of the standard coins of the realm. Prices of most commodities soared during the twenty years which followed, for after Henry's death in 1547, the Duke of Somerset (as protector for the child-king Edward VI) effected a further debasement of the coinage. The partial restoration of the silver content of the pound under Elizabeth in 1560–61, did little to restore the value of money.[61] By that time the inflow of precious metal from America had begun to cheapen silver in England. For the next eighty years prices rose from decade to decade, with only an occasional fall, such as that which accompanied the sharp depression in the cloth trade from 1618 to 1622.

A precipitous rise in prices was more novel for England than for most continental states, where princes, in their efforts to meet mounting expenditures, had made frequent changes in the metallic content of the standard coins during the fourteenth and fifteenth centuries. Before the Reformation in England rents and wages had been firmly fixed by custom and even by law. Consequently, when a rapid increase in English prices began, it was more difficult to bring about an upward adjustment of rents and wages than on the Continent. Fixed rents and fixed wage rates played into the hands of industrialists with capital, who needed land and labor on advantageous terms. During the 1540's and 1550's the owners of most mines and manufactures were able to sell their products at steadily increasing prices without any appreciable rise in their costs. In mining and manufacturing there was apparently no recurrence of this long spell of windfall profits from low wage rates.[62] Once the country had become adjusted to rapid changes in the price level, wage rates were adjusted quickly to higher prices. But the introduction of improved furnaces and machinery (which began in the mid-sixteenth century and became remarkable toward the close of Elizabeth's reign and in the early seventeenth century) reduced the real costs of production, made industrial enterprise extraordinarily profitable, and so facilitated the rapid economic development which we call an "early industrial revolution."

Other even greater incentives to new business activity were provided, as has been suggested, by the break with Rome and the dissolution of the monasteries in 1536 and 1539. Large tracts of church land, often rich in mineral resources, were transferred to the crown. Through action by the Court of Augmentations, created in 1536 to govern these properties and the revenues derived from them, valuable additional lands were frequently put at the disposal of merchants and gentry of mercantile origin, who were eager to develop industrial wealth.[63] After the middle of the sixteenth century the growing inability of the crown to enforce its economic policies, or even to hold its own landed property, also encouraged laymen with capital and with energy for economic enterprise to assert their private interests. They used their wealth and influence partly to develop new and larger industrial ventures. Strong against Rome, the English kingship proved weak, in the course of the hundred years following the break with Rome, against the merchants and industrialists who had gained wealth and influence partly because of the break.[64]

CHAPTER SIX

Restraints on War

· IN SO FAR AS THE PERIOD FROM ABOUT 1494 TO 1648 IS CONCERNED, such constructive consequences as the Europeans derived from military preparations were more than offset by the economic damage caused by these preparations and by war itself. The influence of war was to lower the material standard of living. Population and production grew mainly in those parts of Europe where there was the least fighting. War contributed less than peace to the progress of science and even of industrial technology. War enlarged the scale of economic enterprise mainly by increasing the civil services and the annual expenditures of princes and kings. A concentration of economic power in sovereign states, such as heavy warfare stimulated, had occurred in earlier civilizations than the Western; for example in classical antiquity under the Roman Empire, as Professor Rostovtzeff has shown. Not a concentration of power, but an increase in the independence of economic enterprise within the state — favored by the peaceful condition of Great Britain from 1558 to 1640 — accompanied the genesis of industrial civilization.

If war cannot be considered an important cause for the progress of large-scale industry and for such prosperity as Europe had from 1494 to 1648, what were the relations between the new warfare and the genesis of industrial civilization? War is a disease of human nature, which has afflicted all societies above the lower savagery in various ways and in varying degrees. By seeking and achieving economic improvement, men and women change the means of fighting. The greater their economic success, the greater the risks that economic success brings with it. Peace breeds production, but production breeds war. The pursuit of industrial progress — the particular interest which the Western peoples had from early times in power-driven machinery, their eagerness to exploit the riches of the subsoil — brought as by-products weapons of more devastating kinds in greater abundance. Warlike impulses — fear, hatred, cruelty, revenge, pleasure in destruction and human suffering, together with competition, religious conviction, and the courage and sense of honor aroused by the obligation to fight — are not peculiar to the Western peoples. But their consequences as revealed in modern weapons and in the scale of warfare have been peculiar. Modern war and industrialism are joint products of the same historical forces.

From the time gunpowder came to be extensively used in war, it was evident that the Western Europeans would find it easier than earlier civilized peoples to kill and destroy. Unless the conditions of life or the hearts of men were altered in such ways as to restrain the propensity of nations and factions to do away with one another, there was always a risk that wars with new weapons would put an end to economic progress.

Whether men and women were of more cruel and revengeful disposition when firearms first became the decisive weapons than they have revealed themselves to be in the twentieth century is doubtful. But in the fifteenth and sixteenth centuries physical suffering, capital punishment, and the infliction of excruciating pain by torture and other corporal violence had long been taken for granted to an extent which shocked civilized Western society in the eighteenth and nineteenth centuries. The restraints in customs, laws, and manners on physical cruelty, which were built up after the era of religious wars, seem now to be forsaking the human race. That is partly because recent material progress has made it much easier to kill. During the sixteenth century also, with the increasing use of guns and refined poisons, material progress made killing and injury easier than before for peoples who were more accustomed to pain than their twentieth-century descendants and who were without the strong conventional restrictions upon the infliction of pain that existed among Europeans and Americans at the end of the nineteenth century. Technical developments gave the sixteenth-century Europeans weapons that made it possible to fight to a finish with a smaller cost in physical horror than had been necessary during the Middle Ages. Hand-to-hand combat became less essential. Soldiers could now execute their missions with guns of various sizes at distances sufficient to draw at least a thin veil over the messy results. The gunners who fired the balls which took off two officers' heads as they were dining in the field with Alexander Farnese saw none of the mischief. They felt none of the revulsion which seized the other diners.

It is less personal and less terrifying for most men to kill others at some distance than face to face, where they stare into the eyes of their opponents, witness their agony, or see how they must share the same fate.

As the facilities for killing improved, the will to kill grew, because issues arose which made it possible to represent killing more frequently as a virtue. The increasingly bitter religious struggles over the meaning and the efficacy of the sacraments strengthened the motives for the use of violence. By the 1540's the hopes of the first leaders of the Reformation — Luther and Zwingli — for a new reformed church which could command universal allegiance were doomed. The disagreements were not being settled by rational argument; new disagreements were appearing every year among the reformers themselves. They were not able to unite. The Lutherans developed one form of worship, the Calvinists another, the Church of England another — to speak only of the main Protestant religious allegiances which existed in 1540, less than a generation after Luther in 1517 had challenged the authority of the Pope to sell indulgences. Few ardent religious leaders were willing to accept these divisions and to let each person choose his worship according to the dictate of his conscience. It seemed to many among both the Roman Catholics and the reformers, to the increasingly large number of persons who held strong convictions on behalf of their religious beliefs, that there was nothing to do but settle their differences by force. Some men persuaded themselves, or let others persuade them, that any means of persecution and killing, no matter how frightful, were justified by the purpose of bringing all to adopt *their* worship, *their* recipe for eternal life. As the eminent nineteenth-century historian, J. A. Froude, expressed it, "In the great spiritual struggle of the sixteenth century, religion made humanity a crime." [1]

With religious zeal so little relieved by the supreme Christian virtue of charity, and armed on all sides with weapons unknown to the violent of earlier ages, an almost universal slaughter became possible. Something very like it occurred on a number of occasions — in battles, in the sacking of cities like Antwerp and Magdeburg, in nights of assassination like those in many French towns in 1562 and, a decade later, in Paris during the famous Massacre of Saint Bartholomew. For brief spells, which grew longer as the heat of war was fanned by more war, murder became almost respectable. At times Europe seemed about to become a stage for the Greek tragedy.

It is perhaps easier to explain why there should have been so much slaughter and destruction than to explain why there should not have been more. If there had been much more, no economic advance would have taken place and industrial life would hardly have assumed new features which pointed unmistakably towards the triumph of industrial civilization. The economic progress of the age was a result less of war than of limitations on war.

(1) *The Material Restraints*

A variety of material and accidental circumstances, which it would have been scarcely possible for any European to foresee in the time of Henry VIII and Charles V, combined to give England the respite from serious war which helped to make possible the early "industrial revolution." Prominent among these circumstances, as has been already emphasized, was natural geographical isolation. Another was the jealousy felt for each other by the principal continental powers, France and Spain, especially the jealousy felt by the few persons — the kings and their ministers — who were in charge of the destinies of these powers. As Froude remarked, this "left Elizabeth more free to settle her own difficulties than if the 'ditch' which divided England from the Continent had been the Atlantic itself."

Still other reasons made it easier than in earlier times for England to avoid continental adventures. After the loss of Calais in 1558, the English crown had no longer any territory to hold on the Continent. For a time the desire to reconquer Calais was strong, but the expansive ambitions of the English people now had new objectives. America was one of them. In this recently discovered world of free land, sparsely populated by Indians, there was room all the way from Hudson Bay to the Horn for colonizers from many countries. At this very juncture in English history two remarkably unwarlike sovereigns, Elizabeth and James I, occupied the throne for sixty-seven years. They wanted to keep out of war and they were able to keep out of it almost altogether, in spite of opposition from some of their more belligerently inclined ministers, such as Sir Francis Walsingham.[2] The accidents that protected Elizabeth from disease and the good luck (combined with ministerial vigilance) that protected her from the assassin's dagger or poison gave her long life, with her faculties and her energy unimpaired, and helped prevent the outbreak of civil disturbances [3] which might have delayed the early "industrial revolution," as the Civil War of 1642, following a long period of unparalleled prosperity, probably helped to delay the later, more famous industrial revolution.[4]

These advantages, which allowed Great Britain a long respite from exhausting military effort, were not shared by most European states. Yet terrible as warfare on the Continent became, especially from 1562 to 1648, the devastation and the destruction of life might have been

much greater than they were. It was restraints upon war which prevented a general collapse of European civilization following the
Reformation, a collapse which would have involved Great Britain and
would have prevented the genesis of industrial civilization in the
north of Europe. In spite of the improved facilities for killing and the
spread of religious issues over which men and women of all social
classes were prepared to die and were often determined to kill, conditions intervened to hold the slaughter within bounds.

One of the conditions was a lack of the material resources needed
to carry on the fight. The iron, copper, lead, tin, and other metals
produced were insufficient to enable the commanders to push the
battles to complete destruction. The gradual abandonment of armor as
a part of the equipment of soldiers during the seventeenth century
freed some metal supplies for the manufacture of firearms and missiles.
It would have been hardly possible to furnish the relatively large
armies, raised during the Thirty Years' War, with much armor in addition to the new munitions. As it was, the shortage and high price of
metal, along with the difficulties experienced by princes and kings in
raising money from their subjects, imposed limits upon the extent of
the fighting during the era of religious wars.

In spite of the efforts of the Spanish kings, in spite of the springboard which they possessed in the Netherlands for an advance over
the Meuse and Rhine, in spite of the religious justification they invoked
as defenders of the ancient Christian faith, they were never able to
conquer the United Provinces. Today the Dutch territory can be
snatched by a great power in a few days. But in the sixteenth century
the Dutch defended themselves successfully for eighty years against
the strongest arms in Europe. Their great resources were the sea with
its inlets, the good harbors and rivers, and the inland waterways which
they built.[5] On critical occasions in their wars with Spain, the sea
enabled many Dutchmen to escape the enemy in boats and to flood
the invading armies out of victory. The sea enabled them to become
the carriers for all the nations of northern Europe, and to get from
Sweden, northern Germany, England, and Scotland the materials
which they needed to defend themselves.

The resources of the northern states proved adequate for defense.
They were inadequate for the conquest of the Continent. Europe was
saved from destruction more by its poverty than by its wealth.

(2) *The Intellectual Restraints*

Peace and war were not altogether at the mercy of accident and of
geographical and other material conditions. History is never inde

pendent of the minds of men. It is less independent in an age like that of the religious wars, when men are conscious of their own wickedness and of their responsibilities, than in an age like that of industrialism, when so many among the learned have accepted the thesis that individuals are mere automatons and are the powerless victims of circumstances. The delivery of Western Europe during the sixteenth and early seventeenth centuries from even greater destruction cannot be explained simply by suggesting that a point was reached beyond which it cost more to kill than the Europeans could afford. If the cost was so high, this was partly because the men of genius and of talent whose ideas and whose work counted were not eager to make it cheaper.

Leonardo da Vinci's lack of enthusiasm for the development of weapons, of which he claimed to know the secret, is proverbial. At the time the first atomic bombs were dropped, the papal newspaper in Rome, the *Osservatore Romano,* issued a statement to the effect that Leonardo had refused to give the world knowledge of his destroying engines. As has been suggested, the story of Leonardo as an inventor of machinery and as a humanitarian is not without its apocryphal aspects. Yet this story serves truth by calling attention to an attitude which was not the exclusive property of a great individual genius, but part of the outlook of the European mind. Nor does the story misrepresent Leonardo. His notebooks apparently were not intended for publication. Yet even in them he was unwilling to tell all he knew. When he wrote of an underwater boat, he remarked, "This I do not . . . divulge, on account of the evil nature of men, who would practice assassinations at the bottom of the seas by breaking the ships in their lowest parts and sinking them together with the crews who are in them." [1]

In the era of the Renaissance knowedge was sought in the service of a very human man. His wickedness stared people in the face. His happiness was far more subtle, varied, and individual than statistics can measure. Rabelais, More, and Shakespeare could banish wickedness by literary and poetic invention. Rabelais banished it from his Abbaye de Thélème, over whose gates hung the motto, "Do as you please." All the inmates were good. More created "the newe Yle, called Utopia," where decency and integrity of character prevailed. Shakespeare created another, more magical island in *The Tempest*, where the good, sweet, and charming people came out on top without seriously harming the wicked. These were all consciously constructed dreams. The need for such dreams arose out of the sinfulness of men and women, which the Europeans took for granted. What Shakespeare thought of the prospects for the ideal in the world is made plain in most of his historical plays and still more in his great dramas of the soul — *Hamlet, Lear, Macbeth, Othello* — all of which were written before *The Tempest.* A shrewd historian, Professor J. W. Allen, has given an interesting interpretation of More's *Utopia.* "The real land of More's heart's desire," Allen wrote, "was not of this world. More knew that his Utopia was nowhere and proved nothing. He had declared in effect that, men being what they are, there is no conceivable remedy for social evils except, at all events, one that cannot be adopted." [2] If this can be said of Utopia, it can also be said of Rabelais' miraculous abbey; the rest of *Gargantua* makes clear enough what Rabelais thought human societies were really like.

The idea of original sin — along with other general, agreed-upon conceptions concerning human nature, derived from classical and Christian tradition and experience — was still almost universally held during the sixteenth and early seventeenth centuries, in spite of the multiplying religious divisions. These universal ideas and conceptions were almost invariably binding on work of the mind. Every specialist — whether thinker, craftsman, or artist — embarked on his mission from a common spiritual, moral, and intellectual haven. Whatever his work might be, he remained throughout his life in continuous communication with this haven. Partly for that reason specialization in work of the mind was much less narrow in its spirit and in the consequences that flowed from it than modern specialization has been among the Europeans and their descendants during the past hundred and fifty years.

Genius can flower in one man in many spheres only when his mind sets out from a unity. The minds of the Renaissance had this advantage over contemporary minds. As Sir Kenneth Clark has recently shown, painters and sculptors of the fifteenth and early sixteenth centuries actually created "architectural ideas," something which, Clark writes, would be "incredible today." [3] Painting, sculpture, and architecture were often combined with engraving and through architecture with engineering. Engineering was a part of the art of fortification. All these arts proceeded from a generally accepted theological and philosophical view of man's origin and destiny. Although the administration of the Roman Church and the morals of professing Christians gave rise to increasing scandal, faith in the Founder remained all but universal. Faith was knit with a philosophical outlook derived from the scholastic philosophy of the twelfth and thirteenth centuries. The main assumptions of the philosophy — in close accord with Revelation — were accepted by so characteristic a Renaissance man as Giovanni

Pico della Mirandola (1463–1494),[4] who influenced both More and Zwingli.

Faith and reason combined to provide a common starting point for genius and talent. With the help of classical experience and a new interest in nature, men and women of the Renaissance felt that they were discovering new means of living and of achieving their Christian end. But both the beginning and the end of life were much the same for them as for their medieval ancestors. Their acceptance of a single, venerable view of man's origin and destiny provided them with a foundation, lacking today, for an exercise of their gifts in many lines. The labor of the artist was closely linked with that of the scientist; artistic work involved direct experience with the natural attributes and the technical possibilities of many materials, while scientific work was often concerned directly with the behavior of matter for achieving artistic objectives. It was possible, therefore, for a mind to express its ideas and to develop its sense of form with consistency — and at an equally high level of distinction and sophistication — across almost the whole range of intellectual achievements. Leonardo is a preëminent example. But there were many other men who combined art and science. There was Albrecht Dürer, who was mathematician and engineer as well as painter, engraver, and etcher. There was Bernard Palissy (c. 1510–1589), who renewed the art of ceramics, constructed salt marshes and gardens, and made fundamental contributions to the science of geology.

At the beginning of the sixteenth century scientific and artistic invention were still so close to each other as to be almost part of a single inspiration.[5] They were combined, moreover, with a conception of the variety and wholeness of man's nature within the Christian view of his origin and destiny. It was more difficult, in consequence, for the conscientious intellect to do two things which it came to do with little scruple at the beginning of the twentieth century. One is to treat the intellectual process as purely matter-of-fact and explicable in material terms. The other is to consider the problem of what is morally good or bad as nonexistent or at least as irrelevant to intellectual inquiry. The absence of illusions with respect to human nature, combined with the relegation of hopes for perfect felicity to a world beyond positive experience, made it natural for Europeans in the sixteenth and seventeenth centuries to call human qualities and weaknesses by their names. This helped them to recognize that the most rewarding experiences open to man on earth are derived from his inner life and that this life is transcendental. That is why for them art was a part of life and why they were often able to make life itself an art.

For the artist inspiration invariably remains mysterious. As long as art and science were close together in the minds of men, persons who made scientific or even mechanical discoveries felt a sense of mystery about their works; they were reticent about trying to explain the works fully.[6] Confident of their own powers, while still wary of the uses to which their discoveries might be put in the practical world, Europeans of genius made an effort to control the consequences of their work in the one place where control might be effective, within the mind itself.

The case of John Napier is an example. Theologian, landlord, scientist, and inventor — though known to posterity as mathematician — Napier became alarmed over the danger of a Spanish invasion. An invasion might have turned Great Britain into a battlefield and have brought economic progress to a halt. What concerned Napier was not the economic but the religious consequences of conquest. For many years he had worked on a book which he published in Edinburgh in 1594, when the Spanish danger still weighed on his mind. As a young man he had come under the influence of John Knox and Christopher Goodman, the two leading Scottish Presbyterian preachers who did so much to make popular the new Church of Scotland with its Calvinist roots. Napier's work was based on the last book of the New Testament. *A Plaine Discovery of the Whole Revelation of Saint John*, he called it. The first part is in the form of propositions, presented with almost the same mathematical precision that he was to use so effectively in his later treatise on logarithms. In his theological treatise, Napier aimed to prove two things. First, the day of judgment would fall somewhere between 1688 and 1700. Second, the Pope was Antichrist. It followed that Protestants had the duty of persuading all Roman Catholics to repent of their worship during the short space of three generations that remained.[7]

Holding these convictions with a fervor that appears on almost every page, Napier would stick at nothing to prevent an invasion in the Roman Catholic interest. If successful, such an invasion obviously would reduce the chances of Napier's contemporaries and their descendants to attain salvation, because another political realm would have been won for Antichrist. It was to prevent this that he worked upon the "Secrett Inventionis," which he described in the manuscript of 1596, written shortly after the publication of his *Plaine Discovery*.[8] The document was apparently sent to the English crown by some of the future James I's ambassadors. It found its way into the papers of the Bacon family, already active in the service of Queen Elizabeth. Beyond the tank, which has been already described in Napier's words, and beyond the burning glasses designed to set fire to an enemy's ships at sea [9] (and reminiscent of a weapon attributed with little evidence to Archimedes) Napier referred to a still more terrible weapon, whose exact character he covered up more completely than he hid the nature of his tank. This is what he had to say about it:

> The invention and visible demonstration of a piece of artillery, which, shott, passeth not linallie through the enemie, destroying onlie those that stand on the random thereof, and fra them forth flying idly, as utheris do; but passeth superficially, ranging abrode within the whole appointed place, and not departing furth of the place till it hath executed his whole strength, by destroying those that be within the boundes of the said place.
>
> The use hereof not onlie serveth greatlie against the armie of the enemy on land, but alsoe by sea it serveth to destroy, and cut downe, att one shott the whole mastes and tackling of so many shippes as be within the appointed boundes as well abreid as in large, so long as any strength at all remayneth.[10]

We do not know what this weapon was or whether it could accomplish anything approaching what Napier claimed. Its history was described by another Scot, Sir Thomas Urquhart, the translator of Rabelais. Urquhart was born six years before the death of Napier, whom he idolized. According to Urquhart, Napier "gave proof upon a large plain in Scotland to the destruction of a great many herds of cattel, and flocks of sheep, whereof some were distant from other half a mile on all sides, some a whole mile." Urquhart wrote that this powerful engine, "by vertue of some secret springs, inward resorts, and other implements and materials fit for the purpose," could "clear a field of four miles circumference, of all the living creatures exceeding a foot of height." [11]

Napier had evidently conceived and experimented with some powerful engines of destruction, of which this seems to have been the most remarkable. That he was at pains to conceal their workings is equally evident. Urquhart wrote that an old acquaintance tried to pry from Napier on his deathbed the secret of his new "artillery." Napier is said to have replied: "For the ruin and overthrow of man, there were too many devices already framed, which if he could make to be fewer, he would with all his might endeavour to do; and that therefore seeing the malice and rancor rooted in the heart of mankind will not suffer them to diminish, by any new conceit of his the number of them should never be increased." [12]

However fanciful the story, it is certainly not inconsistent with the known facts of Napier's life [13] or with his deep consciousness — which also emerges from his theological treatise — of the sinfulness of man.

Even if the story were an invention, it was an invention of the era to which Napier belonged, and therefore revealing of an attitude then prevalent and influential. There are some who still hold this attitude in the twentieth century, but it has almost ceased to influence history. The scientists who made the atomic bomb for the United States Government confined themselves to telling the government not to use it.

Napier's conception of his responsibilities had behind it the weight of the classical Greek tradition. In Plutarch's account of the siege of Syracuse by the Romans under Marcellus, we are told how Archimedes (c. 287–212 B.C.), confronted by the invaders, put his vast learning to practical purpose. He employed war engines, hitherto never used, which hurled missiles on a scale and with a frequency that forced the Romans to flee. Plutarch explains that Archimedes refused to "set forth any booke how to make all these warlicke engynes . . . He esteminge all kinde of handy craft and invention to make engines, and generally all maner of sciences bringing common commodity by the use of them, to be but vyle, beggerly, and mercenary drosse: employed his witte and study onely to write thinges, the beawty and subtiltie whereof, were not mingled any thinge at all with necessitie." A few pages earlier, in his account of Archimedes' own intellectual background, Plutarch wrote that Plato had considered it "utterly corrupt" to make "Geometry . . . discende from things not comprehensible, and without body, unto things sencible and materiall, and to bringe it to a palpable substance, where the vile and base handie worke of man is to be employed." [14]

It is evident that for this Greek philosophical tradition the view that powerful war engines could be legitimately realized in material form only for a just defense was bound up with the principle that neither superior knowledge nor wisdom ought properly be used to obtain practical results. (Plutarch wrote of Archimedes as possessing "divine wisdome.") Already in the early seventeenth century, in Napier's old age, Francis Bacon's philosophy challenged the ancient position that there was something base or degrading about putting the most sublime learning at the service of material things. But the views of the British on these issues were then confused. Few, if any, serious writers were willing to relinquish the principle that learning ought not to be put at the service of destruction. In his *History of the World* Sir Walter Raleigh, a contemporary of Napier's, wrote with apparent approval of Archimedes' refusal to reveal the secrets behind his engines: "To enrich a mechanical trade, or teach the art of murdering men, it was beside his purpose." [15] Napier was not opposed to enriching mechanical trades. He apparently made contributions to coal mining and salt manufacturing as well as to agriculture. Yet he shared the ancient prejudice against contributing to the art of murdering men. The question was whether it would be possible for genius to devote itself wholeheartedly to practical improvements without contributing equally to improvements in destruction.

We are not suggesting that Napier had an atomic bomb up his sleeve! But data in manuscripts and printed works of the period from 1450 to 1650 show that ideas of the tank, the submarine, and the airplane were not the monopoly of some rare misunderstood genius, a role in which popular writers have been fond of casting Leonardo da Vinci. Many men had plans for these twentieth-century wonders. Some among them, like Bishop Wilkins,[16] thought they could be realized then and there in the early seventeenth century, when only thirty or forty thousand Englishmen had settled in North America.

What held back their realization for a dozen generations? Apart from the manifold technical difficulties, may not the reticence of the scientists, their reluctance to embody sublime knowledge in concrete forms, their Christian sense of responsibility for the sinfulness of man, have delayed the march of mechanical improvement, especially for military purposes?

No doubt it would have been impossible in the seventeenth century to achieve great destructive power with tanks, submarines, and explosives, even if scientists and engineers had turned the full force of their minds to the exploitation of the new inventions and conceptions. There was too little metal available to produce tanks in any number or to multiply greatly the output of guns, balls, and bullets. Even after the notable expansion in the metallurgical industries at the end of the Middle Ages, the costs of constructing a number of armored vehicles would have been prohibitive. In the seventeenth century the building of a large fleet of iron tanks was materially as insoluble a problem as would be today the construction of a large fleet of silver tanks!

Yet the slow, cautious way in which all practical inventions were exploited, the reluctance of the scientist to put any of his learning unreservedly at the disposal of practical results,[17] cannot be attributed altogether to the backwardness of men's minds or even to the backwardness of the knowledge available for them to draw upon. If the precise scientific knowledge, to which modern universities give their first allegiance, was in fact lacking, this was partly because the greatest minds were then more disposed than now to seek other less precise results. They still thought of knowledge as a means of enriching men's souls, even when, as in England and Holland, they had begun early in the seventeenth century to see the possibility of applying knowledge to the advantage of men's bodies. Sir Walter Raleigh's words show that the prejudice against revealing the secrets of death-dealing engines was bound up with the closely related prejudice that wisdom was more important than knowledge, that knowledge could be properly employed only for higher ends than the material and the practical. Such a prejudice interfered not only with the production of more efficient weapons, but also with the use of scientific learning and even technical knowledge for the production in greater quantities of most commodities, including the base metals upon whose abundance the future of the tank, the submarine, and the airplane depended.

The intellect is always confronted with problems of choice. There was another choice which had much significance for history besides the choice between the search for many-sided, infinitely varied Truth and the search for approximate truths in the interest of material improvement. This other choice was between efficiency and the service of beauty in the material objects produced.

A sensitive English art critic, Geoffrey Scott, who died prematurely in 1929, has taught that the period which began in the early fifteenth century with the architecture of Ghiberti and Brunelleschi and lasted into the eighteenth century was an era during which the claims of delight occupied a more central place in architecture than at any other time in Western history.[18] Renaissance styles were moving not in the direction of the practically efficient, a pursuit indispensable for the triumph of industrial civilization, but toward inutilities which demonstrate constructive powers of a different order. Renaissance artists indulged in constructions which were enchanting but "completely pointless, except in so far as [they created] a beautiful space."[19] This preoccupation with beauty was not confined to architecture, which was frequently combined with painting and sculpture. The claims of delight extended to the making of almost all durable objects from a castle or a fort to a piece of cloth or a lock and key. As technicians and even scientists were in close touch with the workshops, technology and science were influenced by the concern with beauty characteristic of the Renaissance. As much as the classical conception of knowledge as most sublime when independent of material results, the concern with beauty interfered with the modern purpose of turning out commodities cheaply in large quantities. As much as the belief in original sin, it conflicted with the purpose of fashioning efficient weapons to kill.

The effort of the artist to achieve perfection requires an immense amount of thought, time, labor, and patience, and so a society in which the workers are preoccupied with artistic results is deprived of human energy which might be harnessed for military purposes. A Victorian

Englishwoman, Mrs. Mark Pattison, has left an account of the adventures of Palissy as a master potter. Her story illustrates the struggle of the sixteenth-century craftsman and it reveals the love and care which were lavished on art even during the long age of European wars following Columbus' voyages. She wrote:

Palissy now set to work for seven or eight months learning how to make the vessels on which he should employ the discovered enamel. He erected a furnace for himself, being his own mason, tempering his own mortar, carrying on his own back the materials for his work . . . When the toil of baking the pots in this furnace was over, it was succeeded by the terrible hardships of grinding night and day, for a month . . . The vessels previously prepared were then covered with the composition; for six days and nights, Palissy fed the furnace fire, but the enamel would not melt. Suspecting a possible mistake in the proportions of the ingredients, he pounded afresh the same materials, at the same time keeping alight his fire, lest the furnace should cool. His own pots were gone: he bought new ones; but the fire was flagging, his fuel was exhausted, the palings of his garden, the tables, the flooring of his house were cast into the furnace. In his unspeakable anguish he was sustained by a gleam of better fortune: the last trials, though not successful, showed promise of ultimate success.[20]

Mrs. Pattison's lines describe part of a long battle for beauty repeated with variations by craftsmen all over Europe. It was a battle which had nothing to do with war — indeed, which stood in the way of war.

During the fifteenth and early sixteenth centuries the growing disposition of the wealthier Europeans — under the influence of the Italian Renaissance — to seek a more delightful worldly existence, to build anew, to lead more luxurious lives, had stimulated production by the spread of artistic crafts to serve men's new desires. This had been partly responsible for the growing demand for metal. In this way the Renaissance, which in its later phases became, after about 1460, an "industrial" renaissance, had contributed to the spread of firearms and to the development of a fresh "art of war."[21] Yet as long as the industrial workers and craftsmen, together with the artists, were guided in their callings by the ends of art, limits were imposed upon the expansion of output and upon the effective use of industry for military purposes.

As it developed in Italy and Germany during the fifteenth century, particularly during the fifty years preceding the revolutionary changes in warfare, the making of plate armor was an art, pursued in the same spirit as painting and sculpture. Iron was among the materials used in the new Renaissance arts, as it had been used in the medieval arts. In fact, iron was destined to serve the artist well into the eighteenth century,[22] until the costs of producing this metal began to be reduced with revolutionary rapidity. The methods of composition and execution employed in constructing and decorating a suit of armor were no less artistic than those employed in creating a work in stone, oil, bronze, or enamel. As one authority, R. C. Clephan, has written, "The effect of the Italian 'renaissance' was especially seen in profuse and artistic ornamentation, which at length came to be more regarded even than strength itself . . . Much of the armour was covered with embossed figures, engraved, chased and damascened with gold." [23] The ornamentation was combined with purity of line and elegance of form in the suit as a whole. A knight was prepared for battle in a robe of metal that had a perfection in fit and decoration equal to the most elegant dress. The style of Italian armor was in fact a reproduction of late medieval Florentine clothing. "The number of artists and craftsmen, who were employed to design, turn out, and finish a suit of armour . . . was simply legion," Clephan proceeds, "and of course, in the case of enriched suits . . . still more were brought into requisition." There was "the designer, modeller, steel, silver and goldsmith, carvers, enamellers, inlayers, engravers, — workers in hammered work, damasceners, polishers, and hosts of other craftsmen, each contributing his quota of industry and skill to one complete whole."

Like all the arts of the Renaissance, the making of armor enlisted the services of men of universal genius. Such artists as Donatello, Michelangelo, Dürer, Leonardo, and Cellini made designs for armor, and some of them also participated as engravers in its production.[24] It was an age when on the Continent artistry was spreading in the making of objects for use. Even water- and horse-driven machines were wanted to produce more economically the materials needed by artists and other craftsmen in the service of art. With the principle of delight in view, it would hardly have occurred to those whose decisions counted — the Renaissance craftsman, his client, patron, or employer (when he was dependent upon an entrepreneur) — to allow machinery to interfere with the quality of the materials in the interest of a larger output, any more than to allow machinery to interfere with the actual works of art for which materials were needed.

That peacefully minded king, James I, who first united the Scottish and English crowns in 1603, is said to have remarked that armor provided double protection. It secured its wearer against blows and also prevented him from effectively injuring others! A century before James's peaceful reign, the protection afforded by armor began to be shattered. At the very time when the suits reached their greatest perfection as works of art, at the close of the fifteenth century, they fell victim, as we have seen, to new and increasingly numerous guns.[25]

Yet the revolution in weapons failed to end the conflict between delight and destruction. As created by human beings, beauty is the embodiment of transcendental, immaterial conceptions in tangible material forms. These conceptions are concerned not with abundance but with perfection. And for every conception which finds concrete expression, there are always many others which flit about in the mind and influence the lives of the persons who have them. There are almost certainly a much larger number of these transcendental conceptions (relative to the population) in societies where the pursuit of delight is an integral part of most industrial workers' daily labor than in those societies where such daily labor is more routine and mechanical, where machinery determines the form of the objects produced. The societies of the twentieth century are, in this sense, routinized and mechanical. Those of which Western Europe was chiefly composed when gunpowder first came into widespread use, were devoting themselves far more to the service of delight. Ideas of beauty — with its inseparable allies, fancy and wit — were not losing ground as a result of the increasing concern with sense impressions and with classical models, characteristic of the Renaissance. These ideas were vigorous enough and widely enough diffused to carry over into the crafts of making munitions of war, even when great changes occurred, as during the sixteenth century, in the nature of the arms with which men fought. The art that had gone into the fashioning of armor and medieval weapons persisted in the production of new instruments of defense and destruction.

It has been suggested in Chapter III that the building of fortresses in Renaissance Italy was a branch of the art of architecture, as it had been from the eleventh century during the ages of Romanesque and Gothic building. Early in the sixteenth century Sanmichele was one of the first architects partly to adjust his plans to the new danger from cannon fire. Ideas of defense were invariably intermingled in his mind with the conceptions of beauty of position, structure, and decoration. He conceived of the fortification and embellishment of his native Verona as a single task, in the accomplishment of which defense and delight complemented each other.[26] It was not for some generations afterwards, not until the late seventeenth century, that a sharp conflict arose between beauty and the power of armed resistance, and it was not until the late eighteenth century that the conflict began to be resolved in favor of resistance. Only since then have leading fortress builders been disposed to shake off an ancient prejudice, reaffirmed by Europeans of the Renaissance, that a fort should be a work of art.

What was of primary importance in restraining war was the persistence of aesthetic principles even among the makers of the new weapons of attack. Like the fortifications, men-of-war were designed to charm the beholder. The masts, spars, and yards formed, with the hull of the ship, a sketch worthy of a great draftsman. Both masts and hull were richly embellished: the masts with streaming, many-colored pennants, as well as billowing sails; the hull with elaborate decorations at bow and stern and all along the sides.[27] These sides were punctured with rows of cannon's mouths, looking more like the oval windows in the lofts of castles than the belching muzzles of flame which they became when, in sight of enemy vessels, they spit out their balls of destruction. In describing the "Réale" (1644), a flagship of the newly built French navy, a nineteenth-century scholar wrote that it was "very thickly ornamented with sculptures, and covered with rich gildings and paintings, veritable works of art." [28] Such creations were useless for destruction, and Holland and England, states on the defensive during the religious wars, took the initiative after the middle of the seventeenth century in a movement to get rid of them.

The same concern of builders and craftsmen with beauty blunted the force of bullets, shot, balls, and explosives. Princes who controlled the arsenals seem to have stressed the importance of art in connection with the new armament manufacture. For example groups of artists were attached to the large establishment at Nancy known as the "artillerie." The tasks of these artists were to sculpt, mold, and engrave works of art as part of guns and even gun carriages.[29] According to the artful Biringuccio, who wrote about 1535, the part of the gun molds called the breech was always ornamented with some piece of sculpture.[30] Cannon were treated by their makers as objects to contemplate, notwithstanding the gruesome purpose they served. Such treatment got in the way of the purpose.

Arquebuses and muskets for the common soldier were plain, no doubt. But the ornamental work lavished by gunsmiths upon many small firearms, in the interest of pageantry and of the chase, had its effect on the preparation of all offensive weapons and auxiliary equipment. In European societies down into the eighteenth century, hunting and sport played a larger role than today. Compared with more recent times, Europe was still sparsely populated, and besides wolves and other ferocious animals able to tear men to pieces, game of most kinds — wild fowl, deer, and rabbits — was more abundant than in the modern industrial age. Many weapons, from the crossbow to the bayonet, were apparently invented, not for war, but for the chase. According to a recent authority, it was not until the nineteenth century that war replaced sport as the leading stimulus to technical improvements in firearms.[31] Something of the spirit of the chase, including the decoration of weapons, was carried over into war. All the pieces for officers, even for minor officers, were artistically executed. Clephan writes that "the decoration of many of the hand-guns of the sixteenth century was of a most artistic character, the barrels being often enriched with chasings, fine metal incrustations, or damascened, while the stocks were curiously and delicately carved and inlaid. It has been often assumed that the material usually used for inlaying was ivory. It was really bleached stagshorn, and inlaying with tortoiseshell was also not uncommon. . . A great amount of decorative skill was also expended on powder flasks." [32] In Italy gunmakers were regarded as artists at least as late as the 1640's, when John Evelyn noted that Brescia "consists most in artists, every shop abounding in guns, swords, armourers, etc. Most of the workmen come out of Germany." [33]

In the early seventeenth century, when the aristocracy on the continent of Europe was adding to its prestige and when it furnished many army officers, the warlike equipment carried by leaders on campaign was bound to set an example. Whatever the condition of the pieces served out to ordinary foot soldiers, the skill and energy of the armament makers was largely spent upon the solution of aesthetic issues — not, as in the twentieth century, upon problems connected with efficient destruction.

Explosives were scarce; yet the love of pageantry got the better of kings, princes, and nobles, and they were devoted to firework displays, a practice which apparently originated in China — a country which had not gone in for destructive efficiency in its use of gunpowder. If enough effort was spent on pageantry of this kind, the stock of materials indispensable for shooting was reduced and armies might be left without the means of fighting to a finish.

Think of the time wasted on delight in preparing fortifications, in fashioning firearms and auxiliary equipment, and even in pyrotechnics. Precious time it was; it might have been spent, as many now would take for granted it should have been, in making the guns more effective as instruments of death and destruction and in multiplying their output and the output of ammunition as well, so that more men could have used them more often.

The preoccupation of the Europeans with art was also a force in holding back an increase beyond a certain point in the output of metal, indispensable for waging war, especially in those countries — Italy, Switzerland, and France — where industrial progress took the form of quality more than quantity. The idea of expanding indefinitely the production of industrial materials — iron in particular — had not yet got hold of government officers or their economic advisers in most continental states, even to the extent that it had got hold of private adventurers in England and Holland, where economic enterprise was less effectively fettered by the state than in France, Spain, or Italy.

In 1542 and 1543 the French king issued edicts which actually aimed to prevent the increase of iron mills anywhere in France.[34] Repeated efforts were made to enforce these enactments during the hundred years that followed.[35] After 1626 Cardinal Richelieu interested himself in a new edict designed to maintain and improve the quality of French iron.[36] But he apparently took no steps to remove the restrictions upon output.

No doubt the motives of the French king's advisers in restricting the output of iron were complicated. Complaints of deforestation occasionally appear in the state papers of sixteenth-century France, and it is plausible to assume that some fear arose at court lest the multiplication of furnaces, forges, and other mills, by increasing the demand for charcoal, might denude the country of its trees. Yet compared with Great Britain, France was plentifully stocked with woods; it was not France but Great Britain which faced a timber crisis in the late sixteenth and early seventeenth centuries. And in England it was not legislation but the rising price of fuel which checked the growth in the output of metal.[37] Nor was there imminent danger of an exhaustion of the supplies of French ore to account for the legislation; France is rich in iron ore. It is plausible to suppose that other considerations besides actual scarcity influenced French national policy towards the production of iron. What could they have been?

The author of one of the earliest treatises devoted to political economy, Antoine de Montchrétien (1575–1621), who also composed rather dreary plays, showed considerable concern, in his treatise of 1615, over the dominant position gained by Germany and more recently by England, Holland, and Flanders in the production of firearms, locks, and cutlery. If any French writer of the time was likely to be anxious to increase the French output of iron, Montchrétien should have been the one. In 1611 or shortly afterwards, when he returned from exile in England, where he had observed the extraordinary industrial expansion that was going on, he had established a steelworks and a manufacture of knives, lancets, and scythes at Ousonne-sur-Loire. Yet in his book Montchrétien wrote of metalwares as would any characteristic Frenchman of his age. His interest was in improving their quality. Doubtless he assumed that an improvement in quality was the key to the restoration which he sought for the French metal industries to a leading place in Europe. But it never occurred to him to regard metallic ores as a natural resource basic to the whole French economy. For him there were five such fundamental pillars — wheat, wine, wood, flax, and salt.[38]

Montchrétien's views on national economic policy hardly differed from those of the great minister, Sully (1560–1641), who was his older contemporary, and who preceded Richelieu as the architect of French royal absolutism. Sully had written of "husbandry and pasturage" as "the two breasts of France, the true mines and treasures of Peru." It was the products of the soil rather than the subsoil on which the French, like other great peoples before them, were accustomed to base the economic strength of the nation. France remained true to earlier conceptions of civilized life in which rivers of metal had no place. In the late Roman republic, legislation had been passed prohibiting mining in Italy. Ancient philosophical thought had rebelled against the idea of exploiting the riches of the subsoil indiscriminately. This was regarded as a kind of sacrilege. The pillage of mineral treasure seemed to the ancients to violate a higher law to which the pagan peoples, even before the coming of Christ, felt men were bound. Such an attitude formed part of the tradition which the Western Europeans inherited from the classical writers who were so often their mentors. It was an outlook which died harder in France than in Great Britain and Scandinavia, where very likely it had never been as firmly established as in the Latin countries.

Statesmen like Sully or Richelieu were bent on achieving for France political hegemony in Europe. This was sought by consolidating and adding to the French territorial dominions and even by encouraging dissension abroad as a means of diminishing the relative prosperity of other European states. But few efforts were made to divert the national energies from agriculture, or even from the artistic and the luxury industries, in the direction of the kinds of mining and metallurgy which could supply abundant war materials. What were wheat, wine, wool, flax, and salt good for, without metal, in waging battles with gunpowder? Not until peoples were more ready to rob the underworld of its treasures were they likely to have the raw materials, as well as the machinery and the power, necessary to provide the efficient flow of destructive weapons and munitions which would make practicable total war.

If Europe was unable to commit suicide with the help of explosives in early modern times, the survival was not entirely the accidental result of historical forces beating upon the bodies and minds of men. It is startling to reflect that twentieth-century opinion regards as unreasonable, superstitious, and impractical the moral and intellectual scruples and the love of beauty which were still characteristic of Europeans in the early seventeenth century, and which bound them — scientists, artists, craftsmen, governors, and statesmen alike — by a kind of voluntary servitude to make choices which seemed to them pre-eminently rational. Twentieth-century opinion attributes their choices almost entirely to ignorance and backwardness. It is taken for granted in the making of things that the aims of efficiency and abundance alone have value; the utility of the useless has been forgotten.

The machine and the total exploitation of the natural resources of ore and fuel are certainly immediately practical. But may not the immediately practical prove to be in the long run the most impractical of deities to worship? The pursuit of the practical has now made it practicable to destroy most of what the mind has helped to create across a millennium of time. It no longer requires a Napier to prove that the day of judgment is at hand. The new day of judgment is not the work of God but of man.

CHAPTER SEVEN

The Surrender at Breda
and its Background

· THREE HUNDRED YEARS AGO THE PEOPLE OF ENGLAND WERE ENGAGED in a terrible civil war. Among the young men then coming of age was Robert Boyle. Except for Newton, he helped more than any other Englishman of the late seventeenth century to make his country the center of the great school of natural philosophy whose achievements constituted the chief glory of the reigns of the last two Stuarts — Charles II and James II.

Boyle was horrified by the war. In 1646 he wrote about it from London with touches of wisdom astonishing from a boy of nineteen. He had had conversations with a number of partisans of the House of Commons, with men who were destined to be on the winning side. Those who look forward to victory in modern war as the solution of their troubles might meditate to advantage upon his words.

"The greater part of men in these parts," he wrote, "are pleased to flatter themselves with the hopes of a speedy settlement of things; but for my part, that have always looked upon sin as the chief incendiary of the war, and yet have by careful experience observed the war to multiply and heighten those sins, to which it owes its being, as water and ice, which by a reciprocal generation beget one another, I cannot without presumption expect a recovery in that body, where the physic that should cure, but augments the disease." [1]

His words would seem to contain three partial truths. None is original; all deserve repetition. First, the principal cause of war is sin. Second, victory does not solve the difficulties which brought men into battle; it is more likely to accentuate those difficulties. Third, war begets war.

If war begets war, is it not true also that peace begets peace? The historian is confronted with a two-sided problem, toward an understanding of which his knowledge might contribute. Why have not movements toward more total and devastating wars, like the one in which we recently found ourselves, led in the past to universal massacre? Why have not countermovements toward more and more pacific relations, like the one in which our grandfathers found themselves, led to general amity?

History provides examples of these long-term movements toward and away from bellicose conditions. At a certain time in the seventeenth century, perhaps even before Boyle wrote his words in the midst of the special troubles of his country, a turning point was reached on the Continent. After more than a hundred years of atrocious warfare the Europeans bound up their wounds, scowled at, cursed, and dreaded each other, and even continued to fight, but with diminishing fierceness and less destructive consequences. The hundred years preceding, in 1740, the accession of Frederick the Great as king of Prussia and Maria Theresa as archduchess of Austria and queen of Hungary and Bohemia — when the War of the Austrian Succession broke out — were an age during which, in spite of occasional setbacks, the tendency was continuously toward more pacific conditions.

Modern Europe inherited from its Christian past the idea that war among men, particularly war among the Christian peoples of the West, is an evil and that the settlement of disputes and grievances which arise out of man's sinful nature ought not to be left completely at the mercy of the strong. The late Professor Haskins remarked that "the major sport of the Middle Ages was war, with its adjuncts the tournament, the joust, and the judicial duel." [2] Campaigning and fighting were hedged in by customs and conventions. War had its closed seasons. A papal council held under Pope Innocent II, in 1139, placed under an interdict the crossbow, a deadly weapon apparently unknown to the ancient Greeks or Romans, and hitherto used chiefly to kill animals rather than men. The Church held it to be a barbarous instrument, unfit for Christian warfare. Its condemnation was confirmed by Pope Innocent III two generations later.[3] Such limitations on fighting, together with those imposed by the chivalrous etiquette expected from the medieval knight, were frequently broken, as are all restrictions, customs, and laws which men establish to control their violent dispositions. But during the twelfth and thirteenth centuries the faith, and the conventions which surrounded medieval warfare, helped to keep killing and destruction within bounds among peoples whose manners were hardly tender.

For the Christian humanist on the eve of the Reformation, war was a denial of man's rational nature; it drew men down to the level of the animals. No one represented the physical enormity of battle with more horror than Erasmus in *Adagia*. "To clash with violence," he wrote, "is characteristic of beasts and gladiators whom I class with beasts." "Warre or battle," his contemporary and friend Thomas More remarked in *Utopia*, "[is] a thing very beastly, and yet of no kinde of beastes in so muche use as to man." Both Erasmus and More wrote at the time of the revolution in weapons which was helping to break down many of the restraints imposed upon warfare by medieval traditions and customs. Conceived in terms of swords, lances, shields, and armor, chivalry could hardly survive the hail of cannon balls, bullets, shells, and bombs.[4] In *Henry VI*, Part 1, Shakespeare portrays the consternation produced by the death of the Earl of Salisbury from gunfire.

The disappearing reality of the supernatural world of the medieval mind, in which the tangible realities of our passing world of human life had been treated as appearances, was enacted in one of the very greatest creations of an artist — the *Don Quixote* of Shakespeare's remarkable contemporary, Cervantes. The human spirit had played a role in medieval battle; it had lent wings to the knight mounted on his horse. But now this spirit had nothing to tilt against except windmills. In actual battle the spirit was confounded by the fearful hail of the new iron balls and lead bullets. "Blessed be those happy ages," Don Quixote observed in the midst of his exploits, "that were strangers to the dreadful fury of these devilish instruments of artillery, whose inventor I am satisfied is now in hell, receiving the reward of his cursed invention, which is the cause that very often a cowardly base hand takes away the life of the bravest gentleman, and that in the midst of that vigour and resolution which animates and inflames the bold, a chance bullet (shot perhaps by one that fled, and was frighted at the very flash the mischievous piece gave, when it went off) coming nobody knows how, or from whence, in a moment puts a period to the brave designs, and the life of one, that deserved to have survived many years."[5]

To a European at the end of the Middle Ages there was something unfair and fundamentally brutal about killing an armored knight with the new projectiles. At the same time it filled fighting men with new rage and invited the most awful reprisals. A fifteenth-century Italian family, the Vitellis, was made up largely of soldiers of fortune. They had been raised in the traditions of the *condottieri*, for whom war was a kind of combination game and business, having no larger purpose than to serve the petty political intrigue of the rulers of the many small states into which Italy was split. Sport and business enterprise have much in common. Both are played according to conventional rules and with conventional counters. Balls and bullets, fired to kill, were not among the accepted counters in the warfare of Renaissance Italy, which had resembled sport. The response of Gian Paolo Vitelli to a widespread use of firearms by his enemies shows how the new weapons contributed to a new ferocity. Shortly before he was accused of treachery and executed in 1499 at the order of Cesare Borgia, Paolo witnessed in a battle the death of many of his companions by gunfire. Thereupon he began to pluck out the eyes and cut off the hands of all *arquebusiers* whom he could capture, deeming it disgraceful that noble men-at-arms should be shot from a distance by low-born infantrymen. When in 1498 he took Buti, a small town near Pisa, he had the hands of all the gunners of the garrison cut off.[6]

Once conventions and rules of war lose their force there are no limits to reprisals, except those imposed by human revulsion, charity, and compassion, or by fear of counterreprisals. More persons were mowed down each decade by gunfire. In Italy during the twenty-one years following 1494, three commanders-in-chief were casualties; during the fourteen years following 1516, nine were killed.[7] The incentive to retaliate grew; battles degenerated more and more frequently into butchery. The comments of a distinguished French soldier, Guillaume du Bellay, whose brother became a cardinal, suggest that Europeans in the early sixteenth century felt that a degradation was taking place in the conduct of warfare. In 1536 he described the retreat by the Emperor Charles V's army from Aix-en-Provence to Fréjus, back along the route of the easy American advance into southern France in the Second World War. Before most of the retreating troops could escape, the local peasants in the fields abandoned their peaceful occupations. They had few weapons, but they stripped the firearms from dead or dying soldiers of the Emperor. They tore up the paths and roads in the rear of the fleeing army, demolished the bridges over the swollen and impetuous streams flowing from the Alps on one side and the Monts des Maures on the other. To support these efforts of the peasants, the French commanders who were pursuing the Emperor's army sent light horses which continually harassed the rear guard.

The ferocity and craft of the peasants, as hostile to the invader of 1536 as they were benevolent to the invader of 1944, effectively blocked the retreating enemy from finding food for the men or forage for the horses. The defeated soldiers with their beasts could neither get away nor eat. The roads were soon littered with the dead, the sick, and the starving. Abandoned pikes, arquebuses, and harnesses lay on the ground for the peasants to take at will; horses died in their tracks, slowly, like the soldiers. As Du Bellay rode toward Fréjus after the defeat had become a certainty, he was appalled by the heaps of men and animals that he saw, all tangled together pell-mell, the dying with the dead. It was "so horrible and piteous a spectacle," he wrote, "that it made even the most obstinate and intransigent enemies miserable, and those who witnessed the desolation could not conceive it to be less than that which Josephus describes in the destruction of Jerusalem and Thucydides in the Peloponnesian war. I tell you what I saw. On my return to Marseilles, I lay for fifteen days without the strength to lift myself on horseback." [8]

Du Bellay's comparison with Jewish and pagan history suggests that this new warfare struck him as unchristian. Although there was still much reconnoitering, scouting, and maneuvering without an immediate struggle for an issue, when the new armies met battles were likely to be total unless, as often happened, the ammunition of both sides gave out. Some years before the rout of his army in Provence, Charles V in some quiet moment had penned a few notes. They lay for centuries unnoticed in the Vienna archives. Possibly they were written on the eve of the famous battle of Pavia, in 1525, where the Emperor's rival, Francis I of France, was made prisoner and carried off to Spain. In any event the Emperor wrote: " . . . the armies are now very close to one another. A battle in which I shall be either victorious or wholly defeated cannot be postponed for much longer." [9]

In the religious and political wars that followed during the late sixteenth century, pitiful slaughters, like those which marked Charles V's victory at Pavia or his retreat from Aix, became increasingly frequent in the armed clashes which fed the European earth from the Pyrenees to the Carpathians and from Sicily to Flanders. Early in the seventeenth century a French authority on the art of war, Du Praissac by name, in describing the battles of his time used almost the very words of Charles V. Struggles in which "either you are vanquisher or vanquished," Du Praissac observed, were the normal issue of campaigns.[10]

When the conquering soldiers were let loose, the sequel was often more frightful than the battle. Atrocities at the expense of innocent noncombatants, the murder of prisoners, were by-products of the wars.[11] There were few regions on the Continent where the local villagers escaped such sights as obliged even a general, with a sense of humanity, to take to his bed. The horror reached a climax during the Thirty Years' War, particularly in the sack of Magdeburg in 1631 by Tilly. The town was burned to the ground; only the cathedral and some 140 houses were left standing. The greater part of the population of about thirty thousand was slaughtered without regard to age or sex. According to Schiller, it was "a murderous scene for which history can find no words and the art of writing no pen." [12]

How sharp is the contrast presented by the surrender of the Dutch garrison at Breda in 1625. After the defenders had held out against the attacking Spanish armies for eleven months in a new type of fortress, constructed under the influence of Simon Stevin, the Marquis of Spinola accorded his defeated enemy every military honor. He approved an order of capitulation according to which "the governor [of the fortress] with the officers and soldiers, both horse and foot, [were] to march out of the town armed soldier-like, viz. the foot with flying colors, drums beating, completely armed, bullets in mouth, matches lighted on both ends, their charges full of powder and shot. The horse with their trumpets sounding, standards displayed, armed in such sort as when they march towards the enemy. No soldier shall be questioned or detained for any cause or pretext whatsoever, not though he had formerly been in the enemy's service. And it shall be lawful for them to take with them their wives, children, household, household-staffe, horses and carts." The Prince of Orange was allowed to remove his furniture from the castle. Spinola provided wagons to carry the governor of the fortress and his officers to Gertruydenberg, ten miles north on the Rhine delta, and to convey as well all the parrots belonging to the garrison.[13] Men, women, and birds were assured a safe retreat, beyond the water barriers, into the heart of busy Holland.

When we look at Velasquez' great picture of the surrender, we feel ourselves in the presence of a new chivalry — adjusted to novel and horrible weapons, hitherto unused by man. In spite of the religious wars, Europeans had at their disposal remnants of the medieval conception of universal Christian community. They also had remnants of the old chivalry and the pageantry that accompanied it and that had found expression during the sixteenth century in ceremonials. For example, a brilliant pageant took place early in 1526, on the Franco-Spanish frontier between Hendaye and Fontarabia. Francis I, captured the year before in the battle of Pavia, was liberated in exchange for his two small sons who were delivered to Spain as hostages for the fulfillment of the treaty of Madrid, imposed by Charles V. Two splendid barques lavishly bedecked, their masts hung with banners, the one accompanied by twelve costumed French gentlemen and twelve French rowers, the other by twelve equally sumptuously dressed

Spanish gentlemen and twelve Spanish rowers, effected the exchange of royal persons across the bay formed by the mouth of the river Bidassoa separating the two countries.[14] Out of such traditional pageantry as that, and with the help of a polite etiquette and a human tenderness that evolved during the seventeenth century, a code of honor was forged. It was destined to have a pacific influence upon history. The ceremonies that accompanied the surrender at Breda were an early expression of it.

Among all the European forces during the previous century and a quarter, none had acquired a more frightful reputation for ferocity and unscrupulous cruelty than the Spaniards. The leadership by a Genoese of an army enlisted in the Spanish cause in a movement toward more restricted, more restrained and honorable warfare, and the commemoration of the scene by one of the finest Spanish artists in a majestic composition, serve to remind us that the miracle of humane change has not been the monopoly of any nation. Spinola's action was partly the achievement of an individual, who on a critical occasion took responsibility into his hands and acted, not as his contemporaries were constrained by habit to act, but as the magic of grace directed him to lead — toward charity which is neither old nor new, but eternal. Magnanimity without stint, without concern over the consequences, above all magnanimity by the powerful, is a potent force to hold back, and even to thwart, a rising tide of destruction.

The conditions of evolving civilized societies and the acts of an individual soul are never completely unrelated, however mysterious and unfathomable the actual connection may be. Spinola's example at Breda would have been barren of results, had it not appealed to hopes which were held deeply by Europeans on all sides of the religious and political struggles.

At the very time when Breda surrendered, two books appeared, one by a Dutchman, the other by a Frenchman, representing movements in thought which were largely new, and which were to have important influences in mitigating the bloody and cruel political and religious relations which had prevailed for decades among the Europeans. One book became famous. The other remains practically unknown.

One was the work of the remarkable political thinker, Hugo Grotius, born at Delft in Holland in 1583. His *De jure belli et pacis*, written in a French chateau near Senlis and published in 1625, provided a natural-law basis for restricted warfare. According to traditional Christian doctrine, a higher law exists, binding on all men independent of their individual interests, preferences, and circumstances. This is the eternal law, parts of which have been made known by Revelation, to be expounded and developed, according to Roman Catholic doctrine, by the Church. Yet apart from revealed knowledge and apart also from the dogmas and laws of the Church, by virtue of their rational nature, men have the power with their reason to recognize immutable principles, to participate dimly and imperfectly in eternal Truth, and thus to confirm and even to amplify the laws vouchsafed by God to man. It was this power, for example, that had enabled Aristotle, a pagan, to declare in the *Ethics* that murder, theft, and adultery were wrong absolutely. This natural law, as the product of human reason, did not conflict with revealed law, but existed independently of it, and could even stand without it as among the ancient Greeks. In the thought of the great French political philosopher, Jean Bodin (1530–1596), the king, prince, or other political sovereign, in his administration, his lawmaking, and his judicial decisions, was bound to respect the natural law, as well as the law of God.

Grotius set about to show that, as men under God, princes ought properly to be guided by the natural law, not only in their relations with their subjects, but in their relations with other states. If there were to be restrictions on war, a law of nations, such as Grotius aimed to provide, had become indispensable in the seventeenth century, now that the ancient authority of the Roman Church to restrain fighting among Christians had been compromised by the Reformation, the competition between worships, and the wars of religion, with the popes taking sides. No institution had been left to which all sides could appeal, and which could represent the fountainhead of universal justice.

Grotius owed an important debt to the scholastic philosophers, and in particular to Thomas Aquinas; he also owed a debt to his older contemporaries, Robert Bellarmine (1542–1621) and Francisco Suárez (1548–1617). A man of prodigious learning, Grotius brought his encyclopedic knowledge to bear on the judicial problems raised by the wars of which he had read, as well as by those he was living through. What is most significant for subsequent history in his work on war and peace is the insistence that legal principles exist in the human reason, independent of any actual worldly authority, political or religious, yet binding in the world — principles which should govern in all contingencies arising out of breaches of the peace between sovereign states. Before recourse to arms, a country should make a formal declaration of its grievances, and should go to war only if satisfaction could not be obtained through diplomatic negotiations. Wars should be fought according to accepted rules providing for humane treatment of the wounded and the prisoners. Treaties ending wars should also be drawn according to accepted rules which, in effect, precluded the conquest of one of the antagonists by the other and the subjugation of the enemy population.

On the Rights of War and Peace passed through many editions during the hundred years following its publication. Long and difficult to read, it remains one of the prominent books by a European. Grotius' work provided for the first time a civilized code, independent of the Bible as well as of the political authority of particular countries, for the conduct of international relations, including war. It took for granted that some fighting among nations was inevitable. Grotius' purpose was not to eliminate war but to limit it.

The other book, *Le Nouveau Cynée*, went much further. It was written by a Frenchman named Emeric Crucé. An almost exact contemporary of Grotius, Crucé left hardly a trace upon the voluminous historical records of his time. It has been claimed that he was a monk, but so little is known about him that this can neither be denied nor confidently affirmed. Only a few copies of *Le Nouveau Cynée* have survived.

To the old conception which Europe inherited from its medieval past, Crucé added a conception different from that of Grotius, and even fresher. Christian thought had been profoundly influenced by the division set forth by Saint Augustine, early in the fifth century, between the City of God and the city of man. Even though war was an evil, even though it was unchristian, the Europeans had resigned themselves to the inevitability of some war in the actual world where sinful men and women are condemned to live.

The new warfare of the sixteenth century engulfed so much of the life, the work, the thought, and the faith of the European peoples that it became more difficult than in the Middle Ages to reconcile with Christianity organized fighting in the temporal world. At the same time this temporal world had become more real and vital for Europeans at the end of the Middle Ages than it had been for their ancestors in the twelfth century, when the ultimate world of Eternity, to which death was the gate, was a more immediate part of thought, as well as of the imagination. Consequently, what happened in the temporal world of positive experience had taken on a greater importance by the sixteenth century, when organized violence became more widespread and was less redeemed by the practices of chivalry.

As one obscure Frenchman, writing in the midst of the religious wars in France, expressed it, "How piteous a thing is war. I believe that if the saints in paradise went to war they would soon turn into devils." [15] The conception of "just war," prevalent in medieval thought, seemed more of a contradiction in terms than before. If war with fire-arms made men and even saints into devils, battles lost such judicial, moral, and religious value as they had seemed to possess.

While, as Boyle wrote, war begets war, it also begets a distaste and even a horror of war. This distaste grew during the very period when killing for religious purposes increased. Although many Frenchmen fell to fighting with enthusiasm or at least with nonchalance at the out-break of hostilities in 1562, by the 1590's, after a generation of battles and slaughter within their country, the arms may be said to have fallen from their hands, so great was their lassitude.[16] Almost everywhere on the Continent by the middle of the seventeenth century, after another generation of continuous war, the exaltation over death, received or inflicted to prove the strength of religious faith, began to give way to a different kind of exaltation. It came to be felt that such virtue as could be drawn from battle consisted in generous and humane treat-ment of a defeated enemy — treatment of which Spinola gave an example.

If the highest ideal in battle was not death but restraint and mercy, why battle at all? If wars were never just, why have them? What Cruce's book aimed at was nothing less than the abolition of war. He proposed to keep always in existence in some chosen city, such as Venice, an assembly of ambassadors from all the sovereign states not only of Europe but of the entire world. This assembly was to settle peacefully every difference.[17]

Cruce's book made peace seem a possible goal for man, before the eternal life which for the Christian had been and continued to be his natural destiny. Among the early Christians, before the time of Augus-tine, there had been some who looked forward, when all men should be converted, to peace on earth.[18] But the Christian society of medieval Europe, which has been often regarded as a partial realization of the idea of Saint Augustine, had not nourished the hope of pacifism, save for the priesthood who were expected to desist from shedding blood. Now the idea of universal peace was revived by one who is thought to have been a religious. In spite of the vocation of its author, the idea was based not, as the earlier hope had been, on the universality of faith, but on the progress of rational thought and the improvement of economic conditions since the tenth century of our era. Non-Christian states were to be included on equal terms.

Cruce's project for perpetual peace formed an integral part of pro-posals which he put forward for freedom of trade among all nations. In his time, economic thought generally favored restrictions of various kinds on international commerce, from tariffs to prohibitions. It was taken for granted that the economic interests of nations were necessarily in opposition. Commerce itself, which had not completely separated from piracy in the later Middle Ages,[19] was regarded as a form of war by economic writers, virtually all of whom in Crucé's time were nationally minded. They considered war desirable, either as a means of direct enrichment at the expense of other nations or — as with Bodin — as a means of diverting the people within a nation from economically disastrous civil fighting.[20] Crucé's originality as an economic writer consisted in his view that the economic interests of every nation were in peace rather than war.

The future of peace lay with rational restraints upon war, which Grotius promulgated and which Spinola demonstrated in the field. It lay also with changes in the direction of economic thought of which Crucé was the forerunner. If his economic ideas were almost entirely ignored in his time only to become the accepted dogma of political economy a hundred and fifty years afterward, with the publication in 1776 of Adam Smith's *The Wealth of Nations*, this was partly because, in the interval, Europe had moved towards a similarity and a community of historical experience such as had been temporarily lost during the religious wars.

PART TWO

LIMITED WARFARE AND HUMANE CIVILIZATION
Circa 1640 to Circa 1740

CHAPTER EIGHT

Toward European Economic Community

· NO AGE IS MORE IN NEED OF REËXAMINATION THAN THE HUNDRED years which began in England with the outbreak in 1642 of the Civil War and in France with the accession of the infant Louis XIV in 1643. These hundred years were of immense importance in the general history of Europe and of the European colonies, which had been spreading all over the globe since the fifteenth century. In Europe itself a fresh sense of community evolved among the intelligent and the cultured. Men were drawn to exchange ideas concerning natural science, philosophy, and art, with almost no regard to political divisions and eventually with little regard to religious ones. The conviction that rational thought could provide a sound foundation for the unification of Europe and even of the world gained ground, as the disputes over religious dogma and worship ceased to end in violence and eventually lost some of their bitterness.

Although Protestants were sometimes persecuted on the Continent and Catholics in England, wars were no longer fought over religious issues. The principle of religious toleration had won the day in England by the Restoration in 1660.[1] There was a recrudescence of religious persecution in Europe towards the end of the seventeenth century, when the Huguenots were deprived of their privileges in France and when in 1685 the edict of Nantes, which had granted them some civil and religious liberty, was repealed. Bishop Gilbert Burnet (1643–1715), whom James II undertook to prosecute for his intrigues on behalf of the Dutch Prince of Orange (later William III of England), began to write his memoirs at about this time. Burnet understood history since the early sixteenth century much as Napier seems to have understood it a hundred years before, as a struggle in defense of the Reformation against the papists.[2] Yet during Burnet's later years, efforts were ending to root out Protestantism by the force of political authority.

During the early eighteenth century religious persecution notably diminished. Dean Tucker, an Anglican clergyman who has left his mark on the history of thought mainly by his work in economics as a forerunner of Adam Smith, objected to "the Romish religion" mainly on the ground that it was unfavorable to the economic improvement that he had so much at heart and that he associated with the freedom of the merchant. As the merchant class in France was more inclined to Protestantism than members of most other social classes, persecution of any kind by the Roman Church was, in Tucker's estimation, a serious disadvantage to trade. But in 1750 he observed that "the Bigotry of the court of France is not near so great, as it was in former times."[3]

When the Europeans were becoming more tolerant of each other and were drawing together in so many ways, could they have been splitting apart in their economic ways? Were the divergences of the previous hundred years, which had divided Europe territorially into three parts, increasing or diminishing after the mid-seventeenth century?

The two states which emerged as the leading political powers — France and Great Britain — became no less indisputably the leading economic powers. When Louis XIII died in 1643, French industry and trade were in a very depressed state, in spite of the efforts of his principal minister, Richelieu, to encourage agriculture and commerce, foreign as well as domestic. Trade with the Levant had fallen precipitously during the 1620's and 1630's. Notwithstanding Richelieu's success in keeping the country out of the worst fighting of the Thirty Years' War, the north of France was little more prosperous than the south.

It would be a mistake to suppose that the French were growing continually more prosperous between 1643 and 1740. The last decades of the seventeenth century and the first decade of the eighteenth were decades of depression, when the output of many commodities, such as cloth and fuel, apparently receded. There were only two periods of striking industrial and commercial progress: the sixties and seventies of the seventeenth century, when Colbert as Louis XIV's chief minister was responsible for royal policy, and the late twenties and thirties of the eighteenth, after France had recovered from the losses of Louis XIV's last wars and from a financial collapse in 1720.

Yet if the condition of France be compared with 1640, the country was rich at the outbreak of the War of the Austrian Succession in 1740. This was not simply because France had acquired by conquest rich territories, such as Alsace and Franche-Comté. Production had increased both in the old provinces and in the new ones. In the 1730's the basic industries of modern times — mining, metallurgy, and textiles — were all enjoying moderate prosperity, destined to increase during the fifty years preceding the French Revolution.[4] Even at the end of Louis XIV's long wars the consumption of food and foodstuffs of all kinds in Paris had increased by about a fourth since 1634.[5] The French output of coal and iron in 1740 was at least double what it had been in 1640. When Fragonard (1732–1806) was a child the products of the luxury manufactures, in which painters had a hand and for which France had provided the models for Europe ever since the early seventeenth century, were more widely esteemed than ever. Tapestries, furniture, fine metal- and glasswares, magnificent coaches and ornamental work of every kind, as well as paintings and musical instruments, were being turned out in greater profusion than ever before. With the introduction here and there during the early eighteenth century of coal-burning furnaces, industries such as glassmaking, sugar refining, and soap boiling, not yet robust in terms of the volume of output, were taking a new lease on life.

While the volume of industrial production grew at a more rapid rate in France from 1640 to 1740 than from 1540 to 1640, in England the rate of growth slackened with the Civil War. The early English "industrial revolution" came to an end. Although there was a recovery after 1660, and the production of British coal, cloth, and paper grew during the eight decades that followed the Restoration of that year, it was not until at least the 1750's that the rate of increase in English industrial output was again as rapid as during the period 1540–1640.

For England, as for France, the late seventeenth and early eighteenth centuries formed an age of intermittent industrial and commercial prosperity, which ended with the country rather more wealthy than before. Compared with the conditions of material progress to which civilized peoples had been accustomed before the nineteenth century, the growth in production and in the felicity of the upper orders of society, was impressive in both countries. Compared with the astounding expansion in the volume of industrial output and the general rise in the material standard of living which were destined to characterize the nineteenth century, both countries were advancing at a snail's pace.

As the rate of economic growth in the two countries converged, the commodities produced grew more alike. So did the nature of industrial organization and the character of industrial labor, especially after the Peace of Utrecht in 1713. In the Elizabethan age the British had begun to concentrate their efforts upon the production at lower costs of comforts and conveniences, with the help of water- or horse-driven machinery and more powerful furnaces. The French had concentrated upon objects of artistic craftsmanship, whose use and contemplation added to the splendor and style of living. While the British had emphasized economic quantity and efficiency, the French had emphasized aesthetic quality and form. In Great Britain the heavy industries had progressed most rapidly, in France, the artistic.

Early in the eighteenth century, if not before, the more homely but robust commodities of British workmanship began to attract steadily increasing attention in France and other continental countries. In agriculture the French introduced ways of fertilizing and plowing, "in imitation of England." A remarkable Scottish financier and adventurer, John Law, famous for his economic knowledge, had much success in interesting the Duke of Orleans (the regent after Louis XIV's death) in his expert advice, derived from Scottish experience. Law reformed the French national finances and introduced northern methods of banking and economic enterprise. Frenchmen began to be impressed by the firmness of the paper produced by English mills. They tried to imitate it in making playing cards and other commodities. In a few French provinces, especially in the north from Franche-Comté to Flanders, the inhabitants, under pressure from the shortage of wood, began to adopt the British practice of burning coal in place of charcoal and firewood for heating their houses, cooking their food, and brewing their beer. French travelers sought eagerly a knowledge of the methods of mining and of making metal commodities practiced in England and Sweden.

As the French, with the help of the British, were learning to produce practical, substantial commodities, the British were learning from the French how to fashion objects of beauty. The development of baroque architecture in Great Britain owed much to the instruction which English architects had derived from their travels on the Continent. Painting and the visual arts flourished in eighteenth-century England as they had never flourished in the age of Elizabeth. Even the Irish were producing silver and lace wares of remarkable beauty at the very time when some Irishmen, as well as some Scots and more numerous Englishmen, were going to France to help the French to exploit mines and to develop heavy industries. The upper classes in the British Isles were coming to insist upon charm even in the art of cookery, in which France now excelled Italy. While France and Great Britain had grown more apart in their economic ways during the hundred years following the Reformation, with the diminishing violence of religious hatred after 1648, they tended to draw together. A reconciliation took place between the requirements of comfort and efficiency and those of quality and style.

This new approach to a harmonious European economic civilization was based partly on discoveries and technical inventions which, when they had first spread during the sixteenth and early seventeenth centuries, had helped to undermine the earlier harmony of the Middle Ages and the Renaissance. After the mid-seventeenth century most of the other countries of Europe were progressing industrially and commercially to much the same degree and in much the same directions as France and England.

In the 1640's Germany and the rest of central Europe were in the last stages of the Thirty Years' War. After the war ended in 1648 with the Peace of Westphalia, economic conditions began slowly to mend. Before the seventeenth century was over recovery was well under way. By the 1720's and 1730's industrial enterprise in many parts of Germany was beginning to thrive. In the region of the Ruhr, the output of coal, hitherto of slight importance compared with that of England, Scotland, or the prince-bishopric of Liége, doubled between 1700 and 1737.[6] In Prussia the clothmaking industry was encouraged by the crown in order to supply uniforms for the rapidly expanding Prussian army. The so-called "blue cloths" of Berlin acquired some celebrity in Europe; the population of the capital increased from 137,945 in 1723 to 206,520 in 1739. By that time Berlin had taken its place as one of the great cities of Europe.

In the economic development of Prussia, and especially of the Prussian textile manufactures, French bureaucratic methods were followed, regulating the weight and quality of cloth.[7] The encouragement of domestic industry by the king of Prussia and other German princes owed at least as much to French example as to the past experience of the German rulers during the economic expansion which had characterized the late fifteenth and early sixteenth centuries in central Europe.

While the Germans were learning their administrative methods from the French, they were learning new technical processes from the English, whom they had taught during the sixteenth century. At the time of the Reformation central Europe had been the first home of a literature of mechanics. In his work, *De re metallica*, published in 1556, Georgius Agricola (1494-1555), the leading early authority on mining and metallurgy, a physician who had spent some three years of his life taking care of the miners and smelters of Joachimstal, had provided a kind of summa of early mechanical knowledge.

Later German writers leaned upon this and other books of Agricola's. But in the eighteenth century German heavy industry, like French, began to be modeled upon English experience. Although the Germans had had a primitive form of hand-drawn railway carriage in the early sixteenth century, horse-drawn railway wagons were introduced into Germany from England in the eighteenth century. At this time the Germans called the railway an *englischer Kohlenweg*, because of the prevalence of this means of haulage in the English coal-mining districts.[8] Like all knowledge, technical knowledge in the eighteenth century was becoming pan-European.

Extensive borrowing in work of the mind is frequently a sign of intellectual vitality. It is not to be confused with mere copying. If the German countries remained backward economically about 1740 as compared with France and England, their backwardness was less conspicuous than it had been a hundred years before. English travelers making the grand tour were not told, as John Evelyn had been in 1645, that the German part of Europe was barbarous. In the early eighteenth century Germany was being willingly drawn more strongly into the orbit of general European civilization than at any time since the twelfth and thirteenth centuries.

Spain and the Low Countries, the southern part of which were under Spanish control until the Peace of Utrecht in 1713, present something of an exception in the history of substantial progress in industrial output, characteristic of Europe during the century preceding 1740. The collapse of Spanish prosperity during the early seventeenth century had left Spain, like Germany, in an economic backwater compared with most of Europe. Recovery in Spain was delayed even longer than in Germany. It began only after 1700.[9]

Relatively speaking, Holland was perhaps somewhat less important as a European economic power in the 1730's than in the 1630's. It is probable, nevertheless, that the Dutch national output had increased almost as much as the French. The United Provinces had fared much better in a material way than the rest of the Low Countries. They had fared much better than Spain during the second half of the seventeenth century, for the long wars between France and Spain played into the hands of the Dutch, who wrested from the Spaniards a large part of their foreign commerce. The Dutch retained their control of it until the War of the Spanish Succession, which ended in 1713.[10] For John Law and those of his contemporaries who regarded economic progress as the chief goal of life, the Dutch still shared with the English at the beginning of the eighteenth century the economic leadership of Europe.[11]

It was in Holland that the objective of making beautiful commodities was most effectively reconciled and combined with more efficient production. During the lives of Hals (1580–1666) and Rembrandt (1606–1669) the United Provinces became not only the financial and commercial but also the intellectual, artistic, and industrial brokers for all Europe. These two great artists, along with their younger contemporary, Vermeer (1632–1675), and two supreme landscape painters, Ruysdale (1625–1682) and Hobbema (1638–1709), not only equaled but excelled in their exquisite, copious, and profound artistic genius the painters who were their contemporaries in Spain, Belgium, France, and Italy. As for the English, they had no painting of much distinction in the great age of Dutch art. This was partly because of the nature of their early "industrial revolution," which put comfort and security before beauty in the products of workshops and small factories.

Dutch art extended to the making of almost all industrial products, to cloth and to the lovely faïence pottery which took its name from the town of Delft, Vermeer's birthplace. At the very time when the Dutch were conceiving and executing many of the most beautiful objects made in Europe, they were building ships with an economy in labor and an efficient use of machinery that more than matched the economy of their only rivals, the English, and made the Dutch shipyards a marvel to the foreign shipbuilders of the age. It was to the Dutch shipyards especially, with their cranes, their machines and engines for raising weights, and their novel models of vessels, that Colbert directed the attention of French experts in shipbuilding, when he set out in the 1660's to make France strong at sea.[12] Seeking instruction, Peter the Great came from Russia in 1697 and worked as a laborer under an assumed name in the shipyards at Saardam. Using timber, metal, and other materials imported especially from Sweden, Holland launched at lower costs than any nation busses and other fishing boats and freighters of every kind, with what then seemed remarkably ample holdspace. Into this were dumped ever larger quantities of fish, salt, coal, and metal. The number of seamen required to operate a vessel of a given tonnage was nearly halved.

More than any other country, Holland set the example for a reconciliation between the objectives of giving delight and commodity by the products of industry. Such a reconciliation was fundamental in creating the relatively homogenous European civilization of the eighteenth century. More than any other people, the Dutch built the bridge between the economic civilization of the Continent, with its classical and its medieval roots, and the budding industrialism of northern Europe.

Each of the major European countries was learning from the economic experiences of others and was assimilating the experiences into its own ways of farming, mining, manufacturing, and trading. When we compare the industrial histories of the European states from 1540 to 1640, what stand out are the growing contrasts. What stand out from 1640 to 1740 are the growing resemblances. The economic objectives and the economic fortunes of the European countries became more alike in each succeeding decade.

This movement towards economic homogeneity had a close relation to the history of war. When civilized nations are drawing together in their ways of living, in their ways of producing, exchanging, and consuming; when these ways provide men and women with opportunities to employ all their faculties and to taste the joys of life completely lived, they are moving towards a community of outlook which diminishes suspicion, hatred, and fear.

CHAPTER NINE

Less Blood and More Money

· AS THE ECONOMIC EXPERIENCE OF THE VARIOUS EUROPEAN COUN-
tries grew more alike, their military experience grew more alike too.
There was less war in the heart of Western Europe, where war had
been most devastating, and more war on the periphery, especially
upon the seas.

While the continental people were more peaceful from 1640 to
1740 than they had been from 1540 to 1640, the British were less so.
In Great Britain, 1642 marked the outbreak of the most serious fighting
that has ever taken place within the island, in terms of numbers
engaged and of destruction. For the first time the English fought out
their differences with guns and explosives. Their pistols were no longer
mere bottles of sack; they brought a quicker death. This civil war was
short compared with the long and terrible struggles that were ending
in central Europe. But England engaged in wars of one kind and
another more frequently from 1640 to 1740 than during the previous
century. Several years of civil war were followed by three successive
naval wars with the Dutch in the course of the twenty-two years 1652–
1673, and then by two long wars in which England, allied with Holland, joined a European coalition against France — the War of the
Dutch Alliance from 1689 to 1697 and the War of the Spanish Succession from 1702 to 1713. Warfare was still a less important factor in the
normal life of Great Britain from 1640 to 1740 than in that of France
and most other European states, large and small. But the differences
were ceasing to be conspicuous.

For Western Europe as a whole, years of war were still the rule,
years of peace the exception. Yet there was a more or less continuous
moderation in the fierceness of the fighting. Already in 1677 Robert

Boyle's brother, Roger, Earl of Orrery, an army officer who had seen
service under Cromwell against the Irish, observed that "we make
War more like Foxes, than Lyons, and you have twenty Sieges for one
Battel." [1] Two decades after that, when England was making a settled
policy of sending expeditionary forces to intervene in the major continental wars and maintain a balance of power abroad, defensive tactics
and strategy were still more firmly established. As the long War of the
Dutch Alliance came to an indecisive end, Daniel Defoe (1661–1731)
wrote: "Now it is frequent to have armies of fifty thousand men of a
side stand at bay within view of one another, and spend a whole campaign in dodging, or, as it is genteelly called, observing one another,
and then march off into winter quarters." [2] By the time a dynastic quarrel over the succession to the Spanish throne assumed the dimensions
of a general European war, in 1702, commanders of victorious armies
had ceased to aim at the annihilation of a defeated army. They expected the enemy's troops to get away. [3]

It was only in the east of Europe that older conceptions of military
campaigning persisted. Austria waged offensive wars against the Turks.
Charles XII, the remarkable warrior king of Sweden, invaded Saxony
and then embarked upon the first of three modern attempts to conquer
Russia. His exploits ended in disaster before Peter the Great. They
took place when Western Europe was engaged in a separate war, the
War of the Spanish Succession, with France arrayed against a European coalition in which England took a leading part. The treaties of
Utrecht closed that war in 1713. It was followed by three decades more
peaceful for Western Europe as a whole than any since the French
king, Charles VIII, had marched his army into Italy in 1494. For the
great historian, Jules Michelet, the War of the Spanish Succession
brought to an end two centuries of warfare.

In the midst of that long war, with France everywhere on the defensive, Louis XIV issued on April 16, 1705, instructions concerning the
holding of forts. Henceforth the military governor of a fortress was
authorized to surrender, with honor, after a small breach had been
made in the stronghold and a single assault had been repulsed. These
directions replaced others issued three generations before under Louis
XIII, forbidding a commander to surrender until a *wide* breach had
been made in the *main* wall of the fort and *several* assaults had been
repulsed. Louis XIV's instructions remained in force for three generations until 1792, [4] when the citizen armies of the French Revolution
were formed to stop the Prussian invaders as they moved toward Paris.
Then new instructions were issued; the commander of the fortress of
Longwy, in Lorraine, was guillotined, together with his wife, for sur-

rendering to the Prussians after a defense which, though perfunctory, would have satisfied the honor of the nation under Louis XIV.[5]

The long interval of a century and a half between Louis XIII's instructions and those of the revolutionary government was an age of limited warfare. One of the most famous generals of the Revolution, Lazare Carnot, wrote in all seriousness that "what was taught in the military schools was no longer the art of defending strong places, but that of surrendering them honorably, after certain conventional formalities." Moderation in war seems to have gone farthest at about the time *Robinson Crusoe* (1719) appeared containing a panegyric of sober, thrifty, economic life, with the gun an instrument of humane defense used to advance civilization against savages and wolves. A little earlier the author of this wonderful story had summed up the military history of his age by remarking that wars now spent "less blood" and "more money." [6]

For the intellectual community of the early eighteenth century, in which leading minds took increasing pride, war had become litttle more than an accepted hazard that engaged the passions of writers, artists, and natural philosophers hardly more than an earthquake or a spring flood. Battles were fought; on occasions there was even terrible carnage. It would be a mistake to assume that sin greatly diminished as religious toleration grew! Human nature was by no means purged of cruelty and lust. But there were fewer opportunities for venting cruelty and lust, and fewer causes for the fears which goad even peacefully disposed men into battle.

Except among the nobility — who furnished most of the officers and whose code made military service an obligation like the fighting of duels [7] — the task of soldiering, especially among the English, carried with it no special honor like that attached in more recent times to dying for one's country. The only special loyalty felt by the private soldier, even on the Continent, was a personal one to the prince for whom he fought.[8] In the period from the treaties of Utrecht (1713–14) to the French Revolution, battles were localized episodes — usually attempts of a ruling prince to gain some small territorial advantage at the expense of his rivals — without any pan-European plot involving the people generally, as the earlier struggles between Protestants and Catholics had involved them, even those who tried to remain neutral.

By comparison with the century 1540 to 1640, the destruction of life and property was light in proportion to the greatly increased number of soldiers under arms. In 1704, a decisive year for England in the War of the Spanish Succession, the year of three battles famous in

English history — Schellenberg, Blenheim, and Málaga — not more than two thousand British soldiers and sailors fell in action; not more than three thousand others died of wounds, of disease, or of any causes traceable to the war.[9]

The moderate, regulated nature of the new species of warfare is revealed again and again in the practices and the writings of the eighteenth century.[10] Let us take, for example, the memoirs of a cultivated man of the world and a great man of letters, the Italian-born Carlo Goldoni (1707–1793). Like most of the important minds of the early eighteenth century Goldoni was European in his outlook. He wrote plays in Italian and his memoirs in French. In 1733 he was engaged as secretary to the minister of the Venetian Republic in Milan, at the time of the so-called War of Don Carlos, in which the king of Sardinia, on behalf of that Spanish prince, combined his forces with those of France and Spain against the house of Austria. In Vienna the Emperor Charles VI was disposed to resist Don Carlos' claims to the throne of Spain. In spite of his name, there was nothing about this Don Carlos, as there was about Philip II's deranged son who died mysteriously in the midst of the dramatic age of religious wars, to arouse the poetical genius of Schiller or the musical genius of Verdi. The eighteenth-century Don Carlos and his war have almost dropped out of history. But the campaigns, now forgotten, made some stir in their time.

Goldoni was present at the siege of Milan by the allies and several weeks later at Parma, where the rival armies met in a fierce battle outside the town. In neither place were the sympathies of the inhabitants seriously moved by one side or the other. Their only fear was that the troops of either army should get within the gates and pillage. The fear proved groundless. At Parma the citizens ran to the town walls to watch the battle in the open country beyond, much as a modern city crowd would congregate to watch a conflagration which the fire department manages somehow to keep under control.

The relations between the officers of the fighting armies were of a kind that would astonish the participants in modern warfare. Goldoni gives an account of these relations before the armies had reached Parma. He visited the camp of the allies near Crema during a three-day armistice which they had readily granted the Germans who were defending the fortress of Pizzighetone.

A bridge thrown over the breach afforded a communication between the besiegers and the besieged: tables were spread in every quarter, and the officers entertained one another by turns: within and without, under tents and arbours, there was nothing but balls, entertainments and concerts. All the people of the environs flocked there on foot, on horseback, and in carriages: provisions arrived from every quarter; abundance was seen in a moment, and there was no want of stage doctors and tumblers. It was a charming fair, a delightful rendezvous. [11]

After the armistice, the allied army obligingly moved toward Parma, nearer to Venice. Goldoni's diplomatic duties were lightened. He applied himself successfully to what he called the "more agreeable" occupation of completing one of the delightful plays with which he charmed the audiences of his own age and of the nineteenth century.[12]

There was no such reduction in the extent of naval warfare as in land warfare. Peaceful relations between the northern sea powers — Great Britain, Sweden, and the United Provinces — had provided one condition for the economic expansion of northern Europe during the late sixteenth and early seventeenth centuries. These peaceful relations came to an end. Freed from the common danger of invasion by Roman Catholic powers, which had helped to hold England and Holland at peace with each other, the two nations took to fighting over commerce. They had become the leading European countries in the carrying trade by sea. Each nation was concerned to increase its share in this trade. The expanding navy of each power seemed to the other a menace to its commercial interests, because the warships could harass, capture, and even sink merchant vessels, and so increase for their rivals the cost of doing business.

By the time of the first Anglo-Dutch war of 1652–53, the large ships of the line, the mainstay of the new fleets, were launched in a form and size which was still characteristic two centuries later in the early Victorian era. The type was established in 1637, with the building of Phineas Pett's "Sovereign of the Seas," a vessel of 1,200 tons or more, larger than the average country house of the day. In length, breadth, and the number of decks with long rows of muzzle-loading guns, there was no great change in the ships of the line until the advent, about 1840, of screw propulsion and larger guns,[13] and the superseding during the American Civil War of the wooden by the metal battleship. The hull of the old wooden ship of the line "ranged some two hundred feet from the figurehead under the great bowsprit to the ornate windows of the cabin at the [lofty, ornamented] stern." [14] Partly to meet the need in battle for quick turns, vessels of this kind were made to bulge at the sides. They measured at the waterline some fifty feet across, half the breadth of the "Queen Elizabeth," the most stupendous ocean liner launched in the early twentieth century, a vessel made of steel and weighing some 80,000 tons.

For two hundred years, the strategy and tactics of war at sea were determined largely by the number of the ships of the line. With the multiplication of warships during the late seventeenth century, when France, Portugal, and Sweden all developed naval forces rivaling those of Holland and England, engagements at sea became more frequent, at any rate in the northern and western waters about Europe.

The harm caused by the new and increased sea warfare to the economic life of the chief European powers, was not comparable to that caused by the terrible land warfare of the late sixteenth and early seventeenth centuries. After the mid-seventeenth century the lack of enthusiasm among the Europeans for carrying through campaigns relentlessly on land was conspicuous at sea too. As cannon balls became effective in striking enemy vessels at a distance, hand-to-hand fighting became very rare. As early as 1618 an English Commission of Reform for the navy had reported on the changes which had taken place during the previous hundred years, since shooting at sea had first become important. The report contains these words: "Experience teacheth how sea-fights in these days come seldom to boarding, or to great execution of bows, arrows, small shot and the sword, but are chiefly performed by the great artillery breaking down masts, yards, tearing, raking, and bilging the ships." [15] Battles at sea were perhaps more frequent from 1640 to 1740 than they had been from 1540 to 1640, but like the new battles on land, they were less decisive.

In the struggles between Holland and England efforts were made by the Dutch naval commanders to spoil the fishing and other trades in the North Sea,[16] and to block or at least to disrupt the passage from the Tyne and Wear to London. The object was to deprive hundreds of thousands of people in the London area of coal, for the capital had become dependent for adequate supplies of fuel upon the regular movements south of large fleets of colliers.[17] In the spring of 1653, for example, John DeWitt, a famous Dutch admiral, appeared off Flamborough Head, on the coast of the North Riding of Yorkshire, with nineteen or twenty Dutch men-of-war, some having three tiers of guns. He surprised a fleet of three hundred coal hoys on their course from Newcastle to the Thames. The English convoy of nine warships appeared to be no match for the enemy. Its commander, Captain Motham, put in at Scarborough, unloaded the bulk of his powder and mounted cannon on the pier. Had it not been for a sudden offshore wind, DeWitt's squadron might have sent some English hoys to the bottom, or it might have captured part of the fleet of colliers, laden with heaps of coal to relieve the freezing Londoners.[18]

As has almost always been the fate of attempts to win a conclusive victory by blows at the economic life of the enemy, such efforts fell short of their objective. After the second Anglo-Dutch war of 1665–1667 the harm done by hostile craft to the coasting trade of Great Britain diminished.[19] In the long wars which followed from 1689 to 1713, when Holland and England were allies against France, the chief threats were no longer to English coastwise commerce, but to international trade. Much mischief was accomplished by both sides. French privateers, principally the notorious Dunkirk pirates, who had harried shipping for at least a century, captured or sank multitudes of British merchant vessels. In the War of the Spanish Succession the number of prizes taken by the Dunkirkers alone has been estimated at 1,614 vessels.[20] This type of trade war had been carried to its highest pitch under the leadership of Jean Bart, who was born at Dunkirk in 1651. As part of the price of peace in 1713, England insisted that the town's fortifications be demolished and the harbor filled up.

English and Dutch captains, in their turn, warred on French trade. But they encountered many traditional and practical obstacles to thoroughgoing destruction. One important obstacle was the natural reluctance of the Hollanders to give up any part of their own trade. Their commerce had usually thriven in time of war.[21] Interference with normal trading relations by land had played into their hands. It increased the need for sea-borne traffic in food and other necessities. The Dutch regained a measure of their earlier prosperity mainly when wars hindered other countries from trading directly with one another.[22]

It was a part of the new strategy to fight in so far as possible in the interest of industry and commerce.[23] Holland depended more for its economic welfare on foreign trade than any other country, and so it was natural for the Dutch to trade with their enemies through neutral states. Such transactions became a well-recognized and not altogether disreputable form of early eighteenth-century traffic, to which the French gave a special name — "commerce précaire." All belligerents engaged in this kind of trade.[24] The dependence of the Dutch upon their shipping, their role as carriers for other states, had made "business as usual" in wartime their settled policy. For them war had become inseparable from business.[25]

For these reasons, when England and Holland became allies, the English were never able effectively to bind the Dutch to renounce commerce with France. The English themselves were only halfhearted in the effort. They looked back to an age when they had waxed rich in peace. As they were not aiming to conquer and hold large tracts of territory on the continent of Europe, they were committed to only limited victory.

Even postal communications were not successfully restricted for long in wartime. Letters circulated without censorship, with a freedom that astonishes the twentieth-century mind. We are led to wonder whether all the technical improvements in the speed of transportation and in the transmission of sounds have actually increased intimacy and confidence among the Western peoples. The subjects of two warring nations talked to each other if they met, and when they could not meet corresponded, not as enemies but as friends. The modern notion hardly existed that learned subjects of an enemy country are partly accountable for the belligerent acts of their rulers.

Nor had the warring rulers any firm disposition to stop communications with subjects of the enemy. The old inquisitorial practices of espionage in connection with religious worship and belief were disappearing, and no comparable inquisition in connection with political or economic convictions was even contemplated. Passports were originally created to provide safe-conduct in time of war. During most of the eighteenth century it seldom occurred to Europeans to abandon their travels in a foreign country which their own was fighting. In a famous passage, Laurence Sterne (1713–1768) tells how, when he embarked on his *Sentimental Journey*, he "left London with so much precipitation, that it never entered my mind that we were at war with France; and had reached Dover . . . before the idea presented itself; and with this in its train, that there was no getting there without a passport." He got there without one, nevertheless. Instead of being consigned to a bastille, he was actually handed a passport at Versailles by a French count, who remarked that he had obtained it from his master, a duke, apparently the duc de Choiseul himself, the foreign minister who was actively prosecuting the Seven Years' War against England. The count had explained to the duke that he was intervening on behalf of the English king's jester. "Un homme qui rit," said the duke, "ne sera jamais dangereux." [26]

Today travelers no longer visit the country of the enemy in time of war. Passports are insisted on at frontiers in time of what is called peace, with an inexorable seriousness that even Sterne, if he lived, would find hard to circumvent. Peace and war, alike, have ceased to be laughing matters. International relations are based on assumptions of vital hostility which would profoundly shock those Europeans whose ideas of cultured life were in the ascendancy during the eighteenth century.

The curiously ambiguous, almost halfhearted, nature of their wars

— especially as conducted by the Dutch — helped to make the transitions from peace to war scarcely perceptible for traders, as well as for lighthearted travelers. Such conditions and such an outlook fostered a conception of international relations which persisted at the outset of the world struggles of our time: that war and normal business relations were compatible. In August 1914 "business as usual" was proclaimed as British policy when the battalions of the small British expeditionary force landed at Le Havre and marched to be slaughtered beside the more numerous French soldiers. Some of the French were bedecked in gay, brightly colored uniforms, another remnant of the earlier age of limited warfare when organized fighting had been for the officers something like a sport of gentlemen.

At the beginning of the eighteenth century the idea persisted among many writers on economic matters that the economic interests of nations were necessarily in opposition.[27] Political officials generally were still of the opinion that the most effective means of enriching a state were to take some of the territory held by neighboring countries or to damage their trade. As the commercial relations of the Europeans with America and the Far East grew in importance, the object of attacking the overseas trade of rival nations played a leading role in the calculations of statesmen.[28] During the late seventeenth and early eighteenth centuries, fighting with the new weapons was not leading to very satisfactory results either in territory or trade gained. So statesmen turned increasingly to another kind of weapon, to duties and prohibitions upon imports, and to the preferential treatment of colonial traders who dealt with the mother country. It was supposed that by imposing burdens on the goods exported by neighboring nations, manufactured goods in particular, a nation stood to gain. It would be unnecessary to pay the foreigner for his goods; instead they would be made at home by native craftsmen; treasure in the form of bullion and specie would accumulate.

The late seventeenth century was a period when tariffs and other restrictions upon international commerce were increasing. In October 1665 the Lord Mayor of London was told that the English king was so concerned over the sums laid out in purchasing products of foreign manufacture, that he had resolved, "after the mourning for the king of Spain [is] over, [to] wear nothing inside or out that is not of English manufacture, except linen and calicoes,"[29] brought largely from France, then at peace with the English, who were at war with the Dutch. By the 1670's and 1680's duties on the movement of most commodities across national frontiers were high in peacetime.

Such additional barriers to trade as were erected in wartime were seldom effectively enforced. There were several periods during both of the long wars with France, when the restrictions imposed by the normally high tariffs were the only limits set by the English upon the import of wines and other luxuries which the French excelled in preparing. So long as commercial advantage was an important motive for making war,[30] neither side was eager to give up, even in wartime, such trade as was considered advantageous.

At the beginning of the War of the Dutch Alliance, an effort was made by England to prevent neutral states from trading with France, by seizing all ships which sailed from French ports and by turning back all those bound for France.[31] But the convention which the English got Holland to enter on behalf of this effort was a dead letter almost from the start. By the Peace of Ryswick, in 1697, which ended the war, the Dutch reëstablished their old principle of "free ships, free goods." This meant that all neutral trade, except in a few articles declared contraband, was to be permitted in time of war. Of all wars the War of the Spanish Succession, which followed, was noted as the one during which "there was the least infraction of neutral rights." [32]

Wars for the sake of commerce became a contradiction unless they were restricted in scope and purpose.[33] Against what was gained, even the victors had to offset the terrific damage done to trade and to manufacturing. The Earl of Orrery, writing in 1677 on the art of war, praised the Roman military administration. "But then," he added, "I must say, their Trade was war, and I thank God ours is not." [34] On the contrary the commercial powers of northern Europe seem almost to have tried — not altogether successfully — to convert war itself into a form of trade, at a time when international trade, with the duties and prohibitions upon the movement of goods, was made almost a form of war.

Fighting by means of tariffs was certainly not in itself favorable to economic progress. Yet duties and prohibitions were less harmful during the late seventeenth and early eighteenth centuries than they have become during the past hundred and fifty years, because the nations are now far more dependent upon international exchanges for food and other necessities and for many of the raw materials indispensable in manufacturing. Duties and prohibitions moreover are almost always less harmful than heavy war. While they have been a cause for war in recent times, in the late seventeenth and early eighteenth centuries they also provided something of an alternative to war, a sort of supplement to it, which gave the rivals the satisfaction of attacking each other without bloodshed. Duties and prohibitions seem to have played a part in the change from blood to money.

The shift in emphasis from war on land to war at sea worked in the same direction, toward greater moderation in martial affairs. Under the conditions of international politics which prevailed, the influence of naval warfare, with its commercial objectives, was to limit the scope of war. In 1745 an English pamphleteer actually claimed that it was more in the interest of the English merchants to have England at war with France and Spain, "so that war is carried on only by sea, than in a state of peace." [35] As the three great powers of the age — France, Great Britain, and Holland — had no common frontiers, the sea provided a partial alternative to land warfare. By its nature, naval warfare is indecisive and — under the conditions which prevailed in the early eighteenth century — moderate.

The decline in the seriousness of war was reflected in the opinions of Europeans. It seemed hardly more sensible to Voltaire that persons persisted in organized shooting, in this blowing of each other to pieces, than that they engaged in private duels. The use of cannon and muskets to settle scores between nations could not be justified on rational grounds. Unlike Grotius, Voltaire had no conception of a just war. For him there were never conditions under which good could come of war. In this he and Boyle seem to have agreed. Grotius as well as Boyle would have also agreed with Voltaire that, in spite of the horrors of war, there was no hope of establishing perpetual peace among the states of Europe. But Voltaire differed from Boyle and the Christian writers generally about the source of men's belligerency. He denied that the fundamental cause of war was human nature. "Men must have corrupted nature a little," he wrote, "for they were not born wolves, and they have become wolves." [36] The same conception of man is to be found in Rousseau, who assumed that men and women in a state of nature were full of sweetness and light and that civilization had corrupted them. The writers whose influence predominated in the eighteenth century were putting a trust in man's original nature which the Bible does not justify. They refused to believe that man himself was the cause of his own corruption. If man himself was not the cause of war, it was up to him to put an end to war or to run the peril of blaming war on groups of his fellow men, of claiming for his group or nation a monopoly of virtue, and of losing through a return to more ferocious war the happiness that was within his grasp.

To intelligent Europeans of the mid-eighteenth century, such a danger seemed remote. No one went farther in his hopes for the future felicity of the Europeans than Edward Gibbon (1737–1794). His ideas about war, like those of so many of his contemporaries, were formed from the circumstances of the limited warfare which prevailed when he was born. He was convinced that resort to fighting by civilized peoples as an instrument to destroy the independence of other civilized peoples was at an end. He took it for granted that European society had a secure future, under the prevailing political and intellectual conditions. The conquest of the various powerful independent states by anyone among their number did not occur to him as even a distant possibility. The aim of total victory by one civilized country over another was, he thought, alien to civilization itself. The armed forces of Europe were exercised in war "by temperate and undecisive contests," which kept large bodies of armed men in trim, ready to consolidate as a single great army to meet barbarian hordes if any should ever appear. The new weapons which had been invented since the discovery of gunpowder were at the disposal of the civilized; the barbarians could acquire a knowledge of them only at the price of ceasing to be barbarous, and hence at the price of ceasing to want to conquer! [37] "A philosopher," Gibbon wrote, "may be permitted to enlarge his views, and to consider Europe as one great Republic whose various inhabitants have attained almost the same level of politeness and cultivation. The balance of power will continue to fluctuate . . . but . . . partial events cannot essentially injure our general state of happiness, the system of arts and laws and manners, which so advantageously distinguish, above the rest of mankind, the Europeans and their colonies." [38]

What lay behind the extraordinary confidence which eighteenth-century Europeans had come to feel in their civilization and in themselves? Nothing in the life of the mind was so potent a cause for their hopes as the new knowledge expounded by the natural scientists. What were the relations between the history of warfare from 1640 to 1740 and the progress of scientific and mechanical knowledge?

CHAPTER TEN

War and Scientific Progress

· IN 1943, TWO YEARS BEFORE THE FIRST EXPLOSION OF AN ATOMIC bomb, the economist Lionel Edie prepared a paper for the Hercules Powder Company in which he spoke with enthusiasm of "the scientific developments growing out of the war." "In the space of two or three years," he wrote, "you are getting as much scientific progress in this country as you ordinarily get in 40 or 50 years." Dr. Edie made no effort to prove this, nor to explain that the words "scientific progress," as he used them, had a limited meaning, which might be misunderstood.

Even students of history frequently fail to distinguish between fairly obvious divisions of the general subject of science and technology. They speak of "scientific progress" as covering anything from the most general theories to the most narrow and practical aspects of mechanics. Actually the subject is divided into a number of parts, and we cannot take it for granted that progress in one is inevitably accompanied by progress in all.

The matter is complicated further by the fact that technical improvement has various objectives, of which some of the principal ones are the service of beauty, the service of commodity, and the service of abundance. These objectives are by no means identical. They may conflict, because the fashioning of an object designed primarily for contemplation requires different methods and a different spirit from the production of objects intended primarily to accomplish practical tasks, such as shaving with a razor or shooting with a gun.

In Western European history there have been great changes in the emphasis laid by societies upon these different objectives. In early modern times, especially on the Continent, technical invention in the arts was often so closely related to technical invention in the sciences, that technique had a different meaning from the one which now prevails. An artist uses sense impressions derived from the same physical universe which confronts the natural scientist. But the invention of the artist has not necessarily a precise relation to the facts of matter, space, and time; he may ignore the rules of formal logic. Invention of this kind has not been absent from the speculations of the greatest modern scientists. Most of the revolutionary theories concerning nature and the physical world have come from flights of intuition.[1] But all modern scientists have had to justify their visions by positive demonstration. Experiment as a necessary procedure in all scientific work is an innovation of the past four centuries. During that time experiment has become the decisive test of truth in natural science.

Art commands enthusiasm by the delight which it gives, a delight which emerges from truths that transcend positive demonstration. Unlike modern scientists, artists are not concerned with adding to knowledge of the nature and properties of matter and space as such; unlike most modern technicians, artists are not concerned with making commodities merely more convenient to use or with the multiplication of output; they are concerned with using such knowledge as they gain in the service of art. The insistence upon positive demonstration in connection with science has separated science from art. This growing separation, together with the increasing disposition of artists and scientists to specialize, make it necessary, in considering modern "scientific progress," to put art aside, and not to make the increasingly common mistake of treating it as a branch of science or of speaking of science as art raised to a higher stage.

Among the many possible divisions of "scientific progress," three seem especially relevant to an inquiry into the reciprocal relations between modern wars and economic history. First, there are speculations which are primarily of a theoretical and general kind. They depend for verification, as all investigations of matter, space, or time must, upon the direct observation of the biological world, of the physical world as it exists in nature and also as it is modified by farmers, craftsmen, miners, manufacturers, and transport workers. Speculative scientists have sometimes learned from methods of actual work and from mechanical contrivances used in practical life. But the purpose of their speculations has been knowledge — the nature of particular classes of things, how they become what they are, and the relations of some to others. While the knowledge acquired has often tremendous practical consequences, the observations and experiments, like the thought behind them, do not have as a direct objective an increase in the volume of material output, a reduction in human toil, or an improvement in health.

For example, Harvey's discovery, with experimental demonstrations, of the true manner in which the blood circulates in animals was destined to revolutionize the practice of medicine and surgery. Its practical implications struck an adventurous mind almost at once. Descartes discussed it at length in his short *Discourse on Method*, first published at Leiden in 1637. In the same book, Descartes went on to suggest that his own physics might have immense practical consequences. It might help men to understand and then to employ the force and the action of fire, water, air, the stars, and the heavens, and thus render human beings "the masters and possessors of nature." [2] Although Descartes' physics was soon superseded by Newton's, he was clairvoyant in his recognition of the new possibilities for material progress opened to man by science.

Harvey's immediate aim had not been to cure illnesses, to improve health. Still less was Descartes' object in his physics to reduce the manual labor of human beings. Both simply sought for truth — in the case of Harvey, truth about a particular physiological process, the circulation of the blood, central to the maintenance of all life.

As used popularly today the phrase "scientific progress" covers, secondly, investigations helping to solve material problems which are of significance for scientific theory, and which contribute directly or indirectly to general and theoretical knowledge, as well as to practical technological skill: to reductions through invention in the costs of production. In the third place, the phrase covers investigations which have almost no consequence beyond the practical result of providing a new, more efficient technical instrument or process.

It is difficult to draw lines between these kinds of work, especially between the last two, for it is impossible to know what consequences for scientific theory particular technical improvements may have. Yet the mind which seeks practical results for their own sake differs in its attitude toward learning and in its procedures from one which regards these results as properly subordinate in the hierarchy of knowledge to general scientific laws. Technological improvement as such — the invention of new machines and new explosives — generally involves a different kind of thought and different methods from those involved in the disinterested search for truth. It is possible for one mind to combine the two kinds of inquiry. But there is also a conflict between them. In one case men are seeking general truth, which is the property of all the world. In the other they are serving the particular interest or good of a business, a group, a nation, or they are serving a particular side of man's varied nature. Purpose and means are always interrelated in work of the mind. Consequently the spirit behind and the methods employed in the practical application of general knowledge are almost invariably narrower than those at work in the attainment of knowledge itself.

Dr. Edie seems to have had in mind only investigations of the second and third kinds, and almost exclusively investigations of the third kind, devoted to limited, specific results for their own sake. He was thinking mainly of machinery and other devices capable of raising the material standard of living.[3]

We cannot take it for granted, as people commonly do now, that the successful application of scientific knowledge is of service to science in all times and places. Information obtained from the experiences of practical life provide valuable material for the speculative mind. One thing that held back the progress of natural science in medieval Europe was the tradition which kept separate labor of the mind — called the liberal arts — and labor with matter — called the servile arts. The breakdown of the barrier which had separated intellectual from manual work, and therefore science from technology, was of great benefit to science. Scientists were encouraged to make the most of material experiences. But the view, widely held in our time, that there is never any danger to the enlightened pursuit of fundamental theoretical research from an emphasis on technical results, has not been satisfactorily established. There is little historical evidence to support it.

A century ago there was at least one distinguished scientist, Charles Babbage, famous for his precision as a mathematician, who argued that the growing emphasis which scientists were putting on practical improvement was harmful to the advance of scientific knowledge.[4] Babbage reached this conclusion not because of the danger, which is now obvious, that the application of science for destructive purposes might reduce the world in a matter of days from civilization to barbarism. He feared that the growing interest of scientific minds in practical results would lead men to desert those speculative pursuits which had given them insight denied to all earlier civilizations into the nature of the physical universe.

It has been suggested that there exists a symbiosis between speculative scientific inquiry and technological improvements of every kind, in the sense that the two are mutually dependent.[5] The nature of the interrelationship between science and technology remains to be explored. But from what is known already, it appears that symbiosis is not the best word to describe the association. It suggests a union in which modern science depends for its existence upon technological development, no less than technological development depends upon the progress of science. To use the word "symbiosis" in this context is to neglect most of history. Technical improvements of varied kinds have been made by all civilized peoples; the pursuit of experimental science awaited the Western peoples. It was mainly modern science that turned technology toward more practical objectives, and resulted in the unprecedented power which men have now attained to produce, to move, and to destroy. No serious student of the history of modern science will deny that inventions to reduce the labor costs of production have been dependent on the general and theoretical speculations of natural scientists, in the sense that, without a growing body of general scientific knowledge of a very high order, we should never have had technical improvements capable of raising the material standard of living to the levels reached in parts of Europe and America at the beginning of the twentieth century.[6]

In the hands of a completely distinterested genius such as Pasteur, practical inquiries into industries give the world fruitful generalizations of universal value to scientific knowledge. For example it was partly a study of the fermentation of wines and beers, and of diseases of silkworms, that led Pasteur to discover the germ theory of disease, a scientifically demonstrated proposition which proved to be of enormously extensive practical application.[7] But such an issue of practical inquiry is possible only when the inquirer is in no way limited in the scope of his creative work by a practical objective. In so far as the investigator is bound by the terms of his employment or even the terms of his special subject, he is almost certain to move in one channel rather than to explore the varied possibilities opened by a discovery that he makes. So he loses himself in the particular instead of using it, as Pasteur used it, to reveal the universal.

Another distinction between science and technology illustrates even more strikingly the danger in giving equal value to the two, and using the phrase "scientific progress" to cover both. In itself, scientific knowledge can never be destructive. Neither the Newtonian laws of motion nor the modern quantum theory are any use to an invading army or air force. But the technical results derived from scientific knowledge have been devastatingly destructive. They are capable of destroying scientific knowledge.

During the past four hundred years it has been the more philosophical scientific speculations which have provided the intellectual capital on which modern inventors and technicians have drawn, without giving back an equivalent. The more practical "science" becomes, the less new intellectual capital is likely to be provided. And the strength of the intellect depends upon continual exercise; the human mind cannot live on its past. If, then, our object is to examine the relations between wars and scientific progress, we should separate the influence of wars upon technological improvement from their influence upon speculative science. We should not take it for granted that advances in technology, aiming at greater economic efficiency or even better health, invariably advance scientific knowledge. We should not take it for granted that, by themselves, advances in technology are evidence of the vitality of the creative mind.

From a misinterpretation of the Bible, our seventeenth-century ancestors assumed that man's life span had been shortened with the march of history. Under the influence of the modern belief in the inevitability of progress, we are in some danger of assuming that longevity is a distinctive achievement of industrial civilization. The chances for reaching middle life *have* increased enormously with the improvements during the past two hundred years in medicine, sanitation, and surgery, and with the remarkable rise in the material standard of living. Infant mortality and the death rate among all persons up to fifty have been amazingly reduced in the more industrialized countries. But for those who last beyond the fifties, the promise of a long Indian summer is not much better now than it was in the England of Hobbes, who was born in 1588 and lived to be ninety-one, or the France of Fontenelle, Corneille's nephew and perpetual secretary of the French Academy of Science, who was born in 1657 and lived to be a hundred.

It was Fontenelle who pronounced in Paris the funeral oration for Isaac Newton. Among the long-lived men of distinction who appear prominently in seventeenth- and early eighteenth-century history, Newton is the most eminent. He lived from 1642, the year of Galileo's death, until 1727. His life spanned the period during which European warfare grew milder. It may be disputed whether Galileo or Kepler was the greatest scientist of the previous hundred years. But no one would dispute that Newton was the greatest scientist of the age of limited warfare.

During Newton's life, the leadership in natural science passed from Italy to England. In Italy cultivated opinion and public authority had looked with distaste, incredulity, and sometimes with downright distrust on the observations and experiments necessary for modern scientific advances, and on the advances actually achieved by Galileo and other Italians. In England cultivated opinion and public authority warmly welcomed such procedures and treated such results as contributions of the first rank to human happiness. Newton lived his last years venerated as few savants had ever been. As Voltaire wrote, he was buried like a king.

Natural science had gained a prestige in Great Britain among learned men, and also among the curious in all walks of life, such as the subject had never before possessed. The older view, which held the ascendancy in France at least through the late seventeenth century, was expressed by the most celebrated French philosopher of the age, Father Nicholas de Malebranche (1638–1715). "It is legitimate," he suggested, for us "to regard astronomy, chemistry and almost all the other sciences as suitable diversions for a decent man," but we "should not be dazzled by their brilliance or put them before the science of man himself." [8] Malebranche's view had prevailed among the learned prior to his time in Western Europe, in classical Rome, and in Greece. The view against which he protested — that the natural sciences should be given a priority over philosophy and theology as guides to learning and the speculative life — came to prevail in modern times. It was already gaining ground in seventeenth-century England, when scientists were more naturally philosophical in outlook than they have since become.

As England was more deeply engaged in wars during the hundred years which followed 1640 than during the preceding century, persons without sober training in historical sociology, who take the line that war is a great constructive force, might pounce on the growing importance of science in England to support the thesis that Newton, Boyle, Hooke, Halley, and other contemporary English scientists were products of wars. They might build up a case after the fashion of Elie Faure, who concluded from his study of the history of art that great artists and thinkers were in a large measure dependent on wars, because nearly all of them were born or died or lived at least a fraction of their lives when a war was going on. Newton is, in fact, one of a number of examples selected by Faure to support his thesis. *Paradise Lost* and the best works of Hobbes, he remarked, were published after "the last and perhaps the most terrible of English civil wars." [9] And then, as a finishing touch, Faure added, "Isaac Newton saw the light in the very year in which the civil war broke out"! As decades with wars have been much more common in Western European history than decades without them, Faure's thesis is not difficult to support. But is not his argument more of a commentary on the incorrigibly belligerent nature of men and nations than a piece of evidence to support the thesis that war has been responsible for the achievements of the human mind?

Before considering the influence of war on science in the age of Newton, we need to consider its influence on technological development. The late seventeenth and early eighteenth centuries were an age full of "projectors," who devoted their skill to mechanical and other utilitarian improvements.[10] Many technical advances were made. But the most successful involved the perfection and elaboration of methods and processes discovered earlier both on the Continent and in England. For example, boring rods to determine the whereabouts of ores and other minerals had been first introduced between 1600 and 1615 in the Midlands and Northumberland, while it was not until the end of the seventeenth century that the instruments were sufficiently improved to enable prospectors, without sinking shafts, to estimate even the approximate thickness of a seam or to determine its quality.[11]

The early "industrial revolution" of the age of Elizabeth, James I, and Charles I had been possible because of sweeping changes in fundamental industrial technique — of which boring rods were only one among a great number of examples. These changes were predominantly in the interest of commodity and abundance; their object was to reduce labor in mining, manufacturing, and transport. Ever since the eleventh century the Europeans had shown remarkable ingenuity in devising novel labor-saving machinery, furnaces, and other instruments. But never before had a people devoted their inventive skill as exclusively to practical utility, to reducing costs of production, and to ransacking the exhaustible riches of the subsoil, as the English after the 1570's.[12] That is one reason why the period of Elizabeth and the first two Stuarts was of greater significance than any earlier period in the genesis of the industrial civilization which now dominates much of the globe.

On the eve of the Civil War the British had already established an independent and novel technical tradition. They built upon this in the age which followed, when they were more frequently at war. The tradition had been created with the help of the new science and of technical knowledge borrowed from abroad — from the Low Countries, Italy, and above all from central Europe, where the Germans, the Hungarians, the Poles, and the Czechs had excelled during the early sixteenth century in the techniques of mining and metallurgy. During the age of Newton the English projectors were also influenced directly by foreign practice, but the influences were of a different kind. They came mainly from different sources. English technicians were now guided and stimulated more by France than by the states of the disintegrated Holy Roman Empire. As the French began to be impressed with the practical efficiency of the English, England became more concerned with beauty, which the French have always tried to renew in connection with the articles that they make. There was a kind of marriage between the English desire for comfort and material profusion and the French desire for order, proportion, harmony, and grace, combined with convenience, characteristic of the "classicism" which evolved during the long reigns of Louis XIII, Louis XIV, and Louis XV from 1610 to 1774. There was consequently what may almost be described as a return to an older technical tradition, or at least a reconciliation which had not been made during the early "industrial revolution" of the older technical tradition with the new. One explanation for the strong claims of art and taste in English industrial history from 1660 to 1750 or so is to be found in the relatively slow economic progress which followed the early industrial revolution and preceded the more famous one. One explanation for the slowing down of progress toward industrialism in England is to be found in the renewal of an older civilized emphasis on artistic workmanship.

In England the age of Newton was by no means devoid of technical inventions which were portentous of the triumph of industrialism. The two most important were the steam engine and the substitution of coke for charcoal in the blast furnace for producing pig iron. Both were made in the first decade of the eighteenth century.

Neither can be attributed primarily to the pressure of military demands. Early experiments with the force in a jet of steam seem to have had no military motive.[13] The search for a steam engine, together with its actual discovery, is explained first and foremost by the need for draining mines. What made this problem especially acute in Great Britain was the tremendous increase in the demand for coal during and after the Elizabethan age.[14]

A need for metal in the armament industries was not the chief drive behind the discovery, apparently in 1709, of a successful method of producing pig iron with mineral fuel. Serious attempts to solve that problem had begun early in the peaceful reign of James I,[15] before the outbreak of the Thirty Years' War had increased the demand for weapons. As in most cases where attempts were made to substitute coal for wood as fuel, the principal difficulty arose from the harm done the product by contact with fires of raw coal. Coke was the fuel which overcame this difficulty in the ironmaking industry. Coke was first made in connection with the drying of malt, in order to avoid the nasty taste which malt prepared with coal fires had transmitted to beer. It would be difficult to show that war did as much as peace for the extraordinarily rapid expansion of the English brewing industry during the late sixteenth and early seventeenth centuries!

There are several ways in which the performance of tasks set by warfare and the preparation for it contribute to peaceful technological progress. War needs may hasten the adoption of new kinds of furnaces and machines, useful for normal industry and trade as well as for war. Mechanical improvements designed for weapons may indicate methods of technical advance which prove fruitful in time of peace. Finally war may enlist in the service of technological advance minds which would not otherwise have turned to the subject, and so increase the attention paid after the war to improvements which reduce the costs of production.

The wars of the late seventeenth and early eighteenth centuries were accompanied by efforts on the part of technicians, amateur inventors, and even some scientists to improve the weapons of attack and defense. How far were these special inquiries into technological problems leading to mechanical improvements which have been of value to peaceful industrial progress?

Naval engineering, the construction of forts, the improvement of firearms, gunpowder, grenades, bombs, mines, and mortars, engaged much attention both in Great Britain and on the Continent.[16] Some of the knowledge acquired in making weapons contributed to the rise of industrial civilization. For example, boring machines were invented to produce smooth barrels in cannon and were later adapted to the production of parts of steam engines.[17] But military requirements raised fewer technical problems than the more continually insistent needs for powerful machinery, better furnaces, and artificially treated raw materials in connection with industries which flourished more in peace than in war. And while the demands of war raised many new questions for inventors and mechanics, they also diverted attention to some extent from the more numerous questions set by the need for peaceful economic progress.[18]

In Great Britain many men in all walks of life had become interested in these questions of peaceful improvement during the sixty or seventy years preceding the Civil War. The national habits acquired in those two generations account in large measure for the inventiveness of Englishmen during the hundred years that followed. It is hardly probable that if England had continued at peace after 1640, the progress of industrial technique would have suffered. The passion of such persons as John Evelyn to seek direct knowledge of the physical and biological world [19] was inherited from the era of the early "industrial revolution." A remarkable curiosity concerning all natural and mechanical phenomena had undoubtedly caught hold of Evelyn before the Civil War, which broke out when he was twenty-two. An able-bodied young man, he could hardly have escaped military service had he been living in the twentieth century. But in his time it was possible to make the "grand tour" of the Continent, even while the Great Rebellion was going on at home. The record that Evelyn kept of his travels shows that he was already full of the interests which led him to take part in the founding and the development of the Royal Society.

Given the momentum toward improvement gained before the Civil War, what calls for explanation perhaps is why there was not more technical progress between 1640 and 1740, rather than why there was so much. What is puzzling, particularly in connection with the use of coal in ironmaking, is why coke was not substituted for charcoal in the smelting furnace for more than half a century after it had been used for drying malt, and why the new process for smelting iron ores was little used for making pig iron until 1775, some sixty-five years after it had been discovered.[20] What is puzzling is why it was not until 1785, more than two generations after this invention and the invention of the steam engine, that these and other new devices began to revolutionize industrial organization and to bring about a phenomenal increase in industrial output.[21] If war had been the principal taskmaker for the British technician, would he not have accomplished more between about 1625 and 1775 to meet the most urgent need of the armed forces — a great addition to the supplies of metal?

Wars do not seem to have been of decisive importance in the technological progress for which the British were famous on the Continent early in the eighteenth century. Defoe's suggestion that the War of the Dutch Alliance was the chief cause for the "general projecting humour of the nation" during the 1690's is an example of his characteristic habit of overstatement in economic matters. He was far from attributing English economic leadership mainly to war, as is evident from his *Complete English Tradesman*. "War has not done it; no, nor so much as helped or assisted to it."[22]

Defoe's exuberance over "projects" and "projectors" should not obscure the fact that the age of Newton was less important for its technical advances and its inventors than for its fundamental theoretical discoveries and its eminent men of science.[23] To contemporaries no less than to modern historians, the achievements of Newton, Boyle, Hooke, and other leading scientists seemed on a much higher plane than those of the most ingenious projectors or mechanics. Thomas Newcomen (1663–1729) built the first steam engine put to practical use;

the elder Abraham Darby (1677–1717) introduced coke in smelting. No writer of their time would have thought of comparing their intellectual stature with that of any great scientist, and indeed the knowledge of their achievement, especially the achievement of Darby, has come not from their contemporaries but from modern researchers studying neglected old manuscripts.[24] It remained for the popular press of recent times to try to raise technical inventors (such as Edison or Marconi) to the rank of great intellects. Until after the middle of the eighteenth century, such men were classed with mechanics or economic "adventurers."

The age of Newton was perhaps the greatest of all ages for the more philosophical aspects of science. Science had begun to assert a complete independence from the old Aristotelian metaphysics. This it could hardly have done had it not contained metaphysical implications of its own which seemed to be irreconcilable with those of the older metaphysics.[25] Newton was probably the most important synthesizer in the whole of scientific history. The third book of his *Principia* opens with these words: "In the preceding books I have laid down the principles of philosophy. . ." Some of his propositions concerning the physical universe have been modified by the new scientific discoveries of the twentieth century. But Kant and other great metaphysicians who had a profound influence on nineteenth-century thought conformed to the Newtonian propositions and even built their philosophical systems around them. One of the most distinguished philosophical students of our time, Etienne Gilson, has suggested that Kant's main philosophical error consisted in making the Newtonian physics a substitute for philosophy, in confusing the physical world which Newton helped to reveal with the ultimate metaphysical truths which the philosopher seeks.[26]

With Newton's contribution the basic scientific work begun on the Continent in the sixteenth century, and developed especially by Kepler at the beginning of the seventeenth, was carried to a tentative conclusion. The discoveries made by these scientists revealed a physical world of matter and space moving through time, heretofore largely hidden from inspection and consequently from intellectual speculation. New knowledge of the movements of the heavenly bodies, the formulation of definite laws of motion which were believed to govern throughout the physical universe, led the European intelligence to assume that it would be possible for the mind to acquire, step by step, by demonstrable experiences, increasing knowledge even of ultimate reality. Physics became, as with Kant, a key to metaphysics.

Modern scientific speculations have reopened the question of the possible paths which the human mind can follow in its search for Truth. But seventy years ago these revolutionary speculations had hardly begun. It was then still correct to say, as the Swiss historian Jakob Burckhardt said, that the results achieved by the greatest seventeenth-century scientists, above all by Newton, "were the foundation of all later consideration of the universe, indeed, of all thought. Hence they rank with the philosophers." [27]

To what extent were the scientific achievements of Newton's time dependent upon contemporary technological improvements, particularly those relating to weapons? Problems of technology then contributed to the progress of natural science in at least two ways. The interest in improvements to lighten labor grew stronger than ever before among the enterprising financial adventurers, the rising squirearchy, husbandmen, industrial managers, and foremen. Almost all of them looked upon the newly formed Royal Society as the fountainhead of knowledge and the natural recipient for all curious information. Such men sent in accounts of their own experiences and of experiences communicated to them. As almost all the leading scientists became members of the Royal Society, they learned from these exchanges of many remarkable natural phenomena and of new mechanical contrivances. Their minds played about among these data, and as a result their speculative faculties sometimes took new directions which added to general knowledge.

The growing public interest in lightening the labor, increasing the commodity, and improving the health of men and women also strengthened the scientific mind in a less tangible manner. In recent times there has a been a tendency for the creative thinker to suffer something of an eclipse, because of the prevailing emphasis upon results which can be measured in terms of profits, wages, and physical output. But in the seventeenth and early eighteenth centuries, when an enthusiasm for technological improvements first took possession of writers, of travelers like Evelyn, and of most persons in England who had leisure to be curious about the processes of nature and mechanics, the new curiosity added to the prestige of the theoretical scientist. His indirect role as a benefactor of mankind became a subject for poetic enthusiasm in the verses of men of letters like Dryden, Cowley, and Pope. In their admiration the poets were expressing views which were becoming common among the educated, in spite of frequent discordant notes, such as those of Harrington, the political philosopher, and of Swift, the master of disgust.[28] The enthusiasm of educated men, including poets, for the general theoretical achievements of science was linked with the growing interest of country gentlemen and other amateurs in natural history and technological progress, as well as with the growing interest of land improvers, industrial foremen, and business promoters in more efficient methods of farming, mining, manufacturing, and moving commodities of all kinds. At the beginning of the eighteenth century the Royal Society, with Newton as its president for twenty-five years, became almost the center of the national life. The new-found prestige which attached to men of science added to the confidence they felt in their speculative mission and encouraged them to concentrate their powerful minds upon this mission.

The utilitarian view that knowledge can be of enormous practical advantage may be of much value to fundamental scientific progress and to human welfare under such conditions as prevailed in Europe in the lifetime of Newton, when formal logic and book learning comprised the curriculums of the schools. Such a view may be of disservice under the conditions which prevail in the twentieth century, when the value for truth of all reasoning which depends upon the imaginative, the intuitive, faculties of the mind has come to be underestimated. The recognition of the practical significance of science once helped to liberate scientists for the pursuit of general truths. Eventually an overemphasis upon this practical significance harnessed scientists in the service of particular interests, ranging from those of business enterprises to those of social classes or national states.

It is difficult for the historian to keep natural science and practical technology separate in an age like that following the Restoration. The actual relations between them, and the nature of their interdependence, were then more justly understood by the articulate public, at least in Great Britain, than they had been in the Middle Ages or than they are in the twentieth century. In so far as military and naval requirements commanded the attention of "projectors" and successful inventors, the needs were likely to stimulate scientific inquiries. We have seen that the use of firearms of various kinds raised issues concerning the movement of projectiles unknown to the ancients or to medieval scientists. Much was done during the late seventeenth century, especially in France, in the mathematics of naval architecture.[29] War needs provided some of the subject matter and stimulated the development of some of the methods used in the natural sciences. No doubt the new relation, which was felt to exist between science and military or naval success, increased the prestige of the scientists.

Yet the contribution of warfare to natural science in the age of Newton was probably less important than its contribution to practical technology, and we have seen that the latter contribution was not great. Moreover, serious warfare interfered with the growth of scientific knowledge even more than with technological progress.

Among the numerous factors responsible for the rise of modern science, the disinterested search for truth was foremost. The more general and comprehensive the nature of scientific work, the more indispensable to its success, even to its conduct, is the love of truth. It has been observed that the greatest scientists are frequently men of singularly fine character.[30] The driving force behind their labor is a passion for knowledge which resembles the love of the artist for his art, in the sense that the love which both have transcends the self and determines the work done, independently of the ordinary personal motives which are frequently of dominant importance in the lives of more ordinary men. Genius is not at the mercy of circumstance in the same way as talent. It has at once less and more freedom. Genius is not free to enlist in worldly causes because it is already enlisted in a higher cause which transcends time and place.

Warfare — with its excitement, its danger, and its drama — puts some ordinary men on their mettle. It may lead them to outdo (another name for forgetting) themselves even off the field of battle, when they are working on weapons to help achieve victory. For a time, therefore, it may stimulate technical experts and inventors to a higher pitch of thought and labor than they are able to command when their country is at peace. But war is of no help in this way to the very great scientist, any more than to the very great artist. Both are on their mettle, both forget themselves, without the stimulus of war. The driving forces behind the achievements of men like Newton and Boyle were neither emotional excitement nor a sense of imminent danger. Such minds gain nothing from the discipline of war.

They may lose much. War may divert their genius away from the universal to the particular, always against their wishes. The highly sensitive nature and the compassion that are part of intellectual and artistic genius are incompatible with the kind of zeal for contriving new methods of dealing death which can be aroused in men of lesser stature — technical experts and even inventors. This was especially true in the seventeenth century, before specialization and the waning sense of sin made it relatively easy for the scientist to evade responsibility for the consequences of his work.

As European wars became more moderate, warfare interfered with scientific thought less than during the age of the religious wars. Nevertheless, the adverse effects of war and of preparation for war at least partly offset any help which science derived in subject matter, methods, or prestige from problems of military engineering and the attempts made to solve them.

Great creative movements of the human mind, which flower in a number of individual lives, are the product of a cultural preparation stretching back for decades and even for generations. Quick returns are frequently the enemy of great and enduring results, both for individuals and for societies. As the principal scientific work of Newton's age was of the kind in which the speculations of the mind and the procedures of research approached closest to philosophy, this work was necessarily the product of a rich intellectual tradition to a greater degree than the technological advances which accompanied it. To search for its inspiration exclusively in the British history of Newton's lifetime would be to neglect its deeper sources. The "new philosophy," as John Donne (1573–1631) had been among the first to call it, owed much to continental scientists. It owed something to the philosophies of Descartes and Spinoza. But it had germinated in England in the time of Bacon and Donne, when the nation was almost always at peace, and when the court of James I, for all its weaknesses and for all the pedantry of the king, was the only court in Europe where the learned professions were in any degree appreciated.[31] Newton and his contemporaries were heirs to the conception of a famous, unfinished work of Bacon's imagination, the *New Atlantis*, an island over the seas, with a great institute of scientific research guiding human destiny. According to the *New Atlantis*, it was possible to understand and master the physical universe in the interest of God as well as man, without setting out to conquer the civilized peoples of the globe.

In the lifetime of Newton society in Great Britain had behind it a long period of peace. The notion that war is an abnormal and undesirable condition for the nation, had become traditional. For the great philosopher Thomas Hobbes (1588–1679), who was a very aged contemporary of Newton, the principal object of political authority was to keep men from destroying each other and the community to which they belonged by war.

Yet, it may be said, the first rich results of the new philosophy were harvested during what was for Great Britain, compared with the peaceful age of Elizabeth, the relatively warlike period which coincided with Newton's life span. In order to understand the relation of these wars to science, we have to see the technical problems raised by the need to improve weapons in the proper perspective, as only one of many stimuli behind the rise of natural science to a place of preëminence in the intellectual life of the nation. There is virtual agreement among three writers — a Russian, an Englishman, and an

American [32] — that mechanical problems connected with weapons were of much less importance than those provided by peaceful industrial and commercial development in stimulating scientific speculations. The English authority, G. N. Clark, has shown that there were several other stimuli, such as medical progress, problems of the fine arts (musical theory in particular), religious ardor about nature as the work of God, and pure speculation.

In Great Britain the Civil War was the only war of the period 1640–1740 which seriously interrupted the ordinary economic and intellectual life of the country. While some of the wars against the Dutch and French, which followed, turned the attention of scientific groups to military and naval problems, there seems to have been little pressure on individuals to curtail in the interest of victory their more theoretical and general speculations. There is no evidence that any pressure was brought to bear upon Newton to turn to war work. It was in 1665 and 1666, in the midst of war and plague that, according to his own account (written later when he was seventy-three), he "minded mathematics and philosophy more than at any time since." [33] Although England was more actively engaged in war during Newton's lifetime than during the seventy years preceding his birth in 1642, English scientists were still less concerned with military problems than were scientists on the Continent.

The Marquis of Louvois (1641–1691), Colbert's successor after 1683 as Louis XIV's principal minister, prepared France for what became the War of the Dutch Alliance. His martial enthusiasm appeared in the hope he expressed in 1684 that the French Academy of Sciences, founded by his predecessor, would devote itself to what he called its true objective — "the Glory of the King." [34] He was thinking of the king's military conquests. In so far as his advice was heeded, it does not seem to have raised the stature of French scientific thought. The long wars of Louis XIV, especially after 1687, interfered with the abstruse scientific studies begun in the 1660's. [35] It was during the relatively more peaceful decades that followed the king's death in 1715 that a great French school of natural science developed to rival the English.

During the late seventeenth and eighteenth centuries the growing moderation of warfare helped to provide European scientists with more frequent opportunities to concern themselves with those aspects of speculation most congenial to conscientious and intelligent scientists. The European mind was much less heavily engaged than during the religious wars with the issues and the outcome of the fighting. This disinterestedness contributed to the growth of a common Euro-

pean culture favorable to scientific discussion. It encouraged an inter-
change of knowledge between the leading scientists of all nations,
such as occurred continually at meetings of the Royal Society, and
was a fruitful source of the advances in speculative science.

The intellectual life of the distinguished French physicist, Denis
Papin (1647–c. 1712), illustrates the new freedom of international
communications that brought the leading scientific minds of Europe
into direct personal relations, which had been more difficult to achieve
during the religious wars. As a young man in Paris, Papin assisted the
celebrated Dutch scientist, Christiaan Huygens (1629–1695), in his experiments with the air pump. Papin then crossed the Channel to London, where he worked with Boyle in his laboratory and was elected
to the Royal Society. Papin's next move was to Venice, where he participated in the work of the recently founded Academy of the Philosophical and Mathematical Sciences. After another sojourn in London,
he was appointed in 1687 to the chair of mathematics in the University
of Marburg. During the next two decades, when the French were
most heavily engaged in wars, he spent most of his time in Germany.
There he was in continual correspondence over scientific matters with
Leibnitz (1646–1716).

Scientific work proceeded independently of the limited warfare,
and more and more without reference to either the national or the
religious issues which had divided Europe during the hundred years
following the Reformation. No doubt under some conditions a dose
of mild wars can do almost as much to help as to hinder speculative
science. But it is difficult to take the appropriate dose.

CHAPTER ELEVEN

Scientific Progress and War

PERIODS IN THE HISTORY OF WAR WHEN THE ADVANTAGES LIE WITH the defense oscillate with other periods when they lie with the attack. Even in our mechanical age wars are fought by human beings, so these oscillations are not smooth and predictable like those of a swinging pendulum. They are uneven in both extent and time. Some occur in the course of a single battle or campaign, others in the course of a war, still others during a series of wars, like those fought by France under Louis XIV, or like the much smaller wars of the English under Charles II against the Moors, or like those wars, so much vaster in scope, fought by Germany against much of the world at the beginning of the twentieth century.

In European history, have not these short-term oscillations occurred within the orbit of longer ones which cover a century or more? The early Gothic age, from the twelfth to the late thirteenth century, with its wonderful cathedrals and fortified places, was a period during which the attackers in Europe generally met serious and increasing difficulties, because the improvement in the strength of fortresses outran the advance in the power of destruction. Later, with the spread of firearms at the end of the fifteenth century, old fortresses lost their power to resist. An age ensued during which the offense possessed, apart from short-term setbacks, new advantages. Then, during the seventeenth century, especially after about 1660, and until at least the outbreak of the War of the Austrian Succession in 1740, the defense regained much of the ground it had lost since the great medieval fortresses had proved unable to meet the bombardment of the new and more numerous artillery.

The conditions which determine these long-term oscillations are complicated, because such oscillations reflect the historical experience of their age. In the forefront are the technical changes in weapons. Such changes, in their turn, are determined partly by the nature and spirit of scientific inquiry. Consequently, knowledge concerning the influence of technological changes and of scientific speculation upon the weapons used, the means of defense, and so upon the character of warfare, is no less essential to an understanding of the reciprocal relations betwen war and the rise of industrial civilization than knowledge concerning the influence of war upon invention and science.

What had technical invention to do with the growing mildness of European war from 1660 to 1740? What had speculative science to do with it?

In spite of the "projecting" mood which prevailed in Great Britain and which was gaining ground on the Continent, in spite of its frequent direction to improvements in the effectiveness of weapons, the actual advances in the technique of destruction were less remarkable than they had been at any time since firearms had come into widespread use following the introduction of new horse-drawn artillery in 1494. It may be doubted whether all the improvements in weapons made during the hundred years from 1640 to 1740 added as much to the power of an attacking army as the improvements made during the thirty-five years from 1494 to 1529.

After the Restoration in 1660, many ingenious engines of war were described by their sponsors in papers submitted to the English crown. For example, there were in 1664 Captain Samuel Carrington's "fireworks," which he offered to bring over to England or Flanders from Madrid. He promised that they would destroy any enemy vessel in "half an hour." These may have resembled the bomb described by the Marquis of Worcester, the amateur inventor who died in 1667. Worcester's bomb could either be carried surreptitiously by a spy in his pocket and planted in a ship of the enemy, or confided to a diver to fasten to the ship's hull.[1] There was also Erasmus Purling's "warlike engine to row with 100 or 120 oars, and 1000 or 1500 men, secured from shot." This was said to be capable of either burning or sinking an entire fleet, whether at sea or in a fortified harbor, "though 100 sail together."[2]

These destructive implements may have died with their inventors, as the methods for boring cannon of a new metal alloy devised some years later by Prince Rupert (1619–1682) of the Palatinate (James I's grandson, who had fought both in the Thirty Years' War and the English Civil War) are said to have died with him.[3] It is likely that the projects of Carrington and Purling were no more practicable than the majority of secret weapons which have been invariably noised abroad in time of war. Similar weapons had been whispered about for generations, but little had been done with them. Something resembling the small bomb which divers were to plant on the hulls of ships to explode the vessels was mentioned by Leonardo in his letter to Sforza, written in the early 1480's.

The most portentous conceptions of the age — the submarine and the tank or armored car — were not new either. In papers apparently written about 1680, Sir William Petty, an active member of the Royal Society and one of the fathers of modern statistics, put forward plans for large squadrons of "war chariots." As was becoming to his statistical mind, the papers were full of figures giving the expense of outfitting these wagons. But the picture which emerges from these data is of "tanks" which would hardly have been a match for those Napier had described some eighty-five years earlier. Unlike Napier's, Petty's tank was not made of *metal*. Also unlike Napier's, Petty's was to be drawn by a horse. Petty's vehicles seem to have been designed for defensive maneuvering rather than to drive through the hostile lines in battle. His project was to put in the field about a thousand chariots, each manned by nine men and a boy, armed with muskets and pikes. For battle purposes the chariots were to be strung into a series, forming a long line of slow-moving vehicles — resembling the line of sailing battleships which had recently become the approved formation for fighting at sea.[4]

Petty's conception reflects changes which were taking place in the practice of war. Some of the changes looked less toward the efficient destructive engines of the twentieth century, suited to mass attack, than away from them. Nor is there evidence that more was done to implement Petty's proposals than Napier's.

Like the advances in industrial technology for peaceful purposes, most of the actual advances in the structure of warships and other military engines consisted in the perfection and elaboration of devices constructed earlier.[5] New and larger vessels for the English navy had been called for by a Commission of Reform in 1618. Their intellectual father was Phineas Pett, a leading shipwright of King James I's reign. It was not until a generation afterwards that his ideas received, at the time of the first Anglo-Dutch war of 1652–53, a general embodiment in the navy.[6]

During the second half of the seventeenth century, in their attempts to capture strong places, attacking forces began to employ a missile which the English dubbed, somewhat inelegantly, a "stink-pot." These projectiles were tried out in the reign of Charles II in defense of the newly gained English stronghold at Tangier, on the Strait of Gibraltar. The zeal with which the English used stink-pots to resist attacks by the Moors, bent on driving them into the sea, may possibly have had something to do with the fact that the enemy was Mohammedan, not Christian. The missiles were ignited at both ends and hurled into forts, where they were intended to do double mischief. They burst into flame and might therefore set any wooden or other inflammable matter ablaze, while they also spread poisonous fumes, so "that men are sufficated." [7] For all these venomous properties, the stink-pot was a form of hand grenade. Grenades and bombs came into more extensive use in the 1670's, when the technique of throwing them was improved.[8] But the principle of the bomb seems to have been discovered in the early sixteenth century. Effective bombs had been invented in or before 1588, when in the Dutch Gelderland the first bombs were heaved.[9]

Many small improvements were made in firearms and missiles during the hundred years preceding the War of the Austrian Succession. Towards the end of the seventeenth century, for example, the French increased the range of cannon fire, particularly from men-of-war.[10] In 1680 an ingenious naval engineer, Renau d'Eliçagaray (1652–1719), conceived the idea of constructing special ships to hold mortars for hurling explosive shells. He invented the so-called bomb ketch, which was tried out with success in the bombardment of Algiers two years later. In spite of the incredulity of conservative opinion, on one occasion the bombs from these sturdy little vessels buried a large number of the inhabitants in the debris of their houses. On another occasion the bombs carried away the best part of the fortifications protecting the port.[11] That was progress. But it was only piecemeal progress. A few bomb ketches might wreak occasional havoc at some port, but there were never enough of them to prepare the way for a large-scale invasion of any European country from the sea.

Another new method of shooting was the so-called *tir à ricochet*. Cannon were made to spit out projectiles which bounded along a stretch of firm, flat earth, after the manner of smooth stones skipping over water. This device was apparently first employed in 1688, also by the French, at the siege of Philippsburg, near Karlsruhe in Baden.[12]

Muskets and pistols were being adjusted to shoot more easily and frequently. In order to fire the arquebuses and early muskets it had been necessary to ignite the powder with a flaming match. A cigarette smoker who tries to light up in a brisk wind, or in a shower like those that fall so frequently in the north of Europe, will readily recognize the difficulties and delays involved in such a method of shooting. During the seventeenth century firelocks were steadily replacing the clumsy matchlocks, as a means of igniting the powder. Here again there was nothing new about the process itself. The most effective of the two kinds of firelock had been invented in the sixteenth century in Germany, where it was called a *snaphance*.[13] By the 1680's snaphance muskets had apparently become a part of the standard equipment of many English regiments.[14]

At about the same time cartridges replaced the noisy and dangerous bandoleers, picturesque belts made to support the muskets and to contain the charges for loading. Bandoleers often caught in the gun and delayed the shooting. Worn as they were all about the body, they might take fire and explode. The cartridge not only did away with these troubles; it saved time in loading.[15]

As might be expected from the increasingly defensive nature of campaigns, a great deal of attention was paid to fortress construction. In 1701 there was published in London "An Essay on the Usefulness of Mathematical Learning." The tract has been sometimes attributed to John Arbuthnot (1667–1735), the famous English physician and Tory political writer. In it we read that "there [is] a force or resistance in the due measures and proportions of the lines and angles of a fortification, which contributes much toward its strength. This art of fortification has been much studied of late, but I dare not affirm that it has attained its utmost perfection." [16]

This association of mathematics with the building of fortifications is not accidental. Just as France furnished more great mathematical minds than any other country during the seventeenth century — the age of Descartes, Fermat, and Pascal — so France was, with the possible exception of Holland, the nation which paid most attention to the construction of forts. The most remarkable improvements made in their military effectiveness during early modern times have been sometimes associated with a celebrated and learned Frenchman, the Marquis de Vauban (1633–1707). He was carefully trained in geometry and other branches of mathematical learning and his mind touched French classical civilization at many points, but he made no important contribution to mathematical theory. It was not until a later age, toward the end of the eighteenth century, that French mathematicians of the highest rank began seriously to apply their mathematical genius to fortress construction.[17]

Vauban began his career as a private in the era of violent pitched battles. During the early campaigns of Louis XIV's reign, when an older conception of more relentless war still prevailed and when the French were extending their frontiers, Vauban's talents were mainly employed to devise new methods of attack. At that time many strong places in the Low Countries — Lille, Tournai, Dinant, Huy — and in the Rhineland — Nimwegen, Trèves — were occupied by French armies, under Vauban's direction. Vauban introduced the systematic method of approaching forts by parallels, so that the attackers worked their way forward along trenches. He established the formulas necessary for military mining. He first used the *tir à ricochet* as a means of breaking down the defense. One of Vauban's greatest successors in the art of fortification, Lazare Carnot (1753–1823), attributed to him a notable reduction in the time required to capture a stronghold.[18]

Yet Vauban's career and its significance are better understood when it is realized that he had scruples concerning the use of so relatively moderate a new weapon as the *ricochet*. He thought the name suggested a mischievous trickery, and he repudiated trickery in warfare as illegitimate,[19] going farther here perhaps than Thomas Aquinas, who had taught that it is justifiable to lay ambushes against an enemy.[20] Unlike the Prince of Condé (1621–1686) — who, though only twelve years Vauban's senior, represented an earlier age when battles were frequently fought to the death — Vauban considered the first object to be to save the lives of his troops. According to the writer of one of his obituaries, his "natural humanity" led him always to sacrifice a quick victory in order to reduce the number of dead and wounded.[21]

At the time Vauban started his military career, French statesmen had been bent on conquest. But after 1675, when Condé led his last campaign to repel along the Rhine the invasion of an imperial army, this unanimity concerning the desirability of further conquests by the relentless use of soldiers was lost. Henceforth France was more and more concerned with keeping territory already gained. Vauban seems to have been less of an innovator than a faithful servant of this new policy, which was represented at court by such men as the dukes of Saint-Simon, Chevreuse, and Beauvillier, all of whom were opposed to wars of conquest. In 1699 Vauban actually went so far as to suggest a repeal of the high French tariff on coal, arguing that it was counter to the true economic interest of the country. It was consistent with his experience and with the evolution of French foreign policy, which he sought ardently to serve, that his attention as a military engineer turned with the years from attack to defense, a subject which had already engaged much of his attention from 1668, when the Peace of Aix-la-Chapelle brought France twelve fortified towns along the border of the Spanish Netherlands.

Fortress construction, as undertaken in the age of Louis XIV, was especially congenial to the French mind, because it called for the same measure and proportion which the Cartesian philosophy exemplified, and which was practiced in the fine arts by Racine, Couperin, Poussin, and Claude Lorrain, and in the art of life, by Madame de Sévigné, Madame de Lafayette, and the Duke of Chevreuse. From Vauban's own early adventures in attacking, he had learned better how to defend than any other French soldier of the age. With the help of ideas derived from his Dutch predecessor, Stevin, and his slightly younger Dutch contemporary, Menno van Coehoorn (1644–1704), Vauban embroidered the French frontiers with his forts, many of which were new versions of old ones. They shielded the entrances to harbors like Dunkirk [22] and Antibes, as well as the numerous easy passages into northeastern France from the Alps to the North Sea and the English Channel.

There has been much dispute concerning the defensive strength of Vauban's forts. During the last wars of Louis XIV's reign they were often easily captured, after a delay estimated at not more than thirty days on the average.[23] The most gifted French military engineers of the late eighteenth century, when war was again becoming more relentless, denied that Vauban's forts had offered anything approaching an adequate defense against his own newly devised methods of attack.[24] But some of Vauban's modern biographers take the opposite line, and represent his forts as providing the first effective answer to attacking artillery.[25]

It is possible to reconcile the two positions. The security of a fort depends not only on the way it is built and equipped but on the customs of defense and the spirit of the defenders. An Englishman who edited a sixteenth-century Italian treatise in 1715, shortly after Vauban's death, remarked that the discouragement to taking forts always lies "with the great loss of Men's lives and expense of Time and Treasure, not the impossibility." [26] Vauban's own methods of attack reduced remarkably the loss of life among the attackers, while increasing the danger to the defenders, at the very time when the distaste for combat was growing from decade to decade. As a consequence it became conventional to surrender more and more readily during the period when Vauban's forts came into use. It follows that the frequent capture of his forts during the later wars of Louis XIV's reign cannot be confidently ascribed to technical weaknesses in their structure and arrangement.

That Vauban helped to multiply forts is incontestable. With the new conditions of war, his contributions to attack and defense alike encouraged the conception of warfare as a limited enterprise, governed by those very rules of rational prudence and even politeness, of which the political authorities as well as the leading minds of Europe were enamored. The wars which began in 1689 between France and Holland were wars in which both sides were impregnated with a defensive mentality — born partly out of the need for holding naturally defensible frontiers. They might almost be described as wars of forts against forts.

The art of fortification continued to be a part of the art of architecture. The new methods of building forts were not out of keeping with the developing early modern architecture of Europe, which culminated in the baroque. As more of the new low-lying forts were embedded in a way of their own (hardly less firmly than the ancient medieval fortresses) in the terrain which nature had provided, as forts were adapted to the new weapons, as both the attackers and the defenders became more prudent about pressing the fighting to the point of slaughter, the actual destruction of fortifications again became less frequent. At the beginning of the eighteenth century, when the wars of Louis XIV ended, the numerous forts were an expression of renewed Western stability. They seem to express also a rational European unity that had taken the place, after the long interval of religious wars, of the earlier medieval unity, of which the Gothic citadel, like the Gothic cathedral, had been a symbol.[27] The new unity extended over the Atlantic to America. A French fort, with stone bastions many feet thick, was built as far west as the meadows along the Mississippi River, at Chartres in the Illinois country.

In contrast to the hundred and fifty years which preceded, the age of French and English political hegemony following 1640 was noteworthy for lack of enterprise in applying scientific discoveries to effect practical advances in destructive power. "Except for sheathing and pumps," wrote a historian of the evolution of English naval armament, "no important improvement [in naval architecture] was patented between the years 1618 and 1800."[28] When John Muller, perceptor of engineering to the Duke of Gloucester, published his *Treatise of Artillery* in 1768, he remarked that "very little improvement has been made in the proportions of guns since Dilichius, a German, who wrote near 200 years ago."[29] The increase in the striking power of firearms of all kinds, so phenomenal during the early sixteenth century, and the further improvements made by the Dutch at the end of the sixteenth century in the effectiveness of artillery were followed by a long period, lasting from the mid-seventeenth to the mid-eighteenth century, during which progress was not impressive.

What part was played by European thought, especially as represented by the great scientists of the age of Newton, in the development of weapons? It is noticeable that, with the exception of Vauban, who was not a natural philosopher, the men who improved weapons of *attack* were mostly obscure persons. The rational powers of the mind, as represented by the leading men of letters, philosophers, and scientists, were coming to have stronger influences than ever before or since upon educated men and women, including those who were responsible for the government of the European nations. When rational ideas carried such weight in human affairs, the attitude of learned men toward the practical use of knowledge was bound to have effects upon the extent and the nature of technological progress.

The great minds of the age were aware of the possibilities science offered for increasing wealth and improving health. These possibilities encouraged them in their labors. But most of them seem to have been ill equipped for exploiting the practical technological possibilities opened by their theories. Receiving homage from their contemporaries — first in Great Britain, Holland, and Sweden, and then in the early eighteenth century also in France, Germany, and Switzerland — the great natural philosophers were neither dismayed nor much concerned because their discoveries were not actually moving the mountains on this planet, or harnessing the tides. Their genius was for discovering general truths concerning matter and space, moving through time. Their influence was in the world of the mind. At the beginning of the eighteenth century, when educated Europeans were beginning to believe, much more than their medieval ancestors, that the rational processes were of paramount importance for human welfare and that these processes were capable of continual improvement, an influence upon other minds seemed to the natural philosopher of immense importance. Such an influence placed upon him great responsibilities, which most of the scientists recognized.

Among the leading natural philosophers of the later seventeenth century, no one seems to have been more interested in the practical applications of science than Boyle. His voluminous writings suggest that a sense of the role which science could play in material welfare was a spur to his scientific work. It also added zest to the work of some of his contemporaries. The records of the English Royal Society, of which the leading English scientists were members, suggest that the scientists were much interested in the accounts of practical experiences supplied them in abundance by craftsmen and men of affairs with whom they corresponded, and parts of whose papers sometimes found their way into the *Philosophical Transactions*, the first publication of the Society. Discussions of practical problems were probably frequent in their meeting rooms at Gresham College in London.

In both France and England, the crown solicited the help of scientists for the improvement of warships and all sorts of weapons. But this kind of work was not their long suit. For example, in 1711, when the War of the Spanish Succession had been in progress ten years, the government called in some of the leading English scientists for advice on problems of naval construction. They actually built a three-decker bristling with eighty guns, the "Royal Katherine." But this ship proved so deficient in stability that it had to be girdled.[30]

Modern writers on the history of guns have emphasized the extensive study of ballistics made by European scientists from Tartaglia to Newton.[31] Some speculated concerning the trajectory of missiles. Others worked at theoretical problems of chemistry connected with gunpowder. Yet in connection with both most of the scientists exhibited the same inaptitude in the practical realm as in connection with warships. When dealing with materials of destruction they seem to have been guided more often than not by the doctrine that it is more blessed to receive than to give! They seem to have learned more from the new weapons and ammunition than they taught the mechanics who built engines of destruction.

In 1742 an English scientist named Benjamin Robins (1707–1751), whose parents were humble Quakers and therefore presumably pacifistically inclined, published a treatise called *New Principles of Gunnery*.[32] Three years later it was translated into German and published in Berlin with a critical commentary by Leonhard Euler (1707–1783), the eminent Swiss mathematician. In 1751 it was translated into French. It provides a landmark in the interrelations between knowledge and war. It seems to have had a considerable influence on the improvements in the accuracy of cannon fire, which became notable at about this time, when there were already signs, which few could read, that the movement toward ever more moderate warfare was beginning to play itself out. Robins was himself a distinguished mathematician. He was apparently one of the first English natural philosophers to combine, with a good conscience, speculative scientific work and practical engineering for destructive purposes.

Nothing is more revealing of the change in scientific outlook, which took place about the middle of the eighteenth century, than Robins' comments on the labor of his great predecessors who had studied ballistics. Scientists had begun long before to test their speculative theories by experiments and observations. Such a procedure was accepted as indispensable by Gilbert, Galileo, Kepler, and Harvey — all of whom had been born in the sixteenth century, four generations or more before Robins. But, while all of them had offered experimental proofs on many occasions, Robins' book suggests that they had seldom resorted to practical verification when it came to destructive weapons. According to Robins, earlier scientists, including Galileo and Newton, had neglected to test by experiments, by actual observation in the field, the particular theories they had expounded concerning the course followed by balls shot out of cannon or their theories concerning the composition of gunpowder. Apart from four men whose names are scarcely mentioned in the history of science — Collado, William Bourne, Eldred, and Robert Anderson — no previous authorities, according to Robins, had treated the subject of gunnery experimentally. Robins set about in his book to show that the theories of Galileo, Newton, and other eminent scientists were all awry. A late eighteenth-century mathematician, Charles Hutton, referred to *New Principles of Gunnery* as "the first work that can be considered as attempting to establish a practical system of gunnery, and projectiles, on good experiments, on the force of gunpowder, on the resistance of the air, and on the effects of different pieces of artillery." [33]

It has been suggested that Newton was not always eager to prove by actual demonstration results he had arrived at by intuition, and of which he was overwhelmingly confident because of his unique power of concentration. Yet he was able to furnish excellent proofs of all his major scientific discoveries.[34] The fact that he and other great scientists, who were his predecessors and contemporaries, were not putting their destructive knowledge to the test of positive verification, suggests two important characteristics of modern science as it developed until after Newton's death. First, the predilection of the early scientists, trained in classical philosophy, was not for the practical. Second, trained in Christian philosophy and believing in the revelations of the Bible, they still feared, as Napier had feared, the consequences of the application of scientific knowledge for purposes of destruction.

Boyle and Newton had these fears. For all their marvelous insight into natural phenomena, they seem to have been imbued with a deep sense of the reality of the supernatural. This reached a point that more recent Western scientists would regard as superstitious. In his "Articles of Inquiries Concerning Mines," Boyle thought it worth-while to ask, "Do the Diggers ever really meet with subterranean deamons?" [35] For a time at least he believed in the possibility of some of the transmutations promised by the alchemists. He devoted much time to the study of theology and to encouraging the propagation of Christianity in the East.

The case of Newton is still more remarkable. Upwards of a million unpublished words survive in his handwriting. According to the late

Lord Keynes, who purchased a large part of them to deposit with Newton's own Cambridge University, "they are just as *sane* as the *Principia*, if their whole matter and purpose were not magical." They suggest Newton was no less concerned than Napier had been with the mysteries behind the physical universe. Just as Napier applied his great mind to matters later to be called "occult" with equal intensity and in much the same manner as to the discovery of logarithms, so Newton applied his much greater mind to such theological issues as the Trinity with equal intensity and in much the same manner as to the discovery of the principles of natural philosophy. "Newton was not the first of the age of reason," wrote Lord Keynes. "He was the last of the magicians . . . the last great mind which looked out on the visible and intellectual world with the same eyes as those who began to build our intellectual inheritance rather less than 10,000 years ago." He based his theological conclusions entirely on the revealed truth of the Bible, as Napier had done.[36] Yet it is necessary to distinguish his outlook from Napier's. Newton's results were unorthodox; he found no support in the Bible for the Trinitarian doctrine. Partly on that account, but perhaps partly too because the mysterious world beyond positive experience was less real to his contemporaries than to the contemporaries of Napier, Newton concealed the results of his "occult" activities in a box, instead of publishing them as Napier a hundred years before had published his.

The greatest intellects of Newton's age were far from excluding the possibility of intervention in natural and historical phenomena by the God Christ had revealed. Bishop Burnet's thesis in the history of his own time was based on a belief in the actuality of such intervention *against* the Roman Church. Like Napier, the scientists of the Restoration had a conception of human destiny reaching beyond worldly experience.

Recent inquiries into Newton's life leave little doubt that his incredibly powerful mind discovered more about the material world than he cared to reveal. In his lecture at the tercentenary of Newton's birth, Professor Andrade quoted passages from a letter which Newton wrote in 1676, when he was mainly concerned with chemical operations. "I cannot hope to convince the skeptical," Andrade said, "that Newton . . . had some inkling of atomic power, but I do say that [these passages] do not read to me as if all that he meant was that the manufacture of gold would upset world trade." [37]

Boyle was certain that it was no part of a learned man's duty to contribute to the "hellish machines" of war. For many years he paid substantial sums out of his private fortune to keep a certain Dr.

Kuffler from exploiting his invention of some new and dangerous explosive. Boyle's relations with Kuffler went back to the late 1650's when, as a young man, he was introduced to this German by Samuel Hartlib. Of Lithuanian origin, Hartlib's father had been chief merchant to the king of Poland, and Hartlib, who was the issue of his third marriage to a rich Englishwoman, first came to England as a mature man about 1630. By the time the Royal Society was about to form, he was old and sick, but he had become very active in London in steering scientific and technical projects in directions which he regarded as "advantageous to the public." In 1655 John Evelyn called Hartlib "a public spirited and ingenious person, who had promulgated many useful things and arts." He was then in close relation not only with Evelyn but with other of the most brilliant young Englishmen of the age, with Petty and with Christopher Wren (1632–1723), the great architect whose activity as a member of the Royal Society is indicative of its many-sided unity. He was close to Milton; it was at his urgent solicitation that the great man wrote his treatise "Of Education." Like Boyle, he was a liberal giver from his private purse, which he had exhausted before he died.

At a critical juncture in English intellectual history, just after a period of fierce wars, Hartlib used his influence against further improvements in weapons. In 1659 he wrote to Boyle about "Dr. Kuffler" suggesting that Kuffler was "so much in love with" "his secret for improving . . . sandy and barren land" that "if he could get any partners, or any other encouragement or assistant for it, he would willingly desist from all eager pursuits about his dreadful and destroying invention." Boyle seems to have acted on this advice and to have subsidized Kuffler to keep him at work improving husbandry. Twenty years later, in 1680, another of Boyle's correspondents, an elderly contributor to the Royal Society named John Beale, wrote that he had learned from Hartlib long since "how largely, and how often, your bounty hindered Kuffler from vending his destroying artifice." [38]

Such scruples as Boyle's and Hartlib's were by no means uncommon. They were in the tradition of Western European learning, which placed immense responsibilities upon the learned man and took it for granted that the responsibilities should extend to persons who put knowledge to practical use. It was less easy than it has now become to evade these responsibilities simply by ejaculating, "Am I my brother's keeper?"

As long as the sense of the evil inherent in human nature was strong, this acted as a deterrent upon the use of knowledge for objects which might turn out to be destructive. Unlike many of his contemporaries, Samuel Johnson (1709–1784), more than two generations after Boyle, retained a deep consciousness of the wages of sin. Boswell has recorded the frightful fear Dr. Johnson had for his own salvation, on account of some of his relations with women. A major figure in the intellectual life of his age, an age in which writers had an immense influence on such opinion as counted in knowledge and politics, Johnson maintained a position concerning invention which seems to have frequently prevailed in Boyle's time and even in Newton's, but which was losing force in Johnson's time, to be forsaken during the last two hundred years. "If men were all virtuous," remarks the artist in Johnson's *Rasselas*, "I should with great alacrity teach them all to fly. But what would be the security of the good, if the bad could at pleasure invade them from the sky. Against an army sailing through the clouds, neither walls, nor mountains, nor seas, could afford any security." [39]

The case of Pascal (1623–1662) illustrates another aspect of the conflict, resulting from Christian revelation, which helped to hold back the practical use of scientific knowledge — the conflict between the worship of God and devotion to the study of positive experience. There is no evidence of this conflict before the rise of modern experimental science, not even in Roger Bacon (1214–1294), perhaps the most scientific of the scholastic philosophers. After the age of Newton the conflict largely disappeared, especially among the deists, who were inclined towards pantheism. But in Pascal's time the conflict was strong, and his own life was a dramatic enactment of it. As a child he showed a genius for mathematics; as a young man, an almost equal genius for physics. To the infinitesimal calculus, to the theory of probability, and to hydrodynamics, he made enduring contributions of the highest value. Possessed of one of the most remarkable minds in history, different from Newton's mind yet equally powerful, with a clarity of exposition that Newton could not approach, Pascal deserted science at thirty-one after his second "conversion," which it has been often suggested resulted from his delivery when nearly dragged to death by a team of runaway horses. He followed his sister into the seclusion provided near the Jansenist abbey of Port Royal, outside Paris, and used his unsurpassed mental endowments and his disciplined training wholly in the service of the Christian faith. For Pascal, improvements in the fortresses of the temporal world ceased to count. Against the perils of ultimate reality, the right conduct of the human spirit was man's sole protection. Therefore all that mattered was the prior Truth revealed by Christ — Truth beyond the grasp of the human intellect but without which the temporal world and its partial truths could not exist.

In an age of European intellectual unification like the late seventeenth and the early eighteenth century, the attitude of the French toward science was bound to influence other countries, including England. One consequence of this outlook was to interfere with the wholehearted application of scientific knowledge for the attainment of practical results. While the greatest scientists were impressed by the promise for posterity of longer life and more abundance to which their researches might contribute, they were still more disposed to seek final consolation in the Christian faith, with its commandments against murder and unbridled violence, than in the hopes of man's dominion over matter. If tangible advances in physical wealth and health, regardless of the ultimate consequences for material destruction and homicide, are considered the final objectives of science, the main course followed by European minds during the hundred years from 1640 to 1740 will be attributed to perversity, if not to ignorance. "Why were not the men of this age smart enough to invent submarines, airplanes and tanks?" men of the twentieth century ask. But has not the emancipation of the educated during the past two hundred years from the special forms of perversity and ignorance which persisted in the age of Newton produced an enslavement of a new kind? Has it not left the modern mind with a partial view of human nature and of the nature of human happiness, in which men's immediate material aspirations have become the final object of all endeavor? Has it not led us to puff up man's material dimensions to so inordinate and inhuman a size that we are deprived of the imaginative resources to which only humility and restraint give access? Has it not denied men access to the total universe which is still the same as in the era of Pascal and Newton, in spite of the new command of nature which has been obtained by "scientific progress?"

Both in England and on the Continent, the intellect was guiding Europe into less fearful times than those of the preceding age of bloody and devastating wars. The concern of the natural philosophers in the late seventeenth century with universal experience and with the universal significance of every particular discovery, helped reveal to their increasingly numerous followers and admirers how much all men and women had in common. Boyle participated in a movement that was helping to check what had seemed to him in his youth the natural course of history — the tendency of war to beget war.

It is ironic that the very success of this movement toward limited warfare should have filled the Western peoples eventually with a sense of security, should have bred among them a novel confidence in human nature which eventually helped to reconcile the scientific mind to a growing irresponsibility. As wars became more moderate, as they engaged the minds and passions of most Europeans less, a new outlook on firearms and other explosive weapons gradually emerged.

This outlook can be traced back to John Donne, who was in many ways a herald of modern experience. On Christmas Day, 1621, he preached a sermon just after he had been appointed Dean of St. Paul's Cathedral in London. In it he spoke in praise of "reason," upon which the Western peoples in the late seventeenth and eighteenth centuries came to count so heavily as a civilizing force. "So by the benefit of this light of reason," Donne said, "they have found out *Artillery*, by which warres come to quicker ends then heretofore, and the great expence of bloud is avoyded: for the numbers of men slain now, since the invention of Artillery, are much lesse then before, when the sword was the executioner." [40]

No doubt Donne's view was partly the result of the extraordinarily peaceful conditions which had persisted in England during his lifetime; perhaps also he was influenced by the ten-year truce on the Continent that had preceded the Thirty Years' War. His view of the gun as an instrument of civilization came to be widely held two generations later, when bloodshed was actually much reduced throughout Europe. In his letter to Boyle concerning the chemist's bounty to Kuffler, John Beale, who became a parson twenty years before, suggested that the new engines of war — "thundering artillery" and "bombs" — were making war less destructive.[41] At the end of the seventeenth century this opinion was becoming common.[42] During the eighteenth century the Europeans ceased to regard the gun as an invention of the devil and began to think of it as a friend of man.

This new thesis rested mainly on two arguments which are to some extent complementary. The first was put by Gibbon in classic form. The invention of powerful weapons is possible only when the level of civilization is raised, and the more civilized individuals and nations become, the less they are disposed to let force be the final arbiter of their destiny. The second argument is that powerful weapons are capable of such frightful destruction that they will bring a war to a speedy end, or even cause the leaders of the nations to recoil from war altogether. In writing about firearms in 1715, for example, an English editor had this to say: "Perhaps Heaven hath in Judgment inflicted the Cruelty of this Invention, on purpose to fright Men into Amity and Peace, and into an Abhorrence of the Tumult and Inhumanity of War." [43] As these arguments gained adherents the scruples felt by scientists diminished against using their knowledge for practical and even for destructive purposes.

Such arguments seemed more plausible as the ancient Christian faith lost its hold among the Europeans. In the eighteenth century new intellectual leaders like Voltaire and Lessing, whose views commanded a wider audience than had been accessible to the seventeenth-century natural philosophers, suggested that men and women were not naturally addicted to evil, that the dogma of original sin was a myth. Scientists like Joseph Priestley suggested that it could be proved that the soul was material.[44] From this it was a short step to the conclusion that the soul died with the body — a conclusion which denied man's responsibility, especially men's collective responsibility, to God, and relieved men of their sense of guilt.

These changes in the outlook of the intelligence helped to turn the attention of scientists from the universal, from the sublime, to the practical and the useful. The denial of original sin, the growing belief in the perfectibility of human nature, enabled men to contribute with clear consciences to the development of destructive engines. If the invention of more accurate and more powerful weapons simply reflected a higher intelligence, if the intelligent proclaimed that wars were stupid and futile, if men were confident that the states of Europe would be governed more and more intelligently, then the scientist need have little concern over using his discoveries in the service of practical efficiency, whether the object of improvement were a steam engine or a cannon.

Such changes in the outlook of the Europeans on human nature, and on the role which science could play in human happiness, became widespread after about 1740. Most scientists forsook what the twentieth century calls magic and superstition. Many of them forsook the Christian view of human nature. The changes helped to breed Benjamin Robins. He was to have many successors.

CHAPTER TWELVE

War and Economic Progress

· THE INCREASING MODERATION OF WARFARE FROM 1660 TO 1740 WAS not brought about by a reduction in the armaments of the European states. This was the period during which the leading powers first came to maintain large concentrations of troops in peace as well as in time of war, in winter as well as in summer.

During the wars of Louis XIV, the French army was swelled again and again, until it is said to have numbered 446,000 in 1690, when the population of France little exceeded twenty millions. During the relatively peaceful decades following the treaties of Utrecht in 1713, the French army was never allowed to fall below 130,000. It was common to keep from 160,000 to 200,000 men under arms in time of peace,[1] some twelve times as many as at the end of the sixteenth century, when a famous French soldier, the Seigneur de la Noue, advised Henry of Navarre, on the eve of his accession to the French throne, to maintain some regiments of infantry in his service even in peacetime.[2] Although Prussia had hardly a tenth the population of France in the early eighteenth century, the Prussian army was increased from some 28,500 under Frederick William of Hohenzollern, the Great Elector (1640–1688), to 83,486 in 1739, the last year of Frederick William I's reign (1713–1740) as second king of the Prussian state.[3] This was a colossal force for a little power of two million people to maintain when Europeans were still living in an economy dominated by scarcity, as peoples always lived until the late nineteenth century.[4]

Other countries were forming battalions to match; the fleets of England and Holland were expanding; the French fleet, negligible at the beginning of the seventeenth century, was built up to rival the English; the Baltic states, especially Sweden, Denmark, and in the early eighteenth century Russia, were fitting out warships. During the peaceful 1720's and 1730's when there was less fighting than there had been for many generations, the number of European soldiers and sailors kept under arms apparently always exceeded half a million.[5] At this time the population of greater Europe was hardly a fifth as large as at the end of the nineteenth century: perhaps less than a hundred millions all told. The proportion of the inhabitants kept in the armed forces at the beginning of the twentieth century, on the eve of the First World War, was little larger.

In spite of the reductions in the fighting and the casualties, military requirements caused an even greater drain on the financial resources of the European states than during the late sixteenth and early seventeenth centuries. The state expenditure of capital and labor per man under arms was very much greater in the bigger armies and navies of the late seventeenth and early eighteenth centuries. There were many reasons for this.

The sea was more important than ever before in the settlement of European political differences, and by its nature modern naval warfare is expensive as well as indecisive. It cost much more to put a sailor to sea in a man-of-war than to put a soldier on the march. Ships had to be built and repaired at large naval yards and arsenals; these had to be stocked with foodstuffs, fuel, and all kinds of munitions. In 1670, for example, the English navy victualler had to supply food for 25,000 men for an eight-month period, the supplies to be delivered at London for 17,000 men, at Portsmouth for 6,000, at Dover for 1,300, at Plymouth for 500, and at Kinsale in Ireland for 200.[6] The maintenance of effective naval forces created intricate problems of supply, which involved tapping the timber resources of the Scandinavian countries and even of North America. Traders galore and naval officials like Samuel Pepys had to turn their minds and energies to the administration of the Royal Navy. The growth in the relative importance of war at sea shifted a great deal of responsibility for success from fighting officers to civilian administrators, some of whom were merchants and industrial adventurers.

Changes in the nature of both strategy and tactics in land warfare worked in the same direction. The multiplication of forts was helping to make war on land resemble the new war at sea. A fort was a kind of stationary battleship. Unlike the old fortified castles, which had provided residences and headquarters of civil government for princes and lesser lords, the new forts were built, like ships of the line, exclusively for military purposes. The expenditure on them, unlike that on fortified castles during the Middle Ages and the Renaissance, was almost entirely for defense. The correspondence of the French *controleur-générale*, or minister of finance, with the *intendants*, who governed the provinces for the crown, is full of references to the great cost of preparing for war. "The navy and the fortifications" are invariably classed together as the chief items of expense.[7] Both imposed annually an enormous and an increasing burden on the financial resources of the kingdom.

European kings and princes appointed officials to manage the construction of fortifications on behalf of the state. These officials in turn negotiated with various entrepreneurs, or contractors, who undertook to carry the plans of the central government into effect and to find the necessary labor and materials. It was no longer possible, as it had been in the Middle Ages, for the defenders of a fortified place to vanquish the attackers by pouring scalding water on them, as they surged toward the steep thick walls. With the increasingly perfunctory hand-to-hand defense of strong places, the hope of holding a fort for even a short time depended upon a murderous fire of guns. Pressure to increase the number of cannon of various dimensions came from the builders of forts almost as much as from the builders of men-of-war and armed merchantmen. By immobilizing an increasing proportion of the heavy guns made in Western Europe, fortress building — described later by a French officer, the Comte de Guibert, as "the mania" of the age [8]— added greatly to the cost of war.

The expenses of providing the soldiers with food, clothing, and shelter, including sometimes beds and bedding,[9] as well as with munitions, and of providing the cavalry and artillery with horses, fell increasingly upon the central administration of the principal European states. Standing armies were more orderly and less mobile than the armies which had fought all over Europe during the sixteenth and early seventeenth centuries. As the concentrations of troops increased, it became more and more difficult for the soldiers to live off the country. Even before 1640, mules with wicker panniers and wagons drawn by four horses were sometimes provided on the Continent to carry a three-day supply of bread for the army.[10] As time went on supplies were increased, and in the early eighteenth century armies on campaign often had supplies for eighteen days. The uniforms and baggage of the officers, and the equipment of the privates, also grew more complicated. Officers frequently carried the luxury and splendor and the amusements cultivated at the courts of Europe along with them on their campaigns. Carts loaded with materials to improvise balls and festivals, like the one held during the siege of Pizzighetone, lumbered along the muddy roads and paths, beside clumsy gun carriages and wagons of ammunition, drawn by long teams of toiling horses. Monkeys and parrots peered out of their cages, and parrots called to the privates as they moved about the encampments where the trains settled down for weeks and even for months.

The troops of all the European nations were put into uniform. Blouses, coats, trousers, and often shoes as well, were manufactured for the central government according to specifications drawn up by officials and were distributed to tens of thousands of recruits. As armies on campaign remained for an increasing length of time waiting about, huts replaced tents as shelter for the soldiers as well as for the officers.[11] At home, with the rise of standing armies, extensive barracks were erected for the first time; they sometimes formed small towns of their own. Like the inhabitants of towns and the sailors on warships, the inmates of these cantonments had to be fed. Supplies of grain, flour, and bread, beer, wine, or cider, together with some fish or meat, were furnished increasingly under the direction of the state administration by traders and porters who looked to the officials for their profits and wages. Elaborate plans had to be made and carried out for distributing supplies to shipyards, fortresses, and barracks. Capital had to be provided for a great variety of enterprises, large and small, industrial, commercial, and financial.

As standing armies came into being, economic organization assumed in connection with military life an importance that was novel in history. In France the earliest important artillery school was established at Douai in 1679.[12] For the first time the organization of such special schools and of regular medical and religious corps, corps of engineers, and the provision of academies for military exercises were regarded as a necessary part of the preparations for warfare. The building and the operation of these schools and academies added to the capital expended upon military preparations which required a knowledge of economics and a gift for administration rather than military virtues on the field of battle. The center of military responsibility tended to shift from the general to the administrator.

The hundred years preceding the War of the Austrian Succession were years of such extraordinary expansion in the supply services for the armed forces that the period provides a valuable testing ground for the thesis that war has been a leading cause for the rise of industrial civilization. An age when wars draw "less blood" and spend "more money" is the kind of age in which their "constructive" influences might be expected to predominate.

In what manner and to what extent was the new limited warfare

determining the forms of economic enterprise and the general directions taken by European economic development down to about 1740?
What influence had this warfare and the preparation for it upon the
social and political position of the wage earner and of the private
economic adventurer whose passport was his capital? What influence
upon the material prosperity of Europe?

Recruiting men for the armed services has never been a wholesome
occupation. During the late seventeenth and early eighteenth centuries
the old methods of buying and selling the services of soldiers and sailors
persisted. But the system proved inadequate to fill the ranks of the
larger standing armies or to man the ships of the expanding navies.
The price which princes were able and willing to pay was too little to
bring into service enough men. Furthermore patriotic appeals which
went back at least to the time of Machiavelli (who had advocated for
Italy a standing army of native soldiers, with the men trained on
Sundays and holidays) made an increasing impression upon sovereigns
and their ministers during the seventeenth century, and this led some
of them to seek foreign mercenaries only when they could not raise
sufficient forces by other means than money. In consequence all the
states of Europe resorted increasingly to various forms of compulsion.
But only in Prussia was an approach made before the French Revolution to the general conscription of able-bodied males. There the system of conscription was inaugurated early in the eighteenth century
by Frederick William I, the father of Frederick the Great.[13] The more
usual method, which was adopted in France, was to call on each district throughout the kingdom to supply a specified number of men.
Sometimes, as in recruiting for the English and French navies, a hit or
miss procedure was adopted of gathering sailors in the port towns
from among the keelmen, lightermen, and porters, or from among the
seamen serving on commercial vessels.

Whatever the means, the only way of getting many of the privates
and noncommissioned officers into the fighting services, or of keeping
them there, was by ruse or by main force.[14] The French recruiting
agents got young men drunk and had them sign papers of enrollment,
or they picked on men in misery who, ruined sometimes by heavy
taxes, had the alternative of serving or starving. The recruiters also
resorted to threats and physical violence. In 1668 an Englishman engaged in observing the press of seamen in France to man new frigates
(war vessels next in size to the ships of the line) wrote that the poor
men "frequently run away after being pressed, although the King has
passed a severe law against it." These Frenchmen tried to escape the
press by taking passage as seamen aboard English merchant ships. At

about the same time the English were equally hard put to find sailors for their navy. One official wrote that the seamen on warships have "been so cheated of their pay . . . that thousands . . . are resolved rather to be torn to pieces than serve again." [15]

The idea that there is a kind of heroic virtue about participating in a large-scale massacre was imperfectly developed. Modern means — big print, photography, the radio — for driving such a notion into the tissues of the population were lacking. Anesthetics as administered to prospective fighters in the twentieth century by popular singers, newspaper columnists, wives, fiancées, and mothers were unknown to our backward ancestors. Almost the only anesthetic was the club. If, as frequently happened, poor, unsuspecting creatures were knocked senseless near the wharves and dragged into service on men-of-war, all their needs had to be provided for.[16] Unlike the earlier mercenary soldiers, these recruits could not be expected to bring with them much equipment beyond the tattered clothes in which they were waylaid. A French official memoir of 1673, containing instructions for outfitting soldiers who were to be sent in ships to the Levant, specified that each man should receive at the time of enlistment a *justaucorps* (a close-fitting body garment descending to the knees), stockings, a hat, shoes, two shirts, two ties, and a comb.[17]

The rise of standing armies stimulated the manufacture of clothing in standard patterns and colors and in several standard sizes. As muskets generally replaced the clumsy arquebuses, which had varied in their bores, and as every species of ammunition came to be supplied from state arsenals and magazines, a premium was put on making many pieces with a standard bore. When this was done, all the musketeers could serve themselves with standard missiles. The replacement of the pike by the bayonet was a further stimulus to the standardization of weapons, because these daggers had to be attached to the muskets. If each manufacturer made firearms according to his fancy, the problem of fitting the bayonets onto them was greatly complicated. The standardization of one part of a weapon encouraged uniformity in other parts which had to fit it.

Standardization has promoted large-scale production and sales in large lots. As Sombart and others have suggested, standardization has contributed in these ways to the rise of industrial civilization. Yet standardization by itself would hardly have led to industrialism. Standardized products became an important part of economic life in the early Roman Empire without producing an industrial civilization comparable to that which in recent times has taken possession of Europe, America, and most of the world.

The changes which occurred in the nature and strategy of warfare were working in other ways besides standardization toward the concentration of industry, trade, and finance. The growth in the relative importance of naval warfare reduced the number of centers for producing munitions, because these could now be manufactured most effectively close to the chief shipyards. The gradual shift in military strategy on land from wars of movement to wars of position, with more numerous forts, permitted increasing centralization of all supplies. The forts and newly built barracks for soldiers kept the more numerous troops in a relatively small number of places. The cautious wars of position made it less dangerous for rulers, lay and ecclesiastical, to concentrate their stocks of saltpeter, gunpowder, cannon, and small arms, and thus to risk the capture of large stores at a single stroke.

Beginning at least as early as the 1660's and 1670's when Colbert's influence predominated in the economic policies of the French crown, large-scale industrial enterprise made much headway in response to the new demands for supplying the armed forces. As part of a general scheme for state participation in economic development, the crown encouraged the expansion of shipyards and arsenals and the establishment of new and larger armament manufactures, by loans without interest, grants of land, and various other favors. In order to build, arm, and launch the scores of war vessels — ships of the line, frigates, and smaller boats — it was necessary to assemble large quantities of naval stores, from ship timber to bronze, iron, and brass cannon and heavy anchors. The naval yards were expanded; the officials claimed further acres of ground in the leading ports; large storehouses, a hundred and fifty feet or so in length, were put up to hold the materials; new workshops were erected along with homes for the workmen; cranes and other machinery were installed for lifting the timbers and the guns into place. In France the largest of the naval arsenals developed under Colbert's direction from 1659 to 1683 were apparently those at Toulon, Rochefort, and Brest.[18] English visitors were struck by the extraordinary activity in these yards, indicative of the intention of the French to become as powerful at sea as the Dutch or the English. As developed under Colbert, the great Rochefort naval base, with its workshops and auxiliary buildings for naval stores, resembled in extent the ancient arsenal at Venice which had attracted the attention of most travelers since the time of Dante. The English naval arsenals at Deptford, Woolwich, Chatham, and Portsmouth were hardly less impressive than the French. While the number of workers employed in each of them varied according to the demand for new warships, there were frequently many scores. In 1670, for example, 797 workmen were required at the four chief English naval yards.[19]

Louis XIV's repeated military adventures were accompanied by a movement towards the concentration of the saltpeter and especially of the gunpowder manufactures. During the later seventeenth century and at the beginning of the eighteenth considerable establishments, some of which formed part of expanding military arsenals, were replacing the older scattered domestic workshops in France as the principal sources for the supply of ammunition for both the army and the navy. The standard book of the age on artillery was the work of a Frenchman, Surirey de Saint Rémy (1650–1716), with a long record of service under the *grand-maître de l'artillerie*, who coördinated the French munition manufacture and supply. Saint Rémy's book first appeared in 1697; a second edition was published in 1707. As corrected and amplified, his *Mémoires d'artillerie* provided the principal guide in connection with the manufacture of munitions in France and even in other countries, at least until the mid-eighteenth century. A third enlarged French edition was published in 1745, four years after another version of the book had appeared at The Hague. Saint Rémy described the saltpeter manufacture established under Louis XIV at the arsenal in Paris as a vast workshop built upon pillars in the form of a long hall, containing 126 tubs for mixing the ingredients. For heating the mixtures there were many copper boilers, each built upon a brick furnace, so that it was possible to keep the saltpeter mixture from the tubs continually cooking.[20]

Documents in the archives of the modern French department of Aisne refer to considerable gunpowder mills, also developed in the reign of Louis XIV, at La Fère near Laon in Picardy. The wooden buildings were burned down several times, apparently by accidental fires, only to be rebuilt and enlarged. Like the earlier English gunpowder mills of the Evelyn family near London, the enterprise at La Fère was an approach to the factory. Before the mid-eighteenth century such enterprises, rare in the French gunpowder manufacture at the accession of Louis XIV in 1643, seem to have become the rule. In the third edition of Saint Rémy's book, there is a series of tables concerning the distribution of the gunpowder-making industry up to 1744. The tables indicate that, before the death of Louis XIV in 1715, several French gunpowder mills were larger than the mill at La Fère. One of these was just south of Paris at Essonnes, long a center for the manufacture of paper; others were at Limoges, Saint Jean d'Angély, Marseille, Rouen, Saint Omer, Douai, Valenciennes, and Verdun.[21]

The French crown took an active part in developing gunmaking shops and larger cannon foundries at new places, particularly in regions near the northeastern frontiers of France, which were pushed farther by the French conquests and which were made less dangerous by the decline in the power of Spain and of the Holy Roman Empire. The manufacture of muskets and other small firearms was coming to be concentrated not only in the ancient armament center of Saint-Etienne and in Nivernais, but also in the environs of Charleville on the Meuse, in territory which had not been part of France during the Thirty Years' War. Saint Rémy referred to a notable factory for making firearms at Nozon, a suburb of Charleville.[22] Cannon manufacturing was pushed still farther east, in order to produce the heavy pieces, so difficult to move, as near as possible to the enemy. A French foundry was started at Breisach, on the east bank of the Rhine, as we learn from a letter addressed to Saint Rémy by a French royal engineer, named Guillan, in 1702. Guillan had been ordered to destroy the foundry because Louis XIV had just ceded the town of Breisach to the Hapsburg emperor, Leopold I. Before carrying out the king's orders, Guillan transmitted to Saint Rémy the plans and dimensions of the foundry, together with a description of the machinery, tools, and accessories.[23]

Considerable enterprises were established also by the French crown for the manufacture of army uniforms. One of these was at Clermont l'Herault, in Languedoc; the old buildings of this "royal manufacture" still stand, with the king's arms in stone above the entrance gate. Many scores of textile workers were maintained within a large walled enclosure. Most of the workers and their families performed their labor in the small insanitary rooms where they lived. Here was a combination of age-old domestic work with the concentration and some of the discipline of the factory.

Similar developments were taking place in the rest of Europe under the exigencies of war orders. French ways commanded increasing prestige and influence throughout the Continent. The privileges granted in France to manufacturers of munitions, and the methods of organizing the building of barracks and arsenals and of supplying the armies, served as models for many princes, and particularly for Frederick William I. With his large standing army, the military requirements of Prussia played an even more important part in shaping Prussian economic development than the military requirements of France played in shaping French.

The rise of standing armies contributed to the divorce between gainful labor and family life which is a feature of the modern economic order. In the mercenary armies of the sixteenth and early seventeenth centuries, it was the practice for wives and grown daughters to go along on the campaigns to care for their men. The dangerous construction work of digging trenches, throwing up earthworks, breaking paths for the artillery and the infantry had been assigned to poor local peasants. They were forced to assist armies on campaigns and in battles, often at the behest of their bishops and lesser priests who, in France, were required by the king to furnish contingents of these pioneers.[24] But during the age of limited warfare the work done earlier by womenfolk, other camp followers, and impressed local peasants was taken over increasingly by the commissariat, the medical corps, and by combat troops who were expected to serve the expanding corps of engineers. In France, Henry IV had introduced the principle that all military labor, including that of sappers and builders of fortifications, should be performed by actual soldiers. By the beginning of the eighteenth century such a policy was widely applied in the European armies.[25] As these were now becoming large self-contained communities with a continuous existence, the soldiers were separated more and more from the life of the ordinary communities — villages, towns, gilds, parishes, mining centers — which had received from and contributed to the main streams of European culture and civilization from time immemorial.

The soldier or sailor, whether pressed into the army or navy by widely employed deceitful and brutal methods or enticed to serve by promises of good pay, was separated from his family (although when compulsion was practiced young unmarried men were generally taken first). Neither the life in barracks nor the military drill developed ruthlessly in Prussia in the eighteenth century was consistent with the performance of family obligations. New kinds of brutality developed which are characteristic of men separated from their women. Unlike the priest, the soldier or sailor is without duties which enable him to participate in the constructive lives of others. Unlike the monk, he has no divine object of devotion and contemplation; his calling provides no ultimate hope. A species of boredom, rare in early Western European history, became common among soldiers and sailors.

Under the stress of battle, military discipline calls for the highest courage, the greatest willingness to suffer. It also calls for considerable initiative even from the private. But military discipline cannot fill the gaps in existence to which the soldier in a standing army has always been condemned, particularly in periods like the late seventeenth and early eighteenth centuries when there was so much "standing." Such ordinary daily work as was required on the parade grounds, in the ports, and on the warships was for the most part tiresome and mentally debilitating. Except for the calls on the soldier, and occasionally on the sailor, to labor in building harbors, fortifications, barracks, piers, breakwaters, and in some exceptional instances canals and aqueducts,[26] few of the tasks assigned by the army or navy offered the constructive opportunities provided by industry, transportation, and commerce, as well as by farming — still the foremost occupation of the Europeans. The new cantonments were breeding grounds for the unresourceful and irresponsible character of many elements in modern industrial society.

In contrast to the lives of the privates in the early standing armies, the lives of industrial adventurers, traders, financiers — who owed their careers partly or wholly to the new war orders — were often busy, varied, and exciting, even though their risks were heavy. If we are to understand the influence of military preparation and limited war upon the economic, social, and political position of the mercantile classes in Europe, we must recognize how little prestige had been attached to their callings and how little political influence such persons had had during the period of the religious wars, except in Holland and England. While a few merchants serving the sovereigns of France and other continental countries were encouraged by special favors not accorded merchants in England, the English merchants gained during the seventeenth century a much more important privilege: actual power through their influence in the House of Commons over the expenditures and policies of the central government. In the 1630's, with the outcome of the struggle between crown and Parliament uncertain and with Charles I trying to govern without Parliament, Thomas Mun, the wealthy English trader, wrote with concern over the lack of encouragement then received by the merchants in England. At the same time he spoke more than once of the "nobleness" of the private merchant's profession.[27] When comparisons were made, the lack of all "nobility" in this profession as practiced in contemporary France was the striking result. Commerce as such was hardly regarded as an honorable occupation. Mercantile pursuits were valued chiefly as a means of making money with which to buy an official position in the rapidly expanding royal service. When a merchant purchased a place in this service, he became part of a great political construction which covered an ever larger proportion of the national economic life and stretched in an orderly logical array — with officials and subsidiary officials, administrative, legislative, judicial — from the Louvre in Paris to the smallest hamlet in remote provinces such as Languedoc or Dauphiné. But the former merchant was no longer able legally to carry on any business save that of the state.

Early in the seventeenth century the lack of respect for the calling of the merchant began to concern a few Frenchmen, who felt that this constituted a danger to the national welfare. Frenchmen with talent, it was said, were either kept out of economic enterprise altogether or were drawn away from it early in adult life. Cardinal Richelieu was disturbed by this, as his *Testament Politique* shows. He died in 1642 without having effected much improvement in the position of the merchant. Another cleric, Jean Eon, who remains as obscure as Richelieu is famous, suggested in 1646 that the crown create for merchants a new rank, apparently in addition to the old nobility, the *noblesse d'épée*, and the new and les r nobility of officials, the *noblesse de robe*.[28] Eon proposed that the new rank should be called the *noblesse commercante*. The book, *Le Commerce honorable*, in which he set forth his ideas, had little sale. But his ideas, like Richelieu's on the same subject, became influential during and after the sixties and seventies, when Colbert was Louis XIV's principal minister.

If the merchant was without honor in early seventeenth-century France, this was partly because the economic adventurer — especially when the crown had not granted him a special commission of some kind and special privileges — was hedged in by ever tighter rules and regulations. These were enacted and enforced on behalf of the monarch, the municipalities, the gilds, and also on behalf of protected economic groups such as the gentlemen glaziers, who monopolized glassmaking in many provinces.

In no civilized society has the economic adventurer ever had complete freedom from all regulation by political authority. "Perfect" competition is a figment of the world created by the modern economists to enable them to treat economics as a science. In no civilized society has the sovereign authority ever eliminated private initiative altogether. "Perfect socialism" is a figment of another world which proved far more real than that of the economists, because some of its communist sponsors gained political power more absolute than that which a good classical economist wished any man or group of men to exercise.

During the sixteenth and early seventeenth centuries, the sovereign states of Europe, with the important exceptions of Holland and England and to a lesser extent Sweden and Scotland, had moved in the direction of greater control and regulation under the authority of a prince. Before the accession of the five-year-old Louis XIV in May 1643, the French crown had insinuated officials of its choosing into the municipal governments and even the gilds. The gilds were part of the

machinery of town government, because they were normally represented in municipal governing bodies. Once the crown got control
of political authority in a town, it got control over the local gilds. By
legislative enactments, the crown laid down detailed stipulations governing the manufacture of cloth, dyeing materials, iron, soap, and beer.
The gilds were used as instruments for enforcing these regulations,
some of which were designed to safeguard the quality of the products.
In most country districts it was indispensable for adventurers to apply
to the local crown officials for a royal privilege, conceding them the
right to start an industrial enterprise such as a forge for making iron.
The increase in the general powers of the national government, together with its expanding economic regulations and its expanding system of granting privileges, gave the king a more or less extensive supervision over rich industrial enterprises such as mines, furnaces and
forges, large workshops, and manufactures in which the adventurers
put out large quantities of materials and partly finished products to be
labored upon in the domestic precincts of the workers. Artists, craftsmen, and inventors, together with economic adventurers and wage
hands, were in varying degrees dependent for guidance and success
upon the king, his councillors, and other royal officials.[29] By the middle
of the seventeenth century little leeway was left in France, or in most
countries of continental Europe, for further encroachments upon private initiative.

Were the hundred years following the accession of Louis XIV an
age of increasing encroachments upon private initiative in economic
matters, as is the prevailing opinion among historians? I doubt it. The
period should still be regarded as one of increasing interference with
the movement of goods across international frontiers. But, within each
country, as time went on, the tendency was to allow the private adventurer somewhat greater independence than he had previously
possessed in making economic decisions.

These changes in policy were gradual. They are difficult to recognize because there was a sense in which the government of France —
and of other continental states that followed France — was extending
state tutelage farther than ever, particularly over industry. The gild
regulations increased. General codes regulating manufacturing multiplied. Colbert and his immediate successors set about to make the
crown responsible directly or indirectly for the licensing of all new
ventures. The practice of granting privileges to particular industrial
enterpreneurs, begun during the century preceding Louis XIV's accession, was greatly extended as the number of rich industrial ventures
grew. The charmed circle of royal and privileged enterprises, heavily

dependent upon royal favor for success, eventually comprised a considerable proportion of all the mines and manufactures of the kingdom, perhaps a third or even more.

Two things have not been adequately understood about the system frequently associated with Colbert, though it seems to have originated less in his mind than a generation earlier in the mind of Richelieu,[30] and though it had been in the making at least since the reign of Louis XI in the late fifteenth century. First, within the system, economic adventurers gained more freedom than they had been ordinarily allowed before the time of Richelieu. Colbert was well aware of the advantages of independent action by men of business. He was himself the son of a draper in the town of Reims and had risen from the very class whose low estate had aroused the concern of Richelieu and Eon. Like them, he wanted to improve the merchant's status. In his own political testament Colbert recommended that Louis XIV provide "a place apart" for merchants — who were then simple members of the third estate without any royal mark of distinction — and another for husbandmen, because of the usefulness of both occupations in maintaining the national economy in peace and war. Colbert objected to the requirements of the French towns which made it necessary for a prospective merchant to serve an apprenticeship, like a common workman. This rule kept able men out of trade, he pointed out, and he suggested that the king issue a royal ordonnance abrogating it.[31] He also wrote earlier of the importance of giving merchants free rein for their private initiative. He was far less disposed than most modern students of seventeenth-century economic history have represented him as being to control the decisions of those merchants who accepted the general regulations which the state imposed upon industry, trade, and finance.

Second, the mercantile system of regulation itself, as it developed in Colbert's time and during the two generations following his death, actually constituted a step toward granting merchants the political recognition, the rank, which Eon had insisted they so badly needed. No commercial nobility was created. But the merchants and officials who worked within the system sponsored and encouraged by the state were given advantages of various kinds, including immunities from some of the regulations and burdens, notable among which was their exemption from the increasingly onerous direct taxes levied by the crown. The more the crown interfered with business, the more it went in for business on its own account, the more it had to find persons gifted with business skill whom it could entrust with its authority. Under Colbert the private capitalists who came within the widening area of royal and privileged manufactures, and who served the vastly extended interests of the state in commerce and finance, actually had more initiative, they enjoyed more prestige, they were given more royal favors, than had been allotted the mercantile classes in most continental states during the age of the religious wars. As the sphere of government control was extended, the rigor of government interference was relaxed. So far as economic enterprise is concerned, France became more of an absolutism but less of a despotism during the long reign of Louis XIV.

Merchants were a more essential part of the system of government than in earlier times. While French merchants had no direct power over policy, their advice was sought by the leading French royal officials. Their collaboration became a vital necessity when, as frequently happened especially in distant provinces and overseas in the French colonial empire, the principal royal officials were corrupt, were out to make their fortunes at the expense of their royal masters. As their mercantile functions grew, the merchants acquired more respectable social positions under the *ancien régime* than their predecessors had enjoyed. Notwithstanding their father's humble origin, Colbert's beautiful daughters married two of the most distinguished noblemen of the kingdom, the duc de Chevreuse and the duc de Beauvillier. During the financial crisis of the War of the Spanish Succession, Samuel Bernard (1651–1739), the banker, relieved the crown of a part of its burdens by accepting bankruptcy on its behalf. He demonstrated how profitable to private fortune public ignominy could be, for he left thirty-three millions at his death, after he had lived to see his sons installed in two of the most honorable political positions in the royal service and his daughter married to a member of the Molé family who occupied an equally honorable office.[32]

Samuel Bernard's career under the most powerful of the Bourbon kings suggests how the mercantile class in France had gained in security since the Renaissance. The contrast between the felicity of Bernard and the disgrace under Charles VII (1422–1461) of Jacques Coeur, the richest and most famous French merchant of that earlier age, can be explained partly by remarkable changes in the direction of more humane and tender manners. But the growing respect in which merchants were held at court by the principal ministers under Louis XIV, also helps to account for the contrast. It was enough for the Bourbons to use Bernard as a front to help the state out of its financial difficulties, while allowing him his private rewards. Charles VII, whom Jeanne d'Arc defended, ruined Coeur. That great merchant's wealth and influence reached its zenith early in 1451. Yet at the end of July, only a few days after the king had accorded Coeur a new mark of royal favor, he signed an order for his arrest on the flimsiest of pretexts. A year and a half earlier Charles's mistress, Agnès Sorel, had died of an illness which came on suddenly following childbirth. Suspicion first centered on the dauphin, the future Louis XI. But Coeur was imprisoned on the preposterous charge that he had murdered Agnès Sorel. There was no evidence to sustain the charge, which was eventually dropped. In the meantime charges of various financial machinations were brought against the merchant. The real trouble seems to have been that the court was heavily in his debt. He was the creditor of many courtiers and of the king himself, whom he had supplied with money to buy back the crown jewels that the royal lover had lavished on Agnès Sorel. The enemies that Coeur's own good fortune had made him were sufficient to condemn him. In 1453 the king seized his vast properties, including mines of copper, lead, and silver in Lyonnais and Beaujolais. Other property was sold at public auction, and Coeur was forced to flee the country; he died in 1456 on the famous old Greek island of Chios.[33] His calling afforded him no protection against injustice and intrigue. If Samuel Bernard had had equally powerful enemies they could hardly have ruined him without much stronger evidence against him than sufficed to condemn Coeur.

With some modifications, the mercantilist system of the French state, as developed two hundred years after the time of Jacques Coeur, was widely followed on the Continent, in the small states of Italy and central Europe — above all in Prussia, which raised itself to a kingdom in 1701. In those countries, as well as in France, the system tended to give merchants better positions than they had had during the sixteenth and early seventeenth centuries, except in Great Britain and Holland. The Prussian merchants of the early eighteenth century were permitted to purchase exemption from the almost universal military service introduced by Frederick William I. The military value given to their profession seems to have strengthened their social and political status, which had suffered in the economic collapse that the Thirty Years' War had helped to produce.

Compared with the private capitalist of the nineteenth century, the most favored traders of early eighteenth-century France and Prussia were entangled in a host of restrictions. No serious effort was made in France to repeal any of them until the 1720's, a decade after the long wars of Louis XIV's reign had ended. Moreover, the limited freedom which the privileged adventurers were allowed was at the pleasure of the sovereign and of the officials to whom the sovereign entrusted economic authority. If a minister like Colbert's successor

Louvois or a monarch like Frederick William I chose to deny the adventurer the increased initiative which Richelieu and Colbert had advocated for him, he had no appeal under the natural or the divine law, both of which were still considered binding on the sovereign in French seventeenth-century political thought. A merchant or financier could hardly appeal effectively in his own support to customary law, for that had been less adaptable to economic change than the English common law, and economic change itself had exerted less pressure upon law in France than in England, mainly perhaps because there had been less economic change from 1540 to 1640. Unlike the English or the Dutch adventurer, who was represented in assemblies which were coming to share political authority with the sovereign rulers, the French, German, Spanish, or Italian adventurer could find no effective legal support for exercising his initiative.

With these qualifications, the position of the mercantile classes improved after about 1660 in France and in most continental states, and the initiative which the mere possession of capital carried with it increased. How far should we attribute these changes to military needs and to the wars without which the military needs would have been much lighter?

The growth in the size of the armed forces and the much greater growth in the supply services partly explain the extension of state authority over economic enterprise on the Continent. As the sovereign became more responsible for naval yards and arsenals, gunpowder mills and cannon manufactures, for fortifications, for the purchase of food and fuel to sustain the troops, for horses to mount the cavalry and drag the artillery, and for the distribution of all military supplies, kings and their ministers found it increasingly necessary, as we have seen, to delegate their responsibilities. The persons best fitted to exercise administrative authority in matters of military supplies, to advise the government concerning the means of raising the funds to maintain the large armaments, and to lend money for war purposes were industrialists, traders, and financiers. During the 1660's and 1670's, when France was frequently at war with Holland, Dutch merchants showed far more skill than the French in providing military supplies, at a time when an efficient supply service was more essential in war than ever before. Since the Dutch merchant had more freedom than the French and, like the English, had attained a higher social status, French statesmen were naturally drawn by military experience to emulate the Dutch in their policies towards the mercantile class.

One thing which made it feasible to grant French traders and financiers increasing freedom of action was the growing moderation of war in Western Europe. While military requirements helped to make France more of a political absolutism, the restraints on war and the desire for peace helped to make it less of a political despotism.

The initiative of private merchants and bankers increased much more strikingly during the twenty-five years after 1713, when the French armed forces were reduced and when the rapidly expanding Prussian army was not called upon to fight, than during the long European wars of the Dutch Alliance and the Spanish Succession, which had kept armies and navies active almost continuously for some twenty-five years before the Peace of Utrecht. The combination of expanding military supplies with limitations upon their use in war was at the root of the improvement in the social position of the mercantile classes on the Continent. Preparations for war, without the damage done by heavy wars, can be represented as contributing to progress in the direction of industrial civilization.

What needs to be recognized is that the progress toward industrial civilization was not great in Europe during the hundred years from 1640 to 1740, especially during the period before 1713, when the economic burdens of war were especially heavy in France and even in England. If attention is focused upon the stimuli which the new war orders provided for the standardization of products, for the growth in the scale of economic enterprise, for the breakup of family life and the cleavage between capital and labor, there is a danger of exaggerating the contribution made by limited warfare, with its larger navies and its big standing armies, to the rise of industrial civilization. Deeper knowledge of economic history provides an antidote. A movement towards the standardization of building materials for churches and other religious edifices goes back in Western history at least to the fourteenth century. In Chapter IV it has been shown how far the concentration of industrial enterprise in large business units had gone especially in England before the mid-seventeenth century, mainly as a result of peace. An increased demand for war supplies, caused by the rise of standing armies, was not indispensable for the further concentration which took place during the late seventeenth century. The private yards for building merchant vessels at Harwich and other English east-coast ports were probably as large as those for building warships, and there were times when the English naval yards had to depend for work upon the progress of the merchant marine. In 1671 William Hannam, master attendant at Woolwich, wrote to the navy commissioners, "I have known so little to do here that the docks were lent to owners to build and repair [merchant] ships." [34] Large enclosed industrial establishments with many buildings, of the kind founded at Clermont-l'Hérault for the manufacture of army uniforms, where the workers were subject to a factory discipline, were started without the stimulus of war orders. In the reign of Charles II (1660–1685), one of the largest belonged to a London ironmaster named Ambrose Crowley. Within a big enclosure which he built at Winlaton, south of the Tyne, and called a "parallelogram," all kinds of metalwares were produced for nonmilitary purposes. Crowley's regulations for his workpeople have been preserved in the form they were promulgated, in a big book, "The Law Book," confided to the British Museum.[35] There was an early curfew, after which all the inhabitants were bound to remain within the gates. Smoking was forbidden at all hours for men and women alike, although the practice had become common by the late seventeenth century even among women in the country districts of the west of England.[36]

For the large workshops which appeared in the French armament industries during the late seventeenth century there were precedents in France itself, where the progress of the artistic and luxury industries during the reigns of Henry IV (1589–1610) and Louis XIII (1610–1643) had created the types of establishments, under royal tutelage, which were later developed for the manufacture of munitions. Peace, even more than war, was the innovating force in the progress of large-scale manufacturing in France. The growth of the war industries under Louis XIV did not create a new form of industrial enterprise which could serve as a model for the development of manufactures to meet the needs of peaceful consumers. On the contrary, the model already existed. The growth of the war industries provided an alternative outlet for the investment of capital which otherwise would have gone into nonmilitary enterprises with large workshops of their own.

Nor was the rise of the new armed forces during the late seventeenth century the only cause for the segregation of the sexes in their *working* lives. As is shown in the next chapter, such a segregation had begun with the cleavage between capital and labor in mining and other heavy industries and in the transport services. This cleavage had already gone far in England by 1640, before the country became more heavily engaged in wars, and when the older custom of keeping wives and other female companions with the soldiers on campaigns was still prevalent. The separation of work from the home in industry and transport may possibly have provided a kind of precedent for the segregation of men from their women in the armies. In any event the split between employment and family relations both in military and industrial occupations resulted mainly from the historical forces of expansion and individualism which were expressed in all sides of the life and thought of the European peoples.

It is not apparent that war and military preparations were adding conspicuously to the material prosperity of Europe or even to that of particular countries. When, after 1640, England became more heavily engaged in wars, there was a notable slackening in the rate of industrial and commercial growth. This slowing down in the pace of economic progress was reflected even in the coal trade, in spite of the continued substitution of coal for firewood and charcoal in many industries, as well as in domestic heating and cooking. During the seventy-five years from 1550 to 1625 the coal shipments coastwise from the north of England had increased some tenfold or more. During the seventy-five years from 1635 to 1710, when England was engaged much more often in sea warfare, they hardly increased 50 per cent.[37] The difference cannot be explained mainly in terms of political history. But the wars of the second seventy-five-year period undoubtedly held back the growth of shipping.[38] The more frequent naval engagements of the states of northern Europe after the middle of the seventeenth century, partly explain why Great Britain, Holland, and Sweden failed to increase notably the leadership in the development of heavy industry which they had gained over the rest of Europe in the late sixteenth and early seventeenth centuries.

The efforts of Charles XII of Sweden (1682–1718) to become a great conqueror at the expense of Russia led in eastern Europe to the only relentless war of the age of limited warfare. This war was also the most disastrous economically, at ·any rate so far as Sweden was concerned. Montesquieu wisely said of Charles XII that he misunderstood his own military genius and that of his country and tried to become a modern Alexander when he was qualified by his gifts to be only the first soldier in the armies Alexander commanded. Charles XII's orders to employ the restricted Swedish military resources against the unfathomable defenses of Peter the Great were of economic benefit only to Holland, England, and Denmark. As the astute Savary des Bruslons pointed out, shortly after the war had ended, all three countries increased their trade with Russia at the expense of Sweden.[39]

Even in the 1630's the social and political power which the private capitalist exercised through his interest in agriculture, industry, trade, or finance was much more pronounced in Great Britain than it had become in most continental countries sixty years later. At the beginning of the eighteenth century John Law, the Scottish economic adventurer who tried to help the French to become as economically progressive as the British and the Dutch, addressed many papers to the leading royal officials explaining how far France was behind Great Britain and Holland in her economic practices, particularly in the use of credit. If war had been the chief cause for economic progress in early modern times, France might have been expected to be far ahead of England. France had had war almost continuously for two hundred years. After the close of the worst phases of the wars of religion in 1589, the battles had been mainly what the proponents of war as the handmaid of progress would regard as the right kind, the kind you either win or at least do not allow the extensive invasion of your country. France had been little invaded. She had extended her frontiers. Roussillon, Franche-Comté, Alsace, and large parts of Flanders had been added — or according to the French view, "reunited" — to the crown. In Europe, Louis XIV, at the end of his reign in 1715, ruled over at least twenty million subjects, compared with some fourteen or fifteen millions at his accession in 1643. Overseas the claims of the French crown had been pushed with much success both in India and America. For two generations, until the defeat of French colonial armies in the Seven Years' War of 1756 to 1763, the French colonial empire rivaled the British.

During the seventeenth century in France and throughout continental Europe, the spread of polite manners was accompanied by a notable increase in the demand for luxury wares — the products of artistic craftsmanship — and by increases in the demand for articles of comfort and convenience. The growth in the production of luxuries often led to a concentration of capital in new and larger enterprises.. Like the demand for comforts in Elizabethan England, the demand for luxuries in France was promoted by spells of peace and interfered with by spells of war.

Some of the chief enterprises started with the support of the crown at the time when Colbert was active expanded into large workshops or factories only in the early eighteenth century, after the strains imposed on the national economy by the wars of Louis XIV were relaxed. The history of the Van Robais textile venture is a case in point. A family of Dutch origin, the Van Robais had been granted special privileges in 1665 to establish at Abbéville a new manufacture of fine cloth, of a texture made earlier in Holland, Spain, and England. The venture was a large one. Before the end of the seventeenth century, the Van Robais employed some fifteen hundred workers, about half of them women and girls who spun yarn in their off-time from domestic cares. Most of the work was done under the putting-out system, which had been common in clothmaking in medieval Europe and which had developed extensively in England during the early "industrial revolution" from 1540 to 1640. Weaving, as well as spinning, was carried on in rooms or cellars scattered all through the town of Abbéville and in cottages along the rutty roads and cowpaths leading into it. Domestic work was the rule, with fathers, mothers, and children working side by side. Scouring, shearing, and fulling alone were concentrated in buildings erected by the adventurers. These buildings, with their equipment, were valued in 1690 at some 4500 *livres tournois*. Comparable concentrations of capital in the finishing processes of cloth-making had been fairly common in many parts of Europe at least as far back as the beginning of the sixteenth century. At Abbéville in 1690 there were, in addition, two other central buildings, both small. One was a brewery; in the other the soap needed for scouring the wool and the cloth was manufactured.

Not until the War of the Spanish Succession drew to a close was an attempt made to bring all the workpeople, except the spinners, into a central establishment. Between 1708 and 1714 some 150,000 *livres,* thirty times the value of the principal workhouses in 1690, were spent in erecting a new group of buildings, all in one place. Four additional houses were prepared for spinners in another part of town. The total cost of all the buildings and equipment is said to have exceeded 300,000 *livres.*[40] It is probable that the *livre* had at this time a considerably greater value (if such comparisons can be made at all) than the American dollar of 1950.

By bringing the laborers under their direct and continuous supervision, the Van Robais brothers aimed to deal more effectively with disciplinary problems, as well as to produce cloth more cheaply. During the period of new building the weavers had combined into a sort of labor union and had gone on strike. Disturbances continued, for the Van Robais attempted to subject all the workers to rules regulating their hours of labor and even small details of their working methods. Such regimentation had not been feasible when the work was done in private homes. It is not improbable that the labor troubles were intensified by these efforts to enforce factory discipline, which the great majority of the workers had escaped during the first forty years of the enterprise. The most serious strike broke out in 1716. Like the troubles that followed, it led the royal officials to intervene. As has often been the case in more recent economic history, labor troubles accompanied a great expansion in the market, in the returns from which the wage earners felt they should share. The Van Robais' pay rolls were swelled in the 1720's to three and possibly to five thousand persons. The majority were casual laborers, who also worked at husbandry in the Picardy countryside. By the thirties and forties, with a further expansion of the market and with rival adventurers knocking at the doors, the royal officials ceased to support the local monopoly which the crown had guaranteed the Van Robais ever since the establishment of their enterprise. Other considerable ventures were started.[41]

The history of this manufacture at Abbéville was typical of a general development of French industry in the early eighteenth century, especially remarkable in northern and northeastern France. During the twenty-five years following the death of Louis XIV, the concentration of capital and labor in large industrial establishments was perhaps as striking as during the entire seventy-two years of his reign. Labor troubles like those experienced by the Van Robais became frequent under Louis XV (1715–1774). They were indicative both of a new prosperity and of a growing cleavage between capital and labor, which accompanied the establishment of large new enterprises and the expansion of old ones.

Glass manufacturing provides another example of the rising tide of industrial output after the wars of Louis XIV. Apart from the works of the Royal Plate-Glass Company at Tourlaville, near Cherbourg, and at Saint-Gobain in Picardy, practically all the French glassmaking enterprises before 1700 were of an old type. Most of them were owned by actual working masters, known as gentlemen glassmakers because of the special privileges they claimed under ancient concessions from the crown. During the next forty years, and especially in the 1720's and 1730's, more than a score of glassmaking factories were built, comparable in their discipline to the earlier two at Tourlaville and Saint-Gobain, where the workers were under a control resembling that against which the employees of the Van Robais struck. By 1740 a large proportion of all the glassworkers labored as ordinary wage hands in considerable enterprises owned by private capitalists. Most of the new establishments were in the north and east of France.[42] All the factories of the new type for the manufacture of window glass were in Franche-Comté, Alsace, and Lorraine — in country which the armies of Louis XIV had been repeatedly sent out to conquer, to hold, and to use as bases for campaigns farther east. The decrease in fighting after 1713 provided an invitation to the sponsors of new glassworks in these regions, which were excellently situated for obtaining the necessary raw materials and for reaching rich markets.

In so far as political history is concerned, the respite from serious warfare rather than the continuance of war orders accounts for both the movement toward industrial concentration and the growing prosperity of French industry and trade during the decades following the treaties of Utrecht. After 1713 the French army was reduced considerably in number. A part of the burden imposed by war on the French economy was lifted. The markets for plate and window glass, and for the products of most of the other expanding industries — papermaking, lace and elegant cloth manufacturing of various kinds [43] — shrank in time of war and expanded in time of peace. Barracks were not yet supplied with glass windows! The markets for glass, for paper, for elegant textile wares were provided mainly by peaceful consumers, seeking luxuries and also, as time went on, comforts of the sort devised by English industry during the seventeenth century. For the French manufactures along the northeastern frontier, the foreign market to the east was of growing importance. Both this foreign market and the domestic market expanded because of the halt in the age-long struggle for the Rhineland, in which European manhood has been so often wasted. A measure of peace and of stable boundaries between sovereign states facilitated the movement of goods across frontiers. The growth of population and the slight reduction in the burden of taxation, both of which owed something to peace, increased the proportion of the French national income available for the purchase of luxuries and comforts which the new establishments supplied.

The regions between France and Germany — and along the frontiers of the two countries — were the richest in Europe in those industrial resources which provided the basis for modern industrial civilization. Belgium, northern France, Alsace, Lorraine, the valleys of the Meuse, Moselle, Rhine, and Ruhr generally, contained a large proportion of the coal and iron ore of Western Europe. These were regions of frequent fierce fighting; their political status was uncertain and continually changing. If they had possessed anything approaching the peace and political unity of Great Britain from the early sixteenth to the early eighteenth century, industrial development there might have been as remarkable as in Great Britain. In the late nineteenth century, even without political unity, these regions became the leading industrial area of Europe and for a time of the whole world under conditions of relatively free trade and of peace broken only by the Franco-Prussian War in 1870–71. With this historical picture before us, it is difficult to regard even limited warfare as a major force in preparing the way for modern industrial civilization.

If the constructive aspects of war stand out nearly as much as the destructive aspects in this particular age, it is mainly because there was, relatively speaking, so little destruction. The modern conception of putting a nation's economy entirely at the disposal of the war effort was alien to the mind of the age. On the contrary, every effort was made to let war interfere as little as possible with peaceful economic life.[44] These efforts were not always successful. In 1731 the village of Queyras complained to the *intendant* in Dauphiné that troops had been so wanton about destroying the forests that it was necessary to heat the local limekiln with coal.[45] But as the sovereign states of Europe assumed more responsibility for clothing, lodging, and feeding soldiers as well as sailors, lawless pillaging and plundering became less rampant. Moreover a larger proportion of the war effort of the European powers went into maneuvers and battles at sea and into the despatch and the maintenance of forces overseas in America, Africa, and India. On the sea there were no towns to sack, no mines, workshops, and factories to ruin, no trains of pack horses to commandeer, no farms to ravage, no forests to destroy. Overseas the expensive military expeditions ranged about the immense stretches of rich territory in the wilds of North America, mainly in Indian country. They did little direct damage to the budding economic enterprises along the Atlantic seaboard and no direct damage to the economic life of Europe.

The character of war preparations in Europe made war orders relatively stable. They fluctuated less violently than in the period of religious wars. With standing armies and growing navies, war orders became very much heavier in time of peace than ever before. The expansion of orders when actual fighting took place was not to be compared with that to which the large states of the twentieth century have grown accustomed. In consequence the changes from peace to war and back to peace did not disrupt the economic life of Europe as much as they had in the sixteenth and early seventeenth centuries or as they were to disrupt it in the twentieth century.

The constructive economic influences of military history were much more conspicuous, and the destructive influences much less, during the hundred years which began with the English Civil War than during those which began with the Reformation. Yet for an understanding of the eventual triumph of industrial civilization, the more important matter is not the growth and administration of large armies and navies, but rather the conditions which made for limited warfare, for a lessening of the tension between Europeans of different creeds and states, for a softening of harsh manners.

A delicate balance was being established in Europe. This was by no means, as historians have frequently assumed, simply a balance of political power, which made it impracticable for any state to obtain hegemony over all the others. It was also an economic and a cultural balance. The passions and hatreds of men, their love of power, were kept from preponderating, partly by a scarcity of the labor and other economic resources which it was now necessary to command in order to fight a decisive war; partly by improvements in manners, resulting from a growing sense of the common humanity of members of all creeds and nations; partly by a reaffirmation of the earlier restraints imposed on war by the fear of evil and the love of beauty. National policies were increasingly affected by an intense pan-European desire to cultivate the human virtues — intellectual, moral, and aesthetic — as part of daily life and work.

CHAPTER THIRTEEN

Economic Progress and War

· DURING THE LATE SEVENTEENTH AND EARLY EIGHTEENTH CENTURIES the course of economic development imposed brakes upon war for at least three reasons. It tended to discredit the military calling as led by the rank and file. It was not sufficiently rapid to provide the means for wars without stint. It encouraged producers of many objects, including weapons, to retain the ancient concern with fashioning matter into forms designed primarily to give delight and, partly on that account, caused the weapons to prove ineffective instruments of destruction.

Life in Europe during the age of Louis XIV had many agreeable, many civilizing aspects. But the dignity of the wage earner was not among them, especially in heavy industries like mining and metallurgy and the manufacture of glass. With the increase in the number of common laborers in these industries, the social status of the manual worker had deteriorated. Workers were gradually deprived of such rights of self-government as they had once exercised through the gilds and municipal governments, and through special privileged communities like those of free miners in country districts.[1]

In the Middle Ages, especially with the expansion of industry and the growth of towns during and after the late eleventh century, the objects fashioned by craftsmen for religious edifices had instructed the multitude.[2] These objects, including the statues and the glass windows, presented Biblical stories and lessons and illustrated them in terms of contemporary living. The artistic craftsmanship involved in the work engaged large numbers; it required knowledge, thought, and taste as well as manual skill. Even the more menial industrial labor was frequently interesting because of the demands that it made on the mind. The craftsmen who undertook it — makers of cloth and leather for example — were generally independent of direct supervision, even when they worked for wages. They had to take considerable initiative and exercise considerable intelligence in solving the problems of their craft. Miners for valuable ores were in some ways more independent than town craftsmen. Their labor was frequently full of adventure and excitement in hilly and mountainous country, which presented natural obstacles to try their courage and judgment. Their lives were filled with varied and often dramatic labor, sometimes similar to that undertaken by the sporting mountaineer of the late nineteenth century working his way up a rock "chimney" to reach the pinnacle of an *aiguille*. The work of the "mountain" men, as the early miners were called in Germany, aroused a respect for them wherever their exploits were known, even among the mighty.

Between the mid-sixteenth and the mid-eighteenth centuries the shift in mining prosperity from central Europe to Sweden and particularly to Great Britain was accompanied by a shift from the mining of silver-bearing ores to the mining of iron ore and coal, which were more abundant but cheaper. The miners' work lost much of the romance and dignity attached to it in the mining communities of the Middle Ages.

With the growth in the size of enterprise, work in a number of heavy industries became dirtier and less repaying than the work of the crafts had been during the twelfth and thirteenth centuries. The manufacture of alum and saltpeter kept workpeople busy in the collection and preparation of urine and fecal matter. Laborers were becoming more repellent to sensitive eyes as well as to sensitive nostrils. Changes in the diet of the poor at the beginning of the seventeenth century or a little earlier seem to have led to the spread of rickets among children and to the early decay of the teeth among adults.[3] Coal mining and coal carrying, together with work at the coal-burning furnaces, stained the faces and often the bodies of the workpeople. Dirt crept through their scanty clothing when they labored underground or in the heat of strong fires. Dirt spread widely over an increasing number of workers, especially in Great Britain and the Low Countries, where coal was coming to be used extensively in manufactures. There were fewer opportunities than there had been to remove stains. Bathing facilities were probably even less common than before the Reformation. Puritan restrictions on any display of the nude, which followed the extreme licentiousness of the late fifteenth and early sixteenth centuries, were no monopoly of Puritans. Stricter manners interfered with the development of public baths. When coal miners or coal carriers cried, as they were wont to cry in the early eighteenth century when Methodists preached the gospel to them, the tears trickling down their cheeks and necks made visible white streaks.

Partly for these reasons, the workpeople in the expanding heavy industries came to be marked off as a class apart. Even their skins appeared to differ from those of more genteel persons. Legends grew up that miners and coal stokers were black men, not fit for the consideration accorded to the whites. The humane Montesquieu, writing in the 1730's and 1740's, regarded slavery as more appropriate for black men than for white, though he looked upon slavery as an evil and considered it one of the great achievements of the Christian peoples of Europe to have abolished it among themselves.[4]

Ever since the twelfth and thirteenth centuries these peoples, especially in the northern countries of Europe, were becoming more interested than their medieval ancestors had been in trying to penetrate the material mysteries of nature. A man's actual appearance and the character of the products which he handled exercised a stronger influence upon the social status accorded him than in the early Middle Ages. Then men and women had been tougher, more earthy in their tastes, less morose. They had less sensitive noses. Having little access to deodorants or perfumes or to disguises for their hands and faces, they took greater pleasure than their modern descendants in the natural state of their human associates as well as of the world of nature to which they were closer. At the same time, they attached a greater importance to the abstract world accessible to a human mind, above all to a mind whose hopes are fixed on eternal life. Flights of the imagination which make tolerable and sometimes even charming the warts and other blemishes dealt out to men and women were becoming more difficult for the mind to accept in the seventeenth and eighteenth centuries, especially in the north of Europe, where the material sides of life preoccupied more of the population more of the time than ever before. It required the invention of a very great artist to create Don Quixote, a knight whose fancy could make an ill-favored, foul-smelling hag into a paragon of womanly sweetness and beauty. The Don belonged to an earlier world that had disappeared. At the beginning of the seventeenth century Cervantes was writing that world's epitaph.

A century afterwards it was hardly possible even for a poet, at least in Great Britain, to use his genius as Cervantes had done. One of the finest modern poets, T. S. Eliot, has traced the disappearance of "wit" in English letters to the late seventeenth century. Wit may perhaps be defined as a quality of art which depends on a combination of toughness with imagination. Andrew Marvell (1621–1678) and Dryden (1631–1700) both possessed it. But Eliot suggests that their successors in the possession of wit were to be found not in England but on the Continent, especially in France [5] where life remained less industrialized and less artificial, and where it has been easier than in the Anglo-Saxon countries for creative minds to elevate their direct sense impressions beyond the actual world of matter. Already in the early seventeenth century Europeans were coming to look with more literal eyes upon workers in the new industries, at a time when conditions were making these workers less attractive to look upon than the craftsmen, miners, and metallurgical workers of the Middle Ages. Natural beauty, probably rather more rare than in the past, was more esteemed and precious. Efforts increased to achieve an equivalent for natural beauty by artificial means, then accessible to only a few.

During the seventeenth century members of polite society were becoming far nicer in their household manners than the feudal nobility had ever been. The introduction of the fork and the *couvert*, with individual plates and eating utensils, gave to each person at table individuality and distinction of a kind which earlier Europeans had missed. The new sense of form and order, first cultivated with subtle charm by the French, spread at the courts, among the nobility, and also among the wealthier members of the rising middle class, who aped those who were regarded as their betters. The progress of manners was confined mainly to the few, and as these few became more sophisticated and nicer in their tastes, the gulf which seemed to separate them from workers at base tasks in the heavy industries was widened.

It is little wonder that recruits for the new industries often found themselves outside the manorial system, outside the gilds, almost outside the law. They were treated frequently as outcasts, as was not unnatural when vagrants and even criminals were sometimes put to wagework by the local magistrates. In 1606 the tenants of Broseley, in Shropshire, protested that the owner of a new colliery was corrupting the life of the manor by introducing "a number of lewd persons, the Scums and dreggs of many [counties], from whence they have bine driven." Some of them were thieves, the report continued, others "horrible Swearers," others "daillie drunkards, some having towe or three wyves a peece now liveing, others . . . notorious whoremongers." [6]

Wage labor in the heavy industries was coming to be identified,

however unjustly, with the underworld of crime as well as with stained
bodies. What seems to have brought some of the early Methodist
missionary workers to the coal miners was the suggestion that there
was no need for them to go as far afield as America in their efforts to
convert the barbarous heathen: the colliery districts could provide
them with plenty of savages to civilize and to Christianize! [7]

In medieval times the humblest villagers had obtained the rudiments of schooling from the priests and by observing the decorations
of church portals, walls, and windows. But even these rudiments were
apparently inaccessible to many of the new industrial outcasts, the
coal miners in particular. As a Belgian historian, Gonzales Decamps,
observed some sixty years ago, "It is a remarkable thing that the
nearer we approach the nineteenth century, in inverse ratio to material
and political progress, the shades of ignorance [among the wage
earners] seem to darken." [8]

Both the cleavage between capital and labor and the growing
ostracism of wage earners in the heavy industries go back to periods
before the rise of standing armies. The progress of heavy industries,
most of which were little dependent on war orders, was partly responsible for the attitude toward the soldiers and sailors in the new armies
and the larger navies. During the late seventeenth and early eighteenth
centuries, men not unnaturally thought and spoke of pressed and conscripted sailors and soldiers in terms similar to those which had already been applied to coal miners, alum workers, porters, and employees in the new coal-burning glass factories.

Between them, the occupations of heavy industry and military
service created a new low class in society. Workers and soldiers were
coming to constitute a social scum, of which there was little trace
during the early industrial expansion of Europe from the eleventh
through the thirteenth century, at least until the lifetime of Dante
(1265–1321), when large enterprises began to appear in industry
particularly in Italy and Flanders and when the town governments,
which had originally included manual workers as well as traders, first
began to exclude the manual workers. Before Dante's time slavery had
almost entirely disappeared among the Christian peoples of Western
Europe, partly, as Montesquieu later assumed, because the law of
the Church made it inadmissible to reduce to servitude a brother in
Christ.[9] Serfdom was on the decline and, through the religious life,
even the peasant had a share in the common intellectual and cultural
experiences, then inseparable from religion, as well as in the faith.

The worsening in the social and political position of manual workers in Europe, which can be detected at least as far back as the late

thirteenth century, first became striking with the expansion of heavy industry during the sixteenth and seventeenth centuries. Forced labor was not unknown in industry before it became frequent in military service. A species of slavery had appeared in Great Britain, though Montesquieu seems to have had no knowledge of it when he wrote *De l'esprit des lois* (1748). In Scotland coal miners and salters who stoked the furnaces with coal to heat the salt pans along the Firth of Forth were actually reduced to slavery in the early seventeenth century. This slavery was not, as was once supposed, an outgrowth of medieval serfdom. It was the result of early industrialism.[10]

In the late seventeenth century these social changes began to have a pronounced influence on war. Until that period Europeans had engaged in organized fighting mainly for faith, for sport, for honor, for plunder, for national pride, or for money. A hundred years afterwards, with the French Revolution, the calling of the soldier took on a new kind of dignity. In the modern age of growing materialism, war was destined to offer, in a terrible form, something of an escape from a material world which is too much with us. It was destined to provide a crude means whereby men could assert the increasingly neglected power of the spirit over the body. In the interval, during the age of limited warfare, the morale in the fighting services of Western Europe reached a low ebb. Soldiers whose services were purchased felt at least some obligation to render an equivalent for the money they received; those who were tricked or beaten into the armed forces felt no such obligation. Taken from the dregs of society, from the element that was without status or settled occupation, the new recruits were soldiers only because they could not aspire to any better calling. As the armed forces increased in numbers, the proportion of the men who belonged to the "scum" grew. Partly for that reason the calling of arms lost some of the prestige attached to it in medieval and even in sixteenth-century Europe. While pirates and other brigands as well as chivalrous knights had participated in medieval warfare,[11] they at least had the honor which prevails among thieves. By the beginning of the eighteenth century any sense of dignity which a soldier or sailor might feel had to come from within himself under the most unfavorable external conditions, without support from the social elite, from men of letters, or even from political leaders and military commanders. Military service, which the common soldier seldom embarked upon voluntarily, became the bitterest form of forced labor.

The view of the soldier as a social outcast, like the coal miner or the alum worker, imposed a restraint upon the relentless use of force in battle.[12] It is hardly remarkable that the soldiers were reluctant to fight and that the commanding officers were unable to depend on them in battle. Toward the end of the second Anglo-Dutch War of 1665–1667, there were, according to report, some three thousand English and Scottish seamen serving in the Dutch fleet, perhaps 10 per cent of all the men Holland had enlisted. More British seamen were going over to the enemy every day, "they have so much encouragement there, and so little at home." [13] In war on land, mass desertions were not uncommon. In 1671 large units of the French army, formed to invade the Low Countries, melted away. A newsletter written from France on August 26, reported that "10,000 have deserted the service of the King of France, and he has published a general pardon." In 1677 four out of seven soldiers deserted from the army of the duc de Vivonne.[14] Even as late as the American Revolutionary War, when the military calling was beginning to be taken more seriously by the common soldier, "it has been said that the combatants had so little zeal for the struggle that the British and American armies were composed of each other's deserters." [15]

The physical material was as inadequate as the human material for waging heavy war, in spite of (indeed partly because of) the notable increase, after the middle of the seventeenth century, in the warships, forts, guns, ammunition, horses, clothing, and food produced for the armed forces of Europe. In the age of limited warfare, and especially during the twenty-five years of most extensive campaigning from 1689 to 1713, the preparations and the wars of position imposed strains upon the financial, commercial, and industrial resources of Europe almost comparable in magnitude to those imposed earlier in so different a cause by the building of monasteries, cathedrals, and other churches during the twelfth and thirteenth centuries. Religious building had done much to divert the energy and thought of the Europeans from war. Building for war from 1660 to 1740 was leading them only to limited war. How can that be explained?

The three great powers of the age — England, France, and Holland — were claiming empires in America, Africa, India, and the Far East, and so were extending their political responsibilities and commitments from the tiny spots on the map occupied by the mother countries, to the ends of the earth. The problem of providing sufficient supplies to overwhelm and subjugate a major enemy was increased when there were so many new places in which to fight.

After the Peace of Westphalia in 1648 and the Restoration in England in 1660 the expansion of the armed forces caused increasing financial difficulties even when the leading countries were not at war, as they were a large part of the time. The burden of preparing for war fell almost entirely on the national budgets of the European powers, because (as piracy gave way to trade) there were fewer soldiers of fortune than in the past who were prepared to meet any substantial portion of the military expenses out of their own pockets. There were more unsavory persons who made money by selling for slaughter the men they rounded up. But such traffickers in human flesh were not providing capital to clothe or to arm it to the same extent as during the religious wars.[16] Partly on that account and still more on account of the increasing cost of armed preparations, governments were in continual difficulties finding money to pay the persons employed in the armament manufactures. The English state papers from 1660 to 1680 are full of complaints about "the clamorous condition of the workmen" who labored in building warships and preparing the materials and munitions to fit out the vessels.[17] They rarely received their wages when due, and the officials of the navy were at their wits' end to find the money to pay them. During the second Anglo-Dutch War, for example, the shipyards at Harwich were used for the navy, and the men employed there in the royal service were quartered on the townspeople, with the understanding that they would pay for their quarters out of their wages. As the war was ending in 1667, the navy commissioners were informed that the workmen owed "half their wages or more"; if the wages were not paid, "many of the townspeople [would] be undone." [18]

Compared with the sixteenth century or even with the early seventeenth when prices generally rose rapidly, the period from 1660 to 1740 was a time of relatively stable prices, though wide fluctuations occurred from year to year and even from month to month in large commercial centers such as Amsterdam and London. To judge from records at Amsterdam, the large forces raised by France, England, Holland, Austria, Prussia, and other states during the five or six decades preceding the Peace of Utrecht in 1713, were fitted out without any notable increase even in wartime in the prices paid there for the necessary materials — for example, for the various metals, gunpowder, and bullets. There was no conspicuous deviation between the course of prices for war materials and for other commodities at Amsterdam. Prices did not go up in the first decade of the eighteenth century, during the War of the Spanish Succession, nor did they decline notably in the twenty-five years following the treaties of Utrecht, when, comparatively speaking, Europe was so much more peaceful.[19]

The course of these prices suggests that the pressure which had been brought to bear for more than a generation on the producers in

the principal countries to increase the supplies of munitions was not
greatly intensified during the major wars. Yet it is well known that
the last two wars of Louis XIV, the War of the Dutch Alliance and
the War of the Spanish Succession, bled the French nation white
financially. In August 1693, in the midst of the first of these wars, the
Marquis de Vauban, incontestably one of the most patriotic and informed French military leaders, addressed a memoir to Louis XIV
advocating a reduction in the expenditures made for the army and
navy.[20] It can be inferred that the state of the royal finances was such
as to make it difficult, if not impossible, to expand greatly the production of arms and ammunition in time of war. This can be attributed
partly to the backwardness of financial knowledge in France. Holland,
England, and Scotland had become the masters of improved methods
of expanding credit to meet the exigencies of state. When, after the
War of the Spanish Succession, John Law instructed the French authorities in the development of credit and banking,[21] he frequently
referred to the backwardness of French practices in these matters as
compared with the practices of the Dutch and the British. But, if the
governments of Holland and Great Britain knew better than the government of France how to borrow and to expand the means of payment at their disposal, they experienced greater difficulties than the
French royal officials in levying taxes. Unlike the French, the English
and Dutch rulers had to obtain the consent of representative assemblies in order to tax, and these assemblies were strongly representative
of the interests of wealthy merchants, who were generally opposed to
the principle of direct taxation. Their opposition imposed a curb upon
the expansion of the war effort of Great Britain and Holland in no
way inferior to that imposed by the backwardness of the French in
the mysteries of higher finance.

Early in the seventeenth century, as wars were about to become
more moderate, Thomas Mun — the rich merchant whose modern
fame as an economist rested at one time on the importance that he
gave silver and gold as the basis of a nation's wealth — remarked
nevertheless that money could properly be spoken of as the "nerves"
of war only in so far as it furnished at the right time and place human
force, provisions, and munitions. He pointed out that battles are not
fought with precious metal.[22] In the final accounting of economic
assets it is the actual material resources, even more than the ability
of governments to raise money, that have determined the power to
wage wars in modern times.

In *L'Esprit des lois*, published a century after Mun made these
observations, Montesquieu drew attention to what he called "a new

malady" which had seized the princes of Europe and had led them to keep under arms an inordinate number of troops. He remarked, in a footnote, that this very disease was mainly responsible for the prevailing political equilibrium, because it broke (*éreinte*) the backs of the great powers.[23] His words imply that the guns and ammunition which the industry of any nation could make available for its vast navies and armies were inadequate to destroy the equally large armed forces maintained by its enemies. Such destruction would have required a series of decisive battles; that, in turn, would have required such renewals of munitions and military equipment as were beyond the productive capacity of Europe in the late seventeenth and early eighteenth centuries. Prevailing conditions of economic scarcity imposed more decisive limitations on warfare than a lack of money.

The most important materials for producing the flow of munitions necessary to smite the enemy were saltpeter, wood, and the various metals. Now that firearms were the crucial weapons, wars could not be fought effectively either on land or sea without large supplies of gunpowder; gunpowder could not be had without saltpeter. The authorizations issued by kings and princes to saltpeter men to enter private lands and to ransack cellars, stables, birdhouses, and even bedchambers for the necessary decompositions were unpopular. All sorts of stories were spread concerning the callous behavior of these saltpeter men. Some of them were said to have so little respect that they forced their way into the bedrooms of the dying and of women in childbirth. The local inhabitants were naturally reluctant to cooperate with persons whose reputations were odious, and the saltpeter men repeatedly left sovereign princes short of supplies for manufacturing the gunpowder indispensable for war. Indian saltpeter, imported to supplement the domestic product,[24] was hard to obtain in large quantities in a hurry, particularly by states such as Prussia which had no ships. So it was difficult to concentrate what we should now regard as a substantial amount of gunpowder in a particular campaign.

It is little wonder that during the second Anglo-Dutch War of 1665–1667, an English physician, employed by the emperor of Russia, should have written with excitement from Moscow about an English brickmaker there who claimed he had found a means of shooting lead missiles *without* gunpowder. The physician regretted that this mechanic was not in England to help in the war. "Had he learning," wrote the physician, "he would be more famous than Archimedes."[25]

Before the end of Louis XIV's reign the French improved their position with respect to gunpowder. In the earth itself they discovered what were thought to be inexhaustible supplies of saltpeter, and so could get the material they needed without disturbing the privacy of homes or ransacking the preserves of birds and domestic animals.[26] But these discoveries proved inadequate. In 1744 Machault d'Arnouville, the minister of finance, wrote: "Even in time of peace, it is absolutely indispensable to increase the yield of saltpeter in France . . . in order to become independent of foreign supplies." A shortage of saltpeter and gunpowder remained a major concern of the military leaders as late as the French Revolution.[27]

Today the Western peoples have freed themselves from a major dependence on wood in warfare. But in early modern times timber was both the flesh and the bones of men-of-war, as of merchant ships. As early as the late sixteenth century Great Britain had become partly dependent on imports for her supplies. The Dutch never had nearly enough wood within the bounds of Holland to supply their shipyards.

An American scholar of history, Professor R. G. Albion, has described the complicated problems which confronted several generations of British admiralty officials in their efforts to obtain within the island of Great Britain, and especially overseas, the various kinds of timber upon which success in naval war depended.[28] Holland had to build its fleet almost entirely with imported timber, much of which came from the forests of Sweden and the Rhineland. In 1666 Colbert wrote to a Monsieur Courtin, living in Stockholm, asking him to start a large establishment and to construct for the French king six ships of the most excellent quality of wood and iron.[29] But France was more adequately stocked with wood than Great Britain or Holland; French timber was generally of better quality than that imported by the Dutch.[30] This made it the more urgent for England and Holland, which replaced Spain and the Empire after the 1670's as the most dangerous enemies of France, to maintain control in the Baltic and the North Sea of the sea lanes along which ships sailed with timber from Scandinavia, Russia, Poland, and East Prussia, and also from Hamburg, a port which received its supplies from the forests of Bohemia, whence the wood could be floated for several hundred miles down the winding river Elbe.

At the beginning of the eighteenth century France herself began to run seriously short of wood. Many French provinces were faced with a crisis of deforestation resembling the earlier crisis in Great Britain during the reigns of Elizabeth and James I. By 1721 *bois de futaie* in particular, great trees suitable for building large vessels, had become exceedingly rare in the neighborhood of any French shipbuilding town.[31]

The timber crisis of the early eighteenth century was European and it affected armies no less than navies. The smoke from cannonades was nothing to that from the hundreds of furnaces and forges that produced the metal and the ammunition without which cannonades would have been impossible. Much fuel was also required to stoke the kilns in making lime and brick for forts. It was only in Great Britain, and to a lesser degree in the valley of the Meuse, that the progress of the coal industry had emancipated the makers of war materials to any appreciable extent from the general use of charcoal and wood as fuel. Even in Great Britain coal was not extensively used before 1785 in smelting iron ore. Consequently the growing scarcity of wood bore down upon the supply of munitions at least as heavily as upon the supply of ships and transport wagons. Between 1640 and 1740, with the growth in the size of the military forces and the increase in their need for all kinds of equipment which depended in one way or another upon the provision of wood, a scarcity of timber diminished the possibilities for conquest.

With the general adoption of firearms in the late fifteenth and sixteenth centuries, large supplies of base metal became, as has been shown, more vital in war than ever before.[32] During the late seventeenth century, something was done to conserve metal by the elimination of the last vestiges of armor from the equipment of the European soldiers.[33] Even breastplates were abandoned between 1685 and 1705.[34] But the future of the new warfare with explosive materials depended not upon saving but upon production, even upon waste.

Shortages of metal had helped to prevent the so-called wars of religion from becoming even more thorough than they were. Gustavus Adolphus had tried to meet the difficulty of obtaining enough metal for guns by sponsoring two kinds of new light artillery. One was a so-called "leather-gun," consisting of a tube of copper or bronze strengthened by rings of iron and covered by a leather skin. The other was a light iron gun of the same size. This is said to have been invented by one of the Scottish Hamiltons while he was employed in the service of the Swedish king.[35] The leather gun was apparently too weak to be effective. Knowledge of the manufacture of the light iron gun is said to have been lost. It apparently played no part in the increasingly moderate European wars of the late seventeenth century.

As has been suggested, the failure of the European ordnance departments to develop more effective light artillery can be explained partly by a lack of enthusiasm among men of science for military improvements.[36] Whether from ineptitude or from a lack of proper instruction by natural scientists, gunmakers could not divest themselves of the mistaken notion that the longer the cannon were, the farther

they would shoot.[37] Between the early seventeenth and the middle
of the eighteenth century, foundries concentrated on the manufacture
of long heavy guns, in spite of the imperative need for saving metal.[38]

While cannon of cast iron and brass had become common by the
middle of the seventeenth century in the north of Europe — in England and Sweden — on the Continent artillery pieces were still generally made of the more expensive bronze or gun metal, substances
obtained from the ores of copper, tin, and zinc. During the 1670's and
1680's there was some increase, at any rate in the French navy, in
the proportion of the cannon produced with cast or wrought iron.[39]
Yet for various reasons there was a disposition almost everywhere in
Europe during the following five or six decades to revert to gun metal
or bronze as the materials for artillery. Cannon of gun metal were
found to be safer, because they were less likely than iron cannon to
explode when heated by repeated firing.[40] At the same time the economies effected by using iron, instead of brass, bronze, or gun metal,
were reduced. Since more charcoal and wood were required to smelt
the ores of iron than the ores of copper, tin, and zinc, the growing
shortage of wood increased the expense of ironmaking more than the
expense of making these other metals. At the end of the seventeenth
century in England, coal began to be successfully substituted for
charcoal in smelting tin, copper, and lead ores. As a result there was
pressure to save wood by reducing the manufacture of iron cannon in
the very country which had first produced them. Among the leading
European powers, Sweden alone, with its abundant forests, had any
iron to spare.

All other ores were scarce compared with iron ore, and reductions
in the costs of smelting lead, tin, and copper did nothing to make those
ores more plentiful. Ordnance officials found it difficult to increase the
stocks of tin, copper, zinc, and lead suitable for the manufacture of
munitions. At the end of the Middle Ages, central Europe had been
the chief source of supply. But there the readily accessible ores had
been largely worked out during the sixteenth century.

Among the three leading European powers, Holland's position in
respect to munitions was the most precarious. The Dutch got nearly
all their iron cannon from Sweden and a few from Russia. Their bullets
and other ammunition came almost entirely from Sweden and Germany, their tin from the Indies, their copper from Sweden and Japan.[41]
These would be tenuous life lines for a powerful offensive in any age;
they were not less so when the voyages were made in sailing ships!

In the early eighteenth century France and Great Britain were the
only Western states with sufficient man power and materials to fight

long offensive wars on a considerable scale. Both were hard put to find metal. Lead, copper, tin, and zinc had always been scarce in France. Like his predecessors, Louis XIV continually issued authorizations or letters patent granting privileges to persons who would search for these ores in various provinces where, it was claimed, they were to be found "in large quantities and of as good a quality as those which come from Germany, England, and other foreign countries." [42] In the 1720's and 1730's Irishmen and Englishmen, as well as French adventurers, were encouraged by royal officials to undertake large copper mining ventures in Provence and in the Pyrenees. The returns were invariably disappointing.[43] A *mémoire* of 1741 concerning the administration of the mines, says that "the largest part of the enterprises formed in France for mining have failed." [44]

England was rather better stocked than France with copper, tin, lead, and zinc ores. The English had been more successful than the French in exploiting them. Even so during the late seventeenth and early eighteenth centuries the metal problem, which has had an important bearing on the whole course of modern history, was nowhere near the solution in Great Britain which was to make industrialism possible. In 1666, during the second Anglo-Dutch War, a smith named John Ruffhead wrote the navy commissioners that he was unable to complete his work on several warships because he had no Spanish iron. A few months later it was suggested that Swedish iron might serve in place of Spanish. England was so short of metal that technical experts busied themselves trying to find ways of making shot, bullets, grenades, bombs, and other projectiles from the dregs and cinders of iron and other metals. In the 1680's one of the masters of a glassworks claimed that he had learned a method of manufacturing grenades of glass, cheaper and "better for execution" than iron ones.[45] Fifty years later John Fuller, an English gunfounder at Heathfield in Sussex, was protesting that he could not produce enough cannon in time of war to meet the requirements imposed on him by the state. In 1744, in the midst of the War of the Austrian Succession, in which an English expeditionary force participated on the Continent in a coalition against France, Fuller wrote, "A land war will so drain us of money that we shall have little left to pay us at home . . . Our best times are over." In their effort to obtain guns, the English royal officials were driven to the expedient of contracting with inexperienced founders. In 1749, after the War of the Austrian Succession had ended, Fuller's son and successor, who bore the same name, wrote from Heathfield, "The exigency set up numbers of little Foundries which I call Tinkers shops, and supplied the Government with small guns; they contracted slapdash for all sorts." [46] Sombart estimated that by this time England required for the production of artillery 14,000 tons of iron yearly — then nearly half the output of the country. [47]

Lighter guns would have helped not only to save metal but to increase the mobility of the artillery. Gustavus Adolphus' short-lived pieces are said to have been carried by four soldiers. They could be moved easily and cheaply and this apparently contributed to his victories. [48] The cost of hauling the heavy cannon was tremendous. But the cast-iron cannon had to be heavy to withstand the shock of shooting. In 1639 some twenty horses had been employed to pull the largest, which weighed about 5,600 pounds, and an additional twenty-four were required to pull the six wagon loads of ammunition needed for the gun to play only a single day. [49] When under fire the guns were sometimes hauled by men, as at a crucial point at Fontenoy in 1745, when the allied armies engaged the French in a battle which provided a classic example of the polite etiquette of limited war.

Small improvements made between 1640 and 1740 in the awkward gun carriages [50] helped somewhat in moving artillery. But there was no decisive change in the methods of haulage. And in other ways such facilities as there were for moving guns deteriorated. Little was done anywhere in Europe to improve the main roads, or even to keep most of them in repair. The cost of haulage increased. In the absence of any new mechanized force for moving vehicles, a resumption of wars of movement depended upon the provision of great numbers of horses, not only draught animals to drag the artillery, but thoroughbreds to mount the cavalry, the only arm capable of speed. Like other "engines" of war, horses were in short supply in the late seventeenth century. In Colbert's time the French laid out money to buy cavalry horses in England and Portugal. [51]

The shortage of horses and the mounting expenses of transport added to the difficulties of waging extensive war, especially in enemy country. To be of much value, cannon foundries had to be near the scene of battle. Work at the foundry in the Arsenal of Paris was abandoned after 1670 because Louis XIV's armies had pushed the French frontiers away from the capital. If it was difficult to bring large guns from Paris to the new frontiers close to the Rhine, it was equally difficult to bring guns manufactured in the valley of the Meuse into Saxony or Bohemia. So, many new conditions combined to make the concentration of artillery fire deep in enemy country less practicable than during the Thirty Years' War. [52] An army on the defensive, near its cannon foundries and other sources of munitions and protected by numerous forts, obviously had great and increasing advantages over an army that had advanced long distances from home. Partly on account of the slow growth in production — which was an important cause for the rising cost of killing men — partly on account of the comparatively small population of Europe, the huge armies of the age had little elasticity compared to those created in the late nineteenth century. Reserves of men and munitions, even uniforms and shoes, were lacking.

During the hundred years from 1640 to 1740 European states were creating the framework of the armaments for modern total war. They were incapable of providing the substance — the fuel, the metal, the gunpowder, the cheap quick transport of munitions, the swift-moving attack — which would have been required to kill enough men to produce decisive results.[53] The expense of supply bore down on the large unwieldy armed units, comprising for the most part unwilling soldiers or sailors, often badly disciplined and inadequately trained for combat. This expense laid upon the new military forces a heavy weight which might be compared to that imposed by suits of plate armor upon an attacking force of medieval knights. In fact the cost of providing thoroughbred horses, together with the heavy armor and other equipment, for the knights, the decisive force in medieval battles, had held back the expansion of armies and so had restrained war during the Middle Ages.[54] After 1660 the same factor of scarcity operated in new ways, in connection with the weapons brought into widespread use since the voyages of Columbus.

The future of decisive war depended upon a waste of men's lives and a waste of materials without precedent in the annals of mankind. No military leader, however powerful and unscrupulous he might be, could order such a waste unless the men and the materials were available. Their provision depended upon the triumph of an idea of expansion, novel in history. Expansion by conquest is one of the oldest and most elemental of human passions. But the exercise of this passion without stint in civilized Europe, with its Christian origins, depended in a material way upon the general acceptance of a new concept, not in itself military — an idea more humane than belligerent — that a people by economic effort could increase in number and multiply physical output indefinitely without seizing foreign territory. In spite of the early English "industrial revolution," in spite of the hopes expressed by Francis Bacon and Descartes, this idea had not revolutionized the methods of manufacturing in the age of Isaac Newton. Industry was still concerned more with making things well than with the abundance of things.

While manual labor in a few heavy industries — such as alum

making, coal mining, and a number of coal-burning manufactures —
had helped to create a social scum in modern Europe, the workpeople
in these occupations still formed at the beginning of the eighteenth
century only a small minority of the industrial population, even in the
European countries which were economically most advanced. As it
had evolved in the seventeenth century under French leadership,
European civilization was nourished also by industrial work of another
kind, in which art and craftsmanship still predominated and in which
the two were closely related. The old alliance between beauty and
difficult manual labor was given fresh life in connection with the manufacture of furniture, hangings, and decorations for palaces, castles,
town halls, and mansions. Classicism is the name often applied to the
French civilization of the age of Louis XIV. In classical style, conceptions derived from the search in the mind for beauty were an integral part of the industrial work in which the French excelled. Considerations of quantity and even of commodity or utility remained of
secondary importance.

Classicism through its order, logic, and harmony aimed, above all,
at good taste and permanence, and these qualities are not without an
important relation to comfort and convenience. Industrialism aims,
above all, at the manufacture of cheap objects which will sell in large
quantities and will be soon replaced by new objects. Far from preparing the ground for industrialism, the European industrial economy
established in the seventeenth century under French leadership offered a kind of alternative to industrialism.

The conceptions of craftsmanship associated with French civilization had an influence upon the manufacture of weapons. The expanding luxury industries provided the court, the nobility, and the
rich bourgeoisie with the furniture, tapestries, paintings, pieces of
sculpture, musical instruments, pottery, glassware, and other artistic
objects which adorned their palaces and mansions and embellished
their gardens. Ever since the reign of Henry IV, when the religious
wars subsided in France, the crown had sponsored the development of
these luxury and artistic industries, often contributing money or
buildings for the foundation of extensive workshops. The form of these
workshops and the methods employed in them had an important influence upon the manufacture of armaments, which came to be carried
on during the reign of Louis XIV mainly in establishments either directly controlled by the crown or dependent for success on royal favors.

Just as worldly success and truth are different masters, which
cannot be served equally well at the same time, the requirements of
quality and quantity pull in different and often in inconsistent direc-

tions. An emphasis on delight as an objective in manual workmanship was not limited in early modern times to any single nation or class. It was still a habitual, a customary attitude among the Europeans with their common Christian past. Barriers to utility were by no means absent among the workers in the expanding munitions industries, the foremen who directed these workers, and even the private adventurers and royal officials who supplied capital, planned the larger workshops and coördinated all the efforts relating to supplies. Designs for warships and cannon were prepared by leading painters and sculptors.

During 1670 and 1671 a conflict arose between utility and beauty in connection with the vast program of naval construction sponsored by Colbert. It centered around the distinguished sculptor and painter, Pierre Puget (1622–1694), a native of Marseille, to whom had been confided the work of designing the new warships built and launched from the arsenal in Toulon. After examining Puget's designs, a Monsieur Matharel, the *intendant* at Toulon, and Colbert himself, tried to persuade the artist to abandon the more costly and elaborate parts of his plans for decorating the prows and especially the broad sterns of ships of the line, frigates, and smaller vessels. In a letter of September 19, 1670, addressed to Matharel, Colbert urged him to explain to Puget that he should install as few ornaments as possible. "In their present-day naval constructions," Colbert proceeded, "the English and the Dutch have scarcely any ornaments, and they have no arcades at all. All these large pieces of work serve only to make the vessels much heavier and subject to fires. It is therefore necessary to imitate [the English and the Dutch], and, with that object, the sieur Puget should reduce the ornaments on the sterns that remain to be executed, whether the boats are on the stocks or in the water."

Similar efforts were made to change the plans of less famous artists at the other naval arsenals. The efforts were only partly successful. Monsieur Jal, French naval archivist in the mid-nineteenth century, had under his scrutiny the new designs drawn by Puget in India ink after Colbert had written to Matharel. In describing these designs, Jal wrote that "sculpture still counted for something . . . the naval edifice was not deprived of ornament; what remained, well arranged, in a beautiful style, of an ample and firm execution, was still a brilliant accessary in the construction of the ships." Some of Puget's designs for sterns and prows were submitted to none other than Charles Le Brun (1619–1690), a still more influential painter who, at Paris, had been put in charge of the principal manufacture of furniture and other works of art for the royal chateaux. He approved Puget's designs. But then opposition arose from another quarter, from a certain Monsieur d'Alméras, an official of the arsenal at Toulon, who felt that Colbert's directions were being evaded. Alméras expressed the opinion that the king would be well advised to pay Puget the handsome sum of 2,000 *écus* a year on condition "that he never set foot in the arsenal." [55]

Puget only partly mended his ways. While he suppressed the larger statues in his designs for sterns, he retained the somewhat lighter statues of medium height. The other naval designers followed his example, so that this type of sculpture was retained by French warships until at least the time of Napoleon. While the large "gardens" or arcades disappeared, two small arcades in the three-deckers and one in the single-deck ships were projected on the face of the stern, to provide a setting for the statues and other works of art. Over each ship's cutwater was a carving, either a bust or a full length figure; this was called the "figurehead," a word destined to become in English a synonym for what is superfluous.

This effective resistance to modern ideas of utility in naval construction was symptomatic of the attitude which prevailed, in spite of some opposition, in late seventeenth-century France in the production of arms of every kind. What is now considered superfluous was then considered essential. In the type of workshops which were built for the manufacture of saltpeter and the production of cannon, French entrepreneurs seem to have been influenced by the large studios established for artists working with stone, glass, oils, yarn, and cloth. The most authoritative French commercial dictionary of the early eighteenth century stated that "the foundries for cannon, mortars, or other artillery pieces are, as is also said of the foundries for church bells, rather similar to those for making statues, especially with regard to the stone, the wax, the cover straps, the furnaces, and so forth." [56]

It was from the founders of church bells that men had first learned how to cast cannon. The artistic origin of this devastating invention still influenced the makers of guns in the eighteenth century. Bell-founders had formed a special earthen mold for each bell, and when the bell was completed the mold was destroyed. The same procedure was followed in casting bronze guns. Although iron molds were already used in the early sixteenth century for casting the iron cannon balls, it was still common in France two hundred years afterwards to make a new mold in the earth for every gun, even at those foundries where a number of pieces of the same caliber were produced. Not until the late eighteenth century were metal molds widely employed by French gunfounders and a series of cannon produced from the same mold. A number of old foundries were still using the ancient method at the time of the French Revolution. [57]

The founding of church bells provided excellent models for fashioning cannon of beautiful proportions, richly decorated and named not infrequently after saints. Elaborate pieces of sculpture, coats of arms, and insignia were emblazoned on the breech, which ordinarily terminated in the shape of a lion's mouth, a wolf's head, or the muzzle of some other formidable animal whose presence was calculated to arouse the fury of the gun crew. The handles were also embellished with various sculptured ornaments — dolphins, serpents, or dragons — and even the chase surrounding the bore was frequently covered with finely chiseled figures and monograms graciously interlaced. On the barrels it was customary to engrave in relief the arms of the reigning prince, the date of production, and a motto fit to inspire terror among the enemy (who were almost always too far off to read it). In these matters of ornament, the decisions were left to the taste of the purchaser and to the individual genius of the worker.[58]

One needs only to examine the beautiful plates which fill Saint Rémy's three volumes on artillery, to recognize that these cannon were works of art. But their charms were largely irrelevant to the execution they had to do on the fields of battle, while the useless work and the wasted time devoted to decoration, as well as the delays entailed in making new molds, reduced the number of pieces that could be supplied for the navy, the forts, and the field artillery. The spirit of workmanship behind them is well represented by Saint Rémy's discussion of the materials best suited for making cannon. Writing at the juncture of the seventeenth and eighteenth centuries, in the midst of the two long wars of Louis XIV, he favored the production of cannon of wrought iron, according to a recipe of his own. Wrought iron was more expensive than cast iron, but Saint Rémy apparently intended to be lavish in the use of it, in order to avoid the danger of breaking to which less substantial artillery had been subject. Wrought iron had long been an important material for works of art; it is indicative of Saint Rémy's artistic predilection that he gives as one reason for using such iron its resistance to rust and demonstrates this by references to the forged iron grills of gardens and the forged iron portals and crosses of churches. He calls the attention of his readers to the wrought ironwork on the doors of Notre-Dame in Paris, "which have lasted in their entirety for centuries, without any care." [59] The French mind was still aiming at permanence rather than at the replacement and increasing mechanical efficiency essential to victories in modern war.

The same methods of manufacture persisted in connection with small firearms, arquebuses, and muskets. Their bores were of fine wood embellished with divers ornaments in silver or copper, or in fine steel, engraved and chiseled.[60] Such decorations did nothing to help these guns to shoot or to multiply the number produced.

The whole atmosphere of elegance, style, and luxury which prevailed in the armament industries of the greatest European power was reflected in the finery of the commanders of the French armed forces. Thomas Holden, an English observer at Dunkirk in 1671, wrote home describing Louis XIV's army, gathered in connection with the fortification of the harbor. "The nobility and officers . . . are extraordinarily gallant in their apparel, their coats of cloth of gold and cloth of silver, with feathers in their hats. His Majesty himself goes very plain in the Spanish fashion, himself once a day viewing the works and workmen. His guards are in red coats trimmed with [gold?] lace; her Majesty's in blue trimmed with silver lace." [61]

In the age of Louis XIV weapons, like dress, were made to conform to the same principles of artistic inspiration and technique which bound together in a common harmony the architectural lines and decorations of the palace of Versailles; the mirrors, tapestries, and furniture of the *salons* of great ladies; the oil paintings of Watteau, Canaletto, and Hogarth; the music of Corelli, Couperin, and Bach. It is significant that the foundry in the Arsenal at Paris, which had been used for more than a century to produce artillery, was no longer used for that purpose after 1670 and was converted in 1684 into a foundry for the statues which embellished the buildings and gardens of Versailles.[62]

As early as the 1730's Voltaire was scandalized by the inefficiency of various products of French craftsmanship. Neither the knives nor the scissors did their work effectively, he complained. He failed to recognize that, but for similar faults in the manufacture of guns and other munitions, the warfare of his time, which he regarded with disgust, would have been even more frightful than it was.

It is now forgotten that economic development is of various kinds. The only kind that is generally recognized as desirable in the twentieth century is that which multiplies the volume of production and increases the immediate practical utility of the products. Judged by these standards, economic progress was painfully slow in Europe from 1640 to 1740. But the standards of that age were not those which have gained the ascendancy with the triumph of industrialism. In the seventeenth and early eighteenth centuries what the cultured Europeans sought was beauty, substance, and permanence in their country estates, in their cities and towns, in their public buildings and homes, and in the objects of polite living with which they surrounded themselves.

These desires were being satisfied by the work that was done in Europe during the late seventeenth and early eighteenth centuries.

The nature of the work also contributed to the mildness of the wars. It is somewhat ironical that the limitations on fighting should have created among the most distinguished, the most industrious, and the most intelligent Europeans a growing sense of security and even a confidence in the perfectibility of human nature, which left the men of the mid-eighteenth century freer than their ancestors to turn their efforts in the direction of mechanical efficiency and abundance. It was this change in the objectives of work that provided the means of replacing and even of wasting commodities and materials of every kind. Replacement and waste helped to make total war possible.

CHAPTER FOURTEEN

Restraints of European Culture
on Violence

· AMONG THE FACTORS WHICH DETERMINE THE CHARACTER OF WARS, two stand out. One is the means available to wage them. The other is the will for organized fighting which exists among the peoples within range of one another. Each factor is complicated in itself and complicated also because it is always interacting with the other. If the will to war is weak, this is partly for lack of adequate means. If the means are inadequate to produce an annihilating struggle, that is partly because the will is weak.

The role of retarded technical and economic development in decreasing the frightfulness of European wars was something which the leaders of thought in the eighteenth century missed, because they observed that remarkable progress was being made among the European peoples. It was progress of a different kind from that which the modern world expects. It consisted in the improvement of manners, customs, and laws, and in the perfection of thought and of art of many kinds, from letters to music and architecture. With so much improvement before them, many Europeans naturally assumed that there was less fighting because Europe was growing into something approaching a single community of culture. They also assumed that the development of "commerce" (then a word which sometimes included industry as well as trade) [1] was working towards peace.

In making these assumptions, they were right. It must not be supposed that inadequate means provide a complete explanation of the growing mildness of warfare. If the Europeans were living more peaceably at the time of the American Declaration of Independence, than when the first settlements were planted in North America during the religious wars, this was partly because of a growing distaste for violence, of nicer manners among the ruling classes, of a growth in the influence of rational thought upon politics, of an increasing desire for the peaceful exchange of better goods.

The distaste for violence was shown in the reception of the bayonet, the most terrifying of all the weapons introduced during the age of limited warfare. Historians have frequently regarded it as a discovery of the late seventeenth century; yet it probably had an earlier origin. Like so many of the terrible instruments of war, among them the medieval crossbow, it was not invented to pierce men's bodies, but for sport. In a French royal proclamation of 1660, the word *baïonette* is used to describe a sort of dagger which hunters could plug into the ends of their guns to engage at close quarters the animals they chased. Possibly the bayonet had been used in hunting for some time before 1660.[2] After these daggers were plugged in, the piece could not be used for shooting. But when it came to finishing off a stag, a bear, or a boar, there was a notable advantage in having ready a sharp instrument on the end of a long gun, with which to stick the beast, because of the danger that it might claw or hug the hunter to death.

Plug daggers of this kind were probably not issued to troops until after 1660. But as early as the winter of 1683–84 bayonets were served out in large quantities to the musketeers in an English regiment commanded by the young Lord Churchill, the future Duke of Marl-borough.[3] Bayonets were a more common weapon among the English infantry in the 1680's [4] than some authors of modern military histories have supposed. As late as 1690 they were still of the hunting variety and were screwed into the muzzles of the pieces. Probably at about this time the iron ring and then the socket were devised, making it possible to attach the dagger outside the barrel and to fire with the bayonet fixed. The Swedes were apparently the first to shoot in this way, during the invasion of central Europe and Russia at the beginning of the eighteenth century by Charles XII.[5] As better methods were devised for adjusting the weapon to the barrel of the piece, the carrying of the new, and potentially much more effective, bayonet became general for the infantry, first among the French and somewhat later among the other European armies.[6]

The bayonet was the cheapest and potentially the most effective instrument of death introduced during the seventeenth century. The substitution of bayonets for pikes as weapons for infantry might have been expected to offset the growth in the defensive tempers of armies and their commanding officers, because the bayonet made it possible for the same men both to shoot and stab. It was no longer necessary to divide the infantry into pikemen and musketeers.[7] The new musketeers could move more quickly than the old infantrymen, slowed down as they had often been to a pace set by the pikemen. A violent dash against the enemy by large bodies of soldiers moving in unison with bayonets fixed became feasible. The amount of metal in a bayonet was small compared with that in a cannon; unlike a firearm, the bayonet was not a complicated piece with a delicate mechanism. It was more difficult to destroy in battle. It did not have to be loaded. When it had done execution, it could be used again and again, because soldiers could be taught to drive it so that it could be easily withdrawn.

Yet the spread of the bayonet actually coincided with a diminution in combat. Whatever action the weapon may have seen when it was still in an experimental stage it had apparently lost at the end of the seventeenth century, when it became part of standard equipment. Far from encouraging offensive actions, the general adoption of this "demon" of war, as Voltaire called it,[8] proved a strong deterrent. The Chevalier de Folard (1669–1752), a famous soldier actively engaged in Louis XIV's last wars, attributed the increasingly defensive tactics to the suppression of the pike in favor of the bayonet. As the new weapon became available, the French troops were encouraged to keep up a distant fire of musketry, and almost never to close with the enemy. Folard deplored this development. "A mistaken prudence," he wrote, "[was] the manifest cause of all our misfortunes in the late war [of the Spanish Succession]." "We may compare our battles," he proceeded, "to two fleets that cannonade each other during a whole day, and that mutually sink each other and without coming to close quarters." He thought that hand-to-hand combat was better suited to the quick, impatient, ardent French temperament.[9]

Under the conditions of warfare prevailing when Folard was a soldier, the use of the new weapon to press home a charge would have involved a reversion to fighting of a kind which the general employment of firearms had diminished.[10] Guns had made it possible for men to kill and wound one another in considerable numbers at discreet distances, where the targets were impersonal and where the men whose hands caused the mischief seldom witnessed closely and immediately the bloody consequences of their acts — the screams, the agonies of the victims. A bullet usually accomplished its object with less flow of blood and less fuss than a knife.

Robert Boyle's brother, the Earl of Orrery, published his treatise on the "Art of War" in 1672, just before the bayonet came into widespread use. He listed five arms of combat troops: "the Sword, the Pike, the Musket, the Pistol, and the Carrabine." [11] Although the pikes had been shortened since the sixteenth century, they were still long and cumbersome. Sixteen feet was regarded as a suitable length, and the chief use of these pikes was to "keep off or gall the Enemies Horse." "Few ordinary ammunition pistols do certain Execution much farther off." [12]

The abandonment of the pike for the bayonet broke down the hedges between fighting groups. Without a notable improvement in the accuracy of artillery fire and a great increase in the supply of ammunition, there was little to prevent armies closing in upon one another, with bayonets fixed, except the unwillingness or inability of the commanding officers to bring about bloody human butchery on a large scale.

As breastplates were no longer issued at the end of the seventeenth century when bayonets became a standard weapon for the infantry, the troops were deprived of the last vestige of the armored protection afforded the medieval warrior, when hand-to-hand combat had been the accepted order of battle. Consequently general fighting with the bayonet would have exacted from soldiers, who had much less devotion to their calling than the medieval knights, a kind of callous abandon and even a gruesome courage that had been rarely required of the knights. This was more than the generals of the leading Western powers were prepared to exact. If, as seems probable, soldiers in the Swedish armies under the fiery Charles XII sometimes fought with bayonets in impetuous charges against the Poles and the Russians, that is partly explained by the more brutal manners which prevailed in the East, by the traditional European's view of the Slav as less entitled than his own people to civilized treatment, and probably also by the inadequate weapons with which the Poles and Russians could then retaliate. In the East too, and also at the juncture of the seventeenth and eighteenth centuries, the wars waged by the Austrians against the Turks were accompanied by a callous brutality and by copious bloodshed which were becoming rare on the fields of battle farther west. Not until the wars of Frederick the Great, which began in 1740, was any appreciable use made of the bayonet as a weapon of attack west of the Oder.[13] Even Frederick was unable or unwilling to put much dependence on this new dagger as an offensive arm in the hands of soldiers whose morale in battle he could never fully trust. As late as 1775, Hippolyte de Guibert, the French army officer who published a highly esteemed treatise on tactics, remarked that it was under German influence that the custom had been established among the infantry of always carrying the bayonet in drill, on parade, and in reviews. He added, "Since everyone carries it no one ever uses it." [14] Its only extensive use came after the French Revolution, when the military calling was given a new glory and when greatly improved and concentrated artillery fire covered the attacking soldiers, usually leaving them only a comparatively small remnant of the enemy to clean up.

The bayonet increased for the killer the ghastliness of his act, while the horror of being killed by a thrust from this vicious dagger also made the troops recoil from direct encounters. Consequently the spread of the bayonet had a marked effect on tactics and through tactics on strategy. The bayonet, which soldiers were so reluctant to use, helped to keep contending armies apart. It made battles milder. It encouraged cautious wars of position.

This early history of the bayonet would seem to support the thesis to which we have already referred — a thesis in which many took comfort before and after the First World War — that the introduction of more frightful instruments of death might impose limits on wars, or perhaps even lead to the abandonment of war as an instrument of political policy. Such a thesis proved illusory. It neglected the distance from the target at which a weapon can be used, and the ease with which it can be made to execute its bloody and destroying mission. It is not mainly the killing power of new weapons which leads soldiers, commanding officers, and politicians to recoil from using them. It is rather the difficulty and the immediate physical horror and fear which their use entails. Bayonets could be employed to kill men only at tremendous cost both in physical effort and in terror. So, paradoxically, this demoniacal weapon actually stemmed the flow of blood in Europe.

One reason that the bayonet, by itself, was an ineffective means of strengthening the attack, was its inherent frightfulness. Another was a weakening of the will to organized fighting. In the age of Louis XIV the Europeans were less disposed to butchery than their ancestors had been at the time of the Reformation. Torture was diminishing. So was the willingness to kill and maim. Lust for the infliction of pain and death persisted. But since the surrender at Breda, and under the influence of natural law, which made human decency binding on all nations, a recognized code for treating wounded enemy soldiers and for surrendering with honor, was coming to be accepted by all the European rulers. Men could express a total lack of compassion when their opponents were Mohammedans, which they would hardly have adopted when their opponents were Christians. In the English state papers for 1671 there is an account by Rear Admiral Sir Edward Spragg of his destruction of a fleet of Algerine cruisers in Bugia Bay;

he remarked that it was lucky that "all their chirurgeon's chests were burnt on board their ships, that they have not the least medicine to dress a wound with." Three years earlier in these state papers there is a notice from Newcastle-upon-Tyne about a report that a ship of the town "was taken by the French, and the crew tied back to back and thrown into the sea, except one boy, whose tongue was cut out before his being set ashore." But it is added that " the better sort do not believe [the story]." [15]

The decrease in the eagerness to mistreat captured sailors or soldiers, and to kill fellow Europeans in cold blood, was indicative of a growing confidence which the Europeans were acquiring in one another's decency even on the field of battle. This confidence was a result of the course taken by Western civilization during the seventeenth and early eighteenth centuries. With the spread of improved manners went an increasing dislike for physical cruelty and an increasing disgust over the brutalizing effects of administering or witnessing blows and seeing blood spurt. The decks of men-of-war were painted crimson to diminish the fearful effects produced by cannon balls and explosive missiles successfully fired from the enemy's ships. Red uniforms spread in the armies.

The distaste for bloodshed was not merely a result of pusillanimity among the mistreated, undisciplined, and often unwilling soldiers of the age. It was also brought on by a growing sense of humanity among the men whose example counted and whose growing reluctance to inflict pain and death was hardly accompanied by a weakening in their courage to bear both. New efforts were made to follow Christ's example. Missionaries in America met fearful deaths at the hands of savages who scalped them, with an intrepidity worthy of the finest traditions of the soldier, and with a resignation that few soldiers have equaled. Because of the more literal and fleshly nature which reality had been acquiring since the Renaissance, men and women were less able than their ancestors to avert their eyes from physical suffering. From kings, queens, and bishops to simple fathers and mothers, they were less ready to employ corporal punishment. Among those who were in no danger of military service, as well as among the soldiers who were paid or forced to participate, there was much less zeal for war than there had been in the sixteenth century.

What relation had this change in the attitude toward organized fighting to the development of a European community of culture? Armies and navies are instruments for the promotion of the policies of the states which raise them. The ways they are used depend partly on the political objectives of the sovereign authorities. These objectives are determined partly by the nature and the conditions of thought and art, and the social intercourse which has been often affected by both. The influence of thought and art upon politics, like the influence of spiritual life, has varied greatly from age to age. In Western history the influence of religion upon politics was strongest from the eleventh through the thirteenth century; the influence of intellectual and artistic life on politics was strongest in the late seventeenth and eighteenth centuries.

Whether they came under the spell of Bacon, of Descartes, of Newton, or of some of their followers, Europeans were falling in love with the perfections of the mind. In the eighteenth century there was a more intent and, in proportion to the number of people alive (especially to the number of people with political influence), a much larger audience for *serious* thought and art than in the early twentieth century. The so-called middle class was growing more numerous, as well as more affluent, and an increasing proportion of its larger numbers was added to the reading audience, until there was a profitable sale for the works of authors such as Fielding, Richardson, and Voltaire. But it was hardly before the nineteenth century, before the time of Sir Walter Scott, that a concentrated effort was made by editors, publishers, and advertisers to trump up a vast public for books. Not until the twentieth century was the publishing business dominated by artificially inflated sales of "best sellers" to the destruction of serious criticism and thoughtful discussion. So, during most of the eighteenth century, there was no pressure upon men of letters from middlemen to write down to a lower level. When they were not propagandists for a cause, writers sought only to do their best.

As always, there were wide differences of opinion concerning the merit of works of art. The greatest did not always make the widest appeal. Music lovers were slow to recognize the genius of Bach's compositions and later of Mozart's. But the confusion over quality was not between the value of different levels of achievement. For example, with no radios or sensational newspapers, the question never arose whether in reaching many people quickly by broadcasting or writing for a popular press there is some special merit to offset the weaknesses inherent in the hastily composed, shoddy work which conformity to the requirements of such publicity makes inevitable. There were not, as there are now, many kinds of audiences. There were disagreements and disputes galore, many of them stupid, even inane. But the disagreements and disputes were mainly over the degree to which a particular work fulfilled intellectual and artistic purposes which the audience understood better than modern audiences, and which were regarded as much more relevant to the whole of life then than now. When serious art was a part of daily experience extending even to the production of warships, when art and morality, art and faith, art and entertainment were all associated, there was little room for pseudo or counterfeit art.

Many persons with political influence or power formed part of the audience which took thought and art seriously. So the independent mind and the imagination had open channels which led directly to political action. It was not by taking sides on current issues that artists made their impression; it was by shaping the attitude of political leaders toward man, toward God, toward beauty, toward good taste, toward abstract virtues such as justice and righteousness, and toward the appropriate means of working to bring Europeans closer to these virtues.

The attitude of the eighteenth-century intelligence concerning war was partly a reflection of a profound belief in its own art and letters. It has been characteristic of writers in all ages to undervalue contemporary work and to deplore the weakness of their times. In the early eighteenth century, as always, there were complaints about the decadence of human nature and human genius. Yet Voltaire (1694–1778), one of the most critical and satirical men of letters of any age, asked a correspondent in the early 1730's: "In what century has the human spirit made more progress than in ours?" [16] On the eve of the famous battle against Montcalm for Quebec in 1759, James Wolfe, the English commander and one of the best soldiers of his age, repeated in a low voice to the officers about him Gray's "Elegy Written in a Country Churchyard." "Gentlemen," he said, as his recital ended, "I would rather have written those lines than take Quebec." [17] The poet he quoted was his contemporary, still living when the battle was fought. It was an age when contemporary art was a part of contemporary history. The poetic virtues were more respected than the military virtues; great works of art seemed more precious to the cultured Europeans than the causes on behalf of which the principal wars were fought. It was partly for these reasons that the Europeans were no more enthusiastic about the wars than the soldiers who, against their will, were pressed to do the fighting.

What also made history less ferocious, more tender, than in the sixteenth and early seventeenth centuries, was the growing love felt for mankind among the cultured as well as the saintly men of Europe. The combination of human faith and hope, which was strong in the political affairs of early eighteenth-century Europe, can be traced back to great humanists of the Renaissance — to Erasmus, Rabelais, and More — and to great Christian reformers of the early seventeenth century, such as Saint François de Sales (1567–1622) and Jeremy Taylor (1613–1667). Their work was followed by the spread of religious toleration, first in Great Britain and then on the Continent. This left the Europeans without issues capable of arousing enthusiasm for slaughter of any kind, particularly for the kind of mass slaughter inherent in total war with modern weapons.

In a well-known passage, Boswell recorded Samuel Johnson's remark in a company of cultured men: "Patriotism is the last refuge of a scoundrel." Johnson was not what would now be called an internationalist; he was a proud Englishman. The passage in which these words are quoted suggests that, even as late as 1775, political disputes were regarded as affairs of princes and politicians and that such persons acted almost always from interested and not infrequently from dishonest motives.[18] The notion that in international relations disinterestedness and honesty are a monopoly of one's own nation was imperfectly developed. With little at stake that seemed vital to an intelligent and conscientious European, in an age whose leading spokesmen admired the intelligence and honored the conscience, the awkward position in which the conduct of princes and their ministers sometimes placed one's country was incapable of arousing deep fear and hatred of other nations.

As conducted during the late seventeenth and early eighteenth centuries in Europe, war has been frequently described as "the sport of kings." The phrase expresses a partial truth about the political history of the age, of which some contemporaries who served the kings were aware. At a time when France was continually on the point of war against both Austria and Holland, Colbert remarked that he favored having Flanders, hitherto part of Spain, join Holland rather than Austria, because "republics never make conquests, so there is nothing [for us] to fear." [19] The fashion which prevailed among the English, who dearly loved the bottle, of drinking "confusion" not to the nation's but to the *king's* "enemies" made it possible for men and women of breeding, hardly less than for mercenary soldiers (employed now by one side, now by another), to disassociate themselves from the military conflicts more readily than was possible in the nineteenth century, when nationalism became for many the supreme ideal.

A point that needs emphasis also, in connection with war as a sport, is that the territorial ambitions of the leading European princes were never boundless. Kings themselves were deeply affected by the pacifistic positions held by theologians, philosophers, and men of letters. Sometimes these effects were direct, like the influence of Voltaire on Frederick the Great, with whom Voltaire carried on for years an intimate correspondence as intellectual guide and for a time as friend, encouraging and criticizing Frederick's literary efforts. More often the effects were indirect, in the sense that the prince's outlook was not derived from reading or from instruction at the time when policies were settled, but was a reflection of the culture of the ministers who served him, of the priests who looked out for the education and spiritual welfare of his children, and of the nobles who paid him court. With the history before us of Puget's successful resistance to Colbert's suggestion that the French warships be divested of statues and arcades, we recognize that even the most powerful prince in Europe could not move far in directions contrary to the prevailing culture. As principal minister, Colbert simply wrote directions in general terms for the *intendants*, who exercised the royal authority in the provinces. His royal master, Louis XIV, governed little notwithstanding his enthusiasm for absolute power, which amounted to an obsession.

Fénelon (1651–1715), who became archbishop of Cambrai, presented his political views in allegorical form in *Télémaque*, which is ostensibly a modern version of Homer's *Ulysses*. In it the reader learns that a king bent primarily on aggressive war is bound to ruin his people and that it is unnecessary for a good king to cultivate a warlike spirit among his subjects. All he need do is govern well; then his subjects, having become accustomed to good rule, will revolt against the government of a foreign conqueror should he come.

These allusions to current politics were not lost on the society of the French court. Fénelon was the tutor of Louis XIV's grandson, the duc de Bourgogne (1682–1712), and wrote *Télémaque* partly for that young man's instruction. The great courtier, the duc de Saint-Simon (1675–1755), author of long, incomparably interesting memoirs, regarded the premature death of this heir apparent as the greatest tragedy which befell France in his time, because the duc de Bourgogne had displayed a deep love of the Christian virtues, had regarded personal integrity and public justice as the fixed stars set to guide the highest person in the state, and had proved in all ways an apt pupil of Fénelon. Saint-Simon's criticism of Louis XIV was not that he failed to take advice, but that he fell too much under the advice of certain minor Jesuit priests who, in Saint-Simon's judgment, did not represent the Christian intellectual tradition as it descended from Saint Augustine and Saint Thomas. Saint-Simon was at no more pains than Fénelon to conceal the view that the extensive wars undertaken by the king in his old age were a disaster for France.

Louis XIV's great grandson, the only member of the duc de Bourgogne's family who survived when the aged ruler died in 1715, succeeded him to the most powerful throne in Europe. The disposition
of Louis XV to treat war as nothing more vital than a humane "sport,"
is revealed in a report that the king refused to have the French armies
adopt a newly invented gunpowder, with more murderous properties
than the older kinds, on the ground that it was "too destructive of
human life." [20]

Under French leadership, European thinkers and writers were acquiring an increasing sense of responsibility for encouraging in their
rulers habits of conduct derived from both the Christian and the humanist conceptions of the good life. French classical civilization cultivated the idea of appropriate size, not only in the arts but in all aspects of worldly life including politics. To exceed this size seemed to
the French mind excessive, and to a true Frenchman of the *grand
siècle*, the age of Louis XIV — to Molière (1622–1673) for example,
no less than to Aristotle — excess was the enemy of truth, beauty, and
virtue, as well as of common sense. No one since Aristotle had breathed
moderation into his theories of politics, ethics, and jurisprudence with
such strength as Montesquieu. He had a profound understanding of
the part which Christianity, as well as climate, had had in making
possible the moderation that his age possessed. His great book, *L'Esprit
des lois*, composed from 1728 to 1748, is a *summa* not only of the spirit
of the laws, but of the spirit of early eighteenth-century European
universalism.

Moderation, proportion, and reason were the values the French
mind sought. War must not dominate politics. To go beyond a certain
point in political conquests seemed no less disproportionate than to
build an edifice too large for the place it occupied or the function it
was intended to perform. For the logical and imaginative French
mind, France extended naturally to the Pyrenees; it should extend in
the other direction as far as two other natural barriers — the Alps and
the Rhine.[21] The philosophy of moderation was not without its influence upon the Bourbon kings, and in particular upon the one who was
most belligerently disposed, Louis XIV. Cautious historians have
shown that "from the beginning of his reign, Louis XIV . . . appeared
not like an Alexander or a Caesar, who wants to conquer the world,
but as the 'mediator' of Europe." [22] The inclusion of his picture with
the pictures of the great conquerors from Alexander to Hitler in the
recent advertisements of a well-known whisky concern, suggests that
the firm was out to fuddle its clients in more ways than one. In the
considered opinion of a careful mid-nineteenth-century historian, what

Louis XIV lacked in military talent was "inspiration, audacity, the art of communicating these qualities to his troops, and also the necessary simplicity of entourage." [23] Toward the end of his long life he grew increasingly conscious of having overdone the military side of his rule, of having assembled too many soldiers, launched too many campaigns. He reproached himself with the words: "I have been too fond of war."

From the thirteenth to the seventeenth century the gradual disintegration in Europe of imperial power, which had been revived by Charlemagne in the eighth century, hindered the idea of limitless conquest from gaining full possession of any prince during the seventeenth and eighteenth centuries. While colonial empires were at stake in the wars of the mid-eighteenth century, while the French lost India and Canada in the Seven Years' War of 1756 to 1763, in Western Europe itself the campaigns from 1660 to 1763 were devoid of extensive territorial objectives or results. The War of the Spanish Succession led to the transfer from Spanish to Austrian sovereignty of what is modern Belgium, but this part of the Netherlands had come to Spain through the accident that made Charles V king of Spain and also heir through the Hapsburgs to the dominions of the ancient dukes of Burgundy. As there were no longer any sovereign dukes of Burgundy, Belgium was restored to the imperial family into which the daughter and only heir of the last reigning duke, Charles the Bold, had married. The War of the Austrian Succession gave Silesia to Prussia. In the Seven Years' War the principal bone of contention in Europe was this same Silesia, and the Treaty of Paris, which ended the war, left Europe territorially in almost exactly the same position as before.

The growing sense of restraint and proportion in international politics, which characterized the century following the Thirty Years' War, was encouraged by the love of metaphorical truth, of wit not simply as an accessory but as an intimate part of life, a love which the Reformation and the Counter Reformation had threatened to destroy.[24] Wit and lightness of touch have almost disappeared from twentieth-century international relations, along with the last remnants of polite manners. Some twenty years ago, just before the National Socialist despotism took over power in Germany, an American lawyer was summoned to Washington to occupy a high office in the Department of State. While temporarily in charge of foreign policy, he received a frantic dispatch from a chargé d'affaires in an American embassy abroad, concerning a quarrel which had taken place between one of our consuls and a well-known European political leader. The chargé d'affaires asked for instructions. He received three words by cable from the acting secretary of state: "Laugh it off." The embassy was puzzled. Was it a code message? The word "laugh" had disappeared from the vocabulary of international relations.

There is something ominous about a world which has forgotten how to laugh. It is almost certain to be a world which regards tears only as a sign of weakness and fails to recognize that they can spring also from the source of humanity and faith which differentiate men and women from beasts. The eighteenth century knew and understood both laughter and tears and was able to distinguish true ones from the false. In the art which pervaded the age and influenced its political life both laughter and tears had their place.

Among the fictitious eighteenth-century characters who were undermining the social hierarchy on the eve of the French Revolution, none was more influential than Beaumarchais' Figaro. What is it that he says in one of the most arresting passages of the *Barber of Seville*, after the count has asked him who has given him so gay a philosophy? "The habit of sorrow. I hasten to laugh at everything which happens out of fear lest it should oblige me to cry." [25] It was man's need to accept unhappiness as a part of his lot that the industrialized peoples were to forget at the beginning of the twentieth century. It is something of a mockery that the common man, for whose value Beaumarchais felt such sympathy, should have later endorsed leadership completely devoid of the qualities which the society of Beaumarchais possessed — the qualities of knowing how to laugh and how to cry.

The laughter of the twentieth century is mostly hollow or brutal. Sobs of self-pity or screams of physical pain have replaced tears. What so many twentieth-century men and women regard as a common-sense view of reality is an unbalanced notion of reality. It lacks sobriety. It provides no insurance that any of the competing civilizations, which resemble each other so much in the qualities they lack, will perpetuate themselves. After the sullen hardness that had accompanied armed struggles between Catholics and Protestants in the sixteenth century, laughter and tears, and the wit essential to them, became part of the diplomatic vocabulary of Europe under French intellectual leadership. These qualities helped keep violence within bounds.

During the late seventeenth and early eighteenth centuries a doctrine, novel in history, was gaining strength in Europe, the doctrine that the material interests of great states were served better by peace than by war. To call warfare in this age the "sport of kings" conveys a false impression, in spite of the partial truth expressed by the phrase, because it suggests that military affairs were not taken seriously even by the persons responsible for them.[26] In one important respect they were taken more seriously than ever. With the growing emphasis placed by the Europeans on Reason and with the increasing knowledge of contemporary conditions provided by writers on trade and economic statisticians, the advantages and disadvantages of war became more than before a subject for rational calculation among writers, statesmen, and the rulers they advised.

During the seventeenth century the principal causes for warfare had ceased to be religious and had become economic. Nations lived in a continuous atmosphere of commercial conflict, based on the view expressed by most economic writers of the sixteenth and early seventeenth centuries that a nation could improve its material position most successfully at the expense of other nations. Tariffs and prohibitions were one type of weapon in this struggle; cannon balls, bombs, and bullets another. The second simply supplemented the first. The leading purpose of both was the economic advantage of a prince and of the nation which he ruled.

Bishop Huet (1630–1721), a French priest educated in mathematics, Greek, and Hebrew, whose manners were formed in the first of the famous French *salons*, published at the close of the seventeenth century a book devoted entirely to economic subjects. In its English version this work was called *A View of the Dutch Trade in All States, Empires and Kingdoms in the World Shewing Its First Rise and Amazing Progress*. "If we will only remember," wrote Huet, "that *England* and *Holland*, which (by Reason of their Situation) make so great a Figure in the Affairs of *Europe*, regulate their principal Interest always with an Eye to their Commerce; and this was the principal Motive which caused the last Wars; (that is, Security of their Trade,) we shall be entirely satisfied, that Commerce ought to have no mean Place in modern Politicks." [27] When Huet wrote, commerce was already becoming the dominant motive in European politics. Some decades later in the mid-eighteenth century "naval war . . . was a branch of business," according to a recent historian, "not only for the colonists who claimed the protection of the navy, but for the strategists who planned the operations and most of all for the sailors who carried them out." [28]

At least as early as the mid-seventeenth century, statesmen began to calculate the relative advantages of peace and war in terms of political economy — a discipline which developed as a separate branch of knowledge with the progress and triumph of modern industrial civilization. During the 1660's Colbert cited war as one of seven reasons for the ruin of the French cloth manufactures. On another occasion he wrote to the king pointing out the disorders which were being caused in the provinces along the northeastern frontiers by the movements of large bodies of troops; many French peasants had become so disgusted and frightened that they had emigrated, and Colbert begged Louis XIV to remedy this evil. In considering the best policy for France to adopt in the naval war which had just broken out in 1665 between England and Holland, Colbert wrote: "If the King decides to assist the Dutch and to break off relations with England, we shall certainly have to defend our trade by sea . . . and this will not only cause a prodigious reduction in the state revenues from imports and exports, but also in the receipts from the *tailles* and other domestic taxes, because of the falling off in the transport and consumption of provisions." [29]

When the second Anglo-Dutch War ended, a Czech writer of considerable influence, John Amos Comenius (1592–1671), who took a leading part in establishing gentle and humane methods for educating the young, addressed an appeal to the English and Dutch delegates to the peace conference. He called this appeal, which he based on the Christian faith, *The Angel of Peace.* Comenius pointed out that Christian belief could not justify struggles over trade as it could struggles over the form of worship best suited to the attainment of eternal life. "*If . . . the cause of such cruel warfare is indeed (as it is held to be) rivalry and the endeavour to seize from another sea-routes to foreign peoples, and the markets and gain therefrom proceeding,* then so much greater is the abomination and the guilt, that Christian nations (so cultivated in morals, wisdom and religion) should struggle in such a merciless manner over *things pertaining to this life.*" [30]

During the hundred years that followed, this appeal to the Christian conscience was fortified by the conclusions increasingly reached by experts on economic welfare, that the commercial gains from war were mainly illusory. In 1713, treaties were drawn up ending the War of the Spanish Succession. If a French authority on diplomatic history were asked what the major result of that long war had been, he would be likely to reply that "it founded English naval power." [31] But, in fact, English naval power was already founded in the 1660's, when Colbert, following Richelieu, made it part of French policy to challenge the supremacy of both the Dutch and English at sea. The net result of fifty years of competitive naval building in France and England was wasteful expenditure.

This same War of the Spanish Succession deprived Spain of her political authority over the southern Low Countries. But the possession of what is modern Belgium had not prevented the collapse of

Spanish prosperity during the seventeenth century. Spanish statesmen with extensive knowledge of political economy, Jovellanos and Campomanes, thought that notwithstanding its unfavorable political outcome, the War of the Spanish Succession benefited their country.[32] In any event, a strong revival of Spanish prosperity came after Spain had lost the Low Countries to Austria. Under Louis XV (1715-1774) France was unsuccessful in nearly all her wars, especially overseas, but at home her economic progress was more rapid than that of any other European nation.[33]

Such practical lessons were not lost on the Europeans. During the early eighteenth century the idea gained strength that earlier writers had been mistaken in regarding war as a means to commercial prosperity.[34] That view was being replaced by a new one, to which material scarcity (as well as a growing concern with material improvement) undoubtedly contributed, that rationally commerce and war must be regarded as alternatives. "If the spirit of commerce should extend to every quarter," Accarias de Serionne, a minor French economist living in Holland, wrote in 1767, "wars will become less frequent in Europe. Rivalry among the nations will henceforth only excite a general emulation; instead of leading to a clash of power, it will serve only to stimulate industry." [35]

Emeric Crucé's thesis, that the economic interests of rival nations are not fundamentally hostile, gained increasing adherents during the century and a quarter following the publication of his *Le Nouveau Cynée* in 1623.[36] By 1740-1750, even among statesmen and sovereign rulers, it was no longer a generally accepted principle of political policy that the best way to enrich a nation is by impoverishing its neighbors. Much ground had been gained for the view that national economic advantage could be better served by fostering agriculture, trade, and industry within a country's European borders, than by trying to extend those borders through conquest, or by attacking the trade of foreign countries. In spite of Great Britain's repeated wars with France during the eighteenth century, the eminent philosopher and historian, David Hume (1711-1776), pleaded "for the flourishing commerce of Germany, Spain, Italy and even France itself!" [37]

Policies engendered by any kind of economic warfare produced an increasingly complicated tangle of contradictions, because the means employed were ill-adapted to the ends sought. Bullets and even tariffs were dubious engines for enriching a state; its rivals were bound to retaliate with both tariffs and bullets. In international politics the art lay in waging warfare only as far as seemed materially advantageous. But how far was that? In 1723, when Europe was more peace-

ful than she had been for generations, an immense commercial dictionary was published. It was mainly the work of Savary des Bruslons
(1657–1716), who had occupied an important official position in
France as inspector general of manufactures and customs revenue. In
writing these massive volumes, he had collaborated with his brother,
a priest. Their *Dictionary* is pacifistic in tone and content. In discussing
cannon foundries, for example, the authors express regret that the "art"
of manufacturing "such murderous machines" as cannon had ever been
discovered.[38]

If a cannon was too strong a weapon to advance mercantile interests,
why should weapons be used at all? Why not leave quarrels between
monarchs to be settled with the fists, Henry Fielding suggested a
generation later in *Tom Jones* (1749), and use "cold iron" for "digging
no bowels but those of the earth." [39]

Two developments were of much importance in making economic
calculation a pacific force in Europe. One was the tendency after
1640–1660 for all the nations to grow more alike in their economic
experiences.[40] The other was the close relation established between
economic thought and general culture.

During a period like that from 1640 to 1740, when the causes of
war became mainly economic, a growing community of economic experience helped to provide a receptive audience for pacific economic
doctrines. People in all countries found it easier to understand and
share one another's outlook concerning the nature and purpose of
material improvement. Common objectives, common hopes, and common fears are indispensable as a basis for peace. The cultural developments which were leading the Europeans, after their disputes over
religious worship, to seek the same kinds of happiness helped to guide
the economic life of the various countries into similar channels. Economic calculation became the ally of intellectual and artistic distinction, and of the good taste and manners in which Europe was
preëminent. As general culture played a part in forming and spreading
new economic doctrines, the future effectiveness of these doctrines
depended on their becoming part of the general culture.

It was apparently Montesquieu first and foremost who incorporated
the new economic doctrine concerning peace into Western thought.
De l'esprit des lois is one of the few serious attempts ever made to
understand, as a whole, the multiple forces which have governed civilized evolution. It was directly from Montesquieu that Accarias de
Serionne derived his statement concerning the pacific influence of
commerce: "The natural effect of commerce is to lead to peace."
Montesquieu had written: "Two nations which trade with each other

become reciprocally dependent; if it is to the advantage of one to buy, it is to the advantage of the other to sell; and all unions are founded on mutual needs." What is of special interest is that Montesquieu derived this idea from another thesis set forth in his book, that by healing destructive prejudices, commerce contributes to the improvement of manners: "It is almost a general rule that wherever there are tender manners, there is commerce; and wherever there is commerce, there are tender manners." Montesquieu used the word "commerce" as the antithesis of "brigandage," or piracy, and for him and his contemporaries "manners" covered human conduct generally, both public and private.[41]

What Montesquieu has done in De l'esprit des lois is to link the self-interest of nations with virtue — to suggest that the disposition of countries toward "the abomination and the guilt," against which Comenius had pleaded, will diminish with the spread of commerce. During the early eighteenth century a number of other distinguished men thought they had discovered that, with the progress of civilized manners, an old force — self-interest — had come to work toward the good.[42] It seemed to them that such a force, allied to virtue, might be sufficiently powerful to change the course of history, and lead the peoples in their international relations not only to the recognition but to the practice of what is right.

The new significance which eighteenth-century philosophers were finding in economics made it part of the total rational process. Enriched both by the thought of the new experimental sciences and by economic speculation, the total rational process seemed to the Europeans to promise a happier future for the nations and their peoples than had ever been open before to the human race, at the very time when the illustrious German philosopher and scientist, Gottfried Leibnitz (1646–1716) had persuaded many that, however bad the world in which they lived might be, it was "the best of all possible worlds."

The most powerful countries of Europe — France, Great Britain, Holland, and also Prussia, Austria, Spain, and with them Russia — had acquired in the early eighteenth century, for the first time since the thirteenth, something approaching a common universe of customs and beliefs and a common body of concepts and propositions which transcended differences of language. Differences of language were of no great consequence when most cultured persons spoke and wrote easily in three or four tongues, some with almost equal distinction in two, and when all the nations accepted French as the medium for diplomacy. The new community of culture was recognized by nearly all the distinguished men of the age.[43] As the eighteenth century was ending no one described it with more eloquence than its leading orator, Edmund Burke (1730–1797). The European states had come to possess, he wrote, "a system of manners and education that was nearly similar in all this quarter of the globe, and which softened, blended and harmonized the color of the whole . . . From this resemblance in the modes of intercourse and in the whole form and fashion of life no citizen of Europe could be altogether an exile in any part of it . . . When a man travelled . . . from his own country he never felt himself quite abroad." [44]

Such affinities as Burke described provide the true basis for international peace. Their development during the late seventeenth and early eighteenth centuries strengthened the civilized mode of conduct in matters of war and international relations, which Grotius helped to form and which was based on a reaffirmation of the natural law as binding all nations [45] — one of the cardinal tenets in the jurisprudence of Blackstone (1723–1780), the leading English legal mind of his age. With the growing community of culture, it was difficult for the monarchs who still waged war to utilize fully the scarce means which were at their disposal to strengthen their armaments. "Men are not tied to one another by paper and seals," wrote Burke. "They are led to associate by resemblances, by conformities, by sympathies. It is with nations as with individuals. Nothing is so strong a tie of amity between nation and nation as correspondence in laws, customs, manners and habits of life. They are obligations written in the heart. They approximate men to one another without their knowledge and sometimes against their intentions." [46]

Two streams of civilization — one mainly of French origin, the other mainly of English — can almost be spoken of as uniting in the eighteenth century to form a great river, to the enrichment of which all the European peoples contributed. The two countries which alone had material power enough to conquer and subjugate other civilized states were disinclined to carry such an excessive and gruesome business as war to a conclusion. They preferred to leave their European neighbors the liberty to work out their own destinies. Without the development of a European conscience as part of common conditions of life and thought, such deterrents as the inferior morale of the soldiers, the scarcity of materials, the slow progress of technology, the reluctance of scientists to serve practical ends, the restraints imposed by art on efficient production, might not have reduced the seriousness of warfare. After all, when they are sullen and hard and perverse enough, fighters can do each other in with the weapons Nature gave them.

The balance and restraint, the sense of humane responsibility, characteristic of European intercourse in the early eighteenth century, were cultivated mainly by a comparatively few persons, with wealth, social position, intellectual and artistic distinction. For these men and women the realm of rational speculation concerning the physical world had widened greatly since the Middle Ages. That realm had not begun to be narrowed by the specialization of the scholar and cheapened by the vulgarity of the salesman. The multiplication of printed matter had not begun to weaken serious thought or to damage good taste. It had not yet enabled crudeness and irresponsibility to command the great majority of readers. Paper was limited in quantity, but staunch in quality. The deluge of paper, produced from chemical and machine-made pulp instead of rags, came only in the nineteenth and twentieth centuries, when the output among the Western peoples multiplied over a hundredfold. In 1800 in the United Kingdom 11,347 tons of paper were produced, all hand made. A century later 651,650 tons were produced, of which 647,764 tons were machine made.[47] The quality of the paper and the value to civilization of what was on it were destined to decline together. Even if the art of letters in the age of world wars had been able to produce works comparable with the best of the late seventeenth and eighteenth centuries, such works could no longer have made as deep a mark on the intelligence or the politics of mankind. There was too much that was cheap and ill-considered to compete with them.

At the time Montesquieu began to write *De l'esprit des lois*, about 1730, it was plausible for the educated European to assume that wars for "economic advantage" would eventually cease, as wars for religion had ceased. But the causes for war are many; as Robert Boyle had recognized early in life these causes are deeply embedded in human nature. The course of economic progress upon which Europe was embarking in the early eighteenth century provided no insurance against wars for ideas, for fantasies, or merely for the sake of war, especially when economic progress should go far enough to overcome the scarcity that in the age of Newton put brakes on military development and military adventures.

Long before the deluge of paper helped to debase the character of human communications, another weakness in the structure of European society began to undermine the cultural restraints on war. The citizenry of Europe, upon whose affinities Burke laid such hope, was a limited citizenry, which hardly included more than some thousands in countries with over a million people. While these few citizens actually came close to forming all Europe into what Gibbon called "one great Republic," within each nation there was a growing division among the inhabitants. The "great Republic" was a republic of the crust.

The failure of Europe to find a place in its "heavenly city" of rational speculation and cultured delight for the majority of Europeans led to a determination among leaders of the people to create a new society in which every man and woman would be a citizen. This determination provided a new will to battle. After the middle of the eighteenth century even the peacefully disposed citizens at the top were being drawn, almost in spite of themselves, toward war. Peace ceased to beget peace.

PART THREE

INDUSTRIALISM AND TOTAL WAR
Circa 1740 to Circa 1950

CHAPTER FIFTEEN

The Industrial Revolution Reconsidered

WE FIND OURSELVES IN A WORLD OF SWIFT MOVEMENT AND JERKY retirement; a world thronged as never before with people hustling by each other on the sidewalks of huge cities, people brooding or daydreaming in uneasy seclusion in the cells of high apartment buildings; a world of streamlined automobiles, railway cars, and airplanes; sprayed by a din from microphones, bombarded by newspaper headlines and changing scenes of motion pictures and of television. This world is part of an economic regime unique in history — the regime of industrial civilization — now shared by Russians, Americans, and Japanese, even to some extent by Chinese and Indians, as well as by the peoples of Western Europe.

(1) *Nature and Origin of the Concept*

How did industrialism come into existence? In Europe and America the past two generations have been taught that it was the result of an "industrial revolution" which began in England about the middle of the eighteenth century. According to the commonly understood meaning of the phrase, a series of technical inventions, made in rapid succession in Great Britain, converted one industrial process after another from hand labor to machinery, concentrated industry in large mines and factories, and helped to bring about an unprecedented rapid increase both of industrial output and of population. By 1832 most of the changes fundamental to the triumph of modern industrial civilization had taken place.

Knowledge of the manner in which this view of the "industrial revolution" originated should have made the careful scholar wary about treating it as an "open sesame" to modern history and to the constructive study of modern society. As a supposedly scientific generalization, it goes back to the early 1880's, when young Arnold Toynbee delivered some brilliant lectures at Oxford. He died prematurely at thirty. He had spoken without notes. It was decided to make use of notes taken by students who had attended his course. In 1884 a small volume was published posthumously, entitled *Lectures on the Industrial Revolution of the Eighteenth Century in England.* The book soon made a striking impression. In its main lines, Toynbee's argument was accepted and amplified not only in Great Britain, but also in France (where Professor Paul Mantoux tried to write the book he thought that Toynbee might have written had he lived), in the United States, in the British Dominions, and in most of the world.

Because of the chronological framework of Toynbee's lectures, the industrial revolution has been widely represented as beginning in 1760.[1] If any of us as American school children, when our pliable young minds first met the concept, had taken the time to inquire into general political history, we should have seen that his reason for choosing that particular year was that it marked the accession of George III. But, in our youth, we were given to understand that great wars belonged to the past, and that political history was a boring, almost an obsolete subject. We were all too willing to accept this view because it relieved us of a part of our obligation to study. Our attitude toward past events resembled that of the small American boy who pleased his isolationist father, shortly before the United States found itself in the Second World War, by saying, "I hate war." When asked why, he explained, "Because war makes history, and I hate history." So, if young Americans thought about it at all, they assumed that there must be economic reasons for beginning the industrial revolution in 1760, and for ending it in 1832, as Mr. and Mrs. Hammond did in their famous volumes — *The Village Labourer, 1760–1832; The Town Labourer, 1760–1832;* and *The Skilled Labourer, 1760–1832.* But that later date was also selected for reasons of constitutional history. The year 1832 marked the passage in Great Britain of the Reform Act, which extended the suffrage, hitherto limited to a tiny minority.

The phrase "industrial revolution" could hardly have been uncommon in conversation before Toynbee's lectures gave it content. As a phrase it goes back to the early nineteenth century. It was apparently coined by Frenchmen. During the 1820's and 1830's it appeared in print more frequently, and in all probability it was more frequently heard, in France than in England, particularly among engineers and members of chambers of commerce.[2] When these Frenchmen wrote of an "industrial revolution," they usually had in mind phenomenal changes which had been taking place during their lives, especially in England, and which seemed even more remarkable to foreign observers than to the Englishmen who participated more directly in the changes. The phrase was convenient for describing technical innovations which were startling and which spread with extraordinary rapidity from one industry to another.

The germ of the thesis that developments in England during the seventy-two years *from 1760 to 1832* revolutionized the economic life of the world came from a different source. It is to be found in one of the most famous and widely read histories ever written. It is set forth in a conspicuous place, in the justly celebrated third chapter, of Macaulay's *History of England*, first published in 1848. This is what Macaulay wrote:

> It can easily be proved that, in our own land, the national wealth has, during at least six centuries, been almost uninterruptedly increasing; that it was greater under the Tudors than under the Plantagenets; that it was greater under the Stuarts than under the Tudors; that, in spite of battles, sieges, and confiscations, it was greater on the day of the Restoration than on the day that the long Parliament met; that, in spite of maladministration, of extravagance, of public bankruptcy, of two costly and unsuccessful wars, of the pestilence and of the fire, it was greater on the day of the death of Charles the Second than on the day of his Restoration. This progress, having continued during many ages, became at length, about the middle of the eighteenth century, portentously rapid, and has proceeded, during the nineteenth, with accelerated velocity . . . The consequence is that a change to which the history of the old world furnishes no parallel has taken place in our country. Could the England of 1685 be, by some magical process, set before our eyes, we should not know one landscape in a hundred or one building in ten thousand.[3]

Toynbee may well have been influenced directly by this passage (he could hardly have failed to be influenced indirectly) for he lived when the reading public got most of its history from such works as Macaulay's. Now that the substantial histories of the nineteenth century have been superseded by popular biographies and up-to-date textbooks, soon out-of-date, few would think to look to Macaulay as father of the concept of the industrial revolution. By the time Toynbee lectured, modern scientific history was coming into its own. It was beginning to diminish the scope of historical writing, to narrow the treatment of particular subjects acceptable to the learned, to eliminate much of the sparkle and dash from the pages written in the serious hope they might endure. But, whatever research lies behind Toynbee's lectures, his framework of industrial history and the significance which he saw in it are in accord with this passage from Macaulay. And, whatever the merits of Macaulay's *History*, the picture of change which he painted was not derived from an extensive examination of economic documents and statistics, such as the careful modern scholar would demand before he took seriously any generalization like the one made by Macaulay and later by Toynbee.

Ideas influence the conduct of men and the course of history. Many influential ideas have been derived from knowledge of the past. These historical ideas can never be photographs of actual scenes and experiences. When we speak of a historical idea as true, we mean that the impression it conveys corresponds to the relevant facts as these present themselves in the accessible materials. In order to present such an impression, it is not enough to be in possession of a vast quantity of data on some detail of history in some special period; it is necessary to understand the relation of this detail to the history of the period as a whole and to that of preceding periods. The literary range of Macaulay, with his declamatory style, is not enough. But, for generalizations, the precision of a careful twentieth-century scholar like Professor Emile Coornaert of the Collège de France, whose statistics for the early cloth trade of Hondschoote were cited in Chapter V, is not enough either. A combination of the two is needed. Accurate specialization can produce inaccurate history no less than can the historical generalizations which preceded the age of the specialist. Partly for want of a general view of the whole of industrial history, a warped impression, derived from Toynbee and his followers, has prevailed concerning the role of the period from 1760 to 1832 in economic and general history. The idea of the "industrial revolution," common in the early twentieth century, is essentially false and has hindered an understanding of the relation of industrialism to war and to human welfare generally. What can be put in its place?

(2) *Economic Progress c. 1735–c. 1785*

When we compare the economic history of the leading countries of Europe during the later eighteenth century, we find that the resemblances were far more striking than the differences. The movement towards economic community characteristic of the age of Louis XIV and Newton, who died in 1715 and 1727, continued for another two generations, in the sense that the course of economic progress in most parts of Europe was still similar. Yet in all countries changes occurred in the character and pace of economic development. During the previous eighty years, from about 1640 to 1720, there had been a mutual drawing together and interpenetration between the new civilization of Great Britain and other northern countries (with its emphasis upon commodity, abundance, and cheaper costs of production) and the different civilization of the Latin countries led by France (with its emphasis on delight, splendor, style, and the restraint essential to proportion).[1] Then, beginning early in the eighteenth century, the tendency became pronounced for the continental countries — first and foremost among them France herself — to follow in all manner of ways, from farming to politics, the example and methods of Great Britain, the only European country which had already gone through something of an "industrial revolution" since the Reformation. During the eighteenth century the economic development, in which most parts of Europe shared, no longer produced a balanced synthesis of British and continental workmanship, in which the claims of each were given something approaching equal weight. English example began to prevail, with reductions in costs of production the principal object of industrial invention and workmanship. Yet old ways of living and producing change slowly, even when a new spirit is abroad in the minds of men. Decades passed before the new spirit transformed the conditions of work in any country. It may almost be said that, for a time, especially from 1720 to 1750, Great Britain was rather less enamored of her own example than were the neighboring countries of Europe. It was only at the end of the eighteenth century that Great Britain began to make the most of the industrial advantages which the island's head start on the road to industrialism had given it.

In 1697 an ardent English improver, James Puckle, wrote that English "artisans were universally allow'd the best upon Earth for Improvements." [2] His words describe a condition which probably goes back to the time of Charles I. But what was the state of the industrial arts in France during the eighteenth century? Frenchmen like Montesquieu and Voltaire, who were born just before Puckle published his tract, would have agreed with him as late as the 1730's, which is to say when Voltaire was entering middle life. Voltaire's correspondence shows that he regarded as scandalous French ignorance of natural science in general and of the achievements of Newton in particular. "In truth," he wrote of his countrymen in 1735, "we are the whipped cream of Europe." [3] For him the grace, the precision, the sweetness, and the finesse of French culture could not make up for a lack of what he called the more masculine virtues in which the English excelled.[4]

Voltaire's words were a reflection of existing conditions. They were also a lash to drive his countrymen to change these conditions. The lash was not ineffective, for the will to change existed, and had begun already to manifest itself. The suggestions of Colbert that French master craftsmen and artists adopt English methods of building, outfitting, and decorating warships had met with a lukewarm response in the 1670's. But by the beginning of the eighteenth century, there was a notable increase in the receptivity of French industry to English methods. By the 1730's and 1740's when Voltaire and other writers were unstinted in their admiration for the work of English scientists, the phrase "à l'imitation de l'Angleterre" had become a commonplace in French treatises concerning industry, trade, finance, and husbandry.

The year 1749 provides a landmark in the development of this new intellectual outlook. It was then that the Comte de Buffon (1707–1788) published the first three volumes of his *Histoire naturelle*, a work completed in forty-four volumes in 1804. During the last half of the eighteenth century Buffon's influence in France came to resemble that gained earlier in England by the man whose mind Buffon, like Voltaire, admired above all others — Isaac Newton. Frenchmen addressed themselves to scientific progress of every kind with an ardor which equaled that of the contemporary English. Hitherto French preëminence in science had been largely confined to theoretical mathematics. But in Buffon's time, France came to share with England leadership in all the natural sciences. In fact, leadership seemed to be shifting from England to France.[5]

French civilization was changing its goals. The change in direction extended to the policies of the French crown. By the 1720's and 1730's a definite attempt was made to copy English policies, which, it was assumed, had had something to do with the economic leadership attained for British heavy industry.[6] The practical results of this movement in France must not be exaggerated. It was not strong enough before 1789 to bring about any general suppression of the tolls imposed on the transport of raw materials and commodities within the country.[7] It was not strong enough to bring about the suppression of the gilds.[8] But there was a disposition on the part of public officials, in Paris and in the provinces, to disregard the old regulations, both of the gilds and of the central government, when they interfered with the introduction of cheaper methods of mining and manufacturing and with increases in production.

One can see the process at work in Languedoc. Restrictions imposed by the crown on the output of the chief textile enterprises there were withdrawn and each merchant or group of merchants was allowed to decide independently how much cloth to produce for the market in the Levant.[9] The construction of large coal-burning factories for the manufacture of glass bottles was encouraged, even though this was an infringement of the privileges of a closed craft, the gentlemen glassmakers, whose rights had been established by letters patent of 1436, and confirmed by subsequent letters patent of Louis XI in 1475, Louis XIV in 1655, and Louis XV in 1727.[10] A decree of 1744 revoked the exclusive right to refine sugar in the province granted earlier to two successive companies of Montpellier merchants. The decree opened sugar refining to anyone who was disposed to try his fortune in it.[11]

Similar changes in policy may be observed in all provinces. The manner of leasing coal mines throughout the realm was radically changed by a decree of 1744. Previously the crown had granted to various noblemen and others widespread monopolies, often covering a number of provinces. Now concessions for starting collieries at particular places could be obtained by any persons with sufficient capital.[12] Traders, merchants, and landlords, whose passport was their financial resources, found it increasingly easy to enter industry.

At the same time, the burdens imposed by the financial policies of the crown upon the resources of the private merchant were somewhat lightened. After 1725 industrial capital and the profits from industries were largely relieved from the obligation to pay the *vingtième*, a tax imposed to supplement two other direct taxes on property, the *taille* and the *capitation*. The *vingtième* became almost exclusively a tax on land.[13] Until 1725 the intrinsic value (the content in precious metal) of the French standard coin, the *livre tournois*, had been notably reduced in almost every generation, at least since the late fifteenth century. In 1715 the *livre* contained little more than a fourth as much silver as in 1478. After 1725, following the example set by the English in managing their currency, its value was much better maintained. During the sixty years from 1725 to 1785 its silver content was fixed,[14] and the risks to creditors from debasement by the crown, if not from default, were diminished. This was one of the rare periods in which France has had a stable money.

There was only one aspect of industrial life with which French government officials interfered more than in the past. Experience, English experience in particular, seemed to show that, in this case, government interference was needed to promote prosperity. Ministers, *intendants, sousdélégués*, and inspectors of manufactures all helped industrialists to introduce into mining and manufacturing new machinery, new kinds of furnaces, and new chemical processes.[15] The government advanced capital more freely to help in the establishment of new industrial enterprises when their sponsors could convince the royal officials of the improvements they would introduce to cheapen costs of production. The immigration of foreign technicians and capitalists was welcomed as never before. A patent system to encourage and protect inventors, modeled on the one introduced in England during Queen Elizabeth's reign, was not adopted until 1791, after the French Revolution had broken out. But during the last decades of the *ancien régime* much was done by the state to encourage the scientist and the inventor.[16] A change occurred in the attitude of statesmen and lesser governmental officials toward technical improvements designed to increase production or mechanical efficiency. The contrast between the new attitude and that prevalent in seventeenth-century France is likely to strike every reader of history.

No French statesman of the early seventeenth century had had a sounder knowledge of economic processes or a greater eagerness for the financial welfare of the crown and the economic welfare of France than Cardinal Richelieu.[17] But his view of the directions in which it was desirable to encourage industrial work was different from that which came to prevail before the end of the eighteenth century. In 1613 a certain Torelli, the governor of Malta (an island which the Emperor Charles V had ceded to the Knights of Saint John), fitted a ship with paddles which enabled it to pass through the Straits of Messina against the tide. He offered the invention to Richelieu, but the cardinal was not impressed by its possibilities and did nothing to encourage its development.[18]

Various stories, circulated about Richelieu since his time, also suggest that he was not enthusiastic either about cheapening industrial output with the help of technical inventions or about exploiting relentlessly the mineral resources of the realm. One of the stories concerns his relations with the scientist Solomon de Caus. In 1615 De Caus published his treatise containing a description of a machine to raise water by fire, one of many ancestors of the first steam engine put to practical use in coal mining in Staffordshire a century later. De Caus is said to have pestered Richelieu so much with pleas for royal support for his invention, that the statesman, bored by his importunities, declared him crazy and had him locked up near Paris in the Château de Bicêtre.[19]

Shortly before Richelieu's death, a certain Martine de Bertereau, a native of the Loire valley, dedicated a book to him in which she described the search that she and her foreign-born husband had made to discover new mines in various parts of France.[20] The couple were sentenced soon afterwards, on charges of practicing magic, to perpetual imprisonment, the woman in the massive dungeon of Vincennes, the man in the Bastille. It is unlikely that Richelieu was responsible, as

has been sometimes suggested, but there is no evidence that he inter-
ceded on behalf of Martine de Bertereau.[21]

Whether these stories are authentic or not so far as Richelieu is
concerned, they indicate that in early seventeenth-century France the
ancient view prevailed that there is something profane about using
sublime knowledge for inventions whose merit is to increase mechanical efficiency and that there is something indecent about ransacking
the treasures of the underworld for practical use. Persons who sought
with ardor to promote what was merely useful were sometimes treated
as demented.

During the eighteenth century, the new enthusiasm for scientific
inquiry and its practical applications began to influence the attitude of
government officials towards technical improvements. Some years before the French Revolution, we meet, in the course of some correspondence preserved in the French archives, with an expert technician who was admittedly a little mad. He had special gifts for
directing a textile factory and in central France had been put in charge
of one sponsored by the crown. Whenever he entered the halls with
their moving shuttles, an aberration caused him to imagine that the
workers were deriding him, simply because, in the depth of winter,
they coughed and sneezed. It emerged from the correspondence that
officials in the north, who had sent him, had been well aware of his
idiosyncrasy. And now their colleagues farther south arranged the
routine at the factory so as to keep him out of trouble and to make use
of his gifts. In Richelieu's time in France, persons who had a single-
minded enthusiasm for reducing costs of production and increasing
output by more powerful and efficient machinery or by the discovery
and use of more ores were considered queer, if not downright mad.
A hundred and thirty years later, on the eve of the Revolution, officials
of the same absolute government encouraged such persons in their
work, even when they were actually unbalanced.

It was common in the eighteenth century to refer to all persons in
France who adventured their money in industry, trade, and finance by
the generic word "merchant." With the changes in French policy and
outlook during the last half century of the *ancien régime*, the social
as well as the economic position of the merchant improved much more
than it had during the reign of Louis XIV.[22] At the beginning of the
eighteenth century the French merchant was universally regarded as
occupying a position inferior to that of the English merchant. But by
the 1780's some observers, among them a historical writer and pamphleteer, John Andrews, held that the merchant was now hardly less
respected and less influential in France than in Great Britain.

These new developments in French intellectual outlook, economic policy, and social status were accompanied after about 1735 by a remarkable growth in the volume of industrial output and in the number of working people employed in mines and manufactures. Since the thirteenth century, there had been in France no fifty years comparable to those from 1735 to 1785 for rapidity of industrial growth. No fifty years since the half century following the Hundred Years' War had even approached them.

The output of coal and iron grew faster in France than in England, although it must be remembered that England was already a coal-burning country at the beginning of the eighteenth century, while France was not. Compared with the high mounds beside the collieries in Durham and Northumberland, the piles of coal beside the chief French pits resembled ant hills. The ignorance of some educated Frenchmen concerning the nature of mineral fuel will strike the twentieth-century industrialized mind as comical. In 1709 the *intendants* were asked by the *contrôleur général*, or minister of finance, to supply reports on the state of the coal mines. The *intendant* in Lyons, a certain Trudaine, reported on the mines around Saint-Etienne, which were at the time, with those near Lyons in and around Rive-de-Gier, the principal collieries in France. Trudaine sent the *contrôleur général* a pessimistic account, but he combined it with delightful optimism. Production had fallen off by half, he wrote. He attributed this to the exhaustion of the coal mines, but he told the *contrôleur général* not to be troubled. Nature would mend matters. The mines would soon replenish themselves. Often, he wrote, colliers who return to pits they abandoned a few months before find that coal has sprouted in their absence.[23]

Such a misconception of geological processes would have exposed any public man in England or the Low Countries to ridicule even a century earlier. It reminds one of the ignorance of some Roman writers of the Empire, when coal was hardly known except in Britain. Undoubtedly one reason for Trudaine's blunder was the small importance of coal mining in France in the first decade of the eighteenth century. From the reports of the *intendants* in 1709, it appears that the annual output of the entire country amounted to under a hundred thousand tons. Great Britain, a country less than half as populous, was producing in the neighborhood of three million tons.[24]

After about 1715, when the rich coal fields of the north, along the Belgian frontier, were discovered, the progress of the coal-mining industry in France was very rapid. Progress was more rapid still after the decree of 1744, which made it easy for capitalists to get mining concessions on favorable terms. During the ten years preceding the French Revolution, the annual output of coal in France probably exceeded 700,000 tons. It may possibly have amounted to a million tons, or even more.[25] Production had increased, therefore, at least tenfold in eighty years. Meanwhile British production had grown too, but at a slower pace. During the ten years 1781 to 1790, the annual output in Great Britain had hardly reached ten million tons, an increase of at most threefold since the first decade of the eighteenth century.[26]

In spite of the remarkably rapid progress of the French coal industry, France by no means overcame its backwardness. On the eve of the French Revolution, the per capita production of coal was still overwhelmingly greater in England. But in the per capita production of iron, France overtook England.

About the year 1720 England and Wales were producing annually some 25,000 tons of pig iron and 18,000 tons of bar iron, a considerable part of which had passed through the pig-iron stage.[27] The iron output of France at this time is uncertain,[28] but it is doubtful whether it equaled that of England and Wales. Eighteen years later French production had increased; English production had not. Yet in 1738 the French output of iron was only slightly above the English, according to estimates made by some Swedish ironmasters in a memorandum addressed to the Swedish parliament. Their figures, which are probably short of the truth for both countries, gave France an annual output of 40,800 tons, half of which was pig iron.[29] After 1738 the expansion of the French iron manufacture became much more striking. According to the recent authoritative estimate made by the Bourgins, the output of pig iron in France in 1789 was about 136,000 tons, that of bar iron about 94,000 tons.[30] This was well over twice the output of England and Wales at the time. The figures for England and Wales, *plus* Scotland, on the eve of the French Revolution were only 68,000 tons of pig iron and 33,000 tons of bar iron.

All the progress in Great Britain had been made since 1757, most of it since 1775. As late as 1757, the output of iron in England and Wales had been no greater than in 1720; it was only a little greater in 1775.[31] Between 1720 and 1775, while the output of iron hardly increased in Great Britain, it probably more than tripled in France. Between 1720 and 1789, while the output of iron perhaps doubled in Great Britain, it multiplied some fivefold in France.

An abundance of coal and iron was of primary importance in the industrialization of Europe and North America; yet it would not be safe to draw from these figures for coal and iron production generalizations concerning the growth in the total volume of industrial output in the two countries during the half century preceding the French Revolution. France had been backward in the use of coal fuel partly because of her abundant timber supplies. During the eighteenth century in certain provinces the French turned to coal as the English had turned during the Elizabethan age, because of the exhaustion of the forests. But France continued to burn larger quantities per capita of firewood and charcoal than England. The earlier exhaustion of timber in Great Britain is the chief explanation for the stationary condition of iron production there during the first three quarters of the eighteenth century. The course of iron production is, furthermore, an imperfect guide to the progress of the English metal industries. From Scandinavia and America, still plentifully supplied with wood, England imported iron suitable for manufacturing into finished commodities, and such imports were increasing between 1720 and 1775. In England the production of tin, lead, and copper was also growing, largely because these ores were generally smelted in coal fires much sooner than iron ore.

When we consider further manufactures, there is apparently no instance in which the rate of industrial growth from 1735 to 1785 was much more rapid in France than in England. The output of cotton and woolen cloth probably grew at a slower rate in France. Yet English capital, some English labor, and much English technical skill were being introduced into the French textile industry, as they were into the mining, metallurgical, paper, and glassmaking industries. In these and in nearly all the other heavy industries one result was a notable increase in output. Another was a growing cleavage between capital and labor and a growth in the scale of private enterprise.

On the eve of the French Revolution several large plants were in operation in France. Each employed about a thousand or more workmen and represented an investment of many millions of what seem in the mid-twentieth century very valuable francs. There was one such enterprise for mining coal at Anzin in the north, another for metallurgy at Le Creusot in central France, and a third for making glass at Saint-Gobain in Picardy.[32] Anzin was to be the inspiration for Zola's famous novel, *Germinal*; Le Creusot was to come into the hands of the Schneider family and to gain notoriety as the property of men who were called, between the two World Wars, the "merchants of death." Establishments of this size, under the control of private enterprise, were a novelty even in the second half of the eighteenth century, except perhaps in shipbuilding. It is doubtful whether there were any as large in England before the 1780's. Privately owned mines and factories employing more than a hundred workmen in one place were no novelty in either country. In France the number of these increased rapidly during the last fifty years of the *ancien régime*. By 1785 there were scores.

While parts of France were not touched by this remarkable industrial development and England remained the most advanced industrial nation, her lead over France in the volume of output per capita from mines and manufactures was less striking on the eve of the French Revolution than it had been fifty years before. The same may be said of her lead in the use of machinery and large furnaces and in the development of large privately owned enterprises. During the last half century of the *ancien régime*, France was not falling behind England in the expansion of heavy industry, as she had been except for very brief periods since the religious wars. Early in the seventeenth century Montchrétien, after his prolonged visit to England, had expressed the hope that the French would learn from English and Dutch economic experience and again surpass them industrially as in the Middle Ages. On the eve of the French Revolution it seemed that this hope might at last be realized.

Confirmation for the view just presented of the comparative economic progress of France and England during a major part of the eighteenth century is found in the records of commerce and of population. Of course, one should be a little suspicious of official figures, if the ways of gathering them practiced under the exigent demands of Napoleon are typical. Napoleon's minister of the interior, Jean-Antoine Chaptal (1756–1832) — a chemist in his own right at a time when the French had come to rival the English as leaders in the natural sciences — left a warning for posterity about the statistics gathered in the Napoleonic era. Napoleon, he wrote, "sometimes demanded the impossible and insisted on getting data at once. He asked for statistics which, if they were to be exact, would have required several weeks' labor, and he asked for them forthwith because he did not know how to adjourn his needs. . . So it proved better to lie with audacity than to delay in order to tell him the truth. I have seen him affect a great predilection for Regnault de Saint Jean d'Angély, because he answered every question daringly, and would not have been in the least embarrassed if he had been asked how many flies there were in Europe in the month of August. Several times it was on such haphazard foundations as these that the government offered statistics on the condition of manufactures, of agriculture, etc. It was with an equal abandon that France was credited with several billions of commerce and industry in times of acute calamity." [33]

The statistics for the last seventy years of the *ancien régime* were probably not the result of this kind of guesswork; the times were not calamitous enough to require it. Older civil servants did not labor under the pressure of such an impatient taskmaster as Napoleon. "I may often lose a battle," he is said to have remarked, "but I shall never lose a minute." [34] Napoleon's dynamic personality was more in keeping with an age that was coming than with the spirit of the eighteenth century.

For what they are worth, the eighteenth-century statistics for the value of French commerce show an increase in the period 1764–1776 of nearly three and a half fold over the period 1716–1720. The figure for the earlier period is 214.8 millions of *livres* per annum; that for the later period, 724.9.[35] Comparable statistics for England suggest that the rate of growth in English foreign trade was slightly slower than in French between 1720 and 1774. The English figure for 1720 is approximately thirteen million pounds sterling per annum; that for 1774 is 29.2 million pounds sterling.[36]

Adam Smith observed that "the most decisive mark of the prosperity of any country is the increase in the number of its inhabitants." He was not impressed by the rapidity of the increase in Great Britain at the time he wrote,[37] nor was the increase then very rapid. According to the best available figures, which leave much to be desired because they are not based on any census, the population of England and Wales in 1720 was a shade over six millions. In 1790, fourteen years after *The Wealth of Nations* appeared, the population numbered between 8.2 and 8.6 millions.[38]

The figures for France leave even more to be desired. But taking all the departments which comprise the France of 1950, the population in 1720, eight years after the War of the Spanish Succession, was perhaps about twenty millions. This country had not increased in inhabitants since the early fourteenth century. During the latter part of Louis XIV's reign the continual wars waged by the crown against various European coalitions are supposed to have caused a reduction in the population, less the result of deaths in battle than of economic hardships involved in maintaining large armies in the field. But after these wars ended conditions changed. In 1789 the most reasonable figure for the population of the same area is twenty-six millions.[39] During the seventy years from 1720 to 1789 some five million French, as compared to little more than two million English and Welsh, were added to the world's population. This period, when the growth was comparatively slow, is the only stretch of time during the two hundred years preceding the Second World War when the inhabitants of France have multiplied as rapidly as those of the other major European countries.

In Europe early in the eighteenth century a remarkable increase in the human species began, which was destined eventually to lift the population of Western Europe and America from a little more than a hundred to over seven hundred millions. The increase started almost simultaneously in France and England, and also in Spain and Germany.[40] Before the outbreak of the French Revolution economic progress and prosperity in Europe had been general for some fifty years or more. In Great Britain the advance in the rate of industrial growth, characteristic of all the Western nations, seems to have hardly begun before the 1750's,[41] rather later than in France. Great Britain remained the most industrialized country of Europe about 1780, not because of exceptionally rapid progress during most of the eighteenth century, but because she was more industrialized than other countries at the beginning of the century. As the American War of Independence was ending, the island owed its preëminent position in heavy industry to the early leadership gained in the use of coal, cast iron, and power-driven machinery during the reigns of Elizabeth, James I, and Charles I. Unlike the early "industrial revolution" of that period, the "industrial revolution" of the eighteenth century ought not to be regarded as especially English or British, but as European.

A quickening of economic progress was notable almost everywhere on the Continent in the 1730's and 1740's. In Spain industrial development after 1735 was hardly less remarkable than in France.[42] Germany also grew more prosperous during the Prussian kingship of Frederick the Great (1740–1786) and his successor, Frederick William II (1786–1797).[43] New strata of iron ore were discovered and worked in Upper Silesia.[44] The coal mines in Silesia and in the Ruhr took on a considerable importance for the first time; in the Ruhr the output is said to have increased from 52,343 tons in 1764 to 231,788 tons in 1791.[45] In 1788 a writer in the *Encyclopédie méthodique* estimated the number of workers in the Prussian textile industry at 123,000 (out of a total population of only a few millions). According to his estimate one-half of all the cloth was produced for export. He went to some pains to insist that Frederick the Great had protected and favored manufactures in every possible way, especially after the Seven Years' War of 1756 to 1763.[46]

When *The Wealth of Nations* appeared in 1776, the Europeans everywhere were increasing their production and trade. In sparsely settled North America, so much of which had been won fourteen years before for the British crown and so much of which was about to be lost for the same crown, the *rate* of growth was more rapid than in populous Europe. Adam Smith's great book reflects these conditions of general prosperity. "It deserves to be remarked, perhaps," he wrote, "that it is in the progressive state, while the society is advancing to the further acquisition, rather than when it has acquired its full complement of riches, that the condition of the labouring poor, of the great body of the people, seems to be the happiest and the most comfortable. It is hard in the stationary, and miserable in the declining state. The progressive state is in reality the cheerful and the hearty state to all the different orders of society. The stationary is dull; the declining, melancholy." [47]

From the material standpoint, which is not the only one that should be considered (some economists to the contrary notwithstanding), is it not less the total amount of wealth that men have which leads them to rejoice than the fact that their wealth is increasing? If a citizen of the industrialized United States were carried into the eighteenth century by magic (like Ralph Pendrel in Henry James's novel, *The Sense of the Past*) he would doubtless feel lost without the material conveniences to which Americans have become accustomed. It should be remembered that no eighteenth-century man could have made such a comparison. Not having lived in the time of Henry James or amid the bathrooms, the central heating, and the artificial refrigeration of the early twentieth century, he could not form the notion some men now form for him of what he lacked.

In considering the material happiness of the Europeans during the half century preceding the French Revolution, the question that needs an answer, therefore, is whether the economic welfare of most of them was improving. There can be no doubt that in France and England from 1735 to 1785 the volume of industrial output and the volume of trade were increasing more rapidly than the population. The same was true in Spain, Belgium, most of the rest of continental Europe, and Scandinavia. Almost everywhere, then, there was more to distribute per capita.

How was it distributed? Both prices and wages were rising during these fifty years. The recent works of Professor Earl J. Hamilton and Professor C. E. Labrousse indicate that in Spain and France prices rose more rapidly than wage rates. [48] On the other hand, Mrs. Elizabeth Gilboy's statistics, worked out earlier, suggest that there were exceptions to this movement. In the north of England (in Lancashire and the West and North Riding of Yorkshire), where industrial development was most pronounced, wage rates apparently rose more than prices. [49] If, as seems probable, the general tendency in Europe was for prices to climb more than wage rates, were there compensating gains in regularity of employment and in increased opportunities for families to add to their income from other sources than wages? Probably not; probably as industry became relatively more important in the economy of Europe than it had been, the tendency was for wage earners with their families, especially in the industrial districts, to become more dependent upon their wages for livelihood than before. As crowding in industrial towns reduced the land available there for a single family to cultivate, the opportunities were diminishing for families of wage earners to farm — and so to combine industry with husbandry as had once been common. Hamilton has argued forcibly that the real earnings of European wage earners declined during the last half of the eighteenth century.[50]

Whatever the truth may be, wage earners still formed even as late as 1785 a much smaller proportion of the entire population than they do now; the proportion of all the wage earners who depended predominantly on wages for their existence was also much smaller. It is by no means impossible that the material lot of a majority of Europeans was actually improving during the decades immediately preceding the French Revolution, as Tocqueville suggested was the case in France.[51] Even if an older view than his should prove correct, the view that the bulk of the population was made poorer, it is obvious that the real income of most merchants, shopkeepers, and of nearly all persons employing wage earners increased remarkably. For a considerable few, at any rate, society was in a most "progressive state," "advancing to the further acquisition . . . of riches."

Among these few were the persons who courted and sustained philosophers, scientists, artists, and men of letters. The materialism of the eighteenth century was inseparable from speculative thought, art, and cultured enjoyment, at a time when the audience for works of thought and art was larger than ever before. A general impression of growing felicity prevailed in circles like those frequented by Burke, Gibbon, Haydn, Gainsborough, Fragonard, Goya, and Adam Smith — in the circles where intelligent thought and works of art were formed, at a time when thought and art had an immense influence on politics and on political economy. The sense of general felicity helped to diffuse among philosophical and other writers a new confidence in the capacity of the Europeans to bring about further unprecedented material improvements, such as the nineteenth century actually produced, and to combine them with the cultivation of the intellect and with the increasingly civilized intercourse, in which many great men of the eighteenth century took pride.

(3) *The Triumph of Industrial Civilization*

If the phrase "industrial revolution" were retained as a title for the progressive eighteenth century, how could we differentiate this period from a later one during which industrial progress became so much more rapid in rate, so mechanical in nature, so world-wide in scope? Sir William Ashley, one of the two pupils whose notes were used to reconstruct Toynbee's *Lectures*, wrote that the lecturer used the word "revolution" in the sense of "a rapid and sweeping phase" of "evolution." [1] If such a change in the tempo of industrial development is the proper test, the accession of George III in 1760 is not the right date to select for the beginning of the industrial revolution. When was it that the rate of industrial progress became revolutionary in Great Britain? When in Europe generally? When in the world as a whole?

"What a change from 1785 to 1824!" wrote Stendhal. "In the two thousand years of recorded world history, so sharp a revolution in customs, ideas, and beliefs has perhaps never occurred before."[2] During his life, Stendhal's most widely read book was neither of those by which he is now generally known — *La Chartreuse de Parme* and *Le Rouge et le noir*. It was *Racine et Shakespeare*, an essay published in 1825, in which he examined the social changes that were leading in the arts from classicism to romanticism. An unprecedented acceleration of industrial progress began, not in 1750 or 1760, but in the 1780's.[3] It was then also that the movement of industrial labor from domestic to factory manufacture became unprecedentedly rapid. Unlike a modern economist, Stendhal was thinking, as his words indicate, of an upheaval in the whole of European history. Yet if our concern were merely with the rate of industrial growth and the spread of industrial capitalism, there is a good statistical reason for fixing, as Stendhal did in *Racine et Shakespeare*, on 1785 as a crucial date.

The insight of the artist, even when tested by statistics, often turns out to be clearer than that of a long line of professional students of history. One is reminded of some words of the Athenian in Plato's *Laws*: "Poets are a divine race, and often in their strains, by the aid of the Muses and the Graces, they attain the truth of history." [4]

Two technical inventions were of primary importance in bringing about a phenomenal growth in British industrial output: the "puddling" process which made possible the widespread use of coal in the manufacture of bar iron, and the adaption of steam power, hitherto employed only for pumping up water, to manufacturing and in particular to spinning. It was not until 1784 that fresh methods of puddling and rolling were combined and coördinated into a single new process by Henry Cort. James Watt took out a patent for his famous new type of steam engine in 1780. But the late Professor Edwin F. Gay told me that this engine, and the new spinning machinery sponsored by Richard Arkwright, began greatly to stimulate industrial and commercial growth only after the quashing of Watt's and Arkwright's patents by the courts in 1785 had made it possible for any adventurer with capital to develop the new kinds of machine production.[5]

After 1785 the powerful steam-driven machinery and the new methods of making iron with the help of coal came into extensive use for the first time. In Great Britain the critical turning point which differentiated British from continental progress in the production of cotton, coal, iron, and other industrial commodities was the middle eighties. For example, the island was producing little more than a third as much iron as France in 1780. Between 1785 and 1797 the output in Great Britain approximately doubled. During the next eight years, it approximately doubled again, reaching about 250,000 tons in 1805.[6] In 1840–41 it had probably reached 1,500,000 tons,[7] something like a twentyfold increase in half a century. By that time Great Britain was producing three times as much iron as France.

Comprehensive data concerning Great Britain show that iron output is a good barometer of the change after the 1780's in the pace of growth of all industrial output. For the previous four decades the average decennial rate of increase had been 14.88. In the nineties the industrial production of Great Britain was 31.44 per cent higher than in the eighties. For the sixty years 1800–1859, the average decennial figure of increase was 35.6. Then during the sixty years 1860–1919, the decennial rate of increase fell to 21.5.[8] The period during which Great Britain set the pace for Europe and the world, in what became a race to achieve the great industrial state, lasted from about 1785 to about 1860.

Foreign trade figures indicate that the great speeding up in the pace of commercial growth occurred at the same time. British imports during the 1770's hardly increased 40 per cent in volume over the previous decade. In the eighties they increased more than 300 per cent. In the nineties they nearly tripled again.[9]

Twenty-two years after Adam Smith's *Wealth of Nations*, Malthus published in 1798 his celebrated *Essay on the Principle of Population*. During the interval between the appearance of the two books, a striking change had occurred in the rate of increase in the inhabitants of Great Britain, which is reflected in Malthus' fear that before long population will outrun the means of subsistence. It was no longer possible when he wrote in the 1790's, as it had been as late as the early eighties, for serious writers to question whether the British people were increasing.[10]

As a "rapid and sweeping phase" of "evolution" the industrial revolution, which began in Great Britain at the end of the eighteenth century, became a European phenomenon after the fall of Napoleon in 1815, first in Alsace, Belgium, and the north of France. In Germany and most of Europe the industrial revolution hardly began before the 1840's. It became a world phenomenon only in the late nineteenth century.

As nation followed nation into industrial civilization, the production of fuel and metal mounted at a dizzy speed. During the hundred and fifty years following 1785, the world output of coal increased more than a hundredfold. The world output of the iron and steel, for which the gods of war were thirsty, increased at least four hundred fold.[11] As it poured from blast furnaces, the flood of liquid metal came to rival the rising waters of ancient Israel which led Noah to take to the ark. "There was the age of antiquity (and of the Bible). There was the Christian age. There is the modern age," wrote Charles Péguy on the eve of the World War of 1914. The modern age, he went on, not without some historical exaggeration, had come with the Third Republic. At the time of the Franco-Prussian War (1870–71) "an average parish . . . was infinitely closer to a fifteenth century parish, or one of the fourth century — or let us say one of the fifth or eighth centuries — than to one of our present-day parishes." [12]

The progressive state of the eighteenth century, in which Adam Smith lived, was replaced in the nineteenth and early twentieth centuries by the industrial state, first in Great Britain and then in country after country. Never in history has there been a time when the volume of the world's industrial production grew at anything approaching the rate reached between 1815 and 1914. Industrialism swept over the globe. If our descendants take a world view and think of the industrial revolution as a phenomenal speeding up of industrial evolution, they will associate it primarily with the nineteenth and early twentieth centuries, and with the remarkable age of European peace which lasted, with few interruptions, from the fall of Napoleon Bonaparte to the First World War.

In the twelfth and thirteenth centuries again in the late fifteenth and early sixteenth, and yet again in the north of Europe during the period 1570–1640, there had been precedents for a rate of economic growth similar to that of the eighteenth century. Like the industrial expansion of the late sixteenth and early seventeenth centuries, which was confined to a few northern countries, that of the eighteenth century, which was common to all Europe, was an essential preparation for the industrial revolution. But for so rapid an increase in production and population as began after 1785 in Great Britain, there were no precedents. It was the transformations of the nineteenth and early twentieth centuries which produced an economic civilization of a kind unknown to man. The phrase "industrial revolution" ought to be reserved for this unprecedented expansion, with its repercussions on every phase of economic, social, political, military, and intellectual history. The industrial revolution proper led the mining, the manufacturing, and the transport industries to dominate the economic life of nations, and brought a majority of all the workers in these industries to labor for wages away from their homes in establishments with more than a score on their payrolls. It made common for the first time vast industrial enterprises with thousands, even tens of thousands, of employees. It led to the widespread replacement of manual labor by machines, to the regulation of work by machines instead of by the independent decisions of men. It made possible the construction of wagons, boats, airships, and even whole cities in iron, steel, glass, and reinforced concrete. As the materials multiplied, more and more buildings were put up less to endure, than to be replaced. The industrial revolution harnessed much of the world's work to power, artificially obtained from coal, oil, and hydroelectricity, and perhaps eventually from atomic energy. It claimed for mechanically produced and transmitted pictures and sound a large proportion of the leisure of the greatly increased population of the world.

Does this change of dates really matter? What are twenty-five or even fifty years one way or the other in the great ocean of time? The answer is that the conventional date — 1760 — for the beginning of the industrial revolution makes a false break in the economic history of eighteenth-century Europe and misrepresents the relations of economic to general eighteenth-century history. According to the popular misconception English, or at any rate British, industrial development was in sharp contrast to continental industrial development throughout the eighteenth century, and not just at the very end of the century.

There was an immense difference between the economic expansion of the eighteenth century and the industrial revolution, a difference which is missed when the two are artificially run together as if they were one process. In the eighteenth century, in spite of considerable travel to the ends of the earth, Western civilization was confined to a small part of the globe — to Europe and to the Atlantic coast of

North America. In those regions economic progress became universal, and there was much similarity everywhere in the rate of development. The older values of splendor and beauty and polite manners were blended, in almost equal proportions, with the newer values of increased output and mechanical efficiency. All countries were progressing, in a kind of unison, to a degree which had hardly been true of the Western peoples since the thirteenth century, when the stage of economic progress had been still smaller and had included only Europe west of the Oder and the slopes of the Eastern Alps. The common economic experiences, which characterized the "progressive state" of the eighteenth century, were part of a general community of culture (combined with national and regional diversities) which the Europeans had managed to achieve for the first time since the Reformation had produced a cleavage in religious worship.

This community of economic and cultural development was interrupted by the industrial revolution. That was not simply because the tempo of industrial expansion changed and because the newer industrial values superseded the older cultural ones. The tempo was not changing in all parts of Europe at the same time, or in the same degree. Consequently the European countries were ceasing to share the same kinds of economic and cultural experiences. France advanced industrially less rapidly than Great Britain and most other European states; she preserved the older artistic values better. The most populous among the great powers when the industrial revolution began in 1785, France had become the least populous at the beginning of the twentieth century. At the outbreak of the French Revolution about one European in five was French, living either in Europe or overseas. Now hardly one person in sixteen of European origin is French. After the mid-nineteenth century the industrial expansion of Germany became far more rapid than that of any other country in Europe. Such sharp differences in the time, the rate, and the character of industrialization reflected a growing disharmony of intellectual and cultural experience as between one country and another. These increasing differences were a cause of discord; they contributed to the intensification of nationalism.

The industrial revolution weakened the community of economic and cultural development in other ways. The spread of rapid and cheap communications combined with the phenomenal growth in production and population to extend the area economically and culturally interdependent to the entire globe. In the eighteenth century a considerable measure of stability for Western civilization could be attained if a fair degree of harmony prevailed in a small area of the earth's surface — in Western Europe. By the twentieth century such limited harmony was no longer enough. As countries outside Europe became industrialized, what had been mainly a European problem became a world problem. Limited community ceased to be sufficient; the only possible basis for unity and understanding became total community.

Yet as new countries were drawn into the orbit of industrial civilization, differences in cultural experience between the interdependent parts multiplied. During the early twentieth century the population of Japan and of Russia grew more rapidly than ever, while a marked slackening in the rate of growth occurred among the peoples of European origin. The new human elements introduced by the extension of the drama of industrialism to the world stage — the Chinese, the Moslems, the Hindus, the peoples of Africa, and the islands of the oceans -- had few of the traditions of religious, moral, and cultural life out of which the European ruling classes had emerged.

For different reasons this was true also of the new elements of industrial society in Europe itself and in other parts of the world governed by people of European origin, North America especially. The unparalleled prosperity brought by the industrial revolution put abundant material commodities within the grasp of the entire population, and the desire to be rich became almost universal. The classes in society which had been excluded as scum and dregs during the seventeenth and eighteenth centuries from direct participation in the intellectual, social, and political life of Europe were not in the same position concerning religious, moral, and cultural traditions as the Japanese, the Chinese, and the Hindus, or even as the African Negroes and the South Sea Islanders. They had not, as the Chinese and the Hindus had, civilized cultural traditions alternative to those of Western Europe. They had not, as the Africans and the Islanders had, settled primitive customs and habits alternative to those of Western Europe. So far as their manners and habits of thought were governed by traditions at all, their traditions were the same as those of the men or women they thought of as their masters. Most of their ancestors, like the ancestors of these masters, had been part of the Christian community of medieval Europe. But since the late fifteenth century (to some extent since the late thirteenth century) soldiers and workers in the expanding industries had been increasingly cut off from the developing culture of Europe. Since the early sixteenth century the Church had ceased to be the center of intellectual and artistic life. Since the early eighteenth century the Christian religion had lost its hold among all classes of society. Consequently religious services and worship no longer bound the workers and soldiers to their masters.

These excluded classes grew rapidly in numbers until, by the beginning of the twentieth century, they formed the largest part of the European population except in rural districts. With the encouragement of new-found intellectual leaders — social reformers, Marxists, and other socialists — the excluded classes determined to share the increasing wealth and all the benefits which they thought went with it. All men and women had now to be reckoned with if a stable community of culture was to be continued and developed.

For these reasons the industrial revolution had become by the twentieth century an increasingly disruptive force in religion and politics as well as in thought and the arts, which were undermined by the new passion for mechanical progress and the growth in output. While the economic progress of the late seventeenth and eighteenth centuries had been a factor working toward cultural community, the much more rapid and very different progress of the nineteenth and early twentieth centuries became a factor working toward disunity and intellectual confusion.

Consequently the violence done to truth by the false idea of the industrial revolution is not simply a matter of dates. That false idea has left the occidental peoples with an erroneous notion of the historical process that has given them the comforts and conveniences which, under conditions of peace, some of them have enjoyed in abundance. The disposition of most of us to treat the customs, traditions, and beliefs of our ancestors before the late eighteenth century as primitive and outgrown is without a firm historical foundation.

(4) *Its Intellectual and Cultural Foundations*

In the high schools and colleges we were taught at the beginning of the twentieth century to think of this globe as an uncivilized place before the great changes which accompanied the "industrial revolution" had produced a world which was, in every important way, so great an improvement on any before inhabited by human beings that men and women could afford to trust the future of philosophical truth, morality, and beauty to the material progress which increasing industrialization had set in motion. Such views persisted down to the outbreak of the Second World War; nor did they disappear after most of the fighting stopped. "All forces, social or political, which impair . . . productive operations," wrote a well-known economic historian, Professor N. S. B. Gras, "threaten the material and therefore the intellectual welfare of mankind." [1]

When the United States entered the First World War, many of our teachers, all our influential playmates, had left us with the impression that the only important concerns in life were the material conveniences: Pullman cars, electricity, sanitation, remedies against disease, and machinery driven by steam and hydroelectric power. We associated all of them with the changes produced by the "industrial revolution" described in the textbooks. It was taken for granted that the Christian religious beliefs, which had flourished earlier, were simply the superstitions of backward men and women without our advantages. Professor T. N. Carver, the well-known Harvard economist, told us that, if we needed a religion, it ought to be a "religion worth having." [2] He meant what he said; he used the word "worth" in the specific sense given it by contemporary economics. He reduced art, along with religion, to economic terms. Thus the "worth" of a work of art, in the last analysis, was measured by the volume of production which it generated. It might stimulate the wealthy businessman who contemplated it to make more money than he would have received if he had never seen it. A person in the Dresden then intact, gazing at the Sistine Madonna (now in Moscow), might get what the Viennese, in happier days, called a *Stimmung*. This — Professor Carver opined, without giving scientific reasons for his opinion — might put the businessman in a mood to work an extra day at his office, and so lead indirectly to the sinking of a new mining shaft near Villach.[3]

The conventional concept of the "industrial revolution" was one of many notions which contributed to the prevailing early twentieth-century belief which Carver reflected in an extreme form. In the comparatively peaceful decade that opened this century, it seemed to most of the men who looked back on Western European, American, and Russian history that the achievements since the mid-eighteenth century were vastly superior to those of any earlier period of equal duration in music and literature, in philosophy and history, as well as in the science and engineering, the medicine and surgery, which were providing the technical means of producing larger quantities of goods and prolonging life. The "industrial revolution" was treated as an eighteenth-century phenomenon, and so it was assumed that the rise of industrialism was in fact responsible for raising the intellectual stature of men and women. It seemed to follow that if all life and thought revolved on the same axles which multiplied commodities and prolonged life, and if the outlook and the methods of the natural sciences were extended to the study and eventually to the control of human beings in society,[4] talent and genius would increase in every sphere of human endeavor. The idea expressed by Bacon in the *New Atlantis* had become a commonplace — that material progress automatically produces intellectual, moral, and even religious improvement. After the Russian Revolution of 1917 this idea (combined with another, the Marxian, of an inevitable violent struggle between wage earners and private capitalists) became for the communists the basis of a new faith in a terrestrial paradise.

Inferences widely drawn from the false concept of the industrial revolution have led to the assumption that nothing which was done or thought before the mid-eighteenth century is of importance for any present problems. It is assumed that the powerful machinery and the powerful weapons developed recently are indicative of a higher general level of intelligence than existed in the age of Newton. It is common to underestimate the religious and philosophical scruples and the cultural doubts which then beset the innovating mind in seeking material efficiency and abundance as the ends of knowledge, because it has come to be widely believed that efficiency and abundance are the *only* goals which the intelligent mind can seek.

The importance given to more immediate practical goals in modern times can be traced back at least as far as the first half of the seventeenth century. But at that time the cruel and treacherous sides of human nature were as manifest as they had been in the later Middle Ages. The wars of religion, in which these sides of human nature exposed themselves, were made more frightful by the new weapons discovered and used by the Western peoples. Enthusiasm for the single-minded pursuit of efficiency was damped by the spectacle of growing efficiency in killing and destroying. It was also kept within bounds by the renewal, especially on the Continent, of different industrial objectives, above all the objective of delight through art and through the new art of polite living.

After the Peace of Westphalia, as wars and the destruction bred of wars diminished in seriousness, as faith in eternal life through Christ and the dogma of original sin began to lose their hold over the European peoples, the scruples of intelligent men against efficiency for the sake of efficiency and abundance diminished. During the reign of Louis XV (1715–1774), under the influence of the changes in the French attitude toward natural science and mechanics and the absorption of English scientific and technological knowledge on the Continent, the new idea of the unique importance of material progress as a means to happiness spread to all European nations and to all classes.

Considerable political stability, good manners, increased production, faith in the rational powers of the mind, humanitarianism, high moral standards, and love of beauty were indispensable if learned men were to acquire sufficient confidence in the value of all scientific and technical knowledge, to disregard the danger that such knowledge might contribute as much to destruction as to production. Such conditions were also indispensable for the leisure and the calm essential to the best work of the mind in the service of science. The eighteenth century offered the European peoples these conditions; it provided the intellectual, moral, and cultural foundations for the phenomenal industrial progress of the nineteenth century.

Many great thinkers, men of letters, and other artists, and many scientists and inventors, whose lives appear as contemporary with the industrial revolution when that is treated as a phenomenon of the period 1760 to 1832, were actually part of the European civilization which made the industrial revolution possible — a civilization which was largely swept away at the beginning of the twentieth century, with the triumph of industrialism. Johnson, Sterne, and Fielding; Hogarth and Gainsborough; Voltaire, Rousseau, and Diderot; Buffon and Lavoisier (even Kay and Arkwright, who invented the flying shuttle for weaving and the waterframe for spinning); all lived in a pre-industrial revolution world. As rapid industrial progress hardly began in central Europe before the mid-nineteenth century, the same might be said of Kant, Schiller, and Goethe, of Haydn, Mozart, Beethoven, and Schubert.

Economic determinism — the theory that economic conditions are the decisive factor in civilized development — gives a false view of history. But one does not, for that reason, have to assume that the economic environment is without its relation to culture. The work of all these great men of the eighteenth and early nineteenth centuries can be better understood when it is recognized that none of them created his masterpieces in an atmosphere of phenomenally rapid material progress, phenomenally rapid mechanization of industry, or phenomenally rapid change in the speed of transport and communications. None of them created his masterpieces when thought and even belief were expected to change as rapidly as the methods of performing labor changed during the industrial revolution.

Without the civilized and harmonious life of the late seventeenth and eighteenth centuries, without the tradition which made kings subject to divine and then to natural law, without the idea that the growth of commerce was bound to lead to better manners, customs, and laws, without the improvement in the social and political position of the merchant and the financier which fostered the laissez-faire philosophy and stimulated economic enterprise, the industrialization of the world in the nineteenth century would not have taken place with such speed and smoothness as it did. We owe our material comforts and conveniences in a large measure to the intellectual, cultural, political, and social conditions of an age that school children have been taught to look upon as backward. The very restraints on industrial progress, inherited from the Europe of the Middle Ages and developed in new forms during early modern times, helped to create civilized conditions and to impose limits on war without which the actual triumph of industrial civilization might have been impossible.

The scientific revolution, which proved to be of decisive importance in the rise of industrialism, had taken place in Europe mainly before 1785, even before 1740–1760.[5] Consequently the scientific foundations were laid for industrial civilization before the restraints imposed on modern progress by the fear of original sin and the love of beauty had broken down. These restraints were as essential as the new scientific knowledge in the attainment of the comparatively stable European civilization of the early eighteenth century. It was the restraints felt by the early scientists, as much as their scientific discoveries and speculations, which gave the Europeans of the eighteenth century a widespread confidence in their own civilization and its future, and helped to stimulate a belief in the inevitability of civilized progress. Late in the eighteenth century this confidence and this belief began to undermine the restraints upon the practical application of scientific and technical knowledge, and also upon the unlimited pursuit of economic enterprise by private adventurers for the sake of profit. The collapse of the restraints was responsible for the unprecedentedly·rapid economic progress, for the ruthless exploitation of the physical world, and for the general mechanization of life which constitute the industrial revolution. But the collapse of the restraints encouraged the Western peoples to abandon the religious, intellectual, and moral values without which there could have been no industrial revolution. The collapse of the restraints helped to deprive the Western peoples of the human resources of faith, art, and balanced speculation which had been an integral part of European civilization.

During the past hundred and fifty years, and especially the past seventy, the industrial revolution has not changed the nature of human beings. It has only brought into greater prominence aspirations which were always there, such as the desire for comforts, conveniences, and better physical health, while other desires, once more prominent, such as the desire to worship God and to express in work the inner human need to humanize and order through art the materials of nature, have receded into the background.

The conventional idea of the industrial revolution has interposed itself like a dense fog between us and our history. It has contributed to the conceit that the industrialized peoples have emancipated themselves from the irrational and primitive aspects of their nature, instead of having merely changed the character of their aspirations in directions perhaps as irrational as those of their ancestors. The fog which surrounds our past hides from us how irrational we are. It makes it difficult for us to take our bearings and plot our course. A more intelligent knowledge of the past and of the works of great thinkers of the past could help to reveal the unity and essential simplicity of all great intellectual and moral problems. It could help to show that unity and simplicity of outlook essential to thought, to art, and to faith are the products of diversity and independence among peoples, nations, and regions seeking common goals. It could help restore man's consciousness of the wholeness of his nature and so bridge the divisions which have made for individual and collective schizophrenia. It could help to show the true connections between the vast number of special disciplines into which scholarship is now broken. Such knowledge could help us to incorporate the valuable new material, together with the new theories, which recent specialized scholarship provides, into a synthesis in the life of the mind. The need for a synthesis is felt today in many intellectual circles. It cannot be realized by the application of ready-made slogans. It cannot be realized by means of the positive sciences alone. They will have to be combined with philosophy, art, and religion, and with the love without which philosophy, art, and religion are empty.

In the life and thought of the eighteenth century there were common concepts and propositions which artists and learned men throughout Europe understood. The Europeans themselves, and even more their cousins overseas, have largely lost the art of living life as a whole and the art of considering with their minds the whole of man's universe, at the very time when both arts are needed by all the diverse peoples and classes which the industrial revolution has brought into a single interdependent world. The crisis of the twentieth century compels us to reconsider the consequences of the industrial revolution as well as the nature and influence of the community which it helped to destroy.

CHAPTER SIXTEEN

The Enlightenment and the Progress of War

· THE DECADE OF THE 1740'S WAS A TURNING POINT IN POLITICAL history and in the history of science and technology. The period began with the accession of Frederick the Great as the third king of the increasingly powerful Prussian state and with the accession to the ancient imperial throne in Vienna of a woman who became Frederick's most persistent political opponent, the Archduchess Maria Theresa, daughter of the Emperor Charles VI, mother of Joseph II and Marie Antoinette. In France, where the most dramatic changes in European history took place in the seventy-five years that followed, Louis XV, now in his thirties, was coming under the influence of favorites of inconsequential intellectual stature, the most notorious of whom some years later was one of his mistresses, Madame de Pompadour. She hated Frederick, who snubbed her with a rudeness that she considered intolerable, and she had a part during the 1750's in dragging Louis and his ministers of state into the Seven Years' War on the side of Austria against Prussia and England. This war, like the other inconclusive wars of the half century 1740–1789, hardly interfered with the remarkable increase in French industrial production. Partly as a result of growing prosperity, the temper of the French people turned in the mid-eighteenth century toward the social, political, and economic reforms which culminated in the Revolution.

It was in the 1740's that Benjamin Robins, the Quaker mathematician, put the practice of gunnery on a new and much more accurate basis by the publication of his *New Principles of Gunnery*. European scientists were abandoning the superstitious prejudices of Newton, his contemporaries, and his predecessors, which had interfered with the practical applications of their great knowledge. Learned men turned toward material improvement as never before. Scientists generally overcame the hesitation experienced by their predecessors about putting their knowledge freely at the disposition of increased production and more efficient destruction.

Conditions of limited warfare had prevailed in the west of Europe for some three generations preceding the 1740's. They had encouraged feelings of relative security and of confidence in human nature, which were partly specious. In so far as the restrictions on war were the result of circumstances such as the poor morale of the fighting men and the high cost of killing, rather than the result of human virtue and community of understanding, the restrictions were most precarious. By intensifying the social problem of the outcast — whether soldier or industrial worker — the age of limited warfare sowed seeds of class struggle. It divided the Europeans, in spite of the common culture which bound the nations together at the top. This division provided new issues destined to lead the Europeans to take wars more seriously. Again, during the age of limited warfare, the growth in the size of armies and navies had imposed a brake on war because of the scarce means available for supplying them. But once the production and distribution of commodities increased enough to permit the continual renewal of the equipment, the weapons, and the other munitions, heavy fighting by large bodies of soldiers (artillery, infantry, cavalry, and engineers) became more practicable, and decisive battles — seldom witnessed during the late seventeenth and early eighteenth centuries — were waged.

The more complete wars, which began in 1792 in defense of the French Revolution and culminated with Napoleon's attempts to conquer Europe, partly grew out of social conditions which had accompanied the growing moderation of warfare during the eighty years or so before 1740. They also partly grew out of the prosperity and the intellectual changes which characterized European history during the later eighteenth century, especially during the fifty years from 1735 to 1785, when wars were still limited in purpose and scope.

(1) *The Citizen Soldier*

The revival of more bloody warfare in Europe was partly a result of the combination of two different and apparently contradictory attitudes toward the common man. There was a disposition to treat him as a combination of beast and machine — a kind of subhuman creature. There was also a disposition to make him into an abstraction and to attribute to the many represented by the abstraction perennial virtue which had seldom prevailed among the privileged few.

The first treatment was in origin more Prussian than French; the second more French than Prussian. But the outlook and habits of one nation inevitably affect others, even nations which regard themselves as standing for an opposite outlook, as possessing the opposite habits. Nations which are in continuous communication with each other are interdependent. If the people of one country could only see their nation objectively, they would be amazed to discover how closely they resemble their enemies. In the eighteenth century, when travel and the exchange of knowledge had increased, when European society was again much more united than it had been during the age of religious wars, it was impossible to confine either concept of the common man within national frontiers.

The concept which developed primarily in Prussia influenced military conditions first. Unlike the French concept, it had behind it neither a Christian nor a humanitarian sense of responsibility for the humble, for persons ill-favored by worldly fortune. Little support for it could be found anywhere in the extraordinarily influential intellectual and artistic life of eighteenth-century Europe. Frederick William I, king of Prussia from 1713 to 1740, the modern founder of conscription and stern, efficient military discipline, was no thinker. He forced his son and heir, Frederick the Great, to witness the beheading of the son's confidant, Lieutenant von Katte, for the crime of trying to assist the young prince in his own wish to escape from his father's tutelage. In order to perpetrate this cold-blooded horror, the king set aside the more lenient verdict of perpetual imprisonment passed by the court-martial he himself had designated.[1]

In the treatment which Frederick William advocated for the soldiers, this relentless Prussian king made departures from what had been customary in the new and larger standing armies of the late seventeenth century. It was he who introduced the brutal discipline which forced the soldier to choose between battle (with its excitement and possibility for survival) and a fate more ignominious, terrible, and certain than death in action. All kinds of punishments had been inflicted in earlier Western European armies — whipping, running the gauntlet, shooting, hanging, and so on.[2] But they had been inflicted haphazardly rather than methodically; in the French armies flogging had been abolished.[3] Under Frederick William I, execution for desertion and for minor infractions of military regulations, daily flogging of varying degrees of violence, became inexorable rules of army administration[4] rather than casual treatment arising out of local circum-

stances or out of the harshness of particular commanders. It is true
that it was not this king but his son who, after his unhappy childhood
and youth, first made use of the new Prussian war machine.

Frederick II was twenty-eight when he succeeded to the throne
that he was to occupy for forty-six years, until his death in 1786. He
proceeded in a more enlightened and restrained spirit than would
have been possible for his father. This pupil of Voltaire possessed
from his youth a sense of the European culture which, with polite
manners and distaste for bloodshed, had done much to create the
concept and to encourage the practice of limited warfare. One of
Frederick's first acts as king of Prussia was to abolish torture as a
legal means of extracting confessions in the small state which he
governed as an absolute ruler. He was at much pains to encourage
religious toleration.[5] His military objectives were never boundless.
After his disciplined Prussian soldiers, with grim faces and fixed bayonets, had routed the Austrian and Saxon armies in the War of the
Austrian Succession, he contented himself in 1745 with the retention
of Silesia, which Maria Theresa had ceded him three years before.
War was causing more casualties than in the early eighteenth century,
especially in central and eastern Europe. But the wars retained their
dynastic character, their limited objectives, calculated in terms of
economic gain or loss. Frederick the Great was unable or unwilling
to revive the relentless, murderous pursuit of a routed army, a practice not uncommon during the religious wars, but which was almost
entirely abandoned before the end of the seventeenth century.[6]

For all his culture and enlightenment, this famous king of Prussia
retained the harsh army discipline created by his father. He saw to
it that the whole expanding economy of his growing kingdom revolved
around the comprehensive military establishment which was a Prussian innovation, and which was destined to remain Prussia's pride.[7]
There was little exaggeration in the observation made on the eve of
the French Revolution, apparently by the most eloquent revolutionary
orator, the Comte de Mirabeau (1749–1791): "Most States have an
army; the Prussian Army is the only one that has a state." In that
sense Prussia was the first country, after fighting for religion had
ceased, to make a serious business of modern war with gunpowder.

But Frederick the Great was much less belligerent during his old
age than he had been in middle life; his country was still small in
population and territory compared with France, and when he died
three years before the French Revolution, no other European state
had followed Prussia's military example. The position of France is
revealed in the writings of the Comte de Saint-Germain (1707–1778),

one of those eighteenth-century soldiers who served in several foreign armies as well as in the army of his own country. On the advice of Turgot, the famous statesman-economist, Saint-Germain was chosen in 1775 as French minister of war. He sought to revive corporal punishment in the French army and to introduce the Prussian system of military discipline. Yet unlike Frederick, with his relatively small Prussian state and the system of conscription which his father had introduced, Saint-Germain regarded the notion of devoting a nation to war (or even of conscripting the choicest men) as a monstrosity. He retained the view, which had come to prevail in the age of limited warfare, that the armed forces, apart from the officers, must be composed of the men least fitted for peaceful work, that the army should represent the dregs rather than the cream of the national man power. In the memoirs which he composed in retirement on the eve of shouldering the French ministry of war, he wrote: "It would undoubtedly be desirable if we could create an army of dependable and specially selected men of the best type. But in order to make an army we must not destroy the nation; it would be destruction to a nation if it were deprived of its best elements. As things are, the army must inevitably consist of the scum of the people and of all those for whom society has no use." Such had become the practice. In 1772 the Comte de Guibert began his book with the observation that the profession of soldier had been abandoned "to the most vile and miserable class of citizens . . . a soft and timid multitude." [8]

When combined in eighteenth-century Prussia with an approach to universal military service and with the use of mercenaries hired in the most unscrupulous ways from all the states of Europe, brutal military discipline helped to keep soldiers in the ranks and to maintain what was for so small a state an army of formidable size. But harsh discipline was incapable of generating an enthusiasm for fighting such as was needed for the world wars of the twentieth century or even for the Napoleonic wars. Frederick the Great tried to raise the morale of the Prussian army by providing uniforms of good quality and looking out for the physical needs of the soldiers and especially the petty officers. Nevertheless the spirit of his men in the hour of battle was inadequate for the purpose of conquest. With his incomparable gift for recreating bits of eighteenth-century Europe, Thackeray in *Barry Lyndon* painted a picture of the Prussian army in the Seven Years' War. We see a mob of miserable unwilling soldiers, numerous old men among them, held in their places by continual blows (wielded by specially appointed slave drivers, some of them mere boys) and by the threat of a bullet from behind to keep them from turning tail on the enemy.[9] Soldiers fighting for Prussia, as for other states, lacked any sense of a special mission, other than devotion to the prince, which was a very old conception, fostered among ancient peoples and primitive tribes alike. It could be effective only in relatively small armies, when the prince could put himself under the direct scrutiny of the men and could share the hardships of campaigns, as the earlier Swedish king-commanders, Gustavus Adolphus and Charles XII, had shared them in the more primitive battles fought in central and eastern Europe. Frederick the Great was aware of the limitations of this personal bond where large armies, composed of a mixture of conscripts, pressed foreigners, and foreign mercenaries, were concerned. On one occasion he remarked, "If my soldiers began to think, no one would remain in the ranks." [10]

There are limits to the things a man can be made to do by fear alone, limits which can be broken through only by appeals to his dignity, to the peculiarly human side of his nature. One of the most tragic developments of the past two hundred years has been the fostering of the idea that war is an ennobling spiritual experience, appropriate for all men. So far as we are aware, the extension of the heroic view of war to the entire male population is new among civilized peoples. The warrior class was regarded with special esteem, even with something approaching veneration, in some earlier countries: in Sparta, for instance, before the Peloponnesian War, and again in Rome under the early Republic. The German tribes, which overran so much of the Roman Empire, are also represented as warlike by nature and as reserving a full measure of respect for the warrior leader. The early Japanese imposed *Bushido*, a heroic code of honor, upon the *samurai* — a small elite. But in all these cases, it would seem to be only a select group which was esteemed for its military prowess and courage.

A recent classical scholar, A. W. Gomme, has emphasized that in fifth-century Greece the city states were mainly dependent for waging offensive war upon the hoplite class of foot soldiers, heavily armed at much expense, and relatively few in number. "Light-armed fighting, such as it was, was left to the very poor, landless men, despised and neglected." Gomme tells us further that, for all the superb qualities of Greek soldiers at Thermopylae and Marathon, the Greeks "never regarded warfare as anything but a tragic interruption of ordinary life." [11]

In the thought of the scholastic philosophers, as represented by Thomas Aquinas, war was legitimate only when undertaken at the order of a sovereign authority, on behalf of a just cause, and with a rightful intention. On other terms war was sinful. Priests were forbidden to engage in it on any terms, because their calling was above that of the soldier. Their mission was to the ministry of the altar, where the Passion of Christ is represented sacramentally. It was unbecoming, therefore, for them to slay or shed blood; more fitting that, if necessary, they shed their own blood for Christ, so as to imitate in deed what they portrayed in their ministry.[12]

In the late seventeenth and eighteenth centuries, the ancient heroism associated with violence among the elite was losing its spell for the European elite. In compiling the memorials of his family after the Restoration of 1660, one of the Holles went out of his way to deplore "the infinite mischiefe that [the] custome of duells hath brought into the worlde." It "threatens to devide the union betwixt a Christian and a gentleman." [13] In his third great novel, *Sir Charles Grandison*, published in 1753, Samuel Richardson sought to demonstrate that the refusal of a duel could be more gallant than the acceptance of the challenge.

Signs were not lacking that this sensible, good-mannered attitude towards the duel was extending to organized war. On the eve of the Revolution, a writer in the *Encyclopédie méthodique* suggested that in Spain the military profession had fallen into great disrepute since the middle of the eighteenth century. Yet at this juncture of history, the Europeans were on the point not simply of reviving but of universalizing the concept of the military hero. How did this happen? The very attitude toward the lowest and most miserable classes of society which led eighteenth-century military men, like Saint-Germain, to consign them as scum to the army, contained germs of terrible social dissension throughout Europe and, as European civilization spread, throughout the world. It encouraged artificial exclusions of many kinds, based not on moral, intellectual, aesthetic, or spiritual grounds, but simply on circumstances of birth, occupation, or appearance. Such exclusions were not new in civilized history, but economic and military developments which promoted them were especially disturbing after slavery had been eliminated from Europe during the Middle Ages. There was no rational justification for perpetuating a social scum at a time when European thought manifested increasing confidence in the perfectibility of human nature under civilized conditions, and when Voltaire, Rousseau, and other influential men of letters attributed special virtues to man in a state of nature, without wealth or even schooling.

Many writers of the eighteenth century were insisting that the exclusion of the common man from the delights of the age was a blot on an enlightened society, since all men, whatever their birth or circumstances, were by nature much alike. The views of the reformers were conducted, as lightning by rods, among the fairly numerous people who then read widely and carefully and who attended to ideas with passionate enthusiasm. An increasing number of men and women felt the spell of the new message. They began to act in ways designed to improve the status of the common man, to promote social equality. On the eve of the Revolution, the change in habits of dress from silk to cotton was the result in no small measure of a desire among the more favored, instructed, and wealthy classes to give a visible manifestation of their sympathy, even their solidarity, with the less fortunate. Enough persons abandoned soft silky costumes for rougher clothing to bring about an important shift in the French demand from silk to coarser fabrics of cotton and wool. On the eve of the industrial revolution, destined to promote production without stint, this scarce silk, this aristocrat among fabrics, whose cultivation had not been successful in the northern, more industrialized parts of Europe, was being deserted by some of the aristocracy in the more moderate climates of France, where silk making had flourished for generations. At Tours, long one of the principal centers for the manufacture, thousands were thrown out of work as early as 1770, and in villages for miles around the wives and children of craftsmen and peasants, who had prepared the thread and other materials, complained that they had no means of helping their husbands and fathers to pay the heavy direct taxes, the *taille* and the *capitation*.[14]

At the end of the eighteenth century and the beginning of the nineteenth the desire of members of the upper classes to wear more prosaic materials led to long trousers and a uniform attire for men, not unlike the uniform of the private soldier. Eventually even women were to take up nondescript standardized trousers. In the twentieth century everyone came to look more alike in dress. But they were not to look at all like the privileged few of the eighteenth century or even of the later Middle Ages, when splendor, style, and elegance in clothing had been cultivated as part of the art and the manners which were of absorbing interest to Europeans of the upper classes, and which were a part of European culture.

It was contrary to Christian doctrine to bar any group of men and women from the happiness of eternal life because of their low birth or condition. In the late eighteenth century the reality of eternal life was becoming dimmer than it had been for persons in all classes of European society. Men and women were substituting for the heavenly bliss envisaged by their ancestors the hopes and prospects of greater joys on earth. A terrestrial paradise had not seemed beyond the range of possibilities, at any rate since the time of Francis Bacon. Hobbes had envisaged Paradise as an earthly phenomenon to be brought about on this globe on the Day of Judgment. After his time the Day of Judgment lost its reality for most men, but their worldly hopes increased, and these were no less earthly than Hobbes's religious hopes had been. With the diminishing seriousness of warfare in the eighteenth century, with the more progressive economic life which formed the setting for Adam Smith's famous book, heaven seemed in fact to be drawing closer to earth. If Paradise was actually to be transferred to this planet, were large sections of humanity, including the great majority of the Europeans, to be denied an entrance?

When the desire for worldly equality first became widespread, war proved the sphere to which it was easiest to admit all men on something approaching equal terms. Not long after the storming of the Bastille, in 1789, the desire to wipe the social stains from the common man took the form of making him a more willing soldier, by increasing the prestige of the military calling for privates and noncommissioned officers. The revolutionary governments were threatened from abroad by foreign invaders, with Austria and Prussia no longer enemies but allies, and both encouraged by some of the old French nobility as well as by Marie Antoinette, who appealed to her Hapsburg relatives to help her retain her power as queen of France. Under this threat the improvement called for at the time of the French Revolution in the status of the peasant and the common industrial worker was soon mixed up with the improvement of the status of the common soldier.

In England compulsory military service for young men in their twenties had been considered desirable, as a defensive measure, as early as the times of Thomas More. Yet an English soldier of the seventeenth century, the Earl of Orrery, regarded it as an evidence of progress over Roman times that military service was not, in fact, a prerequisite even for the gentry. Men were left free to enter civil affairs at an early age, he remarked, and that was beneficial to society.[15] Later, in France, Marshal Saxe (1696–1750), who commanded French armies during the War of the Austrian Succession, took a different view of the matter. He suggested a five-year service law to take all men during the years of their lives which "are devoted to libertinism . . . and [which are], in general, productive of small comfort to parents." [16] An old European notion, derived especially from experience with the Dutch armies, that republics were never aggressive, left the leaders of the first French Republic with little compunction when they introduced universal military service. A year before the fall of the

Bastille, a contributor to the *Encyclopédie méthodique* had written: "A republic never takes up arms except to defend the law and the fatherland." [17] So it happened that all French citizens were called on to defend their own rights, the "rights of man," and their own liberty, equality, and fraternity.

Under the influence of the great social and political thinkers of eighteenth-century France, many of the nobility were behind the new esteem for the common man. The Comte de Mirabeau and the Marquis de Lafayette, fresh from his exploits on behalf of the American Revolution, were two among many nobles who took part in the first stages of the French Revolution. They helped to overthrow Louis XVI's absolute power, though they had no desire to guillotine him and little to depose him. They wanted to make him a constitutional monarch like the English king, to form a government in which the newly summoned States-General would take a part resembling that taken in England by the House of Commons. But they sought greater consideration for the common man than he had gained in England; they sought it for both the craftsmen and the land-owning peasants, a class that was rapidly disappearing north of the Channel.

The more extreme French reformers, such as Danton and Robespierre (who sponsored the guillotine not only for actual traitors but for some nobles not unfavorable to the Revolution), were disposed to respect the common man not so much for his potentialities as for his actual qualities, or at least for qualities which they attributed to him. But the most immediate tangible result of their intercession on his behalf was to put him into the army, a calling until recently regarded as fit only for the dregs of society. The revolutionary governments rooted out by force any resistance to army service by the peasants, such as was offered in the uprising of La Vendée in western France, an uprising fomented, it has been alleged, mainly by priests and disgruntled nobles.

The influence of the great French thinkers, and of enlightened noblemen impressed by their writings, in bringing about the Revolution is a thrice-told tale. It led the way after most of the thinkers were dead, and most of the noblemen who escaped execution had fled, to the citizen-soldiery and the "Marseillaise," the most blood-tingling of all patriotic war songs, and the one from which the composers of the others drew inspiration. This hymn appeared on April 25, 1792, on the eve of the wars fought in defense of the Revolution. It was composed by Rouget de Lisle, a young officer in the French army of the Rhine, garrisoned at Strasbourg. Forty-four years later, at the close of his life, it was possible for him to remark, without immodesty, "I made the world sing." [18]

Thus two concepts of the common soldier emerged from the eighteenth century to influence the conduct of war in the new world which the industrial revolution helped to create. The first was of a disciplined, mechanized animal. The second was of an inspired, godlike resister trampling here and now on the face of evil.

On September 20, 1792, five months after the appearance of the revolutionary song, the two concepts of the soldier were arrayed against each other in the battle of Valmy. The invaders, under the Duke of Brunswick, confronted the newly formed citizen-battalions of France in Champagne, on the threshold of the Ile de France, which the French have often defended with a special tenacity. The French concept won. It began to make much headway everywhere, even among sensitive and humanely disposed people who instinctively shrank from battle but who, equally instinctively, were inspired by the wonderful hope for human brotherhood, on behalf of which, it was plausible to believe, the battles were fought.

What has always given battle its prestige is the opportunities it presents for the exercise of courage. Admiration for military courage on behalf of what is believed to be a just cause is almost universal. The philosophers behind the French Revolution, Rousseau most of all, created an impression that a cause is necessarily just if the many support it. American thought encouraged them to take this view. Benjamin Franklin (1706–1790) wrote that "the judgment of a whole people, especially of a free people, is looked upon to be infallible." [19] Late eighteenth-century revolutionary thought aroused a kind of mystical faith in the judgments of the many.

A perfect knowledge of justice and right — of a just cause — is only potential in human beings. It is no more likely to repose in the combined minds of many men than in the minds of a few, or in the mind of a single man. Even the hope that the many will be more disinterested than the few, or the one, is often disappointed, though it contains perhaps more substance than the notion that wisdom reposes in the many. Writing with the French Revolution just behind, the great English poet, Samuel Taylor Coleridge (1772–1834), suggested that Rousseau was not himself unaware of the vital distinction between the truth, as such, and the view of any man or group of men as to what the truth is. Rousseau was "compelled by history," according to Coleridge, "to allow even the probability, that the most numerous popular assemblies, nay even whole nations, may at times be hurried away by the same passions [that beset an individual], and under the dominion of a common error. The will of all is then of no more value, than the humours of any one individual; and must therefore be sacredly distinguished from the pure will which flows from universal reason . . . All which is said in the *Contrat Social* of that sovereign will, to which the right of universal legislation appertains, applies to no one human being, to no society or assemblage of human beings, and least of all to the mixed multitude that makes up the people; but entirely and exclusively to reason itself, which, it is true, dwells in every man potentially, but actually and in perfect purity is found in no man and in no body of men."

Earlier Europeans had identified such a sovereign will with God. As men were receding from God, they looked for a new place to locate the sovereign will, which can hardly command widespread allegiance unless it is identified. In 1792 the instinctive enthusiasm which men and women feel for courage put to the test in physical combat got mixed up with the cause of revolutionary assemblies, which were assumed to represent the will of most men, a will that was coming to be widely identified with reason itself. So the common man, hitherto spurned as belonging to the "scum" of society, was given an opportunity to take the battlefield on behalf of justice, as interpreted first by representative assemblies of the Revolution and their political leaders and later by a single man, Napoleon Bonaparte.

Coleridge explained the consequences of this mistaken identity, in their bearing upon a new generation of violence. "The later disciples of Rousseau," he remarked, "wrote and harangued without ceasing of the *volonté générale* — the inalienable sovereignty of the people: and by these high-sounding phrases led on the vain, ignorant, and intoxicated populace to wild excesses and wilder expectations, which entailing on them the bitterness of disappointment, cleared the way for military despotism, for the Satanic government of horror under the Jacobins, and of terror under the Corsican." [20]

Faced with their own defeats, the Prussian militarists of the generation of Heinrich von Kleist (1777–1811), the remarkable German dramatist whose sensitive nature helped to drive him to suicide during the Napoleonic wars, observed that Prussian discipline alone was not an adequate basis for conquest or even for defense. It was necessary to learn from Napoleon and from the French intellectual and cultural world which Napoleon had exploited. As a result, something of the French conception of the common man was incorporated into the German. The liberation of the common man, conceived in the international spirit of the eighteenth century, gave the nationalism, which had lost its sting during the age of limited warfare, a new force, partly because of the more aggressive and extensive warfare of the period from 1792 to 1815. As battles were more frequent, as military campaigns were more extensive and frightful, old hatreds revived and new hatreds were formed.

A French noblewoman, the Marquise de la Tour du Pin, who got on well with the Emperor, described an episode in Spain, such as was repeated in many parts of Europe. A young officer of Napoleon's invading army was miserably assassinated in the headquarters of Marshal Soult. The murderer escaped. "As reprisal the village was left to the fury of the soldiers, who made it a bloody, burning hecatomb." [21]

The social problems, which the enlightened minds of the eighteenth century had sought to solve by generous gestures and political reforms, were intensified. The few rich and the many poor found no basis for unity, except in the grim and transitory bond which joined the peoples of one nation against those of others in the marching armies. It was partly the new spirit among the soldiers, generated by doctrines of the brotherhood of man, that made it feasible for Napoleon to keep in the field larger, more effective armies than any ever before assembled in Western Europe. The objective of his soldiers was the slaughter of their brothers who happened to belong to foreign nations. Slaughter of this kind proved an inadequate means of achieving universal brotherhood. Yet even in the cultured German circles where the supreme music of Western civilization was being composed and played, Napoleon was at first mistaken for a kind of incarnation of the new European hero — the common man, millions strong and ripe for joy. There was a time when Beethoven thought of welcoming Napoleon as the savior of Europe. Beethoven discovered in time that the world had to do with a conqueror who resembled the ancient conquerors of history and not the hero for whom the moving notes of the Eroica Symphony were written. It was not the strains of the "Marseillaise" but the music of Beethoven, most of all as combined with the poetry of Schiller in the Ninth Symphony, which expressed the authentic hopes of humanity as they had been stirred during those dramatic years of history.

The citizen-soldier and the "Marseillaise" are not merely tales thrice told. They were woven into a real and awful story, enacted on an ever vaster scale. A new love of humanity, good in itself, was diverted in the direction of fear and hatred which eventually in the twentieth century divided the Europeans more disastrously than the religious disputes that followed the Reformation. The more efficient military discipline, the new concept of the nation in arms in defense of the right, the rising morale of the soldier brought about in part by the growing respect for the poor and humble, helped to spread more widely than ever before the enthusiasm for battle indispensable for a renewal of heavy wars. These developments helped to bring on an era of destruction such as Gibbon and other Europeans of the eighteenth century thought the advance in civilization had made impossible among the nations of the West.

(2) *The Triumph of Science*

By themselves more and better soldiers could not have made these wars. Weapons, ammunition, horses, and military equipment of all kinds had to be supplied on a scale never before undertaken. The Enlightenment, which had a share in creating the concept of the citizen-soldier and the nation in arms, also had a share in providing the material means for more extensive war.

Restraints of two kinds had been holding back Europeans from exploiting fully the new powers opened to them by the advances in the natural sciences. One was the fear of evil, the sense of the dangers that lurk in human nature and that had been stressed by Christian revelation. The other was the emphasis which artists and craftsmen had laid on elegance and beauty of construction in all their products, at a time when industry, especially on the Continent, was still generally under the influence of artists and craftsmen. During the fifty years preceding the French Revolution, both these restraints were breaking down. Nothing perhaps was doing more to undermine them than the diminution in the fear of evil and the fear of war. The improvement in manners, the abolition by some princes of torture as a means of extracting legal confessions, the growing moderation of warfare, the increasing sense of the solidarity of all Western nations, the charm of cultivated life embellished by poetry, music, and spacious buildings, the new growth which began during the relatively peaceful 1720's and 1730's in the output of goods — all these excellent things conspired to persuade the Europeans with the best intentions that only good could follow from the more efficient and thorough exploitation of natural resources and of the revolutionary scientific discoveries of the previous two hundred years. Material improvement was coming to be thought of as a symptom of increasing intelligence. Increases in intelligence were coming to be considered as harbingers of good will and peace. It followed that scientists could devote their minds to material improvement with free consciences, which had been lacking when the possibilities that science offered for more wealth and longer life had aroused the enthusiasm of Bacon and Descartes. Influential eighteenth-century men felt that the position was being reached for which Pascal had hardly hoped this side of paradise, where might and justice would be on the same side.

The increasing concentration of the intellect upon material improvement and the growing interest in the manufacture of cheaper and more uniform products were almost certain eventually to weaken the concern of the Europeans with the elegance and beauty of the commodities they made. While there is a sense in which delight and efficiency are dependent on each other, a powerful shift in emphasis in the direction of one is almost inevitably at the expense of the other. As low costs of production and immediate practical effectiveness in the objects produced became the main object of work, and of the technical knowledge connected with it, less and less attention was given to beauty and endurance in the products. Thus the restraint imposed by the love of art upon the manufacture of more productive tools and more destructive weapons was beginning to disappear along with the other restraint provided by the fear of evil.

During the last half of the eighteenth century there developed a theory of the inevitability of human improvement. Montesquieu contributed to it by his considered statement that the natural effect of commerce is to improve manners and "to lead to peace." A year after these words of his first appeared in print, the law of progress was stated.[1] In 1749, the year of Buffon's first three volumes, young Anne Robert Jacques Turgot, the future economist and minister of finance, was completing his studies for the priesthood. He took the occasion to deliver an address in which he suggested that there is a law of human societies which makes civilization a continual, if slow, advance toward perfection throughout the world.[2]

These new hopes in civilization were accompanied by sharp changes in man's view of his own nature and the nature of work. The question of his origin and destiny, which had been settled for the Europeans in Christian terms, was reopened. At the very time when he composed his *Progress of the Human Mind*, Turgot commented with some concern on the spread of irreligion during the first half of the eighteenth century.[3] The increasing confidence reposed by the more influential minds of the Enlightenment in human nature, unaided by Christian faith, helped the nations, foremost among them France, to forge the weapons and to provide other material resources for the more numerous and more enthusiastic soldiers to use. This was not the first or the last time that relatively peaceful conditions in Western Europe contributed to bigger wars.

Though few men realized it during the relatively peaceful nineteenth century, the consequences of rapid industrial expansion, which the Western intellect made possible, were foreshadowed in the fighting between French and foreign armies that began in 1792, three years after the storming of the Bastille, and continued until Napoleon had been put safely away on the island of St. Helena in 1815. Bonaparte threatened to absorb into a single populous empire the whole of continental Europe, including European Russia. His career has had many eminent interpreters. What concerns us is not his genius as a military commander and political ruler, but the spirit of conquest that he embodied and the conditions of history that made possible such a career, for which there were no precedents in Western European history. The precedents were Caesar and Alexander, with whose names as generals Napoleon's was linked by our fathers and grandfathers.

How was it possible for Napoleon to continue raising large armies, in spite of the enormous casualties in battles, and to move his armies from France to the Atlantic coast of Portugal, and thousands of miles overland through mountain and across water barriers to Egypt, the Volga, and beyond? How was it possible for him to act with such imprudent precipitation as Chaptal described with regard not only to huge armies but to the entire economies of tens of millions of people? What were the relations between the changing outlook of the mind, together with the growth of industrial output, toward the end of the *ancien régime* and the more extensive warfare that followed the Revolution?

During the half century preceding the Revolution, the intellectual and economic conditions were being prepared in Europe, above all in France, which led from wars of position to wars of movement. Science came to engage more minds of great talent than in the past. As religious speculations and mysteries lost some of their attraction for the intellect, scientists devoted their lives more entirely to the advancement of science. At the same time an enthusiasm, which had sprung up in Great Britain during the early English "industrial revolution," for the application of scientific discoveries to agriculture, transport, mining, and manufacturing, became European.

Hitherto artistic conceptions had imposed limitations upon the production of effective and abundant firearms and other weapons. While the earlier producers of arms had invariably turned to artists, and while artists had insisted, at the expense of military efficiency, on decorations and embellishments for warships, cannon, and small arms, a tendency that was apparently new can be detected in the late eighteenth century. Architects began to include the manufacture of arms on a large scale as a part of their visions as town planners.

The plans drawn up by Claude Nicholas Ledoux (1736–1806) are a case in point. His most grandiose conception was an immense ideal town. He aimed to combine with art the theoretical ideas of Rousseau concerning society and education, and at the same time to reconcile in architecture the classical style with the baroque. In 1773 he was entrusted by J. C. Trudaine, then *intendant des finances*, with the task of repairing and enlarging the buildings of the salt manufacture at Chaux, in Lorraine. It was out of this mission that he formulated his project. Though he was unable fully to realize it, he left drawings which have enabled the historical student to reconstruct the entire town, as Ledoux would have built it.[4] Its purpose was the production of salt. The curious thing is that, in addition to saltworks and auxiliary buildings for making charcoal, a financial exchange, a market, a hospital, public baths, a church, a burial ground, houses for workers and traders, a school, a thermal establishment, and a temple "consecrated to Love," Ledoux had sketches of an enormous cannon foundry, more than a mile long, equipped with furnaces and mills for producing guns of bronze and iron.[5] The time was approaching when an earlier procedure of the age of limited war, the conversion of cannon foundries to foundries for statues, was to be reversed, when the statues of kings were to be melted down for cannon.[6]

Wars among the nations of Western Europe, while mild, were frequent during the fifty years preceding the Revolution. The War of the Austrian Succession from 1740 to 1748 was followed in 1756 by the Seven Years' War, and then from 1775 to 1783 by the Revolutionary War in America, which engaged France to some extent as well as England, and which was accompanied in 1778–79 by the War of the Bavarian Succession in Germany. Frenchmen concerned themselves with the manufacture of munitions. Now that practical improvement carried with it more esteem than ever before in France, older techniques for making weapons and ammunition were likely to be replaced as rapidly as older techniques for producing commodities for peaceful consumption.

The general mobilization of all able-bodied men at the time of the French Revolution would hardly have been feasible without a notable expansion of industrial output, combined with a growing desire to put the work of scientists and engineers to the most efficient practical use. A number of developments were needed to overcome the economic handicaps which had helped to keep warfare within bounds. One was an improvement in the accuracy and frequency of gunfire. Another was an increase in the mobility of artillery and of the wagons to supply the cannon with ammunition. In addition there had to be a notable increase in the output of war materials, especially of the metal required for the guns and ammunition.

The intellectual movement primarily responsible for more effective guns was the development of mathematical knowledge and its deliberate application to practical military purposes. The theories of Benjamin Robins and other mathematicians, combined with the insistence of their authors that speculations be put to the test of experiment with guns and missiles, led to notable improvements in the effectiveness and the power of artillery fire.[7] A new school of mathematics developed under the leadership of Gaspard Monge (1746–1818), the inventor of descriptive geometry.[8] This invention grew directly out of Monge's work as a military engineer. When a young man he was concerned with determining the height of the lines of ramparts or parapets in connection with fortifications. He worked out this "defilement" of a fortress by a geometrical instead of an arithmetical process. Monge obtained his result so quickly that his commandant refused at first to receive it, but the advantages of his method of calculation were soon recognized. Partly as a result of Monge's influence, and still more of that of his contemporary, Lazare Carnot (1753–1823), the old Vauban system of fortifications was supplanted in French military strategy at the close of the eighteenth century by a new scheme called "perpendicular." This fitted in with the quick incisive method of which the new mathematicians were masters.

The principle behind perpendicular fortifications was *active* defense. It involved a concentration of artillery fire which amounted to an attack upon the advancing troops, as distinguished from the earlier defense which concentrated not on the enemy but on his preparations to advance. An older man than either Monge or Carnot, the Marquis de Montalembert (1714–1800), was the founder of the "perpendicular school." His masterpiece, *La Fortification perpendiculaire*, was published from 1776 to 1786, at the same time as Gibbon's *Decline and Fall*. It was under the direction of Carnot that Montalembert's plans were adopted by the French military leaders.

Under the continual threats of invasion, Monge was entrusted by the revolutionary committee of public safety in 1793 and 1794 with drawing up a plan for defense. His plan embodied a new concept of a truly national military effort. He urged that all the French resources be mobilized to produce every possible gun and to provide metal and saltpeter in quantities that could repel the coalition of European powers against France. Under Monge's influence a number of blast furnaces were converted into cannon foundries, a number of large iron forges into boring mills.[9] His eyes were on the religious property which many of the revolutionary leaders proposed to confiscate. His proposals included the melting down of church bells to provide copper and bronze for cannon.[10]

Not content with having learned from the bellmakers how to produce guns, the Europeans were now willing to dispense with the ancient methods of their teachers in the interest of defense and destruction. The last vestiges of their teachings were abandoned. Old cannon foundries, which persisted in making new molds for each gun, were replaced by efficient establishments, in which metal molds were used to turn out a series of cannon of the same caliber.[11] Monge went farther. His *Description de l'art de fabriquer les canons*, which appeared in 1794 in response to the assignment of the committee for public safety, contained proposals for converting village churches and chapels into cannon foundries.[12]

When the soldiers were mobilized to defend the Revolution, Monge was made minister of the navy. Carnot, who was active in the armies of the Revolution from the beginning, became what we should now call chief of staff. Later he became minister of war. Here were two great mathematicians in charge of the French armed forces. Their application of new geometrical knowledge to the actual conduct of war, together with their application of scientific knowledge generally to the problems of supplying adequate munitions, were factors of importance in the shift in Europe from wars of position to wars of movement. It was only a step from their concept of defense to wholesale offensive warfare.

On the eve of the French Revolution speculations and experiments of other scientists and technical experts besides Robins, Monge, and Carnot were helping to reduce the weight of artillery pieces and to improve the gun carriages. Cannon were rendered more mobile.[13] With the relatively peaceful conditions which prevailed in Europe and the increase in industrial output, new commercial pressure arose for improved facilities of transport to make possible the moving of heavy commodities more economically for longer distances and to concentrate industrial enterprises around indispensable natural resources, especially coal and ore. Networks of canals were built. Following English example, notable improvements were made on the Continent in the systems of roads with bridges. Better surfaces were provided for rolling artillery and wagons carrying ammunition. We have seen that the output of iron in France grew some fivefold between 1720 and 1785. France was producing more metal on the eve of the Revolution than any other country, possibly more than had been produced at the beginning of the eighteenth century in the whole of Western Europe, if not in the entire world. As production increased, more munitions, more guns of every description were forthcoming.

With the growth in the scale of military preparations, it became more difficult to distinguish defense from attack and to combine military effectiveness with intellectual restraint, as Archimedes and many Western scientists through the time of Boyle and Newton had done. Europe was discarding the intellectual and moral scruples exemplified by John Napier, a great predecessor of Monge and Carnot in mathematics. With the new confidence in the material destiny and moral perfectibility of man, distinguished scientists felt less compunction to conceal the weapons which their knowledge and genius enabled them to conceive. Instead of worrying about the consequences of bequeathing to their fellows and descendants more powerful destructive instruments, some of them, like Monge and Carnot, rolled up their sleeves in the central offices of military administration. They were putting abstract knowledge at the service of the practical directly, without intermediaries. They were able to direct the disposition of the more numerous cannon, to extend the new methods of using the guns, to plan the general course to be taken by the soldiers and sailors who did the marching, the sailing, the loading, and the shooting.

It is significant that the science they mainly applied to problems of destruction was the most abstract of all. According to C. A. Laisant (1841–1920), a later French *savant* who, like Monge and Carnot, had a military and political career, what distinguishes mathematics from the other sciences is that it borrows from actual experience, from the external world, a *minimum* of notions. Ever since the Renaissance, France had been preëminent among all countries in its contributions to mathematics. But under the influence of Descartes and other French mathematicians of the seventeenth century, the French school had set out to lift mathematics from mechanical and practical applications toward pure speculation, with its traditionally greater dignity. Then in the late eighteenth century mathematical minds in France turned in a different direction with a zest that for a time was hardly equaled in any other country. In the era of the French Revolution it was the French who took the lead in the application of mathematical knowledge to military purposes.

When pure speculation in the realm of mathematics could be harnessed for practical objectives, there was no science which was likely to stand aside either from the war office or the market place. In the late eighteenth century the gap between speculative thought and its practical application was being rapidly closed, not only in France but also in England, where industrial expansion was almost as rapid as in France before 1785, and much more rapid afterwards. Most other European countries were following the lead of these two states.

The possibility of winning battles by calculations in the relative calm surrounding desks, and by the relatively safe movements of munitions, was making warfare no more strenuous and hardly more dangerous for many persons than the ordinary labor of peaceful daily life. For those exercising administrative authority or giving expert advice, military occupations were becoming more exciting and rather more interesting than civilian occupations. War was coming to resemble a game of chess, calling for great ingenuity, in which the pawns were real men. As time went on, as the number of men and horses engaged multiplied, as the distances increased at which killing could be effective, it became more and more difficult for the men in offices to distinguish actual from toy soldiers.

Before the eighteenth century there had been writers who observed that peaceful periods were likely to breed war. Montchrétien had explained that this was because a quiet, tranquil life eventually becomes a trial to brave, enterprising men.[14] But it was not mainly because European life on the eve of the French Revolution was becoming too felicitous and tranquil for men to bear that they forsook the limited warfare by means of which the states of Western Europe had settled their differences for more than a hundred years. There were absorbing opportunities for enterprise in many directions — in art, in science and mechanics, in social and political reform, and in the colonization of distant countries. But the exciting pursuit of new economic enterprise in the interest, as it seemed to the enterprisers, of man's happiness, was reënforcing the motives for fighting, contrary to the intentions and hopes of civilized leaders. The progress of "commerce" might be improving manners and tending toward peace, as Montesquieu suggested, but it was also helping more than ever before to provide more destructive means of waging war.

The extension of an enthusiasm for military exploits to the mass of the population, accompanied by material progress of many kinds, and by the progress of administrative skill, made it feasible to mobilize and utilize a nation's man power on a large scale for purposes of general conquest. It was possible to combine the increased firing power of artillery with a concentration of fire worked out by the perpendicular school of fortifications. Such a combination produced under Napoleon a new tactical principle. On the battlefield fire was concentrated upon a definite point in the ranks of the enemy, until this was ripe for inroads of the infantry.[15] By advancing with fixed bayonets, a weapon of which the French had now become the acknowledged masters and which was more used in the Napoleonic era than ever before,[16] the infantry demoralized large units of soldiers, as the attacking French demoralized the Russians and Austrians at Austerlitz early in December 1805. Simultaneously the cavalry, which was massed in far greater number than in the past, bore down at high speed and in overwhelming force upon an enemy wing in order to overwhelm another element in the defense.[17] With the new resources in metal, and the increasing ease with which cannon were moved, such operations could be repeated several times in the course of a battle, until the defending army was put to rout. Increase in the speed of movement also led to a renewal of the pursuit of a defeated enemy. Battles in which "you are either victor or vanquished" were resumed.

More fighting power was obtained in another way. During the late seventeenth century the growth of large armies had been accompanied by the organization of an extensive transport service, which hauled food and other supplies for the soldiers on campaign. A stock of food for eighteen days was required. Each soldier carried bread to last three days; the bread-wagons of each company had a further six days' supply; the flour-wagons of the commissary had flour for a further nine days. In addition transport was provided for hundreds of tents and for much superfluous baggage belonging to the officers.[18] Then, late in the eighteenth century, the methods of supply changed once more. In spite of the further increase in the size of armies, the soldiers were again made to live largely off the supplies provided by the country they invaded or passed through, as soldiers had lived during the religious wars. The revival of the practice was facilitated by the planting of the potato all over Europe. This vegetable had played no part in the Seven Years' War. Twenty years later the War of the Bavarian Succession was jestingly named "the potato war" because many of the soldiers lived on the new food which they claimed from the fields as they moved along.[19]

The change in methods of supplying the armies made it possible to muster more energy for battle. There was no longer a need for the generals to consider continually how to move and provide for long horse-drawn trains of baggage, trailing in the rear of the moving forces.[20] As the soldiers took lodging where they found it, the practice of carrying tents was abandoned. Horses for provisioning were dispensed with, and so more were available for the cavalry and artillery.

It became possible, with an army of approximately a hundred thousand men, to provide an additional five thousand cavalry or several hundred extra guns. The change was attended by a further marked increase in casualties and in the decisiveness of battles.

Science, especially mathematics, was also working to increase the power of attack in naval war. English naval architects were the first to abandon what the modern expert, bent on efficiency, would call "the absurd and lofty stern, with its costly ornamentation," the charming but expensive and unmilitary constructions which French artists of the late seventeenth century had insisted on retaining. A hundred years later both the English and the French, for whom English technical methods had now a fascination, concentrated their skill on better armed, more effective fighting vessels. Soon after 1750 a succession of able men led inquiry concerning the building of warships into "practical channels." As a careful naval historian has explained, they proved "by actual trial . . . that much of the accepted theory was faulty." [21] Robins' experiments with guns for use on land were repeated in connection with the guns of men-of-war. By the beginning of the nineteenth century, the new knowledge and the new concern with practical efficiency brought results in sea fighting. Typical older battles of the period of limited warfare — Beachy Head in 1690, Malaga in 1704, and Toulon in 1744 — were battles of slow attrition and meager results. By concentrating ships and fire on a section of the enemy line of ships, much as the artillery concentrated on a particular point in the opposing ranks, Rodney, Duncan, and Nelson, the famous English admirals of the Napoleonic period, when England commanded an immense superiority in men-of-war over the French emperor, were able to modify naval tactics, to break up the enemy's fleet, and to win decisive victories at sea,[22] such as had hardly been sought since the Elizabethan age.

After 1792, particularly between 1804 and 1815, huge armies, set in motion especially by Napoleon, swarmed over Europe to fight in masses, thousands of miles from home. The armies thrown into engagements were now four or five times the size of the largest during the religious wars. Hundreds of thousands of young soldiers perished in battle. Hundreds of thousands more died from exposure.

Napoleon is said to have had 612,000 men when he crossed the Russian border in June of 1812. Within two weeks he lost 135,000, almost all through desertion, sickness, and lack of supplies. Three months later, the victorious French emerged from the battle of Borodino with the short road to Moscow open to their gun carriages and their battalions. They emerged with less than half the men who had entered the engagement. About 100,000 French soldiers got to Moscow, with winter soon to set in.[23]

Only a few hundred men had died at Valmy, that "decisive battle," as it is classed in military history, which had opened twenty-four years of battles. But before the Revolutionary and Napoleonic wars were over, the dead had to be counted in millions.[24]

When the massacre was drawing to a close in 1813, the Comte de Saint-Simon, horrified by what had taken place, addressed some questions to the mathematicians, which read a little strangely from the pen of a man who was later to put his hope in science as a solvent for the difficulties of modern civilization. "What right have you," he asked the algebrists and the arithmeticians, "to occupy the post in the vanguard of science? . . . All Europe is cutting its throat; what are you doing to stop this butchery? Nothing. What am I saying? It is you who perfect the means of destruction; you who direct their use in all the armies." [25]

As had happened before and as was destined to happen again, the wars contributed less than nothing, while the preparations for war contributed relatively little, to the economic progress of those nations on the Continent which bore the brunt of the destruction. The industrial revolution started in Great Britain in the 1780's, just before the new warfare began on the Continent. There the industrial revolution started later, after 1815, when the guns had ceased to fire.[26] War was an important cause for the delay.

Military operations interfered with peaceful economic development far more than in the period of limited warfare. Now that invading armies of many hundreds of thousands were let loose without adequate provisions on the defending countries, the disruption of normal industry, commerce, and even agriculture was hardly less intense than during the era of religious wars. The devastation and the accompanying dislocation of economic life were more widespread [27] because the moving numbers were so much larger. Only the improved manners in the conduct of war and the increased provisions resulting from economic improvement kept Europe from a return to the state of depravity which had prevailed in Germany before the end of the Thirty Years' War.

The new warfare imposed burdens upon a country, even while it was victorious, that a state which could remain on the defensive, like Holland, had largely escaped in the early seventeenth century. The defense of the Revolution merged into the conquest of Europe. Napoleon followed and extended the practices of the revolutionary leaders in converting France into a military arsenal. Even in the most tranquil and remote parts of the country, garrisons were stationed and munitions manufactured. At one time the dilapidated buildings of the old abbey of Moissac, near Toulouse, were used for producing ammunition. A saltpeter factory was installed in the abandoned monastery.[28]

With the breakdown of restraints upon the practical use of knowledge, scientific thought was put more directly at the disposal of economic developments of every kind. It is difficult to estimate the share of military and naval "improvements" from 1740 to 1815 in setting problems whose solution contributed to the remarkable industrial advances of the age. While wars were holding back the industrial revolution on the Continent, the intense preparations for war gave rise to some scientific discoveries which contributed to the technical progress leading to the triumph of industrial civilization. Descriptive geometry is a case in point. Yet the principles of descriptive geometry had been anticipated, to a considerable extent, by a seventeenth-century Italian architect, Guarino Guarini (1624–1683). He derived his mathematical knowledge, not from any military source, but from the complicated treatment of space in late baroque architecture.[29] All that can be properly claimed for war in this connection is that it contributed to an early appreciation of the science of descriptive geometry. Military preparations were not indispensable to this science. It may be doubted whether they have been indispensable to any important science.

With the development of the experimental sciences, which have interested the West as they had interested no previous civilization, all practical activities, among them the production and delivery of weapons and other munitions, presented more abundant material than ever before for scientific investigations. The more the peoples of the West devoted their energies to war, the more problems of military preparation provided subjects for scientific investigations.

Yet the success of the British in applying scientific knowledge to economic development from 1785 to 1815 was less the result of pressure to meet military and naval requirements than of the freedom of Great Britain from the fighting. Just as Great Britain laid the foundation for the modern industrialized state partly through its isolation from the religious wars, so partly through its isolation from the Napoleonic wars the island gained its lead over all other nations in what was to become a race for industrial supremacy. As in the early seventeenth century, England got many of the constructive economic benefits of warfare without most of the disadvantages. In order to defend the country it was sufficient to maintain a strong navy and to raise, without conscription, relatively small expeditionary forces to strengthen the continental armies resisting Napoleon.

Opportunities to sell guns to the warring nations on the Continent, and especially to the allies, were not neglected. In 1805 or 1806 a German traveler, Philipp Nemnich, visited the large Carron works in Scotland, where he found that in good years about 5,000 cannon were cast, many for export to Russia and Germany. These cannon were bored with machines driven by water power.[30] But peaceful conditions within the island of Great Britain were more important than war abroad in arousing inventive skill and in stimulating industrial production. At home people lived almost as tranquilly as in the novels Jane Austen was writing. Under her delicate guidance the reader never meets with any mention of the wars. Partly because of the improvement in manners that had taken place since the reign of Queen Elizabeth, the British were more secure among themselves than in that earlier age of extraordinary prosperity and peace, which had lasted through the lives of Shakespeare and Donne. The sensational newspaper had still to put in an appearance. There were still no vehicles of communication to whip up fear and anger among the people.

Such passion as existed for the excitement which war provides found a partial outlet in another direction. A remarkable romantic movement began in English literature as early as 1764, when Horace Walpole published his *Castle of Otranto*. The movement reached an extreme of strange fancy two decades later in William Beckford's extraordinary phantasmagoric Oriental story, *The History of the Caliph Vathek*, written in French and translated into English for its British-born author. Beckford had inherited an immense fortune from his father, a London merchant who had been twice lord mayor. At Fonthill Abbey in Wiltshire, the son with reckless extravagance put £273,000 into building a mysterious house, which it was possible to imagine as the scene of Vathek's adventures.

This movement in English art, of which William Blake's poetry and pictures were another manifestation, was indicative of a need felt by many of the British for exciting romance, which the prosaic nature of the new material improvement could not provide, divorced as it often was from both art and worship. In England, during the wars of the French Revolution and Napoleon, the longings of the spirit among people more comfortable and materially more secure than their ancestors had been were partly satisfied by works such as Walpole's, Beckford's, and Blake's, and then by Walter Scott's medieval romances, with their bows and arrows and armor, described, alas, as the meticulous historical researches of recent times tell us, with appalling technical inaccuracies. In 1812, the very year of Borodino, the very year when England went to war with the United States, Scott had grown rich enough on the stunning sales of the *Lay of the Last Minstrel, Marmion,* and the *Lady of the Lake* to make the first purchases of land at Abbotsford, that peaceful highland retreat, with its echoes of a fanciful past, where he was to squander his book-made fortune in building a castle at once majestic and fairylike. The British were finding alternatives for both religion and war in a world of make-believe.

In spite of their quarrel during the last three years of the Napoleonic era, neither Great Britain nor the United States emerged from the conditions of limited warfare which had helped to inspire the new confidence in the intellect and in civilized life among the Western Europeans. It was natural for the British and the Americans to attribute their increasingly good economic fortunes to special virtue and special intelligence, which they thought of as Anglo-Saxon. But both countries owed their escape from the serious consequences of the new wars partly to the expanse of water which separated each from the Continent of Europe, and which also separated one from the other. Natural isolation encouraged the very confidence which facilitated the expansion of both industry and commerce, a confidence largely denied from 1792 to 1815 to the other leading Western nations.

Thus an important proportion of the Western peoples, including those established in North America, remained outside the orbit of the new military campaigns, the first fierce wars with enormous armies. These were the very peoples whose ancestors in the north of Europe — in Sweden, Holland, and above all Great Britain — had prepared the way for modern industrialism, partly because of the somewhat similar aloofness they had managed to maintain from the religious wars. Through colonization, these northern European peoples had gained control over a large portion of those natural resources of the world needed for the triumph of the industrial state, with its enormously increased life expectancy and its enormously improved material standard of living. The Enlightenment made for bigger wars. But scientific and technical progress was insufficient to make total war possible.

CHAPTER SEVENTEEN

Nineteenth-Century Ramparts against War

· WATERLOO, THE SCENE OF NAPOLEON'S FINAL DEFEAT, WAS THE last tremendous battle fought in Western Europe until the German armies broke across the French frontier fifty-five years later, in 1870, and put several hundred thousand French troops out of action as they moved on to surround Paris and force the city's capitulation after many months of siege. For forty years following Waterloo, until the Crimean War of 1854–55, no major European state engaged in a serious foreign war. Toward the end of this peaceful period in international relations, revolts by the working classes, aiming at an increase in their political rights, were in the air. There was violence, with many deaths, in 1830 and much more of both in 1848 in several countries. These outbreaks of civil war were pregnant with danger to the future of peace, but they were soon over. At the time and for a long time afterwards they seemed to most travelers and men of letters no more alarming for civilized progress than the limited warfare of the eighteenth century had seemed to the travelers and men of letters of that earlier age.

It is instructive to compare Goldoni's description of the battle outside Parma in 1733 with Henry James's account of the arrival in Rome in February 1849 of two prominent American expatriates, the William Wetmore Storys. In the revolt of the previous year the pope had been driven from the Vatican to Gaeta, and a Roman republic had been established. "When our friends reached the scene," wrote James, " . . . apparent order prevailed; but this was not long to last, and their predominant interests and emotions soon enough found a centre in that most incoherent birth of the time, the advance of French troops for the restoration of the Pope, the battle waged against the short-lived 'popular government' of Rome by the scarce longer-lived 'popular government' of Paris. It was at this battle that foreign visitors 'assisted,' as in an opera-box, from anxious Pincian windows, and the diaries of Story and his wife give us still the feeling of the siege. They arrive in time to place themselves well, as it were, for the drama, to get seated and settled before it begins, and were afterwards, doubtless, with whatever memories of alarm or discomfort, to love their old Rome better, or at least know her better, for having seen her at one of the characteristically acute moments of her troubled life." The play ended at the beginning of May, when Mrs. Story's notes read in this way: "The French have retreated; saw through the glass a slight skirmish, but it was so distant we couldn't make it out. Rumour that the Neapolitans are at Albans or Velletri. A glorious day indeed. Margaret [Fuller] came in as we were at breakfast." [1]

The unmilitary atmosphere of Goldoni and Sterne, the same lack of concern with victory or defeat they had expressed in the midst of earlier fighting, seemed in the mid-nineteenth century to have come to stay. Scuffles were replacing the early eighteenth-century battles in a Europe full of people as never before, but still uncrowded and more civilized than ever. Virtually complete peace had replaced limited war. The contrast with the years of unlimited war from 1792 to 1815 could hardly have been more striking. How can we account for the new calm? What were the obstacles that kept the peoples of Europe for so long from their almost habitual state of war? Why should the Napoleonic era have proved no more than a frightful interlude in a long age of relatively peaceful relations among all the peoples of Western civilization — an age lasting at least two hundred years, from the treaties of Utrecht at the beginning of the eighteenth century to the First World War at the beginning of the twentieth?

(1) *The Intellectual Barriers*

The Napoleonic wars were an outgrowth not of the industrial revolution, which began on the Continent after the wars were over, but of the progressive eighteenth-century economy which preceded the industrial revolution. As it developed, that earlier economy added considerably to the material resources and to the potential leisure of the European population. In this way the progressive economy provided more adequate means for making heavy war than had been available before. But the means were much more narrowly limited than they became with the triumph of industrial civilization at the beginning of the twentieth century. For example, with an annual output of some two hundred thousand tons of iron in France and perhaps nearly as much again in the rest of continental Europe, it was possible to scrape together enough metal to triple or quadruple the number of guns of all kinds. But with the spread of the fighting and the tremendous losses of men and materials entailed in the new war of movement with its deadly battles, the problem of renewing the supply of munitions and of men became insoluble. One factor that brought the Napoleonic wars to an end was economic exhaustion. Another was the exhaustion of man power. The people in every country grew more and more tired of the fighting and of the loss of men and property. A halt became almost inevitable once Napoleon was out of the way.

What made the peace that followed 1815 more than a mere halt was largely the culture, the customs, laws, and manners, which had evolved in Europe and had found strong and influential expression in the great philosophical, literary, and artistic works of the eighteenth century. The Napoleonic wars were a sequel to the French Revolution, and for all its abuses, the Revolution was an expression of inspiring hopes in the better sides of human nature, kindled by the new faith in progress. The ideas of the Revolution — human brotherhood, equality, and liberty from the absolute power of sovereign princes — made possible the mass levies of men which fed Napoleon's armies. Eventually they helped make possible mass levies in all the countries of the world. But these ideas also helped to kill the older abusive ways of raising men for military slaughter. The mercenary system, and along with it the hit-or-miss methods of inducting men into armies and navies by violence and subterfuge, hardly survived the era 1792–1815. These methods fell into discredit. So the number of fighting men that could be raised by hire in Europe was reduced at a time when serious war required much larger numbers. After the Congress of Vienna had settled the terms of peace, the gradual disappearance of the hired soldier and of abusive kinds of impressment left the European monarchs without adequate traditional means of raising military forces. Only in Prussia had anything approaching universal military service been associated with kingly rule. Consequently there was little in the principle of monarchical restoration, which the peacemakers invoked as a solvent for revolutionary strife, to encourage new plans for developing large armies.

From 1815 to 1848 the most influential statesman was Prince Metternich (1773–1859), the Austrian foreign minister, widely called "the arbiter of Europe." A product of eighteenth-century taste, as it had flowered in the small German principalities before the Revolution,

Metternich was deaf to the good sides of the Revolution, but the principle of monarchy which he successfully defended for many years was not fundamentally belligerent.

What helped Europe to remain pacific for a considerable time was less the new system of monarchical alliances, which Metternich guarded with care, than the powerful eighteenth-century intellectual tradition, which was at least as responsible for the French Revolution as for the restoration that followed 1815. The humane outlook of the Enlightenment was renewed and developed during the half century after 1815. European thought treated war as an evil, during a period when, with the diminishing belief in the reality of original sin, the hope of conquering evil increased. On the subject of war, there was little difference between the mid-eighteenth-century intellectual fathers of the Revolution, who are usually spoken of as liberals or radicals, and its intellectual opponents, who are usually spoken of as conservatives or reactionaries. A French writer of the twentieth century, Julien Benda, has remarked on the unanimity of pacifistic outlook among men of letters in his own country from 1750 to 1850. "What strikes one," he writes, "in reading the doctrinaire political thinkers . . . Montesquieu, Mably, Rousseau, Bonald, Maistre, Comte, or the texts of the Constitutions of their times, is how outstandingly all of them turned to peace, in the sense that for even the least democratic, war occupies a small place, and is limited to the necessity of the State to defend itself." [2] Much the same could be written of the men of letters who were these men's contemporaries in Great Britain and even in Germany. From Voltaire, Fielding, and Smollett to Schiller, Carlyle, and Thackeray, European writers usually looked upon war with disgust and horror. Unless we are mistaken, nowhere in the works of the most influential European writers of those times is there any glorification of general war on behalf of nations or classes. Even the lesser economists were moving away from a chauvinistic outlook toward a pacifistic one. The notion that war is a necessity for man lost ground.

What was the nature of the hopes for peace as these evolved among philosophical, political, and economic writers during the early nineteenth century? How far and in what ways were these hopes an outgrowth of the eighteenth-century progressive society? How far and in what ways were they related to the industrial revolution which began in England about 1785? What bearing had the work of the European mind on the exceptionally peaceful conditions which prevailed in Europe down to the 1850's?

In the eighteenth century the new freedom felt by intelligent Europeans to explore the possibilities opened by natural science and industrial technology had been based partly on a confidence that wars among civilized peoples were bound to be, as Gibbon had expressed it, "temperate and undecisive." This confidence had been strengthened by the growing sentiment among the leaders of European thought that the rational powers of man, demonstrated tangibly by the remarkable increase of production, were gradually getting control over violence and war. Since the time of Grotius and Crucé, since the surrender at Breda in 1625, a succession of reputable and esteemed Europeans had published projects which aimed to bring universal peace among the nations, or something very like it. The work of the gentle and learned Czech, Comenius, was followed by that of the Saxon, Samuel Pufendorff (1632–1694) and by *Some Reasons for an European State* of the less well-known English Quaker, John Bellers (1654–1725). Pufendorff argued that the state of nature is one of peace, not of war, as Hobbes had supposed, but that this peace is feeble and insecure without international authority. Bellers' European state was to enforce its authority by a federal army at a time when, with the customary practice of recruiting soldiers from all the nations to form armies, such an international force might have been much easier for the Europeans to accept than it became after national military service was generally adopted. These writers were followed by the French priest, C. I. de Saint-Pierre (1658–1743); the Swiss publicist, Emerich Vattel (1714–1767); and many others who looked toward permanent peace among the nations as a real possibility.

At the time when many of the battalions had formed for the new warfare, when generals like Hoche and Bonaparte himself already held prominent military commands, the most influential philosopher of the last two centuries, Immanuel Kant (1724–1804), in the quiet of his native Koenigsberg, issued in 1795 a small tract which he called *Perpetual Peace.* It was translated into English the following year and has had a considerable audience ever since in many countries. Kant argued that history was working toward a pacific world, partly because the "spirit of commerce . . . sooner or later takes hold of every nation, and is incompatible with war." Here he was simply following Montesquieu and some other eighteenth-century writers. The idea that commerce was working for peace was widely held by the time Kant wrote his tract, and it continued to spread with his authority behind it.

What made Kant's tract more important for the nineteenth century than any other plea for general peace was another, far more original idea. He argued that in spite of the undeniable evil inherent in human nature, men were becoming capable, because of continual cultural progress, of acting increasingly on behalf of moral perfection. This idea, expressed in *Perpetual Peace*, was related to Kant's general philosophy, itself a product of the Enlightenment and not of the industrial revolution, which hardly began in Germany until half a century after Kant's death.

Kant affirmed that a realm of general truth, moral and intellectual, exists independent of matter, time, and place, and is binding on all men and women, because their rational faculties transcend their circumstances and their interests and enable them to grasp, partially at least, fixed principles of right and justice. In making this affirmation Kant was much closer to the great Greek and great medieval philosophers than to Hobbes. Hobbes had argued that men's views are in the last analysis nothing more than the opinions of individuals founded on the working of their senses, that such views are bound to diverge and conflict, and that in consequence the only possible agreement among human beings is one based on fear and enforced by worldly authority. If Hobbes's philosophy can be properly regarded as partly a product of the early English "industrial revolution," in the midst of which he lived the first.fifty years of his life, and if Kant's philosophy can be properly regarded as partly a product of the progressive eighteenth-century economy, then it seems that the conditions of measured, balanced progress which prevailed in the later period helped to generate a confidence in the power of the mind to control material conditions for good ends such as men had never had before.

Kant's hope for moral improvement rested, first of all, on his peculiar notion of transcendental truth, which divorced man's mind from the Christian God, to whom Christian philosophers had always related it, and from all the material circumstances of history, to which the Marxian and the pragmatic philosophers of the future were to relate it. "The moral law," wrote Kant, "is in fact for the will of a perfect being a law of *holiness*, but for the will of every finite rational being a law of *duty*, of moral constraint, and of the determination of its actions by *respect* for this law and reverence for its duty. No other subjective principle must be assumed as a motive, else while the action might chance to be such as the law prescribes, yet as it does not proceed from duty, the intention, which is the thing properly in question in this legislation, is not moral." [3] Secondly Kant's hope for moral improvement rested — though more remotely — on his discovery that a criticism of the reasoning process itself is the necessary prerequisite for any possible truths which have the reason as their basis. Without supernatural help man could be guided by a sense of universal "moral principle," of virtue, independent of all private interest or advantage (whether individual or national).

Kant accepted an earlier view, advanced by Spinoza, that peace is a moral virtue.[4] He combined this act of faith with his "categorical imperative," which made it incumbent on a man to work for what is "right"; he combined the categorical imperative with the law of progress, first stated by Turgot. So Kant argued that humanity was bound to move toward peace, because the sense of moral principle is always advancing in man and "rendering more culpable those who violate it." [5] With the continual advance in the criticism of the reasoning process and the increasing publicity given to diplomatic exchanges, which Kant expected, men generally would be better able to detect and protest against propositions or acts of statesmen which were not in the interests of peace.

What actually happened during the twenty years following the appearance of Kant's tract came as a profound shock to the European intelligence. Such slaughter as was brought about by the Napoleonic wars was not at all what had been expected. Still less was it what had been wished for. Apparently something had gone terribly wrong with the hopes that the European mind had come to entertain for the improvement of Western civilization.

Writing in Washington, in the comparative calm that followed another frightful war, the American War between the States, Henry Adams remarked that the romantic Horace Walpole, who died at eighty in 1797, "at his life's close saw about him a world which in many respects was less civilized than when as a boy he made the grand tour of Europe." [6] There was an inescapable contrast between the hopes of the age of reason, of the enlightened eighteenth century, and the fate that had overtaken the generation born during the Enlightenment, thousands of whose heads fell under the guillotine; thousands of whom fled from France to England, Germany, and the United States to escape the terror of 1793–1795; millions of whom died as the result of war. For this degradation, the progress of mines and manufactures, which had become so astonishing in Great Britain, seemed hardly adequate compensation. That intelligent and attractive French noblewoman, the Marquise de la Tour du Pin, who had lived through it all, in health and sickness, suffering the death of those she held closest — her husband and her eldest son — left behind this reflection, apparently recorded about 1830: "If the sentiments and the virtues had made the same progress as industry, we should now be angels, worthy of Paradise. How far we are from that!" [7]

Even leaders who had issued orders which helped to make warfare more deadly, battles more decisive, had looked for different results. Lazare Carnot, who survived until 1823, who has gone down in history as the revolutionary "organizer of victory," consistently opposed the increasing monarchism of Napoleon. In the books which he wrote, especially *De la défense de places fortes* (1810) and *Mémoire sur la fortification primitive*, which was published the year of his death, Carnot stressed the defensive intentions of Montalembert's system of fortifications which he had helped to develop. His last work even gives the misleading impression that Vauban had contributed more to offensive war than the perpendicular school to which Carnot belonged. Nor need we conclude that Carnot was disingenuous. In trying to make total war, his intentions, and those of Monge also,[8] had been defensive. The new methods of fortification and mobilization were adopted by Napoleon and his generals for purposes of attack and conquest which their authors had never contemplated.

After Napoleon's defeat the European conscience, as exemplified by philosophical, political, and economic thinkers, was not overcome by extreme optimism, such as captured the United States after the First World War and helped to bring on the second, nor by fatalistic pessimism, such as now threatens to prevail and to bring on a third world war. Seeking for peace, Europeans were not disposed to find fault with the humanitarian movement, with the enthusiasm for the common man, which had unwittingly facilitated the recruiting of large armies. They found little fault with the knowledge that had made possible the production of the metal, the guns, the general supplies, and the improved roads, without which the rapid advances of large armies could hardly have taken place. They found little fault with the passion for scientific and technological development which had made it much easier than in the past to kill large numbers of men in battle. To most people all this progress seemed excellent. "Commerce," the name they gave to what later generations were to call "economic progress," was regarded more than ever as the ally of peace.

Blame for the new era of wars was put chiefly on the spirit of conquest. Men were disposed to regard this as an aberration in the European mentality, adjusted as it had become to wars for limited objectives. The evil use of ideas and machinery that were good was out of harmony with the new hope in man. It was unlikely to recur if adequate safeguards were provided.

If barbarism had cropped out in the community of European nations, it was not because of the ways in which the Western peoples were becoming civilized. It was because they were not civilized enough.

Napoleon was a Corsican of obscure origin, brought up outside the circles of polite European society, with its admiration for rational thought. For the many who were fired with enthusiasm by his name, and still more by his presence, there were many more who called him a barbarian.

The answer to Napoleon which the European mind was frequently disposed to give was given succinctly by Napoleon's own countryman and contemporary, Benjamin Constant (1767–1830). Despite his early liaison with an elderly Dutch noblewoman, Madame de Charrière, and his long sojourns at Weimar, where he mixed in the Goethe-Schiller circle, Constant was not a disgruntled *émigré*. He was a moderate républicain who supported the Revolution and quarreled only with the extreme forms which it took. A man of wide culture and remarkable literary distinction, he provided intellectually a link between the reformers of the late eighteenth century and the liberals of the nineteenth. Unstable in his love affairs and in his practical life, he never deserted the liberal political principles which he was helping to form.

Constant called the pamphlet in which he commented on Napoleon and his wars, *De l'esprit de conquête et de l'usurpation dans leurs rapports avec la civilisation européenne*. It was written in the autumn of 1813 after the emperor's first serious reverses. One of its leading themes is that the new weapons, especially the improved artillery, have made war unnatural for human beings. Most of the soldiers now die by accident, struck by missiles fired impersonally from a distance. Gone was the excitement of bodily combat, which was gaining more numerous readers for Walter Scott's romances than had been provided ever before for literary works. In real wars there were no longer any Ivanhoes. The choice of those condemned to fall in battle had become so largely a matter of fatality that actual fighting had lost its glory. Conquest had become a monstrosity. It had no roots in the nature of man, and could be attempted only when a barbarian got control of a rich and powerful nation. Conquest was more monstrous still, because it involved the conscription of all able-bodied young men, and condemned them to a semi-barbarous existence at the very age when alone it was possible to form in them habits of delicate and just thought, together with the "tradition of tenderness, nobility, and elegance, which alone distinguishes us from the barbarians." [9]

What, above all, made the spirit of conquest absurd, what condemned that spirit inexorably to extinction, was the simple and obvious historical dialectic to which Montesquieu and Kant had already drawn attention. Constant explained in his pamphlet of 1813 that war and commerce were only different means of arriving at the same end, "to obtain what one desires." Civilized human beings could hardly fail to recognize that commerce was the superior method. Unlike war, it involved little or no destruction. War was the product of savagery, commerce of civilized calculation. Therefore as civilization advanced, as commodities multiplied, commerce was bound to replace war. The sweep of Napoleon's armies over Europe was little more than an anachronism.[10]

There is no evidence in Constant's tract that he, any more than Kant, was aware of the dangers inherent in material abundance for future wars and violence among men. If the progress of commerce actually led toward peace, as the intellectual disciples of Kant and Constant assumed in the early nineteenth century, it was natural to blame the recent wars partly on the backwardness of commerce. There had not been enough of it.

As commerce had made most rapid progress in Great Britain since 1785, it was not unnaturally in Great Britain that the first speculations arose concerning the future opened by the unprecedented growth of wealth, which promised to continue. The industrial revolution gave birth to new hopes and new fears. The hopes were expressed first by Jeremy Bentham (1748–1832); the fears first by Thomas Malthus (1766–1834).

Bentham's name has always been associated with the phrase "the greatest happiness of the greatest number." He did not invent this celebrated motto; he was inclined to believe that he got it from the English chemist Joseph Priestley (1733–1804). Whether or not it originated with Priestley, Bentham's inclination to attribute it to him is revealing, for Priestley was one of the first scientists who claimed he had positive evidence to prove that the soul is material. The Benthamite philosophy, which had great influence from the beginning of the nineteenth century, was completely materialistic, and therefore much closer to Hobbes's thought and the early English "industrial revolution" than to Kant's thought and the Enlightenment. What distinguished Bentham's philosophy from that of Hobbes was the idea that the pursuit by each individual of his self-interest is compatible with peace.

No one perhaps did more by his personal influence to weave Bentham's idea and purpose into the actual social life of early nineteenth-century England than Francis Place (1771–1854). Place started life in poverty as a skilled worker, a journeyman breechesmaker. By dint of very hard labor, he became a moderately wealthy employer, closely associated not only with Bentham but with James Mill (1773–1836), another of Bentham's followers. Place was unimaginative and practical, a man with no aesthetic interests, without literary gifts and with little capacity for sustained speculative thought. His limitations, as well as his qualities, made him the perfect Benthamite. His biographer, the late Professor Graham Wallas, has explained that Bentham and James Mill "believed themselves to have found a common-sense philosophy, by which ordinary selfish men could be convinced that the interests of each invariably coincided with the interests, if not of all, at any rate, of the majority. Pleasures, according to this philosophy, are all of the same kind in so far as they are pleasures, and it happens that the acts which secure the interests of the majority are also the most pleasurable. Every man, therefore, if he were reasonably well educated in his youth, would throughout the rest of his life aim at 'the greatest happiness of the greatest number,' simply because he would recognize that that was the way to gain for himself the greatest amount of 'the pleasure of self approbation,' and because self-approbation, being pure, contained more units of enjoyment per unit of time than any other pleasure. That was Place's position." [11]

There was none of the gaiety and charm of eighteenth-century European culture in their outlook. But it was accompanied in Place's case, as in James Mill's, by high moral integrity and tremendous industry. The early Benthamites were frugal and painstaking; though they were not prohibitionists, none of them drank. It would be a mistake to call Place an optimist in the early twentieth-century American sense; he always regarded life as stern, difficult, and full of disappointments; but he held firmly that with the rapid increase that was taking place in the available "units of enjoyment," it would be possible, by a judicious distribution of the units among the working classes and an extension of political suffrage, to add continually to human felicity, and in this way to obviate the dangers of civil strife which he saw were inherent in the industrialization of the country and the growth of wealth.

What Malthus questioned was whether the "units of enjoyment" could be increased fast enough to keep pace with the increasing number of people. He had so little confidence in the material power of man to go on multiplying at faster rates the output of the goods and services necessary to sustain life that he predicted population would soon outrun the means of subsistence. Writing apparently without much reference to contraceptives, Malthus overestimated the future disposition of the population to reproduce. Place was not unaware of the danger which alarmed Malthus, and toward the end of his life, at a heavy cost in personal reputation, he set about to check a too rapid growth in population by advocating the distribution of information which his biographer described discreetly as "neo-Malthusian." [12] Before many decades had passed, a marked decline occurred in the eagerness of married men and women to have children; the birth rate among the Western peoples fell during almost the entire nineteenth century.

Malthus made extensive calculations concerning the checks to population all over the world. But in what he wrote there is little to suggest that he had any inkling of the capacity of industrialized societies to produce. This was not surprising. There was nothing in history to prepare the mind for the pace of industrial expansion since 1785. Moreover Malthus was basing his calculations, especially in the first edition of *An Essay on the Principle of Population*, which appeared in 1798, largely upon his knowledge of his own country, and the industrial and mechanical opportunities of the tiny island of Great Britain, in spite of its remarkable resources and the genius of its people, were more limited than those of some other parts of the world. The power of other, richer countries — particularly Germany, the United States, and eventually Russia — to adopt and improve the efficiency of the economy developed first in Great Britain made it feasible at the beginning of the twentieth century to supply much more abundantly than ever before some five times as many people of Western European extraction as were alive when Malthus wrote his essay.

The discredit thrown on Malthus' theories of population by the history of the hundred years that followed his death is not unnatural. Yet there were dangers in the rapid growth of the world's inhabitants, of which he made little, but which civilization has by no means escaped. This growth has been a potent cause for war, in two ways. It has led nations which have increased rapidly in numbers to claim foreign territory, at a time when all the world is full of people. It has provided the nations with new reserves of man power to supply the fighting services.

These dangers were hardly perceived during the first half of the nineteenth century. Speculative minds held more strongly than ever to the thesis that economic progress was a factor working toward peace. Auguste Comte (1798–1853) reaffirmed that thesis in his *Cours de philosophie positive*, the last volume of which went to press in the summer of 1842, as we learn from an enthusiastic letter which Comte sent to John Stuart Mill on July 13.[13] Unlike Kant or Constant, Comte wrote with knowledge of the new forces that were accompanying the industrial revolution: the rise of the mass of the population with claims to share in the wealth that had been hitherto a preserve of the few, and the tendency for knowledge to be divided among specialists who had no conception of the relation of their specialty to the whole. Comte's remedy for the dangers inherent in both tendencies was to make a specialty of interrelations, to encourage specialization concerning the connections between the new divisions of knowledge. His notion of the rational processes open to philosophy was limited and narrow, though it seemed to him and his followers liberal and broad. His ideas of intellectual progress were derived from those of the Saint-Simon circle of which he was an early member. As has been recently shown by Professor Hayek, these ideas owed much to the Ecole Polytechnique, the famous French school founded in 1794–95, in the flood of French eighteenth-century enthusiasm for the natural sciences, by the very mathematicians — Monge and Carnot — who had helped to increase the deadliness and enlarge the scope of war. Comte aimed to apply pure scientific methods to the study of society and he failed to realize that this involved treating man as if we knew as little about him as we know about external nature. Comte denied the power of the mind to analyze and criticize itself, which Kant had insisted upon as a first principle of philosophy. For Comte the only valid knowledge was that which could be positively verified; thus his plan for the study of interrelations left little or no place for the rational processes as these had been exercised in theology, philosophy, or art, or even in early political economy. Intoxicated by the new results which positive methods were achieving in the domain of the natural sciences, he failed to see that the universalization of the outlook and the procedures of the natural sciences would discredit the values associated with the results obtained in the other realms of intellectual endeavor which had engaged the civilized peoples throughout their history, and would also diminish and minimize the results achieved in the future in these realms. Thus Comte helped to open the way for the dominance of scientific methods in the schools and universities during the past hundred years.[14]

Comte held firmly that the applications of his positive philosophy to history supplied convincing evidence that the progressive movement which he detected, from the theological to the metaphysical and finally to the positive state of knowledge, was a movement away from war toward industrial riches. A considerable portion of the last part of his *Cours de philosophie positive* is devoted to this theme. "During a long succession of centuries," Comte wrote, "the chief concern was to discover and improve military apparatus, and these efforts were not entirely without value for the progress of industry, which often drew valuable lessons from these warlike preparations. In this matter the social condition of the ancients should be regarded as the reverse

of our modern condition. In antiquity the greatest industrial efforts
were related primarily to war, which gave rise to prodigious inventions, especially in connection with sieges. In modern times, on the
contrary, the system of armaments is relatively less perfected than in
Greek and Roman times, when we take into consideration the great
industrial development." [15]

In these lines we have the germ of the thesis which was developed
later by Herbert Spencer (1820–1903), who set up in his sociology
an antithesis between industrial and military competition — between
the new industrial civilization and older civilizations based on war.[16]
As part of positive philosophy, Comte's doctrine concerning the progress of man toward peace in the industrial state had for him and his
followers, including Spencer (who was inclined to deny the influence
of his master), the validity of a scientific law. It was an aspect of the
law of progress, set forth by Turgot a hundred years before and amplified fifty years after that by Condorcet, with the inspired fervor of
his enthusiasm for the French Revolution personifying justice, in his
Esquisse d'un tableau historique des progrès de l'esprit humain.

During the middle decades of the nineteenth century, it seemed
that all streams of thought were leading in one direction. For a century the doctrines of the leading political economists had lent support
to the view that the pursuit of wealth was properly the object of individuals and of nations, and that peace was much more favorable
than war could be to the increase of the wealth of one's own nation.
In the main this was the position of the French physiocrats, who preceded Adam Smith, as well as of the English so-called "classical
school" of political economy, who followed him, and of Comte, who
aimed to replace economics by his positive philosophy.

François Quesnay (1694–1774) has been regarded as the founder
of the physiocratic school. He held that wars for commerce required
such expensive military establishments that they became ruinous for
all the nations which engaged in them, regardless of the outcome.[17]
"If war enriched some of the peoples of antiquity," remarked a writer
in the *Encyclopédie méthodique*, "it impoverishes and makes miserable the peoples of modern times." [18]

The leading economists from Adam Smith and J. B. Say to John
Stuart Mill and C. F. Bastiat were more and more widely read. Their
works formed a part of the regular fare of a general audience for
books, an audience whose interests still transcended national boundaries. Among this audience ideas were taken seriously. Economic
doctrine as established by the physiocrats and by Adam Smith and
his followers has never had so much influence on thought and political

policy as during the half century or so after 1815, first and foremost in Great Britain, the United States, and the British colonies, but also in France and other Latin countries. In Germany and Austria, the influence, while not so predominant, was nevertheless considerable.

In the English-speaking countries some said and many thought that through his work Adam Smith had done more for human happiness than any other man. Adam Smith and nearly all the economists who were listened to in the early nineteenth century showed that nations had open to them an unparalleled opportunity to increase their wealth by industry and trade, that the older means of adding to the wealth of nations by conquest was by comparison unrepaying. To this view of the national interest, Comte and Spencer (in his early period) added the pacifistic assurance that a scientific law was leading the nations of the world away from the military to the industrial state.

If the pursuit of private advantage by the mercantile classes before the industrial revolution had promoted peace, did it not follow that the pursuit of private advantage by the overwhelmingly more numerous working classes would raise even more powerful barriers against war? That was the hope contained in the doctrines of the political economists and sociologists, from Bentham through Comte, who had direct experience of the industrial revolution. That continued to be a strong hope for the generations that followed. It still lingers as a faint hope in the mid-twentieth century, a hundred years after the death of Comte.

Not all the writers of the early nineteenth century were sanguine that the pursuit of economic advantage was likely to improve human manners, customs, and laws. Not all were sanguine concerning the potentialities of human nature to seek the right in an increasingly commercialized world. Not all were confident that virtue, which so many of the rich had failed to practice, would prevail among the poor, if only the poor grew richer. There were great French artists — notable among them Hugo (1802–1885) and Courbet (1819–1877) — who put high hopes in the people, who were heirs to the spirit of the French Revolution in its most generous aspects. But Stendhal (1783–1842) considered the tranquillity following the Napoleonic campaigns sad, dull, tasteless, and unenduring. Delacroix (1799–1863), who was probably a natural son of Talleyrand, had a distrust for the people that was equaled only by his boredom with bourgeois society. In his great epic of contemporary France at peace, Balzac (1799–1850) painted pictures of greed, jealousy, and depravity, which for their bitterness have few equals in any literature. "Misers have no belief in a world to come," he wrote in *Eugénie Grandet* (1833), "for them the present is everything. To reach a paradise of luxury . . . to petrify the heart and grind the body for the sake of passing possession, as men once suffered martyrdom for the sake of life eternal, is the general idea . . . When this doctrine passes from the bourgeoisie to the people, what will become of our country?"

The writers on behalf of peace during the early nineteenth century were not oblivious of the prevalence of avarice and selfishness. They were far from supposing that peace could be secured if only individuals and nations pursued their economic interests. Few Frenchmen of the generation that made the Revolution were more sanguine concerning the benefits which mankind would derive from engineering and material progress than the Comte de Saint-Simon (1760–1825). Yet, when he laid before the Congress of Vienna proposals for a reorganization of European society in the interest of peace, he wrote that a confederation of states united by common institutions and subject to a single government, above the particular governments of nations, "is the only condition which could repair everything." He put no trust in what he called the "mercantile spirit of calculation" as a substitute for the moral progress on behalf of which Kant had written. (It is not without interest that Saint-Simon thought the Germans exemplified especially the moral qualities necessary to peace, and that he attributed the high level of virtue that he believed to exist in Germany to the country's lack of sea trade.) [19]

Among the Western peoples in Europe and America, the hopes placed in economic progress as a solvent for violence and war were almost invariably coupled, until after the middle of the nineteenth century, with a concept of the need for efforts to achieve moral progress as a kind of Kantian categorical imperative. Whatever their religious faith, whatever their nationality, most responsible thinkers of the period from 1815 to 1860 were in agreement that the good, as such, is a concept of fundamental importance to all men, that it is essential to the welfare of mankind. These thinkers were united also in a determination to strive to inculcate the principle of the good in the peoples of Europe and the entire world. Hitherto philosophers had extolled the value of reason. Now reason on behalf of right must be brought into actual operation, in the parliaments, in the newspapers, in the courts of law.

The author of the most penetrating work ever written about the Americans, Alexis de Tocqueville (1805–1859), derived his principal hope in the rising republic of the United States from the greater sense of moral responsibility which he found among its people. Tocqueville's enthusiasm for the moral qualities of the Americans, like Saint-Simon's for those of the Germans, indicates how anxious the Europeans were to cultivate virtue. Thomas Arnold (1795–1842), who became head master of Rugby in 1828, succeeded in reforming the system of English public schools in the interest of moral perfection. He aimed to extend to the entire nation the system he built up. The means he encouraged were not devoid of violence, but at least his violence was relatively mild and was confined to the reform of the young. It was part of the moral code, which Arnold's teaching embodied, that the mature man and woman, properly educated, had placed themselves beyond violence. That was the message contained in *Tom Brown's Schooldays*, a book which reflected Arnold's practice and which was generally read by young people in Great Britain, the British colonies, and the United States for two generations following its publication in 1857.

Such force as was needed to keep older people in order was confided to the courts of law, and to their recently created arm, the modern police, whose origins in England are associated with the statesman Robert Peel (1788–1850). In 1829 Peel abolished the old London watchmen and created the organization which advertises its author by its members' nickname of "bobby." [20] This new system of maintaining order was extended from London over Great Britain and, with variation, over the world. In Great Britain especially it produced remarkable results. The rate of homicide fell rapidly, along with the general death rate from most other causes. Crimes punishable by death were steadily reduced, until in many countries few persons were executed except for murder. The decline in capital punishment was accompanied by a reduction in the infliction of corporal penalties. The increasing tenderness of manners, customs, and laws, cultivated by humane Europeans for generations, as Montesquieu had observed, was spreading under European example and seemed about to become universal. The march of progress, which the Napoleonic era had interrupted, was resumed. History seemed to demonstrate Turgot's law.

The forty-six years from the fall of Napoleon in 1815 to the outbreak of the American Civil War in 1861 form a period freer from violence, piracy, and almost every kind of crime within Western nations, and from war between Western nations, than any earlier period of equal length. In the trade of the Middle Ages the line between the pirate and the merchant was not clearly drawn, and there was attached to the pursuit of lucre by means of trade a stigma derived partly from the association men made between the mercantile profession and piracy.[21] But in the early nineteenth century pirates were disappearing, along with the cannibals and packs of wolves which had frightened and threatened Robinson Crusoe. Except in frontier areas — with their gold rushes — the practice of the mercantile profession was seldom accompanied by serious violence; codes and customs of law governing trading relations were in force among all the European nations, with comparatively few differences from one country to another. The calling of the merchant had become most respectable under law. In many parts of the world, for example in the Hawaiian Islands, mercantile pursuits not only lost all piratical taint but actually came to be associated with the activities of the missionaries whose purpose was to convert primitive peoples to Christianity and to instruct them in better moral principles.

It was no longer respectable in England, as it had been in the seventeenth century, to attend executions and comment on the ordeal of the victims. Among the Europeans generally murder by poison was, in all probability, becoming much less frequent. The matter is not susceptible to proof, but the disposition of nineteenth-century writers to treat the use of poison as exceptional cannot be attributed entirely to hypocrisy. One should compare the account given by the duc de Saint-Simon (1675–1755), in his celebrated *Memoirs*, of the deaths in 1712 of the heir apparent, the duc de Bourgogne, and his wife and child, with a modern version of the episode, such as that found in the French dictionary *Larousse*, which confidently attributes the tragedy to acute infectious disease. Saint-Simon felt certain that all three were victims of poison. The comparison suggests that nineteenth-century men and women were able to conduct their lives as if death by poison were exceedingly rare, an assumption which could not be made in the time of Louis XIV. "This, it will be remembered, was an epoch of poisoners," wrote Francis Parkman, when he introduced his nineteenth-century readers to the world from which La Salle set out in 1680 to survey the west of North America.[22] During the nineteenth century the cruelties and murders characteristic of most earlier civilizations, as exemplified by the Roman imperial government which Tacitus described in his *Annals*, were disappearing from the relations of the civilized West. The Europeans had ceased to kill for religious reasons. Now they ceased to kill for political ones. Commercial competition, in which bloodshed had no place, absorbed the energy of increasing numbers of men in Europe [23] and in the European settlements throughout the world.

After the fall of Napoleon in 1815 the bulwarks against relentless, unrestrained wars among men gained in firmness, partly because of the spread of more humane manners, laws, and customs. Europe and North America were experiencing one of those cycles of more pacific relations, such as had occurred after the Hundred Years' War and again after the Thirty Years' War. About 1850, after a generation without any serious wars, it seemed entirely possible that military adventures belonged to rougher, barbarous ages of human history which civilized humanity was outgrowing. Unlike earlier pacific cycles, that of the nineteenth century bid fair not simply to limit war but to eliminate it.

(2) *The Origin of the Intellectual Barriers in Christian Humanism*

The growth of commerce and industry, together with the increasing peace among the nations, was brought about by the decreasing violence in manners, by the progress of order under law, by the responsibility which philosophers, writers, priests, parsons, and men of affairs (both political and economic) not infrequently assumed for the general welfare of their neighbors, their countrymen, and indeed of all mankind. The moral and intellectual foundations for the peace essential to the triumph of industrialism are to be found in the Christian and the Humanist traditions of the European people, especially as these traditions had developed in the thought and art of the eighteenth century.

At the root of peace was the concept of a universal human community to which the rational man owed his highest terrestrial allegiance. Of all the precursors of the French Revolution, no one had expressed the concept more clearly than the great Montesquieu, the man whose political views are of most direct value for the builder of a world state. "If I knew of something beneficial to me but harmful to my family," Montesquieu wrote, "I would eject it from my mind. If I knew of something beneficial to my family but not to my country, I would try to forget it. If I knew of something beneficial to my country but harmful to Europe, — or beneficial to Europe but harmful to the human race, I would regard it a crime." [1] One of the tragedies of history was the failure of the diplomats who made peace at Vienna after Napoleon's defeat to embody this concept of an allegiance superior to national patriotism and based on universal culture, in the concrete form of a world government. If the Comte de Saint-Simon's counsel had been followed, a governing body would have been available in Europe, which the peoples of the world could have supported before their national and class allegiances had become fanatical, before industrial progress had become so rapid as to help disrupt the traditional values of the Western peoples, and before the geographical barriers of sea and mountain protecting the countries of the world from each other had been overcome by the application of new scientific discoveries to transport by air and heavy bombing. In the first half of the twentieth century, when attempts were actually made to establish a universal government by the creation of the League of Nations and later of the United Nations, the sense of human community had lost much of its force among the intelligentsia, and the intelligentsia itself had been split up. For both reasons, views resembling those of Montesquieu had ceased to carry weight in affairs of state. Allegiances to country or to class took precedence over the more general allegiance to which he had given supremacy.

During the first half of the nineteenth century the sense of European cultural community was still strong; the idea of high intellectual purpose as one and indivisible had not been destroyed; the power of settled moral principles over the conduct and affairs of men was greater than ever. Even without concrete embodiment in government, the concept of an allegiance to humanity above all nations was of much value in keeping the peace.

The turn to a Europe outwardly more peaceful than ever before can be understood better when we realize that the European culture which had helped to bring about the limited warfare of the eighteenth century was by no means played out at the time of the French Revolution and the American Constitutional Convention. In some ways the expressions of the most influential eighteenth-century philosophers, other men of letters, and also of the musicians, came into their own only in the nineteenth century. History shows that the achievements of the human mind and spirit in thought and art have a practical influence — upon customs and manners and upon the way persons generally envisage the adventure of life — usually one or two, even three or four, generations later. The generous ideas of progressive European society, expressed on the eve of the industrial revolution, concerning the power of mankind to seek the good and to master violence were not destroyed by the long and terrible strife from 1792 to 1815. European culture as it evolved in the eighteenth century not only provided the foundation for the industrial revolution; it nourished that revolution for many decades.

Even during the Napoleonic era, no efficient attempt was made to stamp out the liberty essential to creative work, either at home or in the countries of the enemy. The life of the mind at Weimar, with its wonderful literature, or at Vienna, with its supreme music, was largely untroubled by the wars and their repercussions. The mind at its best was little involved in the struggle. In the eighteenth century thinkers, artists, and men of letters had disengaged themselves from religious quarrels without entering into the political quarrels of kings; in the early nineteenth century they had hardly begun to engage themselves in the political quarrels of nations or of classes.

In spite of the anticlerical nature of the French Revolution, the Christian faith remained powerful among the Western peoples. In no country was it taken more seriously, as Tocqueville observed, than in the rising United States. Almost everyone read the Bible, or heard it read by priests and pastors or in the family circle by father or mother at morning or evening prayers. Missionaries representing all the Christian churches settled in Africa, China, and the rich islands of the oceans. There they read and preached the Gospel to the natives and reconciled it with the new hope that commercial and industrial success would raise the material standard of living everywhere. It has become fashionable to deride these missionaries for seeking worldly fortunes for themselves, as many of them did. But that was less inconsistent in an age that coupled commercial prosperity with virtue than in an age that denied virtue all reality. The missionaries, who like all human beings had their weaknesses, had at least the virtue of teaching the truths of Christianity.

There is little in the Gospel of Christ to encourage war. Now that scientific methods of experiment and other positive proofs had gained authority among the Christian peoples in both learning and teaching, men and women were coming to think more in matter-of-fact, material ways than ever before. They were also much freer than their ancestors had been to accept or reject the Gospel. Whether they accepted or rejected it, they were disposed to take it more literally than most of their ancestors in the matter of moral precepts. As long as they were in good faith in doing so, the process strengthened their moral fiber and their pacifistic and charitable convictions. Those conscientious thinkers who rejected the Gospel were for a time even stronger defenders of its moral teachings than those who accepted it. In circles which abandoned Christian worship, Christian morals and Christian modes of conduct were revered. An idea developed, which had considerable influence for several generations, that mankind would become more "Christian" in conduct if it ceased to be Christian in belief!

Intellectual and artistic life in Europe became even more agnostic during the nineteenth century than it had been during the eighteenth. When in 1749 Turgot presented his Latin dissertation, *On the Historical Progress of the Human Mind*, at the Sorbonne, he accompanied it by another called *On the Benefits Which the Christian Religion Has Conferred on Mankind*. A reader of the two treatises will naturally ask how far Turgot considered Christianity a part of the law of progress. He will find no clear-cut answer, for the relations between the two dissertations are vague, but he cannot reasonably conclude that Turgot thought the spread of Christianity had imposed a burden on the human mind. Yet, a generation afterwards, Gibbon suggested that it had done so. In 1776 Gibbon remarked in *The Decline and Fall of the Roman Empire* that he was describing "the triumph of barbarism and religion." Henceforth the law of progress was increasingly identified with religious skepticism and even with hostility to Christian worship. In his *History of Civilization in England*, Thomas Buckle (1821–1862) prolonged the thesis of Gibbon to the point of suggesting that it was precisely those thinkers and men of letters — beginning with Rabelais and Montaigne — who had questioned some of the tenets of the Christian faith, who had created the humane and wealthy civilization of Western Europe.[2] Comte faced the problem in a different way. Unlike Gibbon, he regarded Christianity as a great civilizing force, at least until the twelfth and thirteenth centuries. But it had now been superseded as a civilizing force by a more advanced view of human experience than either the religious or the metaphysical view — by the view of positive science.

In so far as Christian belief and worship were concerned, the result was much the same whether one followed Gibbon or Comte. Organized religion was treated more and more as the enemy of man and of civilization, so that the Mills, father and son, regarded the God of the Christian creed as the *"ne plus ultra* of wickedness." Yet no one was a stouter champion of the moral code, which is an integral part of the New Testament, than John Stuart Mill (1806–1873). He set out to unmask the prejudice that "unbelief is connected with any bad qualities either of mind or heart," and to affirm that conscientious unbelievers "are more genuinely religious, in the best sense of the word religion, than those who exclusively arrogate to themselves the title." [3] The idea of such men as Mill, however misguided they may have been in their premise, was that the time had come to put into practice the Christian morality in relations between nations, as well as in relations within them. There was a brief period during which the Western people thought and behaved more Christianlike, although they were less punctilious than before in observing any prescribed forms of Christian worship and less persuaded of the miracle of God becoming a man that had had much to do with their own love of virtue, because it revealed virtue as eternal and perfect.

In one of his essays Montaigne wrote that virtue implies a vigorous effort to be good. Virtue is active, not passive.[4] The renunciation of faith in Christ and in the immortality of the soul helped eventually to destroy belief in the Absolute and so in the reality of virtue, which can be firm and binding only if it is absolute, only if it presents a pattern which men must live up to independent of circumstances. But the preliminary consequence of irreligion for moralists was different. Among the people of Europe, who were active and practical to a greater extent than any people before them, the immediate effect was to encourage greater activity on behalf of virtue, as well as on behalf of commerce. As Kant had expected, this combination of economic enterprise with the pursuit of moral perfection contributed to peace.

In France the early socialists, who possessed a respect for liberty of conscience, for freedom of thought and speech (enshrined as these were in the early pronouncements of the Revolution), were all putting forward humanitarian doctrines in one form or another. They derived powerful support from the new republic in America, which offered the foremost example of equality of opportunity. In Great Britain, where the evils of crowding and the concentration of industrial work in large dehumanized units were greatest, humanitarian and moderate socialist doctrines grew stronger than in France. They began to enter into the practice of the market place and even into the plans of the Tory party. As the party's great Jewish leader, Benjamin Disraeli (1804–1881), envisaged these plans in his early political days, they involved the reconciliation of the "two nations," the poor and the rich, along with the protection of the poor.

At the end of the eighteenth century the rise of such doctrines had led in Scotland to the abolition of the slavery which had existed since the beginning of the seventeenth century in the Scottish coal mines and saltworks.[5] During the nineteenth century practical results came in quick succession on behalf of the economic and social welfare of the wage earner, particularly the industrial wage earner. Beginning with the Reform Act of 1832, the suffrage was extended to an ever larger portion of the population in one European country after another. In the United States the powerful antislavery movement eventually found its leader and moderator in Abraham Lincoln. Germany was deeply impressed with these same humanitarian ideas, as the revolution of 1848 showed. That was accompanied and followed by large emigrations of Germans seeking freedom and humanity. The German element played an important part in Lincoln's election to the presidency of the United States. The actions of German reformers in Germany, as well as overseas, revealed a warm generosity and love of man, which had been fostered by the Enlightenment in central Europe as well as in France.

Among the striking results of practical Christianity and humanitarianism was the increasing respect for men and women as physical persons, a respect difficult to reconcile with the use of the body as cannon fodder. The sensitiveness to the horrors of war increased among men and women of all social classes. The tenderness and sweetness developed especially with the unfolding of French civilization, as the shadow of religious wars and persecutions lifted, were becoming an accepted part of domestic manners in ever widening circles all over the globe.

Among the developments which filled the leading minds of Europe and America with hope, was the remarkable progress of wealth and health in every country. Men were becoming, as Descartes had predicted they might become, the "masters and possessors of nature." In Europe freedom of trade and peace were closely identified in the thought, not only of learned men but of political leaders. As the eventual triumph of doctrines of free trade seemed to be assured, except possibly in Germany, peaceful international politics, which had become a sort of corollary of free trade, gained ground. Newspaper editors, who were now more influential than ever before, felt a responsibility, especially in Great Britain, to help in maintaining international peace. They operated their foreign services with a view to that end. Instead of seeking for news at any price and publishing every scandal, foreign correspondents reserved sensational rumors for the private letters they wrote to the editor, who was at pains not to publish them.

Commerce, with its concrete objects of exchange, seemed in fact to be replacing war as a means of satisfying human desires. For the ingenious French social philosopher, Pierre-Joseph Proudhon (1809–1865), war was the oldest of religions, and since, with economic progress, humanity was losing its faith in religion, men were bound to forsake war.[6] In England, Winwood Reade reached a somewhat similar conclusion a little later in his *Martyrdom of Man*, published in 1873. The book had many readers. Reade was impressive because he evoked a tragic, almost apocalyptic interpretation of history, without an appeal to either war or the last judgment. In the final paragraph he wrote that "famine, pestilence, and war are no longer essential for the advancement of the human race." What men were called upon to relinquish was the soul, "the hope in immortality."[7]

The conditions of the mid-nineteenth century seemed to justify the view that recourse to military force as the arbiter of human destinies was no longer natural. The tremendous energy of a rapidly growing population was finding plenty of outlets in the economic conquest of the globe, many parts of which were still sparsely populated. There were unfortified frontiers in many directions, and abundant land and mineral resources beyond for those who had the enterprise to push on to them and the skill and capital to exploit them. Even the fortified frontiers were perfunctorily guarded. During the increasingly numerous years of peace the ordinary traveler was seldom asked to show any identification papers. Gold rushes, railroad building, the struggle to eliminate individual bad men, the outfitting of fleets of steamships, the use of power-driven machinery to triumph over swamp and desert, kept people so busy that they had little time to think of organizing to fight one another. The spirit of conquest was coming to be split up, as knowledge was more and more split up during the mid-nineteenth century. Like knowledge, the spirit of conquest had plenty of un-military objectives. With so much matter and space to go round, every-one was left free to try his luck, as long as he carried the passport of European or American civilization. The frontier was an invitation not a wall.

In 1830, after a short revolution in Paris, Louis Philippe was called to the French throne at the age of fifty-seven to administer a new constitution, promulgated by the Chamber of Deputies. A child of the house of Orléans, he came to be regarded as representative of the bourgeois society in which he lived, partly because he began his reign by accepting in succession for the office of prime minister two finan-ciers: Casimir Périer and Jacques Laffitte, whose name arouses a special pleasure among lovers of claret. The bourgeoisie generally was, in fact, more inclined toward peace than some mentors of the working classes, who gained influence in the nation during the new reign. In spite of the glorious part which Louis Philippe, as the youth-ful duc de Chartres, had played in the battles fought in 1792 at Valmy and Jemappes on behalf of the French Revolution, he acquired as king the reputation of being too pacific in his foreign policy. His habit of moving about the streets of Paris, umbrella in hand, is said to have contributed to this reputation and to his downfall in 1848. The um-brella, a manifestation of the persistent concern of commerce with comfortable improvement, began to acquire a notoriety as a symbol of weakness in international policy which it was not to lose.

Yet the next French ruler, Napoleon III, whose name promised a firmness which Louis Philippe lacked, proved incapable of maintaining a vigorous policy of expansion. Napoleon was forty-two when he established the second French Empire in December 1852. After the termination of the Crimean War of 1854–55, in which France, England, and Piedmont were allied with Turkey against Russia, Napoleon led an army over the Alps in 1859 to aid Piedmont against Austria. The object was to drive the Austrians out and establish a united Italy. Wars on behalf of nationalism began.

Charles Sumner, who was soon to play a part in America in another more terrible war, was traveling in Italy on the eve of the battles, and in Turin he was received by Count Cavour, the principal architect of Italian unity. Sumner reported this interview to William Story, who had made his home in Italy during the decade since the skirmishes of 1848 in Rome. Sumner found Cavour hopeful and the people of Turin "full of confidence and anticipating victory. They say that this is to be their last war and that great armies will no longer be needed." [8]

The words express a hope that was to be repeated often during the century that followed, while the armies got ever larger and the wars became frequent and total. But at the time Sumner wrote, the yearnings for peace had a strong hold on the political leaders, particularly on Napoleon III. His reputation as a general, cast in the mold of the first French emperor, did not survive the summer of 1859. He was nonplussed by the sight of modern war, as it presented its horrible spectacle to him after the French victory on the battlefield of Magenta, where thousands of dead bodies — of intermingled men and horses — lay in disorderly stillness in the midst of the rice fields, vineyards, and groups of mulberry trees of the province of Milan. Two centuries before a similar sight on a smaller scale in Provence had caused Guillaume du Bellay to take to his bed. Napoleon III turned pale with disgust and remorse. He remarked that war no longer fitted into the frame of our civilization.[9] After another battle at Solferino, which shocked him even more, he met the young Austrian emperor, Francis Joseph, to find a way to end the war.

At just this point in history, when Proudhon was about to compose his book on war and peace, the use of guns and bayonets seemed incongruous in conjunction with the new order and compassion which had taken hold of the Europeans since 1815. The weapons were crude because since the industrial revolution had begun in Great Britain two generations earlier the ingenuity spent on engines of production and transportation had far exceeded that spent on engines of destruction.

When Comte composed his *Cours de philosophie positive*, he was an instructor, on yearly appointment, at the Ecole Polytechnique in Paris. Comte hated his post and formed a low opinion of the military skill of his time, partly because of a dislike (which was mutual) for François Arago (1786–1853), a celebrated scientist — later minister of war and marine — who had succeeded Monge in 1808 as director of the school. During the unpleasant experiences with Arago and the Ecole Polytechnique Comte wrote in his celebrated book the passages on the backwardness of military preparations in the modern industrial state.[10] He was acquainted at first hand with the military preparations of his age and had positive evidence to support his contention that in the new industrial state the efforts devoted to the production of weapons of war were proportionately slight compared to the efforts devoted by earlier civilizations, those of antiquity in particular.

When the Civil War broke out in America, it was fought with primitive equipment. There were no uniform guns even in the Union army; any kind of gun was brought into service, even bird-guns.[11] Yet this war was carried through to the end, at a time when an honorable end to a war was still possible. The cost in life was tremendous; in four years the loss was approximately 600,000 men out of a population of little more than thirty-one millions.[12] The Franco-Prussian War, in 1870–71, proved equally deadly while it lasted. It was conducted with efficiency by the German armies, and with a relentlessness that would have astonished the Comte de Saint-Simon, who had placed so much hope in Germany to carry the burdens of the new pacifism.

These two wars were more serious than any fought in Western Europe in the times of Newton and of Gibbon. Both wars were undertaken and finished, nevertheless, for specific and restricted objectives. The Civil War arose out of the unwillingness of the North to permit slavery to extend to the new states that were forming in the West. The South preferred to secede rather than to accept such a limitation of slavery. So the purpose of the victor was not the annihilation of an enemy but the elimination of slavery and the maintenance of the union. Similarly the motives of Prussia as formulated and carried out by Bismarck in the Franco-German War were restricted and clear: the annexation of Alsace-Lorraine and the union of Germany in a single state. For Western civilization in general wars were much fewer and much shorter after 1815 than they had been in the eighteenth century. In comparison with earlier ages, the nineteenth century was the age of "the great peace."

Yet with the two wars of 1861–1865 and of 1870–71 the Western peoples were provided with a foretaste of what war might be, if it were not confined to one nation, like the Civil War, or conducted for a limited objective, like the Franco-Prussian War. Western civilization had reached a parting of the ways. Even without world government, statesmen could follow the paths toward peace that had been suggested by many great Europeans since the seventeenth century. Or statesmen could prepare for a kind of warfare such as no peoples heretofore had ever been in a position to wage. The Civil War and the Franco-Prussian War should have shown how ill-founded was the thesis that industrial civilization was incompatible with war. Under the pressure of battle enormous advances were made in the strength of weapons. In the Civil War the battle of the "Merrimac" and the "Monitor" showed that a wooden fleet without heavy armor was useless. In London *The Times* wrote: "Before this we had . . . 149 first class warships, now we have only two." [13]

What Comte had missed — what all those who, like Spencer, followed him in assuming that industrial progress was leading to peace missed — was this: the relative backwardness of military preparations in the mid-nineteenth century had not been brought about by conditions inherent in the new industrial civilization created by the industrial revolution. What explained this backwardness was the will of the Western peoples as expressed in thought, letters, and art to attain universal peace and culture, a will which had been established independently of the industrial revolution and indeed before it had begun. Industrial civilization inherited its pacifistic temper.

Shortly after Comte published his celebrated work signs began to appear that industrialism was by no means bound to preserve its pacifistic heritage. Six years after the appearance of the last volume of the *Cours de philosophie positive*, a document was issued which was destined to have a far more positive influence than the works of the Positivists — the *Communist Manifesto* of Marx and Engels. These two thinkers by no means rejected the idea of progress. They embraced it. But for them, unlike most of their philosophical predecessors, peace was not a moral virtue in itself. While the idea of progress had been associated with peace ever since it was advanced a hundred years before by Turgot, the authors of the *Communist Manifesto* associated progress with violence. War on behalf of the proletariat was not an evil; it was not the result of sin. Such a war, on the contrary, would be virtuous if it were total, because it would establish a society infinitely better than any that had preceded it.

CHAPTER EIGHTEEN

The Material Road to Total War

· LITTLE MORE THAN FORTY YEARS SEPARATED THE FRANCO-PRUSSIAN War from the First World War. In terms of material welfare, upon which the economists helped to fix man's attention, these were the most successful years in history. The inhabitants of our planet in 1650 have been estimated at half a billion. From 1870 to 1914 nearly half a billion were added.[1] In little more than one generation the world's population grew by almost as much as it had grown during the untold generations which separate Adam, the first man, from Newton, the first man of science of the seventeenth century. According to the enterprising calculations of Colin Clark, the real income per person gainfully employed improved 75 per cent or more from 1870 to 1914, while the hours of work were substantially reduced in the wealthier countries of Western Europe (Great Britain, Sweden, Norway, Germany, France) and in North America.[2] In the United States the per capita output of the manufacturing industries grew nearly four times over.[3] Tawney explains that "during the greater part of history, the normal condition of the world has been one of scarcity . . . [But] as a result of the modernization of production and transport, first in Great Britain, then on the continent of Europe and in North America, then in parts of the Far East, mere scarcity ceased, after the middle of the nineteenth century, to be, except in the last, the haunting terror which till recently it had been." [4]

Important among the conditions which made possible this extraordinary change from scarcity to abundance were the peaceful relations which prevailed in Europe and throughout most of the world since 1815. Never in the history of Western civilization had so large a proportion of the Europeans, both in Europe and overseas, lived with so little fighting over long stretches of time, as from 1815 to 1854 and from 1871 to 1914.

After the general use of gunpowder in war had begun at the end of the fifteenth century, various restraints had prevented the relentless exploitation of the new weapons for the sake of conquest. Christian charity, the fear of sin and its consequences, the consciousness of moral responsibility, the love of beauty in the production of tangible objects, the geographical isolation of leading states, all had imposed limits upon war. These restraints had been also, in varying degrees, restraints upon the multiplication of the volume of manufactured goods, which became phenomenally rapid during the industrial revolution. The collapse of the restraints helped to increase production, but at the same time it helped to create the conditions for total war.

A civilization so extensive, so sophisticated, and by comparison with most earlier civilizations, so gentle in its manners as that of Western Europe and North America had become by about 1900, required for war between large nations overwhelmingly greater and more refined means of destruction than any hitherto available to man. The phenomenal industrial progress of the past hundred years provided them. Behind new possibilities for destruction were the achievements of the inventor, the engineer, and every variety of technical expert. Behind their achievements was the genius of the natural scientist. Industrial civilization proved capable of harnessing for the purposes of more colossal warfare all the practical advances made by the human mind, even those devoted to the improvement of men's material lot — even those intended to maintain his health and postpone his death.

Since the late eighteenth century, and even more since the mid-nineteenth, the possibilities for directing the mind to the conquest of matter have been fostered as never before. Again and again, the ingenious application of machinery to processes hitherto confided to manual labor has reduced the human energy required to produce a given quantity of steel, of glass, of cloth, and to transmute these materials into commodities and instruments for quick and handy use in building, living, moving, and destroying. Machine methods took command not only in mining, manufacturing, and transport, but in finance, communications, and agriculture.[5] Montesquieu had supposed that sugar could never be produced economically from cane except by slave labor. But on large plantations machines now do much of the work of preparing the ground, cutting, and loading the cane. The concentration of the intellect on material improvement has resulted too in so remarkable a conquest of disease by surgery, drugs, sanitation, and new comforts that the average sojourn on earth of children born in the industrialized countries has doubled.

(1) *Growth in the Destructive Power of Arms*

During the nineteenth century the opportunities finally ceased for hiring foreign soldiers, the chief means of filling the ranks during the sixteenth and early seventeenth centuries. Even in Switzerland, the traditional source of mercenaries, recruiting by foreign powers was forbidden by federal law in 1859, at the conclusion of the short war fought by France and Piedmont to drive the Austrians from Italy.[6] Meanwhile, with the increasing reservoirs of man power, it became easy to make up this deficiency. The supply of able-bodied young men available for national service grew rapidly in every country, and after the decade of wars which ended with the German triumph over France in 1871, compulsory military training was decreed by all the principal powers of continental Europe on a basis of the conscription which originated in early eighteenth-century Prussia.

In spite of the larger armies, educated men continued to accept the diagnosis repeatedly made of industrial civilization as nonmilitary. Scientists and engineers especially, and businessmen or advertisers who flourished on sales, held the opinion that the more men and women were provided with better material conditions, the less likely they would be to embark on military adventures. Partly for that reason the interest of the scientific mind in tangible results increased. It sought more than ever before to serve the practical, as measured in terms of increased productivity, better health, longer life. Any invention, any improvement in a technical process, was welcomed with enthusiasm regardless of its implications for the production of more powerful and effective weapons, because it was widely taken for granted that if the standard of living were raised, if life-expectancy were prolonged, nations, together with the peoples they represented, would be ever more disposed to let each other alone and to feel sympathy, if not actual affection, for one another.

As long ago as 1830 the able English mathematician, Charles Babbage, had suggested that the "English practice of leaving reward to private enterprise puts a premium on practical achievement as over against abstract truth, which is never rewarded under the system." [7] What in the beginning had been an English practice became to an increasing extent during the nineteenth century the practice of all the principal countries of Europe and America. For a time the spread of private enterprise strengthened men's desire to improve the human lot. Men with scientific and technical knowledge were encouraged to pour all of it into channels leading to practical results. Still other younger men of talent, hesitating over what career to choose, turned to science, engineering, surgery, and medicine. The appeal of these professions became almost irresistible. Were not the men and women who entered them paid for doing good to others?

For centuries Christians had believed that virtue is rewarded in heaven. From the time of Spinoza until the mid-nineteenth century the view gained ground that virtue is its own reward. Then, toward the end of the nineteenth century, it began to appear that virtue is rewarded here and now.

In 1850, as a young man of thirty, Spencer had written that "progress . . . is not an accident, but a necessity . . . The modifications mankind have undergone, and are still undergoing, result from a law underlying the whole organic creation, and provided the human race continues, and the constitution of things remains the same, those modifications must end in completeness." [8] It was widely assumed that men were demonstrating this law when each specialist cultivated his own garden. The economist, for example, had a duty to show how goods could be produced and exchanged in larger quantities and distributed in the manner best suited to further increases in output. Which peoples were to produce the goods, whether it was desirable in the interest of general human happiness to produce some of them at all, were construed as questions for statesmen or philosophers. It was no part of the economist's responsibility to inquire whether statesmen or philosophers recognized their mission or had the knowledge to settle these questions for the benefit of humanity. Economics itself was dividing into a number of specialties — theory, money and banking, public finance, labor relations, statistics, accounting, economic history, history of economic doctrines — and in the twentieth century each of these claimed an independent place among the multiplying studies in the universities.

With the increasing respectability of agnosticism, most of the direct concern of scientists with religious faith vanished. Some of them were called religious men. But as words multiplied, they lost their older generally accepted content. They acquired many different meanings, and not infrequently some of them were employed without any meaning at all. In his dramatic account of the agnostic inspiration of the French Revolution, Jules Michelet (1798–1874) had made it perfectly clear that a man cannot be properly called a Christian merely because he acknowledges, as the Mohammedans do, that Jesus is a great prophet. But the reception accorded the work of a learned man like Spencer by the generation that followed Michelet, the generation of George Eliot (1819–1880), who turned agnostic partly under the influence of Spencer and Comte,[9] shows how confused people were becoming concerning the meaning of the word "Christian." Spencer concluded the passage in which he reaffirmed the law of progress with these words: "As surely as there is any efficacy in educational culture, or any meaning in such terms as habit, custom, practice . . . so surely must the things we call evil and immorality disappear; so surely must man become perfect." [10] Some years afterwards, during the 1870's, a writer in the *Christian Spectator* said of Spencer's doctrine, it "is so profoundly, so intensely, so overwhelmingly religious, nay, so utterly and entirely Christian, that its true meaning could not be seen for very glory . . . This is Science that has been conversing with God, and brings in her hand His law written on tables of stone."

Among scientists in the twentieth century there was some recrudescence of interest in theological questions. Those who reflected upon these questions were disposed to make the subject of theology into a branch of the natural sciences. Thereby they reversed what had been for many human societies the natural order of knowledge, with theology as the "queen" of the sciences. If any of these "religious" scientists were shown the deep religious faith of their ancestors, it had for them the charm of novelty. A place for worship was the last provision that was thought of in creating the town of Los Alamos, where the first atomic bomb was hatched, while hundreds of scientists and technicians set up housekeeping with their families.

When scientists made excursions into philosophy or theology, it was frequently on the assumption that their special scientific knowledge had provided them with the credentials for judging all knowledge. Hesitant about their own powers in dealing with their special subjects, a few of them felt free to forget the caution of Socrates in the most universal of human inquiries and to assume that they had found wisdom. After the mid-nineteenth century, specialists in the multiplying nonscientific disciplines had less and less with which to dispute the credentials of famous scientists. At the same time the ideas which had originated in France among the Saint-Simonians and with Comte — according to which human societies were subject to scientific laws and should be studied scientifically like physical and biological phenomena — spread in learned circles in all countries. More and more scholars outside the natural sciences aped what they took to be approved scientific methods, applying them to economic, sociological, and even psychological and philosophical problems.

For two principal reasons the natural sciences were almost certain to carry the field in competition of this kind. The methods which the natural scientists depended upon for proofs were actually much better suited to the work they were doing than to that of their colleagues in other specialties. Further and still more decisive as time went on, the natural scientists could show that their discoveries had produced tangible results in mechanics, engineering, medicine, surgery. Achievements whose value was readily demonstrable became more and more the only works of the mind which the public and the political leaders alike were willing to accept without question as authentic. As a result of their increasing prestige, the physical and the biological sciences attracted an ever larger proportion of the intelligent when, with the extraordinary growth in population and the equally extraordinary growth in the opportunities for leisure, there were in fact more potentially good minds available than ever before. Less and less hampered by serious concern over the evil in human nature, which had troubled Napier, Boyle, and Newton; emancipated from the distracting concern with art, which had divided the attention of Leonardo and other great men of the Renaissance; the more and more numerous scientists were free to devote their undivided talent, attention, industry, and genius to revealing the secrets of matter, space, and time.

Along with the public appreciation of the practical usefulness of science went an unstinted enthusiasm, which had begun in the seventeenth century in Great Britain and had spread in the late eighteenth century to all Europe and North America, for engineers and inventors of every kind, for physicians and surgeons, and for administrators capable of organizing technical work efficiently. Technicians gained popular applause denied to many an original scientific mind. The applause might be deafening for those who had a flair for publicity. Such applause was not lost on children playing with toys and on young people seeking a career. By processes similar to those which attracted many of the most intelligent, decent, and humanely inclined men and women of the age to the natural sciences, gifted and conscientious persons, many with extraordinary energy, were drawn as engineers, doctors, experts, and managers into those professions where the discoveries of science were practically applied.

The consequence was to orient civilization in the direction of still more population, a still greater volume of production, and equally greater powers of destruction. Progress was becoming cumulative in a variety of ways. As people's minds were directed more than ever before toward scientific knowledge and practical improvement, and toward pecuniary success, the habit of thinking in these terms spread in the schools and colleges, in the press, in the law courts, even in the churches. As scientific, technological, medical, and surgical knowledge increased, the foundation was continually broadened for further advances. Fresh increments of improvement were much easier to achieve than when, as in the sixteenth and seventeenth centuries, these realms of intellectual exploration had been largely unknown and almost entirely uncharted. Maps and equipment were made available which the early explorers had lacked.

Babbage had suggested that the growing interest in the tangible results of knowledge would cause a decline in "the more difficult and abstract sciences." He rightly pointed out that "those intellectual qualifications which give birth to new principles or to new methods, are of quite a different order from those which are necessary for their practical application." [11] But his fear that interest in the practical applications of science would hinder advances in fundamental scientific knowledge proved premature. The tremendous material success of the late nineteenth century made room for both. Until the era of world wars, scientific speculations retained a position of dignity; they commanded a quiet respect, which they had acquired during the seventeenth century especially in Great Britain, before engineers and technocrats were exalted.

During the nineteenth century an idea arose, which had not been current in the England of Newton, that men of genius were likely to go unrecognized by their contemporaries. Stendhal, for example, reconciled himself to writing for the "happy few," because the many were not inclined to read him. With the growing vulgarity of the popular press, the speculative mind often found advantages in withdrawing from public notice, so long as its possessor was assured a modest income and abundant leisure. The absence of the publicity accorded to prominent engineers and other inventors left the scientist with time for serious thought and with a small audience of peers who could discuss his work. Men whose contributions to *science* were mediocre or nonexistent, but who had spectacular popular success, like Edison with the use of electricity or Marconi with the wireless telegraph, took the public acclaim, accorded the interviews, or went the rounds of dinners and festivities, leaving scientific genius the quiet indispensable to the development of great ideas, like Einstein's modification of what had been thought of hitherto as Newton's universal law of gravity, or Rutherford's discovery that the atom could be split and that matter is not composed of final particles.

The "more difficult and abstract sciences" came into their own on the eve of the First World War. The purity, the elegance, and the originality of the new scientific work resembled that of Newton, his contemporaries, and immediate predecessors, except that the modern scientists had a less cosmic view of knowledge and of man, and except that few of them devoted any serious thought to magic or astrology. The result was the quantum theory, the theory of relativity, and other revolutionary discoveries which have changed men's conceptions of the nature of the physical world.

Like the earlier work of Galileo, Kepler, and Newton, this new work had tremendous practical implications. Unlike the earlier work, it came when the training of the young and the outlook of society had created conditions under which practical implications were likely to be quickly and thoroughly exploited. Results which before the nineteenth century would have required decades and even generations to achieve, could now be obtained in months. With the economic, medical, and military progress already realized, it became possible in the twentieth century to extend man's dominion over matter with a frenzied speed that would have baffled the comparatively modest mid-nineteenth-century prophets of progress. When in 1872 Jules Verne (1828–1905), author of some widely read mechanical romances of the Victorian age, predicted that the tour of the world would be made in eighty days, few of his readers took him seriously. Yet some, then in their childhood, lived until men began to be shot around the world in eighty hours.

Science was now able almost to annihilate space and time. But it was also preparing means for the almost complete annihilation of man. Still strong in the age of Newton, the restraints upon the use of knowledge for purposes of destruction had now largely disappeared. After the era of limited wars and the "great peace" which filled much of the nineteenth century, the leading scientists themselves were less wary about the dangers which might be involved in discreetly telling all they knew. Few intelligent men felt, or, if they felt, dared profess, a serious interest in mystery. With the relegation of mystery to the story-teller, the conjurer, and the charlatan, educated men felt they had no right to keep secret any of their knowledge. The circumstances of private life might still be properly allowed to die, but not the circumstances of scientific discoveries. It became almost a dogma among scientists that their work was public property, that their only obligation before publishing was to make sure, within the limits of their special subjects, that the discoveries were sound.

The advent of total wars dealt blows to their confidence in the benefits that would flow from every advance in scientific knowledge, but these wars failed to make many scientists more reticent. They had been led to suppose that humanity and goodness were the normal products of industrial civilization. Dismayed after 1914 by the evident recrudescence of evil and violence, they attributed the new evil and the new violence to certain groups, certain classes or certain countries. If only one got rid of the Jews, the Nazis, the Fascists, the Communists, or the Capitalists, the Poles, the Germans, the Japanese, the Russians, or the Americans, humanity and goodness would again prevail. The march towards a terrestrial paradise could be resumed.

The construction of any weapon, no matter how total its powers of destruction, was justified in the eyes of most scientists because of the excellence of the cause they believed they served. A few held back, nevertheless, distrusting the purity of the cause. Frederick Soddy, an English inorganic and physical chemist, refrained from assisting in the First World War. Earlier than most men, he saw the danger of extinction to which scientific knowledge might condemn Western civilization, and in the 1920's he turned from science to economics. Beating his wings against the sides of the cage in which the learned were now imprisoned, he labored at his new specialty in hope against hope that his work could help save mankind from "the principle of death," which another scientifically trained Englishman, Wilfred Trotter, an eminent surgeon, had suggested might be embodied in the very structure and substance of all constructive human effort.[12]

The conditions of technological advance had changed since the age of Newton. The abstention of one individual, the doubts of another, had lost much of their influence, now that so many were engaged in scientific research and now that astounding technical results could come from minds chained together.

Until almost the end of the First World War, the military administrators and the generals put their reliance mainly on guns — on the astonishing increase that was obtained after 1850 and especially after 1870 in the speed, accuracy, and quantity of fire with new artillery and new rifled firearms of many kinds. In 1911 Colonel F. N. Maude, who edited an English edition of Clausewitz' treatise *On War*, estimated that in the eighty years since the time of Clausewitz the fire of infantry had increased from three to sixteen rounds a minute, while the range of accuracy from cannon fire had increased from one thousand to five or six thousand yards.[13] The machine gun was introduced into the French army in 1866. A French historian, Camille Rousset, pointed out that it could have a magic effect on the morale of the defender.[14]

So it proved in the war of 1914–1918. The avalanche of metal, especially steel, which came from newly invented furnaces and mills in Europe was more than a hundred times the quantity available a century earlier to Napoleon and his enemies. When massed for an attack, the new and more efficient artillery tore up the earth by its fire and hurled into the air fragments of the bodies of thousands of enemy soldiers hiding in trenches, before the first advancing waves of the attacking infantry went over the top with bayonets fixed to destroy such life as remained. An English military commander, General J. F. C. Fuller, writing ten years after the war, affirmed that in the third battle of Ypres, in 1917, "the gunner personnel numbered no less than 120,000; we dumped at Ypres 321 four-hundred-ton loads of ammunition, and fired this off in a preliminary bombardment which lasted for nineteen days. In this bombardment were fired 4,283,000 shells weighing 107,000 tons."

No matter how efficient the artillery preparation, there were almost invariably surviving machine gunners buried in nests of earth. Their guns spit out a hail of bullets at the advancing infantry, often more deadly than the shells of the artillery, because the human targets were exposed and at nearer range. Mass murder became the order of the day; the reward for the attackers was seldom more than a few miles of trenches, captured while the defenders were improving another prepared network behind what had been the front. Indecisiveness was long the most striking tactical feature of the war, whether on sea or land. General Fuller's account of the third battle of Ypres proceeds: "The ground gained was approximately forty-five square miles, and each square mile cost us 8,222 casualties." [15]

This new indecisive warfare had none of the limiting features of the warfare which had been characteristic of Newton's age. Europe could now afford enormous armies, could replenish and supply them again and again while the fighting proceeded. "More money" was needed to kill than ever before, but the money required turned out to be small in comparison with the money that could be raised (with the help of refined advances in the use and manipulation of credit), and in relation to the quantity of munitions which money and credit could buy. So the war cost "more blood" than any war ever fought before — lakes of blood and hills of dead bodies. The exact figure for the dead is unknown, but it could hardly have been less than eight million young men in four years. [16]

Though nominally a victor, France was harder hit than any other country. With a population of about forty millions, the French lost nearly 1,400,000 soldiers. An additional 4,500,000 were wounded. Three out of every four of the eight million men mobilized by France were casualties. Few Frenchmen of an entire generation were unmarked by wounds which plagued them to their dying day. The number of lives required to defend the Ile de France had multiplied at least a hundredfold between the battle of Valmy and the first battle of the Marne, although the French population had not doubled.

The only way to bring about quick decisive results in war was to devise means of producing havoc at longer distances, and at the same time to find ways of encasing spearheads of men in armor. The fulfillment of the early ideas of the airplane and the tank transferred the advantages overwhelmingly from the defense to the attack. The conception of the infinitely destructive bomb exploding on an ever more extensive target, and wiping out all life in an area many miles in circumference, was finally made into a reality, with the very consequences which early scientists had dreaded.

Almost as many men died in combat during the six years of the Second World War as during the four years of the first. Several millions more were done away with in concentration camps or by mass electrocutions in specially constructed railway carriages. The destruction of buildings and deaths of noncombatants in air raids were overwhelmingly greater than in the First World War. Most of the large German cities, many of the Japanese cities were practically reduced to rubble. In Poland, western Russia, China, northwestern France, Italy, Greece, Austria, Hungary, and Czechoslovakia, Holland, Belgium, and Norway large tracts in some towns were bombed to bits from the air; other tracts were smashed from the land by rapidly moving artillery, which was no longer stopped by trench defenses. Parts of some English towns and cities went the way of the German. In the Civil War of 1936–1938 Spain had had its taste of what was coming; Pablo Picasso in 1938 presented the horror to an incredulous world in his vast painting "Guernica."

During the eighteenth century, when hopes ran high for the happiness of humanity, many intelligent men were shocked out of their optimism by a frightful earthquake which, in 1755, brought down large sections of the picturesque Portuguese town of Lisbon, killing many thousands of the inhabitants. No one was more affected by the reports of destruction than Voltaire. Professor Paul Hazard taught us that this was the decisive episode leading to the composition in 1759 of Voltaire's *Candide*, a short satirical novel on optimism. Lisbon in fire and ruins, the groans and shrieks of the injured and the dying, the pieces of dead bodies scattered about the streets, made a mockery of the influential philosophical doctrine of Leibnitz that everything that happens is for the best.[17]

During the war of 1939–1945 the tragedy of Lisbon became almost a weekly occurrence. It was brought about, not by nature, but by man.

(2) *Growth in the Destructive Possibilities of Society*

In modern times learning has increasingly disregarded the ancient tradition, deeply embodied in Greek philosophy, of the dangers involved in putting sublime knowledge into concrete forms. The consequences of the break with this venerable human prudence are as frightful as ancient wise men had feared. The contributions of new knowledge to ever more colossal warfare were by no means confined to the direct application of science and technology to the improvement of weapons. The application of science to peaceful economic progress also served the gods of war. Industrialism has given all economic life military purposes. Every industry, every profession, every invention, however humane its intent, is of potential military value.[1]

"All politics," wrote Walter Rathenau, with his firsthand experience in both government and business, "is economic politics, or preparation for war."[2] In the nineteenth century railways and telegraphs were seen to be hardly less important for war than guns. All the railway systems of continental Europe were laid out with military purposes in mind, at a time when the United States and even Great Britain were sufficiently isolated to build their railways almost exclusively for purposes of trade.

Contrary to the hopes of Montesquieu, Kant, Constant, and others, economic progress did not continue to subdue war. On the contrary, economic progress forced the two leading commercial and industrial nations — Great Britain and the United States — out of their geographical isolation and put them into the orbit of deadly struggle, from which Great Britain had partly escaped after the Reformation. The view that the progress of commerce works for peace was formed before the industrial revolution, when conditions of scarcity still prevailed. The economic resources available in Montesquieu's time were inadequate to carry on both extensive war and extensive commerce. The great new opportunities provided during the nineteenth century for economic expansion made it less imperative to choose between commerce and war. Commerce ceased to work for peace after conditions of scarcity were replaced by conditions of abundance. By the twentieth century the very technical advances which make possible the production and distribution of food, clothing, and less indispensable comforts to the needy in distant places, were easily diverted to supply, on a scale without precedent, gigantic armed forces, whose mission was the destruction of both the needy and the wealthy in nations bulging with tens of millions of people.

During the Napoleonic wars by far the greatest number of deaths among the troops resulted from illness. When Napoleon hurried soldiers to Belgium to provide a defense against a threatened English invasion, fever swept among them, taking a heavy toll.[3] Such episodes had recurred in armies since the beginning of military history. Every leader had to take them into account in his strategy. In the war of 1854–55, 19 per cent of all the British soldiers sent to the Crimea died of disease, and 27 per cent of all the French. Among the remainder, few escaped a serious siege of illness; a larger proportion of the British than of the French were reported as gravely ill. By comparison casualties in battle were small. More than eight French soldiers died of disease for one killed in action.[4]

Since the Crimean War discoveries in medicine and surgery have made it possible to prevent some diseases and cure others. Economic abundance has provided the population generally with comforts, foods, and hygienic appliances which have diminished the ravages of deadly disease. Among the most advanced Western nations the annual death rate per thousand has been reduced from over thirty to about ten. The death rate from illness in the armed forces has fallen even more, because it is those diseases which formerly destroyed the young and healthy which can now be eliminated or successfully treated.

In earlier wars, more died of wounds than were killed in action. Between the Franco-Prussian War and the First World War, a notable reduction was made in the number of the wounded who died.[5] Now the great majority are saved by the same advances in medicine and surgery that are available to repair the bodies broken in automobile accidents. Large numbers of wounded soldiers and sailors can be flown thousands of miles home to be patched and put back into battle after a short time. Wars are now fought with the help of drugs and surgical instruments as well as with guns and explosives. The humane scientist is faced with a dilemma that is largely novel. Shall he prepare the populations to live that they may destroy each other better? Before the recent advances in science, the choices confronting scientific minds were simpler. It was obvious to Napier which of his inventions could kill if he divulged a knowledge of them. The discoverers of penicillin were faced with an issue much less clear-cut.

At the beginning of the twentieth century the chief powers of Europe had come to maintain in years of peace some four million men under arms. This was almost eight times the number in the standing armies and navies of the early eighteenth century. Meanwhile the European population had grown at least four times over. The really striking change was in the capacity for enlarging the forces when war came. Then the number under arms in Europe increased to thirty or forty millions. Women were conscripted for auxiliary war services.

While casualties among combat troops were enormous in the First World War and high in the second, statistics of dubious authenticity were brought forward by the new experts in propaganda to show that, by and large, more persons were injured in accidents under conditions of peace than were wounded in military service. It was hoped that young people would appreciate the advantages thrust upon them by their removal from the dangers of civilian life.

A recent newspaper calculation puts the total man power available for the armed forces of the two coalitions which now confront and glower at each other at about three hundred million men. The life expectancy of all these men, and of the children who may eventually replace them, is many years longer than that of soldiers in the small armies of a few thousands assembled to fight in the Middle Ages.

The triumph of industrial civilization has made it more difficult to distinguish between aggression and defense. It has reduced the trouble and the anguish involved in killing and being killed. In some countries, it has even encouraged waste on a scale of which our ancestors hardly dreamed, and destruction is the most comprehensive form of waste. Let us consider these three matters in order.

1. It is now more than a century since the German general, Karl von Clausewitz (1780–1831), became famous by publishing a book in which he considered war as a philosophical problem. With the rise of romanticism in thought and letters, writers were becoming less prone than they had been to follow the embarrassing practice of calling human qualities and vices by their names. A generally accepted principle in Western European thought, stated by Grotius, was that "it is not the party who repels by force of arms, but the power who first makes the attack, that violates a peace." But in his book Clausewitz advanced the somewhat surprising doctrine that in a war the real aggressor is the defender. "The *offensive*," he wrote, ". . . has for its absolute object not so much *combat* as the *taking possession of something*." What leads to fighting, what causes a war, are overt acts by the soldiers of the invaded country.[6] This thesis was put to continual use during the period of world wars. It encouraged the military enthusiasm of Clausewitz' countrymen, when no one had actually aimed a blow at their nation. There are Germans who feel sure Germany was attacked in August 1914 by Belgium and in September 1939 by Poland.

With the advances in industrial technology it became increasingly difficult to construe any preparations for war as defensive, when more and more the only means of defending was to attack. Even before the First World War had ended, that ingenious American thinker, Thorstein Veblen, pointed out that "any well designed offensive can effectually reach any given community, in spite of distance or of other natural obstacles. The era of defensive armaments and diplomatic equilibration, as a substitute for peace, has been definitively closed by the modern state of the industrial arts." [7] In earlier times countries or groups had fought on behalf of some religious conviction, to gain trade advantages, or simply to conquer. Now the proclaimed object of every nation which fights is only to defend itself.

The spirit of defense, of resistance, is potent. Since Napoleon's time the instinct to defend, which is universal, has come to operate with more equal force on both sides in war. The instinct requires no sophistication. Primitive, even animal, fear and the hatred bred of fear can arouse the most stupid.

2. No army commander in the Second World War made a more dramatic use of the new "defense" [8] than General George Patton. His soldiers swept across most of northern France in a few days. Months later they swept through southern Germany on into the Tyrol and to Vienna with equal rapidity. Shortly before his death in an automobile accident, General Patton gave a newspaper man his opinion of a gun which was incapable of effective execution at more than sixty yards. "To do much good at that distance," the general is said to have observed, "requires real human courage behind the weapon. And, let me tell you, human courage is spread mighty thin."

Thanks to the progress of the past fifty years, the amount of courage required to kill hosts of the enemy, including noncombatants, or to obliterate his naval forces, has been reduced. In the Second World War the final destruction of the Japanese fleet, built at enormous expense during a generation of time, occurred in the battle of Leyte Gulf, which has been called "by any standard the greatest sea fight of all times." In five days the Japanese lost four huge aircraft carriers, three battleships, six heavy cruisers, and eleven destroyers. Some of the large ships were sent to the bottom in a matter of minutes. Most of the mischief was inflicted by torpedoes directed from distant submarines or by equally impersonal bombs dropped from the air at a great height; there was no major encounter between surface vessels.[9]

Warships costing tens of millions of dollars and carrying thousands of sailors can now be sunk — cities inhabited by a hundred thousand people can be wiped out — from a distance of miles by a mere touch of an executioner who moves his fingers mechanically in accordance with prescribed regulations. He has no clear picture of the persons or the property he is destroying, and at the time of execution, he runs comparatively little risk of bodily injury. A further refinement has been achieved by robot planes and rockets. The human executioner is for practical purposes eliminated. Without men, machines do the work.

The psychological advantages of getting back from the target were emphasized by Clausewitz after civilized Europeans had outgrown the prejudice that, in war, there is something cowardly about killing persons who are too far off to see their murderers. "Weapons with which the enemy can be attacked while he is at a distance," Clausewitz wrote, ". . . allow the feelings, the 'instinct for fighting' properly called, to remain almost at rest, and this so much the more according as the range of their effects is greater. With a sling we can imagine to ourselves a certain degree of anger accompanying the throw, there is less of this feeling in discharging a musket, and still less in firing a cannon shot." [10] How little feeling is left in releasing a blockbuster or in detonating an atomic bomb.

What of the new kind of human target opened by the triumph of modern science? Apparently persons are less terrified by the prospect of receiving a missile when they do not associate its coming with the personal anger or hatred of an individual. In his last great philosophical work, Henri Bergson reported that: "An officer who took part in the [First World] War told us he always noticed that the men dreaded the bullets more than the shells, although artillery-fire was far more deadly. The reason is that with bullets we feel we are aimed at; and each of us, in spite of himself, reasons as follows: 'To produce the effect, which would mean so much to me, of death or a serious wound, there must be a cause of equal importance, there must be intent.' A soldier, who, as it happened, had been hit by a splinter from a shell, told us that his first impulse had been to exclaim: 'How silly!' That this fragment of shell, projected by a purely mechanical cause, and which might just as well have struck anybody, or nobody, should nevertheless have come and struck him, him and not somebody else, appeared to his natural intelligence illogical . . ." [11]

Progress has purged much warfare of the direct personal encounters which accompanied the struggles of olden times; it has dehumanized national conflicts, and the result has been a revolution which forms a striking part of the industrial revolution itself. While experts on military tactics and strategy are prone to say that the object of making war always remains the same — the annihilation of the enemy — it is certain that the character of the enemy to be annihilated and the means of annihilation have been changed. Whole nations are becoming targets. Material abundance has completely altered the stakes of diplomacy; the stakes now are all or nothing; total war, perhaps total death, is the alternative to peace. The god of war has been transformed into a mechanical Moloch, almost as impersonal as nature, but made capable by man's intelligence of swallowing at a gulp nearly all the children of God.

Hand-to-hand fighting became less frequent with the general use of gunpowder during the sixteenth century. It retained some importance nevertheless, especially when decisive battles were fought during and after the Napoleonic wars. But hand-to-hand fighting now seldom plays any serious part in deciding a battle; it plays still less part in deciding a war. Even in the First World War only a negligible proportion of the casualties were from bayonet wounds. The principal use made of this long dagger was to hold sausages in a fire while they cooked, or to open cans of food manufactured hundreds of miles from the front and brought to the soldiers by an increasingly effective commissariat. In the Second World War the journalist Ralph Ingersoll represented a veteran as saying that "he had never seen man-to-man bayonet fighting." [12]

Herodotus, the father of history, calls his readers' attention to the advantages possessed in war by a state comparatively poor but full of courageous citizens. He attributed the strength of the Persians, in their early period of conquest, more to their poverty than to their wealth. Later, when the Persians set out to conquer the Greeks, they were no longer "a poor people with a proud spirit." Herodotus explained the successful resistance of the Greeks in the Persian War partly by their indifference to wealth. He depicted the consternation of a Persian leader of the invading armies, who, in the presence of the famous Xerxes, learned that the Greeks spent years training and preparing their bodies for games in which the reward was only an olive wreath. "Good heavens!" the leader exclaimed, ". . . what manner of men are these against whom thou has brought us to fight? — men who contend with one another, not for money, but for honour." [13]

With the rise of mechanized warfare, the extent to which victory is determined by physical courage has diminished. There has been an immense increase in the extent to which victory is determined by the mere power to organize industrial production, to deliver weapons and missiles in profusion, and to guide by technical rules the hands of the fighters. Technical advantages already played a surprising part on European battlefields in the late nineteenth century,[14] and as long ago as 1928 General Fuller took the position that machines would be the decisive factor in any future war.[15] The history of the Second World War, its conclusion, and its sequel suggest that they are no less decisive than he expected. The fanatical willingness of the best

Japanese troops to give their lives in battle was of little avail against the combined mechanized operations of air, sea, and land conducted by the Americans. It requires incredible daring to dive with one's plane to certain death on the deck of an enemy aircraft carrier, but how meager are the results from such exploits compared to those achieved by guiding mechanically from a distance unaccompanied torpedoes or rockets. These can be turned out by mass production. Courage is more difficult to manufacture.

3. Nearly a hundred years ago, the leading English advocate of free trade among the nations, Richard Cobden (1804–1865), laid down the maxim that war is the greatest of all consumers.[16] With the growing mechanization of industry, with the change noted by Tawney from conditions of scarcity to abundance, finding consumers became a major economic problem. Political leaders in the richest industrial countries were confronted periodically with unprecedented unemployment. Their task was not the more ancient one of providing food and other necessities; it became that of providing jobs, so that more persons would have money with which to buy. One way of accomplishing this was to keep up prices, especially in the case of farm products, so as to hold families on the land. While few producers could afford the small waste involved in fashioning beautiful objects, such as figureheads for the bows of warships and arcades for their sterns, waste on a national scale became for the first time almost a political virtue. In order to keep up prices it was felt necessary often to create an artificial scarcity, sometimes by using government credit to buy and destroy grain and other farm produce, including animals.

Organized war has always been the most effective means of destruction known to man. During the last hundred and fifty years its destructive powers have multiplied a great many fold. All the millions and tens of millions now mobilized in time of war have to be fed, clothed, and provided with increasingly expensive mechanical weapons and conveyances. The introduction of a mechanized air force was followed by the mechanization of the navy and then of the army. Each step enormously increased the consuming power of war. While the expenditure of all the belligerents in the First World War hardly exceeded two hundred billion dollars,[17] the United States alone spent more than this sum in the Second World War.[18]

Tawney pointed out that in wartime "labor, consumption goods and capital all became deficient," [19] and so war recreated the conditions of scarcity which had been the common lot of civilized peoples until the last hundred years. If new wars were to be won, governments had to deal with shortages, such as had been normal before the triumph of industrialism. Once a nation engaged in war, its unemployment problems vanished. Jobs were available for all who wanted them and for many who did not.

There was nothing to rival war as a frightful and temporary solution for the new problems of abundance. "Incapable of emptying its gigantic storehouses," wrote the late Georges Bernanos, "gorged with riches of which its avarice refuses to let go of the least particle except for a profit, prisoner of an economic system which increases production without limit and at the same time closes one by one the outlets for production, the modern world prefers to destroy its stocks with cannon balls than to confess its error and again become human."

In the late seventeenth and early eighteenth centuries the inefficiency of industry in terms of its productive power had helped bring about the era of limited war.[20] At the beginning of the twentieth century, contrary to the wishes of many political leaders, economic conditions provided nations with a temptation to make war; or at least, if war had once begun and had fanned national passions, hatreds, and fears, the nations had now for the first time in history the means to carry the war through to a material conclusion.

(3) *Influences of Total War on Material Progress*

As abundance made total war with explosives economically feasible, a novel notion arose that war itself is economically a constructive force. The advantage of gaining territory and riches by conquest is, of course, one of the oldest justifications for war. But the new idea, brought forward by Sombart on the eve of the First World War, was different. He held that the economic experiences of modern war had actually served to raise the level of industrial efficiency and productivity *within* the participating nations. Is there anything about the triumph of industrial civilization and the revolution in the weapons and conditions of war that has made this thesis more tenable for the twentieth century than for the sixteenth, seventeenth, and eighteenth centuries, to which Sombart mainly applied it?

In its essentials, the industrial revolution had been carried through before 1914. One of the conditions behind the remarkable technical progress that made the industrial revolution possible, was the "great peace." From 1815 to 1914 peaceful requirements were of far greater importance than military ones in eliciting the ingenuity of inventors. We may doubt whether the use of power-driven machinery and the level of technical efficiency would have been appreciably lower in 1914, if the statesmen at the Congress of Vienna had succeeded in establishing Kant's "perpetual peace," and if all military preparations had ceased. For example, we do not owe the invention of the explosives nitroglycerin and dynamite to war. They were intended for mining.[1] Without the effective peace which prevailed in Western Europe for a century, except during the twelve years from 1859 to 1871, there would have been no such demand as occurred for peaceful inventions. In all probability technological improvement would have been very much slower. The industrial revolution might never have been completed.

To a greater degree than any preceding conflicts, the world wars of the past thirty-five years have canalized technical and even scientific ingenuity in the service of war. The preceding hundred years had presented the world with far more practical technical skill than was ever available before, and with a far larger number of expert technicians. Just as vastly more material things were manufactured, so there was also vastly more technical skill to waste if mankind chose to waste it. What have been the consequences of the era of world wars for the technical and scientific progress which helped to make the world wars possible?

As the First World War drew to a close, a German biologist, Dr. G. F. Nicolai, who occupied the chair of physiology in the University of Berlin, addressed himself to this very question. "Of course if a war lasts as long as this one," he wrote, "and absorbs all the intellectual and material forces of the nations, it is not surprising that there should be a few inventions while it is going on. There can be not the slightest doubt, however, that future statistics will prove that the annual number of inventions in Europe during the war was smaller — much smaller in comparison — than in any correspondingly long period we may select in the last few decades." [2]

The position of the United States from 1914 to 1945 resembled that of Great Britain during the Revolutionary and Napoleonic wars from 1792 to 1815. Great Britain was then the only major European power not invaded. In the enormous struggles of the past four decades, the United States was the only major world power that escaped both invasion and destruction. Technical progress in the direction of efficient machine production has continued unabated since 1914. Such progress has been possible because the United States obtained most of the constructive advantages of military preparations without receiving at home any of the direct destructive consequences of warfare. The favorable conditions for mechanical progress which prevailed in Great Britain during the early "industrial revolution" of the Elizabethan Age and again during the early stages of the industrial revolution proper from 1785 to 1815 — when Great Britain carried on war from a base out of range of the enemy — were repeated in the United States from 1914 to 1945, with the help of the enormous accumulation of scientific and technical knowledge and on the basis of the general mechanization of industry, transportation, agriculture, and finance, which occurred from 1815 to 1914. Before and during the Second World War the United States provided an asylum for many of the leading scientific men of Europe and for some of the leading engineers. Aided by the knowledge and the skill which these foreign refugees put with enthusiasm at our disposal, the Americans built upon scientific knowledge and technical achievements which were already historically unique before the era of world wars began. The idea of exploiting the revolutionary scientific discoveries of the age of Rutherford and Einstein to release atomic energy for peaceful industry existed before the war of 1939–1945. It may be plausibly claimed that the actual release of this energy came sooner as a consequence of the war, because of the vast sums assembled by the United States government to carry through the necessary research. But it cannot be claimed that war made the general use of this force for the material *benefit* of humanity more imminent.

Against the maintenance of a high standard of living during the past thirty-five years in the United States and in other countries, such as Switzerland and Sweden, that have managed to stay out of destruction has to be put the fall in the standard of living in much of Europe and Asia, where the wars have been fought. While the opportunities have increased in connection with war for researches which have potential value for peaceful progress, the most elementary intelligence should know that the most striking thing about recent progress in scientific research has been the overwhelming contribution it has made to the destructive power of war. During the first half of the nineteenth century destructive lagged behind constructive ingenuity; during the first half of the twentieth destructive forged ahead of constructive ingenuity. The industrial state, which Comte and Spencer regarded as incompatible with the military state, was transformed into an engine of war.

The role of war in promoting industrial progress had been small compared with the role of industrial progress in bringing on war. Warfare is less a cause for industrialism than its shadow and its nemesis. Even when soldiers no longer live mainly off the country they invade, war is more devastating for economic life than ever before, for a number of reasons. Destruction has become enormously greater, because of the general and often indiscriminate attacks on civilian life in cities and towns. It has also become far greater in the country when there is serious resistance to an invading army. If, by rare luck, a nation escapes destructive attacks, as the United States almost completely escaped them during two world wars, the dislocation of orderly economic development offsets any temporary advantages derived from fuller employment. The very totality of modern wars has made the transitions from peace to war and then from war to peace much more difficult than those of the era of limited warfare. These transitions prevent the discovery of even a partial solution for the problem of abundance, such as a rebirth of faith and a renewed love of art might provide. The more total the wars, the more they comprehend all the nations of the earth, the more they have interfered with progress of every kind including mere abundance. War now threatens to put an end to that.

With conditions what they are in the modern world — with the new kinds of explosives and the mechanized warfare made possible by science — war may destroy science itself. There may be an actual case of killing the goose that laid the golden eggs. Already in 1930, before the Second World War, Ortega y Gasset suggested that there was evidence of the first retrogression in pure scientific research since its inception at the time of the Renaissance. "It is becoming difficult," he wrote, "to attract students to the laboratories of pure science." [3] The prestige suddenly directed toward the laboratories because of their demonstrated powers of destruction, may for a time lead larger numbers into the practical sides of scientific research. This is no substitute for the love of truth. And upon the love of truth the future of even material welfare depends.

The material progress, which accompanied the industrial revolution, has helped to make total war feasible. But this progress has not made warfare constructive. Nearly every day we have impressed upon us — over the radio, on the screen, on the television set, in the newspapers and popular magazines — how much science, technology, medicine, surgery, and efficient business administration have done for man. They have done as much for war.

Fathers and mothers have always been reluctant to entrust their children with knives or guns. But men have now entrusted themselves with powers of destruction which would be safe only in the hands of God the Father.

Since the time of Columbus' voyages, the oceans provided broad moats, more efficacious as barriers to decisive fighting than the water-filled trenches built around strong places in the twelfth and thirteenth centuries. Where the medieval moat had protected only a castle, the channels, seas, and oceans protected large nations. Sparsely settled islands and even continents, beyond range of the guns, offered territory where the disgruntled and the persecuted could find a refuge and where adventurous men could go in search of enterprise. Many of Le Blas's fellow Calvinists in Tournai sailed as refugees to the safety of England. Madame de la Tour du Pin, the French noblewoman who later got on well with Napoleon, escaped the guillotine in the French Revolution. With her husband and children she stole aboard a small vessel at Bordeaux, the very night when agents of the Terror were abroad to capture them, to settle and farm in the lovely Hudson River country near Albany.

All that is ended. In the 1880's the moving frontier ceased to exist in the United States, with a destruction of the pioneer spirit that Tocqueville had predicted and that Professor Frederick Jackson Turner was to describe. Since then one frontier after another has gone the way of the American frontier. It is no longer possible to evade the problem of living with other men, other nations, other races, other cultures. The two billion men and women on this planet are now travelers in a single boat. Everywhere people are crowded together; they no longer have any new place to go, unless it be to the moon.

The conquest of the air, combined with the new transport facilities by land and sea, made possible the rapid movement of hundreds of thousands of marines and soldiers to places hardly accessible to tens of thousands a generation ago. The new means of communication — telephone, telegraph, radio, radar — have made it feasible for commanders-in-chief to control and coördinate the movement of millions of soldiers and marines, many times the numbers which Napoleon, with his military genius, had been able to manage.[4] All the countries of the earth have been brought as closely face to face as were the great powers of Western Europe before the First World War. During the very period of forty years from 1910 to 1950 — when the most diverse races, countries, and cultures have been catapulted into a single entity, when the speck on the map represented by Western Europe has been replaced as a potential battlefield by the globe — the proud civilization of whose essential unity Gibbon wrote with such confidence nearly two hundred years ago found itself less united. The Europeans no longer recognized a common Father in Heaven or a common culture on earth. The principle of nationality, which had been counted on to give divided peoples, such as the Italians and the Germans, a new hope and satisfaction that would make for peace, proved a source of conflict such as the Europeans had not had since the wars of religion. Far from completing the Western community, the principle of nationality and of class struggle, and the fiery enthusiasm generated by both, have divided first the Europeans and then the world into vast armed camps. In each of them is to be found kindling, in the forms of men and munitions, for a holocaust more vast than any the world has faced since Biblical times.

Three hundred years ago Thomas Hobbes foresaw the possible consequences of material progress on a world scale. Imbued as he and many of his generation were with a consciousness of original sin and of the prevalence of evil, Hobbes looked to such a concentration of population and such a unified planet as science and invention have now achieved, not with confident hope, but with fearful awe. "And when all the world is overcharged with Inhabitants," he wrote, "then the last remedy of all is Warre; which provideth for every man, by Victory, or Death." [5]

Everywhere on the sidewalks of enormous cities and in the suburbs that stretch beyond them, man is face to face with his neighbor. In a few hours he can be hurled through space to the most distant island; but there he will find his neighbor close at hand. He may reach the moon; others will reach it too. As Hobbes's words indicate, it is open to him to kill his neighbor. It is also open to him to recognize his neighbor.

CHAPTER NINETEEN

The Intellectual Road to Total War

· IN THE PREAMBLE OF A DOCUMENT OF 1945 FORMING THE UNITED Nations Educational, Scientific and Cultural Organization, it is stated that "wars begin in the minds of men." This is part of the truth. And since it is only with their minds and wills that men can influence human destiny, this is a truth that is in need of continual illustration and emphasis. It needs renewal especially after we have seen with what fateful direction, and with what momentum, material progress has been leading for a century toward colossal wars. Again and again the growth of wealth among human societies has helped to provide men with weapons, and with resources that add to the time they can devote to the luxury of fighting. It does not follow that wars are an inevitable result of the multiplication of commodities. What societies can do with their wealth is in their keeping. The total wars of our time have been the result of a series of intellectual mistakes and spiritual, moral, and aesthetic weaknesses, all of which have influenced the course of material development, while they have been influenced by it. There is nothing except themselves to prevent men and women from using their new-found wealth to establish a world society approaching the millennium in the felicity it would provide.

One of the principal errors which led to world wars was the assumption that material progress is necessarily favorable to peace. This notion gained strength during the fifty years preceding the First World War. The gesture of the Swedish chemist, Alfred Nobel (1833–1896), the inventor of dynamite, in leaving a portion of his immense wealth for the award of an annual peace prize, seemed to provide tangible evidence that both the progress of invention and the amassing of private riches were helped by peace. Nor was this untrue. What was false was the assumption that the nations and the peoples of the world would act according to what were, in the long run, their collective material interests; that they would accept the millennium if it were offered them.

On a globe not yet saturated with people or with consumable commodities, the multiplication of goods and services for a time actually contributed to peace, by absorbing the interests and enlisting the combative instincts of men and women in the service of increased production and trade and better health. But human fears and hatreds were only suspended; economic progress did nothing to solve the problem of evil. Once the hourglass of peace, filled with economic preoccupations, began to run out, the wicked sides of human nature regained the ascendancy. The delicate civilization of the eighteenth and nineteenth centuries had closed many of the ancient vents for human violence. With the increasing ease provided by material success at the juncture of the nineteenth and twentieth centuries, people were left with more empty time on their hands. They were not able to resist the temptation to fill it with dreams and expressions of fear and hatred. At some point, perhaps about 1900, commerce ceased to work mainly for peace and began to encourage a belligerent outlook. Let us try to understand how this happened.

(1) *The Weakening of Moral and Aesthetic Values*

During the decades preceding 1914 the public sentiment in favor of peace seemed to be growing. Men of letters, educators, even statesmen, spoke on behalf of peace. More peace societies were formed every year. At the beginning of the nineteenth century, when the American republic was young, Thomas Jefferson had declared that "peace is our passion." Toward the end of the century peace had become the passion of many women of charm, humanity, and intelligence, of whom the two most remarkable were an Austrian, Bertha von Suttner (1843–1914), and an American, Jane Addams (1860–1935). They worked for peace with an integrity and a fervor which may have aroused the hope of saints in Heaven that they could redeem the sin of Eve and lift from the young men of the world the age-old curse of war.

At the beginning of the twentieth century, when women were claiming equal rights with men to vote and when peace organizations, often inspired by women, were more numerous than ever before in history, the private capitalist retained most of the power and influence he had acquired during the eighteenth and nineteenth centuries. As Marx and Engels had remarked in the *Communist Manifesto*, the interests of what they called the bourgeoisie were inclined to be international. The moderate trade union movement, representative of the industrial working classes before the First World War, was gaining ground in all the nations of the world. Responsible and humanely disposed representatives of the movement, such as John Burns in England and Jean Jaurès in France, were beginning to win seats in the national parliaments, even places in the governments. They made forceful pleas for amity, which sounded much more international in intent than most of the utterances of capitalists, so that the working classes appeared to be more likely than the commercial classes to safeguard peace.

By what seemed to the numerous patrons of progress a strange anomaly, these multiplying professions of pacific hopes and intentions were accompanied by a stupendous growth of armaments. At the start of the twentieth century Great Britain and Germany entered a spectacular race to build as many expensive warships as possible.

In university circles and among many who met at the dinner tables of rich capitalists the issue raised by these military preparations seemed susceptible to a common-sense solution. The case for peace was stated vigorously in 1910 by a young Englishman, Norman Angell, in a book called *The Great Illusion*. It was published simultaneously in many languages in London, New York, Paris, Leipzig, Copenhagen, Madrid, Borgä (Finland), Leiden, Turin, Stockholm, and Tokyo. Fresh from the study of economics, Angell set out to prove, with the help of a wealth of statistics, that any war between two or more major powers was bound to damage economically the victor as well as the vanquished. The "great illusion" was that a nation could gain by war. All that was needed to prevent the coming of a great war, which large standing armies and heavy armaments made possible, was to show enough influential people in the leading countries where private and national self-interest lay. It was hoped that *The Great Illusion* would accomplish that result. Peace could be achieved by rational calculation.[1]

Angell's argument was an outgrowth of the eighteenth-century thesis, which Kant had adopted as part of his argument in *Perpetual Peace*, that "the spirit of commerce . . . is incompatible with war."[2] But when we compare Angell with Kant, we find that there are significant omissions from Angell.

Kant had not entrusted the future of peace entirely to self-interest. He had recognized that there is a subjective "opposition between morality and politics." The real case against war was that war is incompatible with "the idea of right." Kant had counted on the rational development of the human mind to "render it more adapted to realize the idea of right." Thus Kant and his followers recognized that men had moral and intellectual responsibilities for peace and that war was an ever-present danger unless human beings adopted loftier and more humane standards of conduct than ever before. They missed another truth which had been plainer to their Christian ancestors. Man's goodness and even his intelligence are only partly the result of his own efforts and those of his parents, teachers, and associates. Man's specifically human powers result also from gifts that are mysterious and inexplicable in purely human terms. The cost of straining for virtue, truth, and beauty unaided by supernatural guidance, as the nineteenth century was more and more disposed to do, was a loss of contact with the Source, a contact upon which all renewals of the intellect as well as of the soul depend.

The separation of rational speculation from revealed Christian knowledge has been represented as both a spiritual and an intellectual mistake. Whether or not this separation was the cause, the Western peoples in Europe, and still more in North America, during the fifty years or so preceding the era of world wars, divorced all particular knowledge from its common origin in rational philosophical speculation. Hitherto the mind had possessed an inner integrity, a consciousness of its own independence of circumstances and events, which the Kantian philosophy had stated in powerful terms. Good and evil had a central place in the Kantian philosophy even though the Kantian did not accept the Christian explanation of their origin. The mind found an anchorage in truths transcending the positive world of daily living, even though men had grown less ready to identify ultimate Truth with God.

The quest for certainty was not abandoned during the late nineteenth century, as men lost hope in a common metaphysics, but the quest changed its objectives. Thinkers hoped for certainty only in tangible things. Reality was more and more confined to what the senses could identify. If men admitted inner experiences independent of the positive world, they relegated these experiences to a separate realm of fancy and superstition. *Things* were coming to ride not only men's bodies but their minds, to a degree that had never before been true in Western European history. The result was to uproot the human conscience more and more from any common sense of either good or evil as such — because good and evil were only abstract ideas. They lacked the positive content indispensable for the serious investigator. They could not be measured, and Lord Kelvin (1824–1907), a scientist with immense prestige, remarked that what could not be measured was not knowledge. Spencer's view that "evil" was disappearing from the modern world with the help of progress also encouraged men to doubt the existence of evil, especially when material progress seemed to be more rapid than even most optimists had expected. By the beginning of the twentieth century a large proportion of all children were brought up in a new dogma: that good and evil are nebulous terms and that it is in terms of practical utility alone that acts and even ideas are to be judged. Such teaching facilitated the escape by adults from the responsibilities which both the Greek and the Christian rational traditions imposed on them.

Conceptions of virtue and of wickedness have given rise to much hypocrisy. But they have at least done something to nourish the human *conscience*. Historical, sociological, and anthropological inquiry all suggest that the conscience, with its sense of shame manifesting itself physically in the blush, is inherent in human nature, among primitive as well as civilized people.[3] When thinkers and artists of distinction have a strong sense of good and evil, and express this in the works of their minds, they quicken the consciences of those who see, hear, or read their works.

As Dr. Arthur D. Nock of Harvard has suggested, "It is something if conscience makes cowards of men even if it does not make saints."[4] The conscience is partly independent of the intellect and the will, because all human beings are endowed in varying degrees with an instinctive sense of shame. Yet the intellect, and still more the will, have the conscience in their keeping. When they deny the responsibilities of each man and woman (individually as well as collectively) for good and evil, they return the human being to a primitive state where the conscience has nothing to sustain it beyond the sense of shame.

That was the condition encouraged by influential writers throughout the Western world at the beginning of the twentieth century. The conscience was left without intellectual as well as without spiritual nourishment. As the particular natural sciences lost contact with their roots in the rational philosophical tradition, they became what they were bound to be by themselves, neutral concerning all ethical questions. Social studies were approached increasingly in the same scientific spirit that prevailed in the physical and biological sciences, and were deprived of moral foundations. Economics, for example, lost contact with ethics, and became neutral on questions of justice. Like science, political economy was soon available as a tool for any particular state or group.

If nothing is either good or bad except as thinking makes it so, what happens to the old Christian tenet, which Robert Boyle had expressed during the English Civil War, that war among men is caused by sin? The most that Boyle's younger contemporary, Vauban, famous fortress builder and soldier that he was, could say for war was that it is "a necessary evil." "War has self-interest for its father," he remarked, "ambition for its mother, and for its close relatives all those passions which lead us into evil." [5] So long as the Christian conception of morality prevailed, war itself could only be evil, however virtuous might be the conduct of particular men under the rigors of warfare, and however just the cause on behalf of which war was waged. Thus the Thomistic philosophy regarded it as wrong for any priest to engage actively even in a just war.

But to the moral relativist, "justice" or even Kant's "idea of right" was as vacant a concept as evil. The persons who talked and wrote of war as bad increased in number, but so, we shall see, did the persons who talked and wrote of it as good. On what authority could it be decided that the first group was right and the second wrong? No relativist could claim that war was evil or sinful in itself. That could no longer be said even of murder. The relativist also rejected altogether the pre-Christian Aristotelian position that murder, theft, and adultery were evil. And so it came to pass that "self-interest," which Vauban had called the "father" of war, was made, as with Angell, the principal bulwark of peace.

The consequences of the denial of ethical principles were the more harmful to the cause of peace because of changes in the organs of publicity and in the purposes they were coming to serve. In the eighteenth century appeals to public opinion had been made almost invariably on behalf of the traditional sense of the reality of virtue, as a principle, rather than on behalf of particular interests. In *Perpetual Peace*, Kant counted on "publicity" as the means of enforcing among statesmen actions on behalf of the "idea of right." He put forward a proposition which he called "a transcendent formula of public right": "All the actions, relative to the right of another, whose maxim is not susceptible of publicity, are unjust." [6] He suggested that appeals to the conscience of mankind through publicity were bound to tell on behalf of peace. By subjecting the actions and the talk of statesmen and diplomats to public scrutiny, it would be possible to detect and reject the private interest inherent in them. Such hopes persisted through the First World War and were expressed in President Wilson's fourteen points for establishing peace between the states of central Europe and the nations allied against them. Wilson's words were "open covenants openly arrived at." He and his advisers held that diplomacy had led to war largely because it had been secret.

But what if mankind had lost its "conscience"? What if the mentors of "publicity" had ceased to shoulder responsibility for a universal "idea of right"? What if they themselves acted from self-interest in a world which was coming to deny any objective standards of moral values?

During the period from the American Civil War to the First World War the character of the newspapers with rapidly growing circulations changed. In deciding upon the content and appearance of the papers, sales became the main guide for publishers and editors, instead of the purveyance of reliable information and the exposition of responsible, ethically inspired opinions on political issues of public interest.[7] During the first half of the twentieth century, with the coming of motion pictures, picture magazines, radio, and television, the notion prevailed that the number of the identifiable audience provided the final test of success. More and more, publicity catered to the lowest level of intelligence, to the least imaginative human being, on the ground that this was the way to augment profits. The owners and editors of organs of publicity conjured up an irresponsible, vapid, somewhat salacious straw man. By offering bold type, pictures, crime reports, slick stories, and noise — all eventually combined in the American "comics" and the cheap broadcasts — the artillery of publicity helped to batter actual men and women and their children into something which resembled creatures of straw.

"Publicity" had been once a word for copious authentic information, together with the serious or the witty discussion of current issues and the recurring ideas of general interest which helped to clarify these issues. Now only a few papers with comparatively small circulations, such as the *New York Times*, try to supply such information, and only a few others, such as the *Manchester Guardian* or the *Monde*, try to conduct such discussions. "Publicity" has come to mean advertising, getting one's name or photograph prominently displayed to a large number of persons. The context in which one appears matters little; a Nobel prize winner or an assassin are equally valid subjects for "publicity." There is even a recorded case in which the eminent musician, Artur Schnabel, descending from a train in an American city, was shown his own photograph on the front page of the local paper, with the caption: "Murdered in the park last night." [8]

The audience and its new mentors moved in a more or less continuous downward spiral, in search of a common denominator of inanity. Children, and with them the increasingly numerous persons who had reached their second childhood, provided abundant new publics for the reception of paper, pictures, and sound. All these multitudes were given not what they ought to have but what the directors of publicity decided they wanted. The stuff that was offered the newspaper or magazine buyer, or the owner of a radio receiving set, was mostly of kinds that do nothing to kindle the native intelligence, imagination, and taste which men and women possess and which the increase of leisure should have given them an opportunity to improve.

The decline of native intelligence, instinctive wit, and taste, partly caused by the new abundant publicity, led ever larger numbers of potentially gifted persons to prostitute their talents for the sake of making money. Critical standards ceased to be recognized. Mr. Sydney Horler illustrated the new test of competence in a letter he wrote objecting to a criticism of a book of his called *High Hazard*. He saw no need for considering the book on its intrinsic merits. "*High Hazard*," he pointed out, "was written expressly to please a huge public that, in these hagridden days, demands entertainment — and whom, consequently, it is a public service to entertain. . . Decry the public taste as much as you like, but the many millions who have put their money down during the past fifteen years to buy a Horler novel can't all be wrong." [9]

Publicity became available for any particular interest, from that of an individual to a nation, provided the interest seemed to promise profit, fame, or power to those who exploited it. What at first sight appeared to be the harmless occupation of making money by keeping large numbers amused became a vital matter in connection with peace and war when these numbers were made the source, or at least the instrument, of political authority. During the late nineteenth and early twentieth centuries, the right to vote was extended again and again, until the suffrage became wide in all countries, even in Japan, and universal in some, such as the United States and Great Britain. But at this very time less and less respect was being shown for the intelligence of the new electorate. Even in those countries where the voter retained the right to cast his ballot freely, almost any subterfuge was considered legitimate for purposes of propaganda. With such preparation it is little wonder that the public could be manipulated to suit the purpose of unscrupulous men who seized political power by *coups d'état* in Italy and Germany. There the habits of representative and constitutional government were less firmly rooted than among the nations of northern Europe, especially Holland and Great Britain, where constitutionalism had been established as early as the seventeenth century. One reason for the success of National Socialism in Germany was the fact that even university circles, which were still looked to sometimes for guidance, had been impoverished intellec-

tually by the upsurge of moral relativism and cheap publicity. An intelligent refugee from Germany, Julius Kraft, described what happened there during the years which preceded the triumph of the Nazis
in 1933. The minds of university men, Kraft said, were already so "accustomed to nonsense, or (and this is true for the scientists) were so
filled with the spirit of technicism that enthusiasm for universal truth,
even for their special truths, had widely evaporated in them." [10]

Under the conditions that were coming to prevail even before the
First World War and that grew far more prevalent during the late
1920's and the 1930's, Kant's hope evaporated of safeguarding peace
by condemning action which was based on a maxim not susceptible
to "publicity." Anything could be publicized. In Germany the National
Socialists shouted their intentions of massacring the Jews and conquering the world. The concrete is likely to appeal to an audience,
and what could be more concrete than the advice of a Nazi speaker
to a crowded hall: You will find cudgels on the tables as you go out;
take one with you and hit the first Jew you see with it! Far from in-
hibiting violence and war, "publicity" became a potent instrument
for bringing both about.

For the collapse of conscientious opinion, for the waning love of
justice and righteousness, the minds of men have been in no small
measure to blame. The artists, the leaders of society, and the learned
men who earn their living in the universities, have ceased to count for
the good, partly because of the prevalent sense of the weakness of
their own intellects and wills, partly because of a growing cynicism
among businessmen and politicians, who toward the end of the nineteenth century made decadence into a form of elegance.[11] Unlike Kant
and his followers, the generation of intellectuals who grew up on the
eve of the First World War considered that men are helpless to alter
the course of history for the better.

Under the influence, during the nineteenth century, of the growing
belief in a "law of progress," men's sense of helplessness in connection
with history caused most of them little concern. Time could be counted
on to march toward the good, or toward the overthrow of the bourgeoisie, which to many a Marxist was the same thing. When in the
twentieth century the shadow of doubt was cast over the law of progress, it was accompanied by such dark uncertainty about the nature
of the good that men contented themselves with the fact that, at any
rate, they were marching. Mere activity became the justification for
existence. So instead of making history, not always happily, as some
of their great eighteenth-century predecessors made it, writers of the
twentieth century have submitted to the march of time. They have

moved in step with the machines that have come to govern the industrialized economy. The result has been to warp, and so to dehumanize, the mind in a variety of ways, until it is of little service to faith, humanity, or to the rounded conception of happiness which alone could wean the publics from the new "publicity" which has enslaved them.

Another restraint on war, which went the way of conscience and responsible "publicity," was that provided by the love of beauty, tangible as well as intangible, in constructions of every kind, from a piece of cloth to a building, from a letter to a book. The emphasis of political economy upon the maximizing of the returns from relatively scarce means fixed men's thoughts on abundance. The ever wider use of machinery reduced the contribution which human intuition — an essential source of art — could make to the ever more abundant articles produced. The pressure for efficiency and sales put a premium on the manufacture of the tangibly useful and the immediately convenient. Machines and furnaces were regarded as worth preserving only so long as more efficient ones were not available to replace them. The practice of replacement, of tearing down for the sake of building, spread through towns and cities and affected the attitude of men and women toward all buildings, even toward old examples of architecture.[12] The new outlook is exemplified in the report of an episode during the American pursuit of the German armies through northern France in 1944. A newspaper correspondent writing from Domfront, in Normandy, described it as "a turreted medieval place." "There is heavy damage in the middle of the town," he wrote. "About mid-day a single blast broke the stillness. It was a platoon of United States army engineers destroying the town's old Louis XIV arched bridge, deemed unsafe for military travel. . . The officer in charge said it would take two hours to put another bridge in its place, 'after we get this stuff out.'" [13]

The very speed of change was contagious. It infected the art of literature. Mr. T. S. Eliot has suggested that the poet has a duty to prevent language "from changing too rapidly." As he wrote recently, "a development of language at too great a speed would be a development in the sense of a progressive deterioration, and that is our danger today." [14]

An effect of the pursuit of material comfort and convenience, of the multiplication of output, as self-sufficient ends has been to relegate the pursuit of delight to a marginal, unessential place in the life of nations. The arts themselves tended to become esoteric and precious, sometimes in spite of the artist, as in the case of Tolstoy (1828–1910); sometimes with the artist's approval, as in the case of the French poet Mallarmé (1842–1898), who made almost a cult of the unintelligible.

In the early nineteenth century Hector Berlioz (1803–1869) had organized with ease a demonstration in a Paris concert hall against the misplaying of a composition by Gluck. But serious demonstrations on behalf of good taste in art became more and more difficult in the early twentieth century, even in Paris. Instead a perverse enthusiasm broke out for gratuitous acts of violence. Blows were exchanged by a dadaist poet with head waiters in restaurants, precisely because the blows had no meaning. The attacker had no acquaintance with the head waiters, and no grievance against them. But where genuine works of the mind were concerned audiences became passive, and their passivity was indicative of a lack of concern with beauty and thought. If they showed excitement it was over the political implications which they attributed to the works of art. It became difficult for the rising generations to distinguish art from propaganda.

Art arises out of imaginative vision, a special attribute of our human powers. This vision enables men to give tangible form to their sense of harmony, mirth, tragedy, and eternity. Art provides for the artist, and for those who contemplate his work, kinds of satisfaction that cannot be found in objects produced for other masters than art. The more we approach art in our work and in the observation of the objects about us, the more beautiful these objects are, the more we approach a state of contemplative rest, even in the inevitable process of carrying on the daily rounds of activity. Such serenity helps us to conquer the fears, the troubles, and the unhappiness which beset us.

Commodity, abundance, activity, and excitement provide different kinds of satisfaction. But if delight is missing, commodity and abundance, even combined with incessant activity, cannot redeem the loss of joy in contemplation. Apart from the role of art in blunting and delaying the manufacture of efficient weapons, the practice of fine craftsmanship has helped men and women to sublimate their belligerent instincts. Commodity and abundance make different contributions to this sublimation, and if the pursuit of delight leads societies to slight the kinds of labor necessary to physical existence, then this pursuit itself can become a cause for war. But that was not the main trouble in the industrialized societies which have gone to war with each other since 1914. The absence of delight in daily living has helped to leave many lives empty and sterile and so fair game for any excitement, including the most terrific of worldly excitements, that of war.

With the triumph of industrialism during the nineteenth century, the drift away from delight as the guiding principle in production impoverished one side of human nature at the very time when men and women were so drugged by the novelty of material abundance that most of them were unaware of any loss. Yet the almost exclusively utilitarian and practical character of the new industrial civilization, for which there was no precedent, began late in the nineteenth century to be a serious worry to a few reformers. These men, John Ruskin (1819–1900), Matthew Arnold (1822–1888), and William Morris (1834–1896) all emerged in Great Britain, the first state to be fully industrialized. They saw that the new abundance and the new commodity were catering more and more exclusively to the prosaic, matter-of-fact, and dull interests of men and women, were depriving life on earth of some of its savor, at the very time when more and more people were putting all their hopes upon their temporal existence. The hopes themselves were desiccated. With the development of machinery and the multiplication in the output of goods and services, work for the common man and woman became less interesting, less engaging. The love of work for its own sake, for the sake of the direct products of work, diminished, along with the capacity of others to contemplate with happiness the results of good work.

If an American economist happens on the phrase a "love of work," the chances are he will want to correct it. He will suggest that what is meant is not a love of the work, but a love of the things for which the money paid for the work can be exchanged. The products are chiefly appreciated not for their intrinsic qualities but for the physical effort which they save, or for the artificial excitement which they generate among men and women during the leisure time industrial progress has borrowed for them.

During the nineteenth century something was done among children to compensate for the loss of beauty by the spread of fairy tales and toys. The world of make-believe in which some of the English romantics of the late eighteenth century had lived, written, and painted was adapted in new forms for the very young, and a charming literature developed, of which *Alice in Wonderland* is the most famous example. But eventually the result of this movement was to starve still more the imagination of grown people, deprived of artistic work. As growing youths were confronted rudely with the consequences of carrying the personality of Little Lord Fauntleroy into practical life, there was an increasing disposition to regard every kind of fancy as an evidence of immaturity, of lack of the crude roughness or the matter-of-fact outlook which were mistaken for maturity. At the same time, with the development of long-range war, the spread of toys among children — toy soldiers especially — encouraged them in a make-believe attitude toward destruction, which had been facilitated mainly by the increase in the distance of military targets. Some continued to play with destruction when they grew up. During the six years of Nazi domination of Germany preceding the Second World War, Hitler's second in command, Hermann Goering, is said to have taken perverse pleasure in producing collisions between toy trains.

(2) *The Decline of Intellectual Bonds*

During the seventeenth and eighteenth centuries, the development of polite manners among the European peoples, under the aegis of the French, had made for limited warfare. Manners inclined rulers, their ministers, and ambassadors to exercise increasing decorum and restraint in the conduct of diplomatic negotiations. Military officers had been generally recruited from the same social classes as diplomats. Through the officers and the example which they set their men, manners extended to the battlefield and encouraged a dignified and humane treatment of the defeated and the wounded.

The etiquette reached its classic expression in 1745 at Fontenoy, just east of the river Scheldt. There, in the War of the Austrian Succession, a French army led by the decrepit Marshal Saxe, who was unable to mount his horse, defeated an Anglo-Austrian-Dutch army commanded by the Duke of Cumberland, in one of those battles of slow movement characteristic of the age of limited warfare. The French objective was to hinder the allies from relieving the fortress of Tournai. Before the fighting started, Captain Lord Charles Hay, of the Grenadier Guards, ran in front of the allied line, doffed his hat to the French enemy, drank to them out of a pocket flask, shouted a taunt, and called for three cheers from his men. The salute and the cheers were returned by the French, who waited for the English to fire the first shots after Hay had rejoined his company.

Thus, as a prelude to battle, officers went through respectful formalities, understood and accepted by both sides, after the fashion of two gentlemen approaching a doorway. Wars were terminated by formal treaties according to generally recognized rules. It would have been as incorrect to leave the terms of peace unsettled as to withdraw from a *salon* without taking leave of the hostess.

Manners retained their political and military importance during most of the nineteenth century. They were extended to wider circles, both within and between nations. But in the last decades of the nineteenth century signs were not lacking that good etiquette was losing its spell for human societies. During the first half of the twentieth century a wholesale disintegration of manners set in, to which the deterioration in the character of "publicity" contributed. To take a banal example, if it proved inconvenient to doff one's hat, one kept it on. The act was deprived of all transcendental meaning. It is not without significance that this polite custom lost ground in the United States sooner than in France, a country which had been much less rapidly and thoroughly industrialized. With the growing use of machinery, human movements became more mechanical. Art, with its imaginative inspiration and its humanity, rather than mechanics is the foundation and mainstay of manners. As that foundation gave way, the rising working classes in Europe, and the peoples of distant countries, such as India, Russia, and Japan, which were drawn by material progress into a single orbit, met with growing vulgarity and callousness in the very quarters which might have set an example of good form.

One consequence was to loosen the restraints upon war. With the growing material power to make war, what was needed was more politeness, more art, more wit in the conduct of international relations. What came was more grossness.

As early as the 1860's it was discovered, apparently in Prussia, that the effectiveness of army officers was increased if most of them were guided in professional conduct exclusively by the discipline of drill and tactics. "In all other countries," it was observed, "the ideal model for the officer is the gentleman." [1] In Germany such an ideal was thought to interfere with military success. So, partly under the pressure exerted by the increasing scale of military operations, the ideal was less and less recognized. In diplomacy both the spirit and the letter of the code of honor were widely abandoned in the twentieth century. Before 1939 representatives of nations had begun to talk to each other during a period of nominal peace in words and with a tone which earlier Western statesmen would hardly have ventured to use even in time of war. As the polite barriers against the making of war gave way, the nations not unnaturally forgot how to end war. No fixed terms for the reparations payable by the defeated were provided in the treaties of peace signed after the First World War. Following the second, the nations were unable even to make treaties.

The decay of conventions had consequences which were of military importance for all social classes in an age when wars had come to employ for the first time all the people, when victory depended partly upon enlisting strong support from the great majority of the nation. At the beginning of the twentieth century, much scorn was directed to the artificial character of the polite dress and of the elaborate etiquette prescribed for social intercourse during the nineteenth century. No doubt the Victorian customs of dress and of social intercourse had made a contribution to cant; no doubt they afforded an example of what Veblen called "conspicuous waste," in that they served no useful purpose. They also provided those imperfect and very human creatures, men and women, with a remnant of the mystery which human nature not unnaturally seeks, since our beginning and our end are and will remain mysterious. However wasteful life in the late nineteenth century may have been, the waste could hardly compare with that brought on later by total warfare. The elaborate dresses, the many-roomed houses, the conventional formalities surrounding friendship and love, put a value upon intimate human intercourse which contributed to both friendship and love. The semipublic stripping off of clothes, the destruction of etiquette, the blows produced by screaming headlines, radio voices in once quiet bedrooms and even in open fields, the penetrating rays of television, deprived the peoples of the earth of some of the last citadels within which their imaginative faculties could play to the advantage of the generous sentiments and the tender manners which had become part of European culture.

Social reformers of the eighteenth century were followed by humanitarians and socialists of the nineteenth. Most of them put their hopes for an earthly paradise upon the emancipation of the common man from the inferior social and economic position he had occupied. It was widely supposed that the troubles among the civilized peoples had come from economic and social injustice, that the more all men and women were reduced as well as raised to a common level, the more virtue would prevail. But with the spread of industrialism, the kinds of commodities and experiences which men had to share were changing. While the standard of living was rising in many countries, the lives led by men and women were no longer the same. In many ways their lives were made safer, more sanitary, and more comfortable. Yet along with this safety, sanitation, and comfort, something of the sweetness, the charm, the laughter, and the joy which had been cultivated in seventeenth- and eighteenth-century Europe disappeared, and not only among the privileged. Such human vitality and wit persists mainly in those civilized parts of the world which have been little industrialized. It is apparent in rural Mexico, in spite of the poverty of the villagers. High wages in large cities full of the products of the machine provide men and women with remarkable facilities for bathing and disinfecting, for taking care of the body; but they do nothing to restore this vitality, this zest for life, which enables a man or woman to live each day enthusiastically.

The problem of providing a richer existence for the poor and needy, for the many, was envisaged during the late nineteenth century almost entirely in material terms, as was natural in view of the evolution of thought. But it proved to be more than a material problem. Could the common man be brought to participate in the life of the mind and spirit which had distinguished eighteenth-century Europe and had given many distinguished Europeans a confidence in the power of the intellect to work for the good, such as no peoples had had before? Could the common man, and even more perhaps the common woman who was his mate and could become his guide, acquire the good taste, the love of art, the sense of order, and the polite dignity which seemed to the eighteenth-century mind one of the chief glories of European civilization? Could these qualities be acquired not only by the descendants of Europeans but by all the races and peoples of the earth?

Neither the late nineteenth nor the early twentieth century supplied affirmative answers to these questions. Victory was achieved at last in what became at the beginning of the twentieth century a race to draw close to naked, positive reality. Yet, now that nothing is concealed, nothing whole can be seen. Man does not live by positive reality alone. One price of attaining it had been the specialization of work of the mind. This has left each man of learning in the presence of only a tiny patch of reality.

A hundred years ago, the most celebrated nineteenth-century convert to Roman Catholicism, Cardinal Newman (1801–1890), presented an "idea of a university." In this university all the participants were to be given the opportunity to acquire general "intellectual culture." "History . . . shows things as they are," Newman wrote, "that is, the morals and interests of men disfigured and perverted by all their imperfections of passion, folly, and ambition; philosophy strips the picture too much; poetry adorns it too much; the concentrated lights of the three correct the false peculiar colouring of each, and show us the truth. The right mode of thinking upon it is to be had from them taken all three together." [2]

What most university men got during the past seventy-five years was not even one of the three, but some small part frequently for the purpose of serving a practical object at the expense of general culture; the very kind of warped training which Newman had warned against. More children and young people than ever before were sent to schools, colleges, and universities. More men and women became teachers.

There were more professors, more persons who were considered learned. But growing specialization was accompanied by increasing superficiality on all general questions concerning the nature of man and his relation to the universe. The result in the higher learning was a generation of experts.

Among the learned, there were many who were as strongly opposed to war as men of letters in the eighteenth century had been. But with specialization and the rise of the new publicity, their pacifistic utterances were regarded as merely the private expressions of professional men. As experts it was not within their province to decide how and for what purposes their recognized special knowledge should be used.

During the eighteenth century and a part of the nineteenth, a general audience had been the recipient of the best that learning and art had to give. Cheap, vulgar, and even obscene writing there had been in plenty. But this had been earmarked for what it was; it was available only for the special audiences who were willing consciously to debase themselves by seeking it. In the early twentieth century, with the fragmentation of knowledge, the position was reversed. The best that learning and art had to give was for special audiences. The general audience, which had grown overwhelmingly in size, was now provided mainly with the superficial, the noisy, and the vulgar, sometimes with the obscene in disguised and tepid forms which could evade the scrutiny of newly created czars of censorship. The shameful was doctored and concealed until it became respectable. Serious intellectual leadership was confined more and more to specialties which the general audience either could not understand or was not encouraged to try to understand. The intellect made a present of the general to the charlatan, the vulgarian, and the dictator.

As a result the community of culture, which alone can bind human beings everywhere and always, was undermined by a materialism combined with a kind of individualism which severs human beings from each other. As long as man is conceived as dual in his nature, human as well as animal, as long as it is believed that what separates people from each other is the imprisonment of the soul within the body, they have momentous matters to share, matters which are beyond the temporal and the individual. Such matters are a source, not of jealousy, but of charity and love. Once a human being is conceived as fully explicable in terms of his sense experiences, and the effects of these experiences on his physical body, each human being is left unique. He has nothing to unite him to another save his body. And unions of the body cannot endure.

In spite of their abundant contributions to knowledge, the many specialties into which learning and even art were splitting were of little or no service to general culture. But the specialists were drawn, sometimes unwillingly or unwittingly, into the service of war. Since the triumph of industrialism, expert knowledge has been in ever-increasing demand. It was wanted by economic enterprises and by national states. Economic enterprises were concerned, above all, with the extension of sales and the multiplication of output, in order to dispose of ever larger quantities of goods at a profit. With the coming of an era of total wars, national states employed experts especially to help with problems related directly or indirectly to military strength. Every kind of specialist, from the Egyptologist to the social psychologist, was useful now that all parts of the world had been brought within the scope of the military campaigns of leading nations and now that every aspect of national life had a bearing on victory or defeat. As Dr. Carl Binger, a psychiatrist of Cornell University, recently complained, psychologists, other scientists, and every variety of expert are wanted by governments not to help with peace but with war.

The pressure that drove psychologists came to bear down upon the two kinds of specialists — the economists and the natural scientists —whose work was thought to contribute most directly to the increase of wealth, and whose prestige consequently was greater than that of other experts. By the early twentieth century, with the growing success of the new publicity, economics was unable to compete in the freedom of the market place (championed by the fathers of orthodox economics) for the increasingly large general audience which was coming into existence. As a subject designed to bring about the material happiness of mankind, economics was becoming its own nemesis. Not only were the economists unable to gain the audience reached by new cults and fads with the help of cheap paper and newsprint, they split up until their own serious audience eventually shrank. Many of them gave up the hope of influencing policy by objective *thought*. Instead they became experts and gave economic advice on matters of business or government administration and management.

Modern science had grown up as the servant of civilized humanity. Civilized humanity was itself a limited conception. With the triumph of industrialism its limitations became ever more serious. It was no longer possible to leave out barbarians and primitive peoples. At the same time the concept of civilization, in the sense of general culture pertaining to all sides of human endeavor and to all mankind, which had a clear meaning for some eighteenth-century men, like Montesquieu, was beclouded by growing cleavages between nations, and by the rise of powerful states outside the European family. It became increasingly difficult to stretch the earlier concept to cover the world as a whole, when it no longer served the small European world as it had. Its basis was sapped by the rise of groups — the Communists, the Nazis, or the Capitalists; the Russians, the British, the Japanese, the Germans, or the Americans — each claiming an exclusive possession of civilization. However international scientists were in their inclinations, they found themselves pushed more and more to take sides.

The same thing was happening to economics and to economists. Economics had in fact fewer natural powers of resistance than science. In spite of its growing autonomy, science in early modern times had been conceived of as a branch of philosophy. But as it developed before the eighteenth century, economics, as its name "political economy" suggests, was considered primarily a branch of politics. In the early seventeenth century politics was already strongly nationalistic, and, apart from a few exceptional men who commanded little attention, the early political economists were chauvinistically inclined. They supported policies designed to do the maximum damage to the economic welfare of rival nations, on the theory that the economic prosperity of one's own country was dependent upon the economic misery of others. It was one of the great achievements of later political economists, and above all of Adam Smith, to associate economics again with its more ancient origin, with ethics or moral philosophy, the science of what is good for man. Along with the change went a new political point of view — the advantages of which for peace have been already discussed — that the prosperity of one's own nation depended on the prosperity of others.[3]

For all that, economics remained nationalistic to a greater degree than science. The prosperity of foreign nations was sought as a matter of national policy. The conception was no less vulnerable from the point of view of universalism than the notion that "honesty is the best policy." What if honesty should prove not to be the best policy? If it could be effectively claimed that promoting the prosperity of the rest of the world was not the best *policy* for one's own country, then economics could readily again become chauvinistic.

Early nationalism among the Western Europeans — the nationalism of the later Middle Ages, of the sixteenth century, and to some extent of the seventeenth — had been accompanied by the idea that the principal if not the only means of adding to a nation's wealth was by the acquisition of more territory. During the seventeenth, eighteenth, and nineteenth centuries, especially with the extraordinary growth in production which accompanied the industrial revolution, it came to be widely believed that the opportunities for national gain were very much greater in connection with peaceful development at home. But at the beginning of the twentieth century, when Angell put forward this belief as a virtual scientific axiom, it was contested by Sombart's thesis that modern war had been an important element in making the wheels of industry turn *within* each country. This view was extended and perverted by new and unscrupulous political leaders — Hitler first and foremost — to mean that conquest could be a paying proposition if only the conquerors were ruthless enough, if only they returned to the ancient pre-Christian custom, abandoned by Western civilization,[4] of enslaving large numbers of the peoples they conquered.

By providing an alternative to physical combat, high tariffs had to some extent contributed to the more moderate character of warfare in the late seventeenth and early eighteenth centuries, at a time when economic scarcity helped to make total war an unbearable burden for a nation and when national honor could be more readily satisfied by token conflict. But in the twentieth century tariffs became a cause for fiercer warfare because they interfered notably with the growth of wealth in some countries, and so helped make plausible a revival of the early thesis that the most promising means of increasing the wealth of a nation was by conquest. Once it was claimed that more could be got by war than by commerce, commerce became national and particular rather than international. The concept of man as a purchasing instead of a rational animal has not been the obstacle to war that many hoped it might be.

Science and economics seldom welcomed force. Yet each was partial, not only in relation to the new kind of world which emerged from the nineteenth century with the triumph of industrialism, but also in relation to human nature. The pursuit of science or of economics as autonomous subjects led naturally to ever further divisions within each subject. So the scientist and the economist, who were never in a position to speak for man, but only for certain aspects of man, became less and less universal with respect to the human being during the period when both were losing such claims to be international as they had once been able to put forward with a measure of plausibility.

The education of the whole people and their participation in politics as voters were counted on by the pacifists to provide a bulwark against war. It was argued that no nation with universal suffrage would vote itself into a war, because men and women would be unwilling to give their lives or the lives of their sons and husbands for military purposes. But hope in the pacifistic influence of the masses proved at least as disappointing as hope in the pacifistic influence of the business interests to whom Angell appealed. There was little in the instruction, the information, or the entertainment that the masses were given to encourage a sense of responsibility for the material civilization in whose commodities and comforts they shared. In his remarkable books, Ortega y Gasset has suggested that one of the most notable changes that accompanied the triumph of industrialism was the disposition of most men and women to take it for granted that the material goods of life would go on multiplying regardless of the uses to which human beings put their lives. Twenty years ago Ortega wrote that " the common man, finding himself in a world so excellent, technically and socially, believes that it has been produced by nature, and never thinks of the personal efforts of highly-endowed individuals which the creation of this new world presupposed. Still less will he admit the notion that all these facilities still require the support of certain difficult human virtues, the least failure of which would cause the rapid disappearance of the whole magnificent edifice." [5]

Irresponsibility causes more unhappiness than responsibility. During the late nineteenth century and at the beginning of the twentieth, with the fantastically rapid growth in population and in wealth, boredom and uncertainty became more prevalent than at any time in history. A sense of uneasy dissatisfaction took possession of herds of men and women, more and more uprooted from the soil, from any continuous vocational tradition and from any settled abode in or near a city. As it became easier to move, people became increasingly eager to change their residence, often for no better motive than the desire for change. They welcomed almost any distraction as an escape from their surroundings and from themselves. The masses of the people did not want war. But they were ripe for the uneasy fear, the anger, and hatred which boredom and uninteresting labor breed and which lead to war.

Influential writers were not lacking to provide the masses with ideas and data which aroused a mixture of excitement, fear, and hatred. The works of such writers, unlike those of learned specialists, had a wide appeal. Like the doctrines of Luther and Calvin in the early sixteenth century, those of Karl Marx and his followers since the mid-nineteenth century made an impression upon the dissatisfied elements in society, at a time when men and women were better off materially than ever before and when, partly for that reason, the very real economic, social, and legal abuses appeared less tolerable than in periods when there had been more physical suffering. Poverty and even destitution persisted in the new industrial civilization, when the unprecedented abundance was making serious poverty hardly justifiable and destitution not justifiable at all.

The attempts to raise the standard of living through the spread of capitalistic enterprise, or through a class struggle to set up an absolute state of some kind — ranging from National Socialism to Communism — were equally irrelevant as a solvent for the growing problems of spiritual, cultural, and intellectual division. The dislike of one group for another was actually intensified. The concept of a human "scum" ceased to be localized during the nineteenth century. Instead each person or group came to think of those human beings he did not like as the scum. In the age of world wars, groups, races, and nations came to regard other groups, races, and nations — with whom they were brought into contact by progress — as dregs suited only for extermination. One is reminded of the apocryphal American of the 1920's who built a cottage in a remote, almost uninhabited island in the Pacific Ocean. He hung up a sign: "Two hundred per cent American." Unlike his fellow Americans, who hated only the Negroes, the Jews, and the Catholics, he hated "the whole damn human race." This attitude could be easily mobilized against an alleged enemy; it produced mutual fear and hatred where there had been among the Western peoples during the eighteenth and early nineteenth centuries some sense of common purpose in existence.

During the late nineteenth and early twentieth centuries a number of brilliant minds — Marx in England, Dostoevski (1821–1881) in Russia, Nietzsche (1844–1900) in Germany, Freud (1856–1939) in Austria, Proust (1871–1922) in France — were rediscovering the reality and the power of evil, which the eighteenth- and early nineteenth-century intellect had hoped men were outgrowing. Soon after Spencer had predicted the disappearance of evil, these men revealed anew the Messianic and demoniacal attributes of the human soul, which the Jewish and the Christian religions alike had recognized. But, with the exception of Dostoevski, none of them tried to restore the spiritual opportunities which religion had offered the soul for redemption. The result was to bring to men a fresh consciousness of the reality of evil without the means of atonement open to earlier sinners. Sin itself became the only *spiritual* experience of ever larger numbers of men and women.

At the beginning of the twentieth century, this rediscovery of evil combined with the decay of general culture to intensify nationalism and class hatred. As religious and ethical values lost their hold on the Western peoples, both in Europe and America, a blind allegiance to one's nation or one's class offered a substitute for allegiance to God.

Down to the nineteenth century the philosophies of the Western peoples, with their Greek and Christian origins, always had man (not particular men, groups, or nations) as their primary concern. The doctrine of the national state as the final end of existence for the people who compose it was given effective philosophical support for the first time during the late nineteenth and early twentieth centuries. To begin with, the positive assertion of this doctrine in circles of learning and culture was mainly a German accomplishment, if "accomplishment" is a suitable word in this connection. In the early nineteenth century Germany was not yet a single nation. For German thinkers the very process of forming a unified German state became an intellectual experience. Germany came on nationalism late, when it was taken more seriously than before throughout the world. The Germans had no experience of an earlier, more moderate nationalism, like that of the French, the Dutch, or the English. Consequently modern German philosophy, history, and political thought mixed up philosophical speculations with practical patriotic considerations.

The German love of abstract ideas had been manifested earlier not only by thinkers who aspired to universal knowledge, Hegel (1770-1831) foremost among them, but by the historical school of law and politics, by F. C. Savigny (1779–1861), Adam Müller (1779–1829), Friedrich Stahl (1802–1861), and Leopold von Ranke (1795–1886), the great historian. The Comte de Saint-Simon had counted on the German enthusiasm for abstract ideas to help safeguard European peace. None of the early members of the German historical school was interested primarily in the German unity which Bismarck (1815–1898) was to make into a reality. What distinguished German romantic historians, and the whole early nineteenth-century German romantic movement, from the romantic movement in other Western countries was its close and exclusive connection with conservative politics.[6] When conservatism came to be identified with German unity and nationalism, Treitschke (1834–1896) and his followers put history at the service of the nation, and for some time at least Nietzsche and his followers did the same for philosophy. Unlike earlier philosophy German philosophy took, not man, but *German* man as its primary concern. Thus the objective of the mind, which traditionally in Europe had been the universal good, was becoming the particular good of a nation. Such a contraction could easily put the mind at the disposal of groups or individuals.

(3) *The Cult of Violence*

Complementary to the extreme nationalist philosophy, which infected all countries in varying degrees, there grew up among a few intellectual leaders an enthusiasm for war itself as an ennobling spiritual experience. This enthusiasm appealed to the mystical side of man and extended to great numbers of the Western peoples. Thus the mischief caused by the minds of men was not confined to the breakdown of old moral, aesthetic, and intellectual restraints on general war, and to the disintegration, with the decline of European culture, of the idea of a universal human community. A positive will to war was generated during the late nineteenth and early twentieth centuries. It infected the mass of the population (which was obtaining political and economic rights more rapidly than it was assuming political and economic responsibilities). The nearest historical precedent for this general will to war is to be found in the concept of the citizen-soldier, which arose during the French Revolution. But at that time the will to war among the masses was based not on a worship of war for war's sake, but of war on behalf of liberty, equality, fraternity, and the idea of justice.

The new mysticism, which helped to fan the flames of the world wars, seems to have originated in military circles in Germany. It first found expression in Clausewitz. It is absent from the writings of his slightly older German contemporary, the Archduke Charles Louis of Austria (1771–1847), Napoleon's most formidable opponent. Charles called war "the greatest evil which a state or a nation can experience." [1] Unlike Napoleon and his enemy the archduke, Clausewitz was not a remarkably effective officer on the field of battle, and a recent military authority, General Camon, has suggested that "it is impossible to take . . . seriously" Clausewitz' directions concerning the conduct of war.[2] It is reasonable to regard his doctrines concerning the philosophical meaning of war as a product mainly of the mind at work in the study.

Clausewitz and his followers in Germany and eventually in other countries gave warfare an intellectual justification in addition to the emotional justification it derived from the spirit of resistance, of defense, bred in the heat of the French Revolution. Clausewitz' philosophy of war made use of concepts and categories directly derived from the Christian and humanist philosophies of the past, but he put them to a new purpose. For him war became a great exercise, in which the intellectual as well as the moral qualities of man had a unique opportunity for fulfillment. The occasion for the use of the mind was slight, of course, in the case of the private, but even for him there was a respectable place in the new warfare. The choices offered him in great battles called for tremendous grit and for some intelligence. So battles conferred upon the common man a kind of dignity which ordinary economic existence was failing to provide. As one ascended the military hierarchy from the private to the general, the intellectual opportunities increased, until for the commander-in-chief they exceeded those accorded men in other callings.[3]

As all men came to be subject to military service with the triumph of industrialism, such views as those of Clausewitz (even though those of a professional writing about his specialty) took on a weight denied the views of other specialists. The views were adopted also by independent thinkers and writers, who sought to speak not simply on behalf of the military profession or even of a particular nation. During the fifty years preceding the war of 1914, the Western mind encouraged war by making a spiritual value out of organized fighting. At a time when the mind was withdrawing its unequivocal support of both Christian and Greek ethical values, serious writers began to contend that force is philosophically a good in itself. One of the first to expound such a thesis was Proudhon, in his long book on war and peace published in 1861. Proudhon regarded war as a constructive force which had contributed to humanity and the dignity of man. War had reached the height of a religion: "For the masses," Proudhon wrote, "the real Christ is Alexander, Caesar, Charlemagne, Napoleon." [4]

Proudhon's position was ambiguous because he regarded war as an anachronism.[5] With him such enthusiasm as the masses had for force was nostalgic. Ruskin's praise of war is even more ambiguous in its origins and its meaning than Proudhon's. He took up the subject when, in the 1860's, he was asked to lecture to the Royal Military Academy at Woolwich. At this time soldiering in England was still a profession and officering still the preserve of a small group. At the outset of his lecture Ruskin spoke as one specialist, an artist, to other specialists; he spoke with the intention of doing homage to the virtues of the military calling. Art, he suggests, has been a product of war, though he does not make at all clear why he believes this to be so. "I found in brief," he says, "that all great nations learned their truth of word, and strength of thought, in war; that they were nourished in war, and wasted by peace; taught by war, and deceived by peace; trained by war, and betrayed by peace; — in a word that they were born in war, and expired in peace." Yet the further he advances in his speech the more contradictory his remarks become. War is desirable only for persons who have no work to do, he suggests. Of the wars of the Swiss with Austria, of the contests of ambitious nations for extent of power, of the Napoleonic wars and the American Civil War, he has this to say: "None of these forms of war build anything but tombs." Later he remarks that "modern war — scientific war, chemical and mechanic war [is] worse even than the savage's poisoned arrow." He ends with an appeal to women to save the world from war.

Of the ambiguities in these remarks, Ruskin later became aware. In considering the words of his lecture after they had been presented for publication, Ruskin wrote, "I am often accused of inconsistency, but believe myself defensible against the charge with respect to what I have said on nearly every subject except that of war. . . . The conviction on which I act [with respect to war] is, that it causes an incalculable amount of human suffering, and that it ought to cease among Christian nations, and if therefore any of my boy friends desire to be soldiers, I try my utmost to bring them to a better mind. But, on the other hand, I know certainly that the most beautiful characters yet developed among men have been formed in war, — that all great nations have been warrior nations, and that the only kinds of peace which we are likely to get in the present age are ruinous alike to the intellect and the heart." [6]

Neither Proudhon nor Ruskin wrote in the Christian tradition, according to which the roots of war are in sin, nor did they take the position, derived from Christian doctrine, that war is by nature evil and peace by nature virtuous. So both of them helped to remove the barriers which stood in the way of a novel glorification of war as what Ruskin called "a wholesome calamity." As long as man's capacity to rise above his personal likes and interests and to think and act on behalf of accepted absolute values transcending his individual whims was believed in, the infliction of pain had an ethical place in human affairs, private and public alike, as a *means* of enforcing justice. The decline of the belief in absolute values, not subject to positive scientific proof, came in the late nineteenth century at a time when the infliction of corporal penalties of all kinds was diminishing strikingly, and the lovers of peace hoped that the increasing skepticism, which helped to correct many abuses of authority, might lead to the abandonment of force in international affairs. Instead, at the turn of the nineteenth and twentieth centuries, war service began to be treated by some men as an *end* good in itself.

No one in the United States set forth the new creed more effectively than the late Justice Oliver Wendell Holmes, a veteran of the Union army in the Civil War. "I do not know what is true," he told a Memorial Day audience in 1895. "I do not know the meaning of the universe. But in the midst of doubt, in the collapse of creeds, there is one thing I do not doubt, that no man who lives in the same world with most of us can doubt, and that is that the faith is true and adorable which leads a soldier to throw away his life in obedience to a blindly accepted duty, in a cause which he little understands, in a plan of campaign of which he has no notion, under tactics of which he does not see the use." [7] It was the sacrifice, not the cause, which Holmes glorified. In an earlier Memorial Day address, of 1884, he had made plain that he regarded the sacrifice made by the southern soldiers as no less "sacred" than that made by the northern.[8]

A similar veneration for the use of force, combined with an insistence upon the cleansing virtue of the spirit which leads men to fight, is contained in the work of Georges Sorel, a French contemporary of Holmes, and one of the most influential European writers of his time. Sorel's *Reflections on Violence*, which appeared at the beginning of the twentieth century, was translated into English by a brilliant young philosopher with much literary promise, T. E. Hulme, who gave his life in the First World War. Sorel's book is a protest against the widespread view, which had developed among the Western peoples during the eighteenth and nineteenth centuries, that acts of collective and individual violence alike should be regarded as barbarous, that gentleness is the mark of civilization. "The dangers which threaten the world may be avoided," wrote Sorel, "if the proletariat hold on with obstinacy to revolutionary ideas, so as to realize as much as possible Marx's conception. Everything may be saved, if the proletariat, by their use of violence, manage to reëstablish the division into classes, and so restore to the middle class something of its former energy; that is the great aim towards which the whole thought of men — who are not hypnotized by the events of the day but think of the conditions of tomorrow — must be directed. Proletarian violence, carried on as a pure and simple manifestation of the class war, appears there as a very fine and very heroic thing; it is at the service of the immemorial interests of civilization; it is not perhaps the most appropriate method of obtaining material advantages, but it may save the world from barbarism." [9]

Reflections on Violence was partly directed at the socialism of Jaurès. In so far as war is concerned, Jaurès' socialism resembled that of Karl Kautsky in Germany and of John Burns in England. All of them were devoted to the cause of peace among the nations; all of them were mild socialists in the sense that they wanted to prevent relentless class war. For Sorel such an outlook was an evidence of weakness: his philosophy reversed the age-old association of violence with barbarism. For him violence and war become the leading instruments of civilization, because they dedicate men to nonmaterial ends.

The poetry of A. E. Housman, whatever its intention, appealed to the same idea, that civilization itself with its refined ways and its commercial dealings was decadent and materialistic, and that violence and death offered the generation that was growing up at the beginning of the twentieth century a means of demonstrating the nobler power which the soul possesses over the body.[10] In his *A Shropshire Lad*, composed at the juncture of the nineteenth and twentieth centuries, Housman foresaw the destiny of the oncoming generation.

> On the idle hill of summer,
>   Sleepy with the flow of streams,
> Far I hear the steady drummer
>   Drumming like a noise in dreams.
>
> Far and near and low and louder
>   On the roads of earth go by,
> Dear to friends and food for powder,
>   Soldiers marching, all to die.
>
> East and west on fields forgotten
>   Bleach the bones of comrades slain,
> Lovely lads and dead and rotten;
>   None that go return again.
>
> Far the calling bugles hollo,
>   High the screaming fife replies,
> Gay the files of scarlet follow:
>   Woman bore me, I will rise.

In the lines one hears the tramp of the soldiers in the British expeditionary force as they moved through the streets of Le Havre, night after night during August and September of 1914, to meet the invading German armies which were full of the pent-up enthusiasm for the fight that had been denied them in 1911 when the statesmen of Europe had recoiled from war over the Morocco crisis.

In *More Poems*, published in 1936, Housman worked himself into something approaching a perverse ecstasy over the calling of the soldier.

> I did not lose my heart in summer's even,
>   When roses to the moonrise burst apart:
> When plumes were under heel and lead was flying,
>   In blood and smoke and flame I lost my heart.
>
> I lost it to a soldier and a foeman,
>   A chap that did not kill me, but he tried;
> That took the sabre straight and took it striking,
>   And laughed and kissed his hand to me and died.

These appeals went straight to the chords in human nature that desire violence, danger, and excitement, chords less touched than in the past by faith in Christ, homely duty, and compassion. Nietzsche described the human condition which the cult of violence alone could satisfy, on the basis of his experience with the German nation in the wars of the late nineteenth century. "Whenever in our time a war breaks out," he wrote, "there also breaks out, and especially among the most noble members of a people a secret desire: they throw themselves with delight against the new danger of death, because in the sacrifice for the fatherland they believe they have found at last the permission they have been seeking, the permission to evade their human purpose. War is for them a short-cut to suicide, it enables them to commit suicide with a good conscience." [11]

During an age when life among the Europeans was losing its ancient Christian meaning, when men were taking their own lives more frequently than in the past, the works of Nietzsche, Housman, Sorel, and Holmes were a direct summons to the drums that were beating in the human subconscious. The common man was offered, on an unprecedented scale, the opportunity to participate in what seemed a compelling purpose, at a time when all sense of purpose in connection with peace and ordinary living was being lost. In the empty solitude of noise and hustle, he became in the moments of flickering inner life what the recruiting posters were to tell him was "the man of destiny," what the popular magazines had convinced him it would be glorious for him to become, "the man of the year." Again, as in the age of the French Revolution and Napoleon, but on a much wider scale and with a novel pleasure in evil, the mass of men, and even eventually of women, were admitted to complete equality — to the equality of serving and perhaps dying in war. The identification of violence with virtue, with the willingness to make a gratuitous sacrifice of one's life, made it possible not merely to restore the prestige of fighting under conditions of industrialism and mass slaughter, but to extend that prestige to all, to make it as democratic as the suffrage.

Throughout Christian history, respect for the soldier hero had been tempered by the conviction that war is by nature evil, the result of sin. The two ideas were inseparable as long as the revulsion from sin and from evil was strong. But when the existence of sin and evil was denied, heroism in war was left without any counterweight. By the beginning of the twentieth century it was in a position to take the place of both the Christian faith and the Christian morality. War became a moral equivalent for ethics and religion. Is it any wonder that the problem for the lover of peace was, as the first famous pragmatist, William James, expressed it, to find a moral equivalent for war?

Force as the arbiter of national and even of class disputes had a more general appeal than commerce, because the appeal of force was more instinctive and elemental. Force was represented as less corrupt than profit-seeking, and even as providing redemptive possibilities now that redemption through the Christian or the Jewish faith was less sought after.

The cult of violence is actually no substitute for material gain, nor is it an equivalent for redemption. The appeal to force is an extension of greed and so even more corrupt than the profit-seeking systems of the nineteenth century which stopped short of force. Violence is a substitute for redemption in the sense that Hell is a substitute for Heaven.

CHAPTER TWENTY

Conclusion

· AFTER TWO WORLD WARS, THERE IS MUCH TALK ABOUT THE GREAT powers. It is the fashion to reduce them to four, to three, and especially to two. Any such classification is based on the industrial force each can muster: the output of steel, coal, and oil, especially the output per head. An inquiry into the modern crisis of the intellect suggests that such classifications are based on a highly incomplete conception of the meaning of greatness. To a considerable extent the minds that have fostered the triumph of the industrial state have contributed to the decline of the human mind. They have made it partial, special, and irresponsible. The material strength they have helped to create has made the attainment of order, charm, and serenity, in the lives of the humble and the mighty alike, more difficult to achieve than in countries which have devoted themselves less single-mindedly to industrial advance. The happiness men seek is not within their grasp, in spite of all the energy and ingenuity spent in the pursuit of happiness. The very advances men have made are leading them, in spite of themselves, toward wars more devastating than any ever fought by the human race.

When we try to look at industrialism and war from beyond ourselves, we see that the idea that the industrialized state has some special mission to perpetuate by force of arms its particular economy, its particular form of government, is no less grotesque than any of the motives on behalf of which conquests have been attempted in the past. Most people recognize the barrenness of the wars that fill the books of history. As we look back we are glad that the Greeks defended themselves successfully against the Persian invaders, but we see no cause for rejoicing over the success of Alexander of Macedon in conquering much of the classical world, including the Persian Empire. Conquest has glory only for the warrior; it has never taught the conquered or the conquerors much that matters. What made Greek civilization immortal was not its arms but its ideas, its beauty, its truth. The defense at Marathon in 490 B.C. and at Thermopylae ten years later have eternal meaning not because of the battles, but because of what three generations of Greeks made of the independence that these victories insured. The only justification for war is the defense of a culture worth defending, and the states of the modern world have less and less to defend beyond their material comforts, in spite of the claims of some to represent fresh concepts of civilization. The new weapons have made nonsense of defensive war. Peoples have been left without any means of defending except by destroying others, and the destruction is almost certain to be mutual.

Restraints upon men and societies, which made war more humane and reduced the amount of fighting among civilized peoples, were created before the triumph of industrial civilization. They were more a cause for that triumph than a result of it. Industrialism has helped to destroy the restraints. Its future (like the future of general culture and world community, without which industrialism cannot survive) depends upon their renewal. The future of industrialism depends, therefore, not upon states becoming more heavily industrialized than they already are. It depends upon the integration of industrialism, the fruits of which have been abundance, commodity, and sanitation, with style, order, and delight. The goals of ransacking the earth for its mineral treasures and harnessing new sources of physical energy will lead nowhere, unless they are subordinated to the use of these resources for the benefit of a rich human existence, which our ancestors understood better than we do. As Jean Giraudoux's play, *The Madwoman of Chaillot*, suggests, the cost of undermining and destroying Paris in search of oil is too high.

What has this to do with the future of war? Our inquiry shows that in the past there have been limits to the process — the historical cycle — toward greater and greater destruction. Eventually a point has been reached where war ceased to beget war, where the willingness of men to kill and destroy diminished. Like the human capacity to love, the human capacity to fear and to hate is not boundless. But, as the material and intellectual restraints imposed by Western civilization upon war have broken down, one after another, the limits have become much less narrow than they were in the era of the Napoleonic wars, less narrow even than in the era of the religious wars.

Our inquiry shows further that the minds of men have played a part in accentuating or diminishing the constructive and the charitable inclinations of peoples and nations, and also in diminishing or accentuating the destructive and the evil inclinations of peoples and nations. Great turning points away from war, such as those which followed the wars of religion and the wars of Napoleon, have not been exclusively the work of material exhaustion, of fate and circumstance. Men also have been behind them.

It is at least possible that what has happened before will happen again. While the meaning of war has changed with the triumph of industrialism, while the problems of creating a relatively harmonious civilization have grown enormously in size and in difficulty, the actors in the colossal drama of the twentieth century are still men and women. Like their ancestors, they possess faculties for common sense, for rational speculation, for craftsmanship, for art, for love, for charity, for faith. More than ever their future, both as individuals and as members of societies, depends upon the encouragement given them to use these faculties.

A study of the interrelations between war and industrial civilization becomes inevitably a study of the interrelations between both and the history of Western civilization. A study of the triumph of industrialism among the European peoples becomes inevitably a study of the interrelations between these peoples and all the peoples of the earth. We find that never before has a movement towards war assumed such proportions as during the past century and especially the past fifty years.

We also find that the causes for the movement of war to beget war have never been so accessible to the human mind as they are in our time. These causes are partly the result of changes in the directions taken by the mind, especially since the late eighteenth century and particularly during the fifty years preceding 1914. Does it not follow that if men are able to use their intelligence and their will, which have become feeble instruments largely because the good in man has lost confidence in them, they have an opportunity to direct the intellect in ways that would count for peace more not less than in the past? If the mind is to count at all it will have to count more, for the very reason that the task before us is a harder one than it was for our ancestors. We are perhaps better prepared, by our knowledge of history, but the difficulties are far greater. The industrial revolution has led the Western peoples to undertake more perhaps than they can manage. They have to believe as never before in the powers for good of the mind and spirit, and to act upon this belief, at the very time when the directions which the mind has taken are leading not toward peace but toward war; at the very time when the search for material gain and the warped pursuit of spiritual excitement threaten to submerge the intelligence and the love which is the real mother of peace.

War is now even less a separate problem than in earlier times; it is part of the total problem of modern civilization. The seriousness of wars can be mitigated, therefore, only by the growth of a common community of understanding relating to life as a whole, such as existed to some extent among the peoples of Europe in the age of limited wars during the late seventeenth and much of the eighteenth century, such as existed still earlier and on a broader basis in the twelfth and thirteenth centuries when wars among the Christian peoples were few and relatively inconsequential. This community of understanding can no longer be confined, as it then could be, to the Western peoples, for the only community that can preserve Western civilization is a world community, in which both individuals and regions, with their cultures, are given an opportunity to develop their special talents and genius under general law. This community of understanding can no longer be confined, as it was in early modern times to the relatively few in each country and region. It is the many again, as well as the few, who have to become a part of a larger whole even than that offered by the Christian church to the many of the Middle Ages, down through the thirteenth century.

A community of the kind toward which we are groping should be the work of the human mind and spirit, creating now more than ever independently of politics, of the pomp and circumstance of the states which are engaged in threatening each other. Just as the modern purveyors of news and entertainment make a caricature of the common human being and provide fare for this caricature, so modern states represent only caricatures of the public and the public opinion they are supposed to embody in their policies. It is the task of the human mind and spirit to win over these states and the publics they represent by offering them a world totally different from the one which usually confronts them when they pick up the morning paper, switch on the radio, visit the cinema or the prize fighting ring.

The works of the mind and spirit which are needed are not those usually offered by the school teaching, the college instruction, the university lecture, or the weekly sermon which now provide the alternatives to news, sport, and entertainment. Nor is the need for the dicta of a political ruler — seeking national, class, or ideological ascendancy. It is the task of the human mind and spirit, seeking for universality and true redemption, to win over the institutions of instruction, research, and worship as well as the governing institutions. All these institutions have come in the main to treat of the special, the immediate, the practical, the national. The crisis of the intellect suggests that it is precisely these concerns with the special, the immediate, the practical, and the national that have helped to produce not only the weapons needed for total war but the will and the means to use them, without which the general slaughter, destruction, and violence of the last thirty-five years would hardly have occurred.

If we begin our work, as we must, as specialists, as individualists, as modern men, as members of nations and groups, we have to labor not in the light of any of these particular attitudes. We have to labor instead to serve man as a whole everywhere and always. We have to labor in the light of charity, which is eternal, not at the mercy of the fleeting and the practical. We have to labor for the best in the human being, wherever that best may be found, whether it be in Chicago, in Paris, in Mexico, in Moscow, on the steppes, or in some far off African village.

If we focus our minds on the welfare of the human being under God as our objective, the special circumstances of our existence can be made into servants of the universal, rather than remaining, as they now are, servants of the particulars which have divided humanity. Many of the discoveries of the scientists, of the economists, of various historical specialists, are of great value to world community, both as idea and as reality, provided they are approached not with the purpose of the scientist, the economist, or the historian, but provided they are approached with the object of revealing their universal meaning for men everywhere and always. If they were approached in that way the valuable particulars discovered by learning during the past two centuries might be drawn into something resembling a unity. If similarly the artist were to use his special circumstances and environment as a basis for revealing to men the delight which is common to humanity, though presented and received in different ways according to climate, history, and other circumstances, he has the opportunity both of creating works that will endure and of drawing many of many races and countries into a common joy.

These directions are no less natural for men and women than the directions of specialization, particularity, and production, which they have been following. The new directions are in fact at the present juncture of history more natural, because the peoples of the earth have moved an unnatural distance toward the special, toward the prosaic, toward the measurable and the matter-of-fact, toward material quantity, toward fear, hatred, and division. The tragedy is that the material success which has accompanied this orientation has been so extraordinary — above all in the United States and Russia — that neither the peoples nor their leaders have understood that the ransom of this success is total war. The price of peace is likely to seem to feeble human beings still dearer. It is the renunciation, in large measure, of success as the guiding principle of thought, labor, and even of politics.

The hope of peace hardly rests in a final sense with the material and the intellectual sides of man. Men have not only moved an unnatural distance toward division; they have stumbled unwittingly an unnatural distance toward evil, by the very fact of denying its existence or of identifying it exclusively with the human elements they dislike. The remedy is not to be achieved by rational means alone. When the mind of man has presented humanity with weapons that would be safe only in the hands of God, is it not evident that the only hope of staying the power of these weapons lies in redemption through Him?

Let us not hoodwink ourselves with notions of perpetual peace and of the millennium. These only increase the danger of war, for they rest upon a misunderstanding of human nature. Men and women are not angels. It is certainly their duty and their delight to create here on earth, in so far as they can, something that resembles the heaven of their dreams. But they should not confuse this with heaven itself. The result of such confusion will not be the gain of either earth or heaven. It will be the loss of both.

NOTES

Notes

I. A TRIPARTITE DIVISION OF EUROPEAN HISTORY

1. Robert Boyle, "Of the Usefulness of Natural Philosophy," *Works* (London, 1772), II, 65.

2. M. J. Elsas, *Umriss einer Geschichte der Preise und Löhne in Deutschland* (Leiden, 1936), I, 78; C. V. Wedgwood, *The Thirty Years' War* (New Haven, 1939), pp. 512–13, 515–16.

3. Georg Loesche, *Johannes Mathesius* (Gotha, 1895), I, 62, 253–55, and *passim*.

4. J. U. Nef, "Silver Production in Central Europe," *Journal of Political Economy*, XLIX, no. 4 (1941), 590.

5. *Annales* (Paris), II, no. 2 (April–June 1947), 196.

6. Leopold von Ranke, *History of the Popes*, trans. Sarah Austin (2nd ed.; London, 1841), I, 518; III, 70. The most authoritative figures for the population of Italy are to be found in Karl Julius Beloch, *Bevölkerungsgeschichte Italiens* (Berlin, 1937, 1939), I, 152, and *passim*; II, *passim*. The monumental work of Fernand Braudel, *La Méditerranée et le monde méditerranéen à l'époque de Philippe II* (Paris, 1949), shows conclusively that Italy grew more prosperous during the second half of the sixteenth century.

7. *The Works of Francis Bacon* (London, 1803), II, 282.

8. Traugott Geering, *Handel und Industrie der Stadt Basel* (Basel, 1886), pp. 474ff, 517, 521, 523–24, 528–29, 564, and *passim*.

9. *Diary and Correspondence of John Evelyn*, ed. William Bray, (London, 1889), I, 168.

10. Anonymous, *News from Newcastle*, a poem "Upon the Coal-pits about Newcastle-upon-Tine," 1651.

11. Nef, *The Rise of the British Coal Industry* (London, 1932), I, 21.

12. *Ibid.*, pp. 43–48.

13. See Nef, "A Comparison of Industrial Growth in France and England from 1540 to 1640," *JPE*, XLIV (1936), *passim*.

14. Thomas Coryat, *Coryat's Crudities Hastily Gobled Up* (Glasgow, 1905), I, 197, 204.

15. See Nef, *British Coal Industry*, I, 181–84, 218–19.

16. Nef, "Note on the Progress of Iron Production in England, 1540–1640," *JPE*, XLIV (1936), 401–403.

17. See Nef, *British Coal Industry*, I, 156–61.

18. Henry Hamilton, *The English Brass and Copper Industries to 1800* (London, 1926), *passim*.

19. *Victoria County History of Derbyshire*, II, 231, 233, 351; J. W. Gough, *The Mines of Mendip* (Oxford, 1930), pp. 112–15; Nef, *British Coal Industry*, I, 167.

20. Nef, "Industrial Growth," *JPE*, XLIV, 522, n. 66; Hamilton, *English Brass*, pp. 57–58. See also *Calendar of State Papers, Domestic, 1668–69*, p. 140.

21. See Chapter XV.

22. "A Relation of a Short Survey of the Western Counties Made by a Lieutenant of the Military Company in Norwich in 1635," ed. L. G. Wickham Legg, *Camden Miscellany* (London, 1936), XVI, 97.

23. Clarendon, *The History of the Rebellion and Civil Wars in England* (Oxford, 1843), p. 30.

24. N. W. Posthumus, *De Geschiedenis van de Leidsche Lakenindustrie*, ('s Gravenhage, 1939), II, 304.

25. Figures derived from Eli F. Heckscher, *Sveriges Ekonomiska Historia Från Gustav Vasa* (Stockholm, 1935–36), Vol. I (i), p. 157; Vol. I (ii), pp. 473–74.

26. *Ibid.*, Vol. I (i), appendix, pp. 28, 30; Vol. I (ii), pp. 443–44.

27. Henri Hauser, *La Préponderance espagnole (1559-1660)* (Paris, 1933), p. 398.

28. Henri Pirenne, *Histoire de Belgique* (Brussels, 1927), IV, 301–302; Jean Lejeune, *La Formation du capitalisme moderne dans la principauté de Liége au 16e siècle* (Paris, 1939), p. 133, and *passim*; Jean Yernaux, *La Métallurgie liégeoise et son expansion au 17e siècle* (Liége, 1939), especially chapter i.

29. Pirenne, pp. 430–31.

30. Hubert G. R. Reade, *Sidelights on the Thirty Years' War* (London, 1924), III, 34.

31. Nef, *Industry and Government in France and England, 1540–1640* (Philadelphia, 1940), ch. v and *passim*.

32. See Schiller, *Geschichte des dreissigjährigen Kriegs*, in *Sämtliche Werke* (Stuttgart, 1862), IX, 84, 133; *Cambridge Modern History*, IV, ch. i.

33. Reade, *Thirty Years' War*, III, 547.

34. See Frederick Lewis Taylor, *The Art of War in Italy, 1494–1529* (Cambridge, 1921), p. 2.

35. For the period 1540–1600, I have depended on Charles Oman, *A History of the Art of War in the Sixteenth Century* (New York, 1937), especially pp. 703–705; for the period 1601–1640 on G. N. Clark, *The Seventeenth Century* (Oxford, 1929), p. 98.

36. See Otto von Simson, "Rubens and Richelieu," *The Review of Politics*, VI (1944), no. 4, 427.

37. Reade, *Thirty Years' War*, III, 441, 495.

38. See *The Elizabethan Underworld*, ed. A. V. Judges (London, 1930), *passim*, and also Dr. Frank Aydelotte's *Elizabethan Rogues and Vagabonds* (Oxford, 1913).

39. J. A. Froude, *History of England from the Fall of Wolsey to the Defeat of the Spanish Armada* (London, 1870), I, 20.

40. See Froude, *passim*; C. H. Firth, *Cromwell's Army* (London, 1902), pp. 6–7.

41. Lansdowne MSS, 844, f. 513, as printed by Charles Dalton, *Life of Sir Edward Cecil* (London, 1885), II, 394–401.

42. Reade, *Thirty Years' War*, I, 488–89, and *passim*.

II. INVENTION AND FIREARMS

SECTION 1

1. See J. U. Nef, "The Progress of Technology and the Growth of Large-Scale Industry in Great Britain," *Economic History Review*, V (1934), 3–24; "Prices and Industrial Capitalism in France and England," *ibid.*, VII (1937), no. 2, 174.

2. W. H. Prescott, *History of the Reign of Ferdinand and Isabella* (New York, 1838?), II, 29–30; Philippe de Comines, *Mémoires*, ed. Joseph Calmette (Paris, 1925), III, 285.

3. Surirey de Saint Rémy, *Mémoires d'artillerie* (3rd ed.; Paris, 1745), I, p. ix.

4. Prescott, *Ferdinand and Isabella*, I, 267–68.

5. Comines, *Mémoires*, III, 38–40.

6. *Ibid.*, p. 192.

7. Frederick Lewis Taylor, *The Art of War in Italy, 1494–1529* (Cambridge, 1921), pp. 86, 88–90.

8. See Henry W. L. Hime, *The Origin of Artillery* (London, 1915), pp. 104–16.

9. *Ibid.*, pp. 11–24.

10. See Ernst Kantorowicz, *Frederick the Second* (London, 1931), pp. 552–53. See also pp. 167, 199–200, 207–208.

11. Cf. Henri Pirenne, *A History of Europe* (New York, 1939), p. 340.

12. Claude Henri de Saint-Simon, *De la réorganisation de la société européenne* (October 1814), ed. Alfred Pereire (Paris, n.d.), pp. 20–21. See also pp. 7–8, 10, and below, Chapter XVII.

13. J. H. M. Poppe, *Geschichte der Technologie* (Göttingen, 1810), II, 557–58.

14. Robert Boyle, *Works* (London, 1772), II, 65.

15. Hime, *The Origin of Artillery*, pp. 124–27.

16. R. C. Clephan, *The Defensive Armour and Weapons and Engines of War of Mediaeval Times, and of the "Renaissance"* (London, 1900), p. 25.

17. Vannoccio Biringuccio, *Pirotechnia* (1540), ed. Cyril S. Smith (New York, 1942), p. 222n.

18. Gaspard Monge, *Description de l'art de fabriquer les canons* (Paris, 1794), pp. 59–60. See also Charles Ffoulkes, *The Gun-Founders of England* (Cambridge, 1937), p. 2.

19. Tacitus, *The Annals* (Everyman ed.), pp. 346, 353–54 (lvi); M. I. Rostovtzeff, *The Social and Economic History of the Hellenistic World* (Oxford, 1941), I, 152, 588, II, 1203, 1220–21, 1232–33, 1235–36.

20. Raleigh, *The History of the World* (Edinburgh, 1820), V, 398–402 (bk. v, ch. iii, sec. xv). See also John Wilkins, *Mathematicall Magick* (London, 1648), pp. 135–37. For the passage in Livy from which Raleigh probably derived his information, see *The History of Rome*, bk. xxiv, ch. xxxiv; see also Plutarch's *Life of Marcellus*. (I am grateful to my colleague, Dr. P. H. von Blanckenhagen, for calling these two works to my attention.)

21. Clephan, *Defensive Armour*, pp. 216–17; Prescott, *Ferdinand and Isabella*, I, 152; H. B. C. Pollard, *A History of Firearms* (Boston, 1928), p. 9.

22. Clephan, pp. 40, 48–50.

23. See William Ridgeway, *Origin and Influence of the Thoroughbred Horse* (Cambridge, 1905), pp. 354–55. For the replacement of the thegn, or foot soldier, by the knight after the Conquest, see David C. Douglas, "The Norman Conquest and English Feudalism," *EHR*, IX (1939), no. 2, 132.

24. Delbrück, *Geschichte der Kriegskunst im Rahmen der Politischen Geschichte* (Berlin, 1907), III, 669.

25. *Ibid.*, p. 214.

26. Biringuccio, *Pirotechnia*, pp. 226–27. See also Clephan, *Defensive Armour*, p. 226.

27. J. R. Ullman, *High Conquest* (Philadelphia, 1941), pp. 31–32.

28. See W. H. Prescott, *History of the Conquest of Mexico* (1843); Salvador de Madariaga, *Hernán Cortés* (Buenos Aires, 1941).

29. J. A. Froude, *History of England* (London, 1870), VI, 285–87.

30. Max Jähns, *Handbuch einer Geschichte des Kriegswesens von der Urzeit bis zur Renaissance, Technischer Theil* (Leipzig, 1880), p. 1275.

31. See, for example, A. Jal, *Archéologie navale* (Paris, 1840), II, 278–86.

32. For the trained bands in one county see William Bradford Willcox, *Gloucestershire: A Study in Local Government, 1590–1640* (New Haven, 1940), ch. iv.

33. C. H. Firth, *Cromwell's Army* (London, 1902), p. 8.

34. Jähns, *Handbuch*, p. 1056.

35. Lupton, *Warlike Treatise of the Pike* (1642), p. 131, quoted in Firth, *Cromwell's Army*, p. 12.

36. Leopold von Ranke, *History of the Reformation in Germany*, trans. Sarah Austin (London, 1905), p. 394. See also Taylor, *Art of War*, pp. 90, 130.

37. Hermann Foertsch, *The Art of Modern Warfare* (New York, 1940), p. 56.

SECTION 2

1. Leopold von Ranke, *History of the Reformation in Germany*, trans. Sarah Austin (London, 1905), p. 394. See also Frederick Lewis Taylor, *The Art of War in Italy, 1494–1529* (Cambridge, 1921), pp. 90, 130.

2. Vannoccio Biringuccio, *Pirotechnia*, ed. Cyril S. Smith (New York, 1942), p. 225.

3. *Ibid.*, pp. 315–17. See also John Wilkins, *Mathematicall Magick* (London, 1648), pp. 137–38.

4. J. L. Motley, *The Rise of the Dutch Republic* (New York, 1879), III, 555–56.

5. Biringuccio, *Pirotechnia*, pp. 225–26.

6. Wilkins, *Mathematicall Magick*, p. 139.

7. See Surirey de Saint Rémy, *Mémoires d'artillerie* (3rd ed.; Paris, 1745), I, 90–91.

8. J. H. M. Poppe, *Geschichte der Technologie* (Göttingen, 1810), II, 525.

9. Taylor, *Art of War*, pp. 39–40.

10. Martin and Guillaume du Bellay, *Mémoires* (Paris, 1908–1912), I, 189.

11. Ed. de la Barre-Duparcq, "L'Art militaire pendant les Guerres de Religion, 1562–1598," *Séances et Travaux de l'Académie des Sciences morales et politiques*, LXVI (1863), 303, 305.

12. Taylor, *Art of War*, pp. 46–47, 50–51, 76, 107.

13. Pliny, *Natural History*, bk. xxxiii, ch. i. See my forthcoming chapter in *Cambridge Economic History*, II, ch. vii.

14. See J. U. Nef, "Industrial Europe at the Reformation," *Journal of Political Economy*, XLIX (1941), no. 1, 9–10.

15. Such an estimate depends on much guesswork. But the scattered information available indicates that the annual iron production of Europe in the 1520's and 1530's could not yet be counted in several hundreds of thousands of tons, as it could be for the first time at the end of the eighteenth century, when the French Revolution broke out (Chapter XV).

In the early sixteenth century one of the leading iron-producing districts of Europe was Styria, where some eight or nine thousand tons came from the furnaces and forges annually (L. Bittner, "Das Eisenwesen in Innerberg — Eisenerz," *Archiv fur österreichische Geschichte*, LXXXIX [Vienna, 1901], 490, 628–29). Iron was also produced in small quantities in a large number of other districts of the old Empire. In Spain, which had been famous for its iron throughout the Middle Ages, the output of the two most productive provinces, Biscay and Guipuzcoa together, according to a contemporary Spaniard, amounted to about 15,000 tons annually toward the end of the sixteenth century. (James M. Swank, *History of the Manufacture of Iron in all Ages* [Philadelphia, 1892], pp. 22–23). It is improbable that the production had been larger in the 1530's. While I have not been able to master the data on iron production in the Spanish Low Countries in J. A. Goris' book, *Etudes sur les colonies marchandes méridionales à Anvers* (Louvain, 1925; especially pp. 477–79), they suggest that the output there was considerably greater than in Spain itself during the middle decades of the sixteenth century — possibly 30,000 to 40,000 tons in the prince-bishopric of Liége, Namurois, and the region of Charleroi combined. In Great Britain and still more in Sweden the ironmaking industry was backward in the early sixteenth century. The annual iron output in England and Wales at the dissolution of the monasteries, in 1536 and 1539, did not perhaps exceed six or seven thousand tons (Nef, "Note on the Progress of Iron Production in England, 1540–1640," *JPE*, XLIV, no. 3 [1936], 402).

16. At the time of the Reformation most of the leading mining and metallurgical enterprises in central Europe turned out silver and copper as joint products. Between 1450 and 1530 the output of silver in central Europe increased at least fivefold (Nef, "Silver Production in Central Europe," *JPE*, XLIX [1941], 586). During this period the silver was obtained increasingly from argentiferous copper ores instead of from the argentiferous lead ores, the main source of silver in medieval times. The figure 15,000 tons for the annual output of copper in Europe about 1540 is a guess. Records of the Fugger family from 1495 to 1525 show that they alone dealt in some 1500 tons of copper a year (Max Jansen, *Jakob Fugger der Reiche* [Leipzig, 1910], p. 155). At Mansfeld the production of copper reached 2000 tons in good years during the 1530's (Walter Mück, *Der mansfelder Kupferschieferbergau* [Eisleben, 1910], I, 58–59). By this time there were in central Europe some five or six other argentiferous copper-mining centers in the same class with Mansfeld, besides many smaller cen-

ters (see Nef, "Silver," *JPE*, XLIX, *passim*; also my chapter in the forthcoming *Cambridge Economic History*, II).

17. *Ibid.*

18. For this use of water power in England, see E. M. Carus-Wilson, "An Industrial Revolution of the Thirteenth Century," *EHR*, XI (1941), 40, 43–46, 50.

19. Karl Sudhoff, *Beiträge zur Geschichte der Chirurgie im Mittelalter* (Leipzig, 1914), I, plate xxxi. I am grateful to Dr. Lynn White for having called my attention to this plate.

20. Rhys Jenkins, "The Rise and Fall of the Sussex Iron Industry," *Transactions of the Newcomen Society*, 5 ser. I (1920–21), 17.

21. Charles Hutton, *Mathematical Dictionary* (London, 1795), I, 241.

22. Ernest Straker, *Wealden Iron* (London, 1931), pp. 38–43, 141*ff*; L. Stone, "State Control in Sixteenth-Century England," *EHR*, XVII (1947), 112.

23. Frederick Leslie Robertson, *The Evolution of Naval Armament* (London, 1921), p. 73.

24. V. V. Froukje Breedvelt, *Louis de Geer, 1587–1652* (Amsterdam, 1935), pp. 80, 84–86.

25. Violet Barbour, "Dutch and English Merchant Shipping in the Seventeenth Century," *EHR*, II (1930), 261.

26. Breedvelt, p. 113.

27. Biringuccio, *Pirotechnia*, pp. 319–21.

28. Jenkins, p. 17.

29. Straker, pp. 39–43; Biringuccio, pp. 146–48.

30. See Nef, "A Comparison of Industrial Growth in France and England," *JPE*, XLIV (1936), 516–17.

31. Goris, *Etudes*, pp. 477–78.

32. Nef, "Note on Iron," *JPE*, XLIV, 401.

33. See Breedvelt, pp. 118–19.

34. Henri Denifle, *La Désolation des églises, monastères et hôpitaux en France* (Paris, 1899), I, 1.

35. G. N. Clark, *Science and Social Welfare in the Age of Newton* (Oxford, 1937), p. 51.

36. Bernhard Hagedorn, *Die Entwicklung der wichtigsten Schiffstypen bis ins 19 Jahrhundert* (Berlin, 1914), pp. 69–70, 120; A. F. Pollard, *The Political History of England, 1547–1603* (London, 1919), p. 221.

37. See Chapter IV, Section 2.

III. THE BIRTH OF MODERN SCIENCE

1. Galileo, *Two New Sciences*, trans. Henry Crew and Alfonso de Salvio (Chicago, 1939), pp. 255–56.

2. Polydore Virgil, *De inventoribus rerum* (abridged English ed., 1546), bk. ii, ch. vii.

3. Egerton MS (British Museum, London) 2642, f. 150, quoted in Ernest Straker, *Wealden Iron* (London, 1931), p. 143.

4. J. H. M. Poppe, *Geschichte der Technologie* (Göttingen, 1810), II, 541–42.

5. See Frederick Lewis Taylor, *The Art of War in Italy, 1494–1529* (Cambridge, 1921), pp. 137–38.

6. Charles Oman, *A History of the Art of War in the Middle Ages* (2nd ed.; London, 1924), II, esp. bk.

xi, ch. iii; bk. xiii, ch. ii; bk. xiv, conclusion.

7. Niccolò Machiavelli, *The History of Florence*, ed. Henry Morley (London, 1891), p. 273; see also pp. 228, 351.

8. Ferdinand Lot, *L'Art militaire et les armées au moyen âge* (Paris, 1946), I, 429–32.

9. Quoted in Felix Gilbert, "Machiavelli: The Renaissance of the Art of War," in *Makers of Modern Strategy*, ed. E. M. Earle (Princeton, 1943), pp. 7–8.

10. See Chapter VI.

11. Oman, p. 424.

12. *The Notebooks of Leonardo da Vinci*, ed. Edward MacCurdy (New York, 1938), II, 552, and *passim*. See

also Antonina Vallentin, *Leonardo da Vinci*, trans. E. W. Dickes (New York, 1938), pp. 74*ff*.

13. Kenneth Clark, *Leonardo da Vinci* (New York, 1939), p. 56.

14. M. I. Rostovtzeff, *The Social and Economic History of the Hellenistic World* (Oxford, 1941), II, 1232.

15. Vallentin, *Leonardo*, pp. 80–81.

16. Emile Mayer, "Les Tanks et les chars de guerre au moyen âge et sous le second Empire," *Revue des études napoléoniennes*, XX–XXI (1923), 218–20, 231, a reference for which I am indebted to Otto von Simson. Cf. the more moderate description of these "tanks" in Hans Delbrück, *Geschichte der Kriegskunst im Rahmen der Politischen Geschichte* (Berlin, 1907), III, 506–508.

17. Lot, *L'Art militaire*, II, 201–206.

18. See MacCurdy, *Notebooks of Leonardo*, II, 179–200.

19. *Ibid.*, pp. 179, 183, 552.

20. See Karl Brandi, *The Emperor Charles V*, trans. C. V. Wedgwood (New York, 1939), p. 183.

21. *Leonardo da Vinci's Note-Books*, ed. MacCurdy (New York, 1923), pp. 198–99.

22. Clark, *Leonardo*, p. 56.

23. See Chapters VI and XI.

24. See Chapter VI, Section 2.

25. Clark, *Leonardo*, pp. 58–59.

26. Pierre Duhem, *Etudes sur Léonard de Vinci* (Paris, 1906), p. 223, and *passim*.

27. *Ibid.*, pp. 140, 143–44.

28. *Ibid.*, pp. 252–53.

29. *Ibid.*, pp. 245–46.

30. *Ibid.*, p. 225.

31. Paul Valéry, *Introduction à la méthode de Léonard de Vinci* (Paris, 1919), p. 13.

32. See Chapter X.

33. C. S. Sherrington, *The Endeavour of Jean Fernel* (Cambridge, 1946), p. 142.

34. Francis R. Packard, *Life and Times of Ambroise Paré* (New York, 1926), pp. 26–27.

35. Sidney Toy, *Castles: A Short History of Fortifications* (London, 1939), pp. 139–40.

36. See Anonymous, *The State of England* (1600), in *Camden Miscellany*, 3 ser. LII, 43.

37. Taylor, *Art of War*, pp. 152–55.

38. Charles Hutton, *Mathematical Dictionary* (London, 1795), I, 500–501.

39. Michel Steichen, *Mémoire sur la vie et les travaux de Simon Stevin* (Brussels, 1846), p. 119.

40. *Ibid.* See also pp. 113–15.

41. H. Butterfield, *The Origins of Modern Science* (London, 1949), pp. 74, 78.

42. Steichen, *Simon Stevin, passim*.

43. See H. Guerlac, "Vauban," in *Makers of Modern Strategy*, p. 31.

44. See Cyril Stanley Smith, "Biringuccio's 'Pirotechnia' — A Neglected Italian Metallurgical Classic," *Mining and Metallurgy*, XXI (1940), 191–92.

45. I owe my knowledge of this treatise, which is still in MS, to the kindness of Mr. A. R. Hall of Christ's Church, Cambridge. It is entitled "Fundición de artillería" and is preserved in the Cambridge University Library.

46. Rostovtzeff, *The Hellenistic World*, II, 1203, 1212, and *passim*.

47. Taylor, *Art of War*, p. 82; Hutton, *Mathematical Dictionary*, I, 562, II, 563.

48. Galileo, *Two New Sciences*, p. 42.

49. *Ibid.*, pp. 95–107.

50. See F. R. Wegg-Prosser, *Galileo and His Judges* (London, 1889), p. 94, and *passim*.

51. C. F. von Weizsäcker, "The Spirit of Natural Science," *Humanitas*, II (1947), no. 1, 6. See also L. W. Taylor, *Physics, the Pioneer Science* (Boston, 1941), p. 191.

52. Voltaire, *Le Siècle de Louis XIV* (1751), ch. xxxi.

53. MacCurdy, *Notebooks of Leonardo*, II, 552.

54. *Ibid.*, I, 24–25.

55. Vallentin, *Leonardo*, p. 81.

56. Charles Ffoulkes, *The Gun-Founders of England* (Cambridge, 1937), p. 108.

57. Mark Napier, *Memoirs of John Napier of Merchiston* (Edinburgh,

1834), pp. 247–48 (see the facsimile reproduction of the document in these *Memoirs*).

58. Vallentin, *Leonardo*, pp. 275–76.

59. Pedro Calderón, *El Sitio de Breda*, Act II.

60. Napier, *John Napier*, pp. 274–75.

61. See Chapter VI.

62. John Wilkins, *The Discovery of a New World in the Moone* (London, 1638).

63. Wilkins, *Mathematicall Magick* (London, 1648), pp. 154–57, 159, 161, 178–79, 181–82, 187–88, 220.

64. See J. U. Nef, *Industry and Government in France and England, 1540–1640* (Philadelphia, 1940) pp. 118–20, and *The Rise of the British Coal Industry* (London, 1932), I, 255.

65. Etienne Gilson, *The Unity of Philosophical Experience* (New York, 1937), pp. 133–34.

66. *Ibid.*, pp. 152–53, and *passim*, and Gilson, "Descartes, Harvey et la scolastique," *Etudes de philosophie médiévale* (Strasbourg, 1921), pp. 191–245.

67. Robert Willis, *The Works of William Harvey* (London, 1847), p. xlix. I have in hand an essay from which I have drawn the comparisons in this book between the progress in France and England of science and technology (*Essays in Honor of Conyers Read*, in preparation).

68. See J. Michelet, *Histoire de France* (Paris, n.d.), XI, 261–62.

69. Kepler, *Epitome of Copernican Astronomy* (Annapolis, 1939), II, 202.

IV. PROGRESS OF CAPITALIST INDUSTRY

SECTION 1

1. Werner Sombart, *Krieg und Kapitalismus* (Munich, 1913), pp. 4–6, 77.

2. *Ibid.*, *passim*. See also his *Der moderne Kapitalismus* (4th ed.; Munich, 1921), I, 750–59, 906–908; II, 850–51, 874–76, 880–84, 894–96.

3. J.-B. Giraud, *Documents pour servir à l'histoire de l'armement au moyen âge et à la Renaissance* (Lyon, 1899), II, 100–11.

4. G. G. Coulton, *The Medieval Village* (Cambridge, 1926), pp. 65, 441.

5. *The Notebooks of Leonardo da Vinci*, ed. Edward MacCurdy (New York, 1938), II, facing p. 206.

6. M. I. Rostovtzeff, *The Social and Economic History of the Hellenistic World* (Oxford, 1941), II, 1210–11.

7. See my forthcoming article (chapter vii) in *Cambridge Economic History*, II.

8. Tenney Frank, *An Economic History of Rome* (2nd ed.; London, 1925), pp. 220–23, 236–38.

9. F. C. Lane, *Venetian Ships and Shipbuilders of the Renaissance* (Baltimore, 1934), pp. 129–30.

10. Archives départementales du Var (Draguignan), E. 1133, ff. 416–19.

11. J. U. Nef, *Industry and Government in France and England 1540–1640* (Philadelphia, 1940), pp. 63–64, 66–68.

12. *Ibid.*, pp. 66–67, 89–90, 97.

13. Archives communales d'Amiens, FF. 519 [12].

14. *Inventaire des Archives départementales du Gard*, E, II, 223, 232; A. Bardon, *L'Exploitation du bassin houiller d'Alais* (Nîmes, 1898), p. 15.

15. J. H. M. Poppe, *Geschichte der Technologie* (Göttingen, 1810), II, 532.

16. See A. P. Wadsworth and J. de L. Mann, *The Cotton Trade and Industrial Lancashire 1600–1780* (Manchester, 1931), p. 97.

17. H. A. Innis, *The Cod Fisheries* (New Haven, 1940), pp. 10–11, 15–16, 30, and *passim*.

18. Max Prinet, *L'Industrie du sel en Franche-Comté avant la conquête française* (Besançon, 1900), pp. 80, 156–58, 168–70, and *passim*. For Dieuze, see Koch, "Geschichtliche Entwickelung des Bergbaues und Salinenbetriebes in Elsass-Lothringen," *Z. Bergrecht* (1874), p. 163.

19. L. Gollut, *Les Mémoires historiques de la République séquanaise* (Arbois, 1846), bk. ii, chs. xxvi, xxvii.

20. J. U. Nef, "Industrial Europe at the Time of the Reformation," *Journal of Political Economy*, XLIX (1941), 15–16.

21. Lansdowne MSS (British Museum, London), 152, f. 57.

22. Nef, *Industry and Government*, pp. 108–109.

23. Nef, *The Rise of the British Coal Industry* (London, 1932), I, 350–80; II, 139–40.

24. Lansdowne MSS, 59, no. 69; *Calendar of State Papers, Domestic*, 1655, p. 36.

25. "Hooker's Synopsis Chorographical of Devonshire," *Report and Transactions of the Devonshire Association*, 3 ser. VII, 338.

26. Karl Marx, *Das Kapital*, ch. xii, sec. i (Karl Kautsky edition; Berlin, 1922, p. 283).

27. See Henri Hauser, *Les Débuts du capitalisme* (Paris, 1927), pp. 6–8.

28. See, for example, R. H. Tawney, Introduction to Thomas Wilson's *A Discourse upon Usury* (London, 1925), pp. 44–49; Wadsworth and Mann, *Cotton Trade*, pp. 36–53; E. Lipson, *The Economic History of England* (London, 1931), II, 17, and *passim*.

29. Geeraert Brandt, *Verbaal van de Reformatie* (Amsterdam, 1663), pp. 208–10.

30. For the early history of cane growing and sugar refining, see Edmund O. von Lippmann, *Geschichte des Zuckers* (Berlin, 1929).

31. State Papers Domestic (Public Record Office, London) James I, LXXXVII, no. 74 (iv), (v). Mr. F. J. Fisher kindly supplied me with transcripts or summaries of these State Papers relating to sugar.

32. Henri Pirenne, *Histoire de Belgique* (Brussels, 1923), III, 218.

33. State Papers Domestic, Elizabeth, CCXLV, no. 52; William Reed, *The History of Sugar* (London, 1866), p. 9.

34. State Papers Domestic, Elizabeth, CCXLV, nos. 48, 52; CCLIII, no. 95.

35. *Ibid.*, CCXLV, no. 52; see also Nef, "Richard Carmarden's 'A Caveat for the Quene,'" *JPE*, XLI (1933), 33ff.

36. Cf. Henri Denifle, *La Désolation des églises, monastères et hôpitaux en France* (Paris, 1897); Jacques Monicat, *Les Grandes Compagnies en Velay, 1358–1392* (Paris, 1928).

37. Shakespeare, *Henry IV*, Part I, Act V, scene 3.

38. Alfons Müllner, *Geschichte des Eisens in Krain, Görz und Istrien* (Vienna, 1909), p. 727; M. R. von Wolfskron, "Beitrag zur Geschichte der Tiroler Erz-Bergbaues," *Zeitschrift des Ferdinandeums für Tirol und Vorarlberg*, III (1897), 51.

39. J. A. Goris, *Etudes sur les colonies marchandes méridionales à Anvers* (Louvain, 1925), pp. 486–87; Pirenne, *Histoire de Belgique*, IV (1927), 430 (for the truce, see *ibid.*, pp. 239–41); Jean Yernaux, *La Métallurgie liégeoise et son expansion au 17e siècle* (Liége, 1939), *passim*.

40. See Marcel Bulard, "L'Industrie du fer dans la Haute-Marne," *Annales de Géographie*, XIII (1904), 234–35.

41. A. Bardon, *L'Exploitation*, pp. 36–37. See also Nef, "Industrial Growth in France and England," *JPE*, XLIV (1936), 518–19.

42. Nef, "Industrial Growth," p. 519.

43. Pirenne, *Histoire de Belgique*, IV, 431. See also discussion in Chapter I above.

44. V. V. Froukje Breedvelt, *Louis de Geer, 1587–1652* (Amsterdam, 1935), pp. 80, 84. See also pp. 85–86, 113.

45. See Sloane MSS (British Museum, London), 2103, ff. 247–65.

46. Ernest Straker, *Wealden Iron* (London, 1931), pp. 162–63.

47. See A. Jal, *Abraham Duquesne et la marine de son temps* (Paris, 1873), I, 158–60.

48. Eli F. Heckscher, "L'Histoire du fer: le monopole suédois," *Annales*

d'histoire économique et sociale, IV (1932), 134.

49. For estimate see Chapter II, Section 2, note 15.

50. Rhys Jenkins, "Rise and Fall of the Sussex Iron Industry," *Newcomen Society Transactions,* I, 1920–21), quoted in Straker, *Wealden Iron,* p. 147.

51. Nef, "Note on the Progress of Iron Production," *JPE,* XLIV (1936), 398–400.

52. Taylor, "The World Runnes on Wheeles," *All the Workes of John Taylor the Water-poet* (London, 1630), pp. 237, 240.

53. Nef, "The Progress of Technology and the Growth of Large-Scale Industry in Great Britain, 1540–1640," *Economic History Review,* V (1934), 10–14, and the authorities and sources there cited.

54. *Ibid.,* p. 13.

55. Quoted in Henry Hamilton, *The English Brass and Copper Industries to 1800* (London, 1926), p. 55.

SECTION 2

1. Fernand Braudel, "Monnaies et civilisations," *Annales,* no. 1 (1946), pp. 17–18.

2. See *The Autobiography of Phineas Pett,* ed. W. C. Perrin (Navy Records Society, 1918), *passim.*

3. State Papers Domestic, Charles II, CLVII, no. 46; CLVIII, no. 15. See also *Calendar of State Papers, Domestic,* 1665–66, pp. 315, 374.

4. *Ibid.,* 1666–67, pp. 72, 406; 1670, p. 65; 1684–85, pp. 185–86.

5. Bernhard Hagedorn, *Die Entwicklung der wichtigsten Schiffstypen bis ins 19 Jahrhundert* (Berlin, 1914), pp. 69–70; Walter Oakeshott, *Founded upon the Seas* (Cambridge, 1942) pp. 21–22.

6. A. T. Mahan, *The Influence of Sea Power upon History, 1660–1783* (Boston, 1918), pp. 49–53, 81–82, and *passim.*

7. *Ibid.,* p. 28.

8. Quoted by Max Jähns, *Handbuch einer Geschichte des Kriegswesen* (Leipzig, 1880), p. 1288.

9. "Hooker's Synopsis Chorographical of Devonshire," *Report and Transactions of the Devonshire Association,* 3 ser. VII, 1848.

10. Werner Sombart, *Der moderne Kapitalismus* (4th ed.; Munich, 1921), I, 762.

11. J. U. Nef, "A Comparison of Industrial Growth in France and England," *Journal of Political Economy,* XLIV (1936), 308.

12. M. Oppenheim, *A History of the Administration of the Royal Navy* (London, 1896), p. 271.

13. Sombart, *Krieg und Kapitalismus* (Munich, 1913), p. 191.

14. Hagedorn, p. 108.

15. Nef, *The Rise of the British Coal Industry* (London, 1932), I, 391–93, and *passim.*

16. Information which I owe to Mr. S. C. Gilfillan.

V. PROGRESS OF CAPITALIST COMMERCE AND FINANCE

1. Ferdinand Lot, *L'Art militaire et les armées au moyen âge* (Paris, 1946), II, 13–14, 441. See also *passim* for the general evidence on which the statements in the text are based.

2. Ed. de la Barre-Duparcq, "Du Nombre des tués dans les batailles," *Séances et Travaux de l'Académie des Sciences morales et politiques,* XCI (1870), 247.

3. Hubert G. R. Reade, *Sidelights on the Thirty Years' War* (London, 1924), I, 381–82; II, 382.

4. References to active armies of 30,000 and more men in Western Europe in the later Middle Ages (for example, Werner Sombart, *Krieg und Kapitalismus,* Munich, 1913, p. 38) have been discredited by the work of Professor Lot. Sombart's statement that Edward III had an army of 32,000 men at Calais in 1347, on the eve of the battle of Crecy, is refuted by J. H. Ramsay, "The Strength of English Armies in the Middle Ages," *English*

Historical Review, XXIX (1914), 223–24.

5. Victor Loewe, *Die Organisation und Verwaltung der Wallensteinschen Heere* (Leipzig, 1895), p. 6; C. V. Wedgwood, *The Thirty Years' War* (New Haven, 1939), p. 219.

6. See J. Christopher Herold, *The Swiss without Halos* (New York, 1948), ch. iii.

7. More, *Utopia*, ed. George Sampson (London, 1910), p. 37.

8. See Fernand Braudel, "Misère et Banditisme," *Annales*, no. 11 (1947), pp. 130–33, and *passim*.

9. Loewe, pp. 32–33.

10. H. Guerlac, "Vauban – the Impact of Science on War," *Makers of Modern Strategy*, ed. Edward M. Earle (Princeton, 1943), p. 27.

11. See Loewe, pp. 48, 51–54.

12. See Barre-Duparcq, "L'Art militaire pendant les guerres de religion, 1562–1598," *Séances et Travaux*, LXVI (1863), 354.

13. *The Elizabethan Underworld*, ed. A. V. Judges (London, 1930), p. 345.

14. H. Pirenne, *Histoire de Belgique* (Brussels, 1927), IV, 239.

15. Loewe, p. 41; Barre-Duparcq, "L'Art militaire," *Séances et Travaux*, LXVI (1863), 300.

16. Cf. Loewe, pp. 40–41; Wedgwood, *The Thirty Years' War*, p. 132.

17. Barre-Duparcq, "L'Art militaire," *Séances et Travaux*, LXVIII (1864), 93.

18. J. U. Nef, *Industry and Government in France and England, 1540–1640* (Philadelphia, 1940), pp. 66, 88–98.

19. See Surirey de Saint Rémy, *Mémoires d'artillerie* (3rd ed.; Paris, 1745), III, 361–62, *passim*.

20. Richard Ehrenberg, *Capital and Finance in the Age of the Renaissance* (London, 1928), pp. 26ff.

21. *Ibid.*, pp. 76, 83, *passim*.

22. See Georges Espinas, *La Vie économique et sociale au moyen âge* (Fontenay-le-Comte, 1946); Fritz Rorig, *Mittelalterliche Weltwirtschaftsperiode* (Jena, 1933). See also my forthcoming article in *Cambridge Economic History*, II, chapter vii.

23. See A. P. Usher, *The Early History of Deposit Banking in Mediterranean Europe* (Cambridge, Mass., 1943), especially Part I, and the recent works of Dr. Raymond de Roover.

24. See my forthcoming chapter in *Cambridge Economic History*, II.

25. Leopold von Ranke, *History of the Popes*, trans. Sarah Austin (2nd ed.; London, 1841), III, 61–62.

26. Brian Pearce, "Elizabethan Food Policy and the Armed Forces," *Economic History Review*, XII (1942), 40–41, 44–45.

27. Froude, *History of England* (London, 1870), IV, 126–27.

28. Sombart, *Krieg und Kapitalismus*, p. 49.

29. William Bradford Willcox, *Gloucestershire: A Study in Local Government* (New Haven, 1940), pp. 77–79, 91–93, and ch. iv generally.

30. See Pearce, *EHR*, XII (1942), 44.

31. N. S. B. Gras, *The Evolution of the English Corn Market* (Cambridge, Mass., 1915); F. J. Fisher, "The Development of the London Food Market, 1540–1640," *EHR*, V (1935), 46–64.

32. Gras, p. 75.

33. Max Weber, *Wirtschaft und Gesellschaft* (Tübingen, 1925), p. 624.

34. Henri Denifle, *Les Désolation des églises, monastères et hôpitaux en France* (Paris, 1899), I, 1–3.

35. Braudel, *Annales*, no. 11 (1947), pp. 130–33.

36. Cf. Barre-Duparcq, "L'Art militaire," *Séances et Travaux*, LXVIII (1864), pp. 104–107, 265–66; Fernand Braudel, "De l'or du Soudan à l'argent d'Amérique," *Annales*, no. 1 (1946), p. 18; Hubert G. R. Reade, *Sidelights on the Thirty Years' War* (London, 1924), II, 434.

37. See Chapter XII.

38. Nina Bang, *Tables de la navigation et du transport des marchandises passant par le Sund, 1497–1660* (Copenhagen, 1922), II, *passim*.

39. Edward Hughes, *Studies in Administration and Finance, 1558–1825* (Manchester, 1934), p. 37.

40. Bibliothèque Nationale (Paris), Manuscrits français, 18165, f. 467.

41. Bang, *Tables*, *passim*.

42. P. Raveau, *Essai sur la situation économique et l'état social en Poitou au XVIᵉ siècle* (Paris, 1931), pp. 18–21, 41, 43–44, 45.

43. I owe this knowledge to M. Jacques Monicat, who had charge of these books in the Archives Nationales before the outbreak of the Second World War.

44. P. Barrey, "Le Havre transatlantique, 1571–1610," in Julien Hayem, *Mémoires et documents pour servir a l'histoire du commerce et de l'industrie en France* (Vᵉ Série; Paris, 1917), pp. 68–75.

45. *Encyclopédie départementale: Les Bouches-du-Rhone*, ed. Paul Masson (Marseilles, 1920), III, 178–82.

46. Emile Coornaert, *La Draperie-sayetterie d'Hondschoote* (Paris, 1930), pp. 17, 493.

47. *Ibid.*, pp. 493–94.

48. *Ibid.*, pp. 42–43, 46–47, 56–59, 493–95.

49. *Ibid.*, pp. 52–55; H. Pirenne in *EHR*, III (1931), 296–97.

50. E. de Parieu, "Le Siège et la capitulation de Brisach," *Séances et Travaux de l'Académie des Sciences morales et politiques*, CV (1876), 397–98.

51. For the decline in population in Germany, see Chapter I. Apparently there was a similar decline in the population of Franche-Comté (Abbé Berthet, "Un Réactif sociale: le parrainage du XVIᵉ siècle à la Révolution,", *Annales*, no. 1, 1946, pp. 45–47).

52. A. F. Pollard, *The Political History of England 1547–1603* (London, 1919), pp. 285–86.

53. I learned this from the lectures delivered by Professor R. H. Tawney at the University of Chicago in the spring of 1948. I understand that the information was derived from the researches made by Mr. F. J. Fisher in the English port books.

54. G. D. Ramsey, "Industrial Laissez-Faire and the Policy of Cromwell," *EHR*, XVI (1946), 95.

55. J. U. Nef, "A Comparison of Industrial Growth in France and England from 1540 to 1640," *Journal of Political Economy*, XLIV (1936), 296–97, 306–307, 317, 507, 522, 531, 651–52; Nef, *The Rise of the British Coal Industry* (London, 1932), appendix D (i) (a), (iii), and (iv). See also Chapter I.

56. See Thorstein Veblen, *An Inquiry into the Nature of Peace and the Terms of Its Perpetuation* (New York, 1917), p. 13.

57. Descartes, *Discours de la méthode*, Part III.

58. Earl J. Hamilton, "Monetary Disorder and Economic Decadence in Spain 1651–1700," *JPE*, LI (1943), 482. See also his "The Decline of Spain," *EHR*, VIII (1938), 175.

59. Voltaire, *Le Siècle de Louis XIV* (1751), ch. ii; Antoyne de Montchrétien, *Traicté de l'oeconomie politique* (Paris, 1889), p. 315.

60. Hamilton, "American Treasure and the Rise of Capitalism in France and England (1500–1700)," *Economica*, IX (1929), 338–57.

61. A. E. Feaveryear, *The Pound Sterling* (Oxford, 1931), pp. 45, 47*ff*, 78–79, and *passim*.

62. Nef, "Prices and Industrial Capitalism in France and England 1540–1640," *EHR*, VII (1937), 173–74, 184, and *passim*.

63. Kenneth Pickthorn, *Early Tudor Government Henry VIII* (Cambridge, 1934), pp. 280–81, 372–73, 382–83.

64. For a discussion of the influence of the transfer of ecclesiastical property upon the development of the British coal-mining industry, see Nef, *British Coal Industry*, I, 133–56. Subsequent research, which I hope to publish, suggests that these transfers had a similar influence upon the metallurgical and the salt-making industries.

VI. RESTRAINTS ON WAR

SECTION 1

1. J. A. Froude, *History of England* (London, 1870), X, 121.
2. See Conyers Read, *Mr. Secretary Walsingham and the Policy of Queen Elizabeth* (Oxford, 1925), passim.
3. J. E. Neale, *Queen Elizabeth* (London, 1934), passim.
4. See Chapter XII.
5. See Alfred T. Mahan, *The Influence of Sea Power upon History* (Boston, 1918), pp. 25–26.

SECTION 2

1. *The Notebooks of Leonardo da Vinci*, ed. Edward MacCurdy (New York, 1938), I, 25. See the earlier discussion in Chapter III.
2. J. W. Allen, *A History of Political Thought in the Sixteenth Century* (New York, 1928), p. 156.
3. Kenneth Clark, "Architectural Backgrounds in Italian Painting," *The Arts*, no. 1 (1947), pp. 13–24; no. 2, pp. 33–42, esp. p. 39.
4. Avery Dulles, *Princeps Concordiae* (Cambridge, Mass., 1941).
5. See also Chapters III and X.
6. See Mark Napier, *Memoirs of John Napier of Merchiston* (Edinburgh, 1834), p. 255.
7. See John Napier, *A Plaine Discovery of the Whole Revelation of Saint John* (Edinburgh, 1593), pp. 16ff., 34ff., 41ff.
8. See the previous discussion in Chapter III.
9. Mark Napier, pp. 256–64.
10. *Ibid.*, pp. 247–48.
11. *Ibid.*, pp. 245–46.
12. *Ibid.*, p. 246.
13. See *ibid.*, passim, esp. pp. 271–75.
14. Plutarch, "The Life of Marcellus," *The Lives of the Noble Grecians and Romanes*, trans. Thomas North (Oxford, 1928), III, 75, 79.
15. Raleigh, *The History of the World* (Edinburgh, 1820), V, 401.
16. See Chapter III.
17. See Chapter XI.
18. Geoffrey Scott, *The Architecture of Humanism: A Study in the History of Taste* (2nd ed.; New York, 1924), see, for example, p. 34. See also J. U. Nef, "Architecture and Western Civilization," *Review of Politics*, VIII (1946), 201–208.
19. Clark, *The Arts*, no. 1 (1947), p. 23.
20. Mrs. Mark Pattison, *The Renaissance of Art in France* (London, 1879), II, 256–57.
21. Cf. Piero Pieri, *La Crisi militare Italiana Renascimento, vella sue relazioni con la crisi politica ed economica* (Naples, 1934). In this valuable book concerning war and the progress of wealth in Italy during the late fifteenth and early sixteenth centuries, the author appears not to have emphasized the role played by the growth of wealth in making it feasible to wage more extensive wars (see above, Chapter II, Section 2).
22. See Henri René d'Allemagne, *Ferronerie ancienne* (2 vols.; Paris, 1924), passim.
23. R. C. Clephan, *The Defensive Armour and Weapons and Engines of War of Mediaeval Times, and of the "Renaissance"* (London, 1900), p. 70.
24. *Ibid.*, pp. 70, 114–15, 140–41, 155–56, passim.
25. *Ibid.*, pp. 61–62, 114–15; C. H. Ashdown, *British and Foreign Arms and Armour* (Edinburgh, 1909), pp. 242–43.
26. G. Vasari, *Les Vies d'artistes* (1568), French trans. Charles Weiss (Paris, 1919), II, 778–80.
27. See plates in Johan E. Elias, *De Vlootbouw in Nederland, 1596–1655* (Amsterdam, 1933).
28. A. Jal, *Abraham Duquesne et la marine de son temps* (Paris, 1873), p. 139.
29. J.–B. Giraud, *Documents pour servir à l'histoire de l'armement au moyen âge et à la Renaissance* (Lyon, 1899), II, 102.
30. Vannoccio Biringuccio, *Pirotechnia* (1540), ed. Cyril S. Smith (New York, 1942), p. 243.

31. H. B. C. Pollard, *A History of Firearms* (Boston, 1928), p. 23.

32. Clephan, *Defensive Armour*, pp. 227–28. See also pp. 146, 157, and Pollard, pp. 25–26.

33. John Evelyn, *Diary and Correspondence* (London, 1889), I, 230.

34. Archives Départementales de la Côte d'Or (Dijon), B. 11688; Archives Nationales (Paris), X¹ᵃ 8614, ff. 22–23. See also Henri Hauser, *Les Débuts du capitalisme* (Paris, 1927), p. 122, and *Ouvriers du temps passé* (5th ed.; Paris, 1927), pp. 256–57.

35. Archives Nationales, X¹ᵃ 8650, ff. 328–34; KK509; Archives Départementales d'Ille et Vilaine (Rennes), C 2771.

36. *Recueil général des anciennes lois françaises* (Paris, 1829), XVI, 183–91.

37. J. U. Nef, *The Rise of the British Coal Industry* (London, 1932), I, 156–62; see also Nef, "Prices and Industrial Capitalism," *Economic History Review*, VII (1937), 178–83.

38. Antoyne de Montchrétien, *Traicté de l'œconomie politique*, ed. Th. Funck-Brentano (Paris, n.d.), pp. 48–49, 53–54, 239.

VII. THE SURRENDER AT BREDA AND ITS BACKGROUND

1. Robert Boyle, *Works* (London, 1772), I, p. xxxi.

2. C. H. Haskins, *Studies in Mediaeval Culture* (Oxford, 1929), p. 108.

3. C. H. Ashdown, *British and Foreign Arms and Armour* (Edinburgh, 1909), pp. 126–27.

4. See also the discussion in Chapter II, Section 1.

5. Cervantes, *Don Quixote of La Mancha*, trans. Motteux (Edinburgh, 1822), II, 231.

6. Frederick Lewis Taylor, *The Art of War in Italy, 1494–1529* (Cambridge, 1921), p. 56.

7. *Ibid.*, p. 60.

8. *Mémoires de Martin et Guillaume du Bellay*, ed. V.-L. Bourrilly and F. Vindry (Paris, 1912), III, 298–300.

9. Karl Brandi, *The Emperor Charles V*, trans. C. V. Wedgwood (New York, 1939), pp. 219–20.

10. Sieur du Praissac, *Briefe méthode pour résoudre facilement toute question militaire* (Paris, 1614); *Les Questions militaire* (Paris, 1614). The quotation is from the English translation of Praissac's *Les Discours militaires* of 1625 (*The Art of Warre or Militarie Discourses*, ed. John Cruso [Cambridge, 1639], p. 29).

11. For atrocities in early sixteenth-century war, see Du Bellay, *Mémoires*, I, 151, 221, 307.

12. Schiller, in *Sämtliche Werke* (1862), IX, 176–77.

13. John W. Wright, "Sieges and Customs of War at the Opening of the Eighteenth Century," *American Historical Review*, XXXIX (1934), 643–44; Hubert G. R. Reade, *Sidelights on the Thirty Years' War* (London, 1924), II, 432.

14. Du Bellay, *Mémoires*, II, 111–14.

15. Ed. de la Barre-Duparcq, "L'Art militaire pendant les guerres de religion 1562–1598," *Séances et Travaux de l'Académie des Sciences morales et politiques*, LXVI (1863), 277.

16. *Ibid.*, LXVIII, 282–83.

17. Emeric Crucé, *Le Nouveau Cynée* (1623) (Paris, 1919), *passim*. See also Edmond Silberner, *La Guerre dans la pensée économique du XVIᵉ au XVIIIᵉ siècle* (Paris, 1939), esp. p. 135.

18. See, for example, Saint Athanasius, *De incarnatione verbi dei* (c. 325), paras. 51–52.

19. See Henry S. Lucas, "John Crabbe: Flemish Pirate, Merchant, and Adventurer," *Speculum*, XX, no. 3 (1945), 334*ff*.

20. Silberner, *La Guerre*, pp. 11, 24, 35, 65, 108–109, *passim*.

VIII. TOWARD EUROPEAN ECONOMIC COMMUNITY

1. W. K. Jordan, *The Development of Religious Toleration in England, 1640–1660* (London, 1940), IV, 466–67.

2. Burnet, *History of His Own Time* (2 vols.; London, 1724–1734).

3. Josiah Tucker, *A Brief Essay on the Advantages and Disadvantages Which Respectively Attend France and Great Britain with Regard to Trade* (London, 1750), p. 24.

4. See Chapter XV, Section 2.

5. Savary des Bruslons, *Dictionnaire universel de commerce* (Geneva, 1742), I, Part II, 16–17. The comparison is between a *Mémoire* of 1634 and another of 1722, but the latter "paroit avoir été dressé quelques années auparavant," consequently about 1715, the year of Louis XIV's death.

6. J. U. Nef, *The Rise of the British Coal Industry* (London, 1932), I, 127.

7. Leopold von Ranke, *Memoirs of the House of Brandenburg and History of Prussia*, trans. Sir Alexander and Lady Duff Gordon (London, 1849), I, 441–42.

8. A. Wolf, *A History of Science, Technology, and Philosophy in the 16th and 17th Centuries* (London, 1935), pp. 510–512; Ludwig Beck, *Geschichte des Eisen* (Braunschweig, 1884–1903), III, 960. Cf. Nef, *British Coal Industry*, I, 244–45, and *passim*.

9. See Earl J. Hamilton, "The Decline of Spain," *Economic History Review*, VIII (1938), 170–171; "Monetary Disorder and Economic Decadence in Spain, 1651–1700," *Journal of Political Economy*, LI (1943), 492–93; "Money and Economic Recovery in Spain, 1701–1746," *Journal of Modern History*, XV (1943), 192–93, 206.

10. See Savary des Bruslons, *Dictionnaire*, I, Part II, 317.

11. See Charles Wilson, "The Economic Decline of the Netherlands," *EHR*, IX (1939), 111–13, 127; *Anglo-Dutch Commerce and Finance in the Eighteenth Century* (Cambridge, 1941), pp. 16–19, 24, and *passim*. See also G. N. Clark, *The Dutch Alliance and the War Against French Trade, 1688–1697* (Manchester, 1923), p. 133.

12. See, for example, Pierre Clément, *Lettres, instructions et mémoires de Colbert*, III, Part I (Paris, 1864), p. 199.

IX. LESS BLOOD AND MORE MONEY

1. Earl of Orrery, *A Treatise of the Art of War* (London, 1677), p. 15.

2. Defoe, *An Essay upon Projects*, in Henry Morley, *The Earlier Life and the Chief Earlier Works of Daniel Defoe* (London, 1889), p. 135; see also Comte de Guibert, *Essai général de tactique* (Liége, 1775), II, 187–88.

3. See Carl von Noorden, *Europäische Geschichte im achtzehnten Jahrhundert* (Düsseldorf, 1870), I, 575.

4. John W. Wright, "Sieges and Customs of War at the Opening of the Eighteenth Century," *American Historical Review*, XXXIX (1934), 630–31.

5. Lord Acton, *Lectures on the French Revolution* (London, 1932), p. 215.

6. L. N. M. Carnot, *De la défense des places forts* (3rd ed.; Paris, 1812), p. xiii; Defoe, *Essay*.

7. See Ed. de la Barre-Duparcq, "Des Imitations militaires," *Séances et Travaux de l'Académie des Sciences morales et politiques*, LXXVI (1866), 374; *Calendar of State Papers, Domestic*, 1671, p. 287.

8. See Smollett, *Roderick Random*, ch. xliv, and *passim*. See also Boyle, *Works* (London, 1772), I, p. xxix.

9. G. M. Trevelyan, *England under Queen Anne: Blenheim* (London, 1930), I, 433.

10. See A. J. Toynbee, *A Study of History* (London, 1939), IV, 142–50, 158–62; Count Saxe (1696–1750), *Reveries, or Memoirs upon the Art of*

War (London, 1757), p. 85; W. S. Churchill, *Marlborough, His Life and Times* (New York, 1935), III, 97–98.

11. *Memoirs of Goldoni*, trans. John Black (London, 1814), I, 207; a reference for which I am indebted to Professor Ulrich A. Middeldorf. The translation of this passage from the French seems to me to be almost perfect. *Cf. Mémoires de M. Goldoni* (Paris, 1787), I, 246–47.

12. *Memoirs of Goldoni*, I, 201–16; *Mémoires de M. Goldoni*, I, 240–57.

13. R. G. Albion, *Forests and Sea Power: The Timber Problem of the Royal Navy, 1652–1862* (Cambridge, Mass., 1926), pp. vii–viii, 3–5. See also Frederick L. Robertson, *The Evolution of Naval Armament* (London, 1921), pp. 21, 24–25, 31, 50, 246ff.

14. Albion, p. 3.

15. Robertson, p. 21.

16. *Calendar of State Papers, Domestic*, 1665–66, p. 372, and other references too numerous to cite.

17. See J. U. Nef, *The Rise of the British Coal Industry* (London, 1932), II, 263–65, 285, 287–88, 296–98, 301. See also *Calendar of State Papers, Domestic*; for example, 1666–67, p. 327; 1667, pp. xxv, 94, 190, 241, 294, 479–80. See also Chapter I.

18. *Calendar of State Papers, Domestic*, 1653, pp. 257–58, 262, 264, 268, 271–79, 283.

19. Nef, Appendix D(i).

20. Henri Malo, *La Grande Guerre des corsaires, Dunkirk 1702–15* (Paris, 1925), p. 126.

21. *Calendar of State Papers, Domestic*, 1665–66, p. 461.

22. See Charles Wilson, *Anglo-Dutch Commerce and Finance in the Eighteenth Century* (Cambridge, 1941), pp. 16–17, 19; Lemontey, *Essai sur l'établissement monarchique de Louis XIV, Oeuvres* (1829), V, 61, cited in Barre-Duparcq, *Séances et Travaux*, LXXXIII (1868), 252n; *Calendar of State Papers, Domestic*, 1665–66, p. 461.

23. See *Calendar of State Papers, Domestic*, 1665–66, p. 461.

24. Savary des Bruslons, *Dictionnaire universel de commerce* (1723; Geneva, 1742), I, Part II, 12, 243. See Colonel de Rochas, *Vauban, sa famille et ses écrits* (Paris, 1910), II, 126.

25. See P. D. Huet, *A View of the Dutch Trade* (1698; 2nd ed., London, 1722), pp. ii–iii, and *passim.*

26. *A Sentimental Journey through France and Italy* (1768), *The Works of Laurence Sterne* (London, 1808), II, 374, 399, and *passim.*

27. Edmond Silberner, *La Guerre dans la pensée économique du XVIe au XVIIIe siècle* (Paris, 1939), pp. 11, 108–109.

28. See, for example, Savary des Bruslons, *Dictionnaire*, I, Part II, 484, 860, for international jealousy concerning trade in the Far East. And also Richard Pares, *War and Trade in the West Indies, 1739–1763* (Oxford, 1936), *passim.*

29. *Calendar of State Papers, Domestic*, 1665–66, p. 31.

30. See *Calendar of State Papers, Domestic*, 1689–90, p. 93; Pares, pp. viii, 62.

31. See Savary des Bruslons, *Dictionnaire*, I, Part II, 281.

32. G. N. Clark, *The Dutch Alliance and the War Against French Trade, 1688–1697*, pp. 4–7, 63–64, 91–92, 106–19, 139–40; Clark, "War Trade and Trade War, 1701–1713," *Economic History Review*, I (1928), 263–64, 268–70, 274, 276.

33. Jean Lagorgette, *Le Rôle de la guerre* (Paris, 1906), pp. 193, 597; S. T. Coleridge, *The Friend* (London, 1837), II, 89–90; John Houghton, *A Collection for the Improvement of Husbandry and Trade* (London, 1727), I, 204ff, II, 5, 28, 290; *Calendar of State Papers, Domestic*, 1666–67, pp. 46, 161, 202, 550, 589; *ibid.*, 1667, pp. vii, xxx; *ibid.*, 1671, p. 562; *ibid.*, 1677–78, p. 665.

34. Earl of Orrery, *Treatise*, p. 22; see also p. 14.

35. Pares, *War and Trade*, p. 62. See also J. A. Williamson, *The Ocean in English History* (Oxford, 1941), p. 179.

36. Voltaire, *Candide* (1759), ch. iv. See also *Oeuvres complètes de Voltaire, Correspondance* (Paris, 1880), I, 506; L. Walowski, "Le grand dessein de Henri IV," *Séances et Travaux de l'Académie des Sciences morales et politiques* (1860), LIV, 30–59; Silberner, *La Guerre*, p. 167.

37. This view was widely held.

See *Encyclopédie méthodique* (Paris, 1784), IV, 575.

38. Gibbon, *Decline and Fall of the Roman Empire*, ch. xxxviii (Bury ed., IV, 176). See also pp. 175–81, esp. pp. 176, 178, of the Bury edition; passages called to my attention by Dr. Robert M. Hutchins.

X. WAR AND SCIENTIFIC PROGRESS

1. See Lord Keynes, "Newton the Man," and E. N. daC. Andrade, "Newton," in *Newton Tercentenary Celebrations* (Cambridge, 1947), pp. 20, 28–29.

2. Descartes, *Discours de la méthode*, Parts V, VI (Etienne Gilson edition, Paris, 1925, pp. 50–62; the passage from which I quote is cn pp. 61–62). For the shortcomings of Descartes' own method and thought as instruments for the progress of natural science, see Gilson, "Descartes, Harvey et la scolastique," *Études de philosophie mediévale* (Strasbourg, 1921), pp. 244–45.

3. Lionel D. Edie, *What of Postwar?* (Wilmington, Delaware, 1943), pp. 13–14.

4. Charles Babbage, *Reflections on the Decline of Science in England* (London, 1830), pp. vii, 1–2, 14–15, 17–18, 30ff.; a work called to my attention by Dr. Harold A. Innis.

5. See, for example, J. B. Conant, "Lessons from the Past," *Industrial and Engineering Chemistry*, XXXI (1939), 1215–17.

6. See Robert Boyle, *Works* (London, 1772), III, 402–25, 442–55. Views like Boyle's on these matters were common enough among the English scientists who were his contemporaries. References could be multiplied.

7. See René Vallery-Radot, *The Life of Pasteur*, trans. Mrs. R. L. Devonshire (New York, n.d.), I, 274–75, and *passim*.

8. Malebranche, *La Recherche de la vérité* (Paris, 1880), p. 23.

9. Elie Faure, *La Danse sur le feu et l'eau* (Paris, 1920), pp. 50–52, 59–78. I am not suggesting that Faure

is wrong in his insistence upon the tragic element in great art or in his remark that war has been an integral part of civilized history. See my *The Universities Look for Unity* (New York, 1943), pp. 41–42, and the "Comment" in *Measure*, I (1950), no. 1, 89.

10. As used by Defoe, the word "projects" included public works of all kinds. He called Noah's Ark and the Tower of Babel projects! See *An Essay upon Projects* in *The Earlier Life and the Chief Earlier Works of Daniel Defoe*, ed. Henry Morley (London, 1889), p. 38.

11. J. U. Nef, *The Rise of the British Coal Industry* (London, 1932), II, 446–48.

12. J. U. Nef, "The Progress of Technology and the Growth of Large-Scale Industry in Great Britain, 1540–1640," *Economic History Review*, V (1934), 5–18; "Prices and Industrial Capitalism in France and England, 1540–1640," *ibid.*, VII (1937), 174, 184.

13. See W. Stanley Jevons, *The Coal Question*, ed. A. W. Flux (London, 1906), pp. 113ff.

14. Nef, *British Coal Industry*, I, 242–44, 353–58, and *passim*.

15. The armament industry was not the main consumer of English iron at the beginning of the seventeenth century. Its increasing importance as a consumer of iron at the beginning of the eighteenth century resulted partly from a shrinkage in the output of English iron during the late seventeenth century (see Nef, "War and Economic Progress, 1540–1640," *EHR*, XII [1942], 27n). The puzzling prob-

lem is why, with the increasing need for metal in the armament industries, so little should have been done in England during five generations, from say 1620 to 1770, to develop new and cheaper processes of making iron (see Chapters XIII, XIV, XV).

16. See Defoe, *Essay*, pp. 25, 31–32.

17. G. N. Clark, *Science and Social Welfare in the Age of Newton* (Oxford, 1937), p. 51.

18. *Ibid.*, pp. 17–19, 73–74.

19. See Virginia Woolf, *The Common Reader* (London, 1925), p. 111.

20. See T. S. Ashton, *Iron and Steel in the Industrial Revolution* (Manchester, 1924), p. 60, and ch. ii.

21. See Chapter XV, Section 3.

22. Defoe, *Essay*, pp. 25, 31; *The Novels and Miscellaneous Works of Daniel De Foe* (Oxford, 1841), XVII, 248–49.

23. See Babbage, *Reflections*, p. 2.

24. For example, Ashton, *appendix* E; see also pp. 28–36.

25. E. T. Whittaker, "Aristotle, Newton, Einstein," *Science*, XCVIII (1943), no. 2542, 249–53, an article called to my attention by my colleague, Dr. Dallas B. Phemister.

26. Etienne Gilson, *The Unity of Philosophical Experience* (New York, 1937), pp. 224–25, 227–30, and ch. ix generally.

27. Jacob Burckhardt, *Force and Freedom* (New York, 1943), p. 311.

28. The phrase is Mr. T. S. Eliot's.

29. S. C. Gilfillan, *Inventing the Ship* (Chicago, 1935), pp. 249–50.

30. Sir William Bragg, "History in the Archives of the Royal Society," *Science*, LXXXIX (1939), no. 2316, 452–53.

31. Mark Pattison, *Isaac Casaubon* (2nd ed.; Oxford, 1892), pp. 263–64.

32. B. Hessen, "The Social and Economic Roots of Newton's 'Principia,'" *Science at the Crossroads* (London, 1931), pp. 157–74; Clark, *Science and Social Welfare*, pp. 68–91; Nef, *British Coal Industry*, I, 240–56.

33. Quoted in Andrade, "Newton," p. 4.

34. *Histoire de l'Académie Royale des Sciences*, 1666–86, p. 386.

35. Clark, pp. 17, 19, 73–74; L. F. Alfred Maury, *Les Académies d'autrefois: l'ancienne Académie des Sciences* (Paris, 1864), p. 39; Charles Wesley Cole, *Colbert and a Century of French Mercantilism* (New York, 1939), I, 459.

XI. SCIENTIFIC PROGRESS AND WAR

1. Marquis of Worcester, *A Century of Inventions* (1663), ed. John Buddle (Newcastle, 1778), p. 12.

2. *Calendar of State Papers, Domestic*, 1664–65, pp. 112, 146; 1665–66, p. 283. See also *ibid.*, 1673–75, p. 15, and Robert Boyle, *Works* (London, 1772), V, 6. For other new warlike inventions, see Worcester, pp. 13–14, 16–18, 23–25, 28–29.

3. Daniel Defoe, *An Essay upon Projects*, in *The Earlier Life and the Chief Earlier Works of Daniel Defoe*, ed. Henry Morley (London, 1889), p. 40. But see also Roger North, *Examen* (London, 1740), p. 52.

4. *The Petty Papers*, ed. Marquis of Lansdowne (London, 1927), II, 71–76.

5. See *Histoire de l'Académie Royale des Sciences*, 1666–1740, pas-

sim; M. Gallon, *Machines et inventions approuvées par l'Académie Royale des Sciences depuis son établissement jusqu'à présent* (Paris, 1735), I–VI, passim; *Philosophical Transactions*, passim.

6. Frederick Leslie Robertson, *The Evolution of Naval Armament* (London, 1921), pp. 16–20, 24–27.

7. E. M. G. Routh, *Tangier: England's Lost Atlantic Outpost, 1661–84* (London, 1912), pp. 163, 168.

8. François Blondel (1617–1686), the diplomat and architect, published in 1683, a book called *L'Art de jetter les bombes*, a landmark in the development of the technique. See *Histoire de l'Académie Royale des Sciences*, 1707, pp. 120ff; 1716, pp. 79–86; 1731, pp. 72–76.

9. J. H. M. Poppe, *Geschichte der*

Technologie (Göttingen, 1810), II, 554; Clifford Walton, *History of the British Standing Army, 1660–1700* (London, 1894), pp. 350*ff*; R. P. Daniel, *Histoire de la milice françoise* (Paris, 1721), I, 579–80.

10. Robertson, *Naval Armament*, p. 33.

11. *Histoire de l'Académie Royale des Sciences*, 1719, pp. 103–105.

12. Ed. de la Barre-Duparcq, "Des Imitations militaires," *Séances et Travaux de l'Académie des Sciences morales et politiques*, LXXVI (1866), 106. See also John Muller, *A Treatise of Artillery* (2nd ed.; London, 1768), p. 152; L. N. M. Carnot, *Mémoire sur la fortification primitive* (Paris, 1823), p. 40.

13. See C. H. Firth, *Cromwell's Army* (London, 1902), p. 87.

14. See, for example, *Calendar of State Papers, Domestic*, January–June 1683, p. 366; 1683–84, p. 242; 1684–85, p. 95. Matchlock muskets were still used, however (*ibid.*, 1689–90, p. 238).

15. Walton, *The British Standing Army*, p. 338; Firth, pp. 87, 89; Earl of Orrery, *A Treatise of the Art of War* (London, 1677), p. 31; Hermann Foertsch, *The Art of Modern Warfare* (New York, 1940), pp. 62, 65.

16. George A. Aitken, *The Life and Works of John Arbuthnot* (Oxford, 1892), p. 426. The particular essay on mathematical learning, mentioned in the text, has been frequently attributed to Martin Strong. Cf. the article on Arbuthnot in the *Dictionary of National Biography*.

17. See Chapter XVI, Section 2.

18. Carnot, *Mémoire*, pp. x–xi, and *passim*.

19. Barre-Duparcq, *Séances et Travaux*, LXXVI, 106.

20. Aquinas, *Summa theologica*, Part II (ii), q. 40, art. 3.

21. *Histoire de l'Académie Royale des Sciences*, 1707, p. 169; Henri Baudrillart, "Vauban, économiste et réformateur," *Séances et Travaux de l'Académie des Sciences morales et politiques*, LXXXIII, (1868), 73.

22. See *Calendar of State Papers, Domestic*, 1671, pp. 219, 287.

23. Carnot, *Mémoire*, pp. x–xi; see also Marshal Saxe, *Reveries, or Memoirs upon the Art of War* (London, 1757), pp. 90, 108*ff*.

24. Jacques A. H. de Guibert, *Essai général de tactique* (1772; Liége, 1775), I, p. lv (a work called to my attention by Dr. Ulrich Middeldorf); Carnot, pp. xi *ff*.

25. Baudrillart, *Séances et Travaux*, LXXXIII, 71. See also Colonel de Rochas, *Vauban, sa famille, et ses écrits*, I, 120*ff*.

26. Guido Pancirollus (Panciroli), *The History of Many Memorable Things Lost* (English trans.; London, 1715), II, 449–50.

27. See J. U. Nef, "Architecture and Western Civilization," *The Review of Politics*, VIII (1946), 192–222.

28. Robertson, *Naval Armament*, p. 50. According to Mr. S. C. Gilfillan, there was little improvement in naval architecture during this period, at any rate so far as England was concerned (*Inventing the Ship* [Chicago, 1935], pp. 248–53).

29. Muller, *Treatise of Artillery*, p. iii. See also Charles Hutton, *Mathematical Dictionary* (London, 1795), I, 562; Robertson, *Naval Armament*, pp. 89–90; G. von Scharnhorst, *Handbuch für Officiere, Erster Theil Artillerie* (Hanover, 1804), I, 19–20; Savary des Bruslons, *Dictionnaire universel de commerce* (Geneva, 1742), II, 495.

30. Robertson, p. 35.

31. See Chapter III.

32. Benjamin Robins, *New Principles of Gunnery* (new ed.; London, 1805). See also Hutton, *Mathematical Dictionary*, II, 381–83.

33. Hutton, I, 562–70.

34. Lord Keynes, "Newton the Man," *Newton Tercentenary Celebrations* (Cambridge, 1947), pp. 28–29. I am grateful to my colleagues, Professor S. Chandrasekhar and Professor H. C. Urey for calling this work to my attention.

35. *Philosophical Transactions of the Royal Society*, II (1666), 329–43.

36. *Newton Tercentenary Celebrations*, pp. 27, 30–34. See also pp. 18–21.

37. *Newton Tercentenary Celebrations*, p. 19.

38. Henry Dircks, *A Biographical Memoir of Samuel Hartlib* (London, 1865), *passim*; Boyle, *Works*, VI, 118, 441–42.

39. Johnson, *Rasselas* (1759), ch. vi.

40. *Donne's Sermons*, ed. Logan P. Smith (Oxford, 1919), pp. 100–101.

41. Boyle, *Works*, VI, 442.

42. John Houghton, *A Collection for the Improvement of Husbandry and Trade*, ed. Richard Bradley (London, 1727), II, 128.

43. Pancirollus, *Memorable Things Lost*, II, 388.

44. I am grateful to my colleague, Professor Daniel J. Boorstin, for calling my attention to this matter.

XII. WAR AND ECONOMIC PROGRESS

1. Ed. de la Barre-Duparcq, "Des Rapports entre la richesse et la puissance militaire des états," *Séances et Travaux de l'Académie des Sciences morales et politiques*, LXXXIV (1868), 304.

2. François de la Noue, *Discours politiques et militaires* (Basle, 1587), pp. 260*ff*.

3. Leopold von Ranke, *Memoirs of the House of Brandenburg and History of Prussia*, trans. Sir Alexander and Lady Duff Gordon (London, 1849), I, 421.

4. See Chapter XVIII.

5. See *The Cambridge Modern History*, VI, 213.

6. *Calendar of State Papers, Domestic*, 1670, p. 586.

7. A. M. de Boislisle, *Correspondance des contrôleurs généraux des finances avec les intendants des provinces* (3 vols.; Paris, 1874–1897), *passim*.

8. See Jacques A. H. de Guibert, *Essai général de tactique* (Liége, 1775), II, 147–48, 151*ff*., 158.

9. *Calendar of State Papers, Domestic*, 1661–62, p. 8.

10. Lord of Praissac, *The Art of Warre*, trans. John Cruso (Cambridge, 1639), pp. 143–44.

11. Earl of Orrery, *Art of War* (London, 1677), p. 86.

12. Surirey de Saint Rémy, *Mémoires d'artillerie* (3rd ed.; Paris, 1745), I, 40.

13. *Cambridge Modern History*, VI, 215–16.

14. See Smollett, *Roderick Random* (1748), ch. xxiv.

15. A. de Saint Léger and Philippe Sagnac, *La Prépondérance française* (Paris, 1935), pp. 201–202. *Calendar of State Papers, Domestic*, 1667–68, pp. 293, 304.

16. See Clifford Walton, *History of the British Standing Army* (London, 1894), pp. 482–83. See also Smollett, *Roderick Random*, chs. xxiv, xxxiv.

17. Pierre Clément, *Lettres, instructions et mémoires de Colbert* (Paris, 1864), III, Part I, 486, 487n.

18. *Ibid.*, Part II (1865), pp. 39–44, and *passim*.

19. See, for example, *Calendar of State Papers, Domestic*, 1670, p. 507. See also passing references in the various volumes of the *Calendar*.

20. Saint Rémy, *Mémoires*, II, 298.

21. *Ibid.*, pp. 322–23. For the gunpowder mills at Saint Jean d'Angély, see Savary des Bruslons, *Dictionnaire universel de commerce* (1723; 1740 ed.), I, Part II, 150.

22. Saint Rémy, II, 98. See also Clément, *Colbert*, VII, 243.

23. Saint Rémy, II, 228.

24. Michel Chevalier, "Mémoire sur l'application de l'armée aux travaux publics," *Séances et Travaux de l'Académie des Sciences morales et politiques*, 3 ser. XLI (1857), 371–72.

25. *Ibid.*, pp. 371–72.

26. *Ibid.*, p. 373.

27. Thomas Mun, *England's Treasure by Forraign Trade* (1669; reprint Oxford, 1928), pp. 1, 3, 88.

28. Jean Eon, *Le Commerce honorable* (Nantes, 1646). See the quotation from Eon in Stewart L. Mims, *Colbert's West India Policy* (New Haven, 1912), pp. 5–6.

29. See J. U. Nef, *Industry and Government in France and England, 1540–1640* (Philadelphia, 1940), pp. 21, 88, and *passim*.

30. See Henri Hauser, *La Pensée et l'action économique du Cardinal de Richelieu* (Paris, 1944), *passim*.

31. *Recueil des testaments politiques* (Amsterdam, 1749), III, 441, 479–80.

32. See Mouffle d'Angerville, *The Private Life of Louis XV* (London, 1924), pp. 105–108.

33. See Pierre Clément, *Jacques Coeur et Charles VII* (Paris, 1866), pp. 345–46, and *passim*. In the earlier edition of 1853 the discussions of the Agnès Sorel affair and of Jacques Coeur's disgrace is in Vol. II, pp. 132–141, 189–201.

34. *Calendar of State Papers, Domestic,* 1671, p. 530.

35. Additional MSS 34555. See E. Lipson, *The Economic History of England* (London, 1931), II, 178ff.

36. Misson, *Mémoires et observations faites par un voyageur en Angleterre* (La Haye, 1698), p. 390.

37. Nef, *The Rise of the British Coal Industry* (London, 1932), II, appendix D(i).

38. Innumerable references could be cited to the interference war caused to the English coal trade. See, for example, *Calendar of State Papers, Domestic,* 1665–66, p. 57; 1666–67, p. 327.

39. Savary des Bruslons, *Dictionnaire,* I, Part II, 474.

40. Maximilien Courtecuisse, *La Manufacture de draps fin Vanrobais* (Paris, 1920), pp. 2, 70–77; *Inventaire sommaire des archives départementales, Somme* (1888), II, 65–70.

41. Courtecuisse, pp. 72–77, 102–103, 107–126; *Inventaire sommaire des archives départementales, Somme,* II, 70ff.

42. Warren C. Scoville, "The French Glass Industry, 1640–1740," *Journal of Economic History,* I (1941), 158–59, 163–64, 167; "State Policy and the French Glass Industry, 1640–1789," *Quarterly Journal of Economics,* LVI (1942), 430, 432, 446; "Large-Scale Production in the French Plate-Glass Industry, 1665–1789," *Journal of Political Economy,* I (1942), 673–74, 676, 679–80, 685–86, 691–92, 697; "Labor and Labor Conditions in the French Glass Industry, 1643–1789," *Journal of Modern History,* XV (1943), 279–80, 285–86, 288.

43. See Savary des Bruslons, *Dictionnaire,* I, Part II, 194, 197, 218.

44. See Hans Speier, "Militarism in the Eighteenth Century," *Social Research,* III (1936), 309ff.

45. *Inventaire sommaire des archives départementales, Hautes Alpes,* E. no. 494.

XIII. ECONOMIC PROGRESS AND WAR

1. See my forthcoming article in *Cambridge Economic History,* II, ch. vii, section 4.

2. See Emile Mâle, *L'Art religieux du XIII*e *siècle en France* (Paris, 1899), *passim*.

3. J. C. Drummond and Anne Wilbraham, *The Englishman's Food* (London, 1939), pp. 182–99, and *passim*.

4. Montesquieu, *De l'esprit des lois* (Geneva, 1748), bk. xv, chs. v, vii, and *passim*. This book was the fruit of twenty years' labor, Montesquieu tells us in his preface.

5. T. S. Eliot, *Homage to John Dryden* (London, 1927), especially pp. 34–46.

6. Star Chamber Proceedings (Public Record Office, London), James I, 310/16.

7. Robert Southey, *Life of John Wesley* (2nd ed.; London, 1820), pp. 235–39, 416ff.

8. Gonzales Decamps, *Mémoire historique sur l'industrie houillère de*

Mons, "Société des Sciences, des Arts et des Lettres du Hainaut, Publications" (5th series, 1889), I, 201.

9. Marc Bloch, "Comment et pourquoi finit l'esclavage antique," *Annales*, no. 2 (April-June 1947), pp. 163-65, 170.

10. See J. U. Nef, *The Rise of the British Coal Industry* (London, 1932), II, 157-63.

11. See Ferdinand Lot, *L'Art militaire et les armées au moyen-âge en Europe et dans le Proche Orient* (Paris, 1946), I, 410-11.

12. See Hans Speier, "Militarism in the Eighteenth Century," *Social Research*, III (1936), 309-10, 318; an article which gives strong support to my argument concerning military morale since the early eighteenth century, as the argument is developed in Chs. XVI and XIX.

13. *Calendar of State Papers, Domestic*, 1667, p. 207.

14. *Ibid.*, 1671, p. 448; A. de Saint Léger and Philippe Sagnac, *La prépondérance française* (Paris, 1935), p. 202.

15. Speier, *Social Research*, III, 317; see also *Mémoires de M. Goldoni* (Paris, 1787), I, 247.

16. See Thackeray, *The Memoirs of Barry Lyndon, Esq.* (1844), ch. v.

17. *Calendar of State Papers, Domestic*, 1668-69, pp. 119-20.

18. *Ibid.*, 1667, p. 461.

19. N. W. Posthumus, *Inquiry into the History of Prices in Holland* (Leiden, 1946), tables 167-69, 172-76, 178, 180, 184, 190, 213, and *passim*. I am grateful to Professor John B. Wolf, of the University of Minnesota, for calling this work to my attention and for helpful information concerning the costs of outfitting the military forces at the end of the seventeenth and at the beginning of the eighteenth century.

20. Henri Baudrillart, "Vauban, économiste et réformateur," *Séances et Travaux de l'Académie des Sciences morales et politiques*, LXXXIII (1868), 91-92.

21. See discussion in Chapter VIII.

22. Cited in Edmond Silberner, *La Guerre dans la pensée économique du XVI⁰ au XVIII⁰ siècle* (Paris, 1939), p. 99.

23. Montesquieu, *De l'esprit des lois*, bk. xiii, ch. xvii.

24. See *Calendar of State Papers, Domestic*, 1664-65, p. 351; 1670, p. 374; P. D. Huet, *A View of the Dutch Trade* (1698) (2nd English ed.; London, 1722), p. 158.

25. *Calendar of State Papers, Domestic*, 1666-67, p. 442.

26. Savary des Bruslons, *Dictionnaire universel de commerce*, (1723; Geneva, 1742), III, 670.

27. *Inventaire sommaire des Archives départementales, Marne*, C, I (1884), 359; Gaspard Monge, *Description de l'art de fabriquer les canons* (Paris, 1794), pp. i-ii.

28. R. G. Albion, *Forests and Sea Power: The Timber Problem of the Royal Navy, 1652-1862* (Cambridge, Mass., 1926).

29. Pierre Clément, *Lettres, instructions et mémoires de Colbert* (Paris, 1864), III, Part I, 33.

30. *Ibid.*, Part II, pp. 305-307. See also Vol. VII, p. 243.

31. A. M. de Boislisle, *Correspondance des contrôleurs généraux des finances avec les intendants des provinces* (Paris, 1883), Vol. II, no. 355, also appendix, p. 498. See also *Inventaire sommaire des archives départementales, Herault*, C, III (1887), 382; *ibid.*, *Hautes Alpes*, E, II, 234; Marcel Rouff, *Les mines de charbon en France au XVIII⁰ siècle* (Paris, 1922), pp. 21-32; *Histoire de l'Académie Royale des Sciences*, 1721, pp. 244-45.

32. See Chapter II, Section 2, and A. de Montchrétien, *Traicté de l'œconomie politique* (1615), ed. Th. Funck-Brentano (Paris, 1889), p. 58.

33. In 1667, according to Marshal Saxe, *Reveries, or Memoirs upon the Art of War* (London, 1757), p. 45.

34. I am indebted to Professor John B. Wolf for this information.

35. C. H. Firth, *Cromwell's Army* (London, 1902), pp. 146-47. See also Hans Delbrück, *Geschichte der Kriegskunst im Rahmen der politischen Geschichte* (Berlin, 1920), IV, 204.

36. *Histoire de l'Académie Royale des Sciences,* 1753, pp. 103–104.

37. G. von Scharnhorst, *Handbuch für Officiere, Erster Theil, Artillerie* (Hanover, 1804), pp. 19–20.

38. See Saxe, *Reveries,* p. 77.

39. Werner Sombart, *Der moderne Kapitalismus* (5th ed.; Munich, 1921), I, Part II, 751.

40. See Saxe, *Reveries,* pp. 19–20, 279–80, 282–84, and *passim*; John Muller, *A Treatise of Artillery* (2nd ed.; London, 1768), pp. iv, xxii–xxiv; Surirey de Saint Rémy, *Mémoires d'artillerie* (3rd ed.; Paris, 1745), vol. I, pp. viii, 79; Scharnhorst, *Handbuch,* pp. 280–82, and *passim.*

41. Clément, III, Part II, 311.

42. Archives départementales de la Gironde (Bordeaux), IB. 29, f. 9.

43. Archives départementales des Bouches-du-Rhône (Marseille), C. 2301 (Ordonnance of May 3, 1741, and *passim*); *Inventaire sommaire des archives départementales, Gers,* C (1882), pp. 27–28.

44. Archives départementales des Bouches-du-Rhône, C. 2301 (Mémoire sur l'execution de l'arrest rendu au Conseil d'Etat du Roy, January 15, 1741).

45. *Calendar of State Papers, Domestic,* 1665–66, pp. 219, 332; 1680–81, p. 540; 1689–90, pp. 332–33.

46. Herbert Blackman, "Gunfounding at Heathfield in the 18th Century," *Sussex Archeological Collections,* LXVII (1926), 45, 47.

47. Sombart, *Der moderne Kapitalismus,* II, 881.

48. *Histoire de l'Académie Royale des Sciences,* 1753, pp. 103–104.

49. Lord of Praissac, *The Art of Warre,* trans. John Cruso, (Cambridge,

1639), pp. 108*ff.* See John Wilkins, *Mathematicall Magick* (London, 1648), pp. 138–39.

50. Delbrück, *Geschichte der Kriegskunst,* IV, 41–42.

51. Clément, *Colbert,* II, 10. See William Ridgeway, *Origin and Influence of the Thoroughbred Horse* (Cambridge, 1905), p. 424.

52. See W. S. Churchill, *Marlborough, His Life and Times* (New York, 1935), IV, 15.

53. The founder of the French "physiocrat" school of economic thought, François Quesnay (1694–1774), wrote: "Pour soutenir ces enterprises injustes, on faït des efforts extraordinares par des armées si nombreuses et si dispendieuses qu'elles ne doivent avoir d'autres succès qu'un épuisement ignominieux qui flétrit l'héroïsme des nations belligérantes et déconcerte les projets ambitieux de conquête" (*Oeuvres économiques et philosophiques,* ed. A. Oncken [Paris, 1888], p. 658).

54. See Lot, *L'Art militaire,* I, 92–93.

55. A. Jal, *Abraham Duquesne et la marine de son temps* (Paris, 1873), II, 13–15, which is also the authority for the paragraph that follows.

56. Savary des Bruslons, *Dictionnaire,* II, 503.

57. Monge, *Description,* pp. 60, 64–65.

58. Savary des Bruslons, *Dictionnaire,* I, 198; II, 503–504.

59. Saint Rémy, *Mémoires,* I, 90–91.

60. Savary des Bruslons, I, 198–99.

61. *Calendar of State Papers, Domestic,* 1671, p. 287.

62. Savary des Bruslons, II, 495.

XIV. RESTRAINTS OF EUROPEAN CULTURE ON VIOLENCE

1. For a discussion of the use of the word "commerce" in the eighteenth century, see J. U. Nef, "English and French Industrial History after 1540 in Relation to the Constitution," *The Constitution Reconsidered,* ed. Conyers Read (New York, 1938), pp. 97–98.

2. According to J. H. M. Poppe, *Geschichte der Technologie* (Göttingen, 1810), II, 537, the bayonet was invented between 1643 and 1647; according to J. W. Fortescue, *A History of the British Army* (London, 1899), I, 327, in 1640.

3. *Calendar of State Papers, Domestic*, 1683–84, pp. 111, 400.

4. See, for example, *ibid.*, 1684–85, p. 130; 1689–90, pp. 145, 238.

5. Poppe, II, 538.

6. See also Hans Delbrück, *Geschichte der Kriegskunst im Rahmen der politischen Geschichte* (Berlin, 1920), IV, 218, 305–306; James S. D. Scott, *The British Army: Its Origin, Progress, and Equipment* (London, 1868), II, 314–25; Clifford Walton, *History of the British Standing Army, 1660–1700* (London, 1894), pp. 253, 326, 340–49, 436; Francis Grose, *Military Antiquities* (London, 1786), I, 181; Fortescue, I, 327.

7. Walton, pp. 341–43.

8. Voltaire, *La Henriade* (1723), (London, 1728), p. 180.

9. From a translation of Folard, *Commentaires sur Polybe* (1727–30), made for Lord Frankfort de Montmorency (MS volume in the Crerar Library, Chicago), pp. 240–41, 245. Cf. Jacques A. H. de Guibert, *Essai général de tactique* (Liége, 1775), I, lvii.

10. Guibert, I, liii, 244, and *passim*.

11. Earl of Orrery, *A Treatise of the Art of War* (London, 1677), p. 24.

12. *Ibid.*, pp. 27–28.

13. Poppe, II, 538.

14. Guibert, pp. 42–43.

15. *Calendar of State Papers, Domestic*, 1671, p. 235; 1667–68, p. 301.

16. *Oeuvres complètes de Voltaire, Correspondance*, I, 222–23.

17. Francis Parkman, *Montcalm and Wolfe* (Boston, 1927), II, 297.

18. James Boswell, *The Life of Samuel Johnson* (London, 1857), II, 216.

19. Pierre Clément, *Lettres, instructions et mémoires de Colbert* (Paris, 1869), VI, 220.

20. Poppe, II, 564–65.

21. See *Recueil des testaments politiques* (Amsterdam, 1749), III, pp. 396–97, 401–402.

22. A. de Saint Léger and Philippe Sagnac, *La Prepondérance française, 1661–1715* (Paris, 1935), p. 84.

23. Ed. de la Barre-Duparcq, "Reflexions sur les talents militaires de Louis XIV," *Séances et Travaux de l'Académie des Sciences morales et politiques*, LXXIX (1867), 345–46.

24. A point suggested by some lectures on the interrelations of Renaissance art and philosophy given by my colleague, Professor Edgar Wind.

25. Beaumarchais, *Le Barbier de Séville* (1775), Act I, Scene 2.

26. This was suggested to me by my colleague, Professor Jacob Viner.

27. P. D. Huet, *A View of the Dutch Trade* (2nd English ed.; London, 1722), p. ii.

28. Richard Pares, *War and Trade in the West Indies 1739–1763* (Oxford, 1936), p. viii.

29. Clément, II, cclviii, ccxviii; VI, 246. See also VI, 244–47.

30. J. A. Comenius, *The Angel of Peace* (New York, 1944), p. 57.

31. For example that is the principal result of the war mentioned in the French *Petit Larousse Illustré*.

32. I owe this knowledge to Professor Earl J. Hamilton. See his *War and Prices in Spain 1651–1800* (Cambridge, Mass., 1947), p. 145, and *passim*.

33. See Chapter XV, Section 2.

34. On the subject, see Edmond Silberner, *La Guerre dans la pensée économique du XVI⁰ au XVIII⁰ siècle* (Paris, 1939).

35. J. Accarias de Serionne, *Les Intérêts des nations de l'Europe développés relativement au commerce* (Leiden, 1767), I, 8.

36. See Chapter VII.

37. Quoted in Sebastian de Grazia, "Status as a Political Motive," *The Journal of Liberal Religion*, VIII, no. 11 (1947), 101.

38. Savary des Bruslons, *Dictionnaire universel de commerce* (Geneva, 1742), II, 495.

39. Fielding, *Tom Jones*, bk. v, ch. xii.

40. See Chapter VIII.

41. Montesquieu, *De l'esprit des lois*, bk. xx, chs. i, ii.

42. See Nef, in *The Constitution Reconsidered*, pp. 102–103.

43. Paul Hazard, *La Pensée européenne au XVIII*e *siècle* (Paris, 1946), Part II generally, and especially ch. ix.

44. Edmund Burke, *Letters on the Regicide Peace*, ed. E. J. Payne, III, 80–81.

45. Christopher Dawson, *The Judg-ment of the Nations* (New York, 1942), p. 86.

46. Burke, *Letters*.

47. H. A. Innis, *Political Economy in the Modern State* (Toronto, 1946), p. 36.

XV. THE INDUSTRIAL REVOLUTION RECONSIDERED

SECTION 1

1. The chronological framework of Toynbee's lectures was 1760 to 1840 (Arnold Toynbee, *Lectures on the Industrial Revolution* [London, 1927], p. vi), but, according to the late Sir William Ashley, who attended the lectures, the lecturer "did not bring his detailed study much beyond about 1832" (Henry Hamilton, *The English Brass and Copper Industries to 1800* [London, 1926], p. viii).

2. See Anna Bezanson, "The Early Use of the Term Industrial Revolution," *Quarterly Journal of Economics*, XXXVI (1922), 343–46. In various French publications of the first half of the nineteenth century, I have come across numerous references to an "industrial revolution," besides those recorded by Miss Bezanson.

3. Macaulay, *The History of England* (Philadelphia, 1872), I, 291–92.

SECTION 2

1. See Chapter VIII.

2. James Puckle, *A New Dialogue between a Burgermaster and an English Gentleman* (London, 1697), p. 20.

3. Letter of November 30, 1735, to Abbé d'Olivet, *Oeuvres complètes de Voltaire, Correspondance* (Paris, 1880), I, 556.

4. Letter of November 11, 1738, to Abbé Le Blanc, *ibid.*, III, 41.

5. See F. A. von Hayek, "The Counter-Revolution of Science," *Economica* (February 1941), pp. 9–10.

6. See J. U. Nef, "English and French Industrial History after 1540," *The Constitution Reconsidered*, ed. Conyers Read (New York, 1938), pp. 81ff.

7. Eli F. Heckscher, *Mercantilism* (London, 1935), I, 85–87, 106–107.

8. See Henri Sée, *L'Evolution commerciale et industrièlle de la France sous l'ancien régime* (Paris, 1925), pp. 194–99.

9. Archives départementales de l'Hérault (Montpellier), C. 2949 (Mémoire sur le commerce général de la province de Languedoc, 1744).

10. *Inventaire-sommaire des Archives départementales de l'Hérault*, série C, III, 384.

11. Archives départementales de l'Hérault, C. 2698 (Mémoire des intéressés à la raffinerie royale de Séte and Mémoire pour le Sieur Sabatier, propriétaire de la raffinerie de sucre, à Montpellier). For transcripts of these documents, I am indebted to M. de Dainville, the chief archivist at Montpellier, and to his assistant, M. L. Maury.

12. See Marcel Rouff, *Les Mines de charbon en France* (Paris, 1922), Part I, ch. vi, and Part II.

13. See A. Esmein, *Cours élémentaire d'histoire du droit français* (15th ed.; Paris, 1925), pp. 550–51.

14. Henri Hauser, *Recherches et documents sur l'histoire des prix en France de 1500 à 1800* (Paris, 1936), p. 24. For the statement concerning the period 1725 to 1785 I am indebted to Professor Earl J. Hamilton's unrivaled knowledge of the history of prices.

15. See A. P. Wadsworth and J. de L. Mann, *The Cotton Trade and Industrial Lancashire* (Manchester, 1931), pp. 197–99.

16. Nef, in *The Constitution Reconsidered*, p. 96, and Nef, *Industry and Government in France and England, 1540–1640* (Philadelphia, 1940), p. 118.

17. Henri Hauser, *La Pensée et*

l'action économique du Cardinal de Richelieu (Paris, 1944), *passim*.

18. Frederick Leslie Robertson, *The Evolution of Naval Armament* (London, 1921), p. 212.

19. There are apparently several versions of this story, which is highly suspect. One of them speaks of De Caus as still incarcerated in 1641, a long time after he is supposed to have died (J. B. J. Champagnac, *Travail et industrie: le pouvoir de la volonté* [Paris, 1841], p. 68; James Patrick Muirhead, *The Life of James Watt* [New York, 1859], pp. 98–100). Even if the whole story is apocryphal, there is little doubt that it conveys an accurate impression of the temper of the French mind toward practical inventions in the time of Richelieu.

20. Martine de Bertereau, baronne de Beausoleil, *La Restitution de Pluton à Monseigneur l'eminentissime cardinal duc de Richelieu des mines et minières en France* (Paris, 1640).

21. Cf. Hauser, *Richelieu*, p. 150, with the account in some editions of *Dictionnaire Larousse*.

22. See Chapter XII.

23. *Correspondance des Contrôleurs généraux des Finances avec les Intendants des Provinces*, ed. A. M. de Boislisle (Paris, 1897), III, 188 ("il y a une chose heureuse dans ces mines, qui est la reproduction," etc.).

24. Nef, *The Rise of the British Coal Industry* (London, 1932), I, 19–20, 124–26.

25. Rouff, *Les Mines de charbon*, pp. 422–31, especially pp. 424–31. M. Rouff's researches show that the figures ordinarily given for the production of coal in France on the eve of the Revolution are far too low.

26. Ten million tons is the estimate I made some years ago (*British Coal Industry*, I, 20). But most estimates are lower. An estimate of between six and seven million tons has authoritative support (J. H. Clapham, *An Economic History of Modern Britain* [Cambridge, 1926], I, 431) though I regard it as an understatement.

27. T. S. Ashton, *Iron and Steel*

in the Industrial Revolution (Manchester, 1924), pp. 235–36.

28. See Nef, "A Comparison of Industrial Growth in France and England from 1540 to 1640," *Journal of Political Economy*, XLIV (1936), 520.

29. Heckscher, "Un Grand Chapitre de l'histoire du fer: le monopole suedois," *Annales d'histoire économique et sociale*, IV (1932), 130, 132.

30. H. and G. Bourgin, *L'Industrie sidérurgique en France* (Paris, 1920), p. 463; see also Nef, *JPE*, XLIV, 520.

31. Ashton, pp. 60, 97–98, 236.

32. Rouff, *Les Mines de charbon*, pp. 247–49; Bourgin, pp. 411–15; Warren C. Scoville, "Large-Scale Production in the French Plate-Glass Industry, 1665–1789," *JPE*, L (1942), 681–82, and *passim*.

33. Comte Chaptal, *Mes Souvenirs sur Napoléon* (Paris, 1893), pp. 354–55. I was led to this passage by recollection of my conversations with Professor E. F. Gay, who often referred to it to the amusement of his friends.

34. Lord Acton, *Lectures on the French Revolution* (London, 1932), p. 326.

35. Emile Levasseur, *Histoire du commerce de la France* (Paris, 1911), I, 512n.

36. E. Lipson, *The Economic History of England* (London, 1931), II, 189.

37. Adam Smith, *The Wealth of Nations*, bk. i, ch. viii (J. E. Thorold Rogers ed., I, 74).

38. G. Talbot Griffith, *Population Problems of the Age of Malthus* (Cambridge, 1926), pp. 13, 18, 20.

39. Levasseur, *La Population française* (Paris, 1892), III, 503–507. See also Scoville, *JPE*, L, 698.

40. Earl J. Hamilton, *War and Prices in Spain, 1651–1800* (Cambridge, Mass., 1947), p. 220; Leopold von Ranke, *Memoirs of the House of Brandenburg and History of Prussia* (London, 1849), III, 385, 387.

41. Walther Hoffmann, "Ein Index der industriellen Produktion für Grossbritannien seit dem 18. Jahr-

hundert," *Weltwirtschaftliches Archiv,* XL (ii) (1934), 383–98. The statement in the text is based on figures kindly compiled for me by my colleague, Mr. Bert F. Hoselitz.

42. Hamilton, pp. 221–22.

43. Ranke, III, pp. 384*ff.*

44. *The Cambridge Modern History* (Cambridge, 1934), VI, 720.

45. Otto Hue, *Die Bergarbeiter* (Stuttgart, 1910), I, 347; cf. 354*n.*

46. *Encyclopédie méthodique,* pp. 10–11.

47. Smith, *Wealth of Nations,* I, 85–86.

48. Hamilton, pp. 214–16; C.-E. Labrousse, *Esquisse du movement des prix et des revenues en France au XVIIIe siècle* (Paris, 1933), especially II, 361–62, 491–93.

49. Elizabeth W. Gilboy, *Wages in Eighteenth Century England* (Cambridge, Mass., 1934), ch. vii, and pp. 225–27, 242–43. Professor J. H. Clapham's work suggests that the wage earners in the English industrial districts were not growing poorer from 1790 to 1840 (*Economic History of Modern Britain,* I, ch. xiv).

50. Hamilton, pp. 214–16, 223–24; Hamilton, "Profit Inflation and the Industrial Revolution, 1751–1800," *Quarterly Journal of Economics,* LVI (1942), 256–73.

51. Tocqueville, *L'Ancien Régime et la Révolution,* bk. iii, ch. iv.

SECTION 3

1. Henry Hamilton, *The English Brass and Copper Industries to 1800* (London, 1926), p. ix.

2. Stendhal, *Racine et Shakespeare,* ed. Edouard Champion (Paris, 1925), I, 91.

3. It was from the wide knowledge of the late Professor E. F. Gay that I first obtained confirmation of this view, and I gratefully acknowledge my indebtedness to him in this matter of dating the beginning of the industrial revolution.

4. Plato, *The Laws,* 682A, a reference for which I am indebted to Dr. Robert M. Hutchins.

5. See T. S. Ashton, *Iron and* *Steel in the Industrial Revolution* (Manchester, 1924), p. 93; T. H. Marshall, *James Watt* (Edinburgh, 1925), p. 139; Paul Mantoux, *The Industrial Revolution in the Eighteenth Century* (London, 1928), pp. 233–39.

6. Philipp A. Nemnich, *Neueste Reise durch England, Schottland und Ireland, hauptsächlich in Bezug auf Produkte, Fabriken und Handlung* (Tübingen, 1807), p. 46.

7. J. H. Clapham, *An Economic History of Modern Britain* (Cambridge, 1926), I, 425.

8. Walther Hoffmann, "Ein Index der industriellen Produktion für Grossbrittanien seit dem 18. Jahrhundert," *Weltwirtschaftliches Archiv,* XL (ii) (1934), pp. 383–98 (see above, Section 2, note 41).

9. For the figures see L. C. Gray, *History of Agriculture in the Southern United States to 1860* (Washington, 1933), II, 678, a reference for which I am indebted to Professor A. L. Dunham. For the imports of cotton, see Mantoux, p. 258.

10. See Clapham, p. 53.

11. Figures for 1937 from S. B. Clough and C. W. Cole, *Economic History of Europe* (Boston, 1941), p. 766.

12. Charles Péguy, *Basic Verities,* trans. Ann and Julian Green (New York, 1943), pp. 76, 78.

SECTION 4

1. N. S. B. Gras, *Business and Capitalism* (New York, 1939), p. vii.

2. T. N. Carver, *The Religion Worth Having* (Cambridge, Mass., 1912; rev. ed., Los Angeles, 1940).

3. This impression was derived from lectures of his which I attended at Harvard University thirty years ago.

4. See F. A. von Hayek, "The Counter-Revolution of Science," *Economica* (February, May, August, 1941).

5. See Herbert Butterfield, *The Origins of Modern Science, 1300–1800* (London, 1949), and also J. U. Nef, "The Genesis of Industrial Civilization and the Birth of Modern Science," *Essays in Honor of Conyers Read* (Philadelphia, 1950).

XVI. THE ENLIGHTENMENT AND THE PROGRESS OF WAR

SECTION 1

1. Leopold von Ranke, *Memoirs of the House of Brandenburg and History of Prussia*, trans. Sir Alexander and Lady Duff Gordon (London, 1849), I, 291–311.

2. See Charles H. Firth, *Cromwell's Army* (London, 1902), p. 286.

3. *Cambridge Modern History* (Cambridge, 1934), VI, 213, 269.

4. See Robert Ergang, *The Potsdam Führer, Frederick William I, Father of Prussian Militarism* (New York, 1941), pp. 68, 70.

5. Ranke, II, 53, 55*ff*, and *passim*.

6. *Cambridge Modern History*, VI, 261.

7. Ranke, III, 405–406, and *passim*.

8. Hans Speier, "Militarism in the Eighteenth Century," *Social Research*, III (1936), 310–11; J. A. H. Guibert, *Essai général de tactique, précédé d'un discours sur l'état actuel de la politique et de la science militaire en Europe* (Liége, 1772), I, xi–xii.

9. Thackeray, *The Memoirs of Barry Lyndon, Esq.* (Boston, 1889), p. 67, and *passim*.

10. Quoted in G. F. Nicolai, *The Biology of War*, trans. C. and J. Grande (New York, 1918), p. 61.

11. A. W. Gomme, *A Historical Commentary on Thucydides* (Oxford, 1945), I, 14–15; a work kindly' called to my attention by my colleague, Professor David Grene.

12. Aquinas, *Summa Theologica*, pt. ii (ii), q. XL, arts. 1 and 2.

13. *Memorials of the Holles Family*, ed. A. C. Wood (London, 1937), p. 81.

14. "Mémoire sur la manufacture de Tours," 1770, Archives départementales, Indre-et-Loire, C. 1010.

15. Earl of Orrery, *A Treatise of the Art of War* (London, 1677), p. 15.

16. Marshal Saxe, *Reveries, or Memoirs upon the Art of War* (London, 1757), p. 2.

17. *Encyclopédie méthodique*, III (1788), 357.

18. I am grateful to Professor Jean Hugonnot, of the Lycée Claude Bernard in Paris, for calling these facts to my attention. He plans to publish a brochure on the role of the "Marseillaise" in arousing what he calls "the spirit of resistance" among soldiers and officers in national armies throughout the world.

19. See Lord Acton, *Lectures on the French Revolution* (London, 1932), pp. 21–22.

20. Coleridge, *The Friend* (London, 1837), I, 264–65.

21. Marquise de la Tour du Pin, *Journal d'une femme de cinquante ans* (25th ed.; Paris, 1925), II, 246.

SECTION 2

1. Lord Acton, *Lectures on the French Revolution* (London, 1932), pp. 10–11.

2. "Tableau philosophique des progrès successifs de l'esprit humain," *Oeuvres de Turgot*, ed. G. Schelle (Paris, 1913), I, 215.

3. *Ibid.*, p. 214.

4. Marcel Raval, *Claude Nicholas Ledoux* (Paris, 1945), pp. 24–25, 27, 60–65, 157–206. I owe my knowledge of this book to my colleague, Professor Otto von Simson.

5. *Ibid.*, pp. 62, 188–89.

6. In 1792, for example, the equestrian statue of Henry IV, by Lemot, on the Pont-Neuf in Paris, was melted down and converted into cannon.

7. John Muller, *A Treatise of Artillery* (2nd ed.; London, 1768), pp. vi–vii, and *passim*; G. von Scharnhorst, *Handbuch für Officiere* (1804), I, 18, 59*ff*, and *passim*. Cf. Karl von Clausewitz, *On War*, trans. O. J. M. Jolles (New York, 1943), pp. 113, 195–96.

8. I am grateful to Mr. James Ravone Smith, of the Committee on Social Thought, for having called my attention to the part played by descriptive geometry in the development of offensive war.

9. Gaspard Monge, *Description de l'art de fabriquer les canons* (Paris, 1794), p. iii.

10. *Ibid.*, pp. 45, 54*ff*.

11. Monge, pp. 60, 64–65, 67.

12. *Ibid.*, pp. 151–53, plates 27–29.

13. Hans Delbrück, *Geschichte der Kriegskunst* (Berlin, 1920), IV, 474–75.

14. Antoyne de Montchrétien, *Traicté de l'oeconomie politique* (1615), ed. Th. Funck-Brentano (Paris, n.d.), p. 299.

15. Delbrück, IV, 475.

16. *Niles' Weekly Register*, II (1812), no. 35, 146; a reference for which I am indebted to Earl J. Hamilton.

17. George T. Denison, *A History of Cavalry* (2nd ed.; London, 1913), ch. xxiv.

18. Delbrück, IV, 477. See also R. R. Palmer, "Frederick the Great, Guibert, Bülow: From Dynastic to National War," *Makers of Modern Strategy*, ed. E. M. Earle (Princeton, 1943), pp. 69–70.

19. Delbrück, IV, 479.

20. Clausewitz, *On War*, pp. 267–68, 276–77.

21. Frederick Leslie Robertson, *The Evolution of Naval Armament* (London, 1921), p. 37.

22. J. Holland Rose, *The Indecisiveness of Modern War* (London, 1927), p. 2.

23. Delbrück, IV, 510–11.

24. Between two and ten millions according to Jean Lagorgette, *Le Rôle de la guerre* (Paris, 1906), pp. 571ff.

25. *Oeuvres de Saint-Simon et d'Enfantin* (Paris, 1865), I, 54–55. I am grateful to Mr. Rosenstock-Huessy for calling this passage to my attention.

26. See Chapter XV, Section 3.

27. Clausewitz, p. 267.

28. Meyer Shapiro, "The Romanesque Sculpture of Moissac," *Art Bulletin*, XIII, no. 3 (1931), 255.

29. Sigfried Giedion, *Space, Time and Architecture* (Cambridge, Mass., 1941), pp. 55–56.

30. Philipp A. Nemnich, *Neueste Reise durch England, Schottland und Ireland* (Tübingen, 1807), pp. 551–52.

XVII. NINETEENTH-CENTURY RAMPARTS AGAINST WAR

SECTION 1

1. Henry James, *William Wetmore Story and His Friends* (Boston, 1903), I, 107–108, 136.

2. Julien Benda, *La Grande Epreuve des démocraties* (New York, 1942), pp. 63–64.

3. *The Living Thoughts of Kant*, ed. Julien Benda (New York, 1940), p. 129.

4. Benda, *La Grande Épreuve des démocraties*, p. 63.

5. Kant, *Perpetual Peace* (New York, 1932), pp. 37, 57.

6. Henry Adams, *History of the United States, 1801–1805* (New York, 1931), I, 9.

7. Marquise de la Tour du Pin, *Journal d'une femme de cinquante ans* (25th ed.; Paris, 1924), I, 49.

8. Gaspard Monge, *Description de l'art de fabriquer les canons* (Paris, 1794), pp. i ff.

9. Constant, *De l'esprit de conquête* (Paris, 1947), p. 44. I am grateful to Thomas A. Donovan for having recalled this work to my mind at just the moment when I needed to be reminded of it.

10. *Ibid.*, p. 15, and *passim*.

11. Graham Wallas, *The Life of Francis Place* (London, 1898), pp. 89–90.

12. *Ibid.*, pp. 168ff.

13. *Lettres d'Auguste Comte à John Stuart Mill* (Paris, 1877), p. 56.

14. F. A. Hayek, "The Counter-Revolution of Science," *Economica* (February, May, August, 1941), p. 299, and *passim*.

15. Comte, *Cours de philosophie positive*, summarized by Jules Rig (Paris, 1881), II, 221.

16. See Jean Lagorgette, *Le Rôle de la guerre* (Paris, 1906), pp. 498ff.

17. François Quesnay, *Oeuvres économiques et philosophiques*, ed. A. Oncken (Paris, 1888), p. 658.

18. See *Encyclopédie méthodique* (Paris, 1788), IV, 314.

19. C. H. de Saint-Simon, *De la réorganisation de la société européenne* (1814), "Bibliothèque romantique" (Paris, n.d.), pp. 10, 26–27, 89–90, 96,

and *passim*. Young Augustin Thierry, the future historian, was the co-author (Hayek, p. 33).

20. J. L. and Barbara Hammond, *The Town Labourer 1760–1832* (London, 1920), ch. v.

21. Henry S. Lucas, "John Crabbe: Flemish Pirate, Merchant, and Adventurer," *Speculum*, XX (1945), 334ff.

22. Francis Parkman, *La Salle and the Discovery of the Great West* (Boston, 1927), p. 179.

23. See Gustav Schmoller, "Studien über die wirtschaftliche Politik Friedrichs des Grossen," *Jahrbuch für Gesetzgebung, Verwaltung und Volkswirtschaft im Deutschen Reich* (Leipzig, 1884), p. 60.

SECTION 2

1. Montesquieu, *Pensées et fragments inédits* (Bordeaux, 1899), I, 15. I am indebted to Professor Herman Finer for spotting this quotation.

2. Henry Thomas Buckle, *History of Civilization in England* (London, 1934), I, ch. viii, and *passim*.

3. J. S. Mill, *Autobiography* (London, 1873), pp. 41, 45–46, and *passim*.

4. Montaigne, *Essaies*, II, ch. xi.

5. "Slavery in Modern Scotland," *Edinburgh Review*, CLXXXIX (1899), 119ff; Lord Cockburn, *Memorials of His Time* (Edinburgh, 1856), pp. 77–79; J. U. Nef, *The Rise of the British Coal Industry* (London, 1932), II, pp. 157–64.

6. Proudhon, *La Guerre et la paix* (Paris, 1861), p. 103.

7. Winwood Reade, *Martyrdom of Man* (New York, 1874), pp. 542–43.

8. Henry James, *William Wetmore Story and His Friends* (Boston, 1903), II, 36–37.

9. Hans Delbrück, *Geschichte der Kriegskunst* (Berlin, 1926), V, 294–95, 389.

10. See *Lettres d'Auguste Comte à John Stuart Mill* (Paris, 1877), *passim*.

11. Delbrück, VII, 18–19.

12. Liddell Hart, "After the Verdict," *Leader*, February 24, 1945, p. 13.

13. Quoted in Delbrück, VII, 75.

XVIII. THE MATERIAL ROAD TO TOTAL WAR

SECTION 1

1. Albert Demangéon, *Problèmes de géographie humaine* (2nd ed.; Paris, 1943), p. 36; A. M. Carr-Saunders, *World Population* (Oxford, 1936), *passim*.

2. Colin Clark, *The Conditions of Economic Progress* (London, 1940), pp. 79, 83, 87, 91, 144, and charts facing pp. 147–48.

3. Chester W. Wright, *Economic History of the United States* (New York, 1941), pp. 551, 707.

4. R. H. Tawney, "The Abolition of Economic Controls, 1918–1921," *Economic History Review*, XIII (1943), 24.

5. Sigfried Giedion, *Mechanization Takes Command* (New York, 1948).

6. J. Christopher Herold, *The Swiss without Halos* (New York, 1948), pp. 62–63.

7. Charles Babbage, *Reflections*

on the Decline of Science in England (London, 1830), pp. 14–15.

8. Herbert Spencer, *Social Statics, or the Conditions of Human Happiness* (New York, 1886), p. 80.

9. Joan Bennett, *George Eliot, Her Mind and Art* (Cambridge, 1948), pp. 24–25, 60–61, and *passim*.

10. Spencer, p. 80.

11. Babbage, pp. 1, 17.

12. Frederick Soddy, *Wealth, Virtual Wealth and Debt* (2nd ed.; London, 1933), pp. 303–304, and *passim*; W. Trotter, *Instincts of the Herd in Peace and War* (2nd ed.; London, 1919), p. 242.

13. Karl von Clausewitz, *On War*, trans. F. N. Maude (London, 1911), II, 21n. Colonel Maude's note is confusing. He speaks of "thirty rounds a minute," but this is "without aiming." Apparently the "normal rate" was "eight rounds in half a minute," therefore presumably sixteen rounds a minute.

14. Hans Delbrück, *Geschichte der Kriegskunst*, as continued by Emil Daniels and Otto Haintz (Berlin, 1929), VI, 22.

15. J. F. C. Fuller, *On Future Warfare* (London, 1928), p. 62.

16. J. Holland Rose, *The Indecisiveness of Modern War* (London, 1927), p. 1.

17. Paul Hazard, *La Pensée européenne au XVIIIᵉ siècle* (Paris, 1946), II, 60–64.

SECTION 2

1. See Hans Delbrück, *Geschichte der Kriegskunst* (Berlin, 1920), IV, 530.

2. Quoted by R. Ergang, *The Potsdam Führer* (New York, 1941), p. 186.

3. See Marquise de la Tour du Pin, *Journal d'une femme de cinquante ans* (25th ed.; Paris, 1925), II, 299.

4. Delbrück, V (1926), 80–82.

5. *Ibid.*, VI, 201n.

6. Grotius, *The Rights of War and Peace*, trans. A. C. Campbell (New York, 1901), p. 393; Clausewitz, *On War*, trans. O. J. M. Jolles (New York, 1943), p. 339.

7. Thorstein Veblen, *An Inquiry into the Nature of Peace and the Terms of Its Perpetuation* (New York, 1917), p. 203.

8. Clausewitz might have called it an "attack," since it would be possible to trace it back to the Japanese "invasion" of the Hawaiian Islands, though the American "attack" on Japan at that moment proved weak!

9. James A. Field, Jr., *The Japanese at Leyte Gulf* (Princeton, 1947), pp. vii, 50, 87, 134, and *passim*.

10. Clausewitz, *On War*, trans. Maude, III, 250.

11. Bergson, *The Two Sources of Morality and Religion* (New York, 1935), pp. 135–36.

12. *Times Literary Supplement* (November 27, 1943), p. 566.

13. *The History of Herodotus*, trans. Rawlinson, bk. i, paras. 89, 153; bk. viii, para. 26.

14. Hermann Foertsch, *The Art of Modern Warfare* (New York, 1940), p. 77.

15. J. F. C. Fuller, *On Future Warfare* (London, 1928), pp. 62, 155.

16. *Cambridge Modern History* (Cambridge, 1934), VI, 724.

17. *The World Almanac and Encyclopedia*, 1920, p. 684.

18. Edward A. Shils, *The Atomic Bomb and World Politics*, National Peace Council Pamphlet (London, 1948), p. 79.

19. R. H. Tawney, "The Abolition of Economic Controls, 1918–1921," *Economic History Review*, XIII (1943), 24.

20. See Chapter XIII.

SECTION 3

1. G. F. Nicolai, *The Biology of War*, trans. C. and J. Grande (New York, 1918), pp. 200–201.

2. *Ibid.*, p. 197. After perusing an earlier printed version of Part II of my book, my colleague, Professor Theodore W. Schultz, has kindly given me the benefit of some conversations he had recently with an eminent American engineer concerning the matter of modern war and invention. This engineer's opinion was based on recent American experience. He suggested that the armed services have been completely stagnant between wars, that little technological progress is possible during a war, except of the "hothouse" variety, which is forced and superficial, and that whatever gains have been made in military technology have come as a consequence of more general scientific and industrial advances.

3. José Ortega y Gasset, *The Revolt of the Masses* (New York, 1932), pp. 88–89, 91, 94, 119, 126.

4. Cf. Georges Blanchon, *The New Warfare* (New York, 1918), pp. 90–91.

5. Hobbes, *Leviathan*, Part II, ch. 30.

XIX. THE INTELLECTUAL ROAD TO TOTAL WAR

SECTION 1

1. Norman Angell, *The Great Illusion* (London, 1910), pp. 136–37, 336, 372–73, and *passim*.

2. Kant, *Perpetual Peace* (New York, 1938), p. 37.

3. A point first called to my attention by Jacques Maritain in a seminar

he conducted at the University of Chicago.

4. In a letter written to me by Professor Arthur D. Nock, July 28, 1944.

5. De Rochas d'Aiglun, *Vauban, sa famille et ses écrits, ses oisivetés et sa correspondance* (Paris, 1910), I, 267.

6. Kant, pp. 58–59.

7. This view is supported by Professor Harold A. Innis' important studies on the history of communications from ancient Egypt to the present, studies which I have had the advantage of discussing with him. The most comprehensive of these studies yet published is *Empire and Communications* (Oxford, 1950); see especially pp. 206–207, 209, 211–13.

8. Dr. Artur Schnabel has described this episode in his delightful and illuminating reminiscences, lectures which he gave as White Visiting Professor at the University of Chicago in 1944. It is to be hoped that these reminiscences will soon be published.

9. *The New Statesman and Nation*, August 7, 1943.

10. Julius Kraft, "Liberal Education in Europe and America," unpublished speech to the New York Iota chapter of Phi Beta Kappa, January 28, 1944.

11. See André Siegfried, *Mes souvenirs de la IIIᵉ République*, (Paris, 1946), pp. 102–103.

12. See Nef, "Architecture and Western Civilization," *Review of Politics*, VIII, no. 2 (1946), 192–222.

13. Associated Press dispatch, August 16, 1944.

14. T. S. Eliot, *Milton*, "Proceedings of the British Academy" (London, 1947), p. 19.

SECTION 2

1. Hans Delbrück, *Geschichte der Kriegskunst* (Berlin, 1926), V, 432.

2. John Henry Cardinal Newman, *The Idea of a University* (London, 1899), p. 176; see also p. 165.

3. On the subject see Edmond Silberner, *La Guerre dans la pensée*

économique du XVIᵉ au XVIIIᵉ siècle (Paris, 1939).

4. Grotius, *The Rights of War and Peace*, trans. A. C. Campbell (New York, 1901), p. 346.

5. José Ortega y Gasset, *The Revolt of the Masses* (New York, 1932), p. 63. See also pp. 78–79, and *passim*.

6. Franz Borkenau, "The Roots of Modern German Thought," *The Tablet* (London), January 10, 1942, pp. 16–17.

SECTION 3

1. Archduke Charles of Hapsburg, *Grundsätze der hoheren Kriegskunst* in *Aufgewählte Schriften* (1806), Vienna, 1893, p. 3.

2. Alfred H. Burne, "The Clausewitz Myth," *The Sunday Times* (London), May 6, 1945.

3. Karl von Clausewitz, *On War*, trans. O. J. M. Jolles (New York, 1943), pp. 44, 135, 158, and *passim*.

4. Proudhon, *La Guerre et la paix* (Paris, 1861), I, 83; see also pp. 23–24, 32, 37–39, and *passim*.

5. For Proudhon's view that war is no longer constructive, see *ibid.*, pp. 305–306, 344–45, 366, 370.

6. Ruskin, *The Crown of Wild Olive*, "War," and "Notes on the Political Economy of Prussia," in *Ruskin's Works* (Lovell, Coryell and Co., New York, n.d.), pp. 70, 77, 435.

7. O. W. Holmes, Jr., "The Soldier's Faith," in Max Lerner, *The Mind and Faith of Justice Holmes* (Boston, 1943), p. 20. I am grateful to my colleague, Professor Wilber G. Katz, for calling this passage to my attention.

8. *Ibid.*, p. 9.

9. Georges Sorel, *Réflexions sur la violence* (1907) (7th ed.; Paris, 1930), p. 130.

10. Nietzsche, "Die fröhliche Wissenschaft," *Werke* (Leipzig, 1895), V, no. 338. I am grateful to my colleague, Professor Hans Morgenthau, for showing me this passage and translating it.

Index

Index

Index

Index

EUROPEAN HISTORY TITLES IN
NORTON PAPERBOUND EDITIONS